The

Classical Roman
Reader

The
Classical Roman
Reader

NEW ENCOUNTERS
WITH ANCIENT
ROME

EDITED BY
KENNETH J. ATCHITY

ASSOCIATE EDITOR
ROSEMARY MCKENNA

OXFORD UNIVERSITY PRESS
NEW YORK OXFORD

Oxford University Press

Oxford   New York

Athens   Auckland   Bangkok   Bogotá   Buenos Aires   Calcutta
Cape Town   Chennai   Dar es Salaam   Delhi   Florence   Hong Kong   Istanbul
Karachi   Kuala Lumpur   Madrid   Melbourne   Mexico City   Mumbai
Nairobi   Paris   São Paulo   Singapore   Taipei   Tokyo   Toronto   Warsaw

and associated companies in

Berlin   Ibadan

First published in 1997 by Henry Holt and Company, Inc.,
115 West 18th Street, New York, New York 10011

First issued as an Oxford University Press paperback, 1998

Oxford is a registered trademark of Oxford University Press

Library of Congress Cataloging-in-Publication Data
The classical Roman reader : new encounters with Ancient Rome / edited
by Kenneth J. Atchity : associate editor, Rosemary McKenna.
    p.   cm.
Includes bibliographical references and index.
ISBN-13: 978-0-19-512740-9
    1. Latin literature--Translations into English.   2. Civilization,
Classical--Literary collections.   3. Civilization, Classical-
-Sources.   4. Rome--Civilization--Sources.   5. Rome--Literary
collections.   I. Atchity, Kenneth John.   II. McKenna, Rosemary.
PA6163.C58   1998
870.8001--dc21   98-29785

for
Edmund Zieglemeyer, S.J. and
Mario Puricelli, S.J.
in memoriam

CONTENTS

PART III

The Empire (27 B.C.–A.D. 476)

PREFACE

*T*his reader seeks to present the widest possible perspective on early and classical Rome, from its roots in indigenous Italic and Etruscan cultures to Roman assimilation of its conquests beginning with the Greeks to the Empire's ultimate domination of the entire Mediterranean world—as far east as Persia, as far south as Egypt, as far west as Spain, and as far north as Scotland. Rome's imperial achievement is reflected today in the roads and aqueducts that provide Europe with a communications infrastructure; in the organization and deployment of military divisions; in the secularizing impact of atomic theory that can be traced to Lucretius' *On the Nature of Things*; in the vast corpus of Roman jurisprudence that still forms the foundation of legal proceedings throughout the world; and even in Broadway revivals such as *A Funny Thing Happened on the Way to the Forum*. My purpose is to provide the modern reader with direct access to the voices that shaped the Roman mind and spirit.

Students of literature, law, history, political science, art history, city planning, history of religion, psychology, medicine, women's studies, and anthropology will find here sufficient documentation to provoke further explorations of the powerful outpouring of energy and expression associated with the Romans before they were overrun by barbarian northerners. Previous anthologists have sometimes insisted on calling the culture "Latin" rather than "Roman" because relatively few of its contributors, whether living in the capital city or not, were born in Rome: Ennius from Rudiae, Virgil from outside of Mantua, Cicero of Arpinum, Martial of Bilbilis, Ovid of Sulmo, Livy of Patavium, Plautus of Sarsina. Yet "Roman" was their word for it, whether they lived in Córdoba or Tangier, Persepolis or Macedonia.

The collection is admittedly biased, especially in favor of:

Entrance to the theater, at Italica, Spain

- *The positive:* Rome saw more than its fair share of warfare, insanity, misogyny, military brutality, social upheaval, racism, slavery, bloody persecutions and proscriptions, and epidemics. But transcending it all was Rome's awareness of its talent and destiny for conquest, assimilation, and government.
- *The patriarchal:* Just as the patriarchal writers of classical Greece rewrote the myths they inherited to portray the monolithic worldview they preferred, Roman writers and orators created an orthodoxy based on the primacy of the *paterfamilias* and the proper role of the loyal Roman wife. Despite the tantalizing possibility that there were other writers like Sulpicia, classical Rome was male dominated. That so little is known for sure about Sulpicia, even her real name, further underscores this reality. Until Roman women were partially liberated in the late Republic and early Empire, and then wholly liberated by Christianity, they were officially subject to male authority. Women in Roman myth and legend serve the patriarchy as royal wombs, virgin priestesses, and domestic caretakers. Romans saw the household as a contract between the husband in charge of trade and external affairs and the wife in charge of efficiently running the home

and making it a safe haven for all the family and the household gods. Domestic administration, the Roman predecessor of "home economics," was therefore the primary subject matter of female education while men were trained in the arts of rhetoric and of war. Yet the fabulous queens and goddesses of ancient Rome—in their determination, passion, and endurance—play pivotal roles in major events. Roman myth without Rhea Silvia, Dido, the Sabine women, and Camilla, and the history of Rome without Calpurnia and Agrippina, Octavia, Poppaea, and the Julias, would be quite unrecognizable. As unfashionable as the role seems today, Roman women were truly the "power behind the throne."

- *Paganism:* Another bias has led to the omission of most Christian writers, partly for reasons of space, partly to maintain a focus on Roman civilization rather than the Christian European civilization it gave birth to.

Presenting these encounters with Rome in loose chronological order makes it possible to observe the development of important themes, concerns, and motifs. The index and glossary allow the reader to focus on a particular interest. The section entitled "Landmarks of Roman History" allows the historian to chart the progress of events in a linear fashion. Further, each encounter is given perspective with its own introduction so that readers unfamiliar with the period can just as easily peruse this anthology serendipitously. Where previous anthologies have focused almost entirely on literature, here I've attempted to include representative selections from many different realms of human activity. Students of the classical Rome—literature, art history, ethics, political science, philosophy, history, military history, psychology, history of religion—will find here my favorite texts from "Comp. Lit. 101: Classical Survey," without the frustration of having their number or choice limited by an academic calendar. I hope the selections will be used as stepping-stones to deeper investigations. The themes, images, and characteristics discussed in the introduction can be used to map individual routes through the texts here reprinted.

I have selected both contemporary and older translations based on availability and verisimilitude, fully acknowledging that nothing can equal direct experience with the Latin text, which I had the privilege of encountering throughout my Jesuit education at Rockhurst High School and Georgetown College, then continuing at Yale. I'm delighted, after decades of attrition, to see a renewal of interest in the Latin language in elementary and high schools. Latin is, more than any other single linguistic influence, the basis of Western thought, expression, and customs.

As much as possible, I've tried to follow "Roman" spellings without distracting today's reader. Because the Roman Empire stretched from east to west, even in its own time spellings for the same name could be various—sometimes by caprice, sometimes by intention. I've chosen to use "J" for "I" in names like Julius (Iulius) because that is the more common usage today. Gaius is often the same name as Caius, and I've chosen to use the former where tradition offers both. When Greeks mixed with Romans and gained Roman spellings for their names, I've chosen the more familiar of the two. It's helpful to know how tripartite Roman names like Marcus Tullius Cicero or M. Cornelius Fronto were constructed. The first element is called the "praenomen" or personal name, and was often abbreviated: M. for Marcus, D. for Decimus. The "nomen" proper, in second position, indicates the individual's clan: Gaius Julius Caesar, of the family Julia. The third name, or "cognomen," can be a nickname, an honorific, or a self-chosen title. Marcus Vipsanius Agrippa Postumus was nicknamed "Agrippa Postumus" because he was born after his father's death. The honorific "Germanicus" or "Africanus" was taken or given for the individual's relationship, whether natal or military, to the German or African province.

Familiarity to the modern eye and ear has been my ultimate criterion in the names employed in the introductory essays. The glossary and index help the reader conform the variant spellings that appear in the excerpts.

Since the dating of many events in classical Rome is sometimes uncertain, I've aimed at following a consensus of scholarly opinion; or arbitrarily given my own estimate.

I'm grateful to the late Reverend Edmund Zieglemeyer, S.J., then affiliated with Rockhurst College in Kansas City, who waylaid me at the age of ten and began instructing me in the precision of the Latin language; to my Latin mentor at Rockhurst High School, Mario J. Puricelli, S.J., who made us memorize the *Aeneid*; and to R. J. Schork at Georgetown College, who took me from Horace and Catullus to the Virgilian Academy.

The members of the advisory board have been valuable sources of general perspective and particular suggestions.

I wish to also thank the following:

My reference agent, Sandra Watt, and my editor at Holt, Kenneth Wright.

Rosemary McKenna for her research, suggestions, copyright consulting, and commentary.

Chi-Li Wong and Fran Avallone for their patient assistance in putting the manuscript together.

My students at Occidental College for challenging and exploring.

Art Resources for allowing reproduction of the images from their excellent collections.

And Kevin Ohe for his attention to detail and enthusiasm for the Romans.

INTRODUCTION

*I*n the first decade of the fifth century A.D., according to the historian Procopius, the Emperor Honorius was greeted after breakfast by the chamberlain of his palace in Ravenna with the words: "Rome has fallen!"

"Rome fallen?" cried the stricken emperor, rising from his couch. "But it is not one hour since she was feeding from my hand."

The chamberlain hastened to assure his master that the bad news referred to the *city* of Rome, sacked by the Visigoths the previous day, not to his imperial chicken named *Roma*.

"By Jove, my good friend," said the relieved emperor, "I thought you were referring to my prize hen!"

From the ridiculous (Latin *ridiculus*, "inciting laughter") to the sublime (*sublimis*, "on high"), classical Rome is a marvelous study in opposites: mighty and petty, totalitarian in practice and republican in spirit, Stoic and hedonistic, pontifical and self-deprecating, imperially cosmopolitan and urbanely provincial.

On my first arrival in the Eternal City I could sense that the air itself was redolent with the grandeur and greatness of the Empire. After nearly three thousand years of continuous occupation, Rome today basks in an aura of power attenuated, mellowed into roundness without losing its distinctive sharpness and spice. Under the canopy of a midnight sky that appears more indigo than black, the spirit of Rome is one of universal acceptance, permissiveness—of decadence so profound it has become spiritually nurturing and hedonistically provocative. Nothing fazes contemporary Romans. Aware of their ancient heritage because they are still surrounded by its monuments, they are unimpressed equally by the past and future; today's Romans revel in the present

The arch of Titus

moment, challenging it, daring it to unsettle their *figura.* They are at ease with the history of their sprawling city and laugh at it, telling you to join them for a drink at *Il nasone* (the "Big Nose," referring to the imperial water spouts found everywhere in old Rome, still providing free water to the citizens); or translating the inscription "S.P.Q.R.," found everywhere on monuments and pavements and waterworks, as *"Sono porci questi romani"* ("These Romans are pigs") instead of: *"Senatus populusque romanus"* ("the Senate and the Roman people").

Once, with early summer and the smell of cucumbers in the air, I entered a small restaurant in Trastevere with a Roman friend and ordered *"tutti i cetrioli nella cucina"* ("all the cucumbers in the kitchen").

"With vinegar?" the old waiter replied, without missing a beat.

"Of course," we said, and watched him walk away to fulfill our eccentric demand as though he'd been expecting it. I realized at that moment that for all its harking back to the Greeks, the Renaissance owed its *nonchalance* to classical Rome, to a people whose city was the center of the universe. To this day no one is more nonchalant than the Roman, who will tell you, when crisis comes: *"Coraggio—e sangue de pecora"* ("Have courage—and the blood of a sheep"). If a partying emperor demanded spiderwebs, a legion was dispatched to collect them. Leave it to the Greeks to ask the questions, the Romans specialized in answers—in knowing what to do with things, how to do everything.

Though today's Romans are content to rule the details of everyday personal life and leave politics to the transitory whimsies of ambitious madmen, the classical Romans ruled the world. Climbing the Janiculum toward the American Academy, I was back as an undergraduate at Georgetown's Virgilian Academy, memorizing Anchises' prophesies to his son when Aeneas visits him in Hades:

> *For other peoples will, I do not doubt,*
> *still cast their bronze to breathe with softer features,*
> *or draw out of the marble living lines,*
> *plead causes better, trace the ways of heaven*
> *with wands and tell the rising constellations;*
> *but yours will be the rulership of nations,*
> *remember, Roman, these will be your art:*
> *to teach the ways of peace to those you conquer,*
> *to spare defeated peoples, tame the proud.*
>
> [TR. ALLEN MANDELBAUM]

The Romans built the greatest empire ever known, and held it together for centuries, because they understood that empires are constructed from communities and communication; because they believed in civil service and the religion of the state. All roads lead to Rome because the Romans built them that way. Never in Western civilization has a society of proud individualists been so unanimously dedicated to serving a monolithic government. The classical Roman model of the ideal society was the beehive, which Virgil calls in his *Georgics* "a perfect, model state." If the queen bee is aroused, instantaneously the workers' blood boils with ardor to defend the hive even with their lives. Self-definition, to the Roman mind, begins with self-sacrifice.

Primary sacrifice was made to the ultimate classical Roman god, the city-state itself that the emperor as a "living god" personified. Unlike the Greeks, whose civilization fell first to Persia, then to Macedon, then to Rome because their political individualism regularly overcame all practical need for national unity, the Romans instinctively understood the power of civic unanimity, pervasive and unshakable loyalty to a common cause—which they termed *pietas*, the fundamental classical Roman virtue (Aeneas, in Rome's national epic, is called *pius Aeneas*). Public baths, including communal toilets, were central to a Roman township because, from morning until night, Romans believed in doing everything, from the magnificence of ceremonial "triumphs" to the banalities of the morning *toilette*, together. An inscription can still be read on the walls of Pompeii:

> *Sed amicus mingit*
> *aut cum amico mingere*
> *aut mingere fingere.*

> If a friend stands pissing
> either piss with your friend
> or pretend to be pissing.

The Roman imperial motto, *Divide et impera*, "Divide and conquer," reflects the recognition of the wedgelike leverage achieved by unity. So self-confident were the Romans in the righteousness of their monolithic unanimity that, once they overcame the opposition, they invited the conquered to their communion. The Roman city-state, in the minds of its founders, was simply extending its boundaries to encompass the world. When all subjects throughout the empire were made citizens of Rome, the word "suburban" had been "globalized." If, in the end, the world outside Italy was not capable of sustained *pietas* toward mother Rome, the fissures in the monolith had been introduced by the character of the conquerors themselves.

Roman belief in the superiority of Greek models is both a sign of the paradoxical humility ingrained in the Roman mind and an omen of Rome's downfall: Humility led to recognizing and assimilating the "added value" Rome accrued through her conquests of alien economies, laws, and gods. Sophisticated Romans worshipped Attis at the same time with Venus, Cybele with Fortuna. Rome, as it expanded its boundaries to the limits of the known world, welcomed all infusions of novelty, originality, and new blood: embracing wholesale Greek philosophy, importing horses from Arabia, enlisting barbarians in the legions that conquered them.

The term "Roman" became synonymous with "cosmopolitan" as the character of Rome—some warned to its detriment—never ceased evolving. Beneath it all, the Romans were more sincerely moral than the intellectualizing Greeks, both more expressive of and more detached from their own feelings, and of course more practical in all ways. It was second nature for them to put Greek ideas into effect over vast areas of the globe—an opportunity of which the Greeks had deprived themselves by constant civil warfare. Greece has endured to this day in modern consciousness only because it has been conveyed to us by Rome.

Electoral and theatrical graffiti, Pompeii

Relentless assimilation can be dangerous. The fish that swallows all may swallow something indigestible: "Captive Greece took captive her fierce conqueror." Just as Greek thought, taste, manners, and literature were blamed by classical Roman conservatives of every period for the progressive decadence of their society, Christianity—for hundreds of years, alternately dallied with and persecuted, but finally legitimized by the emperor Constantine the Great—transformed pagan Rome into the "Holy Roman Empire" that became the forerunner of modern European civilization.

Perhaps a more accurate way of thinking of it, however, is this: The Romans were the first to proclaim that you are what you eat. Their appetites were voracious. Cultural cannibal, religious chameleon, military shape-shifter, Rome battened on the strength of her victims. Ovid's *Metamorphosis* is a manifesto for the Roman mechanism of evolution through assimilation. Romans ate what they desired: Greek, Gaul, or Christian; and inasmuch as what they ate transformed their thought and social structures, we are still Romans today.

For those of us fortunate enough to live in industrialized countries, what has survived as the character of these people who engineered modern Western civilization is the routine everyday assumption of abundance. The Romans found and celebrated abundance in all things: energy, laws, entrées at banquets, sex, festivals, and spectacles; but also poverty, slavery, executions, prostitution, subjugated peoples. The classical Roman *lanx satura*, "full plate," of first fruits offered as sacrifice to the gods is alive today in the Louisiana custom of *lagniappe*, "a little too much extra," and in every visit to the supermarket offering fruits and foods from every corner of the world. Juvenal reports a banquet menu featuring a giant lobster, festooned with baby asparagus; mullet from Corsica; the best lamprey from the straits of Sicily; goose liver; a capon "as big as a house"; a boar roasted entire, all accentuated with truffles and mushrooms. No wonder Marcus Aurelius stood out among emperors as an anomaly for his adherence to Socratic moderation.

Where the Greeks believed that the Golden Age of myth and legend lay somewhere in the remotest past, and the persecuted Christians placed heavenly paradise in the ultimate future—both insisting that they themselves were living in a diminished era—the classical Romans of the first centuries B.C. and A.D. believed they themselves were living in the Golden Age. Again it was the imperial poet Virgil who gave voice to their belief, in his famous fourth eclogue:

> We have reached the last era in Sibylline song. Time has conceived and the great
> Sequence of the Ages starts afresh. Justice, the Virgin, comes back to dwell with us, and
> the rule of Saturn is restored . . . The Iron Race shall end and Golden Man inherit all
> the world . . . The fates have spoken, in concord with the unalterable decree of destiny.
> "Run, spindles," they have said. "This is the pattern of the age to come."
>
> [TR. E. V. RIEU]

Roman achievement was prodigious and enduring. We in the West continue to develop our architecture, law, arts, and sciences on Roman models, in languages and an alphabet that also came to us from Rome. Although basic English is Anglo-Saxon, educated English is Latin, as this short list demonstrates:

regal	legal	primary	military	region
agriculture	literature	domestic	republic	ratio
terror	art	horror	classic	virgin
imperial	caesarean	operation	medicine	aquarium
nature	religion	decimate	decide	orbit
educate	civilian	suburban	authority	rural
fortune	martial	diversity	province	virtue
imitate	provision	generation	communion	piety
celestial	dignity	regulate	liberty	urban
transfer	amorous	revolution	fraternity	genius
vigilance	society	secession	equestrian	jury
constitution	institute	patriarchy	vitality	furor

The more schooled we are, the more our vocabulary becomes peppered with Latin phrases and abbreviations: status quo; quid pro quo; prima facie; ipso facto; etc. *(et cetera)*; carpe diem; ibid.

(ibidem); i.e. *(id est)*; e.g. *(exempla gratia)*. Physicians today employ the terms and forms used by Soranus and Celsus: stat, Rx, npo; the periodic table utilizes atomic symbols derived from the Latin names for the elements: Au, for gold, from *Aurus*; Fe, for iron, from *Ferrus*.

The Romans, masters of practicality, provided the infrastructure for civilized life and are the true ancestors of today's global community. A unified world would not have surprised them, but is exactly what they envisioned and sought to accomplish. Faced with the Greek philosopher Zeno's statement that it is theoretically impossible for a man to walk across a stadium—because to do so he must first walk halfway, and before that a quarter of the way, and so on indefinitely—therefore motion is an illusion, a Roman engineer responded: *"Solvitur ambulando"* ("The problem is solved by walking"). Though they applauded those who had the patience for theorizing, the Romans had little patience. Turning theory into practice, they redirected Greek philosophy into the everyday morality and legal principles eloquently proclaimed by Lucretius, Augustus, Marcus Aurelius, the emperor Julian, and Justinian.

Instead of pursuing truth for truth's sake, Romans turned their practical energies to founding and stabilizing an empire that lasted nearly a millennium, extended to all shores of the Mediterranean and other seas as well, and left a heritage that readily can be detected in the legal, topographical, and linguistic infrastructure of today's Western societies. Eventually Roman maps would describe the Mediterranean as *mare nostrum* ("our lake"). The classical Romans would rather act than contemplate, though the mighty reach of the Roman Empire is testimony to the thoughtfulness of Roman action. Knowledge, they believed, is useful only as the basis for effective action.

The Roman Empire was based, as well, on discipline (albeit discipline tempered by excess). Between decision and execution (both Roman terms), the classical Greek mind would contemplate; the Roman mind preferred to contemplate before decision and after execution, looking back on triumphs and defeats rather than imagining possibilities. Even defeats were regarded as stepping-stones to victory. By the time the doors of Janus were closed, the imperial Roman eagle held sway from the Atlantic Ocean to the Tigris River, and from the North Sea to the Nile.

When you walk into the ancient Roman Forum today what you see is the jumble of centuries, detritus left by barbarian invaders and modern Italians of what was once the greatest empire the world has ever known. If you make the *giro* from left to right you are following the path of Rome's most powerful orator, Cicero, who taught himself to memorize his eloquently lengthy speeches by associating each peroration with a different monument in the Forum. From this center of administration, the Romans governed their empire, uniting subject provinces, from north Africa to Scotland, from Spain to Persia, with their language, their laws, and their roads. The pages that follow introduce you to the most representative Romans, including:

- **Cicero**, orator *extraordinaire*, but also redoubtable statesman and philosopher whose *Republic, On Friendship, On Old Age,* and *Laws*, ranking among the most incisive documents of Western civilization, were written in the midst of civil wars and revolution that changed the destiny of Rome and led to their author's execution.

- Lucretius. Epicurean-poet-philosopher, whose *On the Nature of Things* proclaimed the cosmic consciousness that is truly the basis of Roman materialism and its "religion of the state": Mankind has no need of the gods (except as symbols of its own prowess) because the infinite universe, including the human mind and soul, is a marvelous mechanism composed of a finite number of indivisible particles, invisible yet solidly material.
- Julius Caesar. Consul for Life. Dictator. *Pontifex Maximus,* "Highest Priest." Conqueror of Gaul. *Imperator,* "Commander in Chief." The father of the Roman Empire was not only one of the greatest military minds of Western history but also one of its most eloquent prose stylists and orators.
- Caesar Augustus "found Rome a city of bricks and left it a city of marble." His energy inexhaustible, his vision unswerving, the young Octavian was forced to come of age by the assassination of his uncle and achieved adulthood through defeating the assassins, expanding Roman military dominance, consolidating domestic power in his hands, and declaring his uncle, and therefore himself, as a god.
- Pliny the Elder. An accomplished civil servant whose hobby made him the greatest encyclopedist of the ancient world and whose insatiable scientific curiosity led to his death of asphyxiation while exploring recently erupted Vesuvius.
- The Emperor Justinian. His indefatigable nostalgia for the greatness of Rome led to his reconquering its lost territories, recodifying its laws, and restoring the former empire for the remainder of his glorious reign.

If the Golden Age of Roman literature can be said to start with Julius Caesar crossing the Rubicon and end with the death of Augustus, certainly its Silver Age spans the first and second centuries, A.D., under Trajan, Hadrian, and Antoninus Pius, when the empire was at its most expansive. Rome's Golden Age recalls the splendors of Periclean Athens and looks forward to the European Renaissance. Writers of this period, perhaps inferior to those of the earlier age in vigor and boldness, were far superior in artistic ability, technical finish, delicacy of sympathy, and beauty of expression. Augustan masterpieces show a perfect harmony between language and subject matter and between the native Italian genius and Greek influences:

- Horace, whose polished odes excelled even their Greek models and who turned down an emperor's invitation in favor of his art.
- The historian Livy, who accomplished the first great history of Rome and set the stage for Roman imperial expansion.
- Catullus, the "new stylist" whose vivid mastery of the personal lyric has influenced poets for two millennia.

- **Virgil**, whose *Georgics* and *Eclogues* led Augustus to commission the *Aeneid* as Rome's national epic.
- **Ovid**, who walked the tightrope between service to the state and celebration of its private vices—and lost his balance when his obscenely naughty *Art of Love* touched an imperial nerve that led Augustus to banish him for life to a remote outpost on the Black Sea.

Even in the Golden Age, the splendidly self-confident surface of Roman expression reveals a contradictory subtext, an underlying and disturbing counterpoint: that of sadness and even dread as the expanding imperialists recognized the diffusion of the staunch old virtues upon which Rome's initial energy was solidly founded. By the Silver Age, when rhetoric emerged as the most important art and writing was shaped for recitation and declamation, the dread had risen to the surface and writers are more overtly pessimistic about the future:

- **Seneca**, demonstrating the inferiority of Stoicism as a creed to rival a vigorous Christianity.
- **Petronius**, founder of the European novel, proclaiming with wonderful profanity the sterility of materialism.
- **Juvenal**, lashing out with acknowledged futility at the excesses of the aristocracy.
- **Tacitus**, depicting the conscienceless Nero using Christians as torches to light his garden parties.

From the earliest days of the Republic to the fall of the capital to invading northerners, these encounters reveal the variegated yet consistent threads of concern that shape the mighty tapestry of the classical Roman mind:

- **Love for the land.** From Varro's *On Agriculture* through Virgil's *Georgics* to Justinian's *Codex*, to be characteristically Roman meant to revere the earth itself, to honor the land and those who hold and nurture it. This characteristic led the early Romans first to secure their homeland from incursions, then to occupy and love more and more land.

  - Agrarian values included rugged individualism, tolerance for hardship, endurance, and discipline.

- **Loyalty to family.** The continuum between private and public life was unbroken through most of Roman history. An epitaph found in the Scipio graveyard reads: "By my behavior I reflected the virtues of my forebears; I sired offspring and strived to equal the accomplishments of my father . . . My deeds have ennobled my stock." The corollaries of Roman family loyalty include:

- Patriarchal *auctoritas*. The authority enjoyed by the *paterfamilias* over his wife and children translated to the very fiber of Roman society: The leader commands the respect and absolute disciplined obedience of the led. Justinian's *Codex* declares: "When a woman is convicted of having secretly had sexual intercourse with her slave, she shall be sentenced to death, and the rascally slave shall perish by fire."
- Yet the considerable power of the Roman matriarch is reflected in the second-century B.C. inscription on the tomb of a wife and mother:

  Friend, I have not much to say; stop and read it. This tomb, which is not fair, is for a fair woman. Her parents gave her the name Claudia. She loved her husband in her heart. She bore two sons, one of whom she left on earth, the other beneath it. She was pleasant to talk with, and she walked with grace. She kept the house and worked in wool. That is all. You may go. Claudia.

- **Roma, Amor.** The Roman *Roma vincit omnia,* "Rome conquers all," was playfully transformed in the Middle Ages to *Amor vincit omnia;* but though the Romans have been thought of as hard-headed and cold-hearted, they were among the most loving of cultures ever known. Ovid's *Loves* and *Art of Love,* as well as Virgil's *Aeneid,* reminded their readers that they were descendants of Venus. Lucretius' *On the Nature of Things* begins with an invocation of the goddess of love, and the *Aeneid* poses history as the strife between Venus and Juno (hate). Generosity toward the subjugated, then, is only an extension of Roman character: Let us conquer you so we can show you how to love.
- **Law.** Family values were reflected in codified Roman law as early as the Twelve Tables, of 450 B.C., which formed the basis of Roman civil law in the centuries that followed. The publication of the ancestral laws in the Roman Forum represented an early victory of the plebeian class. Table IV is devoted to paternal power.
- **Education.** Believing that native intelligence and talent can and should be molded into perfection, the Romans also believed that education distinguishes man from beasts and that even an evil man can be reformed through learning. When a slave showed promise of learning, he was freed and educated; some of the greatest works of Roman literature were written by freedmen like Terence and Syrus. Preschoolers were taught traditional morality by their mothers; letters by their fathers. Education in classical Rome was neither free nor public, but was inexpensive, coeducational, and practical. Aimed at producing polished orators, it focused on respect for authority, the rules of right conduct, knowledge of the law, and discipline. Athletic prowess was developed, not for its own sake as in Greece, but to enhance military accomplishment. Children of aristocrats completed their education in Athens, learning to read the Greek classics in Greek. A

Roman's education never ended: In the camp and in the Forum the citizen continued learning by example and experience the arts of war and politics.

- **Military prowess.** To be Roman was to soldier in the wars for Mother Rome. Relentlessly expanding its circle of conquests, Rome started by conquering its native Latium, then moved to northern and southern Italy, then to Sicily, then north to Gaul, south to northern Africa and Egypt, east to Greece and Mesopotamia, and west to Spain. Totaling 450,000, Rome's was the largest professional army ever assembled.
- **Government.** Rome was a republic since 509 B.C., and Romans came to understand the potential of various political infrastructures all joined by the equalizing force of the statement, *Civus romanus sum,* "I am a Roman citizen." As M. Gwyn Morgan put it: "Rome's real achievement was neither winning nor losing territory but running an empire successfully for several centuries and, in the process, civilizing much of Europe."

- *City planning, civic architecture, civil engineering.* By the second century A.D., more than two million Roman citizens were served by a vast network of effective aqueducts, roads, sewers, baths, temples, circuses, theaters, forums, ports, irrigation systems, coliseums, and triumphal arches—provincial cities throughout the Empire modeling their civic centers on that of Rome. Roman builders mastered the vault and dome, arch and mosaic tile.

Those fortunate enough to have studied Latin know that the Roman mind is richly manifest in the language of the Empire, a language marked by its simplicity, vigor, restraint, precision, economy, sharpness of image, and rhetorical intensity. Latin sentences are direct and to the point, virile, energetic, austere, and dignified. Although modern Italian is forged from Dante's Tuscan, to this day Italians consider their standard of accent and pronunciation *la lingua toscanna in bocca romana,* "the Tuscan tongue in a Roman mouth." The Roman mind, like the language of Rome, was characterized by:

- **Gravitas.** High seriousness—based on profound respect for established institutions and ancestral accomplishments—pervaded Roman politics, morality, literature, and religion.
- **Pietas.** So replete was the Roman calendar with feasts and festivals to the gods and heroes that the term "Roman holiday" became cliché two thousand years ago. The Roman Catholic Church, until recently conducting its services in Latin, inherited its ritual libations, litanies, sacrifices, and sacraments from Roman models.
- **Dignitas.** The combination of *gravitas* and *pietas* may best explain Roman *dignitas,* which compares only superficially to modern Italian *figura,* its diminished offspring. A Roman's dignity may have been expressed with his external appearance and comportment, but it resided in the disciplined earnestness of his soul.

- **Urbanity and cosmopolitanism.** In many ways being Roman was a state of mind. Seneca was a Spaniard, Livy from Padua, Catullus from Verona. Yet they all were joined to Rome by a common language and intent, as the Empire itself was united by roads and uniform coinage. The Roman Empire, at its successful high points, achieved unity in its diversity. The Roman, thriving on stimulation, was at home among the entire spectrum of cultures, races, classes, economies, and religions. Roman urbanity at its best bred tolerance, politeness, easy manners, conversational skill, and social graces. They were a gregarious people: The Roman word for party was *convivium*, "living together." A real experience, a true experience, the best experience, is a shared experience.

- **Humor.** To taste Roman humor we need go no farther than the mall music store for Stephen Sondheim's lyrics to *A Funny Thing Happened on the Way to the Forum*, stolen directly from Plautus as Plautus stole from Menander. Whether we're reading Ovid's nitty-gritty descriptions of effectively seductive makeup and coiffure, or reading the inscriptions on the walls of Pompeii, or hearing about Gaius Caligula's paying lip service to Augustus' retention of Republican institutions by appointing his favorite stallion consul, as we encounter classical Rome we are surrounded everywhere by a sense of humor and wit ranging from the subtle to the outrageous, from supercilious to slapstick.

- **Humanitas.** Cicero argued that men are united to one another by a common bond of humanity that should guide their "good natured" behavior, conversation, and attitude. One of Terence's characters remarks, *Homo sum, humani nil a me alienum puto*: "I am a man, and think nothing human is alien to me." Though the classical Romans believed that men are distinguished from beasts by their ability to reason, and that education leads to virtue, their concept of humanism embraced all corners of human experience. At one end of the spectrum, Romans were fascinated with sexual experimentation, the frontiers of pain and pleasure, extremes of cruelty; yet at the other end they placed high value on sympathy, altruism, kindness, helpfulness, and simple consideration for others. Piety, contrary to later Christian propaganda, was first and foremost a Roman virtue.

Though the European Renaissance looked to the Greeks for inspiration, it was in profound ways more Roman than Greek in its application: Great "Renaissance men" wrote; leaders were writers and writers became leaders, just as Rome's most highly educated men prided themselves in posing as simple citizens doing what must be done for *Mater Roma*. The Roman upperclass's involvement in everyday commerce and political affairs gives today's European civilization its ideal shape: The erudite observations of a François Mitterrand, the diary of Dag Hammerskjöld, even Prince Charles' vacillation between stubborn public service and personal profligacy are legacies of Rome. The modern British and American statesmanlike ideal, to combine public service with written reflection, from Winston Churchill's natural eloquence to Richard Nixon's tortured self-analysis, is much more Roman, in this sense, than it is Anglo-Saxon or Greek.

Roman history is constant witness to dynamic tension, the persistent coexistence of forces at war in the external world of politics and the internal world of the individual Roman psyche. Though they are remembered vividly for their excesses, the Romans are equally famous for the love for moderation that was a constant ironic underpinning to their writing and behavior. *Carpe diem*, "seize the day," was certainly the watchword of these people who invented the "toga party." Yet everywhere, private and public, Roman monuments testified to their striving for *virtus*, in moderation, balance, and harmony. And so they were, like us, filled with paradox: brutality versus sensitivity; addiction to motion versus the longing for rest; invasion versus accommodation; relish for the presence versus pride in the past; Roman roots versus foreign innovations; urban energy versus country refreshment; the centripetal, consolidating force of returning to and reforming Rome versus the centrifugal force of further expansion, reflected in its great leaders' excursions to military victories and triumphal processionals back to the Forum to be acclaimed by the Senate and the mob; respect for age versus celebration of youth; the Apollonian order of Augustus victorious over the Dionysian hedonism of Antony and Cleopatra.

The deepest classical Roman paradox lies in the dynamic tension between unbridled individual genius and reverential service to the religion of the state. For years I began my lectures on the *Aeneid*, Virgil's great national epic commissioned by Augustus, with this fabricated and anachronistic dialogue:

(Relaxed from avenging the assassins of his uncle, and from conquering Egypt and the East, Augustus calls Virgil into his private chambers.)

AUGUSTUS: You know I loved the old-fashioned agrarian values you describe so brilliantly in your *Georgics*. I now have a mission for you, if you choose to accept it.

VIRGIL: Yes, Highness. What do you have in mind?

AUGUSTUS: Of course you won't have to worry about money again.

(Virgil looks—progressively—interested, relieved, and skeptical. At this moment in history it was still all right to be skeptical in the presence of the tolerant Augustus. Horace, after all, had been allowed to turn down the emperor's invitation to serve as his literary secretary. This was years before Ovid would cross the tolerance line that separated Rome from remote Tomis.)

AUGUSTUS: I want you to write me a poem.

VIRGIL: No problem. I've written lots of poems. I love to write poems.

AUGUSTUS: There'll be no more "lots of poems" from you if you write what I have in mind. You'll never have to write another afterward. Not that I would allow it. What I have in mind is a poem to end all poems. I'll read it, publish it, then I'll concentrate on roads and aqueducts. In fact, we may not need any more poets—

(The emperor chuckles. Virgil doesn't know whether he's serious or not.)

AUGUSTUS: Maybe I'll have them all executed. You'd be the sole emperor of poetry.

(I can't believe this is happening to a simple man from Mantua, Virgil is thinking. A chill races up and down his spine. Public challenge. To be used for something larger than yourself! Every artist's fantasy: Lifetime patronage. You have a completion guarantor behind your work; all you have to do is create, and someone else guarantees payment of all the bills.)

AUGUSTUS: Just write this poem. Everyone will love it. I'll make sure.

(Virgil, thinking: Okay. I can do it. I will do it. Of course I'll do it.)

VIRGIL: Yes, Divinity. I will begin immediately.

(He starts for the door, his head swimming: My fame is assured, more enduring than Horace's bronze, stronger than the marble in the Forum. All I have to do is my best. Which I do anyway when I'm freed from financial pressure. But Augustus stops him, snapping his fingers for a cigar. A slave from Numidia brings it, a slave from Macedonia lights it, a slave from Britannia tests it for the emperor, then hands it to him.)

AUGUSTUS: I'm not quite finished yet. I've gotta talk to you a little bit more.

(Virgil turns around, the first artist in history to hear these words.)

AUGUSTUS: I have just a few little ideas I want to tell you about. Think of them as suggestions from a sincere admirer.

VIRGIL: Tell me what you have in mind.

AUGUSTUS: I want you to put your heart into it, and your entire genius. That's why I've chosen you. I believe that whatever you want to write will be just what we're looking for. Your poetry, your vision, can make this happen. And we trust you entirely. Whatever you write will be on the money, except that we would like you to include a couple of things we've jotted down here.

(Virgil, noticing the size of the emperor's papyrus roll, sinks into the couch.)

AUGUSTUS: First, this poem of ours must be an epic that enshrines the greatness of Rome for all eternity. We want a poem as big as our Empire. Second, this epic must provide a philosophy *for* the Empire. A clear and compelling philosophy. Now that we're in charge of the whole world we want everybody to understand exactly how we think things are. Especially these two central points: The individual is born, and raised, and fated—"fated," we love that word—to serve the state. The Republic. Mother Rome.

(Virgil rolls his eyes. Some republic Rome had become—with every breath taken by every senator and tribune controlled by an absolute dictator. He'd thought Augustus' insistence on restoring the institutions of the ancient "republic" a brilliant PR strategy. Now he saw that he was to play a major role in its propagation.)

AUGUSTUS: We know this is a harsh rule, but it *is* our destiny as Romans. And the second point: When you come to speculating about the order of the universe, the answer is simple: Order equals the emperor's will. Neat, simple, and easy to remember? Don't miss that. And fate, too. Fate equals the Imperator's Will. Got it?

VIRGIL: No, I'm not quite getting this. What about Jupiter, whom we worship on the Capitoline Hill? What about Juno? What about the divine structure underlying human affairs?

(The imperial answer comes back: The emperor is not an avatar of Jupiter on earth. Jupiter is a metaphor for the emperor. The true and only god is divus *Augustus,* nephew *of* divus *Julius. The leader is god. [Why don't the gods sound real in the* Aeneid? *Because they have nothing to do with what's going on. They simply act as metaphorical expressions of fate, the emperor's will, which has predetermined everything in the poem.])*

AUGUSTUS: Third, the poem must provide us Romans with a proud background. Now that we've conquered the world, I hear people on the borders asking, "Who *are* you people? How did you *do* this to us?" We want them to know that we did it because we are the maximum. The tops. When they say, "Where'd you come from?" as things are now we have to answer, "By Jove, we're not sure." We have all these fragmented myths: Romulus, Remus, wolf tits, geese on the capital, Etruscan kings, raped Sabine virgins, a white sow. But nobody seems to have the big picture. Your job, Maro, is to find some way to create a myth for us so that when we're talked about people will say, "You guys have everything! You were fated from the beginning of time to do what you've done. The myth of Rome is fantastic." Do you understand that? Make it sound a little Greek, too—nobody can beat the Greeks for myth.

VIRGIL: Whew, that's quite an assignment. How long do you expect me to take with it?

AUGUSTUS: That's the beauty of our situation. We're now officially eternal. Take all the time you want—take the rest of your life! Don't worry about it.

(Virgil would labor at the Aeneid *for ten years, reading the draft of one book after another to the emperor, even would die while he was still polishing his magnum opus; and order it destroyed by his executors—who were prevented from doing so by Augustus. The poet met the emperor's challenge, by making Aeneas the founder of Rome and thereby connecting Rome with the myths of the Trojan War.)*

AUGUSTUS: Finally, and most important, your poem must make it clear, in case you missed this, that everything in history was meant to predict *us*. Me: "He Who Was Coming to Unite All Nations and Put the Whole World at Peace." That kind of thing. But don't put it exactly that way because some folks might resist the concept. We don't want to seem egocentric. So figure out how to do it without naming me more than once or twice. But make no mistake about it: We are the destined ruler. I am the one.

(Virgil would move the Golden Age from the remote past into the present, by having the Age of Augustus predicted in the time of Aeneas. The characters in his epic would prophesy that the Age of Saturn would occur in the time of the man-god Octavius Augustus. The awaited time is the time in which Romans of Virgil's lifetime live; the Promised Land is the Roman Empire. So the pinnacle of the poet's career is masterful propaganda for the emperor—political purpose informing personal art. The Aeneid *would be at the same time the most enduring monument to the poet's ambition and to the emperor's visionary genius. So, at least, it would seem on the surface.)*

AUGUSTUS: You've seen the new statue of us as a god?

(Virgil, overcome with a vision of his tragic place in history, nods.)

AUGUSTUS: Well, we can hardly lug that statue all over the Empire or make sure that every single household has its own.

VIRGIL: But you've introduced a standardized coinage and placed your bust on every coin.

AUGUSTUS: You got that right, but there's not enough room on a coin for enough words to get the job done. But I can publish your poem and get it read in every provincial court from Paris to Palmyra. You get the picture? By the way, Romans we have special affection for—don't forget to make sure they're mentioned, too, okay?

VIRGIL: Okay. Great. I got that too.

(Setting the Aeneid *at the foundation of Rome, Virgil names Rome's "favorite families" by describing their ancestors' participating in the naval race or the funeral games for Anchises so that contemporary readers could say: "Hey that's my ancestor! I knew my family was ancient and noble! We've come from pilgrim stock!"*

Finally, Augustus reaches the end of his cigar, and, exhausted from his notes, dismisses the nearly wilted court poet.

Passing by the porticoes of the Vestal Virgins, Virgil can't understand why he's downhearted. Everybody will read my poem. It might even appear in The Classical Roman Reader*! Then he turns the corner, spies the statues of the Muses, and remembers why he's depressed: What about me? What about the development of my great poetic vision? What about my "individual genius"?)*

As the introduction to the *Aeneid* excerpt (page 100) explains, Rome's greatest poet ultimately managed to find a way of serving both the emperor's dictated vision and his own inspired talent. He shaped the *Aeneid* into a monument of narrative irony. The epic's surface professes the "party line"; its subtext reflects its author's grave doubts about the emperor's ability to hold together the illusion of order. Why does the golden bough hesitate before it allows Aeneas to pluck it from its tree? Why do we sympathize more with Carthaginian Dido than the pious Aeneas, who abandons her to seek the walls of Rome? Why, when Aeneas is given a mighty shield to bear into battle against the Italic tribes, does he recognize nothing of his future (imperial Rome's past) embla-

Entrance to Hadrian's Neapolis ("New City"), Italica, Spain

zoned upon its surface? Why does our hero emerge from the underworld through the gate of false dreams, illusions, and shadows? Why does the epic, considered the most objective and universal of all modes of poetic expression, begin with those paradoxical words: *Arma virumque cano,* "Arms and the man *I* sing," with the poet inserting himself into the imperial narrative?

Virgil found a way to communicate—to those who would understand him in the future—the pressures he faced in the present, and the tragic irony accompanying Roman greatness.

- **Irony.** From the double meanings rampant in the plays of Plautus to the underlying sadness of the *Aeneid,* the Romans were masters of irony, that art of sending two signals on a single message. Beneath the polished, uniform surface, we catch glimpses of the rough and secret threads that undermine the official pattern, someday perhaps to dominate the tapestry of Empire.

PART I

Early Rome

(509–65 B.C.)

(TITUS MACCIUS) PLAUTUS (C. 254–184 B.C.)

The Rope

*T*he greatest, and earliest, surviving Latin comic playwright, Plautus was as powerful in his impact on Latin culture as William Shakespeare was on English—and as mysterious in his private life. It's widely agreed that Plautus was born into humble circumstances in Sarsina, in northern Umbria, and found his way to Rome where he worked as a stagehand in the theater. Forced by near-bankruptcy to work in a baker's mill, he began writing plays in his middle age, finding his forte in adapting Greek comedies for the entertainment of increasingly loyal audiences, both commoners and aristocrats. Twenty-one of the 130 plays originally credited to him, modeled on Menander, Philemon, and Diphilus, survive today based on texts used by actors.

- The plays include:

  - *The Amphitruo,* a burlesque of Jupiter's seduction of Alcmena;
  - *The Pot of Gold (Aulularia),* from Menander's story of an old man who discovers a treasure;
  - *The Twin Menaechmi,* its plot based on the confusion between identical twins;
  - *The Prisoners of War (Captivi),* in which master and slave change places to win back the hero's son from captivity.

- Playwrights as distinguished as Ludovico Ariosto, John Dryden, Gotthold Lessing, Molière, Cole Porter, William Shakespeare, and Bernard Shaw stole freely from Plautus—as freely as he stole from the Greeks. Echoes of Plautus' *Boastful Soldier (Miles gloriosus)* can be heard in *A Funny Thing Happened on the Way to the Forum.* Plautus is the source of such familiar phrases as:

  "A friend in need is a friend indeed."
  "What's yours is mine, what's mine is yours."

Theater tickets, from Pompeii

"Practice what you preach."
"Fish and guests get stale in three days."

- Unlike Terence, who was known for his perfect plotting and realistic naturalism, Plautus' focus was on the *scene,* and upon the fantastic. Into each scene he pours his entire repertoire of farcical inventiveness and dramatic device, with little regard to its relationship to the rest of the story. In all particulars Plautus refused to be hobbled by consistency. The erratic quality of his structure, characterization, and language provides one of the most involving attractions of his work.
- Plautus employed three kinds of dialogue:

  - ordinary conversational prose, called *senarii,* unaccompanied by music;
  - long verse, accompanied by a reed pipe or flute; and
  - *canticum,* sung verse with elaborately imaginative lyrics.

Regardless of which mode he was employing at the time, his language is vivid, colloquial, obscene, perfectly suited to the speaker's character, and unerringly witty. Cicero admired Plautus' command of Latin, and credited him with developing its literary richness.

- Adapted from Diphilus, *The Rope (Rudens)* tells the story of a free-born heroine rescued from shipwreck by a villainous pimp. The salvage of her trinkets lead to her recognition by her father as his long-lost daughter. The play is typical of Plautus, taking comically anachronistic liberties with his Greek model, pushing action to the edge of slapstick and beyond, and unabashedly exploiting to the fullest Latin's potential for bombastic wordplay and startling and appropriate neologisms. Plautus replaced much of the dialogue he found in his models with song, creating a characteristic Roman theater that is the predecessor of comic opera and this century's "musical comedy."

CHARACTERS IN THE PLAY

ARCTURUS, *prologue, "Warder of the Bear"*

SCEPARNIO, *slave of Daemones, "Ax"*

PLESIDIPPUS, *a young man, in love with Palaestra*

DAEMONES, *an old man, from Athens, driven by fortune to live near Cyrene, in Africa*

PALAESTRA, *a young woman, daughter of Daemones, but kidnapped when a child; now owned by Labrax, "Sport"*

AMPELISCA, *a young woman in the possession of Labrax, "Vinette"*

PTOLEMOCRATIA, *elderly priestess of Venus*

FISHERMEN, *poor men from Cyrene who make a meager living by fishing along the shore*

TRACHALIO, *slave of Plesidippus, "Bull-necked"*

LABRAX, *pander and slave dealer, "Bass" (a voracious fish)*

CHARMIDES, *an old man, friend of Labrax*

SLAVES, *belonging to Daemones*

GRIPUS, *fisherman, and slave of Daemones, "Fisher"*

The *characters* are listed in the order of their appearance in the play, according to the Latin custom.

The scene is laid near Cyrene, in northern Africa, and remains the same throughout the play.

Prologue

ARCTURUS: Compatriot am I, from the realms of the immortals, of him who shakes all lands and seas. I am, as you may see, a gleaming constellation bright; and ever in due season I rise. Arcturus am I called, both here and in heaven, and fair I shine at night among the gods; by day I pass the time with mortals, I and other stars that make their way to earth. Our supreme commander, Jove, stations us about the world, to note the ways and deeds of men, their faith, their reverence, to give them aid. Whoever falsely swears, to win his suit, or forswears his obligations, his name is entered forthwith in Jove's book of accounts. And however great his perjured gains, the judge on high reopens the case, and reverses; and soon he loses more than in the courts of men he falsely made. And Jove knows each day whose heart desires the evil course. But virtue finds its name in another column entered. And the evil wretch who hopes by gift and victim to appease the god has his toil for his pains. For Jove cares naught for the perjured offering; while he who keeps faith will ever find leniency from him. One word of advice then, to those who know yourselves good, who keep faith with men and show reverence to the gods: stand steadfast, that hereafter you may reap due reward.

Now hear the reason why I've come. It was the poet's will that the town here by Cyrene; and here too, in a house on a farm hard by the sea, dwells Daemones, an old man far from his native Athens, whose exile here was through no fault of his, for his life was blameless. Rather does he suffer the penalty of a kindly heart, his property lost in the service of his friends. He had a daughter once, but the wretch who stole her, a mere child, sold her to a vile pander, who hither brought her. And now a youth from Athens, sojourning here, seeing her as she returned home from her music school, fell in love with her, approached her master, and for thirty minas bought her. And straightway he made ample deposit upon the purchase and bound the pander by an oath to complete the transfer. But that vile fellow, as one might know, cared nothing for plighted word or oath.

It chanced a friend of his from Sicily, old, vicious, a man who well his own country might betray, was visiting him. He praised the girl's beauty, and likewise that of the other women in the pander's train, and urged to take them all to Sicily, where, thus he declared, men were so given to pleasure that such trade as his would reap great profit. He gained his point. A ship was chartered and all the pander had was secretly placed by night upon it. To the youth who had bought the girl, he told of a vow to Venus (note here her shrine) and bid him to a breakfast here; then clapped sail upon his ship, and cleared the harbor with his women, leaving it to others to let the youth know what had befallen. Who, seeking him at the port, found the ship far out at sea.

Now I, when I saw the maiden's plight, thus stolen, brought aid to her, but ruin to the pander. With wintry blast I raged, and roughened all the surface of the sea. For know that I am Arcturus, of all the constellations none more fierce, whether at the rising, or when, at my course's end, in storm I hide my light. Look you now, both pander and his Sicilian friend cast forth upon the rocks, shipwrecked. But the young girl and a little maid, her friend, all trembling have leaped from the waves into a tiny boat, and the flood bears them landward from the rocks, toward this very cottage, where dwells the old man from Athens; his cottage too, and roof have suffered from the storm. The slave who now comes out is his slave, and soon you shall see with your own eyes the youth who bought the girl. Farewell now, and may your enemies give way before you.

[Act One: Scene 1]

(SCENE: *A road, leading from Cyrene and its harbor, on the right, to the sea-shore, on the left. In the near background is a small area, raised slightly above the shoreline, with a small temple of Venus facing it diagonally, on the right, and the cottage of* DAEMONES, *in a corresponding position, on the left. Between the two buildings, in the center, there is a clear glimpse of the sky line above the sea, extending half the width of the stage; the altar in front of the temple shows against the skyline. At the left front, flanking the side of the cottage, is thick foliage, including bulrushes; the temple, on the other side, is correspondingly flanked by rocks. It is thus possible for persons at the opposite sides of the stage to be visible to the audience, and yet be out of sight of each other, and of the area proper. It is a clear morning after a hard storm, and* SCEPARNIO *comes out of the cottage, carrying a spade, ready to begin the work of the day.*)

SCEPARNIO: Ye gods! What a storm on the sea last night! And how the winds raised the roof! In fact, it was no mere wind, but what Euripides sent to Alcmene; for see how all the tiles are loose or gone: the storm has made windows to let in light!

[Act One: Scene 2]

(*Enter, from the right,* PLESIDIPPUS *with three friends.*)

PLESIDIPPUS: I have brought you from your affairs, and yet have failed in what I sought: the procurer we couldn't catch at the harbor. But I could not bear to lose my hopes through lack of effort, and so have kept you with me all this while. I want now to visit this shrine of Venus, where he said he had a vow to pay.

SCEPARNIO: If I'm wise, I'll be getting this confounded clay dug.

PLESIDIPPUS: Somebody's talking here.

(*Enter* DAEMONES, *from cottage.*)

DAEMONES: Hello, Sceparnio!

SCEPARNIO: Who's calling?

DAEMONES: The man who paid for you.

SCEPARNIO: Hm! You'll be calling me your slave next, Daemones.

DAEMONES: Well, we shall need a lot of clay, so dig the earth up thoroughly. I see the whole house will have to be patched over . . . hm! "whole" is good; it's all holes.

PLESIDIPPUS (*advancing*): Good morning, good father—and to both of you.

DAEMONES: Good morning, sir.

SCEPARNIO: I say, are you a man or a woman, to be calling him father?

PLESIDIPPUS: Why, I am a man.

SCEPARNIO: Then go look for another father.

DAEMONES: I did have a daughter once, you see, but I lost her when she was young; I never had a son.

PLESIDIPPUS: But the gods will surely give you—

SCEPARNIO (*interrupting, to* PLESIDIPPUS): Well, if you ask me, they'll surely give *you* the devil for coming here, whoever you are, to trouble those who've got troubles of their own.

PLESIDIPPUS: Do you live here?

SCEPARNIO: What do you want to know for? Looking up places to rob?

PLESIDIPPUS: That slave of yours must be a privileged character, to talk so much in the presence of his master, and to address a gentleman so uncivilly.

SCEPARNIO: And you must be a bold, nervy fellow, to be butting into other people's houses, where no one owes you anything.

DAEMONES: Keep quiet, Sceparnio. What is it you wish, young man?

PLESIDIPPUS: Well first, a curse on this fellow for not letting his master get in a word first. But, if it is not too much trouble, I should like to ask you a few questions.

DAEMONES: Certainly, although you find me in the midst of work.

SCEPARNIO: Say, why don't you go down to the marsh instead, while the weather's clear, and cut reeds to thatch the house?

DAEMONES: Be quiet. (*to* PLESIDIPPUS) If I can be of assistance, let me know.

PLESIDIPPUS: Please tell me whether you have seen a rascally looking chap, with curly, gray hair, a false, fawning sort of a scoundrel.

DAEMONES: I've seen many of that breed, and it's thanks to such that I lead an unhappy life.

PLESIDIPPUS: I mean *here*—a man who was bringing two women with him to the shrine of Venus, to offer a sacrifice either yesterday or today.

DAEMONES: Emphatically not. I've seen no one sacrificing here for several days, and it would be impossible to do so without my knowledge. For they are always asking at the house for water, or coals, or a knife, or a spit, or a dish, or something—in fact one would think my utensils and well belonged to Venus and not to me.

PLESIDIPPUS: You pronounce death sentence upon me by those words.

DAEMONES: Not I, sir: you may live as long and happily as you wish, as far as I am concerned.

SCEPARNIO: I say, you, who make the rounds of the temples to get your belly full, why don't you have your meals served at home?

DAEMONES: Perhaps you've been invited here to a breakfast, and he who invited you hasn't come?

PLESIDIPPUS: Exactly.

SCEPARNIO: There's no harm, then, in your going home without breakfast. You ought to pray to Ceres rather than to Venus; for she gives you grub, and Venus only love.

PLESIDIPPUS *(to his friends)*: That scoundrel, Labrax, has fooled me shamefully.

DAEMONES: By the gods! Sceparnio, what's that down by the shore?

SCEPARNIO: That's a party invited to a farewell breakfast, I should say.

DAEMONES: How so?

SCEPARNIO: Because they took their bath after dinner yesterday, a sea-bath that is, and so are ready for lunch today.

DAEMONES: Their ship has been wrecked on the sea.

SCEPARNIO: That's true; but so has our house been wrecked on land, by Jove, and the roof too.

DAEMONES: Ah, poor creatures! See how they swim from the wreck!

PLESIDIPPUS: Where are they, pray?

DAEMONES: Off here to the right, along the shore.

PLESIDIPPUS: I see. *(to his friends)* Come on. I hope the man we're looking for is there, curse him. *(to the others)* And you, farewell.

(Exeunt PLESIDIPPUS *and friends, to the right.)*

SCEPARNIO: We can fare well without any help from you. But holy Palaemon, partner of Neptune and Hercules, what a sight!

DAEMONES: What do you see?

SCEPARNIO: Two women sitting alone in a little skiff. How the poor things are tossed about! . . . Good! good! that's fine! The waves have driven the boat off the rocks toward the shore; a pilot couldn't have done better. I never saw the sea so high; but they're safe, if they escape the breakers. . . . Now, now's the danger. One of them is overboard, but she's in shallow water, and will easily get out. Oh, great! Did you see how the waves washed her out? But she's up and coming this way. It's all right now. But the other has jumped from the boat. She's so frightened, she's down on her knees in the waves. No, she's safe now, and out of the water. There, she is safe on the shore. . . . But she's turning now toward the right, to sure death. Oh, she'll be lost there.

DAEMONES: Well, that's no concern of yours.

SCEPARNIO: If she falls down on those rocks where she's headed, it will be the last of her wanderings.

DAEMONES: See here, Sceparnio, if you're going to have your dinner at their expense this evening, it's all right to worry about them; but if you eat here, I want you to get to work.

SCEPARNIO: All right; that's a fair demand.

DAEMONES: Follow me then.

SCEPARNIO: I'm coming. (*Exeunt* DAEMONES *and* SCEPARNIO *into cottage.*)

[Act One: Scene 3]
(*Enter* PALAESTRA, *by the road from the left. She is wet and exhausted, after having been shipwrecked, and unable to go farther, stops at the extreme left of stage, out of sight of the temple area. She sings plaintively.*)

PALAESTRA: Ah, how much more bitter is life than the tales men weave about it. And here am *I*, left like this *(looks at her dress)*, in terror, cast upon an unknown shore, at the will of heaven. Was it for this I was born? Is this the reward of a life without offense? If in piety to parents or to gods I have been lacking, this would be no injustice. But if exactly in this I have been most careful, then you are wrong, immortals, and most unfair. For how will you repay hereafter the impious, if so you honor the innocent? I should not feel so sorry for myself, if either my parents or I were to blame. But it's my vile master, and his impiety, that have got me into this trouble. Well, he has lost everything, his ship included; I am the last remains of his fortune. She who was with me on the boat is gone; I am alone. If only she were left, it would not be so hard. Where shall I turn for help? Alone, by lonely sea and rocks, meeting no one, what I wear my only fortune; no roof, no food, why should I hope to live? Will there be no one who lives nearby to show me a road or pathway out, to relieve me from my uncertainties? Cold, and fear, and all distractions overwhelm me. My poor parents, you know not how wretched is your daughter—in vain born free; for how am I other than slave, or of what help have I ever been to you? (*She sinks down exhausted.*)

[Act One: Scene 4]
(*Enter, from the right,* AMPELISCA, *in the same state of exhaustion as* PALAESTRA. *She has climbed the bluff on the other side of the temple, and stops before catching sight of the area.*)

AMPELISCA: What better can I do than end it all with death? So wretched I am, so consumed by anxiety! I care no longer to live; I have no hope. All the shore along I have searched, and the undergrowth; calling, looking, listening; but no trace of her. And there is none to ask, and I know not where to turn. There never was desert so deserted as this spot. And yet, if she lives, while I live, I shall never stop until I find her.

PALAESTRA (*rising*): Whose voice is that so near? I am afraid.

AMPELISCA: Who's speaking there?

PALAESTRA: Oh, dear hope, do not forsake me.

AMPELISCA: Away from me, fear!

PALAESTRA: It's surely a woman's voice.

AMPELISCA: It's a woman; it's a woman speaking.

PALAESTRA: Can it be Ampelisca?

AMPELISCA: Oh, is it you, Palaestra?

PALAESTRA: Why don't I call out her name? *(She calls.)* Ampelisca!

AMPELISCA: Who is it?

PALAESTRA: It's I, Palaestra.

AMPELISCA: Oh, where are you?

PALAESTRA: Alas, I am in deep trouble.

AMPELISCA: In that I am with you, but I long to see you.

PALAESTRA: That is my one wish too.

AMPELISCA: Then let our voices lead our steps. . . . Now where are you?

PALAESTRA: Here; come over to me.

AMPELISCA: How eagerly I come. *(Crosses quickly over to* PALAESTRA.*)*

PALAESTRA *(almost too overcome to stand)*: Your hand!

AMPELISCA: Take it.

PALAESTRA: Tell me; is it you, and alive?

AMPELISCA: At last I have the will to live, now that I can hold you—or do I hold you? Take me to your arms. My only hope for life is the comfort you give me.

PALAESTRA: How quick you are to outstrip me; your words speak all my thought. Now we have only to leave this place.

AMPELISCA: But how? By what path?

PALAESTRA: We'll follow the shore.

AMPELISCA: I'll follow you anywhere. Shall we go as we are, with our clothing drenched?

PALAESTRA: We shall endure what we must. But do see there, my dear Ampelisca!

AMPELISCA: What?

PALAESTRA: Don't you see the shrine?

AMPELISCA: Where?

PALAESTRA: Back, to the right.

AMPELISCA: I see—a place worthy of the gods.

PALAESTRA: Some one must live near by; it's such a charming spot. *(They advance supplicatingly to the altar, by which they kneel.)* To this divinity, whoever he be, I pray for help from their troubles, for two poor women in want and despair.

[Act One: Scene 5]
(Enter PTOLEMOCRATIA, *aged priestess of Venus, from temple.)*

PTOLEMOCRATIA: Who asks a boon here of my patron goddess? I heard the voice of supplication. They entreat a patron kind and indulgent, who does not grudge her favors.

PALAESTRA: We give you greetings, mother.

PTOLEMOCRATIA: My greetings to you, maidens; and whence come ye in your dripping weeds, so dismally clad?

PALAESTRA: From the sea nearby; but far away is the port from which we sailed.

PTOLEMOCRATIA: You journeyed then over the darkling paths of ocean on the sea-swung wooden steed?

PALAESTRA: Yes, mother.

PTOLEMOCRATIA: It is scarce seemly to approach the shrine as you are, without white garments or victims.

PALAESTRA: I pray you, where should we, but lately cast up from the sea, find victims? *(They embrace the priestess' knees.)* Behold, we who clasp your knees are strangers in an unknown land, hopeless, and in want; we pray for protection and shelter. Take pity on those who need it; we have lost our all, our goods, our homes, our hope even.

PTOLEMOCRATIA: Do not kneel; give me your hands. No one ever had a heart more compassionate than mine. But you will find me poor. My service of Venus here does not give me enough to support life.

AMPELISCA: This is a shrine of Venus, then?

PTOLEMOCRATIA: It is, and I am her priestess. But all I have is at your service. Come with me.

PALAESTRA: You honor us most generously, mother.

PTOLEMOCRATIA: It is my duty. *(Exeunt all into temple.)* . . .

[Act Two: Scene 3]
(Enter AMPELISCA; *she talks back into the temple.)*

AMPELISCA: Yes, I understand—to knock at the cottage next door and ask for water.

TRACHALIO: Now whose voice is that?

AMPELISCA: Who's that man talking there?

TRACHALIO: Is that Ampelisca coming out of the temple?

AMPELISCA: Why, that's surely Plesidippus' man, Trachalio.

TRACHALIO: It is.

AMPELISCA: Of course it is; welcome Trachalio.

TRACHALIO: Well, well, Ampelisca, what are you doing here?

AMPELISCA: I'm passing most unhappily what should be my time of happiness.

TRACHALIO: Don't say that; it will bring bad luck.

AMPELISCA: If we are wise, we admit the truth. But tell me please, where is your master, Plesidippus?

TRACHALIO: As if he were not there with you!

AMPELISCA: Faith, he is not; he hasn't been here.

TRACHALIO: He hasn't?

AMPELISCA: It's the truth you're speaking.

TRACHALIO: That wouldn't be like me, would it, Ampelisca? But I say, when will the breakfast be ready?

AMPELISCA: What breakfast, pray?

TRACHALIO: Aren't you sacrificing here?

AMPELISCA: You're dreaming.

TRACHALIO: Your master, Labrax, certainly invited my master, Plesidippus, to sacrifice and breakfast.

AMPELISCA: Now, isn't that like him? To cheat both gods and men is in his line of business.

TRACHALIO: Neither you nor your master is sacrificing here?

AMPELISCA: Right you are!

TRACHALIO: Then what are you doing here?

AMPELISCA: We have suffered many misfortunes and have been in great danger and fear of our lives, and in our need we were welcomed by the priestess, Palaestra and I.

TRACHALIO: Is Palaestra here, the girl my master loves?

AMPELISCA: Certainly.

TRACHALIO: Oh, that's good news; my dear Ampelisca, that's splendid. But tell me about your hard luck.

AMPELISCA: Our ship was wrecked by the storm last night, Trachalio.

TRACHALIO: What ship? What are you talking about?

AMPELISCA: Haven't you heard how Labrax tried to carry us off secretly to Sicily, along with all his property? And now he's lost everything.

TRACHALIO: Good boy, Neptune! I always said you were a fine dicer; that was a master throw; you've dished the procurer. But where is he?

AMPELISCA: Dead drunk, I think. Too many drinks of sea water last night.

TRACHALIO: Well, he didn't choose the drink, if there was water in it. Ampelisca, your words are a real treat; what a dear you are! But how did you and Palaestra escape?

AMPELISCA: I'll tell you. Although we were terribly afraid, we jumped into the little lifeboat, when we saw the ship making for the rocks, and quickly untied the rope; the men were too frightened to do anything. The storm drove our boat off here to the right. We pitched about in a rough sea all night, in the greatest distress, until the wind at last drove us ashore; we were nearly dead, I can tell you.

TRACHALIO: I know; that's the way of the old sea dog; Neptune is some market inspector, when he gets started—he throws out any goods he doesn't like.

AMPELISCA: Go on now; don't be impudent.

TRACHALIO: Apply that to yourself, please. I told you so! I knew the slave dealer would be acting that way. I think I'll let my hair grow, and set up for a prophet.

AMPELISCA: Well, if you knew so much, why didn't you and your master prevent his getting away?

TRACHALIO: What should he have done?

AMPELISCA: What should he have done? He should have been on the watch day and night. But on my word, I think his care was the exact measure of his regard for her.

TRACHALIO: What do you mean?

AMPELISCA: It's clear enough.

TRACHALIO: See here, Ampelisca; when a man goes to the bathhouse, no matter how sharply he watches out, he sometimes loses his clothing. It's hard to catch the thief when you don't know whom to suspect. But take me to her.

AMPELISCA: Just go into the temple; you'll find her sitting by the statue of Venus, in tears.

TRACHALIO: Oh, that's too bad; what is she crying for?

AMPELISCA: I'll tell you. She had a little casket containing the tokens of identification by which she hoped sometime to find her father. The procurer had taken this from her, and now she's afraid it's lost; that's why she is so distressed.

TRACHALIO: Where was the casket?

AMPELISCA: On the ship with him; he had locked it away in his luggage, just to make sure she shouldn't find her father.

TRACHALIO: What a scurvy trick, to try to keep in slavery a girl who by rights should be free.

AMPELISCA: And now it's gone to the bottom, along with all his gold and silver.

TRACHALIO: Some one has probably gone in by this time and got it.

AMPELISCA: That's why she's so sad; it's the loss of her tokens.

TRACHALIO: All the more reason for my consoling her. She shouldn't distress herself so; things are always happening to people beyond their expectations.

AMPELISCA: And on the other hand, so many people indulge in false hopes.

TRACHALIO: The more need then of keeping up your spirits in the face of troubles. I'll go in, unless you've something else in mind.

AMPELISCA: Go; I'll meanwhile get the water from the house here, as the priestess wished. (*Exit* TRACHALIO *into temple.*) . . .

[Act Two: Scene 6]
(*Enter, from the left,* LABRAX, *followed by* CHARMIDES, *wet and shivering.*)

LABRAX: If you want to be a beggar and down on your luck, just trust yourself to Neptune; after a mixup with him you will look like this. (*Looks at his clothing.*) By Jove, Liberty, you were a bright lass, never to set foot on ship with your pal, Hercules. But where's that friend of mine who played the devil with me so? Here he comes.

CHARMIDES: Where in the deuce are you going in such a hurry, Labrax? This pace is too swift for me.

LABRAX: I wish you'd been hanged in Sicily before I ever set eyes on you. All this trouble comes from you.

CHARMIDES: I wish the day you were bringing me to your house, I had slept in jail instead. I hope to heaven that after this, all your guests will be like yourself; it's no place for an honest man.

LABRAX: It was Bad Luck I had for a guest, when you came. I was a cursed fool when I listened to you. Why did we go away, or get on the ship, where I lost all I had—and more, too?

CHARMIDES: Any ship would sink that carried a rogue like you, and your rogue's fortune.

LABRAX: You got me in bad with your flatteries.

CHARMIDES: That last dinner I had with you was worse than the one served up to Thyestes.

LABRAX (*coughing*): I feel sick myself; hold my head, will you?

CHARMIDES: I hope you'll cough your lungs up.

LABRAX: O Palaestra, Ampelisca, where are you?

CHARMIDES: They're food for the fishes at the present moment.

LABRAX: It's your fault I'm a beggar; it's all from listening to you and your big lies.

CHARMIDES: On the contrary, it's due entirely to me that a man as insipid as you has had a little salt put in him.

LABRAX: Will you get to hell out of here?

CHARMIDES: I'll just return that advice; go to the devil yourself.

LABRAX: Was there ever a man had worse luck than I?

CHARMIDES: I have; much worse.

LABRAX: How do you make that out?

CHARMIDES: Because you deserve it, and I do not.

LABRAX (*going up to bulrushes growing near*): O enviable, water-shedding bulrush, I would I were as dry as you!

CHARMIDES (*his teeth chattering*): Brr! I'm trembling for a skirmish; even my words are jumping about.

LABRAX: Yes, confound it, Neptune does run a cold bathhouse. With all my clothes on I'm cold.

CHARMIDES: He doesn't even serve hot drinks when you go out; nothing but ice water.

LABRAX: Lucky fellows, these blacksmiths; they've always got a fire.

CHARMIDES: Well, I'd like to be a duck myself, so as to be dry after coming out of the water.

LABRAX: I think I'll go to the country fairs and hire out as an ogre.

CHARMIDES: Why so?

LABRAX: Because I'd need no hinge to work my jaws; my chattering teeth would do it.

CHARMIDES: Do you know, I deserved to be cleaned out in this deal.

LABRAX: Why?

CHARMIDES: For daring to get into a boat with a Jonah like you; you're enough to stir up any sea.

LABRAX: It all came from listening to you. Didn't you promise me that a man could pile up wealth there in my business?

CHARMIDES: Did you expect, like a greedy shark, to swallow up the whole island of Sicily?

LABRAX: Well, I'd like to know what shark swallowed up my hamper, with all my gold and silver stored away in it.

CHARMIDES: Probably the same one that got mine, with a purse full of money.

LABRAX: All I've got left is this one shirt and cloak. Oh, me!

CHARMIDES: Well, I'm your partner in that, on even shares.

LABRAX: If I could at least have saved my girls, there'd be some hope. If I ever meet that chap Plesidippus, who gave me part payment for Palaestra, I'll catch it. Oh-h-h!

CHARMIDES: What are you crying about? As long as you've a tongue in your head, you'll never get caught. . . .

(QUINTUS) ENNIUS (239–169 B.C.)

Annals

*O*nly fragments survive of Rome's first major literary figure, the tragic and epic poet Quintus Ennius, known as "the Roman Homer." Born in Rudiae (near modern Brindisi, in Magna Graecia, now Calabria), Ennius was educated in Tarentum in Greek, Oscan, and Latin—his "three hearts." The elder Cato found him writing poetry in the centurions' barracks on Sardinia during the second Punic War and brought him to Rome in 204 B.C. There he worked as a translator, teacher, and playwright, moving in patrician circles despite his life-long poverty, and finally achieving Roman citizenship thanks to the patronage of the consul Fulvius Nobilior and his son.

- Ennius was truly the "father of Roman poetry," in nearly all its aspects:

  - developing the genres pursued by his successors: lyric, epic, tragedy, and comedy;
  - introducing reverence for classic Greek authorities and ancient traditions that shaped Roman literature for the next three hundred years;
  - exemplifying the tone of rhetorical and moral "high seriousness," what the Greek Longinus called "the sublime," which served as model to writers as diverse as Virgil, Tacitus, and Cicero.

- We know the names of twenty plays by Ennius, though only fragments of them survive to show his moral grandeur and brilliant powers of description and rhetoric. The majority of them based on Euripides, they include the *Achilles, Ajax, Alexander, Eumenides,* and *Phoenix.* Ennius also wrote:

  - comedies, with less success;
  - fables;
  - satires, in various meters;
  - a poem in honor of Scipio Africanus;
  - didactic verse on gastronomy *(The Hedyphagetica)*; natural philosophy *(Epicharmus)* influenced by Pythagoras and mythology;
  - and verse epigrams and epitaphs.

- Although Ennius believed he was the reincarnation of Homer, his epic *Annals*—eighteen books of dactylic hexameters composed in his old age to celebrate Rome's early history and legends—hardly equals the *Iliad* and *Odyssey*. Yet it is a major event in Roman literature. Ennius manages to translate Greek quantitative verse into accentual Latin with great dignity and conviction, adding Roman rhetorical devices like alliteration and assonance to Greek simile and Homer's heroic tone.
- Though it was highly regarded in its time for its magnificently patriotic recapitulation of history from the time of Aeneas to Ennius' own time and its reverent insistence on Rome's manifest destiny, the poem has a relentless chronological structure, following stylistic patterns set down by Livius Andronicus, and its lack of a central hero weakens the narrative and prepares the vacuum for Virgil's brilliant *Aeneid* to replace the *Annals* as the true Roman national epic.
- Despite his flaws, Ennius was popular in his own day and reigned without rival over Roman letters for nearly a century. His importation of Greek influence and versatility from one genre to another influenced Lucretius, Seneca, Terence, Virgil, Cicero, as well as other writers of the first-century B.C. Golden Age.

Like a shower of rain
The weapons on the tribune:

They pierce his shield.
The boss is ringing with spears;
From his helmet glances a shrill sound!

Not one of all the adversaries
Can cut down his body
With the gleaming sword.

Always he shatters or strikes
Down the abundant spears.
Sweat bathes his whole body;

He labors greatly
He cannot breathe.

(MARCUS PORCIUS) CATO THE ELDER (234–149 B.C.)

On Farm Management

*T*he earliest surviving complete Latin prose came from the pen of a peasant-born northern Italian whose stern and puritanical upbringing in the countryside near his birthplace in Tusculum shaped his harshly self-disciplined and demanding character. At the age of seventeen, he turned his back on the grueling work in the fields of his small Sabine farm for a military career under Fabius Maximus in the Punic Wars against Hannibal in Sicily, Italy, and Africa. In addition to his military success, Cato was a redoubtable businessman; distinguished orator; politician with the offices of praetor, quaestor, consul, and aedile; and prolific writer. The inflexible severity but unimpeachable integrity with which he discharged his duties as censor earned him the epithet *"Cato Censorius,"* "Cato the Censor." Contentious throughout his career, he was the defendant in dozens of law suits and indictments, though always acquitted; and the plaintiff in even more. He was instrumental in preventing the repeal of the *Lex Oppia,* the Oppian Law that restricted female extravagance; and in passing the *Lex Voconia,* in 169 B.C., which checked the financial freedom of women.

Though he eventually learned Greek from the poet Ennius, whom he imported from Sardinia to Rome, Cato despised the Greek influence on Roman culture as tantamount to decadence. He was a leading opponent of his former military commander the Grecophile Scipio Africanus; and his outrage at the economic and military recovery of Carthage after its two previous wars with Rome was a chief cause of the Third Punic War. "Carthage must be destroyed," he proclaimed.

- Cato was the first Roman to transcribe and publish his speeches, of which Cicero knew 150; fragments of 80 orations by Cato survive to this day. His other writings included letters to his son; an "early history" of Rome *(Origines)*; and manuals on law, rhetoric, military science and discipline, and medicine.
- Only Cato's *On Agriculture* survives, a comprehensive capitalistic farmer's almanac in 162 chapters dealing with horticulture, wine-making recipes, and stock-keeping; but also with religious observances, superstitions, rules of domestic behavior, and cures.

The pursuits of commerce would be as admirable as they are profitable if they were not subject to so great risks: and so, likewise, of banking, if it were always honestly conducted. For our ancestors considered, and so ordained in their laws, that, while the thief should be cast in double damages, the usurer should make four-fold restitution. From this we may judge how much less desirable a citizen they esteemed the banker than the thief. When they sought to commend an honest man, they termed him good husbandman, good farmer. This they rated the superlative of praise. Personally, I think highly of a man actively and diligently engaged in commerce, who seeks thereby to make his fortune, yet, as I have said, his career is full of risks and pitfalls. But it is from the tillers of the soil that spring the best citizens, the stanchest soldiers; and theirs are the enduring rewards which are most grateful and least envied. Such as devote themselves to that pursuit are least of all men given to evil counsels.

And now, to get to my subject, these observations will serve as preface to what I have promised to discuss.

When you have decided to purchase a farm, be careful not to buy rashly; do not spare your visits and be not content with a single tour of inspection. The more you go, the more will the place please you, if it be worth your attention. Give heed to the appearance of the neighborhood,—a flourishing country should show its prosperity. "When you go in, look about, so that, when needs be, you can find your way out."

Take care that you choose a good climate, not subject to destructive storms, and a soil that is naturally strong. If possible, your farm should be at the foot of a mountain, looking to the South, in a healthy situation, where labor and cattle can be had, well watered, near a good sized town, and either on the sea or a navigable river, or else on a good and much frequented road. Choose a place which has not often changed ownership, one which is sold unwillingly, that has buildings in good repair.

Beware that you do not rashly contemn the experience of others. It is better to buy from a man who has farmed successfully and built well.

When you inspect the farm, look to see how many wine presses and storage vats there are; where there are none of these you can judge what the harvest is. On the other hand, it is not the number of farming implements, but what is done with them, that counts. Where you find few tools, it is not an expensive farm to operate. Know that with a farm, as with a man, however productive it may be, if it has the spending habit, not much will be left over.

When you have arrived at your country house and have saluted your household, you should make the rounds of the farm the same day, if possible; if not, then certainly the next day. When you have observed how the field work has progressed, what things have been done, and what remains undone, you should summon your overseer the next day, and should call for a report of what work has been done in good season and why it has not been possible to complete the rest, and what wine and corn and other crops have been gathered. When you are advised on these points you should make your own calculation of the time necessary for the work, if there does not appear to you to have been enough accomplished. The overseer will report that he himself has worked diligently, but that some slaves have been sick and others truant, the weather has been bad, and that it has been necessary to work the public roads. When he has given these and many other excuses, you should recall to his attention the program of work which you had laid out for him on your last visit and compare it with the results attained. If the weather has been bad, count how many stormy days there have been, and rehearse what work could have been done despite the rain, such as washing and pitching the wine vats, cleaning out the barns, sorting the grain, hauling out and composting the manure, cleaning seed, mending the old gear, and making new, mending the smocks and hoods furnished for the hands. On feast days the old ditches should be mended, the public roads worked, briers cut down, the garden dug, the meadow cleaned, the hedges trimmed and the clippings collected and burned, the fish pond cleaned out. On such days, furthermore, the slave's rations should be cut down as compared with what is allowed when they are working in the fields in fine weather.

When this routine has been discussed quietly and with good humor and is thoroughly understood by the overseer, you should give orders for the completion of the work which has been neglected.

The accounts of money, supplies and provisions should then be considered. The overseer should report what wine and oil has been sold, what price he got, what is on hand, and what remains for sale. Security should be taken for such accounts as ought to be secured. All other unsettled matters should be agreed upon. If anything is needed for the coming year, it should be bought; everything which is not needed should be sold. Whatever there is for

lease should be leased. Orders should be given (and take care that they are in writing) for all work which next it is desired to have done on the farm or let to contract. You should go over the cattle and determine what is to be sold. You should sell the oil, if you can get your price, the surplus wine and corn, the old cattle, the worn out oxen, and the cull sheep, the wool and the hides, the old and sick slaves, and if anything else is superfluous you should sell that.

The appetite of the good farmer is to sell, not to buy.

Be a good neighbor. Do not roughly give offense to your own people. If the neighborhood regards you kindly, you will find a readier market for what you have to sell, you will more easily get your work done, either on the place or by contract. If you build, your neighbors will aid you with their services, their cattle and their materials. If any misfortune should overtake you (which God forbid!) they will protect you with kindly interest.

If you ask me what is the best disposition to make of your estate, I would say that should you have bought a farm of one hundred *jugera* all told, in the best situation, it should be planted as follows: 1. a vineyard, if it promises a good yield, 2. an irrigated garden, 3. an osier bed, 4. an olive yard, 5. a meadow, 6. a corn field, 7. a wood lot, 8. a cultivated orchard, and 9. a mast grove.

In his youth, the farmer ought diligently to plant his land, but he should ponder before he builds. Planting does not require reflection, but demands action. It is time enough to build when you have reached your thirty-sixth year, if you have farmed your land well meanwhile. When you do build, let your buildings be proportioned to your estate, and your estate to your buildings. It is fitting that the farm buildings should be well constructed, that you should have ample oil cellars and wine vats, and a good supply of casks, so that you can wait for high prices, something which will redound to your honor, your profit and your self-respect.

Build your dwelling house in accordance with your means. If you build well in a good situation and on good property, and furnish the house suitably for country life, you will come there more often and more willingly. The farm will then be better, fewer mistakes will be made, and you will get larger crops. The face of the master is good for the land.

Plant elm trees along the roads and fence rows, so that you may have the leaves to feed the sheep and cattle, and the timber will be available if you need it. If anywhere there are banks of streams or wet places, there plant reeds; and surround them with willows that the osiers may serve to tie the vines.

It is most convenient to set out the land nearest the house as an orchard, whence fire wood and faggots may be sold and the supply of the master obtained. In this enclosure should be planted everything fitting to the land and vines should be married to the trees.

Near the house lay out also a garden with garland flowers and vegetables of all kinds, and set it about with myrtle hedges, both white and black, as well as Delphic and Cyprian laurel.

An olive farm of two hundred and forty *jugera* ought to be stocked as follows: an overseer, a housekeeper, five laborers, three ox drivers, one swineherd, one ass driver, one shepherd; in all thirteen hands: three pair of oxen, three asses with pack saddles to haul out the manure, one other ass to turn the mill, and one hundred sheep.

These are the duties of the overseer: He should maintain discipline. He should observe the feast days. He should respect the rights of others and steadfastly uphold his own. He should settle all quarrels among the hands; if any one is at fault he should administer the punishment. He should take care that no one on the place is in want, or lacks food or drink; in this respect he can afford to be generous, for he will thus more easily prevent picking and stealing.

Unless the overseer is of evil mind, he will himself do no wrong, but if he permits wrongdoing by others, the master should not suffer such indulgence to pass with impunity. He should show appreciation of courtesy to encourage others to practice it. He should not be given to gadding or conviviality, but should be always sober. He should keep the hands busy, and should see that they do what the master has ordered. He should not think that he knows more than his master. The friends of the master should be his friends, and he should give heed to those whom the master has recommended to him. He should confine his religious practices to the cross roads altar on festival days or to his own house.

He should lend money to no man unbidden by the master, but what the master has lent he should collect. He should never lend any seed reserved for sowing, feed, corn, wine, or oil, but he should have relations with two or three other farms with which he can exchange things needed in emergency. He should state his accounts with his master frequently. He should not keep any hired men or day-hands longer than is necessary. He should not sell anything without the knowledge of the master, nor should he conceal anything from the master. He should not have any hangers-on, nor should he consult any soothsayer, fortune teller, necromancer, or astrologer. He should not spare seed in sowing, for that is bad economy. He should strive to be expert in all kinds of farm work, and, without exhausting himself, often lend a hand. By so doing, he will better understand the point of view of his hands, and they will work more contentedly; moreover, he will have less inclination to gad, his health will be better, and he will sleep more refreshingly.

First up in the morning, he should be the last to go to bed at night; and before he does, he should see that the farm gates are closed, and that each of the hands is in his own bed, that the stock have been fed. He should see that the best of care is taken of the oxen, and should pay the highest compliments to the teamsters who keep their cattle in the best condition. He should see to it that the plows and the plowshares are kept in good repair. Plan all the work in ample time, for so it is with farm work, if one thing is done late, everything will be late.

When it rains try to find something to do indoors. Clean up, rather than remain idle. Remember that while work may stop, expenses still go on.

The overseer should be responsible for the duties of the housekeeper. If the master has given her to you for a wife, you should be satisfied with her, and she should respect you. Require that she be not given to wasteful habits; that she does not gossip with the neighbors and other women. She should not receive visitors either in the kitchen or in her own quarters. She should not go out to parties, nor should she gad about. She should not practice religious observances, nor should she ask others to do so for her without the permission of the master or the mistress. Remember that the master practices religion for the entire household. She should be neat in appearance and should keep the house swept and garnished. Every night before she goes to bed she should see that the hearth is swept and clean. On the Kalends, the Ides, the Nones, and on all feast days, she should hang a garland over the hearth. On those days also she should pray fervently to the household gods. She should take care that she has food cooked for you and for the hands. She should have plenty of chickens and an abundance of eggs. She should diligently put up all kinds of preserves every year.

The following are the customary allowances for food: For the hands, four pecks of meal for the winter, and four and one-half for the summer. For the overseer, the housekeeper, the wagoner, the shepherd, three pecks each. For the slaves, four pounds of bread for the winter, but when they begin to cultivate the vines this is increased to five pounds until the figs are ripe, then return to four pounds.

The sum of the wine allowed for each hand per annum is eight quadrantals, or amphora, but add in the proportion as they do work. Ten quadrantals per annum is not too much to allow them to drink.

Save the wind fall olives as much as possible as relishes for the hands. Later set aside such of the ripe olives as will make the least oil. Be careful to make them go as far as possible. When the olives are all eaten, give them fish pickles and vinegar. One peck of salt per annum is enough for each hand.

Allow each hand a smock and a cloak every other year. As often as you give out a smock or a cloak to any one, take up the old one, so that caps can be made out of it. A pair of heavy wooden shoes should be allowed every other year.

If the land is wet, it should be drained with trough shaped ditches dug three feet wide at the surface and one foot at the bottom and four feet deep. Blind these ditches with rock. If you have no rock, then fill them with green willow poles braced crosswise. If you have no poles, fill them with faggots. Then dig lateral trenches three feet deep and four feet wide in such way that the water will flow from the trenches into the ditches.

In the winter surface water should be drained off the fields. On hillsides, courses should be kept clear for the water to flow off. During the rainy season at the beginning of Autumn is the greatest risk from water. When it begins to rain all the hands should go out with picks and shovels and clear out the drains so that the water may flow off into the roads, and the crops be protected.

What is the first principle of good agriculture? To plow well. What is the second? To plow again; and the third is to manure. When you plow corn land, plow well and in good weather, lest you turn a cloddy furrow. The other things of good agriculture are to sow seed plentifully, to thin the young sprouts, and to hill up the roots with earth.

Never plow rotten land nor drive flocks or carts across it.

If care is not taken about this, the land so abused will be barren for three years.

The flocks and herds should be well supplied with litter and their feet kept clean. If litter is short, haul in oak leaves, they will serve as bedding for sheep and cattle. Beware of scab among the sheep and cattle. This comes from hunger and exposure to rain.

To prevent the oxen from wearing down their hoofs, anoint the bottom of the hoof with liquid pepper before driving them on the highroad.

Take care that during the summer the cattle drink only sweet and fresh water. Their health depends on it.

To prevent scab among sheep, make a mixture of equal parts of well strained amurca, of water in which lupine has been steeped, and of lees of good wine. After shearing, anoint all the flock with this mixture, and let them sweat profusely for two or three days. Then dip them in the sea. If you have no sea water, make salt water and dip them in that. If you will do this they will suffer no scab, they will have more and better wool, and they will not be molested by ticks.

If an ox begins to sicken, give him without delay a raw hen's egg and make him swallow it whole. The next day make him drink from a wooden bowl a measure of wine in which has been scraped the head of an onion. Both the ox and his attendant should do these things fasting and standing upright.

If a serpent shall bite an ox, or any other quadruped, take a cup of that extract of fennel which the physicians call smyrnean, and mix it with a measure of old wine. Inject this through his nostrils, and at the same time poultice the wound with hog's dung. You can treat a man the same way.

If a bone is dislocated it can be made sound by this incantation. Take a green reed four or five feet long, cut it in the middle and let two men hold the pieces against your hips. Begin then to chant as follows:

"In Alio S. F. Motas Vaeta,
Daries Dardaries Astataries Dissunapiter."

and continue until the free ends of the reed are brought slowly together in front of you. Meanwhile wave a knife above the reeds, and when they come together and one touches the other, seize them in your hand and cut them right and left. These pieces of reed bound upon a dislocated or fractured bone will cure it.

But every day repeat the incantation, or in place of it this one:

"Huat Hanat Huat
Ista Pista Sista
Domiabo Damnaustra."

TERENCE (PUBLIUS TERENTIUS AFER) (C. 190–159 B.C.)

The Brothers

❧

*E*arly Rome's second great comic playwright was born in Carthage of Libyan parents and arrived in the capital as the slave of the senator Terentius Lucanus. Because of his dramatic talent Terence was given an education and eventually his freedom. His patrons included the Grecophiles of the "Scipionic circle": Scipio Africanus, Scipio Aemilianus, Gaius Laelius, Furius Philus, Sulpicius Gallus, Quintus Fabius Labeo, Marcus Popilius, and the comic playwright Caecilius Statius. Terence died in a shipwreck enroute back to Rome from Athens, losing with his life his translations of 108 plays by Menander.

Caesar called Terence a *dimidiate Menander,* "Menander by half," for having Menander's polish without his vivacity. Yet his impact on future literature, based on the power of his style, is considerable. His admirers, imitators, and adapters included Cicero, Horace, Caesar, Petrarch, Erasmus, Montaigne, Sainte-Beuve, and Molière.

Theater at Italica

- Terence's first play was produced by the actor Ambivius Turpio at the Ludi Megalenses in 166 B.C., at the instigation of Caecilius. All six of his plays are primarily inventive reworkings of Greek originals, most of them from the repertoire of the New Comic playwright Menander:

  - *The Maid from Andros (Andria),* where an Athenian's long-lost daughter is discovered through the intertwining of two romantic plots;
  - *The Mother-in-Law (Hecyra),* where a husband whose wife is made pregnant by a rape discovers he himself was the perpetrator and father.
  - *The Self-Tormentor (Heauton Timorumenos),* based on the contrasting lives of two fathers of opposite character;
  - *The Eunuch (Eunuchus),* two brothers' love intrigues are brought into comic focus by a braggart soldier and his sycophant;
  - *The Phormio,* a resourceful parasite assists two brothers in overcoming their father's opposition to their foreign lovers; based on a play by Apollodorus.

- Terence is more literary and self-conscious than Plautus, closer—in his delicately realistic characterization—to his model Menander than to his bawdy Roman predecessor. His verse comedies are both more sophisticated than Plautus' and, in direct result, less "comic." Where Plautus roughed up and "romanized" both his characters and settings, Terence faithfully retained the elements of the cultivated Athenian originals; and imitated the classic Attic style in his graceful, eloquent, and authentically Roman Latin.

- His greatest achievement lay in his plots, linking the causality of action to character with a precision that eluded Plautus entirely. Terence's general popularity was erratic; he was content to please the educated patricians in their salons, while outside the Roman mobs continued to prefer Plautus and circuses.

- The typical Terentian prologue deals with issues of literary criticism. The prologue of *The Brothers* alludes to charges by Terence's chauvinistic rival Luscius Lanuvinus that he'd been assisted in his writing by his friends Scipio and Laelius.

- In *The Brothers (Adelphoe),* first produced at the funeral games of Aemilius Paulus (the father of Scipio Africanus) in 160 B.C., Terence contrasts the upbringing of two brothers—one by a strict father, the other by an indulgent uncle—and examines the relative effects of each type of education on their behavior. Though he presents both sides fairly, Terence clearly favors the more tolerant approach to child-rearing, with Aeschinus appearing far the more appealing of the two brothers. The moral of the play is that imperfect fathers produce imperfect sons, and that education is only as effective as the educators are themselves free of defects. His sources were Menander's play by the same name and a play by Diphilus.

CHARACTERS

DEMEA }
MICIO } old Athenians, brothers

HEGIO, old Athenian, a relative of SOSTRATA

SOSTRATA, a widow, mother of PAMPHILA

AESCHINUS, son of DEMEA, adopted by MICIO

CTESIPHO, son of DEMEA, brother of AESCHINUS

SANNIO, a procurer, a slave-dealer in women

GETA, a slave, servant of SOSTRATA

SYRUS }
DROMO } slaves, servants of MICIO

CANTHARA, old nurse in the household of SOSTRATA

Mute Characters

PAMPHILA, a young woman loved by AESCHINUS

BACCHIS, a courtesan loved by CTESIPHO, a lute-girl

PARMENO, a slave, servant of MICIO

Act V: Scene 3
MICIO, DEMEA

DEMEA: Lord, what now? Shall I shout out my complaints?

Great heaven and earth! Great god of all the
seas!

MICIO: Oho, he's found out; that is why he's
yelling—
The case is ready; I must offer help.

DEMEA: Look at him, the corrupter of our
sons!

MICIO: Master your anger, sir; control yourself.

DEMEA: All right. I've got control. No further
outbursts.
Let's think this over. Didn't we agree
(And you proposed it) we'd not interfere
In bringing up our sons?

MICIO: I don't deny it.

DEMEA: Why is he drunk, at your house?
Why do you
Keep him—my boy!—And buy a mistress for
him?
Can't you be fair with me as I with you?
I don't bring up your son; don't bring up mine.

MICIO: That's not fair.

DEMEA: Why?

MICIO: Do you forget the
proverb,
"The truest friends share everything between
them"?

DEMEA: You're quite a wit, but it's too late for
speeches.

MICIO: Now listen, if that isn't too demanding.
First, if what's bothering you is the money
The boys spend, think of it this way, Demea:
You thought you could afford to raise the two
(Your income seemed enough then for them
both)
And in those days, you were quite certain, too
That I would marry. Well, try that again:
Save, scrimp, invest, make every cent you can
To leave to them. That way you'll earn your
glory.
Let them enjoy the windfall of my wealth.
You won't lose anything; don't be alarmed.
My contribution will be profit for you.
Just take your time and think the business
over—
You'll find you've spared us all a lot of grief.

DEMEA: Who cares about the money? It's
their morals.

MICIO: Wait. I will come to that. We all have
traits
By which our character can be assessed.
Let two do the same thing, and you may say,
"One will be harmed, the other go scot-free."
The deed's the same; only the doers differ.
The more I see, the more I trust our boys
To turn out well, for they have common sense,
Good minds, respect, and fondness for each
other.
Give them free rein—they can be checked at
will.
Are you afraid they may be lax in business?
In other matters age can make us wiser—
The single vice it brings out in all men
Is to grow keener than they should for gain.
The passing years will sharpen our lads.

DEMEA: If
Your generalities don't ruin them,
And that permissiveness.

MICIO: Be still; it won't.
Let's have no more such talk; stay here today;
Stop frowning.

DEMEA: If I must, no doubt I must.
All right, but he and I will leave at dawn
Tomorrow for the country.

MICIO: Or tonight—
Just for today, be pleasant.

DEMEA: And I'm taking
The lute-girl with me.

MICIO: You'll have won your
    fight
And won your son besides, no question
    there—
Only be sure you keep her.

DEMEA: I'll see to it;
Out there, she'll cook and grind the meal until
She's full of dust and smoke and ashes. Like-
    wise
I'll send her out to gather grain at noon,
I'll get her sunburned till she's coal-black.

MICIO: Fine!
I'd call that wise. And more: I'd force the boy
Whether he wants or not, to sleep with her.

DEMEA: You mock me. Well, I'm glad that you
    can take it
So easily. I feel—

MICIO: You've said.

DEMEA: I'm through,
    then.

MICIO: Come in; let's spend the day the way
    we should.

Scene 4
DEMEA

DEMEA: Whoever ordered life so well that
    time,
Experience, circumstance, did not change it
And teach him something? You come out not
    knowing
The things you thought you knew; what
    seemed essential
Loses importance when you test it out.
It's been that way with me, too; I'd reject
The life that I've been living all these years,
Now that it's nearly over. Why? I've learned
The hard way that there's nothing really better
For any man than easy-going kindness.
Compare my brother and me, if you need
    proof.
He's lived in leisure; loved society;
Been calm and kind; hurt no one; smiled at
    all;
Lived for himself, and spared no luxury—
Everyone loves him and speaks well of him.
But I—a farmer, rough and mean, hot-
    headed—
I married—that was misery. We had sons:
More worries. So it goes! and in my struggles
To save for them, I've ground away life.
Now that I'm old, the payment for such toil?
Hate—while he lifts no finger and is loved.

They worship him, shun me, confide in him,
Value him, spend time with him, leave me
   lonely.
They wait my death, but pray he'll live for-
   ever.
Those whom I worked to raise he's made his
   own,
And at no cost; he reaps what I have sown.
Well then, it's about-face, and see if I
Can deal in softer words and acts, so chal-
   lenged.
I want my kin to prize and cherish me.
Does that mean gifts and compliments? I'll
   show them!
What's bankruptcy to me, the elder brother?

Scene 5
SYRUS, DEMEA

SYRUS: O sir, your brother begs you not to
   leave.

DEMEA: What's that? My good man, how are
   things? How goes it?

SYRUS: Fine, sir.
                Great! *(aside)* There! three
unaccustomed phrases
Worked in: *my good man, how are things, how
goes it?*

DEMEA: Though you're a slave, there's
   nothing mean about you;
I'd like to do you a good turn.

SYRUS: Why, thanks.

DEMEA: And Syrus—
I really mean this, as you'll soon find out.

Scene 6
GETA, DEMEA

GETA: I thought I'd go see whom they're send-
   ing for
The bride, ma'am—O hello, sir. Here's
   Demea.

DEMEA: Uh—you are—?

GETA: Geta.

DEMEA: Geta, I've de-
   cided
This very day that you're a man to prize;
The worthiest of slaves, I'd say, is one
Whose master's interests are his own, like you.
And so, if there's an opportunity,
I'll do you a good turn. *(aside)* I'm learning tact
And very quickly.

GETA: Sir, you're kind indeed
To speak so.

DEMEA *(aside)*: One by one I win them over.

Scene 7
AESCHINUS, DEMEA, SYRUS, GETA

AESCHINUS: I'm bored to death with all the
   fuss they're making
Over a wedding: They've spent all day preparing.

DEMEA: Something's wrong, Aeschinus?

AESCHINUS: Is that you,
father?

DEMEA: Your father, yes, in blood as well as
spirit,
Who loves you more than life. But why not
bring
Your bride home?

AESCHINUS: O, I want to—
the musicians
Are late, and those who sing the wedding-
hymn.

DEMEA: Take an old man's advice—

AESCHINUS: Yes, sir?

DEMEA: —Forget them,
Guests, torches, music, hymn singing—forget
them,
And have the garden wall pulled down at once.
Then bring her in; make one house out of two,
And all her household part of ours.

AESCHINUS: That's genius,
And you're the best of fathers.

DEMEA: Great! I'm
"best"—
Micio's house will be an open road jammed
With people—and the cost! But I don't care:
I am the favorite. I'm "best." Tell Croesus
To open up his wallet now for you.
Syrus, get going.

SYRUS: Where, sir?

DEMEA: Break the
wall.
Aeschinus, lead them here.

GETA: God bless you,
sir;
I see you have the family's best interests
At heart.

DEMEA: They're worthy of all favors.
Don't you agree?

AESCHINUS: O yes!

DEMEA: Don't have her
carried
Up streets and down, a woman fresh from
childbirth.

AESCHINUS: There couldn't be a better way
than yours, sir.

DEMEA: Leave it to me. But here comes
Micio.

Scene 8
MICIO, DEMEA, AESCHINUS

MICIO: My brother's orders? Where is he?
Come, tell me:
You ordered this?

DEMEA: I did, for in
every way

I'd make our households one—in mutual love,
Support and unity.

AESCHINUS: I beg you, father—

MICIO: I'm not averse.

DEMEA: By heaven, it's our duty.
First off, there's the bride's mother.

MICIO: Yes,
    What then?

DEMEA: A woman of good repute.

MICIO: I've heard.

DEMEA: Not
    young.

MICIO: I know.

DEMEA: She's past the age of bearing
    children:
She's all alone—no one for her to turn to—

MICIO: What's this about?

DEMEA: You've got to marry
    her,
And (to AESCHINUS) it's your business to be
    sure he does.

MICIO: Marry? I?

DEMEA: You.

MICIO: I? Absurd.

DEMEA (to AESCHINUS):   He'd do it.
If you were a man.

AESCHINUS: Father!

MICIO: You heed him?
    Idiot!

AESCHINUS: No use: you must.

MICIO: You're mad.

AESCHINUS: Let
    me beg you—

MICIO: Get out of here, maniac!

AESCHINUS: As a favor,
    father?

MICIO: Are you out of your mind? I marry, at
    sixty-five,
A doddering old woman? This you want?

AESCHINUS: O please—I've promised—

MICIO: Promised?
    You'd better limit
Your generosity to what belongs to you.

DEMEA: He might ask something greater.

MICIO: There
    isn't any.

DEMEA: Give in.

AESCHINUS: You can't refuse.

DEMEA: Your word?

MICIO: Stop
    pestering!

AESCHINUS: Not till you yield.

MICIO: You threaten—?

DEMEA: Be generous.

MICIO: It all seems ill-advised, unnatural,
    mad—
Still, if you're so determined—well, I'll do it.

AESCHINUS: Splendid!

DEMEA: You're worth my love, but—

MICIO: What?

DEMEA: I'll
    tell you,
Now that I've won.

MICIO: Go on.

DEMEA: Their nearest kin,
Our relative as well, is Hegio.
He isn't rich; we should do something for him.

MICIO: What now?

DEMEA: That bit of land you rent
    outside of town—
Let's give it to him!

MICIO: *Bit* of land?

DEMEA: Big, small—
We must. He's been a father to her; also
He is our relative, a good man. O, it's right
To give it. It's your preaching that I practice;
I heard you say it not long since: "Our failing
Is, in old age, to think too much of money."
Let us try not to; it is sound advice.

AESCHINUS: Please—

MICIO: Very well; you ask it,
    he shall have it.

AESCHINUS: Three cheers!

DEMEA: We're brothers in spirit
    as in blood.
(*aside*) I've turned his sword against him!

Scene 9
SYRUS, DEMEA, MICIO, AESCHINUS

SYRUS: Orders done, sir.

DEMEA: Good man! Today I've come to the
    conclusion
That Syrus must be freed.

MICIO: You'll free him?
Why?

DEMEA: Many reasons.

SYRUS: You're a kind man, sir.
I've done my best to bring the two boys up—
Taught them, and scolded them, and given the
    best advice
I could.

DEMEA: That's clear: we trust you to buy
   food,
Bring home a whore, make dinner on short
   notice—
Not everyone can do the like.

SYRUS: O bless you!

DEMEA: Today, take note, he helped to buy
   the lute-girl—
His work. Reward him: watch your slaves
   improve.
Aeschinus wants you to.

MICIO: You do?

AESCHINUS: O yes, sir.

MICIO: Well then, of course. Syrus, come
   here. Be free!

SYRUS: O thank you, thank you all, but mostly
   you.

DEMEA: Delighted.

AESCHINUS: I too—

SYRUS: Yes. To top things
   off, though.
If my wife Phrygia could be free as well—

DEMEA: She's a good woman.

SYRUS: And your grandson, sir—
She's his first nurse.

DEMEA: Why then, I give my
   word,
If she's the first, of course she must go free.

MICIO: For that?

DEMEA: For that. I'll pay for her. That
   ends it.

SYRUS: May heaven grant you everything you
   pray for!

MICIO: Syrus, a good day's work.

DEMEA: And likewise,
   Micio,
If you will do your part and let him have
A little cash to start on, he'll soon pay you.

MICIO: Less than a little.

DEMEA: He's honest.

SYRUS: I'll return
   it—
Just give it.

AESCHINUS: Please do!

MICIO: When I've thought it
   over.

DEMEA: He will.

SYRUS: What a good man!

AESCHINUS: The   best
   of fathers!

MICIO: What is this? Why have you changed
    your ways so sharply?
Is this a whim, this sudden lavishness?

DEMEA: Listen. It is to show that what they
    judge
To be your inborn lovable good nature
Comes, not from character or love of justice,
But from permissiveness, extravagance,
Indulgence. If you scorn my way of life
Since I don't always grant my sons' desires,
Aeschinus, then there's no more I can say.
Pour money forth; buy, do, all that you covet.
But if you'd have some voice—when you are
    lost
For lack of vision, when your appetite

Is stronger than your wisdom—if a voice
Can hold you back, correct you, or agree
If it is right, hear mine.

AESCHINUS: We both bow, father;
You know what's best. But what about my
    brother?

DEMEA: I'll let him have his way—but he
    must know
It's the last time.

MICIO: Well done.

CANTOR: Applaud,
    applaud!

(GAIUS) LUCILIUS (C. 180–102 B.C.)

Epigrams

᠆᠊᠊᠊᠊᠊ᢙ

*T*he caustic epigrams of the first Roman satirist survive only in fragments, but there are more than enough of them to indicate that the thirty books he's known to have composed would offer major insight, if we could recover them, into his life and times. Born of affluent parents in Suessa Aurunca, near Campania, and a distant relative of Pompey, Lucilius soon found his way to Rome, where he became a friend of Laelius and member of Scipio's inner circle, serving with Scipio at the siege of Numantia in 133 B.C. He died in Naples.

- Although in his early work Lucilius, like Ennius before him, experimented metrically, he eventually settled on the dactylic hexameter as his mature verse form and thereby set it as the standard for later Roman satirists like Horace, Persius, and Juvenal. His pungent, uneven, yet vigorous style, wildly eclectic vocabulary, and cosmopolitan viewpoint, for all its unique eccentricity, show the influence of Stoicism and of Greek Old Comedy. His Latin, which admirer Horace criticized for its hastiness, is sprinkled with Greek words. Many of his poems, like those excerpted here, he wrote entirely in Greek.

- The material of Lucilius' verse includes assaults on public and private morality, reproaches to friends and enemies, lampoons against the lifestyle of the rich and famous, forays into popular philosophy, and biting comments on sex, gladiatorial games, intellectuals, and literary style. Through it all his primary subject, like that of twentieth-century satirist Charles Bukowski, is himself: his own likes and dislikes, his acerbic observations about his fellow Romans, his own passions and despairs. After Lucilius, Roman satire was an autobiographical form. His mockery of specific individuals, by name, earned him notoriety and fame that lasted well into the Empire. The rhetorician Quintilian praised him for his witty and cultured invective.

SHOPPING TIP

Lady, you went to the market
and picked up hair, rouge, honey, wax and
teeth.

For a like amount
you might have bought a face.

ON THE HARD LUCK OF DIOPHON

Diophon was being crucified,
but when he saw another near him on a higher
cross,
he died of envy.

LOVE OF LEARNING

Zenonis gives a place in her home to Menandros
a bearded grammarian,

for she has delivered her son to his instruction;
and the bushy pedant even labors into night,
with the mother,
practicing their figures, her dangling participles
and his copulative verb.

A MONEYLOVER

When miserly Kriton wants to ease his cramp-
ing stomach
he sniffs not mint
but a copper penny.

ON HERMON THE MISER

After spending some money in his sleep,
Hermon the miser was so hopping mad,

he hanged himself.

CONTAGION

Demostratis walks in a halo
of armpit aroma,
but worse,
she makes those who smell her
exhale the same he-goat fumes.

A NIGHT CALL

Diophantos went to bed and dreamed of
Dr. Hermogenes,
and though he was wearing a good-luck piece,
he never woke up.

ON THE SAME HERMOGENES

The barber is perplexed.
Where can he start to shave the head
of this hairy Hermogenes
who—from head to toe—
seems to be all head?

A PROSTITUTE BATHING

A girl of a hundred and still in the métier,
Heliodora, you spend hours in the bath.
But I know your dream: you pray to grow young,
like old Pelias, by letting them boil you alive.

INSIDE AN ATOM

So skinny was the pin-head Markos
that he bore a hole
with his own skull
through an atom of Epikouros
and slipped inside.

FIDELITY IN THE ARTS

Eutychos the portrait painter got twenty sons,
but even among his children—never one
likeness.

THE POET DESCENDING

Eutychides the lyric poet is dead.
Escape! you who inhabit the underworld,
for he comes with odes,
and orders thirteen lyres and twenty crates of
music
to burn beside him on his funeral pyre.
Now Charon has you,
for where can you escape
with Eutychides established in Hell?

(MARCUS TERENTIUS) VARRO (116–27 B.C.)

On Agriculture

*C*alled by Quintilian "the most learned of the Romans," Varro was Leonardo da Vinci's model, a prodigious polymath who wrote more than six hundred books on topics as far afield as grammar, archaeology, mathematics, history, religion, law, and agriculture—all while pursuing his political and military career under first Pompey, then Caesar. He was born to a respected senatorial family in Reate, in the Sabine territory, and sent to study in Rome under the philologist Aelius Stilo Praeconinus and in Athens under the Platonist Antiochus of Ascalon. In 47 B.C., Caesar appointed him Rome's first public librarian. In addition to his three-book *On Agriculture,* only six of his twenty-five books on the Latin language survive.

- Other works by Varro included:

  - *Menippean Satires,* a verse and prose satire in 150 books, introducing the form invented by the Greek Cynic Menippus;
  - *Antiquities,* compiling information on ancient Roman political, religious, and household customs, and on the foibles and adventures of the gods and their priests, feasts, and temples;
  - *Imagines,* with seven hundred biographies of notable Greeks and Romans, illustrated with portraits;
  - and *Disciplines,* an encyclopedia of the cultural arts appropriate to the education of a free man; they include grammar, dialectics, rhetoric, geometry, arithmetic, astronomy, music, architecture, and medicine.

- At his villa at Casinum on the river Rapido, Varro wrote his three-book patriotic dialogue *On Agriculture* when he was eighty years old. He draws not only from Greek and ancient Roman sources, but from his own childhood experience. Dedicated to his wife Fundania and intent on evoking a nostalgia for country life in his fellow Romans, the book deals with:

  - agriculture in general;
  - cattle, horse, pig, and sheep husbandry;

▴ minor livestock, including bees, blackbirds, dormice, peacocks, hares, snails, and fish.

The work is our most important source for understanding Roman agriculture. Francesco Petrarca, the "first Renaissance man," placed Varro between Cicero and Virgil as the "third great light of Rome."

CHAPTER II
THE AIM AND SCOPE OF AGRICULTURE

At the Sementivae (Festival of Sowing) I was in the temple of Tellus, on the invitation of the Aeditumus (guardian of the temple), as our ancestors taught us to call him, though now our modern men-about-town correct us, and would have us say *Aedituus*. There I fell in with Caius Fundanius, my father-in-law, C. Agrius, a Roman eques of the Socratic school, and P. Agrasius the tax-farmer. They were looking at a map of Italy traced on the wall. What are you doing here? I said to them, surely the "Sementivae" haven't brought you gentlemen of leisure here as they used to do our fathers and grandfathers!

Our presence has, I imagine, the same cause as yours, said Agrius, an invitation from the Aeditumus, and if I am right—as your nod would indicate—you must wait with us until he returns, or the aedile who has charge of this temple sent for him and he hasn't yet come back, but he left a request that we should wait for him. So, in the meantime, while he is on the way, suppose we apply the ancient proverb— "The Roman wins by sitting still."

A good idea, said Agrius, and thinking that the longest part of a journey is, according to the proverb, the getting to the gate, at once moved forward to the benches; and we followed.

When we were seated Agrasius said: You men who have traveled over many lands, have you ever seen any which was better cultivated than Italy? My opinion is, said Agrius, that there is none that has so little of its land uncultivated. In the first place, as Eratosthenes divided the earth into two halves, the northern and the southern (the most natural division); and since the northern part is incontestably healthier than the southern, and the healthier a place is the more productive it is, we must conclude that Italy, being in the northern half, was originally more suitable for cultivation than Asia. For in the first place Italy is in Europe; secondly, this part of Europe is more temperate than the inner part, where almost perpetual winters reign. And no wonder, since there are districts between the Arctic Circle and the North Pole—the axis of the heavens—where the sun is invisible for six months together. They say, too, that in consequence of this, sailing even is impossible in the Ocean, owing to the sea being frozen.

I say, said Fundanius, you don't suppose, do you, that anything can grow there, or be cultivated if it does? For Pacuvius' saying is true, "If there be perpetual sunlight or night, all the fruits of the earth perish through fiery glow" or cold! For myself, even in this part of the world where night and day follow each other at reasonable intervals, life would be impossible, did I not in summer time break the day by a siesta. How then could sowing, growing, or mowing be possible in that part of the world where there is a six-months night or day?

Contrast with this Italy, where every useful product not merely grows, but grows to perfection. What spelt is comparable with that of Campania, what wheat with the Apulian, what wine with the Falernian, what oil with the Venafrian? Is not Italy so stocked with fruit-trees as to seem one great orchard? Is Phrygia, which Homer calls ἀμπελόεσσαν, more thickly covered with vines than our country? Or is Argos more fruitful, which the same poet calls πολύπυρον? In what other land does the *iugerum* produce fifteen *cullei* of wine, which is the case in some districts of Italy? Does not M. Cato write in his book *Of Origins* as follows: "That part of the Ager Gallicus is called Roman which, lying beyond the Picentine country on this side of Ariminum, was portioned out to settlers. In that land occasionally ten *cullei* of wine are made to the *iugerum.*" And the same remarkable yield is observed in the country about Faventia, for there the vines are called *trecenariae*, on the ground that the *iugerum* is reported to yield 300 *amphorae*. At this point, with a glance at me, he said, At any rate, your head engineer, Libo Marcius, used to assert that the vines on his farm at Faenza produced this quantity.

Two points above all others the inhabitants of Italy seem to have considered in farming: Could they get back a return proportionate to the labor and expense? And was the situation healthy? If either question has to be answered in the negative, and a man still wishes to farm, he is mentally defective, and had better be put in charge of his legal guardians. For no sane man should be willing to go to the trouble and expense of farming if he sees that no return is possible, or that, while he may get a return in crops, they will be destroyed by disease.

But here we have men better qualified than I am to deal with these matters; for I see coming C. Licinius Stolo and Cn. Tremelius Scrofa. It was Stolo's ancestors who proposed the law limiting the land held by one person (for a Stolo originated the well-known law which forbids a Roman citizen to hold more than 500 *iugera*), and Stolo himself through admirable farming made good his right to the Cognomen Stolo, for not a single "sucker" could be found on his estate since he went round his trees digging up such offshoots from the root as sprouted above the soil—and these were called "stolos." C. Licinius of the same *gens*, when he was Tribune of the Plebs, 365 years after the expulsion of the kings, was the first to lead the people, to hear the laws announced, from the Comitium to the Forum, their seven *iugera* of land.

The other whom I see approaching is a colleague of yours, one of the twenty commissioners appointed to apportion the Campanian lands, Cn. Tremelius Scrofa. Universally accomplished, he is also considered the greatest Roman authority on farming. And is he not rightly so considered? said I; for his farms, owing to their fine cultivation, are a pleasanter sight to many than the palatial buildings of others, since people come in his case to see farmhouses, not picture-galleries as at Lucullus', but store-houses stocked with fruit. There is a picture of our friend's orchard, said I, at the top of the Sacra Via, where fruit is being sold for gold.

Meanwhile, the two of whom I was speaking join us. We have not come too late for the dinner, have we? said Stolo, for I don't see L. Fundilius, who invited us to it. Don't be uneasy, said Agrius, for the egg which marks the last course in the four-horse chariot-races at the games of the Circus has not yet been removed; we have not even seen the egg which usually begins the solemn function of dinner. And so, until we can see the latter together, and while the Aeditumus is on his way, tell us what is the chief end of farming—utility, or pleasure, or both; for they tell me that you are now the great agricultural expert, as was Stolo before you.

We must first decide, said Scrofa, whether farming is concerned only with the sowing of land, or with such things also as are brought on to the land, such as sheep and cattle; for I find that those who have written on agriculture in Phoenician, Greek and Latin, have traveled too far afield.

It is my opinion, answered Stolo, that we are not bound to imitate them in every particular, and that certain writers have done better who have kept within a narrower boundary and excluded from it everything irrelevant to the subject. Thus the feeding of stock in general, which most people make a branch of farming, seems more the province of the shepherd than of the farmer; and so the headmen in each case are distinguished by different names, the one being called the bailiff (vilicus), the other the flock-master. The vilicus was appointed to cultivate the ground and was named after the villa, as he conveys the produce into the farm-house, and out of it when it is being sold. Hence the country-folk even to-day say vea for

via (road) owing to the conveyance (vectura) over it, and vella, not villa, for the place to and from which produce is conveyed (vehit). Carriers likewise are said to follow the trade of conveying (velatura).

Certainly, said Fundanius, the feeding of stock is one thing, tilling the land is another, yet they are related, just as the right-hand flute, though different from the left-hand one, is yet in a sense united to it since the song is the same, of which the one leads and the other accompanies the tune. Yes, and you may add, said I, that the shepherd's life is the leading part, the farmer's takes the second—on the authority of the learned Dicaearchus, who, in the picture he has drawn for us of primitive Greek life, shows that in former ages there was a time when men led a pastoral life, with no knowledge of plowing, sowing, or pruning, and that they took up agriculture a degree later in point of time. Agriculture, therefore, plays second to the pastoral life, in that it is lower, like a left-hand flute in relation to the stops of the right-hand one.

Then said Agrius, You and your piping not only rob the farmer of his flock, but the slave, too, of his peculium—the ox which his master allows him to graze, and you do away with the laws for settlers, in which it is written: On land planted with young trees let not the settler pasture the offspring of the she-goat—creatures which even astronomy has removed to a place in the sky not far from the bull.

I am afraid, Agrius, said Fundanius to him, that what you quote is wide of the mark, for in the laws it is also written "certain cattle," and the reason of this is that certain animals, such as the she-goats you mention, are hostile to cultivation and poisonous to plants, for by nibbling at them they ruin all young plants, and not the least, vines and olive trees. And so on this ground, though from different motives, it was ordained that a victim of the goat kind should be led to the altar of one god, but that at another's no such sacrifice should be performed. The loathing in each case was the same—the one god wishing to see the goat dying, the other not wanting to see him at all. Hence to Father Liber—discoverer of the vine—he-goats were sacrificed to the end that they might suffer death for their misdeeds, but to Minerva they sacrificed nothing of the goat kind because of the olive tree, which is said to become barren if bruised by it, for the goat's saliva is poisonous to vegetation. At Athens, too, we are told that on this account goats are not allowed to enter the Acropolis, save once a year for the necessary sacrifice, lest the olive tree, which they say first sprang up there, be touched by a she-goat.

No animals, said I, come within the province of agriculture save those which can help the soil to greater fertility by their labor, as for example those which yoked together can plow the land. If what you say is true, said Agrasius, how are you to disconnect cattle from the land, seeing that dung, which is of the greatest use to it, is furnished by herds of cattle? Then, replied Agrius, we must say that a troop of slaves belongs to agriculture, if we decide to keep one for that purpose. No, the mistake arises from the fact that cattle may be on the land and be productive of revenue on that land; but you must not make this fact an argument [for connecting them with agriculture]; for if you do, other things as well which have nothing to do with land will have to be admitted—as when a farmer has several

weavers on a farm with buildings set apart for weaving, and so on for other craftsmen.

Well, said Scrofa, let us separate stock-raising from farming, and all the other things to which objection may be taken on this ground. Or, said I, am I to follow the books of the Sasernae, father and son, in thinking that the proper working of potteries has more to do with agriculture than the working of silver and other mines which are doubtless to be met with on some land? Potteries however have nothing to do with farming, any more than stone or sand quarries, though we need not on that account neglect to work them and reap profit from them on land where they can be conveniently worked. Just as, to take another instance, if a piece of land borders on a highway, and the spot suits travelers, it is advisable to build inns, though they, however profitable, do not any the more belong to agriculture. For all produce that an owner gets directly or indirectly from his land, ought not to be credited to agriculture, but only such things as have grown from the ground for human consumption after having been sown.

Then Stolo took him up, saying: You are jealous of the illustrious author, and your criticism of his potteries is mere carping, while you say nothing about many excellent passages, for fear of having to praise them, though they are closely connected with agriculture. Scrofa smiled, for he knew the books and thought little of them. Agrasius, thinking himself to be the only one who knew them, asked Scrofa to mention the passages. So Scrofa began, It describes in these words how bugs should be destroyed: "Put a wild cucumber in water, pour the water where you want the result, no bugs will come near. Or, take ox-gall mixed with vinegar; smear your bed with it." Fundanius looked towards Scrofa and said: And yet he speaks the truth, though the statement does occur in a treatise on agriculture. It is as true, I warrant, said Scrofa, as his recipe for a depilatory—he bids you throw a yellow frog into water, which you are to boil until two-thirds are gone, and to anoint your body with what remains. You had better quote, said I, from that book what more nearly concerns Fundanius's health, for our friend's feet often ache, and pucker his forehead with frowns. Please do, said Fundanius, for I had rather hear about my feet than about the proper way of sowing beetroot.

I will quote, said Stolo with a smile, the very words he wrote: "Thus have I heard Tarquenna say, that when a man's feet began to ache, by remembering you he could be cured. I remember you, cure my feet. 'O Earth, keep thou the pain, and health with me remain in my feet.'" He bids one sing this thrice nine times, touch the earth, spit downwards, and sing it fasting. Said I, You will find many other marvels in the book of the Sasernae, all of which have nothing to do with farming, and are for that reason to be rejected. As though, said he, you couldn't find in other writers, too, examples of the same kind. Why, in the book which the great Cato published on agriculture, are there not scores, for example: how to make a *placenta*, or a *libum*, or how to salt hams? You don't give, said Agrius, the remarkable prescription, "If you should wish to drink deep and eat freely at a dinner-party, you ought beforehand to have eaten raw cabbage in vinegar, some five leaves"!

PART II

The Late Republic
(64–27 B.C.)

(MARCUS TULLIUS) CICERO (106–43 B.C.)

The First Oration Against Catiline and *Letters to His Wife and Family in Rome and to Caesar in Gaul*

~~✑

*E*xcellence in oratory has been synonymous with the name Cicero since 80 B.C., when he first made his name known to the Romans under the dictatorship of Sulla by defending Sextus Roscius of Ameria against a charge of parricide. Cicero was born of an affluent family in Arpinum, son of the equestrian Marcus Tullius Cicero and Helvia, who sent him to the capital at an early age to complete his education in Greek, Latin, law, philosophy, and oratory under the poet Archias, the orators Lucius Crassus and Marcus Antonius, the Epicurean philosopher Phaedrus, the Stoic Diodotus, and the Platonist Philo of Larissa. He furthered his Greek studies in Athens and under the rhetorician Molo in Rhodes.

In 77 B.C., Cicero was back in Rome, where he married Terentia. He was elected quaestor of Sicily in 76, by unanimous vote; and, back in Rome, aedile, in 70. In the same year, at the Sicilians' request, Cicero successfully prosecuted Verres for his abuses of their province. His opponent was Hortensius, at the time the most famous advocate in Rome. In 66, he was unanimously elected praetor and gave his first purely political speech, supporting the tribune Manilius' proposal of Pompey as commander of the Roman army against Mithridates. His continuous support of Pompey was based on Cicero's belief that Pompey alone was strong enough to ensure continual government by the Senate.

When, in 64–63, the Roman aristocracy became alarmed at an attempted coup d'état led by Catiline and Lentulus Sura, Cicero, who had made his name as a proponent of law and order, was elected consul. In his four passionately patriotic speeches against Catiline, he overwhelmed all opposition and railroaded the conspirators to their execution before they had been formally condemned by the people of Rome. As a result, Cicero's enemies forced his exile on the grounds of treason against the fundamental laws of jurisprudence.

Subsequently, when he was allowed to return to Rome after ten months, Cicero found allies among only the nobles, losing the support of Pompey and the Roman plebs. When Pompey allied with Caesar and Crassus, Cicero was invited to join them in a "rule of four." His allegiance to the Roman constitution forced him to decline; instead, threatened by the new tribune of the plebs Clodius Pulcher, he went into exile for eighteen months.

When Cicero returned to Rome in 57, he had been reconciled with Pompey and proceeded to do his best to alienate him from Caesar. But Caesar, who had long sought to win Cicero over to his side, gently forced him to back down and to serve him in the Senate. At the outbreak of the Civil War, Cicero went to Greece to join with Pompey's army, but was plagued with illness and did not receive the welcome he had expected. He returned to Italy via Brundisium (modern Brindisi) and waited out the war in virtual retirement from politics. A year went by before Caesar forgave him and asked him back to Rome.

When, on the Ides of March 44 B.C., Caesar was knifed down in the Senate House, Cicero attempted to reconcile Antony with Caesar's assassins Decimus Brutus and Cassius and managed to achieve a general amnesty. But Antony left the capital for Cisalpine Gaul, and Cicero realized his reconciliation efforts were futile. He delivered a series of stinging attacks on Antony in the Senate, the fourteen *Philippics* (borrowing from Demosthenes' classic speeches against Philip II of Macedon), leading to the dispatching of senatorial forces against Antony in Mutina, where he was blockading Brutus.

Those forces, however, were led by Octavian, who recognized Antony's power was greater than that of his senatorial masters. When he allied with Antony, the two drew up an "enemies list," with Cicero's name at the top. Along with hundreds of other senators, he was executed in the bloody year 43 B.C. Though Cicero was often inflexible in politics, he was always courageous.

- In addition to his speeches, which he published himself, Cicero wrote:

  - voluminous letters, published after his death;
  - hexameter verse that influenced Lucretius, Horace, and Catullus; as well as
  - essays on religion, moral and political philosophy, and rhetorical practice.

- His works include:

  - *De oratore,* a treatise on the art of eloquence;
  - *Republic,* outlining the ideal constitution;
  - *Laws,* describing Roman public and religious codes;
  - *De finibus,* comparing and contrasting Greek schools of philosophy regarding the highest good;
  - *On Friendship,* one of his most popular treatises to this day, a dialogue with Laelius;
  - *On Old Age,* celebrating Cato the Elder and offering insight into the Roman reverence for and celebration of the elderly as a source of wisdom crucial to the functioning of a progressive state.

- In a culture distinguished for its oratory, Cicero was the epitome of the rhetorical art combining the strength of Demosthenes with the insight and metaphorical subtlety of Plato. His speeches, still used today in Latin classes as the highest example of the language's eloquence and power, are emotional, witty, piercingly analytical, and as irresistibly compelling as an avalanche.

- Cicero's command of his language was never equaled. His diction is elegantly pure, unmarred by pretentious neologisms or colloquial slang. The predecessor of all Western litigators, Cicero set out to try every cause he spoke for on his own grounds, narrating the facts to prove that his viewpoint was the only way of perceiving the situation.

- One of his most famous speeches, *The First Oration Against Catiline,* has been used for two millennia as the introductory text in "advanced Latin," and for the training of aspiring orators. In it, Cicero condemns Lucius Sergius Catilina, his political rival, for his conspiracy against the Senate. As a result of Cicero's relentless attacks, Catiline was arrested and executed in 62 B.C.

- Cicero's letters to his wife and family, and to Caesar in Gaul, offer insight into the private life of Rome's greatest orator.

- The poet Catullus called him "the most eloquent of all the seed of Romulus, that are, or were, or ever shall be."

THE FIRST ORATION AGAINST CATILINE

How far, I ask, will you try our patience, Catiline? How long will this madness of yours make sport of us? To what length will this unbridled insolence vaunt itself? Have you in no way been disturbed by the night guard on the Palatine, the city watch, the fear of the people, the gathering of all loyal citizens, the convening of the Senate in this highly fortified place, and the expression on the faces of these senators? Do you not perceive that your plans are manifest, do you not see that your conspiracy is already throttled by its being known to all these men? Who of us do you think does not know what you did last night, what the night before that, where you were, whom you called together, what plans you made? O the morals of these times! The Senate understands these facts, the consul sees, but this fellow lives.

Lives? Why, indeed he even comes into the Senate, he becomes a participant in public deliberation, he marks and designates, as he looks about, each one of us for slaughter. But we, brave men, seem to do enough for the Republic if we avoid his madness and his weapons. Long ago, Catiline, you should have been led to death by order of the consul, long ago the destruction which you have been plotting for us all should have been visited upon you. As a matter of fact, did not that very great man, Publius Scipio, the supreme pontiff, although a private citizen, kill Tiberius Gracchus, who was slightly weakening the condition of the Republic? Shall we, the consuls, tolerate Catiline, who desires to devastate the world by slaughter and fire? For I pass over those other instances as too ancient, when Gaius Servilius Ahala killed with his own hand Spurius Maelius who was striving to incite a

Ruins of Roman Forum

revolution. There was, there was once in this Republic such virtue that brave men punished a harmful citizen with harsher punishments than a most bitter enemy. We have an extremely severe decree of the Senate against you, Catiline, and the counsel and authority of this body are not wanting. We, we, the consuls, I say it frankly, are at fault.

Once the Senate decreed that the consul, Lucius Opimius, should see to it that the Republic should suffer no harm. Not a night intervened; Gaius Gracchus, a man of most illustrious father, grandfather, and ancestors, was killed because of certain suspicions of

sedition; and Marcus Fulvius, an ex-consul, was put to death, and his children with him. By a similar decree of the Senate, the Republic was entrusted to the consuls, Gaius Marius and Lucius Valerius. Was the death penalty of the state delayed for one day thereafter in the case of Lucius Saturninus, the tribune of the people, and Gaius Servilius, the praetor? But already for twenty days we have allowed the authority of these senators to grow dull. For we have such a decree of the Senate, shut up in tablets as if hidden in a scabbard. According to this decree of the Senate it was fitting that you should have been killed at once. You live, and you live not to put aside your insolence but to strengthen it. I desire, senators, to be clement, I desire in such great dangers of the Republic not to seem remiss, but I already condemn myself for my inactivity and my negligence. A camp has been pitched in Italy, in the passes of Etruria, against the Roman people. The number of the enemy increases from day to day, but we see the general of that camp and the leader of the enemy, daily attempting some internal harm to the Republic within the walls and even in the Senate. If I presently order you to be seized, Catiline, if I order you to be killed, doubtless I shall have to fear not rather that all good men will say "too late" than that some one man should say "too cruel." But for a certain reason I am not yet induced to do what should fittingly have been done a long time ago. Then finally you will be killed when nobody can be found so wicked, so abandoned, so like you that he will not admit that this has been done legally. You shall live as long as there is anyone who dares to defend you, and you shall live just as you are living, surrounded by my many strong guards so that you cannot stir against the Republic. Furthermore, although you do not perceive it, the eyes and ears of many will be watching and guarding you, as they have done up to this moment.

And indeed, Catiline, what more is there that you can be waiting for, if neither the night with its darkness can shroud your wicked undertakings nor a private home with its walls keep secret the voices of your conspiracy, if everything comes to light, if everything breaks forth? Change now this mind of yours, believe me, forget about fire and slaughter. You are trapped on all sides; all your plans are clearer to me than the light of day. Suppose we now go over these together. Do you remember my saying in the Senate on October 21 that Gaius Manlius, the satellite and accomplice of your boldness, would be in arms on a certain day, and that this day would be October 27? Was I deceived, Catiline, not only about such a great crime, so heinous and so unbelievable, but even about the very day, a point that must cause greater wonder? I also said in the Senate that you had set the massacre of the optimates for October 28, the date when many leaders of the city fled from Rome not so much for the reason that they wished to save themselves as that they wished to foil your plans. Can you deny that on that very day you, hemmed in by my guards and my diligence, were unable to move against the Republic, when at the departure of the rest you kept saying that just the same you would be content with the slaughter of us who had remained? And what about this? When you were confident that you would occupy Praeneste by a night attack on the very first day of November, did you not perceive

that that colony had been fortified at my command with a garrison, sentinels, and a night watch? You do nothing, you undertake nothing, you think of nothing which I fail not only to hear but even to see and clearly perceive.

Review with me, then, that night before last; soon you will perceive that I am far more keenly on the alert for the safety of the Republic than you are for its ruin. I say that you on that night came to the street of the scythemakers (I will not speak vaguely) into the home of Marcus Laeca; that in that same place many companions of your mad crime had come together. Do you dare to deny it? Why are you silent? I shall prove it, if you deny it, for I see here in the Senate certain men who were there together with you. O ye immortal gods! Where in the world are we? In what kind of city do we live, what sort of Republic do we have? Here, here in our number, senators, in this most sacred and most important council in the world, are those who plot the death of us all, who plot the ruin of this city and even of the whole world! I, the consul, see them and I call for their vote on matters of public concern, and I do not yet wound with my voice those whom it would have been fitting to put to the sword! You were, then, at Laeca's house that night, Catiline, you assigned where it suited you for each one to go, you named those whom you would leave at Rome, those whom you would take along with you, you marked off parts of the city for fires, you declared that you yourself would soon leave, you said that even now you were subject to a little delay because I was alive. Two Roman knights were found to free you of this annoyance, and they promised to kill me in my bed that very night a little before daylight. I discovered these facts before your meeting was hardly more than adjourned; I fortified and secured my home with a greater number of guards, and I kept out those whom you had sent in the morning to greet me when those very ones did come whose coming to me at that time I had already predicted to many very important men.

Since these things are so, Catiline, continue the journey you started; at last begone from the city. The gates are open—go! Too long has that camp of Manlius been eagerly awaiting you. And take along with you all your followers, or if not all, as many as possible; purge the city. You will free me of a great fear, if only there is a wall between you and me. You can no longer live with us; I will not bear it, I will not allow it, I will not permit it. Great thanks must be given to the immortal gods and especially to Jupiter himself, the Stayer, the most ancient guard of this city, because we have escaped so many times already this loathsome, this horrible, this deadly plague of the Republic. Not too often must the supreme safety of the Republic be risked in the hands of one man. As often as you insidiously attacked me when I was consul elect, I defended myself not with public help but with private diligence. When at the last consular election you wished to kill me and your competitors in the Campus Martius, I put down your wicked attempts with the support of bands of friends without arousing any public tumult. Finally as often as you attacked me, I resisted you personally, although I saw that injury to me was coupled with great misfortune to the State. But now you attack the entire Republic openly and you involve the temples of the immortal gods, the houses of the city, the

lives of us all, and finally all Italy in ruin and destruction. Wherefore since I do not yet dare to do that which should come first, that which would be in conformity with this nation's power and the discipline of our ancestors, I shall do what is more gentle in point of severity and more useful to the common good. For if I order you to be killed, the rest of the band of conspirators will remain behind in the Republic, but if you go out, as I have been urging you for a long time, a great cesspool of harm in the State, a cesspool made up of your followers, will be drained out of the city. What do you say to this, Catiline? You do not shrink from doing at my command what you were already proposing to do of your own accord. The consul orders an enemy to leave the city. You ask me, if into exile; I do not order it but, if you ask my advice, I urge it.

For what is there, Catiline, that can still delight you in this city in which there is no one, if we except your gang of abandoned men, who does not fear you, no one who does not hate you? What brand of domestic wickedness is not burned into your life, what disgrace of private life does not cling to your reputation, what lust has ever been absent from your eyes, what crime from your hands, what shame from your whole body? To what youth whom you have caught with the snare of your allurements, have you not held out either the sword for boldness or the torch for lust? But what about this? When recently at the death of your former wife you had cleared out your home for a new marriage, did you not pile this on top of that other unbelievable crime, which I pass over and readily allow to be left unuttered lest it seem that in this city there either existed cruelty capable of committing so great a crime or that it went unavenged? I pass over the ruin of your fortune, all of which you will see threatening you on the coming Ides, and I come to those matters which pertain not to the private disgrace of your vices, not to your domestic difficulties and degradation but to the supreme welfare of the Republic and to the life and safety of us all. Can this light of day or breath of the heavens be pleasing to you when you know that there is not one of those here present who is unaware that on the last day of December during the consulship of Lepidus and Tullus, you stood armed in the assembly, that you organized a gang to kill the consuls and leaders of the State, and that not any attitude of mind or fear on your part but the fortune of the Roman people stood in your way? And now I shall pass over those matters (for your later crimes are neither unknown nor few); but how often did you try to kill me the consul elect, how often have you tried to kill me as consul! How often have I escaped your thrusts, so directed that it seemed impossible to avoid them, by a hair's breadth, as they say! You accomplish nothing and yet you will not stop trying and hoping. How often has that dagger of yours been wrested from your hands, how often has it fallen down and slipped from you by some accident! Indeed I do not know by what rites it has been consecrated and vowed by you that you think it necessary to bury it in the body of the consul.

Well now, what sort of life is this of yours? I am going to talk with you now in such a way that I shall seem not motivated by hatred, as I should be, but by mercy, which is not due you. A little while ago you came into the Senate.

Who of this throng, including so many of your friends and relatives, greeted you? If within the memory of man this has never happened to anybody, are you waiting for them to speak their insults when you are already overwhelmed by the most heavy judgment of silence? What do you think of this that at your coming these benches were left unoccupied, that as soon as you sat down all the ex-consuls whom you had very often slated for destruction, left this section of the seats bare and empty? In what state of mind do you think you ought to take this? Heavens! if my servants feared me the way all your fellow citizens fear you, I should think I ought to leave home. Do you not think that you should leave the city? If I saw that I was unjustly made the object of such grave suspicion and dislike by my fellow citizens, I would prefer to be deprived of the sight of them rather than be viewed by the hostile eyes of all. And you, when you recognize in the consciousness of your crimes that the hatred of all is just and already due you for a long time, do you hesitate to avoid the sight and presence of those whose minds and sensibilities you wound? If your parents feared and hated you, and you could not pacify them in any way, I imagine you would go where they would not see you. Now the fatherland, which is the common parent of us all, hates and fears you, and judges that for a long time you have been thinking of nothing except its destruction. Will you not respect its authority, not follow its verdict, not fear its force? The fatherland thus pleads with you, Catiline, and, though silent, seems to speak thus: "For some years now no crime has existed except through you, no disgrace apart from you. The murder of many citizens, the harassing and plundering of the allies have gone unpunished and free in your case alone. You have been able not only to disregard the laws and the courts but also to overturn and utterly destroy them. Those former acts of yours, although they should not have been tolerated, I nevertheless bore as well as I could. Now it must not be tolerated that all of me should be in fear because of you alone, that Catiline be feared if there is the least noise, that it seems impossible for any plot to be entered into against me unless it has a touch of your criminality. Wherefore depart and relieve me of this fear; if it is true, that I may not be overcome, if false that I may finally cease to fear."

If the fatherland should say these things to you, as I have spoken them, should it not obtain its request, even if it cannot employ force? But what of this? You handed yourself over to custody because you said that you wished to live at the home of Manius Lepidus to avoid suspicion. When you were not received by him, you actually dared to come to me and asked that I should keep you at my home. After you had received that reply from me also, namely that I could in no way be safe under the same roof with you, since I was in great danger because we were within the same city walls, you came to Quintus Metellus, the praetor. Turned down by him, you resorted to your bosom friend, a very fine man, Marcus Metellus. Evidently you thought that he would be most diligent in guarding, most shrewd in suspecting, and most brave in avenging. But how far away from prison and chains does it seem that a man should be who has already judged himself worthy of custody? Since these things are so, Catiline, do you hesitate, if you cannot die with equanimity, to go into some other land and entrust to flight and solitude that life of yours, snatched from many justly due punishments?

You say: "Bring the matter before the Senate"—for that is what you demand; and if this body decrees that it is its pleasure that you go into exile, you say that you will obey. I will not put the matter before the Senate, a thing that is inconsistent with my character, but nevertheless I will take measures to make you understand what these senators think of you. Leave the city, Catiline, free the Republic of fear, go into exile, if that is the word you are waiting for. What is the matter, Catiline? Are you listening at all, do you notice the silence of these men? They do not object, they are silent. Why are you awaiting a spoken command from men whose will you perceive in their silence? But if I had said this same thing to this splendid youth, Publius Sestius, or to that very brave man, Marcus Marcellus, the Senate would already have laid violent hands on me, the consul, in this very temple—and with perfect right. But, Catiline, when they are silent about you, they approve; when they are passive, they decide; when they are quiet, they shout, and not only these senators whose authority is evidently dear to you and whose lives very cheap, but also those Roman knights, just, honorable, and good men, and those other very brave citizens who stand about the Senate, whose number you could see, whose will you could perceive and whose voices you could hear a little while ago. I shall easily induce these same men, whose hands and weapons I have for a long time scarcely kept from you, to accompany you to the gates, as you leave this city which for so long you have been striving to destroy.

And yet what is the use of talking? As if anything could break you, anything correct you, as if you were meditating any such thing as flight or considering any such thing as exile! If only the immortal gods would give you that frame of mind! And yet I see that if, terrified by my voice, you make up your mind to go into exile, what a mighty storm of unpopularity threatens me, if not in the present while the remembrance of your crimes is fresh, at any rate in future generations. But it is worth while if this calamity shall affect only an individual and shall be separate from danger to the Republic. But it must not be expected that you be moved by your vices, that you fear the punishments of the laws, that you bow to the exigencies of the nation. Nor are you such a man that shame has ever recalled you from wickedness, fear from danger, or reason from madness. Wherefore, as I have often said already, set out and, if you wish to excite unpopularity against your enemy, as you say you do, go straight into exile. I shall hardly bear the criticism of men if you do so; I shall hardly sustain the weight of this unpopularity if you go into exile at the command of the consul. But if you, on the other hand, prefer to serve my praise and glory, set out with your cruel gang of criminals, betake yourself to Manlius, arouse desperate citizens, separate yourself from good men, wage war against the fatherland, exult in your impious brigandage so that it may seem that you have gone not as though exiled to strangers but rather invited to your own. And yet, why should I invite you when I know that you have already sent armed men ahead to wait at the town of Forum Aurelium, when I know that a day has already been set and agreed upon with Manlius, when I know that that famous silver eagle, which I trust will be ruinous and fatal to you and all your followers and for which you had a shrine set up in your home, has been sent on ahead? How much longer can you be without that eagle which you were accustomed to venerate as you set out for slaughter and from whose altars you often lifted that impious hand of yours to the murder of citizens?

At last you will go whither your unbridled and mad passion has long been hurrying you. But this prospect does not cause you sorrow but a certain unbelievable pleasure. Nature produced you for just this madness, your will strengthened you, and good luck preserved you. Never have you desired, not to mention peace and quiet, not even war unless it was wicked. You have got together a gang of reprobates, recruited from abandoned men and those bereft not only of all their fortune but even of hope. What happiness you will really enjoy here, in what delights you will rejoice, in what great pleasure you will revel when in such a great number of your followers you will neither hear nor see any good man! In the interest of this sort of life, those boasted labors of yours were put forth, lying on the ground not only to accomplish your lewdness but also to effect your wickedness, keeping awake as you hatched plots not only against the sleep of husbands but also against the possessions of the unwary. You have a chance to show your famous endurance of hunger and cold and the need of everything, and by these you will shortly realize you are undone. I accomplished this much when I kept you from the consulship, that you could as an exile assail rather than as consul harass the Republic, and that what was wickedly undertaken by you should be called brigandage rather than war.

Now, senators, to ward off and avert a certain almost justified complaint of the fatherland, listen carefully, I beseech you, to what I say and let it make a deep impression on your minds and souls. For if the fatherland, which is much dearer to me than life itself, if all Italy, if the entire commonwealth were to speak to me, it would say: "Marcus Tullius, what are you doing? Will you permit him to leave whom you have discovered to be an enemy, who you see is going to be a leader of a war, who you realize is waited for as commander in the camp of the enemy, an author of crime, an originator of a conspiracy, a recruiter of slaves and abandoned citizens, so that you seem not to have expelled him from the city but to have let him loose against it? Will you not order that he be led off to prison, hurried off to his death, and punished with the supreme penalty? What, pray, hinders you? Ancestral custom? But very often even private individuals in this State have punished wicked citizens with death. Or do the laws that have been passed concerning the punishment of Roman citizens hinder you? But never in this city have those who failed the Republic held the rights of citizens. Or do you fear the detestation of posterity? Indeed you are making a splendid return to the Roman people who so early raised you, a man known only through yourself, without any commendation of ancestry, to the highest power, through all the gradations of public office, if because of unpopularity or fear of some danger you neglect the safety of your fellow citizens. But if there is any fear of unpopularity, the unpopularity resulting from

strictness and bravery must not be feared as much as that resulting from inactivity and baseness. Or when Italy will be laid waste in war, when cities will be overrun and homes will be afire, do you not think that you will burn in the fire of unpopularity?"

To these most sacred words of the Republic and to the judgment of those men who feel the same way, I shall reply briefly. If I judged this the best course to follow, that Catiline be given the death penalty, I would not have given this gladiator here the enjoyment of one hour of life. And indeed, if the finest men and the most famous citizens not only did not contaminate themselves but even honored themselves by shedding the blood of Saturninus, the Gracchi, Flaccus, and many other men of former times, certainly I should not have to fear that, after this murderer of citizens had been killed, it would redound a little to my unpopularity with posterity. But if this should threaten me ever so much, I would consider unpopularity born of courage to be glory, not unpopularity. And yet there are some in this body who either do not see what threatens or feign not to see, those who have nursed the hopes of Catiline with soft decisions and have strengthened the conspiracy in its infancy by not believing. By reason of the authority of these men many, not only the wicked but also the inexperienced, would say that I had acted like a tyrant and a king, if I had punished him. Now I know, if this fellow goes to the camp of Manlius whither he intends to go, that there will be nobody so stupid as not to see that a conspiracy has been formed, nobody so wicked as not to admit it. I am aware, however, that after the death of this one man, this pest of the Republic can be checked for a little while, but not put down permanently. But if he banishes himself and takes his followers with him, if he brings together all the other derelicts, rounded up from all sides, not only this far advanced destruction of the Republic but even the root and seed of all evils will be removed and destroyed. In fact, senators, for a long time now we have been living in these insidious dangers of conspiracy, but I do not know how it is, somehow or other, that the fullness of all crimes, of ancient fury and boldness, has broken out at the time of my consulship. But if, from such a gang of brigands, this one fellow here will be removed, perhaps for a certain brief period, we shall seem to be relieved of worry and fear, but the danger will remain and be buried deep in the veins and vitals of the Republic. As oftentimes men, ill with a serious disease, when they toss with a high temperature, if they have drunk cold water, at first seem to be relieved, and then are afflicted much more seriously and violently, so this disease in the Republic, if checked by the punishment of this man, will grow worse in a frightful way as long as the rest are alive. Wherefore, let the wicked depart, let them separate themselves from good citizens, let them assemble in one place, and finally, as I have often said before, let them be separated from us by the city wall. Let them cease their treacherous attacks against the consul in his own home, let them cease standing around the tribunal of the city praetor, loafing about the Senate-House with swords, let them cease procuring fire-darts and brands to burn the city. Finally, let it be written on the forehead of everyone what he thinks about the Republic. I promise you this, senators, that there will be such diligence in us, the consuls, such great authority among you, such great valor among the Roman knights, such great agreement among all loyal citizens that at the departure of Catiline you will see all his plotting not only uncovered and brought to light but also suppressed and avenged.

With these omens, Catiline, for the supreme safety of the Republic, for your own destruction and disaster, and the ruin of those who have joined themselves with you in every sort of crime and treason, go forth to your unholy civil war. And thou, O Jupiter, who wert established under the same auspices as this city was by Romulus, thou whom we rightly call the Stayer of this city and the Empire, thou wilt ward off this man and his fellows from thine and the other temples, from the homes and walls of the city, from the lives and fortunes of the citizens, and thou wilt punish these enemies of all loyal citizens, these foes of the fatherland, these robbers of Italy, united in a pact of crime and by a wicked organization, with eternal punishments, both in life and in death.

[TR. KEVIN GUINAGH]

TO HIS WIFE AND FAMILY IN ROME
(FAM. XIV., 2.)
Thessalonica, 58 B.C.

I send this, my dear Terentia, with much love to you, and my little Tullia, and my Marcus.

I hope you will never think that I write longer letters to other people, unless it so happens that any one has written to me about a number of matters that seem to require an answer. In fact, I have nothing to say, nor is there anything just now that I find more difficult. But to you and my dear little girl I cannot write without shedding many tears, when I picture to myself, as plunged in the deepest affliction, you whom my dearest wish has been to see perfectly happy; and this I ought to have secured for you; yes, and I would have secured, but for our being all so faint-hearted.

I am most grateful to our friend Piso for his kind services. I did my best to urge that he would not forget you when I was writing to him; and have now thanked him as in duty bound. I gather that you think there is hope of the new tribunes; that will be a safe thing to depend on, if we may on the profession of Pompeius, but I have my fears of Crassus. It is true I see that everything on your part is done both bravely and lovingly, nor does that surprise me, but what pains me is that it should be my fate to expose you to such severe suffering to relieve my own. For Publius Valerius, who has been most attentive, wrote me word, and it cost me many tears in the reading, how you had been forced to go from the temple of Vesta to the Valerian office. Alas, my light, my love, whom all used once to look up to for relief!—that you, my Terentia, should be treated thus; that you should be thus plunged in tears and misery, and all through my fault! I have indeed preserved others, only for me and mine to perish.

As to what you say about our house—or rather its site—I for my part shall consider my restoration to be complete only when I find that it has been restored to me. But these things are not in our hands: what troubles me is, that in the outlay which must be incurred you, unhappy and impoverished as you are, must necessarily share. However, if we succeed in our object, I shall recover everything; but then, if ill fortune continues to persecute us, are you, my poor dear, to be allowed to throw away what you may have saved from the wreck? As to my expenses, I entreat you, my dearest life, to let other people, who can do so perfectly if they will, relieve you; and be sure as you love me not to let your anxiety injure your health, which you know is so delicate. Night and day you are always before my eyes! I can see you making every exertion on my behalf, and I fear you may not be able to bear it. But I know well that all our hopes are in you. . . .

TO CAESAR IN GAUL
(FAM. VII., 5.)
Rome, 54 B.C.

Cicero greets Caesar, *imperator.* Observe how far I have convinced myself that you are my second self, not only in matters which concern me personally, but even in those which concern my friends. It had been my intention to take Gaius Trebatius with me for whatever destination I should be leaving town, in order to bring him home again honored as much as my zeal and favor could make him. But when Pompey remained home longer than I expected, and a certain hesitation on my part (with which you are not unacquainted) appeared to hinder, or at any rate to retard, my departure, I presumed upon what I will now explain to you. I begin to wish that Trebatius should look to you for what he had hoped from me, and in fact, I have been no more sparing of my promises of goodwill on your part than I had been wont to be of my own. Moreover, an extraordinary coincidence has occurred which seems to support my opinion and to guarantee your kindness. For just as I was speaking to our friend Balbus about this very Trebatius at my house, with more than usual earnestness, a letter from you was handed to me, at the end of which you say: "Miscinius Rufus, whom you recommend to me, I will make king of Gaul, or, if you choose, put him under the care of Lepta. Send me some one else to promote." I and Balbus both lifted our hands in surprise: it came so exactly in the nick of time, that it appeared to be less the result of mere chance than something providential. I therefore send you Trebatius, and on two grounds, first that it was my spontaneous idea to send him, and secondly, because you have invited me to do so. I would beg you, dear Caesar, to receive him with such a display of kindness as to concentrate on his single person all that you can be possibly induced to bestow for my sake upon my friends. As for him I guarantee—not in the sense of that hackneyed expression of mine, at which, when I used it in writing to you about Milo, you very properly jested, but in good Roman language such as sober men use—that no honester, better, or more modest man exists. Added to this, he is at the top of his profession as a jurisconsult, possesses an unequaled memory, and the most profound learning. For such a man I ask neither a tribuneship, prefecture, nor any definite office, I ask only your good-will and liberality: and yet I do not wish to prevent your complimenting him, if it so please you, with even these marks of distinction. In fact, I transfer him entirely from my hand, so to speak, to yours, which is as sure a pledge of good faith as of victory. Excuse my being somewhat importunate, though with a man like you there can hardly be any pretext for it—however, I feel that it will be allowed to pass. Be careful of your health and continue to love me as ever.

(GAIUS JULIUS) CAESAR (100–44 B.C.)

The Gallic War

~⌐

*S*choolchildren for over two millennia who've had the privilege of learning Latin know by heart the opening words: *"Gallia est omnis divisa in partes tres . . ."* ("Gaul is a whole divided into three parts"). The man who penned these elegantly simple words was the father of the Roman Empire, which his nephew Octavius Augustus would found. Accomplished in nearly every aspect of human achievement, Julius Caesar has been called the single most influential man in European history.

His patrician family, the Julii (his father's name was Gaius Caesar, his mother Aurelia of the Cottae *gens*), traced their roots to Trojan hero and founder of the city of Rome, Aeneas Julus, son of Venus; at least four of Julius' ancestors had served as consuls.

He studied under the Gallic teacher of rhetoric Marcus Antonius Gnipho and Molo of Rhodes. Marital alliances with the consul Gaius Marius (Caesar's aunt was his wife) and Marius' lieutenant, the four-time consul Lucius Cornelius Cinna (Caesar's first wife, Cornelia, who died in 68 B.C., was Cinna's daughter), placed Julius Caesar squarely in opposition to the dictator Sulla and to the Senate's growing aspirations for autocracy. His second wife, Sulla's granddaughter Pompeia, he divorced when she was suspected of adultery with Clodius Pulcher, who dressed as a woman to seduce her during the matriarchal Bona Dea festival; and, in 59, Caesar took Calpurnia (daughter of Lucius Piso) as his third wife, whose dream of his assassination he ignored; his lovers were rumored to have included Servilia, mother of Brutus, Pompey's wife Mucia, and King Nicomedes of Bithynia.

Spending extravagantly to enhance his popularity, Caesar served as quaestor, aedile, Pontifex Maximus, and praetor, arguing that the conspirator Catiline should receive the due process accorded any Roman citizen. His fame as an orator, for his command of the simple and elegant Attic style, was second only to Cicero's. But Caesar's destiny, and visionary genius, lay in his talent and energy for conducting warfare and inspiring the unswerving loyalty of his legions. His first military successes were in Spain, where he served a year as governor and defeated the Lusitanians.

Shortly after being elected co-consul with Marcus Calpurnius Bibulus he formed the First Triumvirate by allying with his banker Crassus and Pompey. Pompey married Caesar's daughter (by Cornelia) Julia. With Crassus' wealth and Pompey's storm troopers all senatorial opposition and the power of his rival Bibulus was crushed. Then as proconsul of Gaul and Illyricum, Caesar set out to conquer the rest of Gaul. For nine years, outnumbered by the barbarian tribes—but with discipline, visionary strategy, brilliant tactics, and a sense of timing that would become his most constant characteristic—he overcame all resistance: in Gaul, in Britain, and in Germany.

His military triumphs, the death of Crassus at the battle of Carrhae in 53, the death in childbirth in 54 of Julia, and Pompey's subsequent remarriage to the daughter of Caesar's enemy Metellus Scipio, led inevitably to the Senate's declaring him a public enemy. Caesar defied their decree that he resign his military command and return to Rome alone. He crossed the Rubicon with his army and the Civil War of 49–45 began. The outcome would determine whether the far-flung Roman world would continue to be governed by the undisciplined and decadent aristocracy, or whether it would be reorganized by a dictator dedicated to the old Roman virtues of discipline and tolerance. At Pharsalus, in 48 B.C., against overwhelming odds, Caesar's foot legions defeated the cavalry of Pompey.

When Pompey fled to Egypt, Caesar pursued him—into the heart of the civil war between Ptolemy XIII and his sister Queen Cleopatra. After receiving Pompey's head from Ptolemy and assisting Cleopa-

tra in gaining the throne (and becoming her lover along the way), Caesar returned in triumph to Rome. He held one consulship after another and, because of his victories at the battles of Thapsus (46) and Munda (45), the absolute dictator of Rome—first for ten years; then, in 44, for life. His achievements included:

- Cancellation of farmers' debts;
- Finding homes for his veteran legionnaires and the Roman proletariat by establishing commercial colonies in Corinth and Carthage;
- Establishing the Julian Calendar (January 1, 45 B.C.);
- Ambitious public works throughout Italy;
- Constitutional standardization among the many Italian municipalities;
- Extending Roman citizenship to aliens throughout the provinces;
- Enlarging the Senate to nine hundred and recruiting new senators from the provinces.

But the office of dictator for life was not to last long. On the Ides of March of the same year he received that title and powers, and in which he had declined the title of Rex and the crown offered him by Marc Antony, republican conspirators who called themselves the "Liberators," led by Cassius and Caesar's friend Brutus, assassinated him at the foot of Pompey's statue in the Senate House to put a stop to his increasing despotism. After avenging his uncle by defeating the Liberators, Octavius declared that Julius Caesar was to be worshiped in Rome as a god. The Roman populace was not surprised; they had deified him long ago.

After the battle against the remnants of Pompey's army at Zela, in Asia Minor, Caesar reported his victory to Rome in his most famous epigram: *"Veni, vidi, vici"* ("I came, I saw, I conquered").

- We know that he wrote poems; a diatribe against Marcus Portius Cato Uticensis *(Anticato),* written in response to Cicero's laudatory *Cato*; a book on grammar and the proper formation of words, dedicated to Cicero *(De Analogia)*; and a collection of jokes and proverbs. The only writings that have survived are his commentaries: one his propagandistic view of the Civil War between him and Pompey; the other on his conduct of the Gallic Wars. Accounts credited to him of his Alexandrine War, African War, and Spanish War were written by anonymous officers.
- Caesar's seven books of commentaries on the Gallic Wars, *De Bello Gallico,* were memoirs of his victorious campaigns conducted from 58 to 52 B.C. (published in 51–50) and presented himself as a hard-headed patriot taking care of business for his beloved Rome. Aulus Hirtius, his staff officer, later added an eighth book, taking Caesar's account from 52 to 50 B.C. Written in elegantly simple and impeccable diction, and a sometimes repetitious but generally straightforward third-person style, the commentaries are most distinguished for their vividly forceful and urgent narrative. The spartan nature of Caesar's prose, as though written by an objective eyewitness, reads like dispatches from the front and memorably highlights the events and characters he describes.

BOOK I

Gaul is a whole divided into three parts, one of which is inhabited by the Belgae, another by the Aquitani, and a third by a people called in their own tongue Celtae, in the Latin Galli. All these are different one from another in language, institutions, and laws. The Galli (Gauls) are separated from the Aquitani by the river Garonne, from the Belgae by the Marne and the Seine. Of all these peoples the Belgae are the most courageous, because they are farthest removed from the culture and the civilization of the Province, and least often visited by merchants introducing the commodities that make for effeminacy; and also because they are nearest to the Germans dwelling beyond the Rhine, with whom they are continually at war. For this cause the Helvetii also excel the rest of the Gauls in valour, because they are struggling in almost daily fights with the Germans, either endeavouring to keep them out of Gallic territory or waging an aggressive warfare in German territory. The separate part of the country which, as has been said, is occupied by the Gauls, starts from the river Rhone, and is bounded by the river Garonne, the Ocean, and the territory of the Belgae; moreover, on the side of the Sequani and the Helvetii, it touches the river Rhine; and its general trend is northward. The Belgae, beginning from the edge of the Gallic territory, reach to the lower part of the river Rhine, bearing toward the north and east. Aquitania, starting from the Garonne, reaches to the Pyrenees and to that part of the Ocean which is by Spain: its bearing is between west and north.

Among the Helvetii the noblest man by far and the most wealthy was Orgetorix. In the consulship of Marcus Messalla and Marcus Piso, his desire for the kingship led him to form a conspiracy of the nobility, and he persuaded the community to march out of their territory in full force, urging that as they excelled all in valor it was easy enough to secure the sovereignty of all Gaul. In this he persuaded them the more easily, because the Helvetii are closely confined by the nature of their territory. On one side there is the river Rhine, exceeding broad and deep, which separates the Helvetian territory from the Germans; on another the Jura range, exceeding high, lying between the Sequani and the Helvetii; on the third, the Lake of Geneva and the river Rhone, which separates the Roman Province from the Helvetii. In such circumstances their range of movement was less extensive, and their chances of waging war on their neighbors were less easy; and on this account they were greatly distressed, for they were men that longed for war. Nay, they could not but consider that the territory they occupied—to an extent of 240 miles long and 180 broad—was all too narrow for their population and for their renown of courage in war.

Swayed by these considerations and stirred by the influence of Orgetorix, they determined to collect what they needed for taking the field, to buy up as large a number as they could of draught-cattle and carts, to sow as much corn as possible so as to have a sufficient supply thereof on the march, and to establish peace and amity with the nearest communities. For the accomplishment of these objects they considered that two years were sufficient, and pledged themselves by an ordinance to take the field in the third year. For the accomplishment of these objects Orgetorix was chosen, and he took upon himself an embassage to the communities. In the course of his travels he persuaded Casticus, of the Sequani, son of Catamantaloedes, who had held for many years the kingship of the Sequani, and had been called by the Senate "the friend of the Roman people," to seize in his own state the kingship which his father had held before him; and Dumnorix also, of the Aedui, brother of Diviciacus, at that time holding the chieftaincy of the state and a great favorite with the common people, he persuaded to a like endeavor, and gave him his own daughter in marriage. He convinced them that it was easy enough to accomplish such endeavors, because he himself (so he said) was about to secure the sovereignty of his own state. There was no doubt, he observed, that the Helvetii were the most powerful tribe in all Gaul, and he gave a pledge that he would win them their kingdoms with his own resources and his own army. Swayed by this speech, they gave a mutual pledge, confirming it by oath; and they hoped that when they had seized their kingship they would be able, through the efforts of three most powerful and most steadfast tribes, to master the whole of Gaul.

The design was revealed to the Helvetii by informers. In accordance with their custom they compelled Orgetorix to take his trial in bonds. If he were condemned, the penalty of being burnt alive was the consequence. On the day appointed for his trial Orgetorix gathered from every quarter to the place of judgment all his retainers, to the number of some ten thousand men, and also assembled there all his clients and debtors, of whom he had a great number, and through their means escaped from taking his trial. The state, being incensed at this, essayed to secure its due rights by force of arms, and the magistrates were bringing together a number of men from the country parts, when Orgetorix died, not without suspicion, as the Helvetii think, of suicide.

After his death the Helvetii essayed none the less to accomplish their determination to march forth from their borders. When at length they deemed that they were prepared for that purpose, they set fire to all their strongholds, in number about twelve; their villages, in number about four hundred, and the rest of their private buildings; they burnt up all their corn save that which they were to carry with them, to the intent that by removing all hope of return homeward they might prove the readier to undergo any perils; and they commanded every man to take for himself from home a three months' provision of victuals. They persuaded their neighbors, the Rauraci, the Tulingi, and the Latobrigi, to adopt the same plan, burn up their strongholds and villages, and march out with them; and they received as partners of their alliance the Boii, who had been dwellers beyond the Rhine, but had crossed over into Noricum and attacked Noreia.

There were two routes, and no more, by which they could leave their homeland. One lay through the territory of the Sequani, betwixt the Jura range and the river Rhone, a narrow route and a difficult, where carts could scarce be drawn in single file; with an exceeding high mountain overhanging it, so that a very few men might easily check them. The other route, through the Roman Province, was far more easy and convenient, forasmuch as the Rhone flows between the borders of the Helvetii and the Allobroges (who had lately been brought to peace), and is in some places fordable. The last town of the Allobroges, the nearest to the borders of the Helvetii, is Geneva, from which a bridge stretches across to the Helvetii. These supposed that either they would persuade the Allobroges (deeming them not yet well disposed toward the Roman people), or would compel them perforce to suffer a passage through their borders. Having therefore provided all things for their departure, they named a day by which all should assemble upon the bank of the Rhone. The day was the 28th of March, in the consulship of Lucius Piso and Aulus Gabinius.

When Caesar was informed that they were endeavoring to march through the Roman Province, he made speed to leave Rome, and hastening to Further Gaul by as rapid stages as possible, arrived near Geneva. From the whole

Province he requisitioned the largest possible number of troops (there was in Further Gaul no more than a single legion), and ordered the bridge at Geneva to be broken down. When the Helvetii learned of his coming, they sent as deputies to him the noblest men of the state. Nammeius and Verucloetius held the chief place in the deputation, with instructions to say that their purpose was to march through the Province without any mischief, because they had no other route; and they asked that they might have leave so to do of his good will. Remembering that the consul Lucius Cassius had been slain, and his army routed and sent under the yoke, by the Helvetii, Caesar considered that no concession should be made; nor did he believe that men of unfriendly disposition, if granted an opportunity of marching through the Province, would refrain from outrage and mischief. However, to gain an interval for the assembly of the troops he had levied, he replied to the deputies that he would take a space of time for consideration: if they wished for anything, they were to return on the 13th of April.

In the meanwhile he used the legion which he had with him, and the troops which had concentrated from the Province, to construct a continuous wall, sixteen feet high, and a trench, from the Lake of Geneva, which flows into the river Rhone, to the Jura range, which separates the territory of the Sequani from the Helvetii, a distance of nineteen miles. This work completed, he posted separate garrisons, in entrenched forts, in order that he might more easily be able to stop any attempt of the enemy to cross against his wish. When the day which he had appointed with the deputies arrived, and the deputies returned to him, he said that,

following the custom and precedent of the Roman people, he could not grant anyone a passage through the Province; and he made it plain that he would stop any attempt to force the same. Disappointed of this hope, the Helvetii attempted, sometimes by day, more often by night, to break through, either by joining boats together and making a number of rafts, or by fording the Rhone where the depth of the stream was least. But they were checked by the line of the entrenchment and, as the troops concentrated rapidly, by missiles, and so abandoned the attempt.

There remained one other line of route, through the borders of the Sequani, by which they could not march, on account of the narrow ways, without the consent of the Sequani. When they could not of their own motion persuade the Sequani, they sent deputies to Dumnorix the Aeduan, in order that they might attain their object through his intercession. Now Dumnorix had very great weight with the Sequani, for he was both popular and openhanded, and he was friendly to the Helvetii, because from that state he had taken the daughter of Orgetorix to wife; and, spurred by desire of the kingship, he was anxious for a revolution, and eager to have as many states as might be beholden to his own beneficence. Therefore he accepted the business, and prevailed on the Sequani to suffer the Helvetii to pass through their borders, and arranged that they should give hostages each to other—the Sequani, not to prevent the Helvetii from their march; the Helvetii, to pass through without mischief or outrage.

The news was brought back to Caesar that the Helvetii were minded to march through the land of the Sequani and the Aedui into the borders of the Santones, which are not far removed from the borders of the Tolosates, a state in the Province. He perceived that this event would bring great danger upon the Province; for it would have a warlike tribe, unfriendly to the Roman people, as neighbors to a district which was at once unprotected and very rich in corn. For these reasons he set Titus Labienus, lieutenant-general, in command of the fortification which he had made, and himself hurried by forced marches into Italy. There he enrolled two legions, and brought out of winter quarters three that were wintering about Aquileia; and with these five legions made speed to march by the shortest route to Further Gaul, over the Alps. In that region the Ceutrones, the Graioceli, and the Caturiges, seizing points on the higher ground, essayed to stop the march of his army. They were repulsed in several actions; and on the seventh day he moved from Ocelum, the last station of Hither Gaul, into the borders of the Vocontii in Further Gaul. Thence he led his army into the borders of the Allobroges, and from thence into the country of the Segusiavi, the first tribe outside the Province, across the Rhone.

By this time the Helvetii, having brought their own forces through the defiles and through the borders of the Sequani, had reached the borders of the Aedui, and were engaged in laying waste their lands. Unable to defend their persons and their property from the invaders, the Aedui sent deputies to Caesar to ask for aid. These pleaded that the Aedui had always deserved too well of the Roman people to merit the devastation of their lands, the removal of their children into slavery, and the capture of

their towns, almost in sight of the Roman army. At the same time the Aedui Ambarri, close allies and kinsmen of the Aedui, informed Caesar that their lands had been laid waste, and that they could not easily safeguard their towns from the violence of the enemy. The Allobroges also, who had villages and settlements across the Rhone, fled to Caesar, affirming that they had nothing left to them save the bare ground. All these events drove Caesar to the decision that he must not wait till the Helvetii, having wasted all the substance of the Roman allies, should penetrate into the land of the Santoni.

There is a river Arar (Saône), which flows through the borders of the Aedui and the Sequani into the Rhone: its sluggishness is beyond belief, for the eye cannot determine in which direction the stream flows. This river the Helvetii proceeded to cross by rafts and boats fastened together. When Caesar's scouts informed him that three-quarters of the Helvetian forces had actually crossed, and that about a quarter remained on the near side of the river Saône, he left camp in the third watch with three legions and came up to the division of the enemy which had not yet crossed. He attacked them unawares when they were heavily loaded, and put a great number of them to the sword; the remainder betook themselves to flight and hid in the nearest woods. The name of the canton was the Tigurine; for the whole state of Helvetia is divided into four cantons. In the recollection of the last generation this canton had marched out alone from its homeland, and had slain the consul Lucius Cassius and sent his army under the yoke. And so, whether by accident or by the purpose of the immortal gods, the section of the Helvetian state which had brought so signal a calamity upon the Roman people was the first to pay the penalty in full. Therein Caesar avenged private as well as national outrages; for in the same battle with Cassius the Tigurini had slain Lucius Piso the general, grandfather of Lucius Piso, Caesar's father-in-law.

This action over, he caused a bridge to be made over the Saône and sent his army across thereby, in order to pursue the remainder of the Helvetian forces. Alarmed at his sudden approach—for they perceived that the business of crossing the river, which they themselves had accomplished with the greatest difficulty in twenty days, had been despatched by Caesar in a single one—the Helvetii sent deputies to him. The leader of the deputation was Divico, who had been commander of the Helvetii in the campaign against Cassius. He treated with Caesar as follows: If the Roman people would make peace with the Helvetii, they would go whither and abide where Caesar should determine and desire; if on the other hand he should continue to visit them with war, he was advised to remember the earlier disaster of the Roman people and the ancient valor of the Helvetii. He had attacked one canton unawares, when those who had crossed the river could not bear assistance to their fellows; but that event must not induce him to rate his own valor highly or to despise them. The Helvetii had learnt from their parents and ancestors to fight their battles with courage, not with cunning nor reliance upon stratagem. Caesar therefore must not allow the place of their conference to derive renown or perpetuate remembrance by a disaster to the Roman people and the destruction of an army.

To these remarks Caesar replied as follows: As he remembered well the events which the Helvetian deputies had mentioned, he had therefore the less need to hesitate; and his indignation was the more vehement in proportion as the Roman people had not deserved the misfortune. If the Romans had been conscious of some outrage done, it would not have been hard to take precaution; but they had been misled, because they did not understand that they had done anything to cause them apprehension, and they thought that they should not feel apprehension without cause. And even if he were willing to forget an old affront, could he banish the memory of recent outrages— their attempts to march by force against his will through the Province, their ill-treatment of the Aedui, the Ambarri, the Allobroges? Their insolent boast of their own victory, their surprise that their outrages had gone on so long with impunity, pointed the same way; for it was the wont of the immortal gods to grant a temporary prosperity and a longer impunity to make men whom they purposed to punish for their crime smart the more severely from a change of fortune. Yet, for all this, he would make peace with the Helvetii, if they would offer him hostages to show him that they would perform their promises, and if they would give satisfaction to the Aedui in respect of the outrages inflicted on them and their allies, and likewise to the Allobroges. Divico replied: It was the ancestral practice and the regular custom of the Helvetii to receive, not to offer, hostages; the Roman people was witness thereof. With this reply he departed.

Next day the Helvetii moved their camp from that spot. Caesar did likewise, sending forward the whole of his cavalry, four thousand in number, which he had raised from the whole of the Province, from the Aedui, and from their allies, to observe in which direction the enemy were marching. The cavalry, following up the rearguard too eagerly, engaged in a combat on unfavorable ground with the cavalry of the Helvetii, and a few of ours fell. Elated by this engagement, because five hundred of their horsemen had routed so large a host of ours, the Helvetii began on occasion to make a bolder stand, and with their rearguard to provoke the Romans to a fight. Caesar kept his troops from fighting, accounting it sufficient for the present to prevent the enemy from plundering, foraging, and devastation. The march continued for about a fortnight with no more interval than five or six miles a day between the rearguard of the enemy and the vanguard of the Romans.

Meanwhile Caesar was daily pressing the Aedui for the corn that they had promised as a state. For by reason of cold weather (since Gaul, as has been said above, lies under the northern heaven) not only were the corn-crops in the fields unripe, but there was not even a sufficient supply of forage to be had. At the same time he was less able to use the corn-supply that he had brought up the river Saône in boats, because the Helvetii had diverted their march from the Saône, and he did not wish to lose touch with them. The Aedui put him off day after day, declaring that the corn was being collected, was being brought in, was at hand. He perceived that he was being put off too long, and that the day was close upon him whereon it was proper to issue the corn-ration to the troops: accordingly he summoned together the

Aeduan chiefs, of whom he had a great number in his camp, among them Diviciacus and Liscus, who had the highest magistracy, called Vergobret by the Aedui: the magistrate is elected annually, and holds the power of life and death over his fellow-countrymen. Caesar called them severely to account because they offered no relief in a time of stress, with the enemy close at hand, when corn could neither be purchased nor taken from the fields. And just because he had undertaken the war largely in response to their entreaties, he complained the more severely of their desertion.

Then, and not till then, the remarks of Caesar induced Liscus to reveal a fact concealed before. There were, he said, certain persons, of paramount influence with the common folk, and of more power in their private capacity than the actual magistrates. These persons, by seditious and insolent language, were intimidating the population against the collection of corn as required, on the plea that it was better for the Aedui, if they could not now enjoy the primacy of Gaul, to submit to the commands of Gauls rather than of Romans; for they did not doubt that, if the Romans overcame the Helvetii, they meant to deprive the Aedui of liberty, in common with the rest of Gaul. These, again, were the men, who informed the enemy of the Roman plans and all the doings of the camp; nor had he power to restrain them. Nay, more, he perceived with what risk he had acted in informing Caesar, under sheer force of necessity; and for that reason he had held his peace as long as he could.

Caesar felt that Dumnorix, the brother of Diviciacus, was indicated in these remarks of Liscus; but as he would not have those matters

Temple to Julius Caesar, Roman Forum

threshed out in presence of a company, he speedily dismissed the meeting. He kept Liscus back, and questioned him separately on his statement in the assembly. Liscus now spoke with greater freedom and boldness. Caesar questioned others privately upon the same matters, and found that it was so—that Dumnorix was the man who, unequaled in boldness, and strong in the influence that his generosity gave him over the common folk, desired a revolution. For several years, it was said, he had contracted at a low price for the customs and all the rest of the Aeduan taxes, for the simple reason that when he made a bid none durst bid against him. By this means he had at once

increased his own property and acquired ample resources for bribery; he maintained a considerable body of horse permanently at his own charges, and kept them about his person; not only in his own but even in neighboring states his power was extensive. To secure this power he had given his mother in marriage to the noblest and most powerful man among the Bituriges, he had taken himself a wife from the Helvetii, and had married his half-sister and his female relations to men of other states. This connection made him a zealous supporter of the Helvetii; moreover, he hated Caesar and the Romans on his own account, because their arrival had diminished his power and restored his brother Diviciacus to his ancient place of influence and honor. If anything should happen to the Romans, he entertained the most confident hope of securing the kingship by means of the Helvetii: it was the empire of the Roman people which caused him to despair not only of the kingship, but even of the influence he now possessed. Caesar discovered also in the course of his questioning, as concerning the unsuccessful cavalry engagement of a few days before, that Dumnorix and his horsemen (he was commander of the body of horse sent by the Aedui to the aid of Caesar) had started the retreat, and that by their retreat the remainder of the horse had been stricken with panic.

All this Caesar learnt, and to confirm these suspicions he had indisputable facts. Dumnorix had brought the Helvetii through the borders of the Sequani; he had caused hostages to be given between them; he had done all this not only without orders from his state or from Caesar, but even without the knowledge of either; he was now accused by the magistrate of the Aedui. Caesar deemed all this to be cause enough for him either to punish Dumnorix himself, or to command the state so to do. To all such procedure there was one objection, the knowledge that Diviciacus, the brother of Dumnorix, showed the utmost zeal for the Roman people, the utmost goodwill toward himself, in loyalty, in justice, in prudence alike remarkable; for Caesar apprehended that the punishment of Dumnorix might offend the feelings of Diviciacus. Therefore, before attempting anything in the matter, Caesar ordered Diviciacus to be summoned to his quarters, and, having removed the regular interpreters,

conversed with him through the mouth of Gaius Valerius Procillus, a leading man in the Province of Gaul and his own intimate friend, in whom he had the utmost confidence upon all matters. Caesar related the remarks which had been uttered in his presence as concerning Dumnorix at the assembly of the Gauls, and showed what each person had said severally to him upon the same subject. He asked and urged that without offence to the feelings of Diviciacus he might either hear his case himself and pass judgment upon him, or order the state so to do.

With many tears Diviciacus embraced Caesar, and began to beseech him not to pass too severe a judgment upon his brother. "I know," said he, "that the reports are true, and no one is more pained thereat than I, for at a time when I had very great influence in my own state and in the rest of Gaul, and he very little, by reason of his youth, he owed his rise to me; and now he is using his resources and his strength not only to the diminution of my influence, but almost to my destruction. For all that, I feel the force of brotherly love and public opinion. That is to say, if too severe a fate befalls him at your hands, no one, seeing that I hold this place in your friendship, will opine that it has been done without *my* consent; and this will turn from me the feelings of all Gaul." While he was making this petition at greater length, and with tears, Caesar took him by the hand and consoled him, bidding him end his entreaty, and showing that his influence with Caesar was so great that he excused the injury to Rome and the vexation felt by himself, in consideration for the goodwill and the entreaties of Diviciacus. Then he summoned Dumnorix to his quarters, and in the presence of his brother he pointed out what he had to blame in him; he set forth what he himself perceived, and the complaints of the state; he warned him to avoid all occasions of suspicion for the future, and said that he excused the past in consideration for his brother Diviciacus. . . .

PUBLILIUS (SYRUS) (FL. 50 B.C.)

Maxims

By the time of Caesar and Cicero, Roman drama had deteriorated to pantomime—a silent performance satirizing current leaders and events in the mode of today's political cartoons. Publilius the Syrian, one of Rome's greatest mimes, arrived as a slave in Rome, probably from Antioch in 46 B.C., but was freed and educated by his master when his literary ingeniousness and acting talents became evident. In the theatrical competition sponsored by Julius Caesar in 45, Publilius defeated the popular Laberius.

- He became a masterful writer of mimes, his work dominating the stage after the death of rival Laberius. We know that his plays included *The Pruners* and *Murmurithon*.
- The ever-practical Romans, who preferred proverbs to philosophical treatises, particularly loved him for his ability to turn a phrase. Though his plays were soon forgotten, over six hundred of his maxims survive in schoolbooks to this day.

Love, or hate: a woman knows no third.

Love is not driven out, but slips away.

Scarcely a god can both love and be wise.

To take a kindness is to sell your freedom.

To die at another's will is to die twice.

Good reputation is more safe than wealth.

To be reconciled with foes is never safe.

Danger comes quicker when it is despised.

War long prepared brings rapid victory.

Women know how to tell a lie by weeping.

Kindness is doubled if it is but hastened.

Even a single hair still casts a shadow.

He whom fate cherishes becomes a fool.

Dangerous he who thinks it safe to die!

Poverty needs a little; greed needs all.

(DECIMUS) LABERIUS (C. 105–43 B.C.)
An Old Actor Addresses Julius Caesar

The first Roman to give written form to mimes was controversial among his contemporaries. Cicero found him boring, Horace accused him of being unpoetic and vulgar, and Julius Caesar, whom Laberius had criticized more than once, forced him to face the upstart ex-slave Publilius in a mime contest—which Publilius won. Shortly after, Laberius retired to Puteoli, where he died less than a year after Caesar's assassination.

- Though we know more than forty of his titles, only a hundred or so of his lines survive to testify to his vigorous style and verbal ingenuity. For the first time in Rome, women acted in his mimes.
- The ironic recantation that follows, written in the lofty six-foot iambic senarius meter, served as prologue to the command performance before Caesar when Laberius was sixty years old. Caesar's intention was to humiliate the old knight and thereby heighten his own control over the equestrian order. Laberius used the opportunity to celebrate freedom and condemn tyranny, embarrassing Caesar enough to lead him to give the crown for mime to Laberius' rival Publilius.

Entrance to theater, Italica

AN OLD ACTOR ADDRESSES JULIUS CAESAR

Necessity, the impact of whose sidelong course
Many attempt to escape and only few succeed,
Whither have you thrust down, almost to his
*   wits' ends,*
Him whom flattery, whom never bribery
Could in his youth avail to shake him from his
*   stand?*
But see how easily an old man slips, and
*   shows—*
Moved by the complacency of this most excel-
*   lent man—*
Calm and complaisant, a submissive, fawning
*   speech!*

Yet naught to a conqueror could the gods
*   themselves deny,*
And who then would permit one man to say
*   him nay?*
I who existed sixty long years without stain,
A Roman Knight who went from his paternal
*   gods,*
Now return home a mime. And certainly today
I've lived out one more day than I should have
*   lived.*
Fortune, unrestrained in prosperity and ill,

Were it your pleasure with the lure and praise
*   of letters*
To shatter the very summit of my good name,

Why when I prospered, when my limbs were
green with youth,
When I could satisfy an audience and such a
man,
Did you not bend my suppleness and spit on
me?
Now you cast me? Whither? What brought I to
the stage?

The ornament of beauty, dignity of flesh,
Fire of the spirit, the music of a pleasing
voice?
As twining ivy kills the stout heart of the
tree,
So has senility in time's embrace destroyed
me
And like a sepulchre I keep only a name.

(SEXTUS) PROPERTIUS (C. 50–16 B.C.)

Elegies

~⌐

*N*ative of Umbrian Asisium (modern Assisi), this intriguing Roman elegist was born to an equestrian father, much of whose estate was confiscated by Octavian after Philippi (41–40 B.C.). The impecunious young Propertius arrived in Rome to study the law, but, attracted by Virgil and Ovid, decided to pursue the muse instead. His personality was brooding, his mood characteristically self-centered and morbid. His patron was the famous Gaius Maecenas, who also supported the jealous Horace.

- Propertius' first book of graceful and visually graphic love poetry, known as *Cynthia monobiblos,* was dedicated to his fiery five-year affair with a sophisticated and cruelly whimsical courtesan he called Cynthia (Apuleius reports her real name was Hostia). By his third book of elegies he was self-consciously imitating the overwrought literary ostentatiousness of the Alexandrian poets Callimachus and Philetas, bending the Latin language to his purposes as he strove for universality. Yet despite lapses into mannerism Propertius achieves a unique erratic grandeur.
- First-hand expert in the psychology of passion, Propertius' elegies, uneven in style but always ardent, celebrate the ups and downs of urban love, enthusiasm always undermined by inevitable disillusionment, moods progressing "from ecstasy to baffled rage and dejection." He was the greatest of the elegists.

BEAUTY UNADORNED
(I., 2.)

Dear girl, what boots it thus to dress thy hair,
Or flaunt in silken garment rich and rare,
To reek of perfume from a foreign mart,
And pass thyself for other than thou art—
Thus Nature's gift of beauty to deface
And rob thy own fair form of half its grace?
Trust me, no skill can greater charms impart;
Love is a naked boy and scorns all art.
Bears not the sod unbidden blossoms rare?
The untrained ivy, is it not most fair?
Greenest the shrub on rocks untended grows,
Brightest the rill in unhewn channel flows.

The beach is with unpolished pebbles gay,
And birds untutored trill the sweetest lay.
Not thus the damsels of the golden age
Were wont the hearts of heroes to engage:
Their loveliness was to no jewels due,
But to such tints as once Apelles drew.
From vain coquettish arts they all were free,
Content to charm with simple modesty.
By thee despite to me will ne'er be done;
The woman pleases well who pleases one.

[TR. GOLDWIN SMITH]

TO MAECENAS
(II., 1.)

You ask, why thus my loves I still rehearse,
Whence the soft strain and ever-melting verse?
From Cynthia all that in my numbers shines;
She is my genius, she inspires the lines;
No Phoebus else, no other Muse I know,
She tunes my easy rhyme, and gives the lay to
  flow.

If the loose curls around her forehead play,
Or lawless, o'er their ivory margin stray:
If the thin Coan web her shape reveal,
And half disclose those limbs it should conceal;
Of those loose curls, that ivory front I write;
Of the dear web whole volumes I indite:
Or if to music she the lyre awake,
That the soft subject of my song I make,
And sing with what a careless grace she flings
Her artful hand across the sounding strings.
If sinking into sleep she seem to close
Her languid lids, I favor her repose
With lulling notes, and thousand beauties see
That slumber brings to aid my poetry.
When, less averse, and yielding to desires,
She half accepts, and half rejects, my fires,
While to retain the envious lawn she tries,
And struggles to elude my longing eyes,
The fruitful Muse from that auspicious night
Dates the long Iliad of the amorous fight.
In brief, whate'er she do, or say, or look,
'T is ample matter for a lover's book;
And many a copious narrative you'll see
Big with the important nothing's history.
Yet would the tyrant love permit me raise
My feeble voice, to sound the victor's praise,
To paint the hero's toil, the ranks of war,
The laurell'd triumph and the sculptured car;
No giant race, no tumult of the skies,
No mountain-structures in my verse should rise,
Nor tale of Thebes, nor Ilium there should be,
Nor how the Persian trod th' indignant sea;
Not Marius' Cimbrian wreaths would I relate,
Nor lofty Carthage struggling with her fate.
Here should Augustus great in arms appear,
And thou, Maecenas, be my second care;
Here Mutina from flames and famine free,

And there th' ensanguined wave of Sicily,
And sceptred Alexandria's captive shore,
And sad Philippi, red with Roman gore:
Then, while the vaulted skies loud Ios rend,
In golden chains should loaded monarchs
    bend,
And hoary Nile with pensive aspect seem
To mourn the glories of his sevenfold stream,
While prows, that late in fierce encounter met,
Move through the Sacred Way and vainly
    threat,
Thee too the Muse should consecrate to fame,
And with her garlands weave they ever-faithful
    name.

    But nor Callimachus' enervate strain
May tell of Jove, and Phlegra's blasted plain;
Nor I with unaccustom'd vigor trace
Back to its source divine the Julian race.
Sailors to tell of winds and seas delight,
The shepherd of his flocks, the soldier of the
    fight,
A milder warfare I in verse display;
Each in his proper art should waste the day:
Nor thou my gentle calling disapprove,
To die is glorious in the bonds of love.

    Happy the youth, and not unknown to
    fame,
Whose heart has never felt a second flame.
Oh, might that envied happiness be mine!
To Cynthia all my wishes I confine;
Or if, alas! it be my fate to try
Another love, the quicker let me die:
But she, the mistress of my faithful breast,
Has oft the charms of constancy confessed,
Condemns her fickle sex's fond mistake,
And hates the tale of Troy for Helen's sake.
Me from myself the soft enchantress stole;
Ah! let her ever my desires control,

Or if I fall the victim of her scorn,
From her loved door may my pale corse be
    borne.
The power of herbs can other harms remove,
And find a cure for every ill but love.
The Malian's hurt Machaon could repair,
Heal the slow chief, and send again to war;
To Chiron Phoenix owed his long-lost sight,
And Phoebus' son recall'd Androgeos to the
    light.
Here arts are vain, e'en magic here must fail,
The powerful mixture and the midnight
    spell;
The hand that can my captive heart release,
And to this bosom give its wonted peace,
May the long thirst of Tantalus allay,
Or drive th' infernal vulture from his prey.
For ills unseen what remedy is found?
Or who can probe the undiscover'd wound?
The bed avails not, nor the leech's care,
Nor changing skies can hurt, nor sultry air.
'T is hard th' elusive symptoms to explore;
To-day the lover walks, to-morrow is no more;
A train of mourning friends attend his pall,
And wonder at the sudden funeral.

    When then my fates that breath they gave
    shall claim,
And the short marble but preserve a name,
A little verse my all that shall remain,
Thy passing courser's slacken'd speed restrain,
(Thou envied honor of thy poet's days,
Of all our youth th' ambition and the praise!)
Then to my quiet urn awhile draw near,
And say, while o'er the place you drop a tear,
"Love and the fair were of his life the pride;
He lived, while she was kind; and when she
    frown'd, he died."

                    [TR. THOMAS GRAY]

A CHANGE OF VIEW
(III., 5, 19 seq.)

Long as of youth the joyous hours remain,
Me may Castalia's sweet recess detain,
Fast by th' umbrageous vale lull'd to repose,
Where Aganippe warbles as it flows;
Or roused by sprightly sounds from out the
    trance,
I'd in the ring knit hands, and join the Muses'
    dance.
Give me to send the laughing bowl around,
My soul in Bacchus' pleasing fetters bound;
Let on this head unfading flowers reside,
There bloom the vernal rose's earliest pride;
And when, our flames commission'd to destroy,
Age step 'twixt love and me, and intercept the
    joy;
When my changed head these locks no more
    shall know,
And all its jetty honors turn to snow;
Then let me rightly tell of nature's ways;
To Providence, to Him my thoughts I'd raise,
Who taught this vast machine its steadfast laws,
That first, eternal, universal cause;
Search to what region yonder star retires,
That monthly waning hides her paly fires,
And whence, anew revived, with silver light
Relumes her crescent orb to cheer the dreary
    night:
How rising winds the face of ocean sweep,
Where lie th' eternal fountains of the deep,
And whence the cloudy magazines maintain
Their wintry war, or pour th' autumnal rain;
How flames, perhaps, with dire confusion hurl'd,
Shall sink this beauteous fabric of the world;
What colors paint the vivid arch of Jove;
What wondrous force the solid earth can move,
When Pindus' self approaching ruin dreads,

Shakes all his pines, and bows his hundred
    heads;
Why does yon orb, so exquisitely bright,
Obscure his radiance in a short-lived night;
Whence the seven Sisters' congregated fires,
And what Boötes' lazy wagon tires;
How the rude surge its sandy bounds control;
Who measured out the year and bade the sea-
    sons roll;
If realms beneath those fabled torments know,
Pangs without respite, fires that ever glow,
Earth's monster brood stretch'd on their iron
    bed,
The hissing terrors round Alecto's head,
Scarce to nine acres Tityus' bulk confined,
The triple dog that scares the shadowy kind,
All angry heaven inflicts, or hell can feel,
The pendent rock, Ixion's whirling wheel,
Famine at feasts, and thirst amid the stream;
Or are our fears th' enthusiast's empty dream,
And all the scenes, that hurt the grave's repose,
But pictured horror and poetic woes.

   These soft inglorious joys my hours engage;
Be love my youth's pursuit, and science crown
    my age.
You, whose young bosoms feel a nobler flame,
Redeem what Crassus lost, and vindicate his
    name.

[TR. THOMAS GRAY]

A ROMAN MATRON TO HER HUSBAND
(V., 11.)

Weep no more, Paullus, where thy wife is laid:
At the dark gate thy prayer will beat in vain;
Once let the nether realm receive the shade,
The adamantine bar turns not again.

Prayer may move heaven, but, the sad river
    passed,
The grave relentless gives not back its dead:
Such sentence spake the funeral trumpet's blast,
As sank in funeral flames thy loved one's head.

No honors that on Paullus' consort wait,
No pride of ancestry or storied bust,
Could save Cornelia from her cruel fate:
Now one small hand may hold her grandeur's
    dust.

Shades of the Dead and sluggish fens that
    gloom
Around Hell's murky shores my steps to bind,
Before my hour, but pure in soul, I come,
Then let the Judge of all the Dead be kind.

Call the dread court: let silence reign in Hell;
Set for an hour the damned from torture free,
And still the Guardian Hound. If aught I tell
But truth, fall Hell's worst penalty on me.

Is honor to a glorious lineage due?
What my sires were, Afric and Spain proclaim;
Nor poor the blood I from my mother drew,
For well may Libo's match with Scipio's name.

And when, my virgin vesture laid aside,
They placed the matron's wreath upon my head,
Thine, Paullus, I became, till death thy bride:
"Wedded to one" shall on my tomb be read.

By glory's shrine I swear, great Scipio's tomb,
Where sculptured Afric sits a captive maid,
By him that led the Macedonian home
In chains and all his pride in ruin laid,

Never for me was bent the censor's law;
Never by me wrong to your honor done;
Your scutcheon to Cornelia owes no flaw,
To her your roll of worthy names owes one.

Nor failed my virtue; faithful still I stood,
And stainless from the bridal to the bier.
No law I needed save my noble blood;
The basely born are innocent through fear.

Judge strictly as ye will, within the bound
Of Death's wide realm not one, matron or maid,
Howe'er renowned in story, will be found
To shun communion with Cornelia's shade.

Not she, the wife of purity unstained,
At touch of whose pure hand Cybele moved,
When hands less pure in vain the cable
    strained,
Not she, the virgin of the gods beloved,

For whom, when Vesta's sacred fire was lost,
It from her votary's robe rekindled sprang.
And thou, dear mother, did thy child e'er cost
Thee, save by her untimely fate, a pang?

Short was my span, yet children three I bore,
And in their arms I drew my latest breath;
In these I live although my life is o'er;
Their dear embraces took the sting from death.

Twice did my brother fill the curule chair,
There sat he when I parted. Daughter, thou
Wast born a censor's child; be it thy care
Like me, by wedded troth, his rule to show.

Now I bequeath our children to thy heart,
Husband, though I am dust, that care is mine;
Father and mother too henceforth thou art;
Around one neck now all those arms must twine.

Kiss for thyself and then for her that's gone;
Thy love alone the whole dear burden bears;
If e'er for me thou weepest, weep alone,
And see, to cheat their lips, thou driest thy
  tears.

Be it enough by night thy grief to pour,
By night to commune with Cornelia's shade;
If to my likeness in thy secret bower
Thou speakest, speak as though I answer made.

Should time bring on another wedding day,
And set a stepdame in your mother's place,
My children, let your looks no gloom betray;
Kind ways and loving words will win her
  grace.

Nor speak too much of me; the jealous ear
Of the new wife perchance offence may take;
But ah! if my poor ashes are so dear
That he will live unwedded for my sake,

Learn, children, to forestall your sire's decline,
And let no lonesome thought come near his life;
Add to your years what Fate has reft from mine;
Blest in my children let him bless his wife.

Though brief my day, I have not lived in vain;
Mourning for child of mine I never wore;
When from my home went forth my funeral
  train,
Not one was missing there of all I bore.

My cause is pleaded. Now, ye mourners rise
And witness bear till earth my meed decree;
If worth may claim its guerdon in the skies,
My glorious ancestors may welcome me.

[TR. GOLDWIN SMITH]

SULPICIA (FL. 80 B.C.)

Lyrics

Although we know from secondary sources that Roman women wrote poetry, only the heart-felt elegies of Sulpicia reprinted here survive to allow us to hear the voice of a *docta puella,* learned young woman, of the classical age. She was the ward of the poet Albius Tibullus' friend, the patron and politi-

Fresco, The Aldobrandini Nuptials

cian Valerius Messala Corvinus; and granddaughter of Cicero's friend Servius Sulpicius Rufus, an influential orator and statesman who had been forced to renounce his patrician status and was eventually declared an outlaw and killed because, as a tribune of the plebs, he had favored sweeping reforms.

- Her poems survive in the *Corpus tibullianum,* the books commonly attributed to Tibullus. Her lover's name, "Cerinthus," may be a pseudonym.
- Her subject matter includes hating and loving her birthday, the painful power of gossip, sickness and love-sickness, and her jealousy for her lover's courtesan.

At last love has come. I would be more ashamed
to hide it in cloth than leave it naked.
I prayed to the Muse and won. Venus dropped
   him
in my arms, doing for me what she
had promised. Let my joy be told, let those
who have none tell it in a story.
Personally, I would never send off words
in sealed tablets for none to read.
I delight in sinning and hate to compose a
   mask
for gossip. We met. We are both worthy.

~

Darling, I won't be your hot love
as a few days ago
I thought I was, if in all my youth
I ever did anything
so stupid, which I regret more,
as yesterday
when I left you alone in the night
to conceal my fire.

~

It's nice that though you are casual about me
you keep me from stumbling into a mess.
Your toga and a hustling whore mean more
to you than Sulpicia, Servius' daughter.
Friends worry about me and are upset that
somehow
I might tumble into bed with a nobody.

~

My hated birthday is here, and I must go
to the awful country without Cerinthus.
What is sweeter than Rome? Is a farmhouse
a place for a girl? Stuck in Arezzo
with its icy river and fields? Friend Messalla,
don't worry. Trips are often poorly timed.

They drag me there. I leave my soul and heart
here
and, being forced, I cannot be myself.

~

Do you have a sweet thought, Cerinthus,
for your girl?
Fever shakes my thin body. Unless
I thought
it was your wish, I would not choose
to win
over my sad disease. Why should I
elude death
if when I am sick, your heart
is calm?

~

Have you heard? The troubles
of the road
have vanished from your girl's
sad spirit?
I shall be in Rome for
my birthday.
Let that day be enjoyed
by us both.
It came from nowhere,
luckily for you.

LUCRETIUS (TITUS LUCRETIUS CARUS) (95–55 B.C.)

On the Nature of Things

*E*picurean philosophy received its most eloquent and most influential expression not from its founder, nor even from a Greek, but in a six-book narrative poem of 7,400 lines by the Roman apologist Lucretius, *De rerum natura* (a translation of Epicurus' and Empedocles' poems, both called *Peri physeos*). Lucretius' masterpiece is the first systematic treatment of Greek philosophy in the Latin tongue and the only lengthy verse composition to survive from the republican period.

St. Jerome reports, with questionable authority, that Lucretius went mad after drinking a love potion and committed suicide when he was forty-four. The truth is we know little for certain of Lucretius' life except that he witnessed Caesar's rise to power in the troubled and exciting times of Cicero and Catiline, of Catullus and the New Poets; and that he died on the day Virgil received the *toga virilis*. But we do know his passionate literary ambition from his poem: to liberate humanity from superstitious enslavement to belief in the gods' capriciousness and to the fear of death and the afterlife by explaining the natural origin and destiny of the universe and its atomic components. With all the passion of a convert, Lucretius wrote his mighty poem to convince his friend Gaius Memmius—orator, poet, and patron of Cinna and Catullus—of the truth of Epicurean philosophy: A materialistic worldview liberates humanity from its fear of the gods and of death.

- Lucretius, in the most majestic hexameters written by a Roman, presents a detailed overview of classical atomic theory that had been formulated first by the Eleatic philosophers Leucippus and Democritus, then embraced by Epicurus and made part of his philosophy. Mankind has no need of the gods as explanations of how things came into existence. The infinite universe is mechanically composed of a number of indivisible particles, invisible yet solidly material. These "atoms" possess only size, shape, and mass; yet their consistency is more important than that of anything we can perceive with our senses. Their spontaneity of movement gives play to human free will.

- Along the way, *De rerum natura* deals with atomic explanations for:

  - astronomical and terrestrial aberrations;
  - the nature of mind and soul, which he considers to be material and mortal; unable to exist apart from the body, the soul consists of the tiniest atoms of particular fineness;

- the origins of animal, vegetable, and human life through spontaneous generation;
- the survival of the fittest;
- the evolution of civilization;
- the chemistry and psychology of thought and sensation;
- vision;
- magnetism;
- bodily mechanisms;
- the function of sleep and dreams;
- and the existence of infinite worlds like ours in the universe.

- Lucretius, at the same time that he honors the memory of his master Epicurus, extends Epicurean philosophy in characteristic Roman fashion. Lucretius' view portrays the universe as more regulated than does Epicurus. His fervor for the benefits of Epicureanism as a cure for the random ills of life that are only acerbated by religion is also quite in contrast with Epicurus' detachment. This fervent energy that moves the verse along makes *On the Nature of Things* compelling reading. It is one of the greatest didactic poems in Western literature, powerfully influencing Virgil in both his *Georgics* and the *Aeneid*.

BOOK I

Mother of Romans, joy of gods and men,
Venus, life-giver, who under planet and star
visits the ship-clad sea, the grain-clothed land
always, for through you all that's born and
  breathes
is gotten, created, brought forth to see the sun,
Lady, the storms and clouds of heaven shun you,
You and your advent; Earth, sweet magic-
  maker,
sends up her flowers for you, broad Ocean
  smiles,
and peace glows in the light that fills the sky.
For soon as the year has bared her springtime
  face,
and bars are down for the breeze of growth and
  birth,
in heaven the birds first mark your passage,
  Lady,

and you; your power pulses in their hearts.
Then wild beasts, too, leap over rich, lush
  lands
and swim swift streams; so prisoned by your
  charms
they follow lustily where you lead them on.
Last, over sea and hill and greedy river,
through leaf-clad homes of birds, through fresh
  green fields,
in every creature you sink love's tingling dart,
luring them lustily to create their kind.
Since you, and you only, rule the world of
  nature,
and nothing, without you, comes forth to the
  coasts
of holy light, or makes for joy and love,
I pray you be with me as I write these verses
that I compose about the world of nature
for my friend Memmius, whom, in every hour,

Lady, you wish in all things blessed and great.
Grant then to my words, Lady, a deathless
    charm.
Cause meanwhile that all savage works of war
by land and sea drop off to sleep and rest.
For you alone can bless our mortal race
with peace and calm: though Mars the War
    Lord rules
war's savage works, yet often he throws himself
into your arms, faint with love's deathless
    wound,
and there, with arching neck bent back, looks
    up
and sighs, and feeds a lustful eye on you
and, pillowed, dangles his life's breath from
    your lips.
Then, as he falls back on your sacred body,
Lady, lean over and let sweet utterance pour
from your holy lips—a plea of peace for Rome.
For in my country's hour of trial I cannot
sit calmly writing, nor can Lord Memmius
in such a season fail the common weal.

Now turn attentive ears and thoughtful mind,
by trouble undistraught, to truth and reason;
my gifts displayed for you in loyal love
you must not scorn before you grasp their
    meaning.
For I shall tell you of the highest law
of heaven and god, and show you basic sub-
    stance,
whence nature creates all things and gives
    them growth,
and whither again dissolves them at their
    death.
"Matter," I call it, and "creative bodies,"
and "seeds of things"—such terms I'll often use
in my discourse, and sometimes call the same

"prime bodies," for with them everything
    beings.
    When human life lay foul before men's eyes,
crushed to the dust beneath religion's weight
(from the high realm of heaven she showed her
    face
in hideous grimace of terror to mortal men)
a man of Greece first dared to raise the eye
of mortal against her, first stood ground
    against her.
Not all god's glory, his lightning, heaven's
    rumble
and rage, could stop him; rather they rasped
    his heart
to keener courage, and made him a pioneer
eager to burst the bolts on nature's door.
His quick and cunning intellect won him paths
to freedom beyond the world's far-flaming
    walls;
in mind and thought he marched the boundless
    Whole
and then, victorious, taught us what can be
and what cannot; yes, and what law defines
the power of things, what firm-set boundary
    stone.
And now religion in turn beneath our feet
is trampled; the victory makes us match for
    heaven.
    This troubles me: that you may think
    yourself
beginning to study blasphemy—"that first step
to a life of crime." Why, no! More commonly
religion has prompted vile and vicious acts.
Remember Aulis? How Diana's altar
was shamed and fouled by Iphianassa's blood
spilled by the Lords of Greece—great heroes,
    they!
They coiffed the poor girl for her wedding day;

a ribbon, long braids to hang each side of her
*   face.*
But there by the altar she saw her father
*   standing*
grief-stricken, and near him acolytes hiding
*   knives,*
and people staring at her with tear-stained
*   faces.*
Voiceless with terror she crumpled to her knees.
Poor thing, no help to her in such an hour
that she'd been first to call the king "my
*   father."*
Men led her to the altar, raised her up
all trembling, not to say their sacred office
and carry her home with nuptial shout and
*   song,*
but that her innocence at the bridal hour
fall criminal victim by a father's blow,
that ships might have clear sailing and fair
*   winds.*
So much of evil could religion prompt.

*   And you, at any moment now, in fear*
of hierophantic threats, will seek to leave me.
For think of the endless fantasies your priests
devise, that can subvert all reasoned thought
and turn your life to terror and confusion!
Of course! For if men saw that all their
*   troubles*
must one day end, somehow they'd find the
*   strength*
to stand against the hierophant and his
*   threats.*
But now they can't stand ground nor make reply
for fear of eternal torment after death.
They do not know the nature of the soul—
if it is born or at birth slipped into us;
whether, destroyed by death, it dies with us,
or goes to see hell's broad and lightless pools,

or by some miracle passes to other creatures,
as our loved Ennius sang, who first brought
*   down*
from lovely Helicon garlands ever green
to grow in fame wherever Italians live.
Yet Ennius also claimed the underworld
exists, and told his tale in deathless verse,
a place where neither soul nor flesh lives on
but a sort of "images"—pale and eerie things.
From there the likeness of Homer the Ever-
*   young*
appeared to him (he says), and shedding floods
of salty tears brought word of the world of
*   nature.*
And so we must think with accuracy and care
about the world above—of sun and moon
and how they move, how everything on earth
takes place; but first with all our reasoning
*   power*
we must inspect the nature of soul and mind,
and things that come to fill our hearts with fear
when we lie ill and awake, or tombed in sleep,
making us think we see and hear right there
men who have died, whose bones the earth
*   embraces.*

*   And well do I know Greek science is obscure*
and difficult to explain in Latin verse,
above all when I must work with coined words
where Latin is lacking and the concept new.
But your great goodness and the hoped-for joy
of your sweet friendship bid me bear all toil,
and keep me awake at work through cloudless
*   nights*
seeking not only words but verses, too,
to be bright shining lights before your mind,
that you may see deep into hidden truth.

*   This fright, this night of the mind, must*
*   be dispelled*

not by the rays of the sun, nor day's bright
    spears,
but by the face of nature and her laws.
And this is her first, from which we take our
    start:
nothing was ever by miracle made from
    nothing.
You see, all mortal men are gripped by fear
because they see so many things on earth
and in the sky, yet can't discern their causes
and hence believe that they are acts of god.
But in all this, when we have learned that
    nothing
can come from nothing, then we shall see
    straight through
to what we seek: whence each thing is created
and in what manner made, without god's help.
    If things were made from nothing, then
    all kinds
could spring from any source: they'd need no
    seed.
Man could have burst from ocean, from dry
    land
the bearers of scales, and from thin air the birds;
cows, horses, sheep, and the rest, and all wild
    beasts
would breed untrue, infesting farm and forest.
Nor would one tree produce one kind of fruit;
no, they would change, and all could bear all
    kinds.
For if there were no factors governing birth,
how could we tell who anyone's mother was?
But things are formed, now, from specific seeds,
hence each at birth comes to the coasts of light
from a thing possessed of its essential atoms.
Thus everything cannot spring from anything,
for things are unique: their traits are theirs
    alone.

And why in spring do we see roses, grain
in summer, vines produce at autumn's call,
if not because right atoms in right season
have streamed together to build each thing
    we see,
while weather favors and life-giving earth
brings delicate seedlings safe to land and light?
But if they came from nothing, they'd
    spring up
all helter-skelter in seasons not their own;
for there would be no atoms to be kept
from fertile union at untimely hours.
Nor would things when they grow have need
    of time
for seeds to combine, if they could grow from
    nothing.
Why! Babes in arms would turn into men
    forthwith,
and forests would leap from sprouts new-
    sprung of earth.
Yet clearly such things never occur: all growth
is gradual, regular, from specific seed,
and with identity kept. Hence learn that things
can grow only when proper substance feeds
    them.
To this we add: without her seasonal rains
Earth could not send up offspring rich in joy,
nor, further, could living creatures without food
beget their kind or keep their hold on life.
Better conceive of many atoms shared
by many things, as letters are by words,
than of a single thing not made of atoms.
To continue: why could nature not produce
men of such size that they could cross the seas
on foot, and with bare hands pull hills apart,
and live the lifetime of ten thousand men,
if not because each thing has but one substance
marked and designed to bring it into being?

Admit then: nothing can be made of nothing
since things that are created must have seed
from which to come forth to the gentle breezes.
Finally, since we see tilled fields excel
untilled, and pay more profit on our toil
surely prime bodies must exist in soil.
Plowing the fertile furrow, turning up
the earth, we bring these bodies to the surface.
But if there were none such, everything would
*   grow*
spontaneously, and better, without our labors.
And now add this: nature breaks up all things
into their atoms; no thing dies off to nothing.
For if a thing were mortal in all its parts,
it would be whisked away, just drop from sight,
since there would be no need of force to wrench
one part from another, or to dissolve their
*   bonds.*
But things are made of atoms; they are stable.
Until some force comes, hits them hard, and
*   splits them,*
or seeps to their inner parts and makes them
*   burst,*
nature brings no destruction to our sight.
Besides, take things that time removes through
*   aging:*
if when they died their matter were all con-
*   sumed,*
whence does Venus bring animals forth to life
kind after kind, and earth, the magic-maker,
nourish, increase, and feed them, kind by
*   kind?*
Whence could native fountains and far-flung
*   rivers*
supply the sea? Whence ether feed the stars?
For everything of mortal mass long since
had been used up as boundless time passed by.
But if the stuff of which this sum of things

is built has lasted down through empty ages,
surely it is endowed with deathless nature;
no thing, therefore, can be reduced to nothing.
*   Lastly, one given cause could commonly*
destroy all things, if they were not held firm
by deathless matter, bonded and intertwined.
For death's mere touch would be sufficient
*   cause*
for things not built of everlasting atoms
whose fabric must be broken up by force.
But now, because the bonds between the
*   atoms*
are ever unlike, and matter is eternal,
things will retain their form and mass intact
until they meet a force to match their fabric.
And so no thing reverts to nothing: all
are sundered into particles of matter.
Finally, rains are lost when Father Heaven
has dropped them into the lap of Mother Earth.
But shining grainfields sprout, and twigs grow
*   green*
on trees; the trees grow, too, and bear their
*   fruits;*
hence our kind and the animal kind are fed,
hence we see happy cities bloom with children
and leafy woods all filled with young bird-
*   song;*
hence flocks wearied with fat lay themselves
*   down*
out in the fertile fields, and bright white liquor
leaks from their swollen teats; hence newborn
*   lambs*
gambol on wobbly legs through tender grass,
their baby hearts tipsy with winy milk.
Things seem to perish, then, but they do not:
nature builds one from another, and lets no
*   thing*
be born unless another helps by dying. . . .

(GAIUS VALERIUS) CATULLUS (C. 84–54 B.C.)

Lyrics

The most modern and passionate of Roman lyricists was born of an affluent and aristocratic family in Verona. We know little of his life except that he traveled to Bithynia with the governor Gaius Memmius and, on his way back, visited his brother's tomb in the Troad of Asia Minor. He spent the last ten years of his short life in and around Rome, with his villa near Tibur (Tivoli), where he found immediate acceptance in the capital's artistic inner circle, hobnobbing with Cicero, Cinna, the orator Quintus Hortensius, the poet Licinius Calvus, Cornelius Nepos, Pompey, and even with his father's friend and guest Julius Caesar (whom Catullus castigated roundly in a number of his poems).

- The most important of the innovative and revolutionary *neoteric* New Poets of the late Republic who sought inspiration from Greek models and renovated Latin literature by combining imported meters and aesthetic energy with themes and images from everyday Roman life, Catullus was recognized by his peers and honored through imitation—by Cornelius Gallus, Virgil, Horace, Ovid, Propertius, Tibullus, and Martial.
- The 113 of his conversational and confessional *Carmina* that survive are in various meters and of various lengths. His longer works include the *Marriage of Peleus and Thetis, Attis, Epithalamium of Julia and Manlius,* and *Berenice's Hair.* But most of the *carmina* are loosely constructed love poems, their novelty, wit, sensuality, tenderness, and accomplishment ranking him with the great masters of the European lyric. Twenty-five of them are dedicated to his "brilliant and faithless" married lover called "Lesbia" (identified with the patrician Clodia, sister of Cicero's antagonist Publius Clodius Pulcher and unhappy wife of the consul Metellus Celer; she was ten years older than the poet). Cicero describes her unflatteringly in his speech *Pro Caelio,* defending Marcus Caelius Rufus against her charge that he'd tried to poison her. Others record Catullus' affair with a young man named Juventius.
- Though characterized by critics from his own time to the present as a poet's poet whose self-conscious art was often accessible only to the initiate, Catullus wrote a passionate account of his lovesickness that moved him away from polished imitation of the Alexandrine Callimachus and the Hellenic Sappho of Lesbos to a harsh intensity completely his own and familiar to anyone who's experienced the throes of romantic love. The poet's feelings range from ecstatic and uncontrollable infatuation through twists and turns of clan-

destine encounters and defeated expectations to inevitable heartrending despair and dashed hopes—and finally to vituperative abuse heaped upon the lover who has delighted and destroyed him. Though he presents the light and dark sides of love, the dark side prevails; in this regard, Catullus foreshadows the development of the "romantic consciousness" in the West.

Young Bacchus

dared to present all time in three tomes,
a labor of learning by one man alone.
So here I submit this bit of a book,
such as it is: and, O Maiden, may you
let it survive for an era or two!

2
PASSER, DELICIAE MEAE PUELLAE

Little sparrow, my lover's love,
with whom she plays, permits to lie
within her lap to nip her finger,
biting quickly with that bill,
when my shining light of love
is pleased to play some little game
to lend her care some tender ease—
her fervor then, I'm sure, must cease—
I should like to play with you
as she, and soothe my troubled heart!

1
CUI DONO LEPIDUM NOVUM LIBELLUM

Who gets my new slender volume of verse,
pumice-stone polished? I'll give it to you,
good old Cornelius, who once deigned to think
my trifles were something, when you—
holy Jupiter!—

2a
TAM GRATUM EST MIHI, QUAM FERUNT PUELLAE

. . . .

That would be as pleasant as
they say the golden apple was
to the nimble girl who would
have kept her girdle tied for good.

~

3
LUGETE, O VENERES CUPIDINESQUE

Be blue, every Venus and Cupid
and every sophisticate man;
my sweetheart has lost her sparrow,
her little sparrow has died.
She loved it more than her eyes.
It knew her, this mellowy sparrow,
as well as my girl knew her mother;
it never moved from her bosom,
but hopped about here and there
and chirped to its only mistress.

But now it travels the shadows
to the realm from which none return.
Be damned, you damnable shadows
that swallow all beauty for Hell:
you took such a beautiful sparrow.
O pitiless crime! pitied sparrow!
For you, now, my sweetheart's eyes
are swollen and red as she cries.

~

5
VIVAMUS, MEA LESBIA, ATQUE AMEMUS

Lesbia, let's live and love
without one thought for gossip of
the boys grown old and stern.
Suns go down and can return,
but, once put out our own brief light,
we sleep through one eternal night.
Give me a thousand, a hundred kisses,
another thousand, a second hundred,
a thousand complete, a hundred repeat;

and when we've many thousand more,
we'll scramble them, forget the score
so Malice cannot know how high
the count, and cast its evil eye.

~

6
FLAVI, DELICIAS TUAS CATULLO

Flavius,
you'd want to tell Catullus all
about your girl and couldn't be still
unless she were some silly frill.
But shame forbids you to repeat:
you're doting on some whore in heat.
Perfumed with wreaths and Syrian oils,
your far from silent sofa spoils
the secret of your prostitute,
denies your nights are destitute;
so dented purse and pillow said,
and quaking of your shaking bed.
This silence doesn't hide your game:
your fagged-out flanks would not be lame
without your sorry whoring grind.
So let me in on what you find,
both good and bad; I'll call your flame
in facile verse to heaven fame.

~

7
QUAERIS, QUOT MIHI BASIATIONES

Lesbia,
your question is, How many kisses
should suffice and be supersufficient?
As many as the Libyan sands that lie
on assafoetidal Cyrene,

between Jove's burning oracle and
the sepulchral shrine of old Battus
or as many as are the stars that see
men's secret loves in the silent night:
to kiss you with that many kisses
would suffice and be supersufficient
for crazy Catullus: the curious
could then never count them and curse us.

⁓

8
MISER CATULLE, DESINAS INEPTIRE

Catullus, poor soul, stop playing the fool;
write off as loss what you see has been lost.
There used to be days full of sunshine for you,
when you followed the path laid out by your
    girl.
We loved her as no girl will ever be loved!
Those were the days when we had all the fun
which you dearly wanted and she didn't shun;
those were real days full of sunshine for you.
Now, though, she shuns it; so you, useless,
    don't
chase her and live a poor soul, as she runs:
instead, stick it out with a stubborn heart.
So long, girl; Catullus is sticking it out.
He won't look you up; he won't ask you out.
But you will be sorry when none asks you out.
What life—damn you, slut!—is left now for
    you?
Who'll come to you now or think you're a doll?
Whom now will you love or whose claim to be?
Whom will you kiss? Whose lips will you bite?
But you, then, Catullus, be stubborn; sit tight.

⁓

13
CENABIS BENE, MI FABULLE, APUD ME

Fabullus, you will dine with me,
gods willing, in a day or three,
if you will bring the meal with you,
good and big, a bright girl too,
and wine and salt and lots of laughs.
If you bring this, my friend, why, look,
you will dine well: the pocketbook
of your Catullus is well filled
with cobwebs; but, in turn, you will
be unadulterably thrilled
by pleasure, taste—say what you will:
I'll have a perfume for you here,
which Love Gods proffered to my dear;
on smelling it, you will propose
that gods above make you all nose.

⁓

15
COMMENDO TIBI ME AC MEOS AMORES

Aurelius,
with my boy-love I give you myself
and make this restrained request:
restraining yourself, keep him pure
as you would any hope of your heart.
Not worried by those in the street,
the passersby, here and there,
each bent on his own affair,
I fear only you and your tail,
a terror to any young male.
Outside, let it swish whom you wish,
when or where, I don't care, save for him:
an exception which seems to me
duly made with sufficient restraint.

You crook, if your crooked brain
does bring you to such a crime
that you tear my life with your snares—
Oh, man, you'll be sorrier more
when I spread your legs and run fish
and radishes through your rear door!

~

18
HUNC LUCUM TIBI DEDICO
CONSECROQUE, PRIAPE

Priapus,
this grove I dedicate and consecrate to you,
whose living and whose law are known at
*   Lampsacus:*
for Hellespontia's coast, more oystery than
*   most*
has cities which show special reverence
*   to you.*

~

32
AMABO, MEA DULCIS IPSITILLA

Please, Ipsitilla, sugar,
my doll, kid, baby, please
tell me to come this afternoon;
contribute to my ease
by letting no one lock your door,
by staying where you are; what's more,
get set to soothe me, as I choose,
with nine uninterrupted screws.
Whatever gives, don't make me wait:
I'm lying, filled with all I ate,
watching my tunic stand up straight.

~

33
O FURUM OPTIME
BALNEARIORUM

You're the best of bathhouse burglars,
Vibennius, you and your pathic son
(the father flaunts a fouler hand,
the son a greedier ass):
why don't you prowl perverted lands
as exiles, where the people know
the father's thefts, and, son, where you
can penny-vend your hairy clefts.

~

34
DIANAE SUMUS IN FIDE

We are in Diana's trust,
girls and untouched boys:
(untouched boys and girls,)
let us sing Diana.

Latonia, mighty progeny
of mighty Jupiter,
your mother laid you down
beside the Delian olive

to be thereby the queen of hills,
the queen of greening woods,
the queen of hidden groves
and queen of sounding streams.

Women lost in labor pains
call you Lucina Juno,
powerful Trivia, known as Luna
by your borrowed brilliance.

Goddess measuring out the year
with a menstrual career,
you fill the farmers' rustic homes
with fruits heaped to the roofs.

Whatever name you like the
     best,
be blest in it, sustain the race
of Romulus with precious help,
your customary grace. . . .

~

85
ODI ET AMO. QUARE ID FACIAM,
FORTASSE REQUIRIS
I hate while I love; would you ask how I do it?
     My pain
proves it's true; that's all there is to it.

SALLUST (GAIUS SALLUSTIUS CRISPUS) (86–35 B.C.)
History of Rome

~

The historian Sallust began his public career as an anti-senatorial, pro-Caesar political activist, as tribune of the plebs attacking Cicero and Milo and inciting riots that ended with burning the Senate House nearly to the ground. The censors accused him of immorality and expelled him from the Senate; but he returned to the public eye when Caesar made him first quaestor, then proconsul of Numidia, and restored his senatorial rank in reward for his military effectiveness as commander of a legion. He retired in somewhat of a scandal for feathering his own nest at the expense of his subjects, and spent the rest of his life writing in the serenity of the *horti Sallustiani*, the Quirinal gardens he created with his ill-gotten wealth. He was born in Amiternum, in the land of the Sabines.

- Sallust's five-book *History of Rome* chronicles the period 78–66 B.C. and strongly influenced Tacitus. Very little of Sallust's *History* has survived, and he is known to us primarily for his study of the Catilinian conspiracy of 63 B.C. and the war against Jugurtha, King of Numidia (111–105).
- His monographs *Catiline* and *Jugurtha* won him the distinction of having invented the form. Though he's not particularly careful with his sources and is thought of more as a political propagandist than a philosophical historian, Sallust employed a narrative style dramatic and vividly descriptive, and, like his models Thucydides and Cato the Elder, he was astutely aware of human psychology as the causality behind events.

The Comitium Well, Place of Assembly, Roman Forum

48. CODEX VATICANUS LAT. 3864 (V): SPEECH OF LEPIDUS TO THE ROMAN PEOPLE

(1) Your clemency and your honesty, fellow citizens, qualities which have made you supreme and renowned throughout all other nations, fill me with the greatest fear in dealing with the tyranny of Lucius Sulla. On the one hand I am afraid that you may be tricked through not believing others capable of acts which you yourselves consider abominable—especially since all Sulla's expectations are dependent upon crime and treachery, and he thinks that he cannot be safe unless he has shown himself even worse and more detestable than you fear, so that when you have been completely duped by him your wretchedness may wipe out your concern for freedom. Then again, if you do take precautions, I fear that you may be more occupied in averting dangers than in exacting retribution for wrongs committed. (2) As for his satellites, I cannot adequately express my amazement that men who bear names made great by the most distinguished deeds of their ancestors are willing to pay for dominion over you with their own slavery, and, without regard for equity, prefer this state of affairs to living as free men according to the highest principles of

justice. (3) Distinguished offspring of the Bruti, Aemilii, and Lutatii, born to overthrow what their ancestors acquired by their prowess! (4) For what did these forefathers defend against Pyrrhus, Hannibal, Philip, and Antiochus other than our liberty and each his own dwelling-place and our right of submitting to nothing but the laws? (5) But all of these benefits this caricature of a Romulus of ours holds in his hands as if they had been wrested from foreigners; not fully sated with the destruction of so many armies, consuls, and other leading men whom the fortune of war had destroyed, he shows more cruelty at a time when success turns most men from anger to pity. (6) But more than that, he alone of all within the memory of man has devised punishment for those yet unborn, who are thus assured of outrage before they are assured of life. Worst of all, up to this time he has been protected by the enormity of his crimes while you are being deterred from taking steps to recover your liberty by the fear of an even more cruel servitude.

(7) Now is the time for action, citizens; now is the time to face up to the tyrant in order that your spoils may not be bestowed on him. This is not the time for putting things off, nor for looking for help by prayers to the gods—unless, perchance, you hope he is now weary or ashamed of his tyranny and that what he has seized through crime he will, with even greater danger to himself, let go. (8) On the contrary, he has sunk to the point where he regards no position as illustrious unless it is safe, and considers every device for retaining his supremacy as honorable. (9) And so that state of tranquillity and peace combined with freedom, which many good men used to

choose rather than an active career with honors as a reward, is a thing of the past; (10) in these times, citizens, one must either be slave or master, one must fear or inspire it. (11) For what else is left to us? What human laws are left? What divine laws have not been violated? The Roman people, a short while ago the ruler of nations, now stripped of power, repute, and rights, without the power to administer its own affairs, an object of contempt, does not even retain the rations of slaves. (12) A considerable part of our allies and of the people of Latium are being debarred by this one man from the citizenship granted them by you in return for their many and distinguished services, while a few of his underlings, as a reward for their crimes, have taken possession of the ancestral homes of the guiltless common people. (13) The laws, the courts, the treasury, the provinces, client-kings, nay even the power of life and death over our citizens are in the hands of one man. (14) At the same time you have witnessed human sacrifices and seen tombs stained with the blood of citizens. (15) Is there anything left to those who are truly men except to rid themselves of oppression or to die valiantly? For in truth nature has appointed one and the same end for all, even for those flanked by armed might, and no man waits for the final inevitability doing nothing, unless he has the heart of a woman.

(16) But Sulla says that I am a cause of political turmoil because I protest against the rewards paid to inciters of civil disorder; he calls me a lover of war because I seek to restore the rights which apply in times of peace. (17) Of course I do, since you will not be safe and

fully protected under Sulla's domination unless Vettius of Picenum and the clerk Cornelius may squander the goods which others have honestly acquired; unless you all approve the proscription of innocent men because of their wealth, the torture of distinguished citizens, a city depopulated by exile and murder, the goods of wretched citizens sold or given away as if they were the spoils of the Cimbri. (18) Sulla charges me with having possessions which are derived from the goods of the proscribed, but in fact the very greatest of his crimes is that neither I nor anyone else would have been sufficiently safe if we were doing what was right. Moreover the property which at that time I bought through fear, I am disposed nevertheless to restore to those who, having paid the price, are their rightful owners; it is not my intention to allow any depredations at the expense of citizens. (19) Let it be enough to have endured what our madness has brought upon us—Roman armies pitted against each other, our arms turned away from the enemy and against ourselves. Let there be an end to crime and outrage—of which, however, Sulla is so far from repenting that he counts them among his claims to glory, and, if he were allowed, would even more eagerly do them again.

(20) But now, while I no longer have qualms about what you think of him, I do have fears about how far you are prepared to go. My anxiety is that, while you are waiting for someone else to give a lead, you may be caught, not by his forces which are unreliable and venal, but through your inaction which allows one to continue on a course of robbery with violence and to appear fortunate in proportion to

one's audacity. (21) For, apart from his crime-stained underlings, who has the same aspirations or who does not desire a complete change, retaining only the achievement of victory? Is it, think you, the soldiers at the cost of whose blood riches have been won for slaves such as Tarrula and Scirtus? (22) Or is it those who in seeking office were thought less worthy than Fufidius, a vile wench, the degradation of all honors? And so I place my greatest confidence in that victorious army which has gained nothing by so many wounds and hardships except a tyrant. (23) Unless perchance their mission was the overthrow by force of arms of the power of the tribunes which their forefathers had established by force of arms, and to rob themselves with their own hands of their rights and jurisdiction. Extraordinary indeed the reward they received when, banished to swamps and woods, they find that insult and hatred are their portion, that just a few carry off the prizes. (24) Why then, you might ask, does the tyrant parade about with so great a following and with such assurance? Because success is a wonderful screen for vices; but if success falters he will be despised as much as he is now feared. Or perhaps he acts in this way under the pretext of maintaining peace and harmony, which are the names he has bestowed on his guilt and treason. Furthermore, he declares that the Republic cannot otherwise stand firm and the war be ended unless the common people are permanently driven from their lands, the citizens cruelly plundered, and all rights and jurisdiction which once belonged to the Roman people placed in his own hands. (25) If this seems to you to be peace and order, then show your approval of the utter demoralization and overthrow of the Republic; assent to the laws that have been imposed on you; accept a peace combined with servitude and hand on to future generations a model of how to ruin their country at the price of their own citizens' blood. (26) As far as I am concerned, although by reaching this highest of offices I had done enough to live up to the fame of my ancestors, as well as to secure my own dignity and even my safety, it was not my intention to pursue my private interests; I regarded freedom united with danger preferable to peace with slavery. (27) If you share this view, citizens of Rome, rouse yourselves, and with the good help of the gods follow Marcus Aemilius, your consul, who will be your leader and champion in recovering your freedom. . . .

67. CODEX VATICANUS LAT. 3864 (V): SPEECH OF PHILIPPUS IN THE SENATE

(1) My greatest wish, Fathers of the Senate, would be that our country might be at peace or that in the midst of dangers it might be defended by all of its ablest citizens; or at least that evil designs should cause harm to their contrivers. But on the contrary, everything is in turmoil, the result of civil dissensions fomented by those whose duty it was rather to suppress them; and finally, the wise and the good are forced to do what the worst and most foolish of men have decided. (2) For even though you may detest war and arms, you must nevertheless take them up because it is what Lepidus wants, unless perchance anyone has a policy of preserving peace and at the same time allowing aggression. (3) O ye good gods, who still watch over this city about which we have ceased to worry: Marcus Aemilius, lowest of all criminals—it is difficult to say whether he is more vicious or more cowardly—has an army for the purpose of overthrowing our liberty, and from being an object of contempt has transformed himself into something to be feared. You, meanwhile, mumbling and dithering, look for peace with words and the incantations of soothsayers instead of fighting for it; you do not realize that by your irresolute decisions you are losing your prestige and Lepidus his fear. (4) This is a natural outcome, since he reached a consulship because of his robberies, and obtained a command and an army because of acts of sedition. What might he not have gained by good conduct when you have rewarded his crimes so generously?

(5) But of course it is those who up to the very last have voted for embassies, for peace, for harmony and the like that have won his favor! Quite the opposite. Despised, considered unworthy of a share in government, they are regarded as fair game since fear it was that made them sue for the peace which fear had made them lose. (6) For my own part, from the very outset, when I saw Etruria conspiring, the proscribed being recalled, and the state rent asunder by bribery, I thought there was no time to be wasted, and with a few others I supported the policy of Catulus. But those who extolled the great deeds of the Aemilian clan and who maintained that they had added to the greatness of the Roman people by taking a lenient view said that even at that stage Lepidus had taken no irrevocable step, in spite of the fact that he had taken up arms on his own responsibility to overthrow freedom. And so, while seeking power

or protection for themselves, each of them has suborned the deliberations of the Senate. (7) At that time, however, Lepidus was a brigand at the head of some camp-followers and a few cut-throats, not one of whom could have got a day's pay for his life. Now he is a proconsul with military power which he did not buy but which you gave him, with staff officers who are still bound by law to obey him. The most vicious characters of every social class flock to his standard inflamed by poverty and greed, driven by the consciousness of their crimes, men who find repose in times of discord, disquiet in times of peace. These are the men who sow the seeds of rebellion after rebellion, of war after war, follow-ers once of Saturninus, then of Sulpicius, next of Marius and Damasippus, and now of Lepidus. (8) Moreover, Etruria and all the other smoldering embers of war are aroused; the Spanish provinces are stirred to revolt, Mithridates, in close proxim-ity to those of the tributary peoples from whom we still receive support, is looking for an opportunity for war; in short, for the overthrow of our empire nothing is lacking save a competent leader.

(9) Wherefore, senators, I beg and implore you to watch out; do not allow the unbounded license of crime, like a madness, to infect those who are still sound; for when the wicked are rewarded, it is not easy for anyone to remain virtuous just for virtue's sake. (10) Or are you waiting for Lepidus to come again with an army and enter our city with fire and sword? In truth that eventuality is much nearer the position in which he now finds him-self than is civil war to peace and concord. (11) He has taken up arms against the state in defiance of all human and divine law, not in order to avenge the wrongs inflicted on him-self or the wrongs of those whom he pretends to represent, but to overthrow our laws and our liberty. For he is driven and tormented in mind by ambition and fear resulting from his crimes; uneasy and cut off from advice, he is resorting now to this plan, now to that. He fears peace, hates war; he sees that he must abstain from luxury and license, and mean-time he takes advantage of your indolence. (12) As for your conduct, I lack sufficient wis-dom to know whether I should call it fear or laziness or madness, when each one of you seems to be praying that such great evils which threaten you like a thunderbolt may not touch him, and yet makes no effort to prevent them.

(13) I ask you to reflect how the order of things is reversed: formerly, public mischief was planned secretly, public defense openly, and hence the good easily forestalled the wicked; nowadays peace and harmony are dis-turbed openly, defended secretly; those who desire disorder are in arms, you are in fear. What are you waiting for, unless perchance you are ashamed or weary of doing the right thing? (14) Or is it that the demands of Lep-idus have influenced your thinking? He says that it is his wish to render to each his own and keeps the property belonging to others; to annul laws set up in time of war, while he uses armed compulsion; to validate the citizenship of those from whom he denies it has been taken, and in the interests of harmony to restore the power of the tribunes, from which all our discords have been kindled. (15) O worst and most shameless of all men, are the

poverty and grief of our citizens of any concern to you? To you who have nothing in your possession which was not seized by arms or by injustice? You ask for a second consulship—as if you had ever given up your first! You seek harmony through war, by which the harmony which we had attained is being broken, a traitor to us, unfaithful to your party, the enemy of all good men. That you stand ashamed neither before men nor before the gods, whom you have outraged by your perfidy and your perjury! (16) Since such is your character I urge you to hold to your purpose and to retain your arms, lest by postponing your plans for rebellion, you may be unsettled yourself and keep us in a state of watchful concern. Neither the provinces nor the laws nor your country's gods tolerate you as a citizen. Continue as you have begun, so that you may meet with your deserts as soon as possible.

(17) And you, my fellow senators, how long, by your hesitation, will you allow your country to be undefended, and how long will you continue to meet arms with words? Forces have been levied against you, money extorted from individuals and from the treasury, garrisons removed from some places and stationed in others; laws are being issued in arbitrary fashion, and in the meantime you are thinking about sending envoys and making decrees! But by Hercules, the more eagerly you seek peace, the more bitter will the war be, since he finds that he is being encouraged in his objectives more by your fear than by the justice and righteousness of his cause. (18) For whoever says that he hates turmoil and the death of citizens, and as a consequence keeps you unarmed

while Lepidus is in arms, is really advising you to suffer what the conquered must endure, although you yourselves have the power to inflict such a fate upon others. Such counselors are advising you to keep peace with him and encouraging him to make war upon you. (19) If this is what you want, if such great torpor has stolen upon your spirits that, forgetting the crimes of Cinna upon whose return to our city the flower of this senatorial order perished, you will nevertheless entrust yourselves, your wives, and your children to Lepidus, what need is there of decrees? What need of Catulus' help? (20) Surely it is in vain that he and other good citizens are taking thought for the Republic. But have it your way. Acquire the protection of Cethegus and other traitors who are eager to renew the regime of pillage and fire, and once more to arm their bands against our country's gods. If on the other hand you stand for liberty and for what is good and true, pass decrees worthy of your name and so increase the courage of our brave defenders. (21) A new army is ready, to which are added the colonies of veteran soldiers, all the nobles and the best leaders. Fortune favors the stronger; soon the forces which our negligence has allowed to develop will melt away. (22) Therefore, this is what I recommend: whereas [Marcus] Lepidus, in defiance of the authority of this body, in concert with the worst enemies of their country, is leading against this city an army raised on his own authority, therefore let it be resolved that Appius Claudius the *interrex*, with Quintus Catulus the proconsul and others who have *imperium*, shall defend the city and see to it that the Republic comes to no harm. . . .

VIRGIL (PUBLIUS VERGILIUS MARO) (70–19 B.C.)

Aeneid

*R*oman literature reaches the zenith of its Golden Age with the grand and tragic epic created by Virgil under the patronage of Maecenas and at the behest of Augustus himself. Publius Vergilius Maro was, as Dante Alighieri has memorialized in his *Divine Comedy,* born on his father's farm near the village of Andes (modern Pietole), outside Mantua, probably of Etruscan lineage. He was educated well—first in nearby Cremona, then in Mediolanum (Milan), Neapolis (Naples), and Rome—in rhetoric and in the responsibilities of a senatorial career. Rumored to be homosexual, he never married. When his family lands were confiscated by Octavian's veterans, the emperor himself interceded to restore them.

In Rome, he fell under the influence of Catullus' school; became good friends with Horace, whom he introduced to Maecenas; and revered the Alexandrine school that had influenced Horace as well. Turning his back on politics entirely, Virgil retreated to Neapolis to complete his education in Epicurean philosophy under Siro, whose villa and land at Nola he inherited and whose love for Lucretius deeply affected Virgil's greatest work. Mastering lyric, pastoral, and didactic poetry as well as epic, Virgil is most known for these important works:

- The ten *Eclogues* (also known as *Bucolics*), begun when he was twenty-eight, which imitated the Greek pastoral idylls of Theocritos, brought him instant popularity, which he greeted by further withdrawing from social circles. Though the background and names are generally Greek or Sicilian, the poems are infused with an Italian sensitivity, details of the Campanian countryside, and of Roman politics and everyday life so that they transcend mere translation and become authentically original works. Most famous is Eclogue 4, predicting the coming of a wondrous child at whose birth a Golden Age would begin where lions would lie down with lambs. Debate has raged for centuries about whether Virgil intended the child to be that of Octavian and Scribonia, of Antony and Octavia, or to be Jesus Christ (the last theory first advanced by Constantine). Developing from an imitation of Alexandrine self-consciousness to an authentically Roman poet, Virgil, in his *Eclogues,* created a new and compelling voice.

- The four didactic books of *Georgics,* loosely modeled on the Greek Hesiod's *Works and Days* and Varro's *On Agriculture,* and written at Maecenas' request, celebrated simple ancient Roman rural values and the noble hard-working farmer as the root strength of the Roman state itself. Book 1 dealt with farming and corn cultivation; Book 2 with fruit trees, olives, and vines; Book 3 with animal husbandry (cattle and horses); and Book 4 with beekeeping and honey processing. Virgil read the work, which was influenced both by the Greek Hesiod and the philosopher Lucretius, to Octavian, who applauded it as being in perfect keeping with his plans for agrarian reform. Many consider the *Georgics* to be Virgil's most characteristic, and most consistently successful, work.

- The *Aeneid,* Virgil's epic masterpiece in twelve books of gracefully complex iambic pentameter, was inspired by Augustus' wish to provide for Rome what Homer had done for the Greeks and what Naevius and Ennius had failed to provide before in earlier times: an all-inclusive poetic vision celebrating the city's splendid mythological origins and the worthy ancient character of her people—and, especially, of her godlike emperor. The first six books are modeled on *The Odyssey,* the second six on *The Iliad*; Apollonius of Rhodes' description of Medea's love for Jason in *The Argonautica* influenced Virgil's "Dido and Aeneas."

- Virgil's poem, truly Rome's "national epic," tells the story of the founding of the city by the fleeing Trojan warrior Aeneas, son of the goddess Venus and the mortal Anchises. Like a true Roman, Aeneas brings his father with him on his exodus, carrying him from Troy on his shoulders. Despite dangers and temptations along the way, including the beautiful Carthaginian queen Dido who wants him to remain in Africa as her consort, Aeneas forges on to Latium to fulfill his destiny of founding a city on the Tiber, Alba Longa, whose greatness he sees only in prophecies. The emperor had the poet read Books 2, 4, and 6 to him in his court. Virgil did so reluctantly, not satisfied that the ambitious poem would ever be ready for its public. When Augustus insisted that he return to Italy from Athens, Virgil complied but, at Megara, fell ill. He died at Brundisium (modern Brindisi), having ordered his literary executor Varius to burn his unfinished epic. Before Varius could carry out the order, Augustus rescinded it, and commanded that it be published without editorial meddling. We owe the survival of Rome's greatest poem to its greatest emperor.

- In Book 6 the hero Aeneas, guided by the golden bough plucked at the instruction of the Cumaean sibyl, journeys into hell (following the footsteps of Homer's Odysseus) in order to question the spirits of the dead about his destiny. Where Odysseus meets his mother's ghost in Hades, who tells him about the past and present, the shade of Aeneas' father Anchises reveals to him the magnificent future of Rome; and pious Aeneas (his most frequent epithet), shaken by the burden he must now bear, returns to the world through the gleaming ivory gate of false dreams, not knowing whether what he has seen below is truth or illusion. In the subtle undermining of the narrative with which the storyteller ends Book 6, Virgil captures both the splendor of the new empire and the nagging sense of dread that is already accumulating beneath Rome's powerful excesses—that will someday cause the magnificent empire to collapse upon itself.

BOOK 6
THE UNDERWORLD

He wept as he spoke and commanded his fleet to sail.

At last he glided to shore at Euboean Cumae.

They turned the prows from the sea toward the beach and then

The anchor secured the ships with tenacious teeth.

The sterns curved along the shore like a garment's fringe.

An ardent band of young men darted down

The Hesperian shore; some sought the seeds of flame

Hidden in veins of flint, some scoured the dense

Haunts of wild beasts or showed others the streams they had found.

But loyal Aeneas went up to the heights where Apollo

Presides, and, farther away, to the retreat of the Sibyl,

That dreadful witch, in her monstrous cave, whom the Delian

Prophet has breathed on with mind and spirit and opened

The future to her. Now they entered the grove of Diana,

The cross-roads goddess, her golden temple. . . . The huge side of Euboean

Rock was hewn out as a cave, where a hundred broad paths

Led on and a hundred doors whence as many voices,

The Sibyl's responses, roared forth. They had reached the threshold

When the virgin cried out: "It is time to beseech the Fates.

Look! the god, the god!" As she spoke, there before the entrance

Her face and her color grew different, the hair on her head

Fell uncombed; her breast with sighs and her heart with rage

Were swollen, she seemed much greater than mortal in size

And sound, since the breath of power was loosed upon her

By the god who stood closer to her: "Do you fail to hasten

Your vows and your prayers, Aeneas the Trojan?" she said.

"The doors of this mighty house will not open for you

Before." She spoke and fell silent. A tremor of chill

Ran through the hard bones of the Trojans; the king from the depths

Of his breast poured out prayers:
"O Phoebus, who pitied the heavy

Sorrows of Troy, who directed the weapons of Paris

Into Achilles' body, with you as my leader

I entered so many oceans and lands that lay near them,

The home of the Massyli hidden away, and the plowlands

That border the Syrtes. Now, fleeing, at last we have reached

The boundaries of Italy. May the bad fortune of Troy

Follow me thus far, no farther. O all gods and goddesses,

It is right you should spare the people of Pergamum now,

You gods by whom Ilium and the soaring glory
Of Troy have been hampered. And you, most
  holy priestess,
Knowing the future, allow me (I ask for a
  kingdom
Not unallotted by Fates) to settle the Teucrians
In Latium, my wandering divinities, the
  harassed powers
Of Troy. I shall build a temple of solid marble
To Phoebus and Hecate, declare the days of a
  festival
Named after Phoebus. Great shrines shall
  await you also
In my domain. I shall place there your lots and
  hidden
Fates spoken to my people and consecrate
Men who are chosen to serve you, O fostering
  one.
Do not entrust your songs to the leaves lest the
  rapid
Winds make them whirling playthings, I beg
  you to sing
The prophecies yourself." He made an end of
  his speaking.
      But the priestess, not yet enduring Phoebus'
  huge frenzy,
Raged in her cave and tried to drive out of her
  breast
The great god. All the more did he weary her
  madly raving
Mouth, subdue her wild heart, and mold her
  with pressure.
A hundred wide doors stood open now in her
  household
Of their own accord, and the cries of the priestess were carried
Abroad on the air:
      "O you who have finished at last

The great dangers of ocean (worse dangers
  await you on land)
The Trojans shall come to Lavinium's kingdom
  (put this care
Out of your heart), but they shall wish they
  had not.
Wars, frightful wars I see, and the Tiber
  foaming
With blood. The Simois, Xanthus, the Dorian
  camp
Shall be yours again. Now another Achilles is
  born
In Latium, he too a goddess' son. Nor shall
  Juno,
The Teucrian foe, be absent when you as a sup-
  pliant
In desperate need ask aid of so many Italian
Tribes, and of so many cities. The cause of such
  evil
Again for the Trojans is a foreign wife and
  again
A bride from abroad.
Yet, do not yield to misfortune, but press on
  more boldly
Than your fortune allows you. The first road to
  safety will open
From a Greek city, where you would least
  expect it."

With such words the Sibyl of Cumae from out
  of her sanctum,
Sang frightful mysteries and roared back in
  her cave,
Involving the truth with obscurity. So did
  Apollo
Shake reins upon her until she raved, and twist
  goads
Under her breast. As soon as her fury abated;

*Her raving grew still, then Aeneas the hero
    began:*

*"O virgin, no new or unthought-of likeness of
    sorrow*

*Rises up to assail me, for I have foreseen it and
    pondered*

*Them all in my mind. One thing I beg of you:
    since*

*The gate of the king of darkness is said to be
    here*

*And the shadowy swamp that is Acheron's
    overflow,*

*Let me go to the sight of my dear father, his
    presence;*

*May you show me the way and open the sacred
    doors.*

*I snatched him from flames and a thousand
    pursuing weapons;*

*I carried him out of the enemies' midst on my
    shoulders.*

*My companion upon the way over all of the
    oceans,*

*He bore with me all the threats of both water
    and sky,*

*Though unwell and exhausted beyond the lot
    of old age.*

*Nonetheless, he gave orders that I, as a suppli-
    ant, seek*

*Your threshold and prayed that I should—take
    pity, I beg,*

*On a son and his father, O fostering one; you
    are able*

*To do everything, and not vainly did Hecate
    make you*

*Her mistress in groves of Avernus. If Orpheus
    could*

*Go down to the ghost of his wife with the aid of
    his Thracian*

*Lyre with harpstrings of song, if Pollux could
    rescue*

*His brother by dying for him and could go and
    come back*

*So often the same road—why should I mention
    great Theseus*

*Or Hercules? I too am sprung from the greatest
    Jove."*

    *He prayed in such words and clung with
    his hands to the altar,*

*When the priestess began to speak: "O child of
    the gods' blood,*

*Trojan son of Anchises, the descent to Avernus
    is easy*

*(For the gate of black Dis stands open by day
    and by night),*

But to recall your steps and to reach upper air,

*This is the task, this the labor. Few, born of the
    gods,*

*Whom Jove, who is just, has loved or their
    excellent virtue*

*Has raised to the heavens, have done it. Woods
    stand in the middle*

*Between this temple and Dis, and Cocytus the
    river*

*Winds round with black waters. If you are so
    anxious to see it,*

*Have such a desire to cross twice the Stygian
    lake,*

*To look twice on darkest Tartarus, if it is
    pleasing*

*For you to indulge in mad labor, then listen
    to me:*

*First you must do this. A golden bough there is
    hidden*

*Upon a dark tree thick with leaves and tough
    twigs and branches.*

*It is said to be sacred to Infernal Juno; the
    whole grove
Covers it up in the shade of an obscure valley.
But you cannot go down to the hidden parts of
    the earth
Before you have plucked this golden-leafed
    bough from the tree.
Lovely Proserpina orders this gift to be brought
    her.
Another as golden appears when the first
    bough is torn
Away, and its stem leafs out with the same
    kind of metal.
Then search for it well with your eyes, and
    when once you have found it,
Pluck it off with your hand, for willingly,
    easily too,
It will come if the Fates are calling you;
    otherwise,
No force can detach it or any tough blade
    shear it off.
Moreover, your friend lies dead (ah, you do not
    know it!)
And defiles all the fleet with his lack of a bur-
    ial while
You visit my oracle, linger upon my threshold.
Give him his proper resting place in a tomb.
Lead forth black cattle; let these be your first
    atonement.
Thus after all you will look upon Stygian
    groves
And a kingdom untrodden by live men." She
    spoke, then grew silent.
        Aeneas, his eyes cast down in a mourn-
    ful face,
Stepped forward and left the cave, turning over
    in mind
These obscure events. . . .*

*Then they followed the Sibyl's orders without
    any delay
And wept as they built up an altar, a pyre with
    boughs
Which they tried to raise high as the heavens.
    They went to the ancient
Forest, the deep retreat of the beasts, and
    felled
Pine trees; the holm-oak rang with the blows
    of an ax.
Ash-beams and oaks fit for cutting were riven
    by wedges.
They rolled huge ash trees down from the
    mountain sides.
Aeneas was first at such labors; he cheered on
    his men
As he swung an ax too like the others. But
    these thoughts he turned
About in his sad heart; he looked at the wide
    woods and prayed:
"If now that gold bough would reveal itself
    on the tree
In such a vast grove, since all you have told
    us is true
About Misenus, O prophetess! Only too
    true!"
He had scarcely spoken when twin doves came
    flying by chance
Down from the sky in front of his face and
    alighted
Upon the green turf. The great hero
    recognized
The birds of his mother and joyfully sent up
    this prayer:
"Become our leaders, if there is a way, and
    direct us
Through the groves with your flight to where
    the costly bough darkens the rich earth.*

And, goddess my mother, be with me in difficult fortunes."
So he spoke and slowed pace to observe what
the signs might bring,
And where the birds moved. They fed, as they
flew, at intervals,
Not advancing beyond the sight of the men
who followed.
Then, when they had reached the ill-smelling
jaws of Avernus,
They lightly rose up and gliding through glis-
tening air
They settled on favorite perches in the twin-
natured tree
Where the glitter of gold flashed distinctly
along the branches.
As the mistletoe blossoms each year in the win-
ter's cold
And produces new leaves in the woods, which
the tree does not have,
Surrounding smooth trunks with its growth of
a yellowish-white,
Such was the sight of the golden leafage upon
The dark holm-oak, the thin plate of metal
that rattled
In the soft breeze. Aeneas immediately seized it
And broke it away in his eagerness, though it
resisted,
And carried it into the house of the prophetess
Sibyl. . . .
      This done, Aeneas quickly obeyed Sibyl's
orders.
There was a deep cave that yawned with enor-
mous chasm,
Rocky but sheltered by its black lake and the
shadows
Of forest around. No bird could fly over it
safely,

So deadly the breath it poured from its night-
black jaws
To the vault of the sky. The Greeks called the
place Aornos,
Or "Birdless." The priestess first stationed here
four black bullocks
And poured wine upon their foreheads.
      Between their horns
She cut off the bristles and laid them in sacred
fire,
First fruits of her worship. She called upon
Hecate, mighty
In heaven, and Erebus. Others slashed the
bulls' throats
And collected their warm blood in bowls.
      Aeneas himself
Dispatched with a sword a black lamb to the
mother of Furies,
Black Night, and to her great sister, Earth,
and to you,
Proserpina, sacrificed a cow that was barren.
Then he began the nocturnal rites to Jove Sty-
gian
And laid on the flames the entire bodies of
bulls,
Pouring fat oil on the entrails that hissed as
they burned.
Look! at the first light of the sun when it rose
in the sky,
The earth underfoot began to rumble, the forest
Ridges to move, dogs seemed to howl through
the darkness
While the goddess approached. "Far off, stay
far off, unholy
Men!" cried the prophetess. "Leave this entire
grove!
You, Aeneas, move forward and draw your
sword from its sheath.

Now you need courage, now strong heart."
                                This was all she said
In her frenzy. She entered her open cave; he
    came after
And equaled his steps, unafraid, with those of
    his leader.
        Gods who rule over spirits, O voiceless
    shades,
Chaos and Phlegethon, broad regions of silent
    night,
Let it be proper for me to tell what I've heard
And by your power reveal the secrets deep
    hidden
In earth and sunken in gloom of the lower
    world.
They walked unseen in the lonely night,
    through shadows,
Through Hades' empty house and through his
    realm
Of nothingness, as when the moon shines
    faintly
With fitful, malignant light. The road led
    onward
Through woods where Jove had hidden the sky
    in darkness
And black night drawn day's color away from
    things.
There on the very threshold and in the jaws
Of Hell crouch Sorrow and avenging Cares.
There dwell pale Illnesses, and sad old Age,
And Fear, and Hunger that counsels evil, and
    squalid
Poverty, frightful forms to see, Destruction,
Pain, and Sleep, Death's brother, the sinful joys
Of Lust, and deadly War on the threshold's
    edge,
The Furies' steel-cold bedroom, insane Discord,
Weaving her snaky hair with bloody ribbons.

There in the center a huge and shady elm
Spreads out its aged arms in branches; here
False dreams, they say, reside and cling
    beneath
All of its leaves, and many shapes beside
Of strange wild beasts: the Centaurs in their
    stalls,
Two-formed Scyllas, hundredfold Briareus,
The beast of Lerna, hissing and horrible,
Chimaera armed with flames, the Gorgons,
    Harpies,
The shadow-shape of Geryon, with three
    bodies.
Shaking in sudden fear, Aeneas snatched his
Sword and turned its edge toward their
    approach,
And, if his wiser comrade had not warned him
That they were tenuous incorporeal spirits
Flitting in hollow semblances of forms,
He would have rushed and with vain steel
    slashed shadows.
        From here the way led down to
    Acheron's banks.
A murky whirlpool there boils mud and belches
All of its mass into Cocytus' river.
A frightful boatman guards these flowing
    waters,
Charon, filthy and squalid, whose white hair,
Unkempt, abundant, covers his chin. His
    eyes
Stare wide with flame. His dirty cloak hangs
    down
By a knot from his shoulders. He steers his
    craft with a pole
And runs up its sail and ferries dead bodies
    across
In a dark-blue skiff. His old age is green and
    sturdy.

⟊

Here, toward the banks the entire crowd kept rushing,

Mothers and husbands and heroes great-hearted but dead,

Boys, unmarried girls, and children placed on their pyres

In front of their parents' eyes, as many as when

The leaves in the woods fall down with autumn's first frost,

Or as many as birds who gather on land from deep ocean

When winter has driven them over the water to regions

Where the sun shines. They stood and begged to be first,

Extending their arms in desire of the farther shore.

But the grim ferry man chose now these, now those,

And drove all the rest far back along the beach.

Aeneas (he wondered at seeing the noisy crowd)

Said: "Tell me, O virgin, what does this hub-bub mean

On the river bank? What do these spirits wish?

Why are some left behind, while others are rowed

Across the dark water?" The old priestess briefly replied:

"Son of Anchises, undoubted child of the gods,

You see the deep pools of Cocytus, the Stygian marsh,

By whose power the gods are afraid to foreswear and deceive.

All this poor crowd you see lies still unburied;

That is the ferryman, Charon; the people he carries

Across have been buried. They are not given to him

Or to these gloomy banks with their roaring waters

Until their bones have been laid to rest in graves.

They wander a hundred years and they fly about

These shores; at last accepted, they revisit

The pools they long for." Anchises' son stood still

Deep in his thoughts and pitying their sad lot.

They took up their journey again and came close to the river.

Now the boatman, although at a distance, had seen them approach

As he looked from the Stygian waves, when they turned their steps

Through the silent grove. He spoke to them first and reproved them:

"Whoever you are who come armed to my river, speak up

And tell why you come. Halt there! Don't budge from the spot!

This is the place of Shadows, of Dreams, and of Night

Full of sleep. It is sinful to carry live bodies across

In my Stygian boat. I did not rejoice when I ferried

Hercules over the lake nor Theseus or Pirithous,

Although they were born of the gods and had never been conquered.

Hercules tried to tie up the watchdog of Hades

And drag him off trembling from the very
    throne of the king;
The last two attempted to kidnap the mistress
    of Dis
From her bedroom." The Amphrysian prophet-
    ess spoke in reply:
"There are no such ambushes on foot here: do
    not be disturbed.
These arms have no force. Let the huge watch-
    dog bark in his cave
And frighten pale shadows forever, let chaste
    Proserpina
Remain in her uncle's abode. Aeneas the
    Trojan,
Outstanding in loyalty and in the use of his
    weapons,
Goes down through Erebus' deepest gloom to
    his father.
If the image of such great loyalty does not
    affect you,
Then note well this branch." (She produced it
    from under her robe.)
There abated the swelling anger in Charon's
    heart
And he said no more but admired the worship-
    ful gift
Of the fatal bough, seen once more after long
    interval.
Then turning his blue boat toward them, he
    steered for the shore
And drove off the other souls sitting upon their
    long benches;
He lowered the gangway, received huge Aeneas
    on board.
The sewn-leather skiff groaned under his
    weight; through its cracks
It shipped much swamp water. At last safely
    over the river

He landed both seeress and hero in the dark
    weeds and foul slime.
      From three throats huge Cerberus filled
    this realm with his barking,
Savagely crouched in his cave. The prophetess
    saw
His neck bristle up with serpents. She threw
    him a cake
To bring sleep, made of honey and meal that
    was mingled with drugs.
Rabid with hunger, he opened three throats
    and swallowed
The offering, then loosened huge backs as he
    stretched on the floor
Of the entire cave. Its guardian unconscious,
    Aeneas
Raced to the entrance, escaped from the banks
    of the water
That permits no return.
      At once they heard sounds of loud wailing,
The souls of small children crying upon the
    threshold,
Whom a dark day had snatched from their
    mother's breast and bereft
Of the lot of sweet life and plunged them in
    bitter death.
Beside them were those condemned to die on
    false charges,
Their places assigned through judges
    appointed by lot.
Minos presides at the vote-urn; he calls the
    assembly
Of dead souls and reviews their lives and the
    crimes they are charged with.
The next places were held by sad folk who had
    killed themselves,
Though guiltless; they hated the light of day,
    so they threw

Their lives away. How they wished that in
    upper air
They might now endure both poverty and its
    harsh labors!
Divine law prevents them, the hateful marsh
    with its gloomy
Water restrains them, and Styx, nine times
    encircling.
      Not far away appeared the Mourning
    Fields—
For so they are called—extending in every
    direction.
Here those whom harsh love destroyed with its
    cruel sorrow
Are concealed by secret paths, and a thicket of
    myrtle
Covers them: care does not leave them although
    they are dead.
Here he saw Phaedra and Procris and sad
    Eriphyle,
Pointing at wounds her cruel son had
    inflicted,
And Evadne and Pasiphaë; here Laodamia
Walked as their comrade, and Caeneus, once a
    young woman,
Then a man, but by Fate changed back to her
    earlier form.
Among them Phoenician Dido, with her fresh
    wound,
Went wandering in a great wood. When the
    Trojan hero
Stood at her side and recognized her in the
    shadows,
As one at the first of the month either sees or
    imagines
He sees the moon through the clouds, he wept
    and spoke to her
In sweet love: "Unhappy Dido, was the report

That came to me true, that you had taken the
    last step
And died by the sword? And was I the cause of
    your death?
I swear by the stars, by the gods, by the faith
    there may be
In the depths of the earth, that I left your
    shores, queen, with reluctance.
But the orders of gods which now force me to
    pass through these shadows,
This wasteland of deepest night, compelled and
    commanded.
I could not believe when I left I should bring
    you such sorrow.
Stand still and do not withdraw yourself from
    my sight.
Whom do you flee from? This word that I
    speak is the last
That Fate may allow me." Aeneas attempted to
    soothe
With these words the anger that blazed from
    her eyes and her soul,
As he burst into tears. She fixed her gaze on the
    ground.
Her features averted were not more stirred by
    his speech
Than if they were made of hard flint or
    Marpessian marble.
Then she flung herself off and fled back to the
    shadowy grove,
Still hostile, where her first husband Sychaeus
    replied
To her sorrow with kindness and equaled her
    love with his own.
Shocked by her tragic misfortune, Aeneas came
    after
At a distance and wept for her, pitied her as she
    went on.

Then he took the course given. . . .
  Aeneas looked about him and suddenly
saw
At the foot of a cliff on his left a broad strong-
  hold surrounded
By triple walls which a rapid river flowed round
In a torrent of flame, Tartarean Phlegethon,
Rolling its grinding boulders. A huge gate
  stood near him,
Its columns of solid adamant. No human power
Could destroy them with steel, not even the
  gods themselves.
A tower of steel rose up in the air: Tisiphone
Sat there in a bloody robe and wakefully
  guarded
The vestibule night and day. From within there
  came groans
And the sound of horrible flogging, the shriek-
  ing of steel,
Of chains being dragged. Aeneas stood still,
  terrified
At the noise. "What forms of wrong-doing, O
  virgin, are these
Arising?" The prophetess thus began to reply:
"Famous leader of Teucrians, divine law for-
  bids that the guiltless
Should set foot on the threshold of sinners. But
  when Hecate gave me
Full charge in the groves of Avernus she led me
  all over
And explained each punishment. Rhadaman-
  thus of Cnossus
Rules here, and most harshly. He hears the
  offenses committed,
The facts in each case, whenever a man has
  attempted
To cheat divine law, postponing his punishment
  vainly

Until death, but too late.
                Tisiphone straightway avenges
His crime. With a whip in right hand she beats
  and torments him.
In her left hand she brandishes snakes and
  calls on the savage
Cohorts of her sisters. At last awful doors are
  spread open
To screech on their hinges dread-sounding. You
  see what doorkeeper
Sits in the entrance, what form keeps watch at
  the threshold?
A hydra much worse, with fifty black horrible
  yawning
Mouths. Then Tartarus extends sheer down-
  ward, twice
As far toward the shadows as the distance to
  airy Olympus.
Here the ancient race of Earth, offspring of
  Titans,
Struck by the thunderbolt rolled into uttermost
  depths.
I saw the twin bodies immense of the sons of
  Aloeus,
Who attacked great heaven and tried to thrust
  Jove from his kingdom
With their hands. I saw Salmoneus severely
  punished
For usurping the lightning and thunder of
  Olympian Jove.
Borne by four horses and shaking a torch in
  his hand,
He rode among people of Greece through the
  center of Elis
And its city in triumph, demanding his honors
  divine.
A madman, to simulate thunder and inim-
  itable lightning

With chariot bronze and the horn-footed gallop
    of horses!

The Almighty Father twirl-twisted his weapon
    through dense clouds;

He did not use torches or smoky pitch-pine, but
    he drove him

Headlong in a monstrous whirl.
                I could also see Tityos,

An offspring of all-bearing Earth; over nine
    complete acres

His body lay stretched. A large vulture with
    hooked beak kept plucking

Away at his undying liver and entrails prolific

Of punishment, ripping them, dwelling beneath
    his high chest.

No respite is given these tissues to grow back
    again. . . .
               Not if I had one hundred tongues

And one hundred mouths and a voice of iron
    could I

Recount all the forms of their crimes or run
    over their names."

    When she had thus spoken, the elderly
    priestess of Phoebus

Said: "Come, on your way, and complete the
    task undertaken.

Let us make haste. I see the walls of the Cyclopes

Forged in their furnace, and gates in the arch-
    way before us,

Where we are instructed to lay down our gifts."
    She had spoken.

They walked side by side through the shadowy
    way and then hurried

Across the midspace and approached the doors.
    Here Aeneas

Went inside and sprinkled his body with fresh
    running water

And placed the bough upright upon the thresh-
    old before him.

    When this had been done, their duty
    complete toward the goddess,

They came to the region of joy and the pleas-
    ant green spaces,

Abode of the blessed, and the groves of the for-
    tunate souls.

Here a more generous air clothed the fields
    with a dazzling

Light; they knew their own sun and their own
    stars.

Some of them exercised on a grassy play-
    ground,

Competing at games and wrestling on yellow
    sand.

Some beat with their feet in a chorus and sang
    as they danced.

There Orpheus, singer of Thrace, in a flowing
    robe,

Accompanied them on the seven strings of his
    lyre,

Striking them now with his fingers, now with
    ivory pick.

Here was the ancient race of Teucer, most
    handsome

Descendants and great-hearted heroes born in
    happier times,

Ilus, Assaracus, Dardanus, founder of Troy.

From a distance he marveled to see their arms
    and chariots,

Empty of men; their spears stood fixed in the
    ground;

Their horses, released, pastured here and there
    through the field.

For the pleasure they took in chariots, arms,
　while alive,
Their interest in caring for glossy horses, remain
When their bodies are laid in the earth.
　　　　　　　　He looked at the others
To right and to left on the grass as they feasted
　and sang
A joyful paean in chorus, there in the fragrant
Laurel grove where the great river Eridanus rolls
Through the woods to the upper world.
　　　　　　　　Here was a band
Of men who had suffered wounds while fight-
　ing for country;
Some who were priests and chaste while their
　life remained,
And others loyal seers who spoke things worthy
　of Phoebus,
Some creative in arts which enrich man's life,
And others whose merit had made men remem-
　ber them.
All of them wore a white fillet around their
　temples.
They thronged about as the Sibyl spoke to them
　thus,
To Musaeus above all, for that most populous
　crowd
Looked up as he towered above with his head
　and shoulders:
"Say, happy souls, and you, the best of all
　poets,
What region, what place holds Anchises? We
　came for his sake
And crossed the great rivers of Erebus." To this
　request
The hero gave, briefly, response: "There is no
　fixed home
For anyone. We inhabit the darkling groves

And lie on the cushion-like banks and the
　meadows refreshed
By streams. But you, if that is the wish in your
　hearts,
Climb up on this ridge, and I'll set you an easy
　path."
He spoke and moved on and showed them the
　shining fields
Down below. They descended here from the
　highest summits.
　　　　But Father Anchises, deep in a bloom-
　ing valley,
Examined quite closely those souls which
　would rise to the light,
Reviewing by chance the number of all his
　descendants,
The grandsons so dear, their fates and fortunes
　and deeds,
Their characters too. When he saw Aeneas
　approaching
Toward him through the grass, he stretched
　eager hands toward his son,
His cheeks bathed with tears, and managed to
　utter this word:
"You have come at last, that loyalty which I knew
Has conquered your difficult course. Do I
　really see
Your face, son of mine? Do I hear and reply to
　your words?
So I felt in my heart that I should, and I reck-
　oned the hours
Before you could come: anxiety did not
　deceive me.
What lands and wide seas you have traveled to
　reach me, my son,
And beset by what dangers! How I feared that
　the powers of Libya

Might injure you!" Aeneas spoke: "It was your
    sad image
Appearing again and again that brought me,
    my father,
To this threshold. My ships lie anchored off
    Tyrrhenian shores.
Give me your right hand, father, and do not
    retreat from
My embrace." So speaking he bathed his
    cheeks in tears.
Three times he tried to throw arms round his
    father's neck;
Three times that image escaped the vain grasp
    of his hands
As if it were soft breeze, or most like a fleeting
    dream.
    Meanwhile Aeneas saw in a nook of the
    valley
A secluded grove and rustling thickets in
    timber,
And the river of Lethe that flowed past homes
    that were peaceful.
Races and peoples unnumbered were flitting
    around it,
Just as the bees in meadows when summer is
    peaceful
Alight upon various flowers and swarm round
    white lilies
And fill the whole field with their murmur.
                   Aeneas was startled
To see them so suddenly, and he inquired the
    reasons,
Not knowing what rivers these were or what
    men filled the stream banks
With such a great throng. Then Father
    Anchises gave answer:
"They are souls who are fated to live in a sec-
    ond body.

They are drinking the waters of Lethe that
    make them forget
And free them from care. I have long been
    eager to tell you
Who each of them is and describe each of my
    descendants.
We shall thus find more pleasure together when
    Italy's won."
"Must I suppose, O father, that some of these
    souls
Will ascend to the light and return to their
    slow-moving bodies?
What a dreadful desire to live in the light have
    these wretches!"
"I shall certainly tell you, my son, nor prolong
    your suspense,"
Said Anchises, revealing each detail in proper
    succession.
    "To begin with, the sky and the lands and
    the watery plains,
The luminous globe of the moon, the Titanian
    sun
And the stars, a spirit within them nourishes.
                      Mind
Gives life to the mass, infused through the
    members of each,
And mingles throughout the great body.
    Thence comes the creation
Of men and of beasts and of birds and the
    monsters which ocean
Bears under its shining water. Their vigor is
    fiery,
Divine is the seed of their being as long as
    they are
Not hindered by harmful, slow bodies or limbs
    that are earthly
And members death-bound. Their bodies give
    rise to their dread,

Desire and grief and joy; shut up in their
　　shadows
And windowless prison they cannot catch sight
　　of the air.
Yet even when life has deserted the last light
　　above,
Not all of their evil departs from miserable men,
Nor all bodily ill; for these grow (as they must)
　　with deep roots,
Are ingrained a long time in a marvelous way.
　　They are punished
Therefore and pay penalties for their old sins.
　　Some are offered,
Hung up, to the winds, and others beneath a
　　whirlpool
Have the crimes that infect them washed out,
　　or burned out with fire.
Each of us suffers the lot of death that was
　　fated;
Then we are sent through wide Elysium; few
Of us hold happy fields until a long daytime is
　　ended
And time's circle complete removes the corrup-
　　tion grown ingrained,
Leaving ethereal sense unpolluted and fiery.
When one thousand years have rolled by, god
　　will call all those souls
To the river of Lethe in a long line so that they
　　may
Without memory rise to the vault of the upper
　　world
And begin to desire return to bodies." Anchises
Had spoken. He drew his son and with him the
　　Sibyl
Into the midst of the murmuring crowd, took
　　his place
On a mound where he could survey them all in
　　a long line

Before him and recognize faces of those who
　　came:
　　"Come, I shall tell of the glory to come for
　　Dardanian
Offspring, descendants unborn of Italian race,
Illustrious souls who shall bear our name; I
　　shall show
What your fate shall be. That young man who
　　leans on a spear
Without blade, who holds the nearest place to
　　the light,
Is the first to rise up to the air with a blood
　　that is mingled
Of Trojan and Italian, Silvius, an Alban name,
Your posthumous son; your wife Lavinia shall
Bear him to you in your late old age. In the
　　woods
She shall rear him as king and father of kings,
　　whence our race
Shall rule over Alba Longa. Next to him is
　　Procas,
The glory of Trojan stock, and Capys and
　　Numitor,
And Aeneas Silvius, who will revive your name,
Outstanding alike in loyalty and in the use
Of weapons, if ever he shall succeed to the
　　rule
Of Alba. What young men they are! Look,
　　what strength they display!
How they wear on their brows the civic crown
　　with its shadow!
They shall build on the hills Nomentum and
　　Gabii,
Fidenae the city, Collatia's citadel, build
Pometii, fortress of Inuus, Bola, and Cora,
All places now nameless, but then they shall
　　have these names.
Yes, even Romulus, son of Mars, shall join

His grandfather; his mother Ilia shall rear
    him up
From the blood of Assaracus. Look, how twin
    crests stand high
On his head, how his father now marks him
    with honor to be
Of the gods above! Beneath his auspicious
    omens,
My son, noble Rome shall equal her power with
    earth,
Her might with Olympus, surround her seven
    citadels
With a single wall, happy with offspring of
    men, like the mother
Of Berecyntus borne in her chariot,
Wearing her crown with its towers through
    Phrygian cities,
Happy in sons she has given the gods and
    embracing
One hundred grandsons, all dwellers in heaven
    and all
Having houses on high. Now turn your eyes
    this way to see
This race and your Romans. Here Caesar and
    all of the clan
Of Iulus will come to the great vault of heaven.
    This man,
This is he whom again and again you have
    heard in the promise
Of prophecy, Caesar Augustus, son of a god.
He shall found once again an era of gold in
    the land
Of Latium, throughout the fields that Saturn
    once ruled.
He shall carry his power beyond Garamantes
    and Indians
(A land that shall stretch beyond stars and
    beyond the paths

Of the year and the sun, where sky-bearing
    Atlas shores up
On his shoulders the axis studded with shining
    stars).
Against his arrival, the Caspian kingdom, the
    land
Of Maeotis, already shakes with the holy
    prophetic
Responses of heaven, the trembling mouths of
    the seven-
Fold Nile are astir. Not even Alcides
    traversed
So much of the earth, though he shot the
    bronze-footed deer,
Made peaceful the groves of Erymanthus and
    frightened the hydra
Of Lerna with his bow; not Bacchus, who drove
    as a victor
With reins made of vines on the backs of his
    tigers from Nysa's
High summit. And are we in doubt to extend
    our manhood
Thus far with our deeds? Or do we fear to
    place feet
On the soil of Ausonia? Who is that bearing
    afar
The sign of the olive branch and the equipment
    of worship?
I know his white beard and his hair. He is
    Numa the king,
Who will give our new city its laws; he will
    come from small Cures,
Barren in soil, to great power. Then Tullus will
    follow
To break up the fatherland's ease and to drive
    sluggish men
Toward their weapons and battlelines long
    unacquainted with triumphs.

Next to him follows the rather too arrogant
    Ancus,
Who even now glories too much in the popular
    favor.
Do you wish to see also the Tarquin kings and
    proud spirit
Of Brutus avenger, the fasces that he
    recovered?
He first shall receive the power of consul, the
    axes
So savage; a father, he shall call his sons to
    their doom.
For starting new wars—he shall do this in
    freedom's fair cause.
Unhappy man, however ages that follow may
    speak
Of these deeds, love of country will conquer
    and measureless lust
For praise. But see also, afar off, the Decii and
    Drusi,
Torquatus fierce with his ax, and Camillus
    returning
The standards once lost. But those souls which
    you see with their gleaming
Armor alike are at peace with each other while
    darkness
Of night presses down on them: ah, what a war
    they will stir up,
What clashes of battle, what slaughter, when
    they reach the light
Of life! A father-in-law who descends from the
    Alpine
Ramparts and from the height of Monoecus, a
    son-in-
Law who arranges his battle ranks drawn from
    the East!
Do not, my children, accustom your spirits to
    warfare

So great, nor turn toward the vitals of your
    fatherland
These strong forces! And you, who are sprung
    from Olympus, from my blood,
Be first in your mercy, throw weapons away
    from your hands.
That victor shall drive in his chariot to the
    high Capitol
When Corinth is captured, distinguished for
    slaughter of Greeks.
This one shall uproot both Argos and Mycenae,
    the city
Of Agamemnon, kill Perseus, Achilles'
    descendant,
So mighty in arms, and avenge his forebears
    and Minerva's
Temples at Troy defiled by the Greeks. Who
    would leave you,
Great Cato, or Cossus, unmentioned? The
    Gracchi and their clan,
The twin Scipios, two lightning bolts of war,
    the destruction
Of Africa, or you, Fabricius, rich with a little,
Or Regulus, you, who sowed your furrow
    with seed?
Where do you eagerly drive me, you Fabian
    men?
You are that Maximus, he who alone saved our
    country
By his delaying!
            Others will fashion the molten
Bronze with more skill (at least I believe this),
    will carve from
Marble live faces, will plead cases better, and
    sketch out
The paths of the heavenly bodies with pointers,
    and forecast
The rising of stars.

You, Roman, remember to govern
The peoples with power (these arts shall be
    yours), to establish
The practice of peace, spare the conquered, and
    beat down the haughty."
    Thus Father Anchises, and added these
    words as they marveled:
"See how Marcellus, illustrious with the Best
    Spoils,
Moves forward, a victor who towers above all
    men.
He shall set Rome in place again after the for-
    eign uprising;
The hoofs of his horses shall trample the Poeni,
    the Gallic
Rebel; to Father Quirinus he'll offer the captured
Arms for the third time." And here Aeneas
    addressed him
As he saw a young man, most handsome and
    shining in armor,
Walking beside Marcellus, but with face and eyes
Cast down and unhappy: "Who, father, is that
    who comes with him?
A son or some other from your long line of
    descendants?
What a shouting of comrades! What genuine
    greatness is in him!
But black night envelopes his head with its
    gloomy shadow."
Then Father Anchises replied, with tears in
    his eyes:
"O son, do not search into the great sorrow
    of our
Descendants. The Fates will merely show him
    the earth
But forbid him to live there further. O gods
    above,

Rome's stock would appear too powerful if your
    gifts
Should remain among men. What groans shall
    the Field of Mars
Carry to that great city, what funeral rites
Shall you see, river Tiber, when you flow past
    his fresh-made
Tomb! No other boy of the Ilian clan shall exalt
His Latin ancestors with such high hopes, in
    none
Of its offshoots shall Romulus' land take so
    great a pride.
Alas for his loyalty! Alas for his ancient
    faith,
His right hand still in war unconquered!
    None
Unscathed could have brought arms against
    him, whether
On foot or spurring a foaming horse's flanks.
Alas, you piteous boy, if ever you could
Break out against your Fates!
                You shall be a Marcellus!
Give lilies with full hands; I too shall scatter
Bright flowers, heap gifts of these at least
    for my
Descendant's soul, perform an empty honor!"

    Thus did they wander through that
    entire land,
In wide and misty fields, reviewed its features.
But when Anchises had led his son about
Among these sights and fired his soul with love
Of fame to come, he told his hero-heir
The wars which must be waged and described
    the peoples
Of Laurentum, Latinus' city, and how he might
    flee

From each trial, or bear it.
             There are twin gates of sleep.
One is of horn, they say, where an easy exit
Is given to shades which are true; the other is
    white
And perfect, of gleaming ivory. Through it the
    Ghosts
Of the Underworld send false dreams to the
    light. Anchises,

His words completed, went with his son and the
    Sibyl
And sent them out through the ivory gate. Aeneas
Made his way to the ships and rejoined his
    comrades, then sailed
Along the straight shore to Caieta's harbor.
                          The anchor
Was thrown from the prow; the ships stood on
    the beach.

HORACE (QUINTUS HORATIUS FLACCUS) (65–8 B.C.)

Ars Poetica

Classical Rome's most elegantly polished lyricist and satirist and most quoted author was a native of Venusia (modern Venosa), in Apulia, born of a freedman tax collector-auctioneer. At considerable sacrifice to his father he was given a first-class aristocratic education, first in Rome under the grammarian Orbilius Pupillus, then in Athens. After fighting on Brutus' side as a *tribunus militum* at Philippi, Horace was pardoned by Octavian who, at the same time, reduced him to poverty by confiscating his family property. But Horace's early poems caught the attention of Virgil and Varius; they introduced him to Maecenas, whose patronage and friendship assured attention and publication. In 33 B.C., Maecenas granted Horace a farm in the Sabine Hills near Tibur (modern Tivoli) and introduced him to Augustus, who asked him to serve as his private secretary; Horace declined the emperor, preferring to continue his career in poetry. Short, fat, cheerful, and pot-bellied, he has been called "the first European" and is certainly the most eloquent spokesman for the Golden Age of Augustan culture. Testimony to his mastery, recognized even among his contemporaries, all of Horace's poetry has survived:

- *Satires* (also known as *Sermones*), modeled on Lucilius and derived from fable, oral tradition, memories, and anecdotes. Two books of colloquial Latin hexameters, some written in dialogue form, dealing humorously with various topics, from moral philosophy and literary criticism to food, sex, success, scenes from the rough-and-tumble of everyday Rome, and eulogizing memories of his father. It was published between 35 and 30 B.C.

- *Epodes.* Seventeen short poems (most of them invectives in the iambic meter) on love and politics modeled on the cantankerous early Greek lyric poet Archilochos, published in 30 B.C.
- *Odes* (also known as *Carmina*). Four books of 103 passionately sophisticated lyrics, dedicated to Maecenas, on various subjects, in a variety of meters; many of them inspired by the Greeks Alcaeus, Anacreon, and Pindar, and many of them filled with praise for the contemporary greatness of Augustan Rome; published between 23 and 13 B.C. In these wonderful expressions of Horace's poetic maturity, the first to successfully use the refined stylistic techniques of the Alexandrine poets in Latin, we read about wine and good company, love passing from youth to middle age, the serenity of the Italian countryside, and the transitory splendors of spring. Mistresses addressed in these poems include Lydia, Tyndaris, Lyce, Glycera, and Chloe.
- *Carmen Saeculare.* A hymn to Diana and Apollo, commissioned by Augustus, acknowledging Horace as poet laureate, for the *Ludi saeculares* ("Secular Games") in 17 B.C. Designed to be sung, this is a stately poem treating the achievements of Augustus with almost religious reverence.
- *Epistles* (or *Letters*). Two books of hexameter letters to friends and notables (including Augustus, Aristius Fuscus, Tiberius, Manlius Torquatus, Tibullus, Maecenas, and Lollius), published between 20 and 15 B.C. and dealing with such issues as etiquette, morality, social relationships, and contemporary politics.
- One of these epistles, that called by Quintilian the *Art of Poetry (Ars Poetica),* Horace's longest poem, is addressed to the father and sons Piso and advises them about the pursuit of literature especially commenting on drama and epic. Following the model of Aristotle's *Poetics,* the work is an outline of literary criticism, theory, and interpretation. Its influence lasted well into the Renaissance; its humor and vitality are characteristic of Horace.

3

Suppose a painter chose to place a human head
upon a horse's neck, to lay feathers of all colors
on organs gathered from all over, to make his figure
a black, disgusting fish below, on top a lovely girl.
Given a private view, my friends, how couldn't you laugh?

Believe me, Pisos, this painting and a kind of poem
are very similar, one like an image in a sick man's dream,
a fever image whose head and foot can't possibly belong
upon the same physique. "The painters and the poets both
have always shared the right of doing what they like."

the Rhine and rainbow are all described at
    length.
But they shouldn't be, not out of place. Per-
    haps a cypress
is your specialty, but what if you've been hired
    to paint
a hopeless swimmer, after a shipwreck? An
    amphora began
to grow—why does the whirling wheel bring
    forth a jug?
In short, make an unbroken unity of every work
    you try.
Most poets, father and young men deserving
    such a father,
go wrong in trying to be right: I struggle for
    concision,
I wind up being obscure; others try for
    smoothness
and lose strength, or for sublimity, and get gas.
One poet, too cautious, fears storms and crawls
    along,
the other craves bizarre variety in a single sub-
    ject
and paints a dolphin in a forest, a boar among
    the waves.
Fear of criticism leads to faults if we lack art.
Near the Aemilian School a sculptor lives, a
    clever man
at shaping fingernails and catching flowing
    hair in bronze,
but the total effect is weak; he can't create a
    whole,
he doesn't know how. If I cared about good
    composition,
I'd no more copy him than like living with a
    crooked nose
even if dark eyes and hair still made me worth
    a look.

Roman Temple

Yes, we seek this indulgence and we grant it in
    return,
but not to couple fierce and gentle creatures,
    not to
pair together snakes and birds or lambs and
    tigers.
Quite often works heroically begun and very
    promising
have here and there a widely gleaming purple
    patch
stitched to them, so that Diana's grove and
    altar,
the quick stream flowing through the pleasant
    fields,

*Writers, choose a subject for which your talent
    is a match*

*and take your time considering what your
    shoulders can't*

*and can endure; a man who picks what suits
    his powers*

*won't find himself deserted by eloquence or by
    clear order.*

*Order has a special quality and charm, in my
    opinion:*

*the poet says right now exactly what he must
    say now*

*and postpones other things which for the
    moment he ignores.*

*Do as much in every line; be both careful and
    precise*

*with any promised poem, choosing this word,
    spurning that.*

*You've written very well if, by placing it with
    skill,*

*you make a known word new. If, by chance, it's
    necessary*

*to shed light on something recent requiring
    new expressions,*

*you can fashion words the belted Cethegi never
    heard.*

We shouldn't overuse this license, but we have it.

Words newly made are well received if flowing

*from Greek sources in a narrow stream. But
    why*

*does Rome grant Plautus and Caecilius what
    it won't*

*to Vergil and to Varius? Why am I offending if
    I add*

*the few I have? Didn't the speech of Ennius
    and Cato*

*enrich the language of our land and invent
    new names*

*to give to things? It has been and always will
    be right*

*that words are coined which bear the imprint of
    the present.*

*As forests change their leaves with every pass-
    ing year,*

*the old ones falling down, so, as older words
    die out,*

*the newborn, like all children, grow and
    strengthen.*

*Death has a claim on us and all we have. Now
    Neptune*

*is received on land to guard our ships from
    northern winds,*

*a regal work; a swamp, long sterile, which only
    oars*

*could cross, feeds nearby towns and feels the
    heavy plow;*

*a river inhospitable to crops is taught a better
    route*

*and flows along it. But all that mortals make
    will die,*

*and language has yet a briefer span of pleas-
    ing, lovely life.*

*Many words now fallen will be reborn and
    others fall*

*that now hold worthy places; use determines
    this,*

*it controls the judging, law, and standard of
    our speech.*

*Exploits of kings and warrior chiefs, disastrous
    wars—*

*Homer made clear the meter one should use for
    these.*

*The couplet with unequal lines first enclosed
    laments,*

*and then was used in giving thanks for
    granted prayers;*

but just what poet first composed the little elegy
scholars keep disputing, and the case remains
    in court.
Archilochus' furious rage armed him with the
    iamb,
the meter both the sock and buskin took as
    theirs;
it was perfect for trading speeches and over-
    coming
the noises of the crowd, and with action it went
    well.
The subjects given by the Muse for singing on
    the lyre
were the gods and their children, the victories
    of boxers
and of steeds, young love affairs, and carefree
    drinking.
Since the poetic forms and styles are definitely
    set,
why call me a poet if I don't know how to fol-
    low them?
Why am I ignorant through false pride when I
    could learn?
Tragic lines don't give comic themes a setting
    they enjoy;
equally resented is comic speech, words almost
    proper
for the sock, when used to sing about Thyestes'
    feast.
Each literary kind should keep its rightful place.
Yet occasions come when comedy will raise its
    voice
and raging Chremes swell his mouth and
    fiercely scold;
at times a tragic figure will lament in common
    speech
(as do Telephus and Peleus, both poor and in
    exile,

abandoning their bombast and sesquipedalian
    words),
if he wants his misery to touch his audience's
    heart.
It isn't enough to make lines pretty; they must
    move,
and affect the hearer's soul exactly as the poet
    wants.
Just as laughter inspires laughter, tears bring
    tears
to human faces; if you want my tears, you first
    must
weep yourself. Then your agonies will hurt
    me too,
Telephus or Peleus. But if your lines don't fit
    you,
I may sleep, or I may laugh. Sad words go
    with gloom
upon a face, words full of threats fit angry
    looks.
Light chatter suits a smile, serious talk a
    frown.
For nature moves us inwardly in response to
    every guise
that fortune wears; it brings us pleasure, fuels
    our wrath,
crushes us to earth beneath our sorrow, tortures
    us,
and then, with speech, brings out the motions
    of the soul.
If a character's words aren't proper for his
    place,
Roman knights and infantry alike will loudly
    boo.
A hero and a god should speak quite differently,
so should a vigorous old man and a fiery youth
in bloom, a matron of high station and a busy
    nurse,

a roving merchant and the tiller of a thriving
   field,
a Colchian and an Assyrian, an Argive and a
   Theban.
Either be traditional or make the characters
   consistent.
Writer, if you've chosen to show great Achilles
   once again,
active, angry, inexorable, have him fiercely
   deny
law's hold on him and claim by violence what
   he likes.
Let Medea be savage and relentless, Ino full of
   tears,
Ixion treacherous, Io far-wandering, Orestes
   sad.
But if, in trying something new on stage, you
   dare
invent a character, keep him to the very end
as he was at his first entrance, entirely consis-
   tent.
It's hard to express the universal in your own
   way,
and you'll do better spinning Troy's story into
   plays
than being first to stage events unvoiced and
   overlooked.
Public subjects will become your private prop-
   erty, if
you neither plod along the common, easy, cir-
   cling path
nor strain to match your model word for word,
   too close
in your translation; for imitating will put you
   in a trap
where you'll be kept, either by your pride or by
   generic law.
Don't begin like this, as the cyclic poets used to:

"Of Priam's destiny I'll sing, and of the war
   renowned."
What can this big-mouthed boaster bring to
   equal that?
The mountains heave and give birth to a tiny
   mouse.
Another poet does much better without the
   clumsy start.
"Tell me, Muse, about the man who, when Troy
   had fallen,
saw the cities and the ways of life of many
   peoples."
To give, not smoke from roaring flame, but
   light from smoke
is his intention, and so he offers us amazing
   creatures,
Antiphates and Scylla, the Cyclops and
   Charybdis.
He doesn't begin Diomedes' return with Melea-
   ger's death
or the Trojan War with the egg that hatched
   the twins.
Always he goes right to the point, midway in
   the action,
as if all his readers knew what went before; he
   grips us,
and if he can't make something shine, he cuts
   it out.
He lies in such a way, making truth and fiction
   blend,
that beginning and middle, middle and end
   won't disagree.
Poet, hear what I, and the people too,
   require
if you want to keep us in our seats until the
   curtain,
all set to clap when the singer tells us, "Now
   applaud."

*Correctly represent the marks of every phase of
     life,*
*and give your characters what suits their vary-
     ing years.*
*A little boy, a recent talker who firmly plants
     his feet*
*upon the ground, loves playing with his
     friends, flies*
*in and out of rages for no reason, and changes
     every hour.*
*A young man, still beardless, but finally on his
     own,*
*loves dogs and horses and the sunny, grassy
     field.*
*He's wax for vice to shape, thorny to good
     advice,*
*slow to acquire things he needs, careless with
     cash,*
*proud and demanding, quick to drop what he
     once loved.*
*An adult has concerns that fit his grown-up
     mind;*
*a slave to his position, he seeks power and
     connections,*
*avoids commitments that later may be difficult
     to change.*
*An old man's life is full of irritation, for
     either*
*he's greedy and miserable, afraid to use his
     savings,*
*or he worries and delays no matter what he
     does.*
*He stalls, keeps hoping, does nothing, wants to
     stay alive,*
*grouches and complains; he's a praiser of the
     vanished past*
*when he was young, censurer and critic of
     those young now.*

*Much that we enjoy comes with the years as
     they advance.*
*Much, as they recede, goes with them. Rather
     than give*
*old men's lines to young men or adult roles to
     boys,*
*always be sure that every age receives its proper
     traits.*
*Action either happens on the stage or is
     reported there.*
*Anything we learn of through the ear less
     moves the mind*
*than something shown our trusted eyes, offered
     firsthand*
to the spectator. But if a scene belongs offstage,
*don't push it on; many things aren't suitable
     for eyes*
*which an actor soon appearing can vividly
     describe.*
*For Medea shouldn't kill her sons before the
     audience*
or evil Atreus cook human guts in public view,
*or Procne be transformed to a bird, Cadmus to
     a snake.*
*Anything like that you show me I'll disbelieve
     and hate.*
*Neither drop below nor raise past five the acts
     presented*
*in a play if you want it to be called for and
     shown again.*
*Let no god meddle without a knot that no one
     but a god*
*could loose, and don't let fourth characters
     butt in.*
*The chorus should work like an actor, with a
     real role,*
*and not step out of it by singing intermission
     songs*

*which don't help the play go forward and fit in
   well.*
*It should support the good and offer friendly
   counsel,*
*calm down furious men, cherish those who dis-
   like vice;*
*it should praise plain living, praise healthful
   justice*
*and law, as well as the peace that comes with
   open doors.*
*Have it keep confidences safe and ask the gods
   in prayers*
*that favor be returned to humble men and
   leave the proud.*
*The pipe, not the modern, brass-ringed version,
   rival*
*to the horn, but with few holes and thin and
   simple,*
*once aided and accompanied the chorus by
   itself, and*
*its music filled the theater, then not too
   crowded.*
*The people gathered there in numbers you
   could count,*
*and they were decent and modest in their
   tastes.*
*But after becoming conquerors, gaining new
   land, enlarging*
*their growing city's walls, they drank at festi-
   vals by day*
*to celebrate the Genius of each man and went
   unpunished.*
*Then greater liberty was given to rhythm and
   to meter.*
*What did they know? A mixed bag of holiday-
   ing rubes*
*and city people, of aristocrats and common
   clods.*

*So to the ancient art the piper added luxury
   and dance*
*and trailed his flowing robes as he swept across
   the stage;*
*so the lyre, once such a simple thing, increased
   its notes,*
*and rhetoric without restraint produced a novel
   style*
*while profound remarks and prophecies were
   uttered*
*that in meaning were no clearer than the ora-
   cles of Delphi.*
*A competitor in tragic song who sought to win
   the goat*
*soon took away the forest satyrs' clothes
   (though crude,*
*he kept his dignity through all the fooling)
   because*
*that was the bait and pleasing freshness which
   could hold*
*a viewer with his sacrifices made, drunk and
   feeling wild.*
*But be careful how you represent your laugh-
   ing jokers,*
*the satyrs, and how you move from serious to
   funny.*
*Don't let any god that you might show, or any
   hero*
*who just appeared dressed royally in gold and
   purple,*
*sound as if he always spent his time in crummy
   bars,*
*or, if he avoids the dirt, reach out for clouds
   and air.*
*Spouting funny lines is below the place of
   tragedy.*
*She's like a fine lady at a festival who has to
   dance,*

*and nothing like the satyrs; she's bashful,
    they're loud.*
I wouldn't reject all words but the very simplest
and plainest, if, Pisos, I ever wrote a satyr play,
*or try so hard to make my style consistently
    untragic*
*that Davus wouldn't differ when he speaks
    from reckless*
*Pythias, who pulled Simo's nose and took his
    money,*
*or from Silenus, tutor and servant to a youthful
    god.*
*I'd make my poem of known materials, so that
    anyone*
*might hope to match me, but he'd work and
    sweat in vain*
*if he dared try: that's the power of order and
    arrangement,*
*that is the effect of style when working with the
    ordinary.*
*Fauns brought from the forest to the stage, in
    my opinion,*
*shouldn't turn into natives of the streets, almost
    the Forum,*
*either by behaving like young studs in love and
    crooning*
*or by firing out a fusillade of disgusting dirty
    jokes.*
*That's how you anger men with horses, fathers,
    and money,*
*and though the pea and nut gallery might
    enjoy the play,*
*the others won't sit still for it, let alone
    crown it.*
*Long syllable following short is called an
    iamb,*
*a quick foot; so the iambic line (as the iamb
    asked)*

*was called a "trimeter" although it held six
    beats*
*arranged the same from start to finish. But
    recently,*
*to reach the ear more slowly with slightly
    greater force,*
*it became a father to adopted sons, slow
    spondees,*
*and was considerate and kind, though more
    than equal,*
*for it kept the second and fourth feet. But
    Accius*
*in his famed trimeters used the iamb rarely,
    and Ennius*
*delivered to the stage lines burdened by enor-
    mous weight.*
*Either he was too hasty a worker, and too
    imprecise,*
*or he had no sense of art; his few iambs
    accuse him.*
*Not all critics recognize bad meter when they
    see it,*
*and pardons are given undeserved to Roman
    poets.*
*So, should I scrawl and ramble as I like? Or
    assume*
*that everyone will spot my errors and play it
    safe,*
*pardonable and cautious? I'd dodge attacks
    by doing that,*
*but I wouldn't merit praise. Make your models
    Greek,*
*and turn their pages nightly; turn them
    daily too.*
*I know your ancestors praised Plautus, for his
    meter*
*and his jokes; they were too charitable on
    either count*

*(I won't say stupid). Well, they liked him. But
   you and I,*
*we understand how a coarse line differs from a
   clever one,*
*and our ears or fingers tell us if the meter is
   correct.*
*The invention of the tragic genre, unknown till
   then,*
*is credited to Thespis, who used wagons for his
   stages*
*where players sang and acted, their faces
   smeared with lees.*
*After him came the creator of the tragic mask
   and robe,*
*Aeschylus, also first to raise the stage a bit on
   beams*
*and to teach actors to project and wear high
   buskins.*
*Next Old Comedy arrived and gained no small
   amount*
*of praise; but its freedom slid to vice, to vio-
   lence*
*needing law's restraint. Law was imposed, the
   chorus*
*silenced and ashamed, and it lost its right to
   wound.*
*Not a single opportunity did our poets leave
   untried,*
*nor were they least successful when they dared
   to step*
*from Greece's path and sing about Italian
   themes*
*in tragedies and comedies attired in Roman
   clothes.*
*No stronger in our courage or in our glorious
   arms*
*would Latium be than in our language, except
   that every*

*single poet hates slow going and working with
   a file.*
*Sons of Pompilius, reject any poem which
   much time*
*and much erasing haven't carefully refined,
   and which*
*they haven't smoothed ten times to meet the
   testing nail.*
*Since genius seems a pleasanter thing than
   painful art,*
*as Democritus believed (who then excluded all
   sane bards*
*from Helicon), most men who write trim nei-
   ther nails*
*nor beards; they seek out hiding places, shun
   the baths.*
*For anyone can win a poet's name and with it
   the rewards*
*if he never brings his head, too mad for Anti-
   cyra tripled,*
*to Licinus the barber. What makes me such a
   fool?*
*I purge myself of bile at the start of every
   spring.*
*No poet could outwrite me if I didn't. But
   since*
*nothing's worth that, I'll be a whetstone and
   restore*
*the edge to others' blades, do no cutting for
   myself.*
*I won't write, but I'll teach the writer's trade
   and duties:*
*where to get material, what feeds and forms a
   poet,*
*what is right, what isn't, where truth and error
   lead.*
*Good writing has its source, its origin, in good
   thinking.*

Your subject you can find revealed in Socrates'
 pages;
your words will follow the subject without
 being forced.
A poet must learn what is owed to country and
 to friends,
how a parent is loved, and a brother, and a
 guest,
what the duties are of senator and judge, what
 tasks
a general has when sent to war; with all this
 understood,
the poet is equipped to make each character
 authentic.
I'll order this learned imitator to take life, real
 manners,
for his model, and draw living voices from that
 source.
Sometimes a few good speeches that fit the
 speakers
make a graceless play without fine language
 or much style,
have stronger appeal and more interest for the
 people
than one with pointless verses and tuneful little
 frills.
Greek genius and Greek mastery of words were
 given
by the Muse to a nation greedy just for
 fame.
Roman boys have calculation drill based on
 the penny
and learn to divide it by a hundred. "Next
 question,
Albinus Jr. If from five-twelfths, you take away
 one,
what's left? Come on, you know it." "A third?"
 "Great!

You're in business! Now add a twelfth instead.
 What then?"
"One-half." But this concern with money rusts
 our souls
and once they're ruined, what poems can we
 expect to write
worth coating with protective oils and storing
 in fine wood?
Poets intend to give either pleasure or
 instruction
or to combine the pleasing and instructive in
 one poem.
Be concise in all you teach, so that attentive
 minds
can quickly see your point and remember it
 correctly;
everything poured into a full memory will flow
 back out.
Inventions made for pleasure must seem quite
 probable:
your story shouldn't ask belief for anything it
 likes,
and extract a living boy from Lamia's belly
 after lunch.
The ranks of older men sneer at poems without
 a message,
haughtily young knights reject the poems they
 find austere.
The poet winning every vote blends the useful
 with the sweet,
giving pleasure to his reader while he offers
 him advice.
His book will make the Sosii money and travel
 overseas,
and far into the years ahead extend its author's
 name.
There are some errors that we're willing to
 ignore:

a tone the ear and mind desire can falter on
  the string,
and when seeking a low note we so often get a
  shrill.
No bow aimed at a target can hit it every time.
So when most of a poem shines brilliantly, I'm
  not bothered
by its spots, the few that inattention chanced to
  spill
or human weakness didn't see. But here's my
  point:
A scribe who makes the same mistake through-
  out his copy,
though often warned, receives no pardon, and
  a singer
raises laughter at himself by always missing
  the same note.
Any poet who keeps slipping up is a Choerilus
  to me;
his few good lines are such a shock I laugh; I
  also
find I get upset whenever worthy Homer dozes
  off,
but into works that long a little sleep must steal.
Poems are like pictures: the closer you stand to
  one,
the better it holds you; another gains as you
  withdraw.
This one loves shadow, this likes being seen in
  light
and fears no critic's wit, no matter how well
  honed.
One pleases once, one always will, though seen
  ten times.
Older brother, though you've learned from your
  father
and have wisdom of your own, let me offer you
  these words

to keep in mind: in some fields "average" will
  suffice,
there's no disputing that. A legal adviser and
  attorney
of moderate skill, not a great speaker like
  Messalla
and not in Aulus Cascellius' class for
  learning,
can still be useful. But poets of moderate
  skill
neither gods nor men endure; neither do
  publishers.
At a generally good dinner, inharmonious
  table music,
heavy ointments, and bitter honey on the poppy
  seeds
are most offensive, since no dinner has to have
  them,
and a poem, something born and meant to
  please the mind,
that falls a bit below the top comes too near
  bottom.
A man who knows no sports won't touch its
  armory;
without training he lets discus, hoop, and spear
  alone
rather than be laughed at by a crowd no one
  would blame.
But a man who knows no poetry will dare to
  write. Why not?
He's free and freeborn; most importantly, he's
  rich,
rich enough to be a knight, and morally
  impeccable.
But you will do or say nothing Minerva
  wouldn't like.
Make this your judgment, this your plan. So, if
  someday

you write a poem, give it to stern Maecius'
    ears,
and your father's and mine; then for nine years
    keep it
safely withindoors. Making changes is quite
    allowable,
before you publish. Once freed, words can't
    return.
The gods sent Orpheus to savage mankind in
    the woods
to stop their murdering and refine their bar-
    barous food,
and so our legends say he tamed fierce lions
    and tigers;
the legends also say that Amphion, who
    founded Thebes,
upraised its stones with lyre music and with
    charming words
could place them where he wished. This was
    the old wisdom
which divided public from private, sacred from
    secular,
outlawed free coupling, made marriage rites
    for man and wife,
erected cities, and carved codes of law on
    wooden tablets.
Therefore fame and honor came to our inspired
    bards
and to their songs. Following them, noble
    Homer
and Tyrtaeus sent virile souls to Mars and
    battle,
rousing men with verse. Oracles were made in
    meter,
and life's road was carefully described. Lyric
    sought
respect from kings, and dramatic festivals
    arose to mark

the end of long, hard work. So, the skillful lyric
    Muse
and Apollo the singer need never make you feel
    ashamed.
Does nature make a poem worth praising or
    does art?
An old question. I don't see the purpose either
    of art
without raw talent or of genius unrefined; for
    each thing
seeks the other's help, and the two combine as
    friends.
A runner who really wants to finish first across
    the line
trained hard and suffered as a boy; he froze
    and sweated,
shunned wine and women. The contestant on
    the pipe
at Delphi first learned his art and feared his
    teacher.
It's not enough to say, "I just gush gorgeous
    poems.
Losers? they stink. It would disgrace me to be
    passed
or to admit I just don't know an art I never
    learned."
Like a crowd that swarms around a spieling
    auctioneer,
yes men seeking bargains obey the summons of
    a poet
rich in land and rich in cash he loans at
    interest.
If, moreover, he can put a fancy dinner on the
    table,
deliver deadbeats and untie friends from legal
    knots
that pinch, it would amaze me if he ever
    learned,

*the lucky stiff, to tell a real friend from a
    fake.*
*If you've given or if you plan to give a man a
    present,*
*don't bring your poetry to him, not when he's
    filled*
*with joy: of course he'll rave: "Lovely! Perfect!
    Great!"*
*He'll turn pale at the right places, even dribble
    tears*
*from sympathetic eyes; he'll jump up, stomp the
    ground.*
*Just as hired mourners at a funeral lament
    and carry on*
*with almost greater passion than those whose
    hearts are sad,*
*your phonies will seem more moved than givers
    of true praise.*
*We hear how kings will urge a man to drink
    repeated cups*
*and twist the truth with wine from anyone they
    probe,*
*eager to learn his value as a friend. If you
    write poems,*
*never be deceived by foxy souls who flatter
    subtly.*
*If you recited to Quintilius, he'd say, "Please
    change*
*this line and that." Should you say you
    couldn't do it,*
*after making two or three attempts in vain,
    he'd order you*
*to take those malformed lines and return them
    to the anvil.*
*If you preferred defending what was wrong to
    changing it,*
*not one more word or bit of useless help would
    he expend*

*to turn you from your matchless love of self
    and work.*
*A good man with good judgment is hard on
    flat, dull lines,*
*condemns those that are rough, marks each
    confusing phrase*
*with a black slash of his pen. He chops away at
    frills,*
*demands that light be shed on anything not
    clear,*
*points out ambiguities, notes what must be
    changed,*
*acts like Aristarchus, and never says, "Why
    irritate*
*my friend with little things?" Little things can
    ruin him*
*if they bring about one rude reception, one
    public sneer.*
*Like a frantic sufferer from severest mange or
    jaundice,*
*or the wild priestly dancers and those Diana's
    driven mad,*
*the crazy poet makes all fear his touch and run
    away,*
*all wise men, though reckless boys harass and
    follow him.*
*And if, while wandering, staring into space
    and burbling verses,*
*as intent on them as is a hunter on a bird, he
    tumbled down*
*inside a well or ditch, although his bellow car-
    ried far, "Help!*
*Romans, help!," no one there would want to
    pull him out.*
*If, however, someone did, and prepared to drop
    a line,*
*I would suggest, "Who knows he didn't jump
    down there,*

and would rather not be saved?" The Sicilian
    poet's fate
I'd then describe: desiring to be thought a
    deathless god,
ice-cold Empedocles took up a pose on Aetna's
    fiery brink
and dropped. Stand up for poets' rights and let
    them die.
Save a man against his will? That's just like
    killing him.
He's tried before; nor will he, if he's saved,
    now
be a man and lay aside this love he has for
    famous deaths.

It isn't clear what makes him go on writing;
    perhaps
he urinated on his father's ashes or by some
    scandal
befouled holy ground. He's surely mad and,
    like a bear
with strength enough to break the bars that
    keep him in,
the fierce reciter makes learned and unlearned
    run in fear.
Any victim that he grabs, he holds, and kills by
    reading,
for he never leaves the skin till filled with
    blood—a leech.

PART III

The Empire
(27 B.C.–A.D. 476)

LIVY (TITUS LIVIUS) (C. 59 B.C.–A.D. 17)

Early History of Rome

～ᗡ

*B*orn in Patavium (modern Padua), Livy was given a stern republican education in rhetoric and philosophy in this famous northern Italian city before his readings in Rome caught the attention of Octavian, shortly after the battle of Actium. Augustus, though he teasingly referred to him as a "Pompeian," recognized Livy's ability to provide the imperially minded Rome with a suitably moral and patriotic account of its history. In this regard, the grandeur of Livy's self-imposed assignment, to which he dedicated nearly his entire productive life, parallels that of Virgil in his *Aeneid*. He was the only major Roman professional historian, with no other occupation but that of chronicler. One of the many legends surrounding his name is that of the citizen of Cádiz, in Spain, who traveled to Rome just to catch a glimpse of the great historian.

- Livy's annalistic *History of Rome* comprises 142 books, of which only 35 survive. Beginning with the Trojan hero Aeneas' arrival in Italy in search of a new home and ending with the death of Drusus, it has been called "the greatest prose work of the Augustan Age." Livy incorporates in his mighty and vibrant canvas the work of all previous historiographers, swallowing them whole.
- Following the principles of Cicero and the Greek Thucydides and Isocrates, Livy sought not only to record but also to embody Roman history literarily, to make it resonate with didactic immediacy. His eloquent re-creation, in a pioneering Latin style Quintilian called "milky rich," of the atmosphere surrounding important events and the psychology of the men involved with them gives his account epic authority.
- His military inexperience, erratic use of sources, and lack of knowledge of Roman institutions are primary flaws in Livy's work marking it to critical contemporaries as provincial; yet his northern Italian upbringing gave him a greater affinity with early Roman virtues than a Roman living in the capital at the time would have been capable of. As a result, his history is as much exhortation as chronicle, serving well the new emperor's purposes.

Drinking fountain, Neapolis, Italica

The task of writing a history of our nation from Rome's earliest days fills me, I confess, with some misgiving, and even were I confident in the value of my work, I should hesitate to say so. I am aware that for historians to make extravagant claims is, and always has been, all too common: every writer on history tends to look down his nose at his less cultivated predecessors, happily persuaded that he will better them in point of style, or bring new facts to light. But however that may be, I shall find satisfaction in contributing—not, I hope, ignobly—to the labor of putting on record the story of the greatest nation in the world.

Countless others have written on this theme and it may be that I shall pass unnoticed amongst them; if so, I must comfort myself with the greatness and splendor of my rivals, whose work will rob my own of recognition.

My task, moreover, is an immensely laborious one. I shall have to go back more than seven hundred years, and trace my story from its small beginnings up to these recent times when its ramifications are so vast that any adequate treatment is hardly possible. I am aware, too, that most readers will take less pleasure in my account of how Rome began and in her early history; they will wish to hurry on to more modern times and to read of the period, already a long one, in which the might of an imperial people is beginning to work its own ruin. My own feeling is different; I shall find antiquity a rewarding study, if only because, while I am absorbed in it, I shall be able to turn my eyes from the troubles which for so long have tormented the modern world, and to write without any of that over-anxious consideration which may well plague a writer on contemporary life, even if it does not lead him to conceal the truth.

Events before Rome was born or thought of have come to us in old tales with more of the charm of poetry than of a sound historical record, and such traditions I propose neither to affirm nor refute. There is no reason, I feel, to object when antiquity draws no hard line between the human and the supernatural: it adds dignity to the past, and, if any nation deserves the privilege of claiming a divine ancestry, that nation is our own; and so great is the glory won by the Roman people in their wars that, when they declare that Mars himself was their first parent and father of the man who founded their city, all the nations of the world might well allow the claim as readily as they accept Rome's imperial dominion.

These, however, are comparatively trivial matters and I set little store by them. I invite the reader's attention to the much more serious consideration of the kind of lives our ancestors lived, of who were the men, and what the means both in politics and war by which Rome's power was first acquired and subsequently expanded; I would then have him trace the process of our moral decline, to watch, first, the sinking of the foundations of morality as the old teaching was allowed to lapse, then the rapidly increasing disintegration, then the final collapse of the whole edifice, and the dark dawning of our modern day when we can neither endure our vices nor face the remedies needed to cure them. The study of history is the best medicine for a sick mind; for in history you have a record of the infinite variety of human experience plainly set out for all to see; and in that record you can find for yourself and your country both examples and warnings: fine things to take as models, base things, rotten through and through, to avoid.

I hope my passion for Rome's past has not impaired my judgment; for I do honestly believe that no country has ever been greater or purer than ours or richer in good citizens and noble deeds; none has been free for so many generations from the vices of avarice and luxury; nowhere have thrift and plain living been for so long held in such esteem. Indeed, poverty, with us, went hand in hand with contentment. Of late years wealth has made us greedy, and self-indulgence has brought us, through every form of sensual excess, to be, if I

may so put it, in love with death both individual and collective.

But bitter comments of this sort are not likely to find favor, even when they have to be made. Let us have no more of them, at least at the beginning of our great story. On the contrary, I should prefer to borrow from the poets and begin with good omens and with prayers to all the host of heaven to grant a successful issue to the work which lies before me.

It is generally accepted that after the fall of Troy the Greeks kept up hostilities against all the Trojans except Aeneas and Antenor. These two men had worked consistently for peace and the restoration of Helen, and for that reason, added to certain personal connexions of long standing, they were allowed to go unmolested. Each had various adventures. Antenor joined forces with the Eneti, who had been driven out of Paphlagonia and, having lost their king, Pylaemenes, at Troy, wanted someone to lead them as well as somewhere to settle. He penetrated to the head of the Adriatic and expelled the Euganei, a tribe living between the Alps and the sea, and occupied that territory with a mixed population of Trojans and Eneti. The spot where they landed is called Troy and the neighboring country the Trojan district. The combined peoples came to be known as Venetians.

Aeneas was forced into exile by similar troubles; he, however, was destined to lay the foundations of a greater future. He went first to Macedonia, then in his search for a new home sailed to Sicily, and from Sicily to the territory of Laurentum. This part of Italy too, like the spot where Antenor landed, is known as Troy. Aeneas' men in the course of their almost interminable wanderings had lost all they possessed except their ships and their swords; once on shore, they set about scouring the countryside for what they could find, and while thus engaged they were met by a force of armed natives who, under their king Latinus, came hurrying up from the town and the surrounding country to protect themselves from the invaders. There are two versions of what happened next: according to one, there was a fight in which Latinus was beaten; he then came to terms with Aeneas and cemented the alliance by giving him his daughter in marriage. According to the other, the battle was about to begin when Latinus, before the trumpets could sound the charge, came forward with his captains and invited the foreign leader to a parley. He then asked Aeneas who his men were and where they had come from, why they had left their homes and what was their object in landing on Laurentian territory. He was told in reply that the men were Trojans, their leader Aeneas, the son of Anchises and Venus; that their native town had been burnt to the ground and now they were fugitives in search of some place where they could build a new town to settle in. Latinus, hearing their story, was so deeply impressed by the noble bearing of the strangers and by their leader's high courage either for peace or war, that he gave Aeneas his hand in pledge of friendship from that moment onward. A treaty was made; the two armies exchanged signs of mutual respect; Aeneas accepted the hospitality of Latinus, who gave him his daughter in marriage, thus further confirming the treaty of alliance by a private and domestic bond

solemnly entered into in the presence of the Gods of his hearth.

The Trojans could no longer doubt that at last their travels were over and that they had found a permanent home. They began to build a settlement, which Aeneas named Lavinium after his wife Lavinia. A child was soon born of the marriage: a boy, who was given the name Ascanius.

The Trojans and the Latins were soon jointly involved in war. Turnus, prince of the Rutuli, to whom Latinus' daughter Lavinia had been pledged before Aeneas' arrival, angered by the insult of having to step down in favor of a stranger, attacked the combined forces of Aeneas and Latinus. Both sides suffered in the subsequent struggle: the Rutuli were defeated, but the victors lost their leader Latinus. Turnus and his people, in their anxiety for the future, then looked ·for help to Mezentius, king of the rich and powerful Etruscans, whose seat of government was at Caere, at that time a wealthy town. Mezentius needed little persuasion to join the Rutuli, as from the outset he had been far from pleased by the rise of the new settlement, and now felt that the Trojan power was growing much more rapidly than was safe for its neighbors. In this dangerous situation Aeneas conferred the native name of Latins upon his own people; the sharing of a common name as well as a common polity would, he felt, strengthen the bond between the two peoples. As a result of this step the original settlers were no less loyal to their king Aeneas than were the Trojans themselves. Trojans and Latins were rapidly becoming one people, and this gave

Aeneas confidence to make an active move against the Etruscans, in spite of their great strength. Etruria, indeed, had at this time both by sea and land filled the whole length of Italy from the Alps to the Sicilian strait with the noise of her name; none the less Aeneas refused to act on the defensive and marched out to meet the enemy. The Latins were victorious, and for Aeneas the battle was the last of his labors in this world. He lies buried on the river Numicus. Was he man or god? However it be, men call him Jupiter Indiges—the local Jove.

Aeneas's son Ascanius was still too young for a position of authority; Lavinia, however, was a woman of great character, and acted as regent until Ascanius came of age and was able to assume power as the successor of his father and grandfather. There is some doubt—and no one can pretend to certainty on something so deeply buried in the mists of time—about who precisely this Ascanius was. Was it the one I have been discussing, or was it an elder brother, the son of Creusa, who was born before the sack of Troy and was with Aeneas in his escape from the burning city—the Iulus, in fact, whom the Julian family claim as their eponym? It is at any rate certain that Aeneas was his father, and—whatever the answer to the other question may be—it can be taken as a fact that he left Lavinium to found a new settlement. Lavinium was by then a populous and, for those days, a rich and flourishing town, and Ascanius left it in charge of his mother (or stepmother, if you will) and went off to found his new settlement on the Alban hills. This town, strung out as it was along a ridge, was named Alba Longa. Its foundation took place about thirty years after that of Lavinium; but the Latins had already grown so strong, especially since the defeat of the Etruscans, that neither Mezentius, the Etruscan king, nor any other neighboring people dared to attack them, even when Aeneas died and the control of things passed temporarily into the hands of a woman, and Ascanius was still a child learning the elements of kingship. By the terms of the treaty between the Latins and Etruscans the river Albula (now the Tiber) became the boundary between the two territories.

Ascanius was succeeded by his son Silvius—"born in the woods"—and he by his son Aeneas Silvius, whose heir was Latinus Silvius. By him several new settlements were made, and given the name of Old Latins. All the kings of Alba subsequently kept the cognomen Silvius. Next in succession to Latinus was Alba; then Atys, then Capys, then Capetus, then Tiberinus—who was drowned crossing the Albula and gave that river the name by which succeeding generations have always known it. Tiberinus was succeeded by Agrippa, Agrippa by his son Romulus Silvius, who was struck by lightning and bequeathed his power to Aventinus. Aventinus was buried on the hill, now a part of the city of Rome, and still bearing his name. Proca, the next king, had two sons, Numitor and Amulius, to the elder of whom, Numitor, he left the hereditary realm of the Silvian family; that, at least, was his intention, but respect for seniority was flouted, the father's will ignored and Amulius drove out his brother and seized the throne. One act of violence led to another; he proceeded to murder his brother's male children, and made his niece, Rhea Silvia, a Vestal, ostensibly to do her honor, but actually by condemning her to perpetual virginity to preclude the possibility of issue.

But (I must believe) it was already written in the book of fate that this great city of ours should arise, and the first steps be taken to the founding of the mightiest empire the world has known—next to God's. The Vestal Virgin was raped and gave birth to twin boys. Mars, she declared, was their father—perhaps she believed it, perhaps she was merely hoping by the pretence to palliate her guilt. Whatever the truth of the matter, neither gods nor men could save her or her babes from the savage hands of the king. The mother was bound and flung into prison; the boys, by the king's order, were condemned to be drowned in the river. Destiny, however, intervened; the Tiber had overflowed its banks; because of the flooded ground it was impossible to get to the actual river, and the men entrusted to do the deed thought that the flood-water, sluggish though it was, would serve their purpose. Accordingly they made shift to carry out the king's orders by leaving the infants on the edge of the first flood-water they came to, at the spot where now stands the Ruminal fig-tree—said to have once been known as the fig-tree of Romulus. In those days the country thereabouts was all wild and uncultivated, and the story goes that when the basket in which the infants had been exposed was left high and dry by the receding water, a she-wolf, coming down from the neighboring hills to quench her thirst, heard the children crying and made her way to where they were. She offered them her teats to suck and treated

them with such gentleness that Faustulus, the king's herdsman, found her licking them with her tongue. Faustulus took them to his hut and gave them to his wife Larentia to nurse. Some think that the origin of this fable was the fact that Larentia was a common whore and was called Wolf by the shepherds.

Such, then, was the birth and upbringing of the twins. By the time they were grown boys, they employed themselves actively on the farm and with the flocks and began to go hunting in the woods; their strength grew with their resolution, until not content only with the chase they took to attacking robbers and sharing their stolen goods with their friends the shepherds. Other young fellows joined them, and they and the shepherds would fleet the time together, now in serious talk, now in jollity.

Even in that remote age the Palatine hill (which got its name from the Arcadian settlement Pallanteum) is supposed to have been the scene of the gay festival of the Lupercalia. The Arcadian Evander, who many years before held that region, is said to have instituted there the old Arcadian practice of holding an annual festival in honour of Lycean Pan (afterward called Inuus by the Romans), in which young men ran about naked and disported themselves in various pranks and fooleries. The day of the festival was common knowledge, and on one occasion when it was in full swing some brigands, incensed at the loss of their ill-gotten gains, laid a trap for Romulus and Remus. Romulus successfully defended himself, but Remus was caught and handed over to Amulius. The brigands laid a complaint against their prisoner, the main charge being that he and his brother were in the habit of raiding Numitor's land with an organized gang of ruffians and stealing the cattle. Thereupon Remus was handed over for punishment to Numitor.

Now Faustulus had suspected all along that the boys he was bringing up were of royal blood. He knew that two infants had been exposed by the king's orders, and the rescue of his own two fitted perfectly in point of time. Hitherto, however, he had been unwilling to declare what he knew, until either a suitable opportunity occurred or circumstances compelled him. Now the truth could no longer be concealed, so in his alarm he told Romulus the whole story; Numitor, too, when he had Remus in custody and was told that the brothers were twins, was set thinking about his grandsons; the young men's age and character, so different from the lowly born, confirmed his suspicions; and further inquiries led him to the same conclusion, until he was on the point of acknowledging Remus. The net was closing in, and Romulus acted. He was not strong enough for open hostilities, so he instructed a number of the herdsmen to meet at the king's house by different routes at a preordained time; this was done, and with the help of Remus, at the head of another body of men, the king was surprised and killed. Before the first blows were struck, Numitor gave it out that an enemy had broken into the town and attacked the palace; he then drew off all the men of military age to garrison the inner fortress, and, as soon as he saw Romulus and Remus, their purpose accomplished, coming to congratulate him, he summoned a meeting of the people and laid the

facts before it: Amulius's crime against himself, the birth of his grandsons, and the circumstances attending it, how they were brought up and ultimately recognized, and, finally, the murder of the king for which he himself assumed responsibility. The two brothers marched through the crowd at the head of their men and saluted their grandfather as king, and by a shout of unanimous consent his royal title was confirmed.

Romulus and Remus, after the control of Alba had passed to Numitor in the way I have described, were suddenly seized by an urge to found a new settlement on the spot where they had been left to drown as infants and had been subsequently brought up. There was, in point of fact, already an excess of population at Alba, what with the Albans themselves, the Latins, and the addition of the herdsmen: enough, indeed, to justify the hope that Alba and Lavinium would one day be small places compared with the proposed new settlement. Unhappily the brothers' plans for the future were marred by the same curse which had divided their grandfather and Amulius—jealousy and ambition. A disgraceful quarrel arose from a matter in itself trivial. As the brothers were twins and all question of seniority was thereby precluded, they determined to ask the tutelary gods of the countryside to declare by augury which of them should govern the new town once it was founded, and give his name to it. For this purpose Romulus took the Palatine hill and Remus the Aventine as their respective stations from which to observe the auspices. Remus, the story goes, was the first to receive a sign—six vultures; and no sooner was this made known to the people than double the number of birds appeared to Romulus. The followers of each promptly saluted their master as king, one side basing its claim upon priority, the other upon number. Angry words ensued, followed all too soon by blows, and in the course of the affray Remus was killed. There is another story, a commoner one, according to which Remus, by way of jeering at his brother, jumped over the half-built walls of the new settlement, whereupon Romulus killed him in a fit of rage, adding the threat, "So perish whoever else shall overleap my battlements."

This, then was how Romulus obtained the sole power. The newly built city was called by its founder's name. . . .

(ALBIUS) TIBULLUS (54–19 B.C.)

Elegies

Born to an equestrian and affluent family in Latium's Pedum, Tibullus found stylish friendship and literary acceptance in Rome from fellow poets Ovid and Horace as well as from Maecenas' rival M. Valerius Messala Corvinus. He developed his craft as a follower of the Alexandrine school. Ovid writes about the death of Tibullus in his *Amores* (Book 3). Though he lost his ancestral property during the Civil War, he seems to have recovered it, perhaps with Messala's help. His surviving three books of panegyrics and elegies reflect a sensitive, conservative, and retiring nature; Tibullus' favorite subjects are romantic love and the pastoral life. He names his mistresses "Delia" and "Nemesis." Quintilian praised Tibullus' dry eloquence, and his contemporaries recognized the art beneath his apparent simplicity. His translator calls him "a dreamer of dreams, eternally weaving vague fantasies of love and of the peace and quiet of rural seclusion." His fourth book of elegies preserves the poems by Sulpicia, celebrating her love affair with Cerinthus, though some scholars think Tibullus wrote them himself.

Processional Staircase, Roman Forum, Temple to Avenging Mars

THE POET'S IDEAL
(I. 1.)

The glittering ore let others vainly heap,
O'er fertile vales extend th' enclosing mound;
With dread of neighb'ring foes forsake their
    sleep,
And start aghast at every trumpet's sound.

Me humbler scenes delight, and calmer days;
A tranquil life fair poverty secure;
Then boast, my hearth, a small but cheerful
    blaze,
And, riches grasp who will, let me be poor.

Nor yet be hope a stranger to my door,
But o'er my roof, bright goddess, still
    preside!
With many a bounteous autumn heap my
    floor,
And swell my vats with must, a purple
    tide.

My tender vines I'll plant with early care,
And choicest apples with a skillful hand;
Nor blush, a rustic, oft to guide the
    share,
Or goad the sturdy ox along the land.

Let me, a simple swain, with honest pride,
If chance a lambkin from its dam should roam,
Or sportful kid, the little wanderer chide,
And in my bosom bear exulting home.

Here Pales I bedew with milky showers,
Lustrations yearly for my shepherd pay,
Revere each antique stone bedeck'd with flowers
That bounds the field, or points the doubtful
    way.

My grateful fruits, the earliest of the year,
Before the rural god shall duly wait.
From Ceres' gifts I'll cull each browner ear,
And hang a wheaten wreath before her gate.

The ruddy god shall save my fruit from stealth,
And far away each little plunderer scare;
And you, the guardians once of ampler wealth,
My household gods, shall still my off'rings
    share.

My numerous herds that wanton'd o'er the mead
The choicest fatling then could richly yield;
Now scarce I spare a little lamb to bleed
A mighty victim for my scanty field.

And yet a lamb shall bleed, while, ranged
    around,
The village youths shall stand in order meet,
With rustic hymns, ye gods, your praise resound,
And future crops and future wines entreat.

Then come, ye powers, nor scorn my frugal
    board,
Nor yet the gifts clean earthen bowls convey;
With these the first of men the gods adored,
And form'd their simple shape of ductile clay.

My little flock, ye wolves, ye robbers, spare,
Too mean a plunder to deserve your toil;
For wealthier herds the nightly theft prepare;
There seek a nobler prey, and richer spoil.

For treasured wealth, nor stores of golden
    wheat,
The hoard of frugal sires, I vainly call;
A little farm be mine, a cottage neat,
And wonted couch where balmy sleep may
    fall.

What joy to hear the tempest howl in vain,
And clasp a fearful mistress to my breast;
Or lull'd to slumber by the beating rain,
Secure and happy sink at last to rest.

These joys be mine!—O grant me only these,
And give to others bags of shining gold,
Whose steely heart can brave the boist'rous
    seas,
The storm wide-wasting, or the stiff'ning cold.

Content with little, I would rather stay
Than spend long months amid the wat'ry
    waste;
In cooling shades elude the scorching ray,
Beside some fountain's gliding waters placed.

Oh perish rather all that's rich and rare,
The diamond quarry, and the golden vein,
Than that my absence cost one precious tear,
Or give some gentle maid a moment's pain.

With glittering spoils, Messala, gild thy dome,
Be thine the noble task to lead the brave;
A lovely foe me captive holds at home,
Chain'd to her scornful gate, a watchful slave.

Inglorious post!—and yet I heed not fame:
Th' applause of crowds for Delia I'd resign:
To live with thee I'd bear the coward's name,
Nor 'midst the scorn of nations once repine.

With thee to live I'd mock the ploughman's
 toil,
Or on some lonely mountain tend my sheep;
At night I'd lay me on the flinty soil,
And happy 'midst thy dear embraces sleep.

What drooping lover heeds the Tyrian bed,
While the long night is pass'd with many a
 sigh;
Nor softest down with richest carpets spread,
Nor whisp'ring rills can close the weeping eye.

Of threefold iron were his rugged frame,
Who, when he might thy yielding heart obtain,
Could yet attend the calls of empty fame,
Or follow arms in quest of sordid gain.

Unenvied let him drive the vanquished host,
Through captive lands his conquering armies
 lead;
Unenvied wear the robe with gold emboss'd,
And guide with solemn state his foaming steed.

Oh may I view thee with life's parting ray,
And thy dear hand with dying ardor press:
Sure thou wilt weep—and on thy lover's clay,
With breaking heart, print many a tender
 kiss!

Sure thou wilt weep—and woes unutter'd feel,
When on the pile thou seest thy lover laid!
For well I know, nor flint, nor ruthless steel
Can arm the breast of such a gentle maid.

From the sad pomp, what youth, what pitying
 fair,
Returning slow, can tender tears refrain?
O Delia, spare thy cheeks, thy tresses spare,
Nor give my ling'ring shade a world of pain.

But now while smiling hours the Fates
 bestow,
Let love, dear maid, our gentle hearts unite!
Soon death will come and strike the fatal
 blow;
Unseen his head, and veil'd in shades of
 night.

Soon creeping age will bow the lover's frame,
And tear the myrtle chaplet from his brow:
With hoary locks ill suits the youthful
 flame,
The soft persuasion, or the ardent vow.

Now the fair queen of gay desire is ours,
And lends our follies an indulgent smile:
'T is lavish youth's t' enjoy the frolic hours,
The wanton revel and the midnight broil.

Your chief, my friends and fellow-soldiers, I
To these light wars will lead you boldly on:
Far hence, ye trumpets, sound, and banners
 fly;
To those who covet wounds and fame begone.

And bear them fame and wounds; and riches
 bear;
There are that fame and wounds and riches
 prize.
For me, while I possess one plenteous year,
I'll wealth and meagre want alike despise.

                              [TR. JAMES GRAINGER]

SENECA THE ELDER (LUCIUS ANNAEUS SENECA) (55 B.C.–A.D. 40)

Suasoriae

∽

*O*rator, historian, and teacher of rhetoric, Seneca the Elder was born of a stern equestrian family in Córdoba, Spain, and, like Quintilian, came to Rome as a young man to seek his education and find his fortune. He succeeded admirably in both. He was the father, by his wife Helvia, of Seneca the Younger, and grandfather of the poet Lucan.

- He wrote a history of Rome from the civil wars to the death of Tiberius; none of it has survived. Seneca's lifelong career in oratory forms the basis of ten books on legal cases and rhetoric, known as the *Controversiae,* and the two books called *Suasoriae,* mock debates with historical characters, such as "Alexander debates whether to sail the Ocean."
- Seneca's style reflects his admiration for the discipline of Cicero. His writings are invaluable for the historical perspective and critical judgment they provide on the Silver Age of Latin literature and its authors, and for their insight into the state of rhetoric under Augustus and Tiberius.

1

ALEXANDER DEBATES WHETHER TO SAIL THE OCEAN

. . . allow: to whatever thing nature has granted size she has granted a limit as well; nothing is infinite except the Ocean.—They say that in the Ocean there lie fertile lands, while beyond it in turn are born new shores, a new world: that nature stops nowhere—always it appears in a fresh guise just at the point where one thinks it had come to a halt. These are fictions easy of invention—for the Ocean cannot be sailed.—Let Alexander be content to have conquered as far as the world is content to have light. It was within the limits of the known world that Hercules won his claim to heaven. —There, motionless, stands the sea, an inert mass of nature failing, as it were, at its own limits: strange and frightening shapes, monsters great even for the Ocean, nurtured by that desolate depth, light plunged in the deepest gloom, day cut off by darkness, the sea itself heavy and stationary, stars either vanished or unfamiliar. Such, Alexander, is nature: beyond all, the Ocean; beyond the Ocean, nothing.

ARGENTARIUS. Stop: the world that is yours calls you back. We have conquered wherever light shines.—There is nothing worth my seeking if the cost is peril to Alexander.

POMPEIUS SILO. Alexander, the longed-for day has come—the day on which nothing should remain for you to do. Your empire and the world have the same limits.

MOSCHUS. It is time for Alexander to come to a halt where world and sun halt.—"What I knew, I conquered. Now I desire what I do not know."—What tribes so barbarous that they have not worshipped Alexander on bended knee? What mountains so rude that their ridges have not been trodden by his victorious soldiery? We have halted beyond the trophies set up by Father Liber.—We are not in search of a world—we are losing one.—Here is a measureless sea, untried by human adventure, that encircles the whole world and guards the earth, a waste undisturbed by oars, shores now disquieted as the waves rage, now deserted as they retreat. A horrid darkness weighs on the breakers; strangely, what nature has removed from men's sight is shrouded by everlasting night.

MUSA. Loathsome the vast monsters, unmoving the deep. Evidence is before you, Alexander, that nothing lies beyond for you to conquer. Go back.

ALBUCIUS SILUS. Even the earth has its end; the very universe has its setting. Nothing is infinite. *You* must give greatness its limits, seeing that Fortune does not.—It is the sign of a great spirit to be moderate in prosperity.—Fortune makes the limit of your victories the same as the limit of nature: your empire is closed by the Ocean.—How far has your greatness surpassed even nature! Alexander is great for the earth: for Alexander the earth is cramped.—Even greatness has some end; the heavens do not proceed beyond their fixed limits, the seas toss within their bounds.—Whatever has reached its peak leaves no room for increase.—We know nothing beyond Alexander, just as we know nothing beyond Ocean.

MARULLUS. We are in pursuit of the seas: to whom are we entrusting the land?—"I am looking for a world I do not know, I am leaving the world I have conquered."

FABIANUS. Can you imagine that this darkness cast over all the sea admits navigation when it excludes even the view ahead?—This is not India, nor that fearful assembly of beasts. Imagine the savage monsters. Look how the sea rages with squalls and waves, look at the breakers it drives shoreward: such is the conflict of the winds, such the raving of a sea churned up from its depths. Sailors have here no ready haven, nothing to save them, nothing they know. All that is primitive and incomplete in nature has retreated to this far refuge. These seas were not the goal even of those who fled from Alexander. It was as something holy that the Ocean was poured round the world by nature. Those who have by now calculated the movements of the stars, and reduced to fixed laws the yearly changes of winter and summer, men to whom no part of the universe is a mystery, are still in doubt as to the Ocean. Does it shut off the earth like a band, or does it go round in a circle of its own, seething into those gulfs that are navigable as into breathing holes serving its great size? Beyond it is there fire, which it itself goes to increase, or air? What are you about, fellow-soldiers? Are you letting the conqueror of the human race, great Alexander, enter something whose very nature is still in dispute?—Remember, Alexander: you are leaving your mother in a world that is still subdued rather than pacified.

Division

Cestius used to say that this type of *suasoria* should be declaimed differently in different places. "One's opinion should be stated in one way in a free country, in another before kings, who need to be given even salutary advice in such a way as to give them pleasure. And even among kings distinctions are to be made. Some can tolerate the truth better than others. Alexander is to be classed among those who are by tradition particularly proud, puffed up beyond mortal standards. Finally, leaving aside other proofs, the terms of the *suasoria* in themselves demonstrate his arrogance; the world that is his is not enough for him."

Cestius accordingly used to say that nothing should be said that did not show the highest respect toward the king, in case the speaker should meet with the same fate as Alexander's tutor, a cousin of Aristotle, whom the king killed because of a witticism that was both outspoken and untimely. Alexander wanted to be regarded as god; once he was wounded, and, seeing his blood, the tutor said he was surprised that it was not the "ichor, such as flows in the veins of the blessed gods." Alexander used the spear to get revenge for this joke.

The point is neatly made in a letter of Cassius to Cicero: after a good deal of pleasantry about the stupidity of the young Pompey, who recruited an army in Spain and was defeated at the battle of Munda, he says: "Here we are deriding him—but I'm afraid he may have his sneer back—with his sword." In dealings with every king, one has to be shy of this sort of wit.

Cestius, then, used to say that in Alexander's presence one's opinion must be given in such a way that his feelings were soothed by lavish flattery, though some moderation must be preserved so as to give an impression not of flattery but of due respect, to avoid the fate of the Athenians on one occasion, when their publicly expressed blandishments were not only detected but punished. For Antony once wanted to be known as Father Liber, ordering this name to be inscribed on the base of statues to him and aping Liber in his dress and attendants. Athenians came to him on his arrival with their wives and children, and saluted him as Dionysus. It would have been better for them if their Attic wit had stopped there. But they went on to say that they were offering him their Minerva in marriage, and asked him to marry her. Antony said that he would do so, but that as dowry he ordered them to contribute a thousand talents. Then one of the Greeklings said: "Lord, Zeus took your mother Semele without a dowry." *He* got away with that; but the Athenians' betrothal cost them a thousand talents. When the sum was demanded, several abusive lampoons were put about, and some even reached the eyes of Antony himself: for example the one written on the base of a statue of his because he had both Octavia and Cleopatra to wife: "Octavia and Athena to

Antony: take your property." The best thing was said by Dellius. He was called by Messala Corvinus the "vaulter" of the civil wars, because he deserted from Dolabella to Cassius on the promise of immunity if he killed Dolabella, then crossed from Cassius to Antony, and finally went over from Antony to Caesar. This is the Dellius whose obscene letters to Cleopatra are in circulation. Now when the Athenians were asking time to get the money together, and not being given it, Dellius said: "Still, you can say they owe you this day next year, two years hence, three years hence."

However, I have got too far from the point in my delight in stories. I must return to my theme.

Cestius used to say that this advice to Alexander should be accompanied by the highest praises of him. His division went like this. First, even if the Ocean could be sailed, it should not be—Alexander had won enough glory; he should rule and put in order what he had conquered *en passant,* have some consideration for soldiers tired out by so many victories, and take thought for his mother: and he added several other reasons. Then he went on to argue that the Ocean could *not* be sailed.

Fabianus the philosopher put the same point first: Even if the Ocean could be sailed, it should not be. But his first reason was different: a limit must be set to prosperity. Here he spoke this epigram: "The only great felicity is that which stops of its own will." He then spoke the commonplace on the variability of Fortune. He described how nothing is stable, everything fluid, now raised, now depressed in unpredictable change, lands being swallowed, seas drained, mountains subsiding. He gave exam-

ples of kings who have been tumbled from the height of their power. Then he added: "Allow nature rather than your fortune to run out."

His treatment of the second point was also different. His arrangement was first to say that there are no habitable lands in the Ocean or beyond it, then that, even if there were, they could not be reached. Here he spoke of the difficulty of navigation, the unknown sea that was such as to permit of no sailing. Finally, even if it were possible to reach them, it was not worth the trouble. Here he said that uncertainty lay ahead, certainty was being left behind. The world would rise in revolt if it became known that Alexander had crossed nature's limits. He brought in Alexander's mother, saying of her: "How she trembled even when Alexander was going to cross the Granicus!"

Glycon's epigram is familiar: "This is not Simois or Granicus. If this were not an evil thing, it would not lie at the end of the world." Everyone wanted to imitate this. Plution said: "It is greatest just because *it* is beyond all— and beyond *it* is nothing." Artemon said: "We are discussing whether we should sail across. We are not standing on the shores of the Hellespont, or the Pamphylian sea, awaiting the ebb within its own time. This is not Euphrates or Indus, but the end of the world, the boundary of nature, the oldest element or the origin of the gods: in any case, it is water too holy for ships."

Apaturius said: "This way the ship will go in one course to the dawn: that way to the unseen setting-place of the sun."

Cestius' description went like this: "The Ocean roars, as though angry that you are leaving the land behind."

It was generally agreed that the most decadent thing said since the eloquent began to go mad was a remark of Dorion paraphrasing Homer, where the blinded Cyclops flings a rock into the sea. Maecenas used to say that you could tell from Virgil how this, instead of being decadent, could be made grand and yet sane at the same time. It is bombastic to say: "Mountain is torn from mountain." So what does Virgil say? His character seizes "no small part of a mountain." He keeps size in mind without ill-advised departure from the truth. It is inflated to say: "and an island is picked up and flung." What does Virgil say of ships? "You might suppose there floated the Cyclades uptorn." He doesn't say it does happen—but that it seems to happen. However incredible it may be, anything excused before it is uttered is received with favor.

I have come across in this same *suasoria* a much more decadent epigram by one Menestratus, a declaimer of some repute in his day, when he was describing the huge size of the monsters bred in the Ocean . . . The result of the epigram is that I am ready to forgive Musa for something more monstrous even than Scylla and Charybdis: "Charybdis, wrecker of the sea itself." And, so as to avoid an isolated folly on the same topic, he said: "What can be safe where even the sea perishes?"

Damas, exploiting character, brought in words of Alexander's mother when describing how new dangers had piled themselves constantly on old: . . .

Barbarus, after introducing the Macedonian soldiers making excuses, expressed this idea: . . .

Arellius Fuscus said: "I swear that your world is deserting you sooner than your soldiers."

Latro spoke this epigram while sitting down; he did not excuse the soldiers, but said: "Lead, I am following. Who offers me enemy, land, day, light, sea? Give me somewhere to pitch camp and fight a battle."—"I have parents and children back home. I want some furlough: is it too soon, when I am on the shores of the Ocean?"

Latin declaimers were not particularly vigorous in their description of the Ocean. They either described too little, or too fussily. None of them could match the verve of Pedo on Germanicus at sea:

"And now they see day and sun long left
behind;
Banished from the familiar limits of the world
They dare to pass through forbidden shades
To the bounds of things, the remotest shores of
the world.
Now they think Ocean, that breeds beneath its
sluggish waves
Terrible monsters, savage sea-beasts everywhere,
And dogs of the sea, is rising, taking the ships
with it
(The very noise increases their fears): now they
think the vessels
Are sinking in the mud, the fleet deserted by
the swift wind,
Themselves left by indolent fate to the sea-
beasts,
To be torn apart unhappily.
Someone high on the prow struggles to break
Through the blinding mist, his sight battling.

He can discern nothing—the world has been
  snatched away.
He pours his frustrated heart into words:
'Where are we being carried? Day itself is in
  flight,
Furthest nature shuts off in everlasting shadows
The world we have left. Are we looking for races
Beyond, in another clime, a new world
  untouched by breezes?
The Gods call us back, forbid us to know the
  end of creation
With mortal eyes. Why do our oars violate seas
  that are not ours,
Waters that are holy? Why do we disturb the
  quiet home of the Gods?' "

No Greek declaimer had better success in this *suasoria* than Glyco. But the decadent passages were as frequent as the sublime. I shall let you sample both. My intention was to try you out by not adding my own views, and not separating the sound from the corrupt. It might have been that you praised the mad more. But that *may* happen even if I make a distinction. This was nicely said: . . . But as usual he spoiled his epigram with a superfluous and bombastic appendage. For he added: . . . Some people find it difficult to assess the following, though *I* don't hesitate to cast my vote against: "Farewell, land; farewell, sun. The Macedonians are darting off into Chaos."

(GAIUS JULIUS CAESAR OCTAVIANUS) AUGUSTUS (63 B.C.–A.D. 14)

Acts

～⌇

*T*he founder of the Roman Empire, son of the senator and praetor Gaius Octavius and Julius Caesar's niece Atia (daughter of Julia), Gaius Octavian was adopted by his great uncle when it became apparent that Caesar would have no heir from his body. He made his first public appearance at the age of twelve, delivering a funeral oration for his grandmother Julia. Despite his frail constitution, he served with Caesar in Spain in 45 B.C., then was sent to Apollonia, in Epirus (modern Albania), with his best friends Marcus Agrippa and Marcus Rufus to continue his study of Greek language and philosophy, and military strategy.

Upon his return to Rome after the assassination of his uncle, he was recognized at the age of eighteen as Caesar's adopted son and heir. He was first married to a relative of the pirate Sextus Pompeius (Pompey the Great's son), Scribonia (mother of Julia), whom he divorced in 39 B.C.; later to Livia Drusilla, from 38 until his death in A.D. 14.

Cautious at first, Octavian was encouraged by Cicero to move against Marc Antony, who was unwilling to relinquish his control of Caesar's estate. The young man sponsored Victory Games in honor of Caesar and, when popular response was overwhelming, was invited to join the Senate. After he defeated Marc Antony's legions at Mutina (modern Modena), in 43 B.C., and was accorded consular rank by a reluctant Senate, he changed his name to Gaius Julius Caesar Octavianus.

Seeking a truce among the warring parties, Octavian then formed a Second Triumvirate with Antony and Marcus Lepidus in 43 B.C., reserving for himself rule of Africa, Sicily, and Sardinia. After executing an enemies' list that included three hundred senators, one of them Cicero, and two thousand *equites,* in 42 B.C. the new alliance defeated the Liberators at Philippi, thereby avenging Caesar's death. As Caesar had been declared a god that same year, Octavian was now *filius divi* ("son of a god").

The treaty of Tarentum, in 37 B.C., renewed the Triumvirate and assigned the West to Octavian, the East to Antony, and Africa to Lepidus. Octavian married his sister Octavia to Antony, who was already dallying with Cleopatra. When Lepidus revolted against his partners, Octavian stripped him of his army and relegated him to the honorary role of Pontifex Maximus. Rome's Sicilian frontier now secured against Pompeius in 38–36, Octavian declared himself *Imperator.* He made his friend Agrippa aedile, and ordered him to begin a beautification program for the capital city. Now the Roman populace shared his outrage at Antony's divorce of his sister Octavia.

The Senate declared war against Cleopatra. When Octavian and Agrippa defeated her and Antony at Actium in 31 B.C., Octavian became the unrivaled head of the Roman world. When he returned to conquer Egypt in 30, Antony and Cleopatra killed themselves rather than face him. Seizing her treasury and executing Caesarion (Cleopatra's son, allegedly by Julius Caesar), Augustus declared Egypt a Roman province.

Augustus' popularity among artists and intellectuals was profound, leading to the richest expression of the Roman imagination by luminaries like Virgil and Horace, Propertius, Ovid, and Livy. Although he officially restored the Republic and its traditions and institutions in 27 B.C., he held nearly absolute power until his death at Nola. His rule was focused on peace and reform, secure trade and easy communication. As he set about with his ruthless drive and unflagging energy to transform a decadent Republic into a vigorous empire with centuries ahead of it, his achievements included:

- Defining, expanding, and preserving the frontiers, and imposing a system of provincial taxation.
- Conducting a census that led to his reorganizing the unruly Senate and reducing its numbers first to eight hundred, then to six hundred. Octavian became the "principal senator."

- Reviving the old Roman religion, including building the great temple to Jupiter on the Capitoline Hill, and temples to Mars the Avenger and to Apollo on the Palatine Hill, and restoring the college of the Vestal Virgins.
- Buttressing old Roman family values by creating laws dealing with excessive luxury, adultery, marriage, and remarriage of the widowed.
- Construction of the magnificent Forum of Augustus, with the help of Marcus Agrippa and Marcius Phillipus.
- Construction of a massive road program throughout the Empire, and a commercial and military fleet to patrol the Mediterranean.
- Dividing the city of Rome into fourteen wards, organized around the traditional *lares.*
- Organizing the Praetorian Guards, an imperial bodyguard stationed in Rome and other Italian cities.
- Creating "civil service" roles for the equestrians and freedmen in the routines of government.

If Octavian was unlucky in anything other than his health it was in his constant search for a successor. His nephew Marcellus, married to his daughter Julia, died in 23 B.C. Julia then married Agrippa, and bore him three sons: Gaius, Lucius, and Agrippa Posthumus. Agrippa and his sons were adopted by Octavian in 17 B.C. to give them imperial legitimacy. Since Agrippa, because of his origins, wasn't eligible for the throne, and his sons were not of age, Octavian appointed Tiberius, son of his wife Livia by her former husband, Tiberius Claudius Nero, as imperial assistant. By 3 A.D., Gaius and Lucius had died, and Agrippa Posthumus and Octavian's daughter Julia had been exiled. Only Tiberius remained available. In 13 A.D. Augustus invested him with imperial powers and filed his will in the temple of the Vestal Virgins. Augustus died in 14. Tiberius, called back from his mission to Illyricum, became the second Roman emperor.

After his death, Augustus was deified and enshrined, with his uncle, among the Roman gods. He said: "I left Rome a city of marble, though I found it a city of bricks."

- Though they haven't survived, we know that Augustus wrote a poem, *Sicily,* in hexameters; a life of Drusus; an autobiography in thirteen books (the *Commentaries,* dedicated to Maecenas and Agrippa); and a tragedy, *Ajax,* which he himself ordered destroyed.
- The only extant writing by Augustus, filed with his will and later inscribed on stone tablets by order of Tiberius, is the *Record of His Enterprises,* usually referred to as the *Acts (Res Gestae* or *Monumentum Ancyranum).* Written in simple and straightforward yet commanding style, this is Augustus' own account of his long service to the Roman state, intended to be displayed in the Campus Martius. The remarkable document covers the honors he amassed, the personal monies he spent on public works and monuments, a report of his military triumphs, and a statement of his position as *pater patriae,* "father of his country," and restorer of the Republic.

1. At the age of nineteen, on my own initiative and at my own expense, I raised an army by means of which I restored liberty to the Republic, which had been oppressed by the tyranny of a faction. For which service the Senate, with complimentary resolutions, enrolled me in its order, in the consulship of Gaius Pansa and Aulus Hirtius, giving me at the same time consular precedence in voting; it also gave me the *imperium*. As propraetor it ordered me, along with the consuls, "to see that the Republic suffered no harm." In the same year, moreover, as both consuls had fallen in war, the people elected me consul and a triumvir for settling the constitution.

2. Those who slew my father I drove into exile, punishing their deed by due process of law, and afterward when they waged war upon the Republic I twice defeated them in battle.

3. Wars, both civil and foreign, I undertook throughout the world, on sea and land, and when victorious I spared all citizens who sued for pardon. The foreign nations which could with safety be pardoned I preferred to save rather than to destroy. The number of Roman citizens who bound themselves to me by military oath was about 500,000. Of these I settled in colonies or sent back into their own towns, after their term of service, something more than 300,000, and to all I assigned lands, or gave money as a reward for military service. I captured six hundred ships, over and above those which were smaller than triremes.

4. Twice I triumphed with an ovation, thrice I celebrated curule triumphs, and was saluted as imperator twenty-one times. Although the Senate decreed me additional triumphs I set them aside. When I had performed the vows which I had undertaken in each war I deposited upon the Capitol the laurels which adorned my fasces. For successful operations on land and sea, conducted either by myself or by my lieutenants under my auspices, the Senate on fifty-five occasions decreed that thanks should be rendered to the immortal gods. The days on which such thanks were rendered by decree of the Senate numbered 890. In my triumphs there were led before my chariot nine kings or children of kings. At the time of writing these words I had been thirteen times consul, and was in the thirty-seventh year of my tribunician power.

5. The dictatorship offered me by the people and the Roman Senate, in my absence and later when present, in the consulship of Marcus Marcellus and Lucius Arruntius I did not accept. I did not decline at a time of the greatest scarcity of grain the charge of the grain-supply, which I so administered that, within a few days, I freed the entire people, at my own expense, from the fear and danger in which they were. The consulship, either yearly or for life, then offered me I did not accept.

6. In the consulship of Marcus Vinucius and Quintus Lucretius, and afterward in that of Publius and Gnaeus Lentulus, and a third time in that of Paullus Fabius Maximus and Quintus Tubero, when the Senate and the Roman people unanimously agreed [that I should be elected overseer of laws and morals, without a colleague and with the fullest power, I refused to accept any power offered me which was contrary to the traditions of our ancestors. Those things which at that time the Senate wished me to administer I carried out by virtue of my tribunician power. And even in this office I five

The statue of Augustus Caesar at Prima Porta

times received from the Senate a colleague at my own request.

7. For ten years in succession I was one of the triumvirs for the re-establishment of the constitution]. To the day of writing this I have been *princeps senatus* for forty years. I have been Pontifex Maximus, augur, a member of the fifteen commissioners for performing sacred rites, one of the seven for sacred feasts, an arval brother, a *sodalis Titius*, a fetial priest.

8. As consul for the fifth time, by order of the people and the Senate I increased the number of the patricians. Three times I revised the roll of the Senate. In my sixth consulship, with Marcus Agrippa as my colleague, I made a census of the people. I performed the *lustrum* after an interval of forty-one years. In this lustration 4,063,000 Roman citizens were entered on the census roll. A second time, in the consulship of Gaius Censorinus and Gaius Asinius, I again performed the *lustrum* alone, with the consular imperium. In this *lustrum* 4,233,000 Roman citizens were entered on the census roll. A third time, with the consular imperium, and with my son Tiberius Caesar as my colleague, I performed the *lustrum* in the consulship of Sextus Pompeius and Sextus Apulcius. In this *lustrum* 4,937,000 Roman citizens were entered on the census roll. By the passage of new laws I restored many traditions of our ancestors which were then falling into disuse, and I myself set precedents in many things for posterity to imitate.

9. The Senate decreed that every fifth year vows should be undertaken for my health by the consuls and the priests. In fulfilment of these vows games were often held in my lifetime, sometimes by the four chief colleges of priests, sometimes by the consuls. In addition the entire body of citizens with one accord, both individually and by municipalities, performed continued sacrifices for my health at all the couches of the gods.

10. By decree of the Senate my name was included in the Salian hymn, and it was enacted by law that my person should be sacred in perpetuity and that so long as I lived I should hold the tribunician power. I declined to be made Pontifex Maximus in succession to a colleague still living, when the people tendered me that priesthood which my father had held. Several years later I accepted that sacred office when he at last was dead who, taking advantage of a time of civil disturbance, had seized it for himself, such a multitude from all

Italy assembling for my election, in the consulship of Publius Sulpicius and Gaius Valgius, as is never recorded to have been in Rome before.

11. The Senate consecrated in honor of my return an altar to Fortuna Redux at the Porta Capena, near the temple of Honor and Virtue, on which it ordered the pontiffs and the Vestal Virgins to perform a yearly sacrifice on the anniversary of the day on which I returned to the city from Syria, in the consulship of Lucius Lucretius and Marcus Vinucius, and named the day, after my cognomen, the Augustalia.

12. At the same time, by decree of the Senate, part of the praetors and of the tribunes of the people, together with the consul Quintus Lucretius and the leading men of the state, were sent to Campania to meet me, an honor which up to the present time has been decreed to no one except myself. When I returned from Spain and Gaul, in the consulship of Tiberius Nero and Publius Quintilius, after successful operations in those provinces, the Senate voted in honor of my return the consecration of an altar to Pax Augusta in the Campus Martius, and on this altar it ordered the magistrates and priests and Vestal Virgins to make annual sacrifice.

13. Janus Quirinus, which our ancestors ordered to be closed whenever there was peace, secured by victory, throughout the whole domain of the Roman people on land and sea, and which, before my birth is recorded to have been closed but twice in all since the foundation of the city, the Senate ordered to be closed thrice while I was princeps.

14. My sons Gaius and Lucius Caesar, whom fortune snatched away from me in their youth, the Senate and the Roman people to do me honor made consuls designate, each in his fifteenth year, providing that each should enter upon that office after a period of five years. The Senate decreed that from the day on which they were introduced to the forum they should take part in the counsels of state. Moreover, the entire body of Roman knights gave each of them the title of *princeps iuventutis* and presented them with silver shields and spears.

15. To the Roman plebs I paid out three hundred sesterces per man in accordance with the will of my father, and in my own name in my fifth consulship I gave four hundred sesterces apiece from the spoils of war; a second time, moreover, in my tenth consulship I paid out of my own patrimony four hundred sesterces per man by way of bounty, and in my eleventh consulship I made twelve distributions of food from grain bought at my own expense, and in the twelfth year of my tribunician power I gave for the third time four hundred sesterces to each man. These largesses of mine reached a number of persons never less than two hundred and fifty thousand. In the eighteenth year of my tribunician power, as consul for the twelfth time, I gave to three hundred and twenty thousand of the city plebs sixty denarii apiece. In the colonies of my soldiers, as consul for the fifth time, I gave one thousand sesterces to each man from the spoils of war; about one hundred and twenty thousand men in the colonies received this triumphal largesse. When consul for the thirteenth time I gave sixty denarii apiece to the plebs who were then receiving public grain; these were a little more than two hundred thousand persons.

16. To the municipal towns I paid money for the lands which I assigned to soldiers in my own

fourth consulship and afterward in the consulship of Marcus Crassus and Gnaeus Lentulus the augur. The sum which I paid for estates in Italy was about six hundred million sesterces, and the amount which I paid for lands in the provinces was about two hundred and sixty million. I was the first and only one to do this of all those who up to my time settled colonies of soldiers in Italy or in the provinces. And later, in the consulship of Tiberius Nero and Gnaeus Piso, likewise in the consulship of Gaius Antistius and Decimus Laelius, and of Gaius Calvisius and Lucius Pasienus, and of Lucius Lentulus and Marcus Messalla, and of Lucius Caninius and Quintus Fabricius, I paid cash gratuities to the soldiers whom I settled in their own towns at the expiration of their service, and for this purpose I expended four hundred million sesterces as an act of grace.

17. Four times I aided the public treasury with my own money, paying out in this manner to those in charge of the treasury one hundred and fifty million sesterces. And in the consulship of Marcus Lepidus and Lucius Arruntius I contributed one hundred and seventy million sesterces out of my own patrimony to the military treasury, which was established on my advice that from it gratuities might be paid to soldiers who had seen twenty or more years of service.

18. Beginning with the year in which Gnaeus and Publius Lentulus were consuls, whenever taxes were in arrears, I furnished from my own purse and my own patrimony tickets for grain and money, sometimes to a hundred thousand persons, sometimes to many more.

19. I built the curia and the Chalcidicum adjoining it, the temple of Apollo on the Palatine with its porticoes, the temple of the deified Julius, the Lupercal, the portico at the Circus Flaminius which I allowed to be called Octavia after the name of him who had constructed an earlier one on the same site, the state box at the Circus Maximus, the temples on the capitol of Jupiter Feretrius and Jupiter Tonans, the temple of Quirinus, the temples of Minerva, of Juno the Queen, and of Jupiter Libertas, on the Aventine, the temple of the Lares at the highest point of the Sacra Via, the temple of the Di Penates on the Velia, the temple of Youth, and the temple of the Great Mother on the Palatine.

20. The Capitolium and the theater of Pompey, both works involving great expense, I rebuilt without any inscription of my own name. I restored the channels of the aqueducts which in several places were falling into disrepair through age, and doubled the capacity of the aqueduct called the Marcia by turning a new spring into its channel. I completed the Julian Forum and the basilica which was between the temple of Castor and the temple of Saturn, works begun and far advanced by my father, and when the same basilica was destroyed by fire I began its reconstruction on an enlarged site, to be inscribed with the names of my sons, and ordered that in case I should not live to complete it, it should be completed by my heirs. In my sixth consulship, in accordance with a decree of the Senate, I rebuilt in the city eighty-two temples of the gods, omitting none which at that time stood in need of repair. As consul for the seventh time I constructed the Via Flaminia from the city to Ariminum, and all the bridges except the Mulvian and the Minucian.

21. On my own ground I built the temple of Mars Ultor and the Augustan Forum from the

spoils of war. On ground purchased for the most part from private owners I built the theater near the temple of Apollo which was to bear the name of my son-in-law Marcus Marcellus. From the spoils of war I consecrated offerings on the Capitol, and in the temple of the divine Julius, and in the temple of Apollo, and in the temple of Vesta, and in the temple of Mars Ultor, which cost me about one hundred million sesterces. In my fifth consulship I remitted thirty-five thousand pounds weight of coronary gold contributed by the municipia and the colonies of Italy, and thereafter, whenever I was saluted as imperator, I did not accept the coronary gold, although the municipia and colonies voted it in the same kindly spirit as before.

22. Three times in my own name I gave a show of gladiators, and five times in the name of my sons or grandsons; in these shows there fought about ten thousand men. Twice in my own name I furnished for the people an exhibition of athletes gathered from all parts of the world, and a third time in the name of my grandson. Four times I gave games in my own name; as representing other magistrates twenty-three times. For the college of quindecemvirs, as master of that college and with Marcus Agrippa as my colleague, I conducted the Secular Games in the consulship of Gaius Furnius and Marcus Silanus. In my thirteenth consulship I gave, for the first time, the games of Mars, which, since that time, the consuls by decree of the Senate have given in successive years in conjunction with me. In my own name, or that of my sons or grandsons, on twenty-six occasions I gave to the people, in the circus, in the forum, or in the amphitheatre, hunts of African wild beasts, in which about three thousand five hundred beasts were slain.

23. I gave the people the spectacle of a naval battle beyond the Tiber, at the place where now stands the grove of the Caesars, the ground having been excavated for a length of eighteen hundred and a breadth of twelve hundred feet. In this spectacle thirty beaked ships, triremes or biremes, and a large number of smaller vessels met in conflict. In these fleets there fought about three thousand men exclusive of the rowers.

24. After my victory I replaced in the temples in all the cities of the province of Asia the ornaments which my antagonist in the war, when he despoiled the temples, had appropriated to his private use. Silver statues of me, on foot, on horseback, and in chariots were erected in the city to the number of about eighty; these I myself removed, and from the money thus obtained I placed in the temple of Apollo golden offerings in my own name and in the name of those who had paid me the honor of a statue.

25. I freed the sea from pirates. About thirty thousand slaves, captured in that war, who had run away from their masters and had taken up arms against the Republic, I delivered to their masters for punishment. The whole of Italy voluntarily took oath of allegiance to me and demanded me as its leader in the war in which I was victorious at Actium. The provinces of the Spains, the Gauls, Africa, Sicily, and Sardinia took the same oath of allegiance. Those who served under my standards at that time included more than 700 senators, and among them eighty-three who had previously or have

since been consuls up to the day on which these words were written, and about 170 have been priests.

26. I extended the boundaries of all the provinces which were bordered by races not yet subject to our Empire. The provinces of the Gauls, the Spains, and Germany, bounded by the ocean from Gades to the mouth of the Elbe, I reduced to a state of peace. The Alps, from the region which lies nearest to the Adriatic as far as the Tuscan Sea, I brought to a state of peace without waging on any tribe an unjust war. My fleet sailed from the mouth of the Rhine eastward as far as the lands of the Cimbri to which, up to that time, no Roman had ever penetrated either by land or by sea, and the Cimbri and Charydes and Semnones and other peoples of the Germans of that same region through their envoys sought my friendship and that of the Roman people. On my order and under my auspices two armies were led, at almost the same time, into Ethiopia and into Arabia which is called the "Happy," and very large forces of the enemy of both races were cut to pieces in battle and many towns were captured. Ethiopia was penetrated as far as the town of Nabata, which is next to Meroë. In Arabia the army advanced into the territories of the Sabaei to the town of Mariba.

27. Egypt I added to the Empire of the Roman people. In the case of Greater Armenia, though I might have made it a province after the assassination of its King Artaxes, I preferred, following the precedent of our fathers, to hand that kingdom over to Tigranes, the son of King Artavasdes, and grandson of King Tigranes, through Tiberius Nero who was then

my stepson. And later, when the same people revolted and rebelled, and was subdued by my son Gaius, I gave it over to King Ariobarzanes the son of Artabazus, King of the Medes, to rule, and after his death to his son Artavasdes. When he was murdered I sent into that kingdom Tigranes, who was sprung from the royal family of the Armenians. I recovered all the provinces extending eastward beyond the Adriatic Sea, and Cyrenae, which were then for the most part in possession of kings, and, at an earlier time, Sicily and Sardinia, which had been seized in the servile war.

28. I settled colonies of soldiers in Africa, Sicily, Macedonia, both Spains, Achaia, Asia, Syria, Gallia Narbonensis, Pisidia. Moreover, Italy has twenty-eight colonies founded under my auspices which have grown to be famous and populous during my lifetime.

29. From Spain, Gaul, and the Dalmatians, I recovered, after conquering the enemy, many military standards which had been lost by other generals. The Parthians I compelled to restore to me the spoils and standards of three Roman armies, and to seek as suppliants the friendship of the Roman people. These standards I deposited in the inner shrine which is in the Temple of Mars Ultor.

30. The tribes of the Pannonians, to which no army of the Roman people had ever penetrated before my principate, having been subdued by Tiberius Nero who was then my stepson and my legate, I brought under the sovereignty of the Roman people, and I pushed forward the frontier of Illyricum as far as the bank of the river Danube. An army of Dacians which crossed to the south of that river was, under my

auspices, defeated and crushed, and afterward my own army was led across the Danube and compelled the tribes of the Dacians to submit to the orders of the Roman people.

31. Embassies were often sent to me from the kings of India, a thing never seen before in the camp of any general of the Romans. Our friendship was sought, through ambassadors, by the Bastarnae and Scythians, and by the kings of the Sarmatians who live on either side of the river Tanais, and by the king of the Albani and of the Hiberi and of the Medes.

32. Kings of the Parthians, Tiridates, and later Phrates, the son of King Phrates, took refuge with me as suppliants; of the Medes, Artavasdes; of the Adiabeni, Artaxares; of the Britons, Dumnobellaunus and Tim . . . ; of the Sugambri, Maelo; of the Marcomanni and Suevi. . . . rus. Phrates, son of Orodes, king of the Parthians, sent all his sons and grandsons to me in Italy, not because he had been conquered in war, but rather seeking our friendship by means of his own children as pledges. And a large number of other nations experienced the good faith of the Roman people during my principate who never before had had any interchange of embassies or of friendship with the Roman people.

33. From me the peoples of the Parthians and of the Medes received the kings for whom they asked through ambassadors, the chief men of those peoples; the Parthians Vonones, son of King Phrates, grandson of King Orodes; the Medes Ariobarzanes, the son of King Artavazdes, grandson of King Ariobarzanes.

34. In my sixth and seventh consulships, when I had extinguished the flames of civil war, after receiving by universal consent the absolute control of affairs, I transferred the Republic from my own control to the will of the Senate and the Roman people. For this service on my part I was given the title of Augustus by decree of the Senate, and the doorposts of my house were covered with laurels by public act, and a civic crown was fixed above my door, and a golden shield was placed in the Curia Julia whose inscription testified that the Senate and the Roman people gave me this in recognition of my valor, my clemency, my justice, and my piety. After that time I took precedence of all in rank, but of power I possessed no more than those who were my colleagues in any magistracy.

35. While I was administering my thirteenth consulship the Senate and the equestrian order and the entire Roman people gave me the title of Father of my Country, and decreed that this title should be inscribed upon the vestibule of my house and in the Senate-House and in the Forum Augustum beneath the quadriga erected in my honor by decree of the Senate. At the time of writing this I was in my seventy-sixth year. . . .

(MARCUS) VITRUVIUS (POLLIO) (FL. 1ST CENTURY B.C.)

On Architecture

*V*itruvius' *On Architecture* has remained—throughout the Renaissance, Baroque, and Neoclassical periods and indeed to this day—a fundamental handbook of the classical principles of one of humanity's mightiest arts. We know all too little of the author's life. Vitruvius probably served as a military engineer during the civil wars and Caesar's African wars and was, as his writings indicate, well educated and well traveled.

- Although he is known to have built a temple at Fanum (modern Fano), his fame resides in writing. His prejudice clearly lies in favor of the Greeks; his desire, to preserve their classical designs for temples and public monuments. Despite Vitruvius' education, the Latin of his ten-volume *De Architectura* is often inelegant and sometimes obscure.
- In his remarkably exhaustive treatise, inspired by Greek models and dedicated to Augustus, Vitruvius examines:

  - the education of architects and history of architecture;
  - city planning and civil engineering;
  - construction methods and materials for edifices of all kinds—from private dwellings to theaters and baths;
  - the "four orders" of capitals: Ionian, Corinthian, Doric, and Tuscan;
  - floor paving and ornamental plaster-work;
  - water supply and aqueducts;
  - the relationship between building and place;
  - environmental factors that might affect longevity; and
  - military engines.

The prefaces to various books disparage the contemporary decline of architectural standards, which Vitruvius hopes to remedy with his survey. His influence on Donato Bramante, Michelangelo, and Leon Battista Alberti can be seen in buildings throughout Europe.

Diocletian's palace at Spalato

CHAPTER II
OF WHAT THINGS ARCHITEC-
TURE CONSISTS

1. Now architecture consists of Order, which in Greek is called *taxis,* and of Arrangement, which the Greeks name *diathesis,* and of Proportion and Symmetry and Decor and Distribution which in Greek is called *oeconomia.*

2. Order is the balanced adjustment of the details of the work separately, and, as to the whole, the arrangement of the proportion with a view to a symmetrical result. This is made up of Dimension, which in Greek is called *posotes.* Now Dimension is the taking of modules from the parts of the work; and the suitable effect of the whole work arising from the several subdivisions of the parts.

Arrangement, however, is the fit assemblage of details, and, arising from this assemblage, the elegant effect of the work and its dimensions, along with a certain quality or character. The kinds of the arrangement (which in Greek are called *ideae)* are these: ichnography (plan); orthography (elevation); scenography (perspective). Ichnography (plan) demands the competent use of compass and rule; by these plans are laid out upon the sites provided. Orthography (elevation), however, is the vertical image of the front, and a figure slightly tinted to show the lines of the future work. Scenography (perspective) also is the shading of the front and the retreating sides, and the correspondence of all lines to the vanishing point, which is the center of a circle.

These three (plan, elevation and perspective) arise from imagination and invention. Imagination rests upon the attention directed with minute and observant fervor to the charming effect proposed. Invention, however, is the solution of obscure problems; the treatment of a new undertaking disclosed by an active intelligence. Such are the outlines of Arrangement.

3. Proportion implies a graceful semblance; the suitable display of details in their context. This is attained when the details of the work are of a height suitable to their breadth, of a breadth suitable to their length; in a word, when everything has a symmetrical correspondence.

4. Symmetry also is the appropriate harmony arising out of the details of the work itself; the correspondence of each given detail among the separate details to the form of the design as a whole. As in the human body, from cubit, foot, palm, inch and other small parts comes the symmetric quality of eurhythmy; so is it in the completed building. First, in sacred buildings, either from the thickness of columns, or a triglyph, or the module; of a balista by the perforation which the Greeks call *peritreton*; by the space between the rowlocks in a ship which is called *dipechyaia*: so also the calculation of symmetries, in the case of other works, is found from the details.

5. Decor demands the faultless ensemble of a work composed, in accordance with precedent, of approved details. It obeys convention, which in Greek is called *thematismos,* or custom or nature. Convention is obeyed when buildings are put up in the open and hypethral to Jupiter of the Lightning, to Heaven, the Sun, the Moon; for of these gods, both the appearance and effect we see present in the open, the

world of light. To Minerva, Mars and Hercules, Doric temples will be built; for to these gods, because of their might, buildings ought to be erected without embellishments. Temples designed in the Corinthian style will seem to have details suited to Venus, Flora, Proserpine, Fountains, Nymphs; for to these goddesses, on account of their gentleness, works constructed with slighter proportions and adorned with flowers, foliage, spirals and volutes will seem to gain in a just decor. To Juno, Diana and Father Bacchus, and the other gods who are of the same likeness, if Ionic temples are erected, account will be taken of their middle quality; because the determinate character of their temples will avoid the severe manner of the Doric and the softer manner of the Corinthian. 6. With reference to fashion, decor is thus expressed; when to magnificent interiors vestibules also are made harmonious and elegant. For if the interior apartments present an elegant appearance, while the approaches are low and uncomely, they will not be accompanied by fitness. Again, if, in Doric entablatures, dentils are carved on the cornices, or if with voluted capitals and Ionic entablatures, triglyphs are applied, characteristics are transferred from one style to another: the work as a whole will jar upon us, since it includes details foreign to the order. 7. There will be a natural decor: first, if for all temples there shall be chosen the most healthy sites with suitable springs in those places in which shrines are to be set up; secondly and especially for Aesculapius and Salus; and generally for those gods by whose medical power sick persons are manifestly healed. For when sick persons are moved from a pestilent to a healthy place and the water supply is from wholesome fountains, they will more quickly recover. So will it happen that the divinity (from the nature of the site) will gain a greater and higher reputation and authority. . . .

CHAPTER IV
ON THE SALUBRITY OF SITES

1. In the case of the walls these will be the main points:—First, the choice of the most healthy site. Now this will be high and free from clouds and hoar frost, with an aspect neither hot nor cold but temperate. Besides, in this way a marshy neighborhood shall be avoided. For when the morning breezes come with the rising sun to a town, and clouds rising from these shall be conjoined, and, with their blast, shall sprinkle on the bodies of the inhabitants the poisoned breaths of marsh animals, they will make the site pestilential. Also if the walls are along the coast and shall look to the south or west they will not be wholesome, because through the summer the southern sky is warmed by the rising sun and burns at midday. Also that which looks to the western sun is warm at sunrise, hot at noon, burns in the evening. 2. Therefore by the changes of heat and cold, bodies which are in these places will be infected. We may even perceive this from those bodies which are not animal. For in wine stores no one takes light from the south or west but from the north, because that quarter at no time admits changes, but is continuously fixed and unchangeable. So also those granaries which look toward the sun's course quickly change their goodness; and fish and fruit

which are not placed in that quarter which is turned away from the sun's course do not keep long. 3. For always, when heat cooks the strength out of the atmosphere and with warm vapors removes by suction the natural virtues, it dissolves and renders them weak, as they become softened by warmth. Moreover, we see the same thing in iron, which is hard by nature, and yet when it is heated through in furnaces, by the vapor of fire becomes so soft that it is easily fashioned into every kind of shape; and when, being soft and red-hot, it is chilled and steeped in cold water, it hardens again and is restored to its previous character. 4. We may also consider that this is so from the fact that in summer, not only in pestilential, but in salubrious districts, all bodies become weak by the heat; and also, through the winter, even the regions which are most pestilential, are rendered salubrious because they are rendered solid by freezing. Not less also the bodies which are transferred from cold to warm regions cannot endure but are dissolved; while those which are transferred from warm places under the northern regions not only do not suffer in health by the change of place but even are strengthened. 5. Wherefore in laying out walls we must beware of those regions which by their heat can diffuse vapors over human bodies. For according as from the elements (which the Greeks call *stoecheia*) all bodies are composed, that is from heat and moisture and earth and air, just so by these mixtures, owing to natural temperament, the qualities of all animals are figured in the world according to their kind. 6. Therefore in whatsoever bodies, one of their principles, heat, is predominant, it then kills them and by its fervency dissolves the rest. Now a hot sky from certain quarters produces these defects; since it settles into the open veins more than the body permits by its natural temperament or admixture. Again, if moisture had filled the veins of bodies and altered their dimensions, the other elements, as though decomposed by liquid, are diluted and the virtues dependent on their proportion are dissolved. So also from the chilling of moisture of winds and breezes, vices are infused into bodies. Not less the natural proportion of air and also of the earthy element by increase or diminution weakens the other elements; the earthy by repletion of food, the aerial, by the heavy climate. 7. But if anyone wishes carefully to apprehend these things by perception, let him regard and attend to the natures of birds and fishes and land animals, and he will so consider differences of temperament or admixture. For the race of birds has one temperament, fishes another, far otherwise the nature of land animals. Birds have less of the earthy, less of moisture, moderate heat, much air. Therefore being compounded of the lighter principles, they rise more easily against the onrush of the air. But fishes with their watery nature (because they are tempered by heat and are compounded of much air and earth, but have remarkably little moisture), the less they have of the principles of moisture in their frame, the more easily they persist in moisture; and so when they are brought to land they lose their life along with the water. Terrestrial animals, also, because they have a moderate degree of the elements of air and heat, and have less of the earthy and more moisture,

inasmuch as they abound in moisture, cannot keep alive long in water. 8. Therefore if these matters are accepted as we have set forth, and if we apprehend by perception that the bodies of animals are compounded of elements, and if we judge that they suffer and are dissolved by excess or defect of them, we do not doubt that we must diligently seek to choose the most temperate regions of climate, since we have to seek healthiness in laying out the walls of cities.

ON INSPECTING THE LIVERS OF ANIMALS FOR TESTING THE QUALITY OF THE AIR

9. Therefore emphatically I vote for the revival of the old method. For the ancients sacrificed the beasts which were feeding in those places where towns or fixed camps were being placed, and they used to inspect the livers, which if at the first trial they were livid and faulty, they went on to sacrifice others, doubting whether they were injured by disease or faulty diet. When they had made trial of many, and had tested the entire and solid nature of the livers in accordance with the water and pasture they established there the fortifications; if, however, they found them faulty, by analogy they judged: that the supply of food and water which was to be found in these places would be pestilential in the case of human bodies. And so they removed elsewhere and changed their quarters, seeking salubrity in every respect. 10. But that it comes about that the salubrious properties of the soil are indicated by fodder and diet, we may take note and learn from the districts of

Crete which are about the river Pothereus, which flows between the two towns Cnossus and Gortyna. For cattle feed on the right and left bank of that river. But of these, the cattle which feed next Cnossus have, and those on the other side have not, an enlarged spleen. Whence also physicians inquiring about this matter have found in these places a plant which the cattle bellow for and, by it, lessen their spleens. So they gather this plant and use this medicine to cure the splenetic, which also the Cretans call *asplenon.* Hence we may know by food and water whether the properties of places are pestilential or salubrious.

11. So also if in marshes walls are laid out, and these marshes are along the sea, and they look toward the north or between the north and east, and these marshes are higher than the sea-coast, they will seem to be reasonably laid out. For if dykes are cut, there is made an outlet of water to the beach; and when the sea is swollen by storms, there is an overflow into the marshes, which being stirred and moved about and mixed with sea salt, does not permit the various kinds of marsh creatures to be born there; moreover, those which, by swimming from higher parts, arrive near the coast, are killed by the unfamiliar saltness. An instance of this may be found in the Gallic marshes which are round Altinum, Ravenna, Aquileia and other townships in like places which are nearest the marshes. For owing to these causes, they have an incredible salubrity. 12. Those places, however, which have stagnant marshes, and lack flowing outlets, whether rivers or by dykes, like the Pomptine marshes, by standing become foul and send forth heavy and pestilent moisture. . . .

CHAPTER V
ON THE FOUNDATIONS OF WALLS AND THE ESTABLISHMENT OF TOWNS

1. When, therefore, by these methods there shall be ensured healthiness in the laying out of the walls; and districts shall be chosen abounding in fruit to feed the citizens; and roads duly laid out, or convenient rivers, or supplies by sea through the harbors, shall have ready transport to the ramparts: then the foundations of the towers and walls are to be laid. If such foundations can be found, they are to be dug down to the solid and in the solid, as may seem proportionate to the amplitude of the work, of a breadth greater than that of the walls which shall be above the ground; and these foundations are to be filled with as solid structure as possible. 2. Towers, moreover, are to be projected on the outer side, in order that when the enemy wishes to approach the wall in an attack, he may be wounded on his exposed flanks by weapons on the right and left from the towers. And it seems that care must especially be taken that the approach be not easy for an enemy blockading the wall. The approach must be made to wind along the steep places, and so devised that the ways to the gates are not straight, but on the left of the wall. For when it is so done, then as the troops approach, their right side will be next the wall and will not be protected by the shield. Moreover, towns are not to be planned square nor with projecting angles, but on the round, so that the enemy be seen from several sides. For when angles run out, defence is difficult, because the angle defends the enemy rather than the townsmen. 3. But I think the width of the wall should be so made that armed men

meeting one another above can pass without hindrance. Then, in the width, through-timbers of charred olive wood should be put very frequently, in order that both fronts of the wall, being tied together by these timbers, as though by pins, may have everlasting strength. For such timber cannot be injured by decay or weather or age; even when it is covered with soil or placed in water, it remains unimpaired and useful for ever. And so not only the city wall, but the substructures, and those dividing walls which are made to be of the thickness of fortifications, when united in this manner, will not quickly be decayed. 4. The distances between the towers are so to be made that one is not further from another than a bowshot; so that if a tower is besieged anywhere, then, by "scorpions" and other missile engines from the towers right and left, the enemy may be thrown back. And also opposite the lower part of the towers, the wall is to be divided by intervals as wide as a tower; and these intervals opposite the interior parts of the towers shall be joined with planks. These, however, are not to be fixed with iron nails. For if the enemy occupies any part of the wall, the defenders shall cut them down, and if they manage it quickly, they will not suffer the enemy to penetrate the rest of the towers and wall, unless he is willing to throw himself headlong. . . .

(PUBLIUS OVIDIUS NASO) OVID (43 B.C.–A.D. 18)

Metamorphoses and *The Art of Love*

~~◡~~

*O*ne of Rome's most prolific and most interesting poets ended his life in bleak exile in Tomis (modern Constanta), a small Rumanian town on the Black Sea where he was banished at the height of his career by Augustus for an error against the emperor himself, which remains unclear to this day. Born east of Rome in Sulmo, Ovid had begun his poetic career—after an education at Rome under Porcius Latro and Arellius Fuscus and at Athens in law and oratory, and after a period of civil service—in the circle of Messalla, Tibullus, Propertius, Cornelius Gallus, and Horace. He was the last of the *neoterici* ("New Poets"). Speculation is that Augustus was so upset with his promiscuous daughter Julia, whom he'd been forced to send into exile, that he directed his rage against Ovid's cynical and licentious *The Art of Love,* which had appeared a few years earlier and epitomized all that Octavian loathed about the citizens of Rome.

Ovid's lost tragedy, *Medea,* praised by Quintilian and by Tacitus, may have influenced Seneca. Ovid's most important surviving works, showing his mastery of the elegiac style of the Alexandrine school, include:

- *Amores (The Loves).* Five books of fifty playful love poems chronicling his affair with "Corinna," published from about 20 to 16 B.C.
- *Heroides* (also known as *Epistulae Heroidum; Letters of the Heroines*). Heartsick letters in the form of dramatic monologues from the great heroines of myth to their husbands and lovers.
- *Metamorphoses (Transformations).* These fifteen books of "transformations" form his most ambitious work. Written in graceful and polished epic dactylic hexameters and brilliantly elaborating on the theme of chaos turned to order through passion (the passion of the gods brings creation out of chaos; the passion of Julius Caesar brings order out of civil war), they record Greek and Roman myths from the beginning of time to the deification of Caesar.
- *Tristia (Book of Sorrows).* A moving plea for justice and forgiveness, and a testimony to the power of poetry, in the guise of fifteen elegiac letters written from exile.
- *Ars Amatoria (The Art of Love).* The three books of light-hearted instruction for men and women on the ins and outs of flirtation, seduction, and the politics of love and sex are, then as now, Ovid's most popular work—not only for their antireformist subject matter but also for the ingenuity and wit by which they parody didactic treatises. Virgil had declared the warrior-founder Aeneas the son of Venus. Ovid tells the Romans they must live up to their heritage, perfecting the arts of venery. He also wrote a mock recantation, *Remedia amoris* (*Cures for Love*; published in 1 B.C.), instructing readers on how to free themselves from love's snares; and a small treatise, *On Make-Up.* Ovid's perspective and advice on amorous behavior in the capital offer the most vivid insight we have of the decadence Octavian sought in vain to temper with traditional Roman virtues.

FROM CREATION
Metamorphoses I, 1–88
My soul would sing of metamorphoses.
But since, o gods, you were the source of
* these*

bodies becoming other bodies, breathe
your breath into my book of changes: may
the song I sing be seamless as its way
weaves from the world's beginning to our
* day.*

Before the sea and lands began to be,
before the sky had mantled everything,
then all of nature's face was featureless—
what men call chaos: undigested mass
of crude, inert, and scumbled elements,
a heap of seeds that clashed, of things mis-
matched.
There was no Titan Sun to light the world,
no crescent Moon—no Phoebe—to renew
her slender horns; in the surrounding air,
the Earth's own weight did not yet balance her;
and Amphitrite's arms had not yet stretched
along the farthest margins of the land.
For though the waves and soil and air were
there,
the land could not be walked upon, the waves
could not be swum, the air was without splendor:
no thing maintained its shape; all were at war;
in one same body cold and hot would battle;
the damp contended with the dry, things hard
with soft, and weighty things with weightless
parts.

A god—and Nature, now become benign—
ended this strife. He separated sky
and earth, and earth and waves, and he defined
pure air and thicker air. Unraveling
these things from their blind heap, assigning
each
its place—distinct—he linked them all in peace.
Fire, the weightless force of heaven's dome,
shot up; it occupied the highest zone.
Just under fire, the light air found its place.
The earth, more dense, attracted elements
more gross; its own mass made it sink below.
And water, flowing, filled the final space;
it held the solid world in its embrace.

When he—whichever god it was—arrayed
that swarm, aligned, designed, allotted, made
each part into a portion of a whole,
then he, that earth might be symmetrical,
first shaped its sides into a giant ball.
He then commanded seas to stretch beneath
high winds, to swell, to coil, to reach and ring
shorelines and inlets. And he added springs
and lakes and endless marshes and confined
descending streams in banks that slope and
twine:
these rivers flow across their own terrains;
their waters sink into the ground or gain
the sea and are received by that wide plain
of freer waters—there, they beat no more
against their banks, but pound the shoals and
shores.

A bronze mirror from Pompeii

At his command, the fields enlarged their reach,
the valleys sank, the woods were clothed with
   leaves,
and rocky mountains rose. And as the sky
divides into two zones on its right side,
with just as many on the left, to which
the hottest zone is added as a fifth,
the god provided regions that divide
the mass the heavens wrap, and he impressed
as many zones upon the earth. Of these,
the middle zone, because of its fierce heat,
is uninhabitable; and thick snows
cover two outer zones; between them, he
aligned two other regions—and to these
he gave a clement climate, mixing heat
and cold. Above, the air extends; and for
as much as earth is heavier than water,
so is the air more ponderous than fire.
He ordered fog and clouds to gather there—
in air—and thunder, which would terrify
the human mind; there too, the god assigned
the winds that, from colliding clouds, breed
   lightning.

Yet he who was the world's artificer
did not allow the winds to rule the air
unchecked, set free to riot everywhere.
(But while each wind received a separate
   tract,
it still is difficult to curb their blasts,
to keep the world, which they would rend,
   intact—
though they are brothers, they forever clash.)
Eurus retreated toward Aurora's lands:
into the Nabataeans' kingdom and
to Persia, where the rays of morning meet
the mountain crests. And Zephyrus now went
to shorelines warm with sunset, in the west.

To Scythia, beneath the northern Wain,
swept horrid Boreas. Incessant rain
and mist that drench the southlands opposite—
this was the work of Auster. The god placed
above these winds, the ether, without weight,
a fluid free of earth's impurity.

No sooner had he set all things within
defining limits than the stars, long hid
beneath the crushing darkness, could begin
to gleam throughout the heavens. That no
   region
be left without its share of living things,
stars and the forms of gods then occupied
the porch of heaven; and the waters shared
their dwelling with the gleaming fishes; earth
received the beasts, and restless air, the birds.

An animal more noble, able, one
with higher intellect, one who could rule
the rest—that living thing was lacking yet.
Then man was born. Either the artifex
of all, begetter of a better world,
created man from seed divine—or else
Prometheus, the son of Iapetus,
mixing the new-made earth with fresh rainwater
(that earth which only recently had been
divided from high ether, and preserved
seeds of the sky, remains of their shared birth),
made man and molded him as likeness of
the masters of all things, the gods. And while
all other animals are bent, head down,
and fix their gaze upon the ground, to man
he gave a face that is held high; he had
man stand erect, his eyes upon the stars.
So was the earth, which until then had been
so rough and indistinct, transformed: it wore
a thing unknown before—the human form.

THE ART OF LOVE
Book III

*I gave arms to the Greeks against the Amazon
 forces:*

*Arms for the Amazons now; turn about is fair
 play.*

*Go to the wars, well-matched, and win by the
 blessing of Venus,*

*Win by the grace of her son, flying all over the
 world.*

*It would be most unfair for the naked to fight
 men in armor;*

*That is no victory, men; you would regard it
 with shame.*

*I can hear somebody say: "Are you furnishing
 serpents with poison,*

*Turning the mad she-wolves loose on the
 innocent fold?"*

*Don't impute to them all the crimes of a few
 wicked women;*

Give a fair hearing to all, let their merits decide.

*If Menelaus had good warrant for railing at
 Helen,*

If Agamemnon's queen killed in adulterous lust,

*If Amphiaraus drove his car to the Stygian
 caverns,*

*Through Eriphyle's crime, bought with a
 necklace of gold,*

*Did not Penelope keep true faith while her
 crafty Ulysses*

*Fought ten years in the war, added ten wan-
 dering years?*

*Think of Alcestis, who gave her days for the life
 of Admetus,*

*Think of Evadne's love, true in the flames of
 the pyre.*

*Virtue herself is portrayed in modest robes, as a
 woman;*

*Virtue, in modest white, has her own people to
 please.*

*Leave her subjects to her: I make no claim on
 her province:*

*My diminutive craft speeds with the slightest of
 sail.*

*I teach nothing but love, in its naughtier mani-
 festations—*

*How should a woman be loved? Ovid will show
 you the way.*

*Women do not hurl flames, nor aim any ven-
 omous arrows,*

*Seldom I see their arms torturing innocent
 men.*

*Men are the ones who deceive, men are contin-
 ual liars;*

*Search for deceitful girls, they are not easy to
 find.*

*Jason's perfidy doomed Medea, already a
 mother,*

*When the second bride came to his eager
 embrace.*

*Theseus abandoned a girl to the lonely shores
 of the sea birds,*

Ariadne was left fearful on Naxos, alone.

*Ask why they call one way Nine Ways, and
 learn about Phyllis,*

Losing Demophoon, left, pitiful even to trees.

*Pious Aeneas we know, that guest with the
 great reputation,*

*Leaving to Dido the sword, leaving the cause of
 her doom.*

*What destroyed them all? Nothing but ignorant
 loving,*

*They were unversed in the art; love requires art
 to survive.*

*I would let them alone, but Venus has bidden
 me teach them,*

Venus herself has appeared, standing before my
    eyes,
Saying to me, "Poor girls! what have they
    done to deserve it,
Weak and defenseless, a throng thrown on the
    mercy of men?
You have written two books arming the men
    with instruction;
Now let the other side have some help and
    advice.
Stesichorus, who made, at first, a song against
    Helen,
Later extolled her praise, strumming a happier
    lyre.
If I know you well, as long as you live, you will
    seek them,
Girls with a cultured flair; do not be mean to
    them now."
So she spoke, and bestowed on me the leaves of
    the myrtle,
Myrtle, torn from her hair, and a few berries as
    well.
As I received them I knew, I felt the power of
    her godhead,
Air had a purer shine, gloom went away from
    my heart.
While I am under her spell, O girls, receive my
    instruction,
Granted by Venus' grace, granted by warrant
    of law.

Have your fun while you may, rejoice in the
    bloom of your springtime,
Years go by like the waves, rapidly streaming
    away.
Waves that are once gone by are past the hope
    of recalling,
Hours that are once gone by surely will never
    return.

Take advantage of time; time is a swift-footed
    glider,
Nor can the good days to come equal the ones
    that have fled.
Violets wither and fade; I have seen their color
    turn ashen,
Only the stems are left out of the garlands I
    wore.
There will come a day when you, the excluder
    of lovers,
Lie in the lonely night, cold, an old woman,
    alone.
No one will batter your door or break it with
    brawls in the nighttime,
You will not find in the dawn roses thrown
    down on the stone.
Most unhappily true—the body is furrowed
    with wrinkles,
Shining complexions lose all their bright radi-
    ant hues.
Those white hairs which you say you always
    had, from your girlhood,
Thicken and multiply fast, covering all of your
    head.
Serpents put off old age by sloughing their
    skins with the season,
Nor do the antlers lost tell the true years of the
    stag.
All our good things go, and we can do nothing
    about it,
Only gather the flower; soon the blossom will
    fall.
Childbearing shortens your days, the hours of
    your youthful allotment—
Does not the harvest field age from continual
    yield?
Do as the goddesses did, the Moon with her
    darling from Latmos,

Or the rosy Dawn, blushing for Cephalus' love.

Venus mourns, it is true, and never had her
 Adonis,

Still, Anchises and Mars gave her a daughter,
 a son.

Study those ways of theirs, mortals, and from
 their example

Do not deny to your men pleasures their eagerness craves.

They will deceive you at last, but what have
 you lost by it? Nothing.

Taking a thousand joys, still they take nothing
 away.

Iron is worn away and flint-stones lessened by
 usage;

That part need not fear loss or attrition from
 time.

Who would forbid us to take light from a light
 that is offered,

Who keep account of the waves in the domain
 of the sea?

So when a woman tells a man, "It doesn't seem
 proper!"

What is she doing but waste what her own
 thirst will require?

I do not want you to be cheap and promiscuous; only

Fearful of unreal loss: what you are giving you
 keep.

More of this later on: we still, it seems, are in
 harbor;

Here let a fluttering breeze ruffle the swell of
 the sail.

Cultivation comes first, the proper care of the
 body—

From the well-tended vine comes the most
 exquisite wine.

Beauty's a gift from the gods, too rare for
 many to boast of:

Most of you (pardon me, dears) don't have so
 precious a boon.

So, take pains to improve the endowments
 nature has given;

With sufficient neglect, Venus would look like a
 hag.

If, in the olden days, girls took no care of their
 persons,

What did it matter? Of old, men were as crude
 and uncouth.

If Andromache wore a one-piece garment of
 burlap,

What was so strange about that? She was a
 warrior's spouse.

How would you like to be dressed like the wife
 of Ajax, in leather,

Seven layers of hide for your protection from
 cold?

Simple and rude, those days, but Rome, in our
 era, is golden,

Ruler of conquered tribes, holding the wealth
 of the world.

Look at the Capitol now, and see, in imagination,

What it used to be, home of a different Jove.

We have a Senate-House worthy of Caesar
 Augustus,

Fashioned, in Tatius' reign, out of wattles and
 clay.

On the Palatine Hill, where Apollo dwells with
 our princes,

What did there use to be? Pasture for oxen to
 browse.

Let others rave about those ancient days; I am
 happy

Over the date of my birth: this is the era for me.

*Not because we mine the stubborn gold from
  the mountains,*
*Not because rare shells come from the farthest
  of shores,*
*Not because the hills decrease as we plunder
  the marble,*
*Not because sea walls bar raids of the dark-
  blue sea,*
*Not for reasons like these, but because our age
  has developed*
*Manners, culture and taste, all the old crudi-
  ties gone.*

*Do not burden your ears with precious stones
  from the Indies,*
Lifted by dusky men out of the watery green;
*Don't stagger under the weight of gold in the
  seams of your garments—*
*Too conspicuous wealth frequently puts us to
  flight.*
*What we cannot resist is elegance: don't let
  your hair blow*
*Wild in the wind, employ just the right touch of
  the hand.*
*There are, of course, many styles and pleasing
  ways of adornment;*
*Look in your mirror and choose which is most
  seemly to use.*
*If your face is long, you should part your hair
  in the middle;*
*If your features are round, then let your hair be
  a crown.*
*Somebody else might look best with the locks
  falling over each shoulder;*
That was Apollo's way, god of the resonant lyre.
*Still another might try a braid, in the mode of
  Diana,*
*Huntress of fugitive game, roaming through
  woodland and glade.*

*Here is a girl who should run her hands
  through her hair, keep it fluffy;*
*There is another whose style calls for the plain
  and severe.*
*One might do well with her combs mottled with
  tortoise-shell markings,*
Others do equally well using a wavy design,
*But it is foolish to count the acorns that hang
  on the oak-tree,*
*Count the bees in the hive, number the fish in
  the sea,*
*So I cannot keep track of all the vagaries of
  fashion,*
Every day, so it seems, brings in a different style.
*Even neglected hair might prove becoming to
  many,*
*Something of yesterday's charm contradicting
  the comb.*
*Art may resemble chance, a hint of coincidence
  in it,*
*Art has an off-hand look, sometimes, that mul-
  tiplies charm.*
*Think how Iole was seen, in a captured town;
  in a moment*
*Hercules knew, at first sight, she was the
  woman for him.*
*Think of the girl from Crete, Ariadne, aban-
  doned on Naxos,*
*Lifted in Bacchus' car, cheered by his reveling
  band.*
*Nature is fond of you, girls, and generous in
  her indulgence,*
*Offering infinite ways, nice compensations for
  time.*
*We poor men, when our hair falls out, are dis-
  gustingly naked,*
*Bare as the boughs when the wind seizes the
  wintering leaves.*

Women can dye their hair, when it whitens,
    with Germany's juices,
Nature improved by art, color surpassing the
    true.
Women can walk along under a bundle of tresses
Purchased in any store, new locks replacing
    the old,
Nor do they blush at the thought; the sales are
    made in the open,
Under the Muses' eyes, close to the temple they
    own.

Now shall I talk about clothes? I do not recom-
    mend flounces,
Do not endorse the wools reddened with Tyrian
    dye.
When you have such a choice of cheaper and
    pleasanter colors
You would be crazy to use only one costly dis-
    play.
There is the color of sky, light-blue, with no
    cloud in the heavens,
There is the hue of the ram, wearing the
    golden fleece,
There is the color of wave, the hue of the
    Nereids' raiment,
There is the saffron glow worn by Aurora at
    dawn,
All kinds of colors: swans-down, amethyst,
    emerald, myrtle,
Almond, chestnut, and rose, yellow of wax,
    honey-pale—
Colors as many as flowers born from new earth
    in the springtime,
When the buds of the vine swell, and old winter
    has fled,
So many colors, or more, the wool absorbs;
    choose the right ones—

Not every color will suit everyone's differing
    need.
If your complexion is fair, dark-gray is a suit-
    able color;
Briseis, taken in war, pleased in her gown of
    dark-gray.
If you are dark, dress in white; such was
    Andromeda's raiment
When the envious gods punished her island
    abode.

Should I warn you to keep the rank goat out of
    your armpits,
Warn you to keep your legs free of coarse
    bristling hair?
No: I am not teaching girls from the rugged
    Caucasian mountains;
Those in my school do not drink out of some
    Mysian mere.
Also, I need not remind you to brush your teeth
    night and morning,
Need not remind you your face ought to be
    washed when you rise.
You know what to apply to acquire a brighter
    complexion—
Nature's pallidest rose blushes with suitable art.
Art supplies the means for patching an incom-
    plete eyebrow,
Art, or a beauty-spot, aids cheeks that have
    never a flaw.
There is nothing amiss in darkening eyes with
    mascara,
Ash, or the saffron that comes out of Cilician
    soil.
I wrote a book about this, The Art of Beauty, I
    called it,
Not a big book, I must say; still, it took labor
    and time.

Read it, and find the cure for any defect in
your beauty—
In your interest, you see, mine is a diligent
art,

Don't let your lover find the boxes displayed on
your dresser,
Art that dissembles art gives the most happy
effect. . . .

SENECA THE YOUNGER (LUCIUS ANNAEUS SENECA) (4 B.C.–A.D. 65)

Pumpkinification of Claudius

*T*he second son of Helvia and his famous father, Seneca the Younger was in his own right a distinguished politician, philosopher, and *literatus*. He has been called the "most important thinker and writer" after Tacitus in the post-Augustan empire. Like his father, born in Spanish Córdoba, he also went to Rome for his education under Attalus the Stoic, Fabianus, Sotion, and Demetrius the Cynic. He was hated by Caligula and banished by Claudius and Messalina to Corsica either because the emperor envied his brilliance or for having an affair with Gaius' sister Julia Livilla (daughter of Germanicus) but was recalled to Rome in A.D. 49 by Agrippina, who appointed him tutor to the eleven-year-old Nero.

That appointment, ingratiating him as it did with the profligate emperor-to-be, turned out to be the beginning of the end for Seneca. With Burrus, captain of the guard, he served as Nero's close confidant and adviser during the five stable years of his reign; but when the Emperor arranged the murder of Agrippina in A.D. 59, Seneca's compromise-based influence suddenly became dangerous. Though at the death of Burrus, Seneca fled Rome into retirement to avoid the fallout from Agrippina's murder, which he allegedly had helped the Emperor to justify, Seneca was ordered to commit suicide for allegedly taking part in Piso's unsuccessful conspiracy. True to his Stoicism, he complied, in 65, slitting his wrists. His beautiful wife Paulina did the same, though she survived.

- Both his prose and verse come down to us, including popular works on philosophy and Stoic morality; essays on various subjects such as "the brevity of life" and the "tranquillity of the soul"; *Questions on Nature,* speeches written for delivery by Nero; and 124 letter-sermons

Temple of Saturn, Roman Forum

inspired by Cicero's letters. He also wrote nine melodramatic, contemplative, declamatory, and laborious "closet dramas," all tragedies based on Greek models, including *Medea, Phaedra, Agamemnon, Oedipus,* and *Hercules Enraged.* No one knew the darkest recesses of the human heart more thoroughly than Seneca, whose writing in all its forms reflects the hope and despair of a progressively decadent empire.

- One of Seneca's most mordantly amusing pieces is his Menippean satire known as the *Apocolocyntosis* or *Pumpkinification of Claudius,* a mock first-hand account of what happened in the heavenly court of Jupiter when the emperor Claudius sought postmortem deification.

. . . And indeed he did go up the flume, and from that moment ceased to appear to be alive. He expired, moreover, while listening to comic actors; so you understand it isn't without reason that I am afraid of those fellows. His last words that were heard among men were these, after a louder utterance in the locality where he expressed himself the more easily: "Oh, dear! I think I have hurt myself." Whether he had, I don't know; at any rate he was in the habit of hurting everything.

What happened afterward on earth it is superfluous to describe. For you know very well, and there is no danger that things which the universal joy has impressed upon the memory will slip from it; no one forgets his own good fortune. Listen to what happened in heaven: it is on the authority of the narrator. The news was brought to Jupiter that somebody had come, a rather tall man, quite gray-headed; that he was threatening something or other, for he kept shaking his head; and that he limped with his right foot. The messenger said he had asked of what nation he was, but his answer was mumbled in some kind of an incoherent noise; he didn't recognize the man's language, but he wasn't either Greek or Roman or of any known race. Then Jupiter told Hercules, who had traveled all over the world and was supposed to be acquainted with all the nations, to go and find out what sort of a man it was. Hercules at the first sight was a good deal disturbed, even though he was one who didn't fear any sort of monsters. When he beheld the aspect of this unknown specimen, its extraordinary gait, its voice belonging to no earthly creature but more like that of the monsters of the deep, hoarse and inarticulate, he thought that a thirteenth labor had come to him. When he looked more carefully, however, it appeared to be a man. He approached him and thus spoke, as was easiest for a Greek chap:

Who and whence art thou, and where are thy city and parents?

Claudius was delighted to find literary people there, hoping there would be some place for his histories. So he, too, in a Homeric verse, indicating himself to be Caesar, said:

Hence from Ilium the winds have among the Cicones cast me.

But the following verse would have been truer, and equally Homeric:

There their city I wasted; the people I slaughtered.

And he would have imposed upon the guileless Hercules, had not Fever been there, who alone had left her shrine and come with him. All the other divinities he had left behind at Rome. She said, "It is simple nonsense that he is giving you. I tell you—I who have lived with him for so many years—he was born at Lugudunum; you behold one of Marcus' citizens. As I'm telling you, he was born sixteen miles from Vienna, a genuine Gaul. And so as a Gaul ought to do, he captured Rome. Take my word for it, he was born at Lugudunum, where Licinus reigned for many years. But you, who have tramped more lands than any wandering muleteer, ought to know men from Lugudunum and that there are a good many miles between the Xanthus and the Rhone." At this point Claudius fired up and angrily grumbled as loudly as he could. What he was saying, nobody understood, except that he commanded Fever to be led away to punishment. With the familiar gesture of his limp hand, that was steady enough for the one purpose of decapitating people as he was accustomed, he had ordered her head to be struck off. You would suppose all those present were his freedmen, so little attention did any one pay him. Then Hercules said, "Listen to me and stop talking nonsense. You have come to a place where the mice gnaw iron. Tell me the truth, quick, or I'll knock the silliness out of you." And in order to be more terrifying, he struck the attitude of a tragedian and said:

"Declare at once the place you call your natal
    town,
Or else, by this tough cudgel smitten, down
    you go!
This club has slaughtered many a mighty
    potentate.
What's that, that in a muffled voice you're try-
    ing to say?
Where is the land or race to own your shaky
    head?
Speak out. Oh, I remember when afar I sought
The triple-bodied king's domains, whose
    famous herd
From the western sea I drove to the city of
    Inachus,
I saw a hill above two rivers, towering high
In face of Phoebus rising each day opposite,
Where the broad Rhone pours by in swiftly
    moving flood,
And Arar, pausing ere it lets its waters go,
Silently laves the borders of its quiet pools.
Is that the land that nursed you when you first
    drew breath?"

These things he said with spirit, and boldly enough. All the same, he was inwardly a good deal afraid of the *madman's blow.* Claudius, seeing the mighty hero, forgot his nonsense and perceived that while no one had been a match for him at Rome, here he didn't have the same advantage; a cock is master only on his own dunghill. So, as well as could be made out, this is what he appeared to say: "I did hope that you, Hercules, bravest of the gods, would stand by me before the others, and if any one had asked me who could vouch for me, I should have named you, who know me best. For if you recall, I was the one who held court before your temple all day long during the months of July and August. You know how many troubles I had there, listening to the lawyers day and night; and if you had fallen among those fellows, though you may think that you are pretty courageous, you would have preferred to clean Augeas' stables. I have cleaned out much more filth. But since I want"—

"It's no wonder you have made an assault upon the Senate-House; nothing is closed to you. Only tell us what sort of a god you want him to be made. He cannot be an *Epicurean god, neither having himself any care nor causing any to others.* A Stoic? How can he be 'round,' as Varro says, 'without head or prepuce'? Yet there is something in him of the Stoic god, now I see. He has neither heart nor head. By Hercules, though, if he had asked this favor of Saturn, whose festival month the Saturnalian prince kept going the whole year long, he wouldn't have got it; and surely he wouldn't of Jove, whom so far as he possibly could he convicted of incest. For he put to death Silanus his son-in-law, just because the man preferred that his sister, prettiest of all the girls, so that everybody called her Venus, should be called his Juno. 'Why his sister?' you say,—in fact, I ask it. Think, you block-head. At Athens that sort of thing is halfway allowed; at Alexandria altogether. 'But since at Rome,' you say, 'the mice live on dainties.' He's going to straighten our crooked ways! He doesn't know what goes on in his own chamber, and now 'he searches the regions of heaven.' He wants to become a god. Isn't he satisfied that he has a temple in Britain; that the bar-barians worship him and beseech him as a god that they may *find him a merciful madman?*"

At length it occurred to Jove that while ordinary persons are staying in the Senate-House it is not permitted to express an opinion nor to argue. "I had allowed you to ask ques-tions, Conscript Fathers," he said, "but you have brought out simply rubbish. I want you to observe the rules of the Senate. What will this person, whoever he is, think of us?"

When the said individual had been sent out, Father Janus was the first to be asked his opinion. He had been elected afternoon consul for the first of July, being a very shrewd man, who always sees *at once both forward and backward*. He spoke at some length, and flu-ently, because he lives in the Forum; but the stenographer could not follow, and therefore I do not report him, for fear of misquoting what he said. He said a good deal about the impor-tance of the gods, and that this honor ought not to be given commonly. "Once," said he, "it was a great thing to be made a god, but now you have made the distinction a farce. And so lest my remarks seem to be dealing with personali-ties rather than with the case, I move that from

this day forward no one shall be made a god, from among all those who *eat the fruit of the corn-land*, or those whom the *fruitful corn-land* feeds. Whoever contrary to this decree of the Senate shall be made, called, or depicted as god, is to be given to the hobgoblins, and to get a thrashing among the newly hired gladiators at the next show."

The next to be asked his opinion was Diespiter the son of Vica Pota, who was himself also a consul elect, and a money-changer; by this business he supported himself, and he was accustomed to sell citizenships in a small way. Hercules approached him politely and gave him an admonitory touch on the ear. Accord-ingly he expressed his opinion in these words: "Whereas the divine Claudius is by blood related to the divine Augustus and no less also to the divine Augusta, his grandmother, who was made a goddess by his own orders, and whereas he far surpasses all mortals in wis-dom, and it is for the public interest that there be some one who can join Romulus in 'eating of boiling-hot turnips,' I move that from this day the divine Claudius be a god, with title equally as good as that of any one who has been made so before him, and that this event be added to the Metamorphoses of Ovid."

The opinions were various, and Claudius seemed to be winning the vote. For Hercules, who saw that his iron was in the fire, kept run-ning to this one and that one, saying, "Don't go back on me; this is my personal affair. And then if you want anything, I'll do it in my turn. One hand washes the other."

Then the divine Augustus arose at the point for expressing his opinion, and discoursed with the utmost eloquence. "I call you to witness,

Conscript Fathers," said he, "that since I was made a god, I have never addressed you; I always mind my own business. And I can no longer disguise my feelings nor conceal the distress that shame makes all the greater. Was it for this that I secured peace on land and sea? For this did I make an end of civil wars? For this did I found the city on a basis of law, adorn it with monuments, that—what to say, Conscript Fathers, I cannot discover. All words are beneath my indignation. So in desperation I must take to the phrase of that most clever man, Messala Corvinus, 'I am ashamed of my authority.' This fellow, Conscript Fathers, who doesn't seem to you as if he could disturb a fly, used to kill people as easily as a dog stops to rest. But why should I enumerate the many great men? I have no heart to lament public calamities when I behold those of my own family. And so I will pass over the former and describe these. For I know, even if my sister doesn't know [as they say in Greek], *my knee is nearer than my shin.* That fellow whom you see there, hiding under my name for so many years, has shown his gratitude to me by slaying the two Julias, my great-granddaughters, one by the sword, the other by starvation, and L. Silanus, one of my great-great-grandsons. We shall see, Jupiter, whether in a bad case, and one which is certainly your own, you are going to be just. Tell me, divine Claudius, why you condemned any one of the men and women whom you put to death before you understood their cases, or even listened to them. Where is this kind of thing customary? It's not the way in heaven. Here is Jupiter, now, who has been ruling for so many years. One person's leg he has broken, Vulcan's, whom

Snatching him by the foot, he hurled
from the heavenly threshold;

and he got angry at his wife and hung her up, but he didn't kill her, did he? But you have put to death Messalina, to whom I was as much a great-uncle as I was to you. 'I don't know,' you say? May the gods be hard on you! It is more shameful that you didn't know it than that you killed her. He has never ceased to follow up the dead-and-gone C. Caesar. The latter had killed his father-in-law; Claudius here, his son-in-law besides. Gaius forbade the son of Crassus to be called Magnus; this man returned him the name, but took off his head. He killed in one household Crassus, Magnus, Scribonia, the Tristionias, and Assario; and they were aristocrats too, and Crassus besides so stupid that he was even qualified to reign. Now do you want to make this man a god? Look at his body, born when the gods were angry. And finally, if he can say three consecutive words together, he can have me as his slave. Who will worship this god? Who will believe in him? As long as you make such gods as he, nobody will believe you are gods yourselves. In short, Conscript Fathers, if I have behaved myself honorably among you, if I have not answered anybody in an ungentlemanly manner, avenge my injuries. This is the resolution which I have to offer;" and he read as follows from his tablet: "Since the divine Claudius has killed his father-in-law Appius Silanus, his two sons-in-law Magnus Pompeius and L. Silanus, his daughter's father-in-law Crassus Frugi, a man as like himself as one egg is to another, Scribonia his daughter's mother-in-law, his wife Messalina, and others too numerous to mention, I propose that strict punishment be meted out to him, that he be granted no rest from adjudicating cases, and that he be got out of the way as soon as possible, departing from heaven within thirty days and from Olympus within three."

There was a division of the house, and this resolution was carried. Without delay the Cyllenian dragged him by the nape of his neck off from heaven toward the lower regions,

"Whence they say no man returns." . . .

(AULUS [A.K.A. AURELIUS] CORNELIUS) CELSUS (A.D. 14–37)

On Medicine

*A*lthough we know that his *Artes* was a wide-ranging encyclopedia modeled on Varro's *Disciplines* and covering everything from agriculture (which influenced Julius Graecinus) to war (influencing Vegetius), law, philosophy, and rhetoric, only Books 7–13, on medicine, written during the reign of Tiberius, survive.

- According to Celsus, the four telltale signs of inflammation were heat, pain, redness, and swelling. Among other things, his treatise discusses the history of medicine, diet and regimen, fevers, ulcers, venereal disease, facial plastic surgery using skin transplants, antiseptics, eye surgery, surgical hygiene, heart disease, the use of ligatures to stop arterial hemorrhage, insanity, hydrotherapy, tonsillectomy, oral and dental surgery, and the removal of bladder stones.
- Rediscovered by Pope Nicholas V, the *De Medicina* was among the first medical texts to be published, in 1478, by the printing press. Though the influence of the Greek Hippocrates and Asclepiades' protégé Themison is everywhere evident and much of his work is a reconstruction of Hellenistic medical practices, well into the Renaissance Celsus enjoyed the reputation

Reconstructed Roman pharmacy, in Castel Sant'Angelo

of being the most important Roman medical writer, "the Hippocrates of the Romans." For the eloquent clarity of his style he became the model for Renaissance writers who proclaimed him "the Cicero of physicians."

BOOK II

Prooemium

Of impending disorders there are many signs, in explaining which I shall not hesitate to make use of the authority of ancient men, and especially of Hippocrates; for although more recent practitioners have made some changes in methods of treatment, they allow none the less that the ancients prognosticated best. Before I note, however, those preceding symptoms which suggest fear of disease, it does not seem unfitting to set out: the seasons of the year, the sorts of weather, periods of life and temperaments which may be in particular safe or open to risks, and what kind of disorders is most to be apprehended in each. Not that men may not sicken and die at any season, in any sort of weather, at any age, whatever their temperament, from any kind of disease, but since certain kinds occur less ... but some kinds occur more often, so it is of use that everyone should recognize against what, and when, he should be most on his guard.

II

1. So then spring is the most salubrious, next after it comes winter; summer is rather more dangerous than salubrious, autumn is by far the most dangerous. But as regards weather the best is that which is settled, whether cold or hot, the worst that which is the most changeable, and that is why autumn brings down the greatest number. For generally about midday there is heat, but at night and in the early morning, cold, as also in the evening. Thus the body, relaxed by the preceding summer, and now by the midday heat, is caught by the sudden cold. But while this chiefly occurs at this season, so whenever the like happens harm is done.

In settled weather fine days are the most salubrious, rainy better than foggy or cloudy days; and in winter the best days are those in which there is an entire absence of wind, in summer those in which westerly winds blow. As for the other winds, the northerly are more salubrious than those from the sunrising or south, nevertheless, these vary somewhat according to the character of the district. For almost everywhere wind when coming from inland is salubrious, and injurious when from the sea. And not only is health more assured in settled weather, but preexisting diseases too, if

there have been any, are milder and more quickly terminated. But the worst weather for the sick man is that which has caused his sickness, so much so that a change to weather of a naturally worse sort may be, in his condition, salutary.

The middle period of life is the safest, for it is not disturbed by the heat of youth, nor by the chill of age. Old age is more exposed to chronic diseases, youth to acute ones. The square-built frame, neither thin nor fat, is the fittest; for tallness, as it is graceful in youth, shrinks in the fulness of age; a thin frame is weak, a fat one sluggish.

In spring those diseases are usually to be apprehended which are stirred up anew by movement of humor. Consequently there tend to arise running from the eyes, pustules, hemorrhages, congestions in the body, which the Greeks call *apostemata*, black bile which they call μελανχολία, madness, fits, angina, choked nostrils, runnings from the nose. Also those diseases which affect joints and sinews, being at one time troublesome, at another quiescent, then especially both begin and recur.

But summer, while not wholly exempt from most of the foregoing maladies, adds to them fevers whether continued or ardent or tertian, vomitings, diarrheas, earaches, oral ulcerations, cankers which occur on other parts but especially upon the pudenda, and whatever exhausts the patient by sweating.

In autumn there is scarcely one of the foregoing which does not happen; but at this season in addition there arise irregular fevers, splenic pain, subcutaneous dropsy, consumption, called by the Greeks *phthisis*, urinary difficulty, which they call *strangury*, the small intestine malady which they term *ileos,* the intestinal lubricity which they call *leienteria,* hip-pains, fits. Autumn too is a season fatal to those exhausted by chronic diseases and overwhelmed by the heat just past, others it weakens by fresh maladies; and it involves some in very chronic ones, especially quartan fevers, which may last even through the winter. Nor is any other period of the year more exposed to pestilence of whatever sort; although it is harmful in a variety of ways.

Winter provokes headache, coughs, and all the affections which attack the throat, and the sides of the chest and lungs.

Of the various sorts of weather, the north wind excites cough, irritates the throat, constipates the bowels, suppresses the urine, excites shiverings, as also pain of the lungs and chest. Nevertheless it is bracing to a healthy body, rendering it more mobile and brisk. The south wind dulls hearing, blunts the senses, produces headache, loosens the bowels; the body as a whole is rendered sluggish, humid, languid. The other winds, as they approximate to the north or south wind, produce affections corresponding to the one or other. Moreover, any hot weather inflates the liver and spleen, and dulls the mind; the result is that there are faintings, that there is an outburst of blood. Cold on the other hand brings about: at times tenseness of sinews which the Greeks call *spasmos,* at times the rigor which they call *tetanos,* the blackening of ulcerations, shiverings in fevers. In times of drought there arise acute fevers, runnings from the eyes, dysenteries, urinary difficulty, articular pains. In wet weather there occur chronic fevers, diarrheas, angina, canker, fits, and the loosening of sinews which the Greeks call *paralysis.* Not only does the weather of the day but also of the preceding days matter. If a dry winter has been accompanied by north winds, or again a spring by south winds and rain, generally there ensue runnings from the eye, dysenteries, fevers, and most of all in more delicate bodies, hence especially in women. If on the other hand south winds and rain have prevailed during winter, and the spring is cold and dry, pregnant women near their confinement are in danger of miscarrying; those indeed who reach term, give birth only to weaklings hardly alive. Other people are attacked by dry ophthalmia, and if elderly by choked nostrils and runnings from the nose. But when the south wind prevails from the beginning of winter to the end of spring, side pains, also the insanity of those in fever which is called phrenesis, are very rapidly fatal. And when hot weather begins in the spring, and lasts through the summer, severe sweating must ensue in cases of fever. If a summer has been kept dry by northerly winds, but in the autumn there are showers and south winds, there may then arise cough, runnings from the nose, hoarseness, and indeed in some, consumption. But if the autumn is dry owing to a north wind continuing to blow, all those with more delicate bodies, among whom, as I have mentioned, are women, enjoy good health. The harder constitutions, however, may possibly be attacked by dry ophthalmias, and by fevers, some acute, some chronic, also by those maladies which arise from black bile.

As regards the various times of life, children and adolescents enjoy the best health in spring, and are safest in early summer; old people are at their best during summer and the beginning of autumn; young and middle-aged adults in winter. Winter is worst for the aged, summer for young adults. At these periods should any indisposition arise, it is very probable that infants and children still of tender age should suffer from the creeping ulcerations of the mouth which the Greeks call *aphthas,* vomiting, insomnia, discharges from the ear, and inflammations about the navel. Especially in those teething there arise ulcerations of the gums, slight fevers, sometimes spasms, diarrhea; and they suffer as the canine teeth in particular are growing up; the most well-nourished children, and those constipated, are especially in danger. In those somewhat older there occur affections of the tonsils, various spinal curvatures, swelling in the neck, the painful kind of warts which the Greeks call *acrochordones,* and a number of other swellings. At the commencement of puberty, in addition to many of the above troubles, there occur chronic fevers and also nosebleedings. Throughout childhood there are special dangers, first about the fortieth day, then in the seventh month, next in the seventh year, and after that about puberty. The sorts of affections which occur in infancy, when not ended by the time of puberty, or of the first coitions, or of the first menstruations in the females, generally become chronic; more often, however, puerile affections, after persisting for a rather long while, come to an end. Adolescence is liable to acute diseases, such as fits, especially to consumption; those who spit blood are generally youths. After that age come on pain in the side and lung, lethargy, cholera, madness, and outpourings of blood from certain mouths of veins which the Greeks call *hemor-*

rhoids. In old age there occur breathing and urinary difficulties, choked nostrils, joint and renal pains, paralysis, the bad habit of body which the Greeks call *cachexia,* insomnias, the more chronic maladies of the ears, eyes, also of the nostrils, and especially looseness of the bowels with its sequences, dysentery, intestinal lubricity, and the other ills due to bowel looseness. In addition thin people are fatigued by consumption, diarrhea, running from the nose, pain in the lung and side. The obese, many of them, are throttled by acute diseases and difficult breathing; they die often suddenly, which rarely happens in a thinner person.

2. Now antecedent to illness, as I have stated above, certain signs arise, all of which have this in common, that the body becomes altered from its accustomed state, and that not only for the worse, but it may be even for the better. Hence when a man has become fatter and better looking and with a higher color, he should regard with suspicion these gains of his; for, because they can neither remain in the same state nor advance further, as a rule they fall back in a sort of collapse. Still it is a worse sign when anyone, contrary to his habit, becomes thinner, and loses his color and good looks; for when there is a superfluity of flesh there is something for the disease to draw upon; when there is a deficiency, there is nothing to hold out against the disease itself. Further, there should be apprehension at once: if the limbs become heavier, if frequent ulcerations arise, if the body feels hotter than customary; if heavier sleep oppresses, if there are tumultuous dreams, if anyone wakes up oftener than usual, then falls asleep again; if the body of the sleeper has partial sweats in

unaccustomed places, and especially about the chest or neck or legs or knees or hips. Again, if the spirit flags, if he is reluctant to talk or move about, if the body is torpid; if there is pain over the heart or over all the chest, or of the head as happens in most; if the mouth becomes filled with saliva, if there is pain in turning the eyes, if the temples are constricted, when the limbs shiver, if the breathing becomes more labored; if the blood-vessels of the forehead are distended and throb, if there are frequent yawns; if the knees feel as if fatigued, or the whole body feels weary. Of these signs, many are often, some always, antecedents of fever. The first thing, however, to be considered is, whether any of these signs happen somewhat frequently, yet no bodily trouble has followed it. For there are some peculiarities of persons, without knowledge of which it is not easy for anybody to prognosticate what is going to happen. Consequently anyone may readily be at ease in the case of happenings which he has frequently escaped without harm: the man who ought to be anxious is the one to whom these signs are new, or who has never found them free from danger unless he has taken precautions.

3. But when fever has actually seized upon a man, it may be known that he is not in danger: if he lies upon his side, whether on his right or left, just as suits him, with his legs a little drawn up, as is generally the way with a healthy person when lying down; if the patient turns readily in bed, if he sleeps through the night, and keeps awake by day; if he breathes easily; if he does not toss about; if the skin around the navel and pubes is plump; if the parts below the ribs on the two sides are uniformly soft, without any sensation of pain; for even although they are somewhat tumid, so long as they yield to pressure by the fingers, and are not tender, this illness, though it will continue for some time, yet will be safe. There is promise of freedom from anxiety when the body in general is uniformly soft and warm, and it sweats uniformly all over, and if with this sweating the touch of fever comes to an end. Among good signs are: sneezing, also a desire for food, whether maintained from the first, or even beginning after a distaste for food.

VALERIUS MAXIMUS (FL. A.D. 31)
Noteworthy Words and Deeds

After traveling with the proconsul Sextus Pompeius to Asia in A.D. 27, the philosopher-historian Valerius Maximus returned to Rome to compile, in the style of a rhetorical handbook, his trove of historical miscellany and moral anecdotes purportedly to illustrate human vice and virtue (though they hardly serve that end). Topics included omens, nationalism, cruelty, moderation, manners, gratitude, and chastity; sources range from Varro, Livy, Sallust, and Cicero, to the Greek writers. In this rambling and superficial *Memorabilia,* dedicated with great obsequiousness to Tiberius and written in exaggeration of Silver Age style, Valerius Maximus selected three women as paradigms of female virtue. Obviously, their choice is based primarily on the acts of loyalty to their husbands.

Tertia Aemilia, the wife of Scipio Africanus and the mother of Cornelia, was a woman of such kindness and patience that, although she knew that her husband was carrying on with a little serving girl, she looked the other way, [as she thought it unseemly for] a woman to prosecute her great husband, Africanus, a conqueror of the world, for a dalliance. So little was she interested in revenge that, after Scipio's death, she freed the girl and gave her in marriage to one of her own freedmen.

When Quintus Lucretius [Vespillo] was proscribed by the triumvirs, his wife Thuria hid him in her bedroom above the rafters. A single maidservant knew the secret. At great risk to herself, she kept him safe from imminent death.

So rare was her loyalty that, while the other men who had been proscribed found themselves in foreign, hostile places, barely managing to escape the worst tortures of body and soul, Lucretius was safe in that bedroom in the arms of his wife.

Sulpicia, despite the very close watch her mother Julia was keeping on her so that she would not follow her husband to Sicily (he was Lentulus Cruscellio, proscribed by the triumvirs), nevertheless put on slave's clothing and, taking two maids and the same number of manservants, fled secretly and went to him. She was not afraid to risk proscription herself, and her fidelity to her proscribed spouse was firm.

PLINY THE ELDER (GAIUS PLINIUS SECUNDUS)
(A.D. 23–79)
Natural History

*T*hough he wrote copiously on rhetoric, military maneuvers, biography, and history, the elder Pliny is remembered for his single surviving work: thirty-seven books on natural history. Born in Novum Comum (Como), he was educated in military matters at an early age and distinguished himself as a cavalry commander under Claudius; under Vespasian, as administrative governor in the German frontier; and under Titus as commander of the Roman fleet at Misenum (the Bay of Naples).

- Pliny's learning was encyclopedic, his scientific curiosity as insatiable as his industriousness was, apparently, unlimited. The prototype of the culturally accomplished civil servant, whose hobby was research and writing, Pliny died of asphyxiation exploring the recently erupted Vesuvius.

- Pliny's plain style *Natural History,* dedicated to Titus and first published in A.D. 77, comprises 20,000 noteworthy facts about "the nature of things, that is, life," compiled from 474 previous Roman and non-Roman sources—from Aristotle to folklore and oral tradition. His list of "authors consulted" includes dozens of names that would be otherwise unknown to us. A scientific miscellany, superficial rather than analytical, it nonetheless offers unique insight into Roman knowledge of natural phenomena including:

  - cosmology and astronomy;
  - physical and historical geography;
  - ethnography;
  - physiology;
  - zoology of animals, fish, birds, and insects;
  - botany of trees, plants, flowers, and herbs with pharmacological properties;
  - pharmacological properties of certain animals and fish;
  - metallurgy and geology; and
  - the use of minerals in painting, sculpture, engraving of gems, and medicine.

- Our knowledge of Roman gardens, of plant species introduced to Italy from abroad, of crop rotation methods, and farm management and harvesting methods owes much to Pliny's reports.
- His influence extended to the Renaissance, where his indiscriminate observations were as much based on wonder as upon accuracy. Pliny's principle of compilation seems to have been: When in doubt, include it. Yet Pliny's comprehensiveness and storyteller's love for his material, like that of the Greek Herodotus, provides us with invaluable insight and perspective into the merits and defects of Roman scientific knowledge and methodology.

BOOK II
AN ACCOUNT OF THE WORLD AND THE ELEMENTS

Chap. 1. (1.)—Whether the World Be Finite, and Whether There Be More Than One World

The world, and whatever that be which we otherwise call the heavens, by the vault of which all things are enclosed, we must conceive to be a Deity, to be eternal, without bounds, neither created, nor subject, at any time, to destruction. To inquire what is beyond it is no concern of man, nor can the human mind form any conjecture respecting it. It is sacred, eternal, and without bounds, all in all; indeed including everything in itself; finite, yet like what is infinite; the most certain of all things, yet like what is uncertain, externally and internally embracing all things in itself; it is the work of nature, and itself constitutes nature.

It is madness to harass the mind, as some have done, with attempts to measure the world, and to publish these attempts; or, like others, to argue from what they have made out, that there are innumerable other worlds, and that we must believe there to be so many other natures, or that, if only one nature produced the whole, there will be so many suns and so many moons, and that each of them will have immense trains of other heavenly bodies. As if the same question would not recur at every step of our inquiry, anxious as we must be to arrive at some termination; or, as if this infinity, which we ascribe to nature, the former of all things, cannot be more easily comprehended by one single formation, especially when that is so extensive. It is madness, perfect madness, to go out of this world and to search for what is beyond it, as if one who is ignorant of his own dimensions could ascertain the measure of any thing else, or as if the human mind could see what the world itself cannot contain.

Chap. 2. (2.)—Of the Form of the World

That it has the form of a perfect globe we learn from the name which has been uniformly given to it, as well as from numerous natural arguments. For not only does a figure of this kind return everywhere into itself and sustain itself, also including itself, requiring no adjustments, not sensible of either end or beginning in any of its parts, and is best fitted for that motion, with which, as will appear hereafter, it is continually

The Grand Fountain, Pompeii

turning round; but still more, because we perceive it, by the evidence of the sight, to be, in every part, convex and central, which could not be the case were it of any other figure.

Chap. 3. (3.)—Of Its Nature; Whence the Name Is Derived

The rising and the setting of the sun clearly prove, that this globe is carried round in the space of twenty-four hours, in an eternal and never-ceasing circuit, and with incredible swiftness. I am not able to say, whether the sound caused by the whirling about of so great a mass be excessive, and, therefore, far beyond what our ears can perceive, nor, indeed, whether the resounding of so many stars, all carried along at the same time and revolving in their orbits, may not produce a kind of delightful harmony of incredible sweetness. To us, who are in the interior, the world appears to glide silently along, both by day and by night.

Various circumstances in nature prove to us, that there are impressed on the heavens innumerable figures of animals and of all kinds of objects, and that its surface is not perfectly polished like the eggs of birds, as some celebrated authors assert. For we find that the seeds of all bodies fall down from it, principally into the ocean, and, being mixed together, that a variety of monstrous forms are in this way frequently produced. And, indeed, this is evident to the eye; for, in one part, we have the figure of a wain, in another of a bear, of a bull, and of a letter; while, in the middle of them, over our heads, there is a white circle.

(4.) With respect to the name, I am influenced by the unanimous opinions of all nations. For what the Greeks, from its being ornamented, have termed κόσμος, we, from its perfect and complete elegance, have termed *mundus*. The name *cœlum*, no doubt, refers to its being engraven, as it were, with the stars, as Varro suggests. In confirmation of this idea we may adduce the Zodiac, in which are twelve figures of animals; through them it is that the sun has continued its course for so many ages.

Chap. 4. (5.)—Of the Elements and the Planets

I do not find that any one has doubted that there are four elements. The highest of these is supposed to be fire, and hence proceed the eyes of so many glittering stars. The next is that spirit, which both the Greeks and ourselves call by the same name, air. It is by the force of this vital principle, pervading all things and mingling with all, that the earth, together with the fourth element, water, is balanced in the middle of space. These are mutually bound together, the lighter being restrained by the heavier, so that they cannot fly off; while, on the contrary, from the lighter tending upward, the heavier are so suspended, that they cannot fall down. Thus, by an equal tendency in an opposite direction, each of them remains in its appropriate place, bound together by the never-ceasing revolution of the world, which always turning on itself, the earth falls to the lowest part and is in the middle of the whole, while it remains suspended in the center, and, as it were, balancing this center, in which it is suspended. So that it alone remains immoveable, whilst all things revolve round it, being connected with every other part, whilst they all rest upon it.

(6.) Between this body and the heavens there are suspended, in this aërial spirit, seven stars, separated by determinate spaces, which, on account of their motion, we call wandering, although, in reality, none are less so. The sun is carried along in the midst of these, a body of great size and power, the ruler, not only of the seasons and of the different climates, but also of the stars themselves and of the heavens. When we consider his operations, we must regard him as the life, or rather the mind of the universe, the chief regulator and the God of nature; he also lends his light to the other stars. He is most illustrious and excellent, beholding all things and hearing all things, which, I perceive, is ascribed to him exclusively by the prince of poets, Homer.

Chap. 5. (7.)—Of God

I consider it, therefore, an indication of human weakness to inquire into the figure and form of God. For whatever God be, if there be any other God, and wherever he exists, he is all sense, all sight, all hearing, all life, all mind, and all within himself. To believe that there are a number of Gods, derived from the virtues and vices of man, as Chastity, Concord, Understanding, Hope, Honor, Clemency, and Fidelity; or, according to the opinion of Democritius, that there are only two, Punishment and Reward, indicates still greater folly. Human nature, weak and frail as it is, mindful of its own infirmity, has made these divisions, so that every one might have recourse to that which he supposed himself to stand more particularly in need of. Hence we find different names employed by different nations; the inferior deities are arranged in classes, and diseases and plagues are deitied, in consequence of our anxious wish to propitiate them. It was from this cause that a temple was dedicated to Fever, at the public expense, on the Palatine Hill, and to Orbona, near the Temple of the Lares, and that an altar was elected to Good Fortune on the Esquiline. Hence we may understand how it comes to pass that there is a greater population of the Celestials than of human beings, since each individual makes a separate God for himself, adopting his own Juno and his own Genius. And there are nations who make Gods of certain animals, and even certain obscene things, which are not to be spoken of, swearing by stinking meats and such like. To suppose that marriages are contracted between the Gods, and that, during so long a period, there should have been no issue from them, that some of them should be old and always gray-headed and others young and like children, some of a dark complexion, winged, lame, produced from eggs, living and dying on alternate days, is sufficiently puerile and foolish. But it is the height of impudence to imagine, that adultery takes place between them, that they have contests and quarrels, and that there are Gods of theft and of various crimes. To assist man is to be a God; this is the path to eternal glory. This is the path which the Roman nobles formerly pursued, and this is the path which is now pursued by the greatest ruler of our age, Vespasian Augustus, he who has come to the relief of an exhausted empire, as well as by his sons. This was the ancient mode of remunerating those who deserved it, to regard them as Gods. For the names of all the Gods, as well as of the stars that I have mentioned above, have been derived from their services to mankind. And with respect to Jupiter and Mercury, and the rest of the celestial nomenclature, who does not admit that they have reference to certain natural phenomena?

But it is ridiculous to suppose, that the great head of all things, whatever it be, pays any regard to human affairs. Can we believe, or rather can there be any doubt, that it is not polluted by such a disagreeable and complicated office? It is not easy to determine which opinion would be most for the advantage of mankind, since we observe some who have no respect for the Gods, and others who carry it to a scandalous excess. They are slaves to foreign ceremonies; they carry on their fingers the Gods and the monsters whom they worship; they condemn and they lay great stress on certain kinds of food; they impose on themselves dreadful ordinances, not even sleeping quietly. They do not marry or adopt children, or indeed do anything else, without the sanction of their sacred rites. There are others, on the contrary, who will cheat in the very Capitol, and will forswear themselves even by Jupiter Tonans, and while these thrive in their crimes, the others torment themselves with their superstitions to no purpose.

Among these discordant opinions mankind have discovered for themselves a kind of intermediate deity, by which our scepticism concerning God is still increased. For all over the world, in all places, and at all times, Fortune is the only god whom every one invokes; she alone is spoken of, she alone is accused and is supposed to be guilty; she alone is in our thoughts, is praised and blamed, and is loaded with reproaches; wavering as she is, conceived by the generality of mankind to be blind, wandering, inconstant, uncertain, variable, and often favoring the unworthy. To her are referred all our losses and all our gains, and in casting up the accounts of mortals she alone balances the two pages of our sheet. We are so much in the power of chance, that change itself is considered as a God, and the existence of God becomes doubtful.

But there are others who reject this principle and assign events to the influence of the stars, and to the laws of our nativity; they suppose that God, once for all, issues his decrees and never afterward interferes. This opinion begins to gain ground, and both the learned and the unlearned vulgar are falling into it. Hence we have the admonitions of thunder, the warnings of oracles, the predictions of soothsayers, and things too trifling to be mentioned, as sneezing and stumbling with the feet reckoned among omens. The late emperor Augustus relates, that he put the left shoe on the wrong foot, the day when he was near being assaulted by his soldiers. And such things as these so embarrass improvident mortals, that among all of them this alone is certain, that there is nothing certain, and that there is nothing more proud or more wretched than man. For other animals have no care but to provide for their subsistence, for which the spontaneous kindness of nature is all-sufficient; and this one circumstance renders their lot more especially preferable, that they never think about glory, or money, or ambition, and, above all, that they never reflect on death.

The belief, however, that on these points the Gods superintend human affairs is useful to us, as well as that the punishment of crimes, although sometimes tardy, from the Deity being occupied with such a mass of business, is never entirely remitted, and that the human race was not made the next in rank to himself, in order that they might be degraded like brutes. And indeed this constitutes the great comfort in this imperfect state of man, that even the Deity cannot do everything. For he cannot procure death for himself, even if he wished it, which, so numerous are the evils of life, has been granted to man as our chief good. Nor can he make mortals immortal, or recall to life those who are dead; nor can he effect, that he who has once lived shall not have lived, or that he who has enjoyed honors shall not have enjoyed them; nor has he any influence over past events but to cause them to be forgotten. And, if we illustrate the nature of our connection with God by a less serious argument, he cannot make twice ten not to be twenty, and many other things of this kind. By these considerations the power of Nature is clearly proved, and is shown to be what we call God. It is not foreign to the subject to have digressed into these matters, familiar as they are to every one, from the continual discussions that take place respecting God.

Chap. 6. (8.)—Of the Nature of the Stars; of the Motion of the Planets

Let us return from this digression to the other parts of nature. The stars which are described as fixed in the heavens, are not, as the vulgar suppose, attached each of them to different individuals, the brighter to the rich, those that are less so to the poor, and the dim to the aged, shining according to the lot of the individual, and separately assigned to mortals; for they have neither come into existence, nor do they perish in connection with particular persons, nor does a falling star indicate that any one is dead. We are not so closely connected with the heavens as that the shining of the stars is affected by our death. When they are supposed to shoot or fall, they throw out, by the force of their fire, as if from an excess of nutriment, the superabundance of the humor which they have absorbed, as we observe to take place from the oil in our lamps, when they are burning. The nature of the celestial bodies is eternal, being interwoven, as it were, with the world, and, by this union, rendering it solid; but they exert their most powerful influence on the earth. This, notwithstanding its subtilty, may be known by the clearness and the magnitude of the effect, as we shall point out in the proper place. The account of the circles of the heavens will be better understood when we come to speak of the earth, since they have all a reference to it; except what has been discovered respecting the Zodiac, which I shall now detail.

Anaximander the Milesian, in the 58th olympiad, is said to have been the first who understood its obliquity, and thus opened the road to a correct knowledge of the subject. Afterward Cleostratus made the signs in it, first marking those of Aries and Sagittarius; Atlas had formed the sphere long before this time. But now, leaving the further consideration of this subject, we must treat of the bodies that are situated between the earth and the heavens.

It is certain that the star called Saturn is the highest, and therefore appears the smallest, that he passes through the largest circuit, and that he is at least thirty years in completing it. The course of all the planets, and among others of the Sun, and the Moon, is in the contrary direction to that of the heavens, that is toward the left, while the heavens are rapidly carried about to the right. And although, by the stars constantly revolving with immense velocity, they are raised up, and hurried on to the part where they set, yet they are all forced, by a motion of their own, in an opposite direction; and this is so ordered, lest the air, being always moved in the same direction, by the constant whirling of the heavens, should accumulate into one mass, whereas now it is divided and separated and beaten into small pieces, by the opposite motion of the different stars. Saturn is a star of a cold and rigid nature, while the orbit of Jupiter is much lower, and is carried round in twelve years. The next star, Mars, which some persons call Hercules, is of a fiery and burning nature, and from its nearness to the sun is carried round in little less than two years. In consequence of the excessive heat of this star and the rigidity of Saturn, Jupiter, which is interposed between the two, is tempered by both of them, and is thus rendered salutary. The path of the Sun consists of 360 degrees; but, in order that the shadow may return to the same point of the dial, we are obliged to add, in each year, five days and the fourth part of a day. On this account an intercalary day is given to every fifth year, that the period of the seasons may agree with that of the Sun.

Below the Sun revolves the great star called Venus, wandering with an alternate motion, and, even in its surnames, rivaling the Sun and the Moon. For when it precedes the day and rises in the morning, it receives the name of Lucifer, as if it were another sun, hastening on the day. On the contrary, when it shines in the west, it is named Vesper, as prolonging the light, and performing the office of the moon. Pythagoras, the Samian, was the first who discovered its nature, about the 62nd olympiad, in the 222nd year of the City. It excels all the other stars in size, and its brilliancy is so considerable, that it is the only star which produces a shadow by its rays. There has, consequently, been great interest made for its name; some have called it the star of Juno, others of Isis, and others of the Mother of the Gods. By its influence everything in the earth is generated. For, as it rises in either direction, it sprinkles everything with its genial dew, and not only matures the productions of the earth, but stimulates all living things. It completes the circuit of the zodiac in 348 days, never receding from the sun more than 46 degrees, according to Timæus.

Similarly circumstanced, but by no means equal in size and in power, next to it, is the star Mercury, by some called Apollo; it is carried in a lower orbit, and moves in a course which is quicker by nine days, shining sometimes before the rising of the sun, and at other times after its setting, but never going farther from it than 23 degrees, as we learn from Timæus and Sosigenes. The nature of these two stars is peculiar, and is not the same with those mentioned above, for those are seen to recede from the sun through one-third or one-fourth part of the heavens, and are often seen opposite to it. They have also other larger circuits, in which they make their complete revolutions, as will be described in the account of the great year.

(9.) But the Moon, which is the last of the stars, and the one the most connected with the earth, the remedy provided by nature for darkness, excels all the others in its admirable qualities. By the variety of appearances which it assumes, it puzzles the observers, mortified that they should be the most ignorant concerning that star which is the nearest to them. She is always either waxing or waning; sometimes her disc is curved into horns, sometimes it is divided into two equal portions, and at other times it is swelled out into a full orb; sometimes she appears spotted and suddenly becomes very bright; she appears very large with her full orb and suddenly becomes invisible; now continuing during all the night, now rising late, and now aiding the light of the sun during a part of the day; becoming eclipsed and yet being visible while she is eclipsed; concealing herself at the end of the month and yet not supposed to be eclipsed. Sometimes she is low down, sometimes she is high up, and that not according to one uniform course, being at one time raised up to the heavens, at other times almost contiguous to the mountains; now elevated in the north, now depressed in the south; all which circumstances having been noticed by Endymion, a report was spread about, that he was in love with the moon. We are not indeed sufficiently grateful to those, who, with so much labor and care, have enlightened us with this light; while, so diseased is the human mind, that we take pleasure in writing the annals of blood and slaughter, in order that the crimes of men may be made known to those who are ignorant of the constitution of the world itself.

Being nearest to the axis, and therefore having the smallest orbit, the Moon passes in twenty-seven days and the one-third part of a day, through the same space for which Saturn, the highest of the planets, as was stated above, requires thirty years. After remaining for two days in conjunction with the sun, on the thirtieth day she again very slowly emerges to pursue her accustomed course. I know not whether she ought not to be considered as our instructress in everything that can be known respecting the heavens; as that the year is divided into the twelve divisions of the months, since she follows the sun for the same number of times, until he returns to the commencement of his course; and that her brightness, as well as that of the other stars, is regulated by that of the sun, if indeed they all of them shine by light borrowed from him, such as we see floating about, when it is reflected from the surface of water. On this account it is that she dissolves so much moisture, by a gentle and less perfect force, and adds to the quantity of that which the rays of the sun consume. On this account she appears with an unequal light, because being full only when she is in opposition, on all the remaining days she shows only so much of herself to the earth as she receives light from the sun. She is not seen in conjunction, because, at that time, she sends back the whole stream of light to the source whence she has derived it. That the stars generally are nourished by the terrestrial moisture is evident, because, when the moon is only half visible she is sometimes seen spotted, her power of absorbing moisture not having been powerful enough; for the spots are nothing else than the dregs of the earth drawn up along with the moisture. (10.) But her eclipses and those of the sun, the most wonderful of all the phenomena of nature, and which are like prodigies, serve to indicate the magnitude of these bodies and the shadow which they cast.

Chap. 7.—Of the Eclipses of the Moon and the Sun

For it is evident that the sun is hid by the intervention of the moon, and the moon by the opposition of the earth, and that these changes are mutual, the moon, by her interposition, taking the rays of the sun from the earth, and the earth from the moon. As she advances darkness is suddenly produced, and again the sun is obscured by her shade; for night is nothing more than the shade of the earth. The figure of this shade is like that of a pyramid or an inverted top; and the moon enters it only near its point, and it does not exceed the height of the moon, for there is no other star which is obscured in the same manner, while a figure of this kind always terminates in a point. The flight of birds, when very lofty, shows that shadows do not extend beyond a certain distance; their limit appears to be the termination of the air and the commencement of the ether. Above the moon everything is pure and full of an eternal light. The stars are visible to us in the night, in the same way that other luminous bodies are seen in the dark. It is from these causes that the moon is eclipsed during the night. The two kinds of eclipses are not, however, at the stated monthly periods, on account of the obliquity of the zodiac, and the irregularly wandering course of the moon, as stated above; besides that the motions of these stars do not always occur exactly at the same points. . . .

SILIUS ITALICUS (TIBERIUS CATIUS ASCONIUS SILIUS ITALICUS) (A.D. 26–101)

Punica

~❯

*T*he author of the longest Latin poem, the *Punica,* Silius, probably born in Patavium (Padua), distinguished himself as a plaintiff's litigator in the Roman courts before serving as consul in A.D. 68 when Nero died, supporting Vitellius in the civil war. He overcame the shame of having been an informer for Nero by distinguished service as administrator of Asia in A.D. 77. A noted Stoic, friend of Epictetus, Cornutus, Pliny the Younger, and Martial, Silius was also a patron of the arts, bibliophile, and art collector. He divided his high-society retirement between Rome and a country house in Tusculum, which he bought from Cicero, where he worked on his poetry. He starved himself to death in true Stoic fashion when he learned that his illness was terminal.

The *Punica,* a seventeen-book, 12,200-verse historical epic based on the Second Punic War from Hannibal's oath to Scipio's ultimate victory, is inspired by Virgil—whom Silius held in such reverence that he refurbished his great predecessor's tomb in Neapolis (Naples). He also followed Homer, Lucan, Livy, Varro, Posidonius, and Hyginus. The poem, written "with more diligence than talent" according to Pliny, has been criticized for its excessive epithets and catalogs, overuse of rhetoric, unpoetic language, and gruesomely vivid battle accounts; it is nonetheless distinguished for the vigor of its verse, clear and lifelike similes, and straightforward description. Though Scipio is the designated hero of the epic, Hannibal is more sympathetic.

BOOK I

Here I begin the war by which the fame of the Aeneadae was raised to heaven and proud Carthage submitted to the rule of Italy. Grant me, O Muse, to record the splendid achievements of Italy in ancient days, and to tell of all those heroes whom Rome brought forth for the strife, when the people of Cadmus broke their solemn bond and began the contest for sovereignty; and for long it remained uncertain, on which of the two citadels Fortune would establish the capital of the world. Thrice over with unholy warfare did the Carthaginian leaders violate their compact with the Senate and the treaty they had sworn by Jupiter to observe; and thrice over the lawless sword induced them wantonly to break the peace they had approved. But in the second war each nation strove to destroy and exterminate her rival, and those to whom victory was granted came nearer to destruction: in it a Roman general stormed the citadel of Carthage, the Palatine was surrounded and besieged by Hannibal, and Rome made good her safety by her walls alone.

The causes of such fierce anger, the hatred maintained with unabated fury, the war bequeathed by sire to son and by son to grandson—these things I am permitted to reveal, and to disclose the purposes of Heaven. And now I shall begin by tracing the origin of this great upheaval.

When Dido long ago fled across the sea from the land of Pygmalion, leaving behind her the realm polluted by her brother's guilt, she landed on the destined shore of Libya. There she bought land for a price and founded a new city, where she was permitted to lay strips of a bull's hide round the strand. Here—so remote antiquity believed—Juno elected to found for the exiles a nation to last for ever, preferring it to Argos, and to Mycenae, the city of Agamemnon and her chosen dwelling-place. But when she saw Rome lifting her head high among aspiring cities, and even sending fleets across the sea to carry her victorious standards over all the earth, then the goddess felt the danger close and stirred up in the minds of the Phoenicians a frenzy for war. But the effort of

Gladiators' corridor, amphitheater at Italica, Spain

together with his household gods—deities that were twice taken prisoners; and he gained a victory and founded a kingdom for the Teucrians at Lavinium. That may pass—provided that the banks of the Ticinus cannot contain the Roman dead, and that the Trebia, obedient to me, shall flow backward through the fields of Gaul, blocked by the blood of Romans and their weapons and the corpses of men; provided that Lake Trasimene shall be terrified by its own pools darkened with streams of gore, and that I shall see from heaven Cannae, the grave of Italy, and the Iapygian plain inundated with Roman blood, while the Aufidus, doubtful of its course as its banks close in, can hardly force a passage to the Adriatic shore through shields and helmets and severed limbs of men." With these words she fired the youthful warrior for deeds of battle.

By nature he was eager for action and faithless to his plighted word, a past master in cunning but a strayer from justice. Once armed, he had no respect for Heaven; he was brave for evil and despised the glory of peace; and a thirst for human blood burned in his inmost heart. Besides all this, his youthful vigor longed to blot out the Aegates, the shame of the last generation, and to drown the treaty of peace in the Sicilian sea. Juno inspired him and tormented his spirit with ambition. Already, in visions of the night, he either stormed the Capitol or marched at speed over the summits of the Alps. Often too the servants who slept at his door were roused and terrified by a fierce cry that broke the desolate silence, and found their master dripping with sweat, while he fought battles still to come and waged imaginary warfare.

their first campaign was crushed, and the enterprise of the Carthaginians was wrecked on the Sicilian sea; and then Juno took up the sword again for a fresh conflict. When she upset all things on earth and was preparing to stir up the sea, she found a sufficient instrument in a single leader.

Now warlike Hannibal clothed himself with all the wrath of the goddess; his single arm she dared to match against destiny. Then, rejoicing in that man of blood, and aware of the fierce storm of disasters in store for the realm of Latinus, she spoke thus: "In defiance of me, the exile from Troy brought Dardania to Latium,

When he was a mere child, his father's passion had kindled in Hannibal this frenzy against Italy and the realm of Saturn, and started him on his glorious career. Hamilcar, sprung from the Tyrian house of ancient Barcas, reckoned his long descent from Belus. For, when Dido lost her husband and fled from a Tyre reduced to slavery, the young scion of Belus had escaped the unrighteous sword of the dread tyrant, and had joined his fortunes with hers for weal or woe. Thus nobly born and a proved warrior, Hamilcar, as soon as Hannibal could speak and utter his first distinct words, sowed war with Rome in the boy's heart; and well he knew how to feed angry passions.

In the center of Carthage stood a temple, sacred to the spirit of Elissa, the foundress, and regarded with hereditary awe by the people. Round it stood yew-trees and pines with their melancholy shade, which hid it and kept away the light of heaven. Here, as it was reported, the queen had cast off long ago the ills that flesh is heir to. Statues of mournful marble stood there—Belus, the founder of the race, and all the line descended from Belus; Agenor also, the nation's boast, and Phoenix who gave a lasting name to his country. There Dido herself was seated, at last united for ever to Sychaeus; and at her feet lay the Trojan sword. A hundred altars stood here in order, sacred to the gods of heaven and the lord of Erebus. Here the priestess with streaming hair and Stygian garb calls up Acheron and the divinity of Henna's goddess. The earth rumbles in the gloom and breaks forth into awesome hissings; and fire blazes unkindled upon the altars. The dead also are called up by magic spells and flit through empty space; and the marble face of Elissa sweats. To this shrine Hannibal was brought by his father's command; and, when he had entered, Hamilcar examined the boy's face and bearing. No terrors for him had the Massylian priestess, raving in her frenzy, or the horrid rites of the temple, the blood-bespattered doors, and the flames that mounted at the sound of incantation. His father stroked the boy's head and kissed him; then he raised his courage by exhortation and thus inspired him:

"The restored race of Phrygians is oppressing with unjust treaties the people of Cadmean stock. If fate does not permit my right hand to avert this dishonor from our land, you, my son, must choose this as your field of fame. Be quick to swear a war that shall bring destruction to the Laurentines; let the Tuscan people already dread your birth; and when you, my son, arise, let Latian mothers refuse to rear their offspring."

With these incentives he spurred on the boy and then dictated a vow not easy to utter: "When I come to age, I shall pursue the Romans with fire and sword and enact again the doom of Troy. The gods shall not stop my career, nor the treaty that bars the sword, neither the lofty Alps nor the Tarpeian rock. I swear to this purpose by the divinity of our native god of war, and by the shade of Elissa." Then a black victim was sacrificed to the goddess of triple shape; and the priestess, seeking an oracle, quickly opened the still breathing body and questioned the spirit, as it fled from the inward parts that she had laid bare in haste.

But when, following the custom of her ancient art, she had entered into the mind of the gods whom she inquired of, thus she spoke aloud: "I see the Aetolian fields covered far and wide with soldiers' corpses, and lakes red with Trojan blood. How huge the rampart of cliffs that rises far toward heaven! And on its airy summit your camp is perched. Now the army rushes down from the mountains; terrified cities send up smoke, and the land that lies beneath the western heavens blazes with Punic fires. See! the river Po runs blood. Fierce is that face that lies on a heap of arms and men—the face of him who was the third to carry in triumph choice spoils to the Thunder-god. Ah! what wild storm is this that rages with sudden downpour, while the sky is rent asunder and the fiery ether flashes! The gods are preparing mighty things, the throne of high heaven thunders, and I see Jupiter in arms." Then Juno forbade her to learn more of coming events, and the victims suddenly became dumb. The dangers and the endless hardships were concealed.

So Hamilcar left his design of war concealed in his secret heart, and made for Calpe and Gades, the limit of the world; but, while carrying the standards of Africa to the Pillars of Hercules, he fell in a hard-fought battle.

Meanwhile the direction of affairs was handed over to Hasdrubal; and he harried with savage cruelty the wealth of the western world, the people of Spain, and the dwellers beside the Baetis. Hard was the general's heart, and nothing could mitigate his ferocious temper; power he valued because it gave him the opportunity to be cruel. Thirst for blood hardened his heart; and he had the folly to believe that to be feared is glory. Nor was he willing to sate his rage with ordinary punishments.

Tagus, a man of ancient race, remarkable for beauty and of proved valor, Hasdrubal, defying gods and men, fastened high on a wooden cross, and displayed in triumph to the sorrowing natives the unburied body of their king. Tagus, who had taken his name from the gold-bearing river, was mourned by the Nymphs of Spain through all their caves and banks; nor would he have preferred the river of Maeonia and the pools of Lydia, nor the plain watered by flowing gold and turned yellow by the sands of Hermus pouring over it. Ever first to enter the battle and last to lay down the sword, when he sat high on his steed and urged it on with loosened reins, no sword could stop him nor spear hurled from far; on he flew in triumph, and the golden armor of Tagus was well known throughout both armies. Then a servant, when he saw that hideous death and the body of Tagus hanging on the fatal tree, stole his master's favorite sword and rushed into the palace, where he smote that savage breast once and again. Carthaginians are cruel; and now, in their anger and grief, they made haste to bring the tortures. Every device was used—fire and white-hot steel, scourges that cut the body to ribbons with a rain of blows past counting, the hands of the torturers, the agony driven home into the marrow, the flame burning in the heart of the wound. Dreadful to see and even to relate, the limbs were expanded by the torturers' ingenuity and grew as much as the torment required; and, when all the blood had gushed forth, the bones still smoked and burned on, after the limbs were consumed. But the man's spirit remained unbroken; he was the master still and despised the suffering; like a mere

looker-on he blamed the myrmidons of the tor-
turer for flagging in their task and loudly
demanded to be crucified like his master.

While this piteous punishment was inflicted on a victim who made light of it, the soldiers, disturbed by the loss of their general,
with one voice and with eager enthusiasm
demanded Hannibal for their leader. Their
favor was due to many causes—the reflection
in him of his father's valor; the report, broad-
cast among the nations, that he was the sworn
enemy of Rome; his youth eager for action and
the fiery spirit that well became him; his heart
equipped with guile, and his native eloquence.

The Libyans were first to hail him with
applause as their leader, and the Pyrenean
tribes and warlike Spaniards followed them. At
once his heart swelled with pride and satisfaction that so much of land and sea had come
under his sway. Libya lies under the burning
sign of Cancer, and is parched by the south
winds of Aeolus and the sun's disk. It is either a
huge offshoot of Asia, or a third continent of the
world. It is bounded on the rosy east by the
river of Lagus, which strikes the swollen sea
with seven streams. But, where the land in
milder mood faces the opposing Bears, it is cut
off by the straits of Hercules, and, though
parted from them, looks on the lands of Europe
from its adjacent heights; the ocean blocks its
further extension, and Atlas forbids its name to
be carried further—Atlas, who would bring
down the sky, if he withdrew his shoulders. His
cloud-capt head supports the stars, and his
soaring neck for ever holds aloft the firmament
of heaven. His beard is white with frost, and
pine-forests crown his brow with their vast

shade; winds ravage his hollow temples, and
foaming rivers rush down from his streaming
open jaws. Moreover, the deep seas assail the
cliffs on both his flanks, and, when the weary
Titan has bathed his panting steeds, hide his
flaming car in the steaming ocean. But, where
Africa spreads her untilled plains, the burnt-up
land bears nothing but the poison of snakes in
plenty; though, where a temperate strip blesses
the fields, her fertility is not surpassed by the
crops of Henna nor by the Egyptian husbandman. Here, the Numidians rove at large, a
nation that knows not the bridle; for the light
switch they ply between its ears turns the horse
about in their sport, no less effectively than the
bit. This land breeds wars and warriors; nor do
they trust to the naked sword but use guile also.

A second camp was filled with Spanish
troops, European allies whom the victories of
Hamilcar had gained. Here the war-horse
filled the plains with his neighings, and here
high-mettled steeds drew along chariots of war;
not even the drivers at Olympia could dash
over the course with more fiery haste. That
people recks little of life, and they are most
ready to anticipate death. For, when a man has
passed the years of youthful strength, he cannot bear to live on and disdains acquaintance
with old age; and his span of life depends on
his own right arm. All metals are found here:
there are veins of electrum, whose yellow hue
shows their double origin, and the rugged soil
feeds the black crop of iron. Heaven covered
up the incentives to crime; but the covetous
Asturian plunges deep into the bowels of the
mangled earth, and the wretch returns with a
face as yellow as the gold he has dug out. The

Durius and the Tagus of this land challenge the Pactolus; and so does the river which rolls its glittering sands over the land of the Gravii and reproduces for the inhabitants the forgetfulness of Lethe in the nether world. Spain is not unfit for corn-crops nor unfriendly to the vine; and there is no land in which the tree of Pallas rises higher.

When these peoples had yielded to the Tyrian ruler and he had received the reins of government, then with his father's craft he gained men's friendship; by arms or by bribes he caused them to reverse the Senate's decrees. He was ever first to undertake hardship, first to march on foot, and first to bear a hand when the rampart was reared in haste. In all other things that spur a man on to glory he was untiring: denying sleep to nature, he would pass the whole night armed and awake, lying sometimes upon the ground; distinguished by the general's cloak, he vied with the hardy soldiers of the Libyan army; or mounted high he rode as leader of the long line; again he endured bare-headed the fury of the rains and the crashing of the sky. The Carthaginians looked on and the Asturians trembled for fear, when he rode his startled horse through the bolts hurled by Jupiter, the lightnings flashing amid the rain, and the fires driven forth by the blasts of the winds; he was never wearied by the dusty march nor weakened by the fiery star of Sirius. When the earth was burnt and cracked by fiery rays, and when the heat of noon parched the sky with its blazing orb, he thought it womanish to lie down in the shade where the ground was moist; he practiced thirst and looked on a spring only to leave it. He would grasp the reins also and break in for battle the steed that tried to throw him; he

sought the glory of a death-dealing arm; he would swim through the rattling boulders of an unknown river and then summon his comrades from the opposite bank. He was first also to stand on the rampart of a city stormed; and, whenever he dashed over the plain where fierce battle was joined, a broad red lane was left on the field, wherever he hurled his spear. Therefore he pressed hard upon the heels of Fortune; and, resolved as he was to break the treaty, he rejoiced meantime to involve Rome, as far as he could, in war; and from the end of the world he struck at the Capitol.

His war-trumpets sounded first before the gates of dismayed Saguntum, and he chose this war in his eagerness for a greater war to come. The city, founded by Hercules, rises on a gentle slope not far from the coast, and owes its sacred and famous name to Zacynthus, who is buried there on the lofty hill. For he was on the march back to Thebes in company with Hercules, after the slaying of Geryon, and was praising the exploit up to the skies. That monster was furnished with three lives and three right arms in a single body, and carried a head on each of three necks. Never did earth see another man whom a single death could not destroy—for whom the stern Sisters span a third lease of life when the thread had twice been snapped. Zacynthus displayed in triumph the prize taken from Geryon, and was calling the cattle to the water in the heat of noon, when a serpent that he trod on discharged from its swollen throat poison envenomed by the sun. The wound was fatal, and the Greek hero lay dead on Spanish soil. At a later time exiled colonists sailed hither before the wind—sons of Zacynthus, the island surrounded by the

Ionian sea that once formed part of the kingdom of Laertes. These small beginnings were afterward strengthened by men of Daunia in search of a habitation; they were sent forth by Ardea of famous name—a city ruled by heroic kings, and rich in the number of her sons. The freedom of the inhabitants and their ancestral glory were preserved by treaty; and by it the Carthaginians were forbidden to rule the city.

The Carthaginian leader broke the treaty and brought his camp-fires close and shook the wide plains with his marching host. He himself, shaking his head in fury, rode round the walls on his panting steed, taking the measure of the terrified buildings. He bade them open their gates at once and desert their rampart; he told them that, now they were besieged, their treaties and Italy would be far away, and that they could not hope for quarter, if defeated: "Decrees of the Senate," he cried, "law and justice, honor and Providence, are all in my hand now." In eager haste he confirmed his taunts by hurling his javelin and struck Caicus through his armor, as he stood on the wall and uttered idle threats. Pierced right through the middle, down he fell;

his body at once slipped down from the steep rampart; and in death he restored to his conqueror the spear warmed with his blood. Then with loud shouting the soldiers followed the example of their leader, and wrapped the walls round with a black cloud of missiles. Their prowess was seen and not hidden by their numbers; turning his face to the general, each man fought as if he were the only combatant. One hurled volleys of bullets with Balearic sling: standing erect, he brandished the light thong thrice round his head, and launched his missile in the air, for the winds to carry; another poised whizzing stones with strong arm; a third threw a lance speeded by a light strap. In front of them all their leader, conspicuous in his father's armor, now hurls a brand smoking with pitchy flame, now presses on unwearied with stake or javelin or stone, or shoots arrows from the string—missiles dipped in serpent's poison and doubly fatal—and exults in the guile of his quiver. So the Dacian, in the warlike region of the Getic country, delighting to sharpen his arrows with the poison of his native land, pours them forth in sudden showers on the banks of the Hister, the river of two names. . . .

QUINTILIAN (MARCUS FABIUS QUINTILIANUS)
(A.D. 35–100)
Education of an Orator

∼◗

The greatest Roman teacher of rhetoric, the son of an orator, was Spanish, born in Calagurris (modern Calahorra), but sent to Rome as a boy to study under the orators Domitius Afer, Remmius Palaemon, and Julius Africanus. The emperors Vespasian and Domitian acknowledged him as an outstanding teacher and legal advocate, and became the patrons of a public school of rhetoric that Quintilian opened. He was the first rhetorician to receive a salary and to become affluent from his teaching. Quintilian's students included Pliny the Younger, Juvenal, Martial, and the nephews of Domitian. For his skills he was awarded consular rank. When he retired from public teaching in A.D. 88, Quintilian collected his teaching in the *Institutio oratoria (Education of an Orator)* to assist him in teaching his own children and the sons of Flavius Clemens and Flavia Domitilla, heirs to the emperor Domitian. Unfortunately both Quintilian's sons died young, so Quintilian dedicated his completed work to his friend the orator Victorius Marcellus for the instruction of his son Geta.

- *Education,* in twelve books, heavily influenced by Cicero, covers the training of the ideal orator from infancy to adulthood, insisting that morality and good citizenship are the underlying foundations for great oratory. The orator must first of all be a good man. Quintilian's purpose was not to invent new principles but to choose among established ones for the most effective and most worthy. He believed that no education is complete until a man has shaped his rhetorical skills, just as he believed that theoretical knowledge without practical know-how is useless. *Education* was published shortly before the assassination of Domitian.
- None of Quintilian's speeches or other writings survive, though we know they included *On the Causes of Corrupted Eloquence* and his lecture notes, *Two Books on the Art of Rhetoric.* Quintilian's contribution to educational theory, rhetoric, and literary criticism made him important throughout the Middle Ages and Renaissance, influencing, among others, Desiderius Erasmus, Ben Jonson, and Juan Vives.
- He advises the teacher:

  ▲ to adapt his methods to the ability and personality of each student;
  ▲ to make learning enjoyable;

- ▲ to avoid corporal punishment and excessive severity; and
- ▲ to take a parent's responsibility (*in loco parentis*).

- Quintilian's vigorous, clear, unaffected, yet classical "Silver-aged Ciceronian" style conveys his wisdom and enthusiasm, his "optimistic cynicism," making it apparent that he was friend as well as teacher to those in his charge.

. . . For my part, I have undertaken the task of molding the ideal orator, and as my first desire is that he should be a good man, I will return to those who have sounder opinions on the subject. Some however identify rhetoric with politics, Cicero calls it a *department of the science of politics* (and science of politics and philosophy are identical terms), while others again call it a *branch of philosophy*, among them Isocrates. The definition which best suits its real character is that which makes rhetoric the *science of speaking well*. For this definition includes all the virtues of oratory and the character of the orator as well, since no man can speak well who is not good himself. The definition given by Chrysippus, who derived it from Cleanthes, to the effect that it is the *science of speaking rightly*, amounts to the same thing. The same philosopher also gives other definitions, but they concern problems of a different character from that on which we are now engaged. Another definition defines oratory as the power of *persuading men to do what ought to be done*, and yields practically the same sense save that it limits the art to the result which it produces. Areus again defines it well as *speaking according to the excellence of speech*. Those who regard it as the science of political obligations, also exclude men of bad character from the title of orator, if by science

they mean virtue, but restrict it overmuch by confining it to political problems. Albutius, a distinguished author and professor of rhetoric, agrees that rhetoric is the science of speaking well, but makes a mistake in imposing restrictions by the addition of the words *on political questions* and *with credibility*; with both of these restrictions I have already dealt. Finally those critics who hold that the aim of rhetoric is *to think and speak rightly*, were on the correct track.

These are practically all the most celebrated and most discussed definitions of rhetoric. It would be both irrelevant and beyond my power to deal with all. For I strongly disapprove of the custom which has come to prevail among writers of text-books of refusing to define anything in the same terms as have been employed by some previous writer. I will have nothing to do with such ostentation. What I say will not necessarily be my own invention, but it will be what I believe to be the right view, as for instance that oratory is the science of speaking well. For when the most satisfactory definition has been found, he who seeks another, is merely looking for a worse one.

Thus much being admitted we are now in a position to see clearly what is the end, the highest aim, the ultimate goal of rhetoric, that τέλος in fact which every art must possess. For if rhetoric is the science of speaking well, its end and highest aim is to speak well.

XVI. There follows the question as to whether rhetoric is useful. Some are in the habit of denouncing it most violently and of shamelessly employing the powers of oratory to accuse oratory itself. "It is eloquence," they say, "that snatches criminals from the penalties of the law, eloquence that from time to time secures the condemnation of the innocent and leads deliberation astray, eloquence that stirs up not merely sedition and popular tumult, but wars beyond all expiation, and that is most effective when it makes falsehood prevail over the truth." The comic poets even accuse Socrates of teaching how to make the worse cause seem the better, while Plato says that Gorgias and Tisias made similar professions. And to these they add further examples drawn from the history of Rome and Greece, enumerating all those who used their pernicious eloquence not merely against individuals but against whole states and threw an ordered commonwealth into a state of turmoil or even brought it to utter ruin; and they point out that for this very reason rhetoric was banished from Sparta, while its powers were cut down at Athens itself by the fact that an orator was forbidden to stir the passions of his audience. On the showing of these critics not only orators but generals, magistrates, medicine and philosophy itself will all be useless. For Flaminius was a general, while men such as the Gracchi, Saturninus and Glaucia were magistrates. Doctors have been caught using poisons, and those who falsely assume the name of philosopher have occasionally been detected in the gravest crimes. Let us give up eating, it often makes us ill; let us never go inside houses, for sometimes they collapse on their occupants; let never a sword be forged for a soldier, since it might be used by a robber. And who does not realize that fire and water, both necessities of life, and, to leave mere earthly things, even the sun and moon, the greatest of the heavenly bodies, are occasionally capable of doing harm.

On the other hand will it be denied that it was by his gift of speech that Appius the Blind broke off the dishonorable peace which was on the point of being concluded with Pyrrhus? Did not the divine eloquence of Cicero win popular applause even when he denounced the Agrarian laws, did it not crush the audacious plots of Catiline and win, while he still wore the garb of civil life, the highest honor that can be conferred on a victorious general, a public thanksgiving to heaven? Has not oratory often revived the courage of a panic-stricken army and persuaded the soldier faced by all the perils of war that glory is a fairer thing than life itself? Nor shall the history of Sparta and Athens move me more than that of the Roman people, who have always held the orator in highest honor. Never in my opinion would the founders of cities have induced their unsettled multitudes to form communities had they not moved them by the magic of their eloquence: never without the highest gifts of oratory would the great legislators have constrained mankind to submit themselves to the yoke of law. Nay, even the principles which should guide our life, however fair they may be by nature, yet have greater power to mold the mind to virtue, when the beauty of things is illumined by the splendor of eloquence. Wherefore, although the weapons of oratory may be used either for good or ill, it is unfair to regard that as an evil which can be employed for good.

These problems, however, may be left to those who hold that rhetoric is the power to persuade. If our definition of rhetoric as the science of speaking well implies that an orator must be a good man, there can be no doubt about its usefulness. And in truth that god, who was in the beginning, the father of all things and the architect of the universe, distinguished man from all other living creatures that are subject to death, by nothing more than this, that he gave him the gift of speech. For as regards physical bulk, strength, robustness, endurance or speed, man is surpassed in certain cases by dumb beasts, who also are far more independent of external assistance. They know by instinct without need of any teacher how to move rapidly, to feed themselves and swim. Many too have their bodies clothed against cold, possess natural weapons and have not to search for their food, whereas in all these respects man's life is full of toil. Reason then was the greatest gift of the Almighty, who willed that we should share its possession with the immortal gods. But reason by itself would help us but little and would be far less evident in us, had we not the power to express our thoughts in speech; for it is the lack of this power rather than thought and understanding, which they do to a certain extent possess, that is the great defect in other living things. The construction

of a soft lair, the weaving of nests, the hatching and rearing of their young, and even the storing up of food for the coming winter, together with certain other achievements which we cannot imitate, such as the making of honey and wax, all these perhaps indicate the possession of a certain degree of reason; but since the creatures that do these things lack the gift of speech they are called dumb and unreasoning beasts. Finally, how little the heavenly boon of reason avails those who are born dumb. If therefore we have received no fairer gift from heaven than speech, what shall we regard as so worthy of laborious cultivation, or in what should we sooner desire to excel our fellow-men, than that in which mankind excels all other living things? And we should be all the more eager to do so, since there is no art which yields a more grateful recompense for the labor bestowed upon it. This will be abundantly clear if we consider the origins of oratory and the progress it has made; and it is capable of advancing still further. I will not stop to point out how useful and how becoming a task it is for a good man to defend his friends, to guide the Senate by his counsels, and to lead peoples or armies to follow his bidding; I merely ask, is it not a noble thing, by employing the understanding which is common to mankind and the words that are used by all, to win such honor and glory that you seem not to speak or plead, but rather, as was said of Pericles, to thunder and lighten?

(FLAVIUS) JOSEPHUS (A.D. 38–C.100)

The Jewish War

~~⌐

*J*ewish historian Josephus was born Joseph Ben Matthias in Jerusalem, of a priestly family, and pre-cociously educated in Judaic law. In A.D. 64, he was sent on an embassy to Rome, where he was befriended by Poppaea Sabina, Nero's wife. The military strength of Rome was thoroughly impressed on him during his visit. When he returned to Judaea and joined the Pharisees, at first he tried to stop the Zealots' rebellion against the Empire. Then, at the request of the Sanhedrin, he reluctantly joined the revolt. Captured in Galilee, he was immediately given protection by the Roman commander Titus Flavius Vespasian because Josephus had predicted his accession as emperor. When Vespasian, after Nero's death, was proclaimed emperor by his troops and returned to Rome, Josephus went with him and eventually enjoyed his patronage and that of Titus and Domitian, receiving a teaching stipend and full Roman citizenship.

- His two most important works, the twenty-book *Jewish Antiquities* and the seven-book *The Jewish War,* were composed in Aramaic, then translated into Greek at Titus' request. Although he spent his literary career defending the Jews and their heritage, he had no use for nation-alistic extremists and favored the stability and religious tolerance he saw in Roman rule.
- His description of the siege of Jerusalem in A.D. 70, the destruction of the Temple and of the great city itself, is among the most vivid first-hand accounts we have of a Roman military operation. According to Josephus, who was present in the retinue of the conquering Titus, the Jews themselves were at fault for this destruction and Caesar showed almost superhuman restraint in his attempt to save the great temple from his rampaging soldiers. Josephus was loathed by the Jews as a turncoat and traitor.

CHAPTER 21
THE TEMPLE BURNT AND THE CITY TAKEN

By now two of the legions had completed their platforms, and on the 8th of Loös Titus ordered the Rams to be brought up opposite the western arcade of the Outer Temple. For six days before they arrived the most powerful Batterer of all had pounded the wall incessantly without result: this like the others made no impression on stones so huge and so perfectly bonded. At the northern gate a second team attempted to undermine the foundations, and by tremendous efforts they did lever out the stones in front; but the inner stones supported the weight and the gate stood firm, till despairing of all attempts with engines and crowbars they set up ladders against the colonnades. The Jews were in no hurry to stop them, but when they climbed up they were violently assailed; some were pushed backward and sent headlong, others clashed with the defenders and were killed; many as they stepped off the ladders were unable to get behind their shields before they were run through with swords, while a few ladders crowded with heavy infantry were pushed sideways at the top and overturned; the Jews too suffered severe losses. Those who had brought up the standards fought hard for them, knowing that it would be a terrible disgrace if they were captured; but in the end the Jews even captured the standards, destroying every man who climbed up. The rest, demoralized by the fate of the fallen, withdrew. On the Roman side not a man died till he had accomplished something; of the partisans all who had distinguished themselves in earlier battles shone once more in this, as did Eleazar, nephew of the party chief Simon. Titus, seeing that his attempts to spare a foreign temple meant injury and death to his soldiers, ordered the gates to be set on fire.

At this time two men deserted to him, Ananus from Emmaus, the most bloodthirsty of Simon's henchmen, and Archelaus son of Magadatus, expecting a free pardon as they were quitting the Jews when they were getting the better of it. Denouncing this as another of their dirty tricks and aware of their habitual cruelty to their own people, Titus was strongly inclined to kill them both, pointing out that they had been forced to it by necessity and had not come by free choice, and that men did not deserve to live if they first set their own city on fire and then jumped clear. However, anger could not stand against his own pledged word and he let the men go, though he did not grant them the same privileges as the others.

By now the soldiers were piling fire against the gates. The silver melted and ran, quickly exposing the woodwork to the flames, which were carried from there in a solid wall and fastened on to the colonnades. When the Jews saw the ring of fire they lost all power of body and mind; such was their consternation that not a finger was raised to keep out or quench the flames; they stood looking on in utter helplessness. Yet their dismay at the present destruction made them no wiser for the future, but as if the Sanctuary itself was already in flames they whipped up their rage against the Romans. All that day and the following night the flames were in possession: the colonnades could not be fired all at once but only bit by bit.

The next day Titus ordered a section of his army to put out the fire, and to make a road close to the gates for the easier ascent of the legions. Then he summoned a council of war, attended by the six senior generals—Tiberius Alexander, the chief of staff; Sextus Cerealius, Larcius Lepidus, and Titus Phrygius, commanding the Fifth, Tenth, and Fifteenth Legions respectively; Aeternius Fronto, tribune in charge of the two legions from Alexandria; and Marcus Antonius Julianus, procurator of Judaea. After these the other procurators and tribunes were brought in, and Titus invited opinions on the question of the Sanctuary. Some insisted that they should enforce the law of war, there would be continual revolts while the Temple remained as a rallying-point for Jews all over the world. Others argued that if the Jews evacuated it and no armed man was allowed on it, it should be spared, but if they climbed on it for military purposes it should be burnt down. It would in that case be a fortress, not a sanctuary, and from then on the impiety would be blameable not on the Romans but on those who forced their hands. Titus replied that even if the Jews did climb on it for military purposes he would not make war on inanimate objects instead of men, or whatever happened burn down such a work of art: it was the Romans who would lose thereby, just as their Empire would gain an ornament if it was preserved. Fronto, Alexander, and Cerealius now confidently came over to this opinion. Titus thereupon adjourned the meeting, and instructing the officers to give the remainder of the army time for rest, so that he should find them full of new vigor when fighting was resumed, he ordered the picked men of all the cohorts to make a road through the ruins and put out the fire.

All that day exhaustion and consternation subdued the enterprise of the Jews; but on the next, having recovered both strength and confidence, they made a sortie through the East Gate against the garrison of the Outer Temple at about 8 A.M. Their onslaught met with stubborn resistance from the Romans, who sheltered behind a wall of steel and closed their ranks, though it was obvious that they could not hold together long as the raiding party surpassed them in numbers and determination. Anticipating the collapse of the line, Caesar, who was watching from Antonia, came to the rescue with his picked horsemen. The Jews broke before their onset, and when the front-rank men fell the rest withdrew. But whenever the Romans gave ground they whipped round and pressed them hard: when the Romans turned about they retreated again, till at about eleven o'clock they were overpowered and shut up in the Inner Temple.

Titus retired to Antonia, intending at stand-to next day to launch a full-scale attack and surround the Sanctuary completely. It had however been condemned to the flames by God long ago: by the turning of time's wheel the fated day had now come, the 10th of Loös, the day which centuries before had seen it burnt by the king of Babylon. But it was the Jews themselves who caused and started this conflagration. When Titus had retired the partisans remained quiet for a time, then again attacked the Romans, the garrison of the Sanctuary clashing with those who were putting out the fire in the Inner Temple, and who routed the Jews and chased them as far as the Sanctuary. Then one of the soldiers, without waiting for orders and without a qualm for the terrible consequences of his action but urged on by some unseen force, snatched up a blazing piece of wood and climbing on another soldier's back hurled the brand through a golden aperture giving access on the north side to the chambers built round the Sanctuary. As the flames shot into the air the Jews sent up a cry that matched the calamity and dashed to the rescue, with no thought now of saving their lives or husbanding their strength; for that which hitherto they had guarded so devotedly was disappearing before their eyes.

A runner brought the news to Titus as he was resting in his tent after the battle. He leapt up as he was and ran to the Sanctuary to extinguish the blaze. His whole staff panted after him, followed by the excited legions with all the shouting and confusion inseparable from the disorganized rush of an immense army. Caesar shouted and waved to the combatants to put out the fire; but his shouts were unheard as their ears were deafened with a greater din, and his hand-signals went unheeded amid the distractions of battle and bloodshed. As the legions charged in, neither persuasion nor threat could check their impetuosity: passion alone was in command. Crowded together round the entrances many were trampled by their friends, many fell among the still hot and smoking ruins of the colonnades and died as miserably as the defeated. As they neared the Sanctuary they pretended not even to hear Caesar's commands and urged the men in front to throw in more firebrands. The partisans were no longer in a position to help; everywhere was slaughter and flight. Most of the victims were peaceful citizens, weak, and unarmed, butchered wherever they were caught. Round the Altar the heap of corpses grew higher and higher, while down the Sanctuary steps poured a river of blood and the bodies of those killed at the top slithered to the bottom. The soldiers were like men possessed and there was no holding them, nor was there any arguing with the fire. Caesar therefore led his staff inside the building and viewed the Holy Place of the Sanctuary with its furnishings, which went far beyond the accounts circulating in foreign countries, and fully justified their splendid reputation in our own. The flames were not yet effecting an entry from any direction but were feeding on the chambers built round the Sanctuary; so realizing that there was still time

to save the glorious edifice, Titus dashed out and by personal efforts strove to persuade his men to put out the fire, instructing Liberalius, a centurion of his bodyguard of spearmen, to lay his staff across the shoulders of any who disobeyed. But their respect for Caesar and their fear of the centurion's staff were powerless against their fury, their detestation of the Jews, and an uncontrollable lust for battle. Most of them again were spurred on by the expectation of loot, being convinced that the interior was bursting with money and seeing that everything outside was of gold. But they were forestalled by one of those who had gone in. He, when Caesar dashed out to restrain his men, pushed a firebrand into the hinges of the gate. Then from within a flame suddenly shot up, Caesar and his staff withdrew, and those outside were free to start what fires they liked. Thus the Sanctuary in defiance of Caesar's wishes was set on fire.

Grief might well be bitter for the destruction of the most wonderful edifice ever seen or heard of, both for its size and construction and for the lavish perfection of detail and the glory of its holy places; yet we find very real comfort in the thought that Fate is inexorable, not only toward living beings but also toward buildings and sites. We may wonder too at the exactness of the cycle of Fate: she kept, as I said, to the very month and day which centuries before had seen the Sanctuary burnt by the Babylonians. From its first foundation by King Solomon to its present destruction, which occurred in the second year of Vespasian's reign, was a period of 1,130 years, 7 months, 15 days; from its rebuilding in the second year of King Cyrus, for which Haggai was responsible, to its capture under Vespasian was 639 years, 45 days.

While the Sanctuary was burning, looting went on right and left and all who were caught were put to the sword. There was no pity for age, no regard for rank; little children and old men, laymen and priests alike were butchered; every class was held in the iron embrace of war, whether they defended themselves or cried for mercy. Through the roar of the flames as they swept relentlessly on could be heard the groans of the falling: such were the height of the hill and the vastness of the blazing edifice that the entire city seemed to be on fire, while as for the noise, nothing could be imagined more shattering or more horrifying. There was the war-cry of the Roman Legions as they converged; the yells of the partisans encircled with fire and sword; the panic flight into the arms of the enemy of the people cut off above, their shrieks as the end approached. The cries from the hill were answered from the crowded streets; and now many who were wasted with hunger and beyond speech, when they saw the Sanctuary in flames, found strength to moan and wail. Back from Peraea and the mountains round about came the echo in a thunderous bass.

Yet more terrible than the din were the sights that met the eye. The Temple Hill, enveloped in flames from top to bottom, appeared to be boiling up from its very roots; yet the sea of flame was nothing to the ocean of blood, or the companies of killers to the armies of killed: nowhere could the ground be seen between the corpses, and the soldiers climbed over heaps of bodies as they chased the fugitives. The partisan horde pushed the Romans back, and by a violent struggle burst through into the Outer Temple and from there into the City, the few surviving members of the public taking refuge on the outer colonnade. Some of the priests at first tore up from the Sanctuary the spikes with their lead sockets and threw them at the Romans. Then as they were no better off and the flames were leaping toward them, they retired to the wall, which was twelve feet wide, and stayed there. However, two men of note, in a position either to save their lives by going over to the Romans or to face with the others whatever came their way, threw themselves into the fire and were burnt to ashes with the Sanctuary—Meirus, son of Belgas, and Joseph, son of Dalaeus.

The Romans, judging it useless to spare the outbuildings now that the Sanctuary was in flames, set fire to them all—what remained of the colonnades and all the gates except two, one on the east end, the other on the south, both of which they later demolished. They also burnt the treasuries which housed huge sums of money, huge quantities of clothing, and other precious things; here, in fact, all the wealth of the Jews was piled up, for the rich had dismantled their houses and brought the contents here for safe keeping. Next they came to the last surviving colonnade of the Outer Temple. On this women and children and a mixed crowd of citizens had found a refuge— 6,000 in all. Before Caesar could reach a decision about them or instruct his officers, the soldiers, carried away by their fury, fired the colonnade from below; as a result some flung themselves out of the flames to their death, others perished in the blaze: of that vast number there escaped not one. Their destruction was due to a false prophet who that very day had declared to the people in the City that God commanded them to go up into the Temple to receive the signs of their deliverance. A number of hireling prophets had been put up in recent days by the party chiefs to deceive the people by exhorting them to await help from God, and so reduce the number of deserters and buoy up with hope those who were above fear and anxiety. Man is readily persuaded in adversity: when the deceiver actually promises deliverance from the miseries that envelope him, then the sufferer becomes the willing slave of hope. So it was that the unhappy people were beguiled at that stage by cheats and false messengers of God, while the unmistakable portents that foreshadowed the coming desolation they treated with indifference and incredulity, disregarding God's warnings as if they were moonstruck, blind and senseless. First a star stood over the City, very like a broadsword, and a comet that remained a whole year. Then before the revolt and the movement to war, while the people were assembling for the Feast of Unleavened Bread, on the 8th of Xanthicos at three in the morning so bright a light shone round the Altar and the Sanctuary that it might have been midday. This lasted half an hour. The inexperienced took it for a good omen, but the sacred scribes at once gave an interpretation which the event proved right. During the same feast a cow brought by someone to be sacrificed gave birth to a lamb in the middle of the Temple courts, while at midnight it was observed that the East Gate of the Inner Sanctuary had opened of its own accord—a gate made of bronze and so solid that every evening twenty strong men were required to shut it, fastened with iron-bound bars and secured by bolts which were lowered a long way into a threshold fashioned from a

single slab of stone. The temple-guards ran with the news to the Captain, who came up and by a great effort managed to shut it. This like the other seemed to the laity to be the best of omens: had not God opened to them the gate of happiness? But the learned perceived that the security of the Sanctuary was dissolving of its own accord, and that the opening of the gate was a gift to the enemy; and they admitted in their hearts that the sign was a portent of desolation.

A few days after the Feast, on the 21st of Artemisios, a supernatural apparition was seen, too amazing to be believed. What I have to relate would, I suppose, have been dismissed as an invention had it not been vouched for by eyewitnesses and followed by disasters that bore out the signs. Before sunset there were seen in the sky over the whole country, chariots and regiments in arms speeding through the clouds and encircling the towns. Again, at the Feast of Pentecost, when the priests had gone into the Inner Temple at night to perform the usual ceremonies, they declared that they were aware, first of a violent movement and a loud crash, then of a concerted cry: "Let us go hence."

An incident more alarming still had occurred four years before the war at a time of exceptional peace and prosperity for the City. One Jeshua son of Ananias, a very ordinary yokel, came to the feast at which every Jew is expected to set up a tabernacle for God. As he stood in the Temple he suddenly began to shout: "A voice from the east, a voice from the west, a voice from the four winds, a voice against Jerusalem and the Sanctuary, a voice against bridegrooms and brides, a voice against the whole people." Day and night he uttered this cry as he went through all the streets. Some of the more prominent citizens, very annoyed at these ominous words, laid hold of the fellow and beat him savagely. Without saying a word in his own defense or for the private information of his persecutors, he persisted in shouting the same warning as before. The Jewish authorities, rightly concluding that some supernatural force was responsible for the man's behavior, took him before the Roman procurator. There, though scourged till his flesh hung in ribbons, he neither begged for mercy nor shed a tear, but lowering his voice to the most mournful of tones answered every blow with "Woe to Jerusalem!" When Albinus—for that was the procurator's name—demanded to know who he was, where he came from and why he uttered such cries, he made no reply whatever to the questions but endlessly repeated his lament over the City, till Albinus decided he was a madman and released him. All the time till the war broke out he never approached another citizen or was seen in conversation, but daily as if he had learnt a prayer by heart he recited his lament: "Woe to Jerusalem!" Those who daily cursed him he never cursed; those who gave him food he never thanked: his only response to anyone was that dismal foreboding. His voice was heard most of all at the feasts. For seven years and five months he went on ceaselessly, his voice as strong as ever and his vigor unabated,

till during the siege after seeing the fulfillment of his foreboding he was silenced. He was going round on the wall uttering his piercing cry: "Woe again to the City, the people, and the Sanctuary!" and as he added a last word: "Woe to me also!" a stone shot from an engine struck him, killing him instantly. Thus he uttered those same forebodings to the very end.

Anyone who ponders these things will find that God cares for mankind and in all possible ways foreshows to His people the means of salvation, and that it is through folly and evils of their own choosing that they come to destruction. Thus the Jews after pulling down Antonia made the Temple square, in spite of the warning in their prophetic books that when the Temple became a square the City and Sanctuary would fall. But their chief inducement to go to war was an equivocal oracle also found in their sacred writings, announcing that at that time a man from their country would become monarch of the whole world. This they took to mean the triumph of their own race, and many of their scholars were wildly out in their interpretation. In fact the oracle pointed to the accession of Vespasian; for it was in Judaea he was proclaimed emperor. But it is not possible for men to escape from fate even if they see it coming. The Jews interpreted some of the prophecies to suit themselves and laughed the others off, till by the fall of their city and their own destruction their folly stood revealed. . . .

LUCAN (MARCUS ANNAEUS LUCANUS) (A.D. 39–65)
Pharsalia

*T*he epic poet Lucan was, like his relatives the Senecas, born in Spanish Córdoba; he moved with his family to Rome at the age of one. His father, M. Annaeus Mela, Seneca the Younger's brother, was a Roman knight; his mother's name was Acilia. In Rome Lucan received the finest education available, studying philosophy, and Greek and Latin literature and rhetoric with L. Annaeus Cornutus and with the satirist Persius. He continued his studies in Athens, until he was ordered back to Rome by Nero and appointed quaestor. In A.D. 60, he married Polla Argentaria. But his passion for Stoicism, and the attention his poetry was getting, alienated him from the jealous emperor, who forbade him to give public recitations; and when, in reaction, Lucan took part in Piso's conspiracy he was forced to commit suicide.

- Lucan's uncompleted epic *Bellum civile* (also known as the *Pharsalia*), deals with the Civil War between Caesar and Pompey from the war's causes and the crossing of the Rubicon to the fall of Alexandria. The first three of its ten proposed books, its history heavily influenced by Livy and its poetry by Virgil, were published in A.D. 62. Lucan's estrangement from the emperor provokes him to the fullest expression of his republican values, and Caesar receives unfair treatment.
- Lucan's Stoicism expresses itself in his substitution of an impersonal Fate for the gods and goddesses that Virgil's *Aeneid* pays lip service to. The hero of the poem is more the republican love for freedom than the designated Cato who is meant to embody that love as he continues to fight for the cause after Pompey's death. Pompey is the character closest to being a sympathetic hero, albeit a tragic one. Although Lucan's relentlessly chronological presentation of his story becomes monotonous, and his verse often deteriorates into bombastic exaggeration and maudlin pathos, the power of his metrical eloquence and his brilliant use of epigrams made him a strong influence on future writers, including Corneille, Dante, Housman, Samuel Johnson, Macaulay, Marlowe, Shelley, and Southey.

BOOK ONE

The theme of my poem is the Civil War which was decided on the plains of Pharsalus in Thessaly; yet "Civil War" is an understatement, since Pompey and Caesar, the opposing leaders, were not only fellow-citizens but relatives: the whole struggle was indeed no better than one of licensed fratricide. I shall here describe how, after the breakdown of the First Triumvirate, Rome turned the imperial sword against her own breast: how kinsman faced kinsman on the field of battle, each line of legionaries armed with identical javelins and carrying the same familiar eagle-standards as its opponents; and how the civilized world reeled under this contest in iniquity.

What made our forefathers embark on such an orgy of self-destruction? And why were their hated enemies permitted to enjoy the spectacle? Why was proud Parthia not first obliged to disgorge the Eagles taken from Crassus, whose ghost still wandered unavenged over her plains? That should have been Rome's immediate duty. It is bitter indeed to reflect how much of the earth's surface—from the lands of sunrise to those of sunset, from the burning Equator to the perpetually frozen seas of northernmost Scythia—could have been bought for Rome with the lives so fruitlessly squandered. We might well have brought the Chinese under our yoke, and the wild men of the Araxes, and whatever human creatures live at the sources of the Nile. Granted that Romans have an insatiable craving for war, why could we not have waited at least until all foreign nations had become subject to our laws before entering upon this criminal career? It is not as though Rome ever lacked enemies. If now, in Italian cities, even some of the most venerable, the walls of empty houses still bulge outward under broken roofs; if the streets are littered with huge stones; if no porters stand at the doorways and only a rare inhabitant wanders among the ruins; if the fields lie fallow year after year,

bristling with thorns and pleading in vain for the plough—who, pray, is to blame? Not Pyrrhus, not Hannibal! Neither of those proud antagonists succeeded in wounding Rome so deeply as she wounded herself. Only when brothers fall out is the sword driven home.

However, if the Fates could not prepare for Nero's advent by any other means—if eternal empire may not be bought except at a heavy price, as when of old a War of the Giants was needed to secure Juppiter's throne—then I naturally abstain from further complaints: the end may here be offered as sufficient justification of the means—including all the crimes

Archives, Forum, Rome

committed during the troubles. What if merciless fighting at Pharsalus heaped the plain with corpses, if at Thapsus rivers of blood glutted the thirst of Hannibal's revengeful shade, and if the final battle at Munda proved no less costly in life? And what if we must add to these horrific annals the famine at Perusia, the ghastly struggle at Mutina, the seafight near the rocky island of Leucas, the defeat of Sextus Pompey's slave-manned fleet within view of burning Etna? Even so, it is arguable that Rome has greatly profited from her Civil Wars: were they not fought, Caesar, that you might reign to-day?

And O, great Prince, when your watch among men ends, and you finally rise skyward, the celestial palace of your choice will receive you amid the loud acclamations of Heaven. I cannot venture to prophesy whether you will assume Juppiter's scepter, or prefer to mount Apollo's fiery chariot and survey the earth from it as you drive along—an earth quite untroubled by the change of divine charioteers. But this much is certain: every deity will shrink humbly back, while Mother Nature waits for you to decide which god to be, and where to establish your seat of power. As for that, I beseech you not to choose the Arctic Circle, or the torrid southern skies, from either of which your light would beam only squintingly on Rome. And, if you put too much weight on any single portion of the limitless ether, you will endanger its balance; it would be best to take up your stance in the very center of Heaven and thus preserve universal equipoise. May that region remain serene and cloudless, affording us an uninterrupted view of our Emperor!

One further wish: may mankind ground arms and consult its own welfare in an epoch of international love: may Peace, sent flying about the world, keep the iron gates of Janus' Temple tight shut. For my part I have already come to regard you as a god; and if your divine afflatus enters my breast and provokes me to verse, I shall not ask to be visited by either Apollo of Delphi or Bacchus of Mount Nysa. You are sufficient inspiration for any Roman poet.

I must now provide the historical background of these tremendous events. It is indeed a formidable task to explain how it came about that our nation ran so frantically to arms and drove Peace from the world. The fact is that long-lasting national supremacy soon attracts the resentment of Fate; and Rome, top-heavy with her own greatness, had grown ripe for a spectacular collapse. Call it, if you will, a foretaste of what must happen when the framework of the world buckles and its long cycles suddenly end; when chaos supervenes; when the constellations collide and dash themselves in pieces; when Earth heaves up her shores and shakes off the stream of Ocean; when the Moon in her two-horse gig usurps the daylight course of her brother's four-horse chariot; and when the mechanism of the Universe gets thrown out of gear, to the utter annulment of all natural law.

As great edifices collapse of their own weight, so Heaven sets a similar limit to the growth of prosperous states. In this case, however, no foreign nation acted as the instrument of divine Nemesis: it was the Romans, now supreme on land and sea, who foolishly brought doom on themselves when they consented to be governed by a triumvirate. They should have known that supreme sovereignty had never been divided among so many as three men except with bloody results. Alas, in this case too, the partners, all disastrously pledged to the same purpose but each blinded by his own ambitions, joined hands in common mischief. Never so long as earth supports sea, or air supports earth, or the Sun makes his perennial journey through the signs of the Zodiac, or night follows day—never will loyalty be found among fellow-despots! It is a law of Nature that every great man inevitably resents a partner in greatness. And why quote foreign history to prove my thesis? Romulus bathed the rising walls of Rome with the blood of his brother Remus, and was not even rewarded for this madness by an empire stretching over land and sea. He gained the mere chieftainship of a small community recruited from runaway slaves and criminals who had taken sanctuary in a near-by grove.

For awhile an unnatural harmony reigned in the Triumvirate: Crassus' mediation somehow kept his pugnacious colleagues from flying at each other's throats. One may liken Crassus to the narrow Isthmus of Corinth which barely prevents a head-on collision between the Ionian and Aegean Seas; if it disappeared, what a welter of water would result! So when Crassus disappeared, falling miserably at Carrhae—where the Syrian soil was dyed with the blood of our legions—his colleagues at once felt free to impose their madness on the world. The Arsacid dynasty of Parthia had, in fact, gained far more at Carrhae than they realized then: civil war had been let loose on the enemy, by severing the bond which united the three tyrants. It soon became apparent that even a powerful Empire, spread across the whole civilized earth, did not provide enough elbow-room for both of them!

The unfortunate death of Caesar's daughter Julia had been ominous of the coming breach; the same bridal torches which welcomed her in bridal array to Pompey's house presently lighted her corpse to the pyre. And with Julia went the last ties that bound these two great men together. Had it been her destiny to live a few years longer, she and she alone might have prevented the quarrel. Julia could have forced her husband and her father to fling away the swords they had drawn against each other—as the kidnapped Sabine women did long ago when their kinsmen marched against Rome. But, as it chanced, Julia's death dissolved the league of friendship sealed by this union: the ambitious rivals now felt at liberty to embark on their struggle for power.

Pompey feared that Caesar's recent conquest of Gaul might put into the shade his own famous suppression of the Cilician pirates. Caesar, for his part, was encouraged to prosecute the military career in which he had now won valuable experience and the favors of Fortune. He disdained to accept a subordinate position at Rome. In a word, Pompey could allow no man to be his equal, and Caesar no man to be his superior. Who am I to judge which of the two had more right on his side? Each could claim the support of a high authority: for the winning cause pleased the Gods, but the losing cause pleased Cato.

Pompey and Caesar met on unequal terms. Pompey, now past middle age, had not taken the field for some years. His main preoccupation was to keep his fame alive by courting the favor of the common people; he distributed largesse, provided costly spectacles, and exulted in the applause that greeted him when he entered the great theater which he had himself built. Resting on his well-earned laurels, he made no attempt to win fresh ones, but basked in the glory of his surname, "the Great," which had been officially bestowed on him by the Senate. It was as when an oak towering above a lush meadow—the repository of votive offerings and enemy spoils hung on its branches by bygone tribal chieftains—ceases to derive any support from the roots, but relies merely on its bulk to keep it upright. Leafless boughs protrude into the sky, it throws no more than a skeletal shadow and totters in the breeze: the first north-easter will send it crashing down. How strange that though many nearby trees are still green and firmly rooted, this hollow oak alone is an object of veneration!

Caesar, on the other hand, had not only won the reputation of a successful general, but was burned with so restless a desire for conquest that he felt disgraced by inactivity. Headstrong, fierce, and never hesitating to flesh his sword, he stood prepared to lead his troops wherever hope of glory or personal resentment offered a battlefield. Confident in Fortune's continued favors, he would follow up each advantage gained; thrusting aside all obstacles that barred his march to supreme power, and rejoicing in the havoc he occasioned. Caesar may, indeed, be justly compared to lightning. Discharged by the winds from a pack of clouds, it darts out jaggedly with a crash that splits the daylight skies, dazzling every eye, striking terror into every heart, and blasting its own airy seats. Nothing may stand against it, either during that furious progress through the clouds, or when it bursts against the earth and at once recomposes its scattered fires.

So much for the opposing leaders; but the people too had a secret propensity for war, characteristic of every sovereign race. The Romans had become masters of the world and were endowed by Fortune with such an excess of wealth that it corrupted their public morality. Spoils won in war tempted them to extravagance; they all felt entitled to possess as much money and as many houses as they pleased and to despise dishes that once tempted their palate. Men adopted a luxurious style of dress unsuitable even for married women; and because the poverty which had once bred a virile stock now seemed odious, they rifled every foreign land of whatever product had most contributed to its downfall. Great estates were formed; and employers entrusted the very soil once laboriously ploughed by Marcus Furius Camillus, or dug by Marius Curius Dentatus, to laborers whose very names they never troubled to learn. No such nation could be satisfied to hang up its arms and grow fat in the free enjoyment of peace and tranquility. Frequent breaches of the peace resulted, as did also vile crimes prompted by the unequal distribution of wealth. To be above the laws of one's own country became a distinction worth winning; and might was right. Hence the unconstitutional measures which both Consuls and Tribunes of the People enacted. Hence the bribes offered by candidates for high office; and the disgraceful yearly scene on the Campus Martius, where the Commons sold their votes to the highest bidder. Hence also usury with its avaricious counting of the days until payment became due; one result of which was the destruction of credit and a ready recourse to arms for the settlement of debts.

Caesar had crossed the icy Alps before he began to consider the disastrous and far-reaching effects of this war; but on his arrival at the Rubicon, a small river which divides the pastures of Gaul from the cornfields of Italy, he was granted a night vision of Rome, his own distressed motherland. She stood bare-armed, her features expressing profound sorrow and her white hairs streaming disheveled from underneath a mural crown. "Where are you bound, soldiers?" she asked, sighing deeply. "Where are you carrying my standards? If you are honest, law-abiding men, you will halt at this stream!" Caesar trembled, his scalp crawled with horror and his feet dragged; yet he edged nearer to the bank and prayed aloud to Juppiter: "O Thunderer, as you gaze down at the great walls of Rome from your temple beside the Tarpeian Rock; and you, Household-gods of the Julian clan, whose images my ancestor Aeneas saved from burning Troy; and you, Romulus, our founder, mysteriously elevated to Heaven as the God Quirinius; and you, Latin Juppiter, in your shrine on the Alban Mount; and you, Vesta, whose sacred fire our virgins tend; and you, too, Goddess of Rome, whose power equals that of any major deity—favor my enterprise! Ah, Rome, I wage no frantic war against you! I am Caesar, the soldier who won great victories for you on land and sea, and who will continue to be your champion while you consent. If any blood is destined to flow, let it fall on the head of the villain who has falsely represented me as your enemy!"

With these words, Caesar unleashed war by hurrying his standards over the rushing stream.

It was as when a lion crouches in the parched fields of Libya, uncertain whether or not to spring on the enemy whom he has sighted. He rouses himself to fury by lashing his cruel tail and uttering a loud, cavernous roar. The nimble Moor may then contrive to wound him with an assegai, but what of that? Even if a hunting-spear should pierce the beast's broad chest, he will continue to attack, driving the weapon yet deeper into his own body.

The rust-colored Rubicon issues from an insignificant spring, and when it crawls along its valley-bed in hot summer, the stream is scanty enough. On this occasion, however, not only was it swollen by three nights and days of winter rain following a change of moon, but damp, warm winds had melted the Alpine snows and greatly increased the force of the current. Caesar therefore made the cavalry form up slantwise across the stream, which the rest of the army then forded without difficulty under the protection of this improvised break-water. Finally Caesar himself crossed, and made a speech from the forbidden Italian bank.

"Men, I am here leaving peace behind me, and defying the Roman Constitution. Henceforth let the Goddess Fortune be my guide. Enough of solemn covenants; I have observed them too carefully by far. Only war can now decide between Pompey and myself."

He brusquely signaled the advance, and his army moved forward through the night, swift as a bolt from a Balearic sling or a Parthian horse-archer's parting arrow. They swooped down on Rimini at dawn, when only the morning-star still shone in the sky, and caused panic in the town. The weather on this first day of conflict was appropriately gloomy—perhaps the gods themselves had ordered the South Wind to drive up those murky clouds. Caesar's men occupied the local Forum without opposition and halted to plant their standards. Blaring trumpets and bugles, and braying horns, sounded the alarm of Civil War and roused the drowsy inhabitants from sleep. The men snatched down the arms hanging in their household shrines: tattered shields, javelins with bent or broken points, swords blunted by old rust—mute witnesses of a long-unbroken peace. But when they saw the shining Roman Eagles and lesser standards, and recognized Caesar seated on a charger at the head of his troops, they stood motionless in cold terror. Every man thought: "This was an unlucky site to choose for a town, so close to Gaul! Profound peace reigns throughout the rest of the world, yet we are the victims of a mad uprising: ours is the first place to be occupied by the rebels. If only we lived somewhere else—in the Far East, say, or in the icy north, or among the nomads of the Steppes—anywhere else but here, at the gateway to Italy. First it was the Sennonian Gauls, next it was Hannibal's Carthaginians, and then came the furious Teutons and Cimbrians; whenever Rome is threatened, the invader always chooses this route." Yet not a man among them dared do more than groan inaudibly, however great his anxiety or sorrow. The consequent silence recalled that of the countryside when winter strikes all singing birds dumb; or of the high seas during a calm.

It was broad daylight, and if Caesar still wavered in his resolution, or felt tempted to compromise, the Goddess Fortune gave him a new incentive to battle. She had decided on providing occasions which would clearly jus-

tify the revolt. Now, when Caesar offered to resign his command on reaching Rome, if Pompey would do the same, two Tribunes of the People had hotly supported his proposal; but the Consuls, in violation of the law which made the Tribunes' persons sacrosanct, threatened them with the fate of the Gracchi unless they kept silent. The Tribunes thereupon fled from Rome to the protection of Caesar's army in Gaul, but found him already across the frontier. With them came bold Caius Scribonius Curio, the man whose eloquence was reputedly on public sale; a spokesman of the people and a champion of their liberties, he had dared reduce armed dignitaries to the level of private citizens. Realizing now that Caesar was still in two minds about which course to follow, he said: "Caesar, while I could continue to defend your party, despite our opponents in the Senate, I did so, and even persuaded the wavering to vote a five years' extension of your command in Gaul. But the Constitution has since been suspended, on the ground that Civil War threatens, and these two Tribunes and I find ourselves driven from Rome. We are, however, prepared to endure exile until your victory restores our rights as citizens. The City is in a turmoil, and it would be folly to let your enemies consolidate their power; procrastination is always dangerous once a man is ready to act. You have campaigned ten years in Gaul to win only an insignificant part of this earth's surface; to-day it will cost you little more exertion or anxiety to gain vastly greater rewards. Fight two or three extra battles, and Rome will be found to have conquered the world for your sake alone. Here lies your only hope of being rewarded with a triumph when you reach the

City, and wearing consecrated laurels in a procession to the Capitol. Envy gnaws at your son-in-law's heart and he has decided to cheat you of the honors that you have long been owed; in fact, you will be lucky to escape being punished for your conquests. Very well: since he withholds your half-share of the world, why not claim his in addition to yours?"

Caesar was already eager to let the sword decide between himself and Pompey, but Curio's words added new fuel to his anger. He resembled a race-horse at Olympia, straining at the closed wooden gates of the barrier, and trying to work the bolts loose with its head; the shouting of the spectators excites it still more. At once he rallied his infantry around the standards and, with set face and raised arm, soon quieted their bustle. This is what he told them: "Men, you have faced the enemy with me a thousand times, and in the last ten years we have never known defeat. But what will your reward be for the blood you shed on Northern battlefields, and for the cold winters you spent beyond the Alps? Such frantic military preparations are in progress at Rome to-day that this might be Hannibal's army, not mine. Every battalion there is being brought up to strength with picked recruits, forests are being felled to build ships, and orders have gone out that I am to be harried ashore and afloat. I wonder what would have happened if we had lost the war and were being pursued by a victorious Gallic army? It is only because Fortune has proved kind, and the Gods have summoned us to the high places of this earth, that our enemies are offering this challenge. Well, we are ready to accept it. Their leader, Pompey, once arranged a triumph for himself before he had reached

legal age, but long years of peace have made him flabby. Let him by all means lead his hastily raised troops against us—and such unwarlike hangers-on as Marcellus the Talker, and fellows like Cato who have nothing to boast about but their names. Do you think it right that Pompey should once more be allowed to renew his despotic power—awarded him over and over again without a break by the dregs of the people whose votes he has bought? Should he never be forced to disgorge the dignities which he has usurped? And is it nothing that he has now assumed control of the world's corn supplies and can make famine a political instrument? Or that his troops have illegally broken into the Courts of Justice—you remember Milo's trial?—and terrorized juries with their glittering standards and swords?

"Once again Pompey is preparing for Civil War; he hopes, no doubt, to postpone his inglorious return to private life. He learned this wicked lesson from Sulla, and is now bent on outdoing his master. The man reminds me of a savage tiger reared by his dam in the Hyrcanian jungle and taught to lap the blood of slaughtered cattle. Pompey used once to lick the blood of Sulla's sword blade, and has never since lost the craving for it. But a diet of human blood turns a man into a savage; so why should we suppose that he will ever lay down his badges of office and end this long history of crime? There was one honorable lesson at least that Sulla might have taught the wretch: the duty of eventual abdication. Yes, I am aware of his successes against the elusive Cilicians, and against King Mithridates of Pontus who, though exhausted by forty years of war with Rome, had at last to be removed ingloriously enough, by poison, not force of arms. But shall Pompey crown his career with a triumph over Caesar— Caesar, who has had the audacity to insist on his constitutional right of entering Rome at the head of these victorious legions? Very well, let me be defrauded of my hard-earned triumph; but I shall never allow you veterans to be denied yours. You shall march in, I swear, under some commander or other, never mind whom. And what of my re-enlisted men? What settlement will be made for those brave veterans when they retire? Can they expect awards of public land and a fortified town to shelter them in their old age? Or will Pompey grant them less even than his defeated pirates won? You will remember that he settled them all over the Empire, not only in their native Cilicia, but in Achaea, and in Italy itself!

"Lift high those victorious standards, men! We must make good use of the strength we have built up; for the proverb runs: 'Deny a strong man his due, and he will take all he can get.' And you may count on divine favor; since my object is neither plunder nor power, but only to rid Rome of the tyrant who dominates her."

Caesar's speech was not, however, greeted with immediate applause. On the contrary, a doubtful whispering spread through the ranks. Though fierce-hearted, and proud of their battle record, the soldiers were too patriotic not to hesitate awhile before supporting Caesar's cause. Yet a passion for fighting, combined with the fear of offending him, soon tipped the balance. Laelius, a leading centurion, winner of an oak-leaf badge for saving a comrade's life in battle, raised his voice.

"My lord Caesar," he shouted, "may I be given leave to speak? To be frank, our complaint is that you have been far too patient and held back too long. Knowing you for the finest general in the army, we could suppose only that our loyalty had ceased to inspire your confidence. For how could you fail to call on us while we still had blood in our veins, and strength to hurl the javelin? We asked ourselves: 'Will he submit to the tyranny of the Senate and disgrace himself by tamely putting on a toga? Is victory in a civil war, after all, so fearful a fate?' My lord, we have always been ready to follow wherever you lead: even against the Scythian hordes, or around the inhospitable Gulf of Sirte, or across the thirsty midsummer deserts of Libya. You led us forward through conquered Gaul, and we consolidated our gains as we went; we took ship and rowed over the Ocean Stream to Britain; we navigated the turbulent mouth of the Rhine. If I may speak of myself for a moment, loyal performance of the tasks you impose has become second nature to me. Command the trumpets to blow the assault against whatever General you please, and I will deny that he is my fellow-countryman. And I swear by these standards, victorious in ten campaigns, and by your future triumphs—it is no business of mine over what enemy they are gained—that this sword-arm will continue to obey your orders even where they may happen to conflict with my rooted inclinations. Tell me to plunge a sword into my brother's breast, my father's throat, or the belly of my wife, now great with child, and I will not fail you. Or to plunder the temples of the gods and set them on fire; I will gladly break up the sacred images and melt them into coin for your war-chest. Instruct me to encamp my men beside the Tiber; I will unhesitatingly mark out the tent-lines across the familiar fields of home. Whenever you wish to level a city wall, call upon me; I will help to swing the battering-ram and send huge stones crashing down—though they be the walls of Rome herself!" . . .

THE STOIC'S WEDDING

Meanwhile, as chilly night gave way to dawn,
A knocking sounded: leaving her husband's
    tomb,
There entered Marcia, filled with pious grief.
A nobler husband took her maidenhood,
Then, when the rich reward of marriage grew
To a third child, another home received her
To fill it too with offspring, a fertile mother
Linking the houses. Now her husband's ashes
Laid in the urn, she came in pitiful stress,
Tearing disheveled locks, beating her bosom
With blow on blow, defiled by funeral ash—
For thus she would please Cato. She addressed
    him:
"While strong and fertile blood was in me,
    Cato,
I did your bidding, gave two husbands children.
My womb is tired now: let me return to you
And let no other husband take me. Grant
Again our early union; let my tomb
Bear the vain title Marcia, wife of Cato.
Let future ages know whether I left you
As a gift or as a castaway from marriage.
You will not share prosperity and peace
With me; I come to share your cares and
    labors.
So let me follow your camp. Must I be left
Further than Pompey's wife from the Civil War?"
Her pleading moved her husband's heart. The
    crisis,

The fates crying "To arms!" were strange for
    marriage;
Yet simple union and a sober wedlock,
With gods alone to witness, pleased their
    thought.
No crowned threshold and hanging garlands
    of joy,
No gay white ribbon linking door and posts,
No torch-procession, couch with ivory dais,
No coverlet of gold embroidery,
No towering marriage-crown, no solemn
    entrance
Of the bride, stepping across the threshold
    lightly;
No saffron veil shielding her downcast face—
A flimsy garment for her modesty—
No jeweled belt girding her flowing garments,
Necklace, or scarf resting light on her shoulders
And flying freely from her slender arms.
She kept the state of grief: she gave her husband
Only the embrace a mother gives her sons.
Her simple robe was veiled with funeral weeds.
There was no marriage-jesting, and the husband
Did not submit to the gay old Sabine songs.
No kin, no family faces smiled on them;
They wed in silence, with one witness—Brutus.
And Cato neither freed his solemn face
Of shaggy hair, nor would admit a smile—
When he first saw the fatal weapons raised,
He suffered his unshorn gray locks to hang
Over his brow, and his beard mourned on his
    cheeks;
For he alone, free of ambition and hate,
Wept for the human race—nor did he now
Resume his nuptial rights: even a just love
His strength refused. Such was the rule of Cato,
Such his unyielding will—to keep sure limits,
To follow nature, spend his life for his country,

To live not for himself but for the world.
To conquer hunger was a feast; a palace
For him was a plain roof; a precious garment
For him was the rough-haired toga of the
   Roman

In time of peace; the only use of love
Was offspring: he begot and loved for Rome.
Justice and rigid honor—these he worshipped,
And virtue serving the world. No act of Cato
Was touched by pleasure and the greedy self.

MARTIAL (MARCUS VALERIUS MARTIALIS)
(C. A.D. 40–C. 104)
Epigrams

Born at the start of Claudius' reign, at Bilbilis, in the Spanish province of Tarraconensis, Martial, the most important Latin epigrammist, was the son of Fronto and Flaccilla, and named for his March 1 birthday. By the time he was twenty-four he was in Nero's Rome, sent there to continue his studies in grammar, rhetoric, and law but finding reputation instead from his poetry. He lived in Rome the majority of his productive years, enjoying the circle of the Senecas, Lucan, Frontinus, Juvenal, Silius Italicus, Gaius Calpurnius Piso, Quintilian, and Pliny the Younger, as well as the patronage of Domitian, whom he flattered shamelessly, and Titus. Shortly after Trajan took the throne, Martial retired to his hometown where he died around 104.

- In his own lifetime, Martial enjoyed fame that had extended far beyond the capital, his works in demand in Gaul, Germany, and Britain. He wrote a book of dramatic criticism, *The Book of Spectacles,* based on performances in the amphitheater of Flavian and written to celebrate the opening of the Colosseum in A.D. 80 by the Emperor Titus. He also wrote two books of "greeting card verse" for Saturnalia gift exchanges.
- Nearly 1,500 of his short and incisive poems survive, in fourteen books. He is the father of the modern epigram, which Samuel Coleridge defined as "a dwarfish whole: its body brevity and wit its soul." Martial shaped epigram into an art form rarely equaled by his imitators.

Aside from their penetrating revelations about human vice, folly, and emotions, his poetic portraits of the men and women of his time provide us with a wealth of information about Roman life in the first-century A.D. Silver Age.

- Martial's epigrams, his most important contribution, were mostly written in elegiac or iambic meter and show the influence of Ovid and Catullus. Like the *Characters* of Athenian philosopher Theophrastus, Martial's epigrams provide us with direct observation of a cross-section of society during his time:

  - the physician-undertaker Diaulus, and Tongilius who feigns illness to get attention;
  - Ligurinus, who holds dinner parties so that he can read his poetry to captive guests;
  - medical student Symmachus, who leaves his patient worse than when he found him; and
  - sycophant Selius, who roams the town searching for his next free meal.

At the same time that they display Roman wit at its sharpest and most profane, Martial's epigrams never fail to mirror an underlying humanity that proves the heart as well as the head has influenced his satirical vision.

I.1

He unto whom thou art so partial,
O reader, is the well-known Martial,
The epigrammatist: while living,
Give him the fame thou wouldst be giving
So shall he hear, and feel, and know it:
Post-obits rarely reach a poet.

[TR. GEORGE GORDON, LORD BYRON]

Nor use the words for hymning him?
We clothe ourselves at Flora's feast,
In chaste stole let whores go dressed?
One rule for witty songs like these:
They may not, without prurience, please.
Then stifle primness, I must ask;
Take not my toys and jests to task.
Nor bowdlerize my pretty verses—
Than Priapic Gallus naught there's worse is.

[TR. PETER WHIGHAM]

I.35

Cornelius sighs . . . the lines I write
Are such no dominie would recite:
They are not "prim" . . . but epigrams,
As men for wives, no pleasure can
Procure without what makes a man.
You'd have me write a Hymen hymn

I.57

My taste in women, Flaccus? Give me one
Neither too slow nor yet too quick to bed.
For me, the middle sort: I've not the will
To be Love's Martyr—nor his Glutton either.

[TR. PETER WHIGHAM]

II.5

Believe me, sir, I'd like to spend whole days,
Yes, and whole evenings in your company,
But the two miles between your house and
    mine
Are four miles when I go there and come back.
You're seldom home, and when you are deny it,
Engrossed with business or with yourself.
Now, I don't mind the two mile trip to see you;
What I do mind is going four to not to.

              [TR. J. V. CUNNINGHAM]

II.8

The breath of balm from foreign branches
    pressed;
The effluence that falling saffron brings;
The scent of apples ripening in a chest;
Or the rich foliage of a field in Spring;
Imperial silken robes from Palatine;
Or amber, warming in a virgin's hand;
The far-off smell of spilt Falernian wine;
A bee-loud garden in Sicilian land;
Odor, which spice and altar-incense send;
Or wreath of flowerets from a rich brow drawn;
Why speak of these? Words fail. Their perfect
    blend
Resemble my boy's kiss at early dawn.
You ask his name? Only to kiss him? Well!
You swear as much? Sabinus, I won't tell!

              [TR. ANTHONY REID]

II.59

Look round: You see a little supper room;
But from my window, lo! great Caesar's tomb!
And the great dead themselves, with jovial
    breath,
Bid you be merry and remember death.

        [TR. ROBERT LOUIS STEVENSON]

II.89

Gaurus, you have a fault for which
I freely pardon you:
You love to drink too much, too late;
That vice was Cato's too.
I'll even praise your scribbling
Verses, instead of prose,
With NO help from the Muses, for
That fault was Cicero's.
You vomit: so did Antony,
You squander: records may show
Apicius as your model—now,
Who led you to fellatio?

            [TR. DOROTHEA WENDER]

II.90

O chief director of the growing race,
Of Rome the glory and of Rome the grace,
Me, O Quintilian, may you not forgive
Though, far from labor, I make haste to live?
Some burn to gather wealth, lay hands on rule,
Or with white statues fill the atrium full.
The talking hearth, the rafters swart with smoke,
Live fountains and rough grass, my love invokes:
A sturdy slave: a not too learned wife:
Nights filled with slumber, and a quiet life.

        [TR. ROBERT LOUIS STEVENSON]

(SEXTUS JULIUS) FRONTINUS (C. A.D. 40–103)

On the Conveyance of Water

〰

*N*othing is more characteristically Roman than the practical details of constructing roads and aqueducts. Frontinus' distinguished career in government included a praetorship under Vespasian and a consulship. He served as governor of Britannia from A.D. 74 to 77, replacing his former commander Peillius Cerealis; and waged war successfully against the Silures in South Wales until he himself was replaced by Agricola. Frontinus, under Domitian, retired to his estate in Campania to pursue his writings, but was called back into service as Rome's *curator acquarum* ("superintendent of waterworks") around the year A.D. 97 by the emperor Nerva. Later he served as *augur* and again as consul under Trajan.

- His writings included three books on applied and historical military science, *Strategemata*, which influenced Vegetius; and a work of agronomy referred to as *On Land-Surveying*. His plain, logical, and straightforward style is a model of practical professional prose.
- Frontinus began his new assignment for Nerva by setting about to survey the history and status of the water system of the city of Rome and to record, based on his own inspection and engineering reports, existing regulations, maintenance, and requirements for improvements. The two books of his *De aquae ductu (On the Conveyance of Water)* are the result of his undertaking.

---

11. I do not rightly perceive the motives which caused Augustus, that most cautious ruler, to bring in the Alsietinian water, called Augusta, since it has nothing to commend it; and is, on the contrary, so unwholesome, that on this account it is delivered nowhere for the use of the people; unless it be that, when he undertook to construct his Naumachia, he brought in this water to avoid drawing upon the better sources of supply, and left the surplus of the Naumachia for the adjacent gardens, and for the use of private parties for irrigation. It is customary, however, to draw from it in emergencies, and thus to eke out the supply of the public fountains in the ward beyond the Tiber, whenever the bridges are undergoing repairs and no water can be delivered from this side of the river. The intake is out of the Alsietinian Lake, on the Claudian Way, at the fourteenth mile-stone, on a cross-road, 6,500 paces to the

right. Its conduit has a length of 22,172 paces; of which 358 paces are on arches.

12. Augustus also conducted another water of equal quality through an underground conduit to the channel of Marcia, for supplementing Marcia during droughts, which conduit is called Augusta after its designer. The intake is further away than that of Marcia; from the intake to its junction with Marcia is a distance of 800 paces.

13. After this, C. Caesar, the successor of Tiberius, because the seven aqueducts did not seem to be sufficient to meet either the public needs or the demands of private luxury, commenced the construction of two aqueducts in the second year of his reign, under the consulate of M. Aquila Julianus, and P. Nonius Asprenas in the year 789 after the founding of the city. This work was completed in the most splendid manner by Claudius, and was formally dedicated under the consulate of Sulla and Titianus, in the year 803 after the founding of the city, on the first of August. One water, which had its source in the Caerulean and Curtian springs, was called Claudia. This one most nearly equals Marcia in good quality. To

Rome in the time of Constantine

the other was given the name of New Anio, so as to distinguish it the better, since now two aqueducts were in use, both called Anio. To the first Anio was given the surname Old.

14. The intake of Claudia is on the Sublacensian Way, at the thirty-eighth mile-stone, on a cross-road, three hundred paces to the left, taking in two very capacious and beautiful wells, the Caerulian (blue one), so called from its appearance, and the Curtian. Claudia also takes in a spring called Albudinus, which is of such purity that whenever there is need of supplementing Marcia, it answers so perfectly, that it in no wise changes the character of Marcia by mixing with it. The spring of Augusta was turned into Claudia, because Marcia seemed plainly to be of sufficient volume by itself; but Augusta remained, nevertheless, a reserve supply to Marcia, the understanding being that Augusta should run into Claudia only when the conduit of Marcia could not carry it. Claudia has a length of 46,406 paces; of which, 36,230 are underground conduit, 10,176 above-ground; of which at various points in the upper reaches 3,076 paces are on arches, and near the city, beginning at the seventh mile-stone, 609 paces on masonry substructure, and 6,491 on arches.

15. The intake of New Anio is on the Sublacensian Way, at the forty-second mile-stone, in the Simbruinum, and from the river; which flows muddy and discolored even without the effect of rainstorms, because it has rich and cultivated lands adjoining, and, as a result, loose banks; for this reason a settling reservoir was built upstream from the intake, so that in it and between the river and the conduit the water might come to rest and clarify itself. But

in spite of this construction the water reaches the city in a discolored condition, whenever there are heavy rains. The Herculanean Brook, which has its source on the same Way, at the thirty-eighth mile-stone, opposite the springs of Claudia and beyond the river and the highway, joins it, being of itself exceedingly clear, but losing the charm of its purity by admixture. The conduit of New Anio measures 58,700 paces; of which 49,300 are underground, 9,400 above-ground; of which at various points in the upper reaches are 2,300 paces on masonry substructure or on arches; and nearer the city, beginning at the seventh mile-stone, 609 paces on masonry substructure, 6,491 paces on arches. These are the highest arches, and at some points are 109 feet high.

16. Will anybody compare the idle Pyramids, or those other useless though much renowned works of the Greeks with these aqueducts, with these many indispensable structures?

17. It has seemed to me not superfluous to examine consecutively the lengths of channel of each aqueduct in its several parts, and in detail;—this because the maintenance of the works is the most important part of the duties of this office, wherefore it is necessary that whoever is placed in charge of them should know which of them are in need of having money spent upon them. But my zeal was not satisfied by a mere personal examination in detail; I also had plans made of the aqueducts, from which it may be seen where there are valleys and how wide they are, and where rivers have been crossed; also where the conduits laid on the hillsides need an extended and continued care for their protection and maintenance. In this

way we reap the advantage of having, as it were, the works referred to directly before us, and of being able to study them, as though we stood by their side.

18. The several aqueducts reach the city at different elevations. Whence it comes that some deliver water on higher grounds, while others cannot elevate themselves to the higher summits; for the hills have gradually grown higher on account of the accumulation of rubbish produced by the frequent fires. There are five aqueducts whose waters rise to all parts of the city, though some are forced up by a greater, others by a lesser head.

New Anio goes the highest; next to it comes Claudia; the third rank is taken by Julia, the fourth by Tepula; this is followed by Marcia, which equals in height at the intake even Claudia.

The ancients laid the lines of their aqueducts at a lower elevation, be it because the art of leveling had not been highly developed, or because they purposely sunk the aqueducts into the ground, in order that they might not readily be destroyed by the enemy, during the frequent wars with the Italians. But now, whenever an aqueduct has succumbed to old age, to save length, they are in certain parts either placed on a masonry substructure or on arches, at the same time avoiding the subterranean loops originally put around the heads of the valleys. The sixth rank in height is taken by Old Anio, which would likewise be able to supply the higher portions of the city if it were raised up on masonry substructures or on arches, wherever the situation of the valleys and low places made it necessary. Its elevation is followed by that of Virgo, then by that of Appia; both of which, since they were brought from points near the city, were unable to reach such high elevations. Lowest of all is Alsietina, which supplies the ward beyond the Tiber, and the very lowest districts.

19. Of these waters, six are drawn into covered catch-basins, this side of the seventh mile-stone, in which, resting as it were from their run and taking a new breath, they deposit their sediment. Their volume is also determined by gauges set up in these basins. Thence onward, Julia, Marcia, and Tepula run on the same line; of which Tepula, which was turned, as has above been shown, into the same conduit with Julia, now leaves the basin of Julia and receives its volume from it, and flows in its own conduit and under its own name. These three run on top of the same arches from the basins onward. The uppermost is Julia; next comes Tepula; then Marcia. These waters, going underground at the elevation of the Viminal Hill, flow up to the Viminal Gate. There they again see the light of day. But first, a portion of Julia is distributed to the delivery tanks of the Caelian Hill, having been diverted at Spes Vetus. But Marcia pours a portion of its waters into the so-called Herculanean Channel, behind the Pallantian Gardens; and though this is conducted along the Caelian Hill, it fails to supply anything to this hill by reason of too low elevation, and ends over Porta Capena.

20. The New Anio and Claudia are carried on high arches from the basins, Anio being the higher of the two. Their arches end behind the Pallantian Gardens, and their waters are distributed thence to the city through pipes. But Claudia first delivers a portion of its waters

over the so-called Neronian Arches, at Spes Vetus. These pass along the Caelian Hill and end near the temple of Divus Claudius. Both aqueducts deliver the water which they bring partly upon the Caelian Hill, partly upon the Palatine and Aventine, and to the ward over the Tiber.

21. Old Anio, this side of the fourth milestone, passes under the arches of New Anio, which crosses from the Latin Way to the Labican, and has there its catch-basin. It then delivers a part of its supply to the Octavian conduit this side of the second mile-stone, and reaches up to the Asinian Gardens in the vicinity of the New Way, whence it is distributed throughout the surrounding district. But the main conduit which passes Spes Vetus comes within the Esquiline Gate, whence it is distributed within the city in high-lying conduits.

22. Neither Virgo, nor Appia, nor Alsietina has a receiving reservoir or catch-basin. The arches of Virgo commence under the Lucullan Gardens, and end on the Field of Mars in front of the Voting Booths. The conduit of Appia, running along the base of the Caelian and the Aventine, emerges again into daylight, as we have said, under the Publician Steps (acclivity). The conduit of Alsietina ends behind the Naumachia, for the supply of which it seems to have been constructed.

23. Having now given the builders and the age of each aqueduct, also their sources, lengths of channel, and order of heights, it seems to me not out of keeping to go more into detail, and to demonstrate how large is the quantity of water which is allotted to public and to private uses, as well as for luxury; and

Detail of sewer system, Italica

through how many tanks it is conveyed, and in what wards these are located; how much water is distributed within the city walls, how much without, how much is used for water basins, how much for fountains, how much for public structures, how much on account of the State, how much by private consumers. But before I mention the names *quinaria, centenaria,* and those of the other ajutages by which water is gauged, I deem it expedient to state what is their origin, what their bulk (areas of cross-section), and what each name means; and to show, after presenting the rules according to which their proportions and capacity are computed, how I discovered their discrepancies, and the way I set about to correct them.

24. The ajutages to measure water are arranged either according to digits or inches. Digits are used down to the present day in Campania, and in very many places in Italy; inches in Apulia and elsewhere. The digit, according to common agreement, is the one sixteenth part of a foot, the inch the twelfth; but even as there is a difference between the inch and the digit, so also digits differ among themselves; some are called square, others round. The square digit is greater than the round digit by three fourteenths of itself; the round digit is smaller than the square digit by three elevenths, obviously because the corners are lopped off. . . .

(PUBLIUS PAPINIUS) STATIUS (C. A.D. 45–96)

Thebaid

~~⌒~~

*D*ante Alighieri and Geoffrey Chaucer considered Statius one of the greatest epic poets, second only to Virgil. Born in Neapolis (Naples), he went to Rome when his poet-schoolmaster father transferred his grammar school there. Before long, Statius, under his father's tutelage, was reciting his verses and orating extemporaneously around town. He earned the attention of the emperor Domitian himself, who awarded him a prize at the Alban Games in A.D. 90. Eventually, with his wife, Claudia, he retired to Neapolis.

- Statius was working on a second epic, the *Achilleid,* celebrating the life and death of the Greek hero of the Trojan War, when he died. He completed only two of twelve proposed books. He also composed thirty-two informal "occasional pieces" known as the *Silvae,* all but six in lyric hexameters. Their subject matter deals with the daily life of the rich and famous in the reign of Domitian: funerals, weddings, anniversaries, illnesses, deaths, festivals, art works, pets, baths, villas, and slaves.

- His *Thebaid,* in twelve books, was published between A.D. 90 and 92. Dedicated to Domitian, the poem is heavily influenced by Virgil's *Aeneid.* It tells the story of Oedipus' curse on his sons, leading to the campaign of the Seven Against Thebes and the fatal duel between Eteocles and Polyneices.
- Although the action of the epic is oddly disjointed and its ornate Silver Age style overly artificial to the modern taste, the poem's strengths include its imaginative action, compelling narrative, and colorfully dramatic descriptiveness.

BOOK I

A certain noble, revered, and honorable king, had assumed sway and proprietorship over the pleasant and splendid capital city of Thebes in Greece. His name was Laius; and he had a son, Oedipus; and from that Oedipus sprang the two fair distinguished sons, to wit, Polynices and Eteocles. They are those brothers that killed one another in the great war between the Thebans and the Greeks, as they contended on each side for the sovereignty of Thebes, the capital city.

Now at that time it came into the mind of Statius the well-born eminent poet of the Franks to describe the origin of the Thebans, how they sprang from Cadmus, son of Agenor, that Agenor who was high-king of Tyre and Sidon, and whose daughter was the well-born maiden named Europa. With her Jove fell deeply in love so that he must needs go in the shape of a bull to fetch her over expanse of sea and ocean. And when he had crossed that sea to Crete, he returned to his own shape, and he held that maiden in great affection, and to that maiden Jove gave the great reward that Europe, one of the three principal divisions of the world, should be named from her.

As for Agenor, however, anger, intense rage, and deep grief took possession of him when he discovered the loss of his well-beloved daughter Europa. Now the plan Agenor then took was to send his well-beloved son over sea and land to seek his sister throughout the world, and he told him, unless he found his sister, not to come again or be seen by him. Then indeed Cadmus searched the world's fastnesses and the wondrous isles of the vast ocean that girds the globe, and he experienced a deal of toil, trouble, and perils of sea and land throughout the world both by sea and by land, and found not the maiden during all that time, though he suffered much tribulation, and for that the reason was that he might not cross Jupiter the son of Saturn, head of the gods, to make known against him his stolen love. And since he found not his sister, the plan he formed in his mind through his wisdom was this, to go to the temple of Apollo, the god of prophecy, and ask of him information and direction where the maiden was. And this Apollo told him, not to seek her, for he would not find her, but to fare forth tomorrow away on the delicately flowering level far-extended plain, "and a horned ever-beautiful cow would meet you on that delicately beautiful plain. Follow her until she lie down, and where she will lie down let a fair-built city be built by you, with great vast walls, with very spacious palaces, and with mild sollers bright with light," so that that city might be the city of the pomp and assembly of the Greeks, and that its name might be Boeotia or Thebes, owing to the power and the oracle of the god Apollo.

Cadmus remained there, and experienced thirst; and a trusty messenger was sent by him for a draught, with a beautiful brazen vessel embossed around with gold and silver, unto a vast darksome cave that was near him, in the midst of an overhanging grove, with a very beautiful earth-cool well in the midst of it. When the messenger had reached the well, and dipped his vessel down into the water, from the back of the cave there came a venomous serpent, with four huge heads upon it, and with three rows of teeth in each several head, and of monstrous shape from tail to head. When it saw the messenger above the well, it at once dealt him a blow with its muzzle, and he was left there lifeless. Afterward when Cadmus, son of Agenor, deemed his servant tarried long, he sent another of his following unto the cave and unto the water, and the serpent meted out the same treatment to him. Nay, fifty youths of his following fell thus. Then Cadmus, son of Agenor, rose, donned his armor, and prepared his arms with a soldier's heat, a lion's rage, and a serpent's venom, going to the door of the cave to avenge him on the man that had killed his retainers. And when he arrived, he saw the unspeakable huge serpent, and it made a great arched coil of itself from tail to head, like a mast of a very huge ship. When it saw the great man come nigh it, they fought together there a bloody, wounding, gory, blood-dripping fight then, and the serpent fell at last, and its poison came to nought. Thereafter he proceeded to the temple of Apollo, and the gods told him to plough the plain whereon the serpent had been killed, and from the sowing of that tilth with the serpent's teeth men arose under arms upon the hill. He tilled the soil before him, and they fought fiercely, furiously, angrily; and each one of them killed the other save a single quintette only, and Thebes was built by that quintette along with Cadmus, son of Agenor. That quintette was an illustrious unity, to wit Echion, who was engaged in building Thebes along with Cadmus, son of Agenor.

Well! Thebes was thus built by Cadmus, son of Agenor, and he dwelt in it for a long time prosperously and in wealth, till ill-luck found him in the end. For he himself and his wife were turned into serpent-shapes for the space of seven years, until the heart of the gods turned to them in the end, and then they got back into their own bodies, and of that man's seed sprang all the great and pure Theban kings, and of his seed was Oedipus, son of Laius. That Laius was in the sovereignty and occupation of Thebes for a long time, and of him prophets and wizards had foretold that when he should see any one of his children, his life would last no longer; so that on this account it was usually so done that in the case of every man-child that might be born to him, they were all destroyed. Then it chanced upon a time that Oedipus, son of Laius, was born of the witch Jocasta and after his birth he was carried to a very great wood near by, and his mother gave orders that he should not be lost or destroyed but lifted up into a very high and smooth tree-trunk in the wood; and Oedipus was left thus, and when he was left alone, he sang his childish little strain.

A certain king's son, however, who was engaged in plunder and rapine, that lad's name by which he was named was Polybus, heard that plaint of the infant bound in the tree. That man came forward toward the infant, and saw the infant in the plight in which it was. He conceived an exceeding great love for it, and carried it away with him to be nursed and reared as a son originally his own. Then Polybus assumed the sovereignty of his own land and country, and he committed the government of his state to the boy who had been brought up by him, to wit, Oedipus, son of Laius. Then that Oedipus chanced on one occasion after that untowardly, unexpectedly to fall in with his father Laius; and Laius knew not that it was Oedipus that met him, and no more did Oedipus know that it was his father Laius that was facing him. And each of them was demanding from the other his name, and neither of them would give the other his name. Then they fought a fierce and angry duel, and his father Laius fell by Oedipus through ignorance and want of guidance.

And Oedipus took his father's land, and on assuming sovereignty espoused his mother as a fitting consort, and knew nothing of that fact till the attention of Queen Jocasta fell upon Oedipus the king's naked feet, for thus they were with a hole through each of them. The queen asked: "What has pierced thy feet?" said she then. "Not hard," said he. "Thus was I found in the middle of a wood in a very high tree in the forest, with a nail through each of my feet keeping me in the tree, and I do not know who had placed me there in that fashion. But I was nursed and brought up by Polybus as his own son, and I knew not that it was not so,

till I was reproached therefor, and I was told that I was a bastard waif, with no knowledge of my father or my mother. I ascertained of Polybus that he could not tell me how he had found me: and what I did was to go to Apollo, the god of prophecy, and to ascertain from him where I should find my fatherland. Apollo told me to make my name known to no man, and to do battle with the first man that met me there, and I should obtain tidings of my father and my mother thereby. And the first man that chanced to approach me thereafter was Laius, wandering in hunting near the city of Phocis, and he fell by me, as ye have heard." "That is sad indeed," said Jocasta; "that Laius was in truth thy father, and I am thy mother; and it is I that gave orders that thou shouldest be bound in the tree and not killed, so much did I love thee; and it is I that bore thee these four children, Eteocles and Polynices, Antigone and Ismene being the two daughters." "Hard is that for me," said Oedipus, "that they should be born, and that these misdeeds should be done by me, though it be through ignorance and want of guidance that they happened." Then, moreover, Oedipus with his two hands seized his two eyes at once, and plucked them out of his head, to the end he might never look on anyone owing to the greatness of his shame in consequence of his committing those great sins, that no hosts or multitude might look upon him.

Now regarding the two sons of Oedipus, Eteocles and Polynices, envy and a strong contention arose between them about the sovereignty of Thebes so that neither of them could allow the other an equal share of the city or the tribe after the blinding of their father. They accorded no honor or distinction to their father, but were themselves with pride and ill-nature consuming their patrimony and the estate; and each one of the sons deems it should be himself that will be king there.

Now as to Oedipus after that, he dwelt gloomily and dejectedly in a cave-dwelling of the earth, with no kingdom or empire since his mutilating and destroying of himself. Then he made a great lamentation and an irresistible appeal to the dread gods of hell, and to the fiendish mad goddess, Tisiphone, in especial, and said: "Thou hast so reared and bred me that I have done many diverse ills through thine instigation and incitement. I have slain my decrepit long-lived sire at the city which is named Phocis, and by thine aid I solved the difficult insoluble riddles of the monster which was called Sphinx, and that is the monster that dwelt in the land of the Thebans, and 'tis it that used to ask this of every one that chanced to come nigh it: 'Which is the four-footed, two-footed, and three-footed animal?' And whoever could not give it a solution for the riddle, these were all slain, until I came to it, while I was in search of my father, and the monster asked the same riddles of me and I told it that the answer was man, inasmuch as he is four-footed in his infancy, to wit, as he moves about with his two feet and his two hands at the same time: two-footed, however, in his youth, to wit, and in his manhood, to wit, having only his two feet as he journeys: three-footed, however, in his old age and eld, to wit, having his two feet and his staff as he journeys. And when I had rede those riddles, we fought a fierce, wary, manly duel, and in consequence thereof the monster fell in the end." Then moreover Oedipus said: "It is by

thine aid and help that I have done these deeds, both slain my sire, and wronged my mother; and through thine instigation I have plucked my wide gray liquid-cool eyes out of my head, and thereafter thou hast awakened a fury of bitter rage between these my sons, to wit, Eteocles and Polynices, that they have rent and violently disrupted the kingdom, so that the one of them can have no headship or control of the other; for pride and folly have filled them by reason of the dishonor and contempt they have shown to me because of my living blind and dark in a cave-dwelling of earth."

Now when Tisiphone had heard these words of Oedipus, then the fiendish mad Fury arose with her locks of venomous serpents about her head, puffing, croaking, whistling, fluttering, and sucking the welling fiery stream named Cocytus, because upon the borders of that stream her dwelling-place was. Then she leaped swiftly impatiently madly from the stream like darting fiery levin, or like a swift star lighting up the quivering firmament; and this was the way she came, through the fierce idle and fiendish rabble, and through the weak and sad assemblies of souls that dwelt in the gravelly abodes of hell, so that horror and vast fear seized them as they beheld the fiendish dusky face of that fiery red-lipped scald of war. And thereupon she advanced forth through Taenaros, baleful door of hell. And when she had arrived, thick darkness like night overspread all earth's face, so that terror and intense fear seized the people of the bounds and districts before her; and then she came by the well-known and excellent road on hilly sloping glens, till she arrived at Thebes. Then a hundred venomous and hostile serpents with crests and stings arose about her head. Her colored and dark-gray eyes were sucked and swallowed into the depths of her head and crown. Then she arose and shook the venomous serpent that was in her hand at the hosts, so that the sound and crash thereof were heard throughout the four quarters of Greece, to wit, as far as Mount Parnassus in the East, the river Eurotas in the West, fair Mount Oete in the South, and to the fringed borders of Isthmos in the North. And that sound, distinct, well marked and very loud, reached the brave contentious envious Theban stock, and Oedipus' large fair sons, to wit, Eteocles and Polynices, so that a lasting feud and intense mutual jealousy about the sovereignty arose through Tisiphone's instigation between those two sons, like two strong, vicious, envious bulls under a huge intolerable yoke, so that they strained and weakened their bonds and fetters, as they mutually strove and pulled one against another.

PLINY THE YOUNGER (GAIUS PLINIUS CAECILIUS SECUNDUS) (A.D. 61 OR 62–114)

Letters

Nephew of Pliny the Elder, Pliny was adopted by his famous uncle after his father, L. Caecilius Cilo, died when he was still a boy. Like his uncle, born in Novum Comum (Como), he was given the best possible legal education in Rome and studied under Quintilian and Nicetes. Arguing his first case when he was only nineteen, Pliny specialized in property law and quickly became distinguished for both his argumentative and administrative skills.

His public offices, starting in the reign of Domitian and promoted by his well-placed friends Julius Frontinus and Verginius Rufus, included serving as military tribune in Syria, quaestor, tribune of the plebs, prefect of the military treasury, praetor, prefect of the civil treasury, consul, superintendent of Rome's drainage system, public prosecutor, and augur. His last appointment was as imperial legate to Bithynia, where he died in A.D. 114, two years after taking office.

- Pliny's *Panegyricus,* a highly rhetorical and flowery oration delivered before the Senate in A.D. 100 to express his gratitude to the emperor Trajan for the consulship bestowed on him, gives invaluable insight into Trajan's early reign and contrasts the emperor's heroism with his despised predecessor Domitian.
- But he's best remembered for his ten books of 247 "newsletters," filled with compelling, succinct, and eloquent images of this sophisticated Roman century. From these pages, written in a readable and informal yet impeccably literary Ciceronic style ("letters written with special care"), we learn about Pliny's kindly personality, his vanity, his studies, his business, his political and judicial victories, weather conditions, senatorial proceedings, his sincere though pedantic interest in literature, the public life and high society of his times, moral concerns, and the doings of Pliny's associates—Quintilian, his good friend Tacitus, Suetonius, Silius Italicus, and Martial.
- Letters to and from Trajan, which comprise the tenth book of Pliny's correspondence, remain a primary source for understanding the day-to-day workings of the Roman Empire, including an account of the early Christians.

TO CORNELIUS TACITUS
(I., 6.)

You will laugh, and I give you leave to. You know what sort of sportsman I am, but I, even I, have bagged three boars, each one of them a perfect beauty. "What!" you will say, "you!" Yes, I, and that too without any violent departure from my usual lazy ways. I was sitting by the nets; I had by my side not a hunting spear and a dart, but my pen and writing tablets. I was engaged in some composition and jotting down notes, so that I might have full tablets to take home with me, even though my hands were empty. You need not shrug your shoulders at study under such conditions. It is really surprising how the mind is stimulated by bodily movement and exercise. I find the most powerful incentive to thought in having the woods all about me, in the solitude and the silence which is observed in hunting. So when next you go hunting, take my advice and carry your writing tablets with you as well as your luncheon basket and your flask. You will find that Minerva loves to wander on the mountains quite as much as Diana. Farewell.

TO SOSIUS SENECIO
(I., 13.)

This year has brought us a fine crop of poets: right through April hardly a day passed without some recital or other. I am delighted that literature is so flourishing and that men are giving such open proofs of brains, even though audiences are found so slow in coming together. People as a rule lounge in the squares and waste the time in gossip when they should be listening to the recital. They get some one to come and tell them whether the reciter has entered the hall yet, whether he has got through his introduction, or whether he has nearly reached the end of his reading. Not until then do they enter the room, and even then they come in slowly and languidly. Nor do they sit it out; no, before the close of the recital they slip away, some sidling out so as not to attract attention, others rising openly and walking out bodily. And yet, by Hercules, our fathers tell a story of how Claudius Caesar one day while walking up and down in the palace, happened to hear some clapping of hands, and on inquiring the cause and being told that Nonianus was giving a reading, he suddenly joined the company to every one's surprise. But nowadays even those who have most time on their hands, after receiving early notices and frequent reminders, either fail to put in an appearance, or if they do come they complain that they have wasted a day just because they have not wasted it. All the more praise and credit, therefore, is due to those who do not allow their love of writing and reciting to be damped either by the laziness or the fastidiousness of their audiences. For my own part, I have hardly ever failed to attend. True, the authors are mostly my friends, for almost all the literary people are also friends of mine, and for this reason I have spent more time in Rome than I had intended. But now I can betake myself to my country retreat and compose something, though not for a public recital, lest those whose readings I attended should think I went not so much to hear their works as to get a claim on them to come and hear mine. As in everything else, if you lend a man your ears, all the grace of the act vanishes if you ask for his in return. Farewell.

TO TACITUS
(VI., 16.)

You ask me to send you an account of my uncle's death, so that you may be able to give posterity an accurate description of it. I am much obliged to you, for I can see that the immortality of his fame is well assured, if you take in hand to write of it. For although he perished in a disaster which devastated some of the fairest regions of the land, and though he is sure of eternal remembrance like the peoples and cities that fell with him in that memorable calamity, though, too, he had written a large number of works of lasting value, yet the undying fame of which your writings are assured will secure for his a still further lease of life. For my part, I think that those people are highly favored by Providence who are capable either of performing deeds worthy of the historian's pen or of writing histories worthy of being read, but that they are peculiarly favored who can do both. Among the latter I may class my uncle, thanks to his own writings and to yours. So I am all the more ready to fulfill your injunctions, nay, I am even prepared to beg to be allowed to undertake them.

My uncle was stationed at Misenum, where he was in active command of the fleet, with full powers. On the 23d of August, about the seventh hour, my mother drew his attention to the fact that a cloud of unusual size and shape had made its appearance. He had taken his sun bath, followed by a cold one, and after a light meal he was lying down and reading. Yet he called for his sandals, and climbed up to a spot from which he could command a good view of the curious phenomenon. Those who were looking at the cloud from some distance could not make out from which mountain it was rising—it was afterward discovered to have been Mount Vesuvius—but in likeness and form it more resembled a pine-tree than anything else, for what corresponded to the trunk was of great length and height, and then spread out into a number of branches, the reason being, I imagine, that while the vapor was fresh, the cloud was borne upward, but when the vapor became wasted, it lost its motion, or even became dissipated by its own weight and spread out laterally. At times it looked white, and at other times dirty and spotted, according to the quantity of earth and cinders that were shot up.

To a man of my uncle's learning, the phenomenon appeared one of great importance, which deserved a close study. He ordered a Liburnian galley to be got ready, and offered to take me with him, if I desired to accompany him, but I replied that I preferred to go on with my studies, and it so happened that he assigned me some writing to do. He was just leaving the house when he received a written message from Rectina, the wife of Tascus, who was terrified at the peril threatening her—for her villa lay just beneath the mountain, and there were no means of escape save by shipboard—begging him to save her from her perilous position. So he changed his plan and carried out with the greatest fortitude the ideas which had occurred to him as a student.

He had the galleys launched and went on board himself, in the hope of succoring, not only Rectina, but many others, for there were a number of people living along the shore, owing to its delightful situation. He hastened, therefore, toward the place whence others were flying, and steering a direct course, kept the helm straight for the point of danger, so utterly devoid of fear that every movement of the looming portent and every change in its appearance he described and had noted down by his secretary, as soon as his eyes detected it. Already ashes were beginning to fall upon the ships, hotter and in thicker showers as they approached more nearly, with pumice-stones and black flints, charred and cracked by the heat of the flames, while their way was barred by the sudden shoaling of the sea bottom and the litter of the mountain on the shore. He hesitated for a moment whether to turn back, and then, when the helmsman warned him to do so, he exclaimed, "Fortune favors the bold; try to reach Pomponianus." The latter was at Stabiae, separated by the whole width of the bay, for the sea there pours in upon a gently rounded and curving shore. Although the danger was not yet close upon him, it was none the less clearly seen, and it traveled quickly as it came nearer, so Pomponianus had got his baggage together on shipboard, and had determined upon flight, and was waiting for the wind which was blowing on shore to fall. My uncle sailed in with the wind fair behind him, and embraced Pomponianus, who was in a state of fright, comforting and cheering him at the same time. Then in order to calm his friend's fears by showing how composed he was himself, he ordered the servants to carry him to his bath, and, after his ablutions, he sat down and had dinner in the best of spirits, or with that assumption of good spirits which is quite as remarkable as the reality.

In the meantime broad sheets of flame, which rose high in the air, were breaking out in a number of places on Mount Vesuvius and lighting up the sky, and the glare and brightness seemed all the more striking owing to the darkness of the night. My uncle, in order to allay the fear of his companions, kept declaring that the country people in their terror had left their fires burning, and that the conflagration they saw arose from the blazing and empty villas. Then he betook himself to rest and enjoyed a very deep sleep, for his breathing, which, owing to his bulk, was rather heavy and loud, was heard by those who were waiting at the door of his chamber. But by this time the courtyard leading to the room he occupied was so full of ashes and pumice-stones mingled together, and covered to such a depth, that if he had delayed any longer in the bed-chamber there would have been no means of escape. So my uncle was aroused, and came out and joined Pomponianus and the rest who had been keeping watch. They held a consultation whether they should remain indoors or wander forth in the open; for the buildings were beginning to shake with the repeated and intensely severe shocks of earthquake, and seemed to be rocking to and fro, as though they had been torn from their foundations. Outside again there was danger to be apprehended from the pumice-stones, though these were light and nearly burnt through, and thus, after weighing the two perils, the latter course was determined upon. With my uncle it was a choice of reasons which prevailed, with the rest a choice of fears.

They placed pillows on their heads and secured them with napkins, as a precaution against the falling bodies. Elsewhere the day had dawned by this time, but there it was still night, and the darkness was blacker and thicker than any ordinary night. This, however, they relieved as best they could by a number of torches and other kinds of lights. They decided to make their way to the shore, and to see from the nearest point whether the sea would enable them to put out, but it was still running high and contrary. A sheet was spread on the ground, and on this my uncle lay, and twice he called for a draught of cold water, which he drank. Then the flames, and the smell of sulphur which gave warning of them, scattered the others in flight and roused him. Leaning on two slaves, he rose to his feet and immediately fell down again, owing, as I think, to his breathing being obstructed by the thickness of the fumes and congestion of the stomach, that organ being naturally weak and narrow, and subject to inflammation. When daylight returned—which was three days after his death—his body was found untouched, uninjured, and covered, dressed just as he had been in life. The corpse suggested a person asleep rather than a dead man.

Meanwhile my mother and I were at Misenum. But that is of no consequence for the purposes of history, nor indeed did you express a wish to be told anything except of my uncle's death. So I will say no more, except to add that I have given you a full account both of the incidents which I myself witnessed and of those narrated to me immediately afterward, when, as a rule, one gets the truest account of what has happened. You will pick out what you think will answer your purpose best, for to write a letter is a different thing from writing a history, and to write to a friend is not like writing to all and sundry. Farewell.

TO SURA
(VII., 27.)

The leisure we are both of us enjoying gives you an opportunity of imparting, and me an opportunity of receiving, information. So I should very much like to know whether in your opinion there are such things as ghosts, whether you think they have a shape of their own and a touch of the supernatural in them, or whether you consider they are vain, empty shadows and mere creatures of the imaginations. For my own part, I feel led to believe that they have a real existence, and this mainly from what befell Curtius Rufus.

In the days when he was still poor and obscure, he had attached himself to the person of the governor of Africa. One evening at sundown he was walking in the portico, when the figure of a woman—but taller and more beautiful than mortal woman—presented itself before him and told Rufus, who was terrified with fright, that she was Africa and could foretell the future. She declared that he would go to Rome and hold high offices of state, and that he would also return with plenary powers as governor to that same province, and there meet his death. All these details were fulfilled. Moreover, when he was entering Carthage and just stepping out of his ship, the same figure is said to have met him on the beach. Certain it is that when he was attacked by illness, he interpreted the future by the past, and his coming adversity by his

present prosperity, and, though none of his people were despairing of his recovery, he cast aside all hope of getting better.

Now I want you to consider whether the following story, which I shall tell you just as I heard it, is not even more terrifying and no less wonderful than the other. There stood at Athens a spacious and roomy house, but it had an evil reputation of being fatal to those who lived in it. In the silence of the night the clank of iron and, if you listened with closer attention, the rattle of chains were heard, the sound coming first from a distance and afterward quite close at hand. Then appeared the ghostly form of an old man, emaciated, filthy, decrepit, with a flowing beard and hair on end, with fetters round his legs and chains on his hands, which he kept shaking. The terrified inmates passed sleepless nights of fearful terror, and following upon their sleeplessness came disease and then death, as their fears increased. For every now and again, though the ghost had vanished, memory conjured up the vision before their eyes, and their fright remained longer than the apparition which had caused it. Then the house was deserted and condemned to stand empty, and was wholly abandoned to the specter, while the authorities forbade that it should be sold or let to any one wishing to take it, not knowing under what a curse it lay.

The philosopher Athenodorus came to Athens, read the notice board, and on hearing the price, hesitated, because the low rent made him suspicious. Then he was told the whole story, and, so far from being deterred, he became the more eager to rent it. When evening began to fall, he ordered his people to make him up a bed in the front part of the house, and asked for his tablets, a pen, and a lamp. Dismissing all his servants to the inner rooms, he applied mind, eyes, and hand to the task of writing, lest by having nothing to think about he might begin to conjure up the apparition of which he had been told and other idle fears. At first the night was just as still there as elsewhere, then the iron was rattled and the chains clanked. Athenodorus did not raise his eyes, nor cease to write, but fortified his resolution and closed his ears. The noise became louder and drew nearer, and was heard now on the threshold and then within the room itself. He turned his head, and saw and recognized the ghost which had been described to him. It stood and beckoned with its finger, as if calling him; but Athenodorus merely motioned with his hand, as if to bid it wait a little, and once more bent over his tablets and plied his pen. As he wrote the specter rattled its chains over his head, and looking round he saw that it was beckoning as before, so, without further delay, he took up the lamp and followed. The specter walked with slow steps, as though burdened by the chains, then it turned off into the courtyard of the house and suddenly vanished, leaving its companion alone, who thereupon plucked some grass and foliage to mark the place. On the following day he went to the magistrates and advised them to give orders that the place should be dug up. Bones were found with chains wound round them. Time and the action of the soil had made the flesh moulder, and left the bones bare and eaten away by the chains, but the remains were collected and given a public burial. Ever afterward the house was free of the ghost, which had been thus laid with due ceremony.

I quite believe those who vouch for these details, but the following story I can vouch for to others. I have a freedman who is a man of some education. A younger brother of his was sleeping with him in the same bed, and he thought he saw some one sitting upon the bed, and applying a pair of shears to his head, and even cutting off some hair from his crown, and the locks were found lying close by. A little time elapsed, and a similar incident occurred to make people believe the other story was true. A young slave of mine was sleeping with a number of others in the dormitory, when, according to his story, two men clothed in white tunics entered by the window and cut his hair as he slept, retiring by the way they came. Daylight revealed that his hair had been cut, and the locks lay scattered around. No incident of any note followed, unless it was that I escaped prosecution, as I should not have done if Domitian, in whose reign these incidents had taken place, had lived any longer than he did. For in his writing-desk there was discovered a document sent in by Carus which denounced me. This gives rise to the conjecture that, as it is the custom for accused persons to let their hair go untrimmed, the fact that the hair of my slaves was cut was a sign that the peril overhanging me had passed away.

I beg of you to bring your erudition to bear on these stories. The matter is one which is worth long and careful consideration, nor am I altogether undeserving of your imparting to me your plentiful knowledge. I will let you follow your usual habit of arguing on both sides of the case, but be sure that you take up one side more strongly than the other, so that I may not go away in suspense and uncertainty, when the reason I asked your advice was just this—that you put an end to my doubts. Farewell.

TO TRAJAN
(96.)

It is my custom, Sire, to refer to you in all cases where I do not feel sure, for who can better direct my doubts or inform my ignorance? I have never been present at any legal examination of the Christians, and I do not know, therefore, what are the usual penalties passed upon them, or the limits of those penalties, or how searching an inquiry should be made. I have hesitated a great deal in considering whether any distinctions should be drawn according to the ages of the accused; whether the weak should be punished as severely as the more robust; whether if they renounce their faith they should be pardoned, or whether the man who has once been a Christian should gain nothing by recanting; whether the name itself, even though otherwise innocent of crime, should be punished, or only the crimes that gather round it.

In the mean time, this is the plan which I have adopted in the case of those Christians who have been brought before me. I ask them whether they are Christians; if they say yes, then I repeat the question a second and a third time, warning them of the penalties it entails, and if they still persist, I order them to be taken to prison. For I do not doubt that, whatever the character of the crime may be which they confess, their pertinacity and inflexible obstinacy certainly ought to be

punished. There were others who showed similar mad folly whom I reserved to be sent to Rome, as they were Roman citizens. Subsequently, as is usually the way, the very fact of my taking up this question led to a great increase of accusations, and a variety of cases were brought before me. A pamphlet was issued anonymously, containing the names of a number of people. Those who denied that they were or had been Christians and called upon the gods in the usual formula, reciting the words after me, those who offered incense and wine before your image, which I had given orders to be brought forward for this purpose, together with the statues of the deities—all such I considered should be discharged, especially as they cursed the name of Christ, which, it is said, those who are really Christians cannot be induced to do. Others, whose names were given me by an informer, first said that they were Christians and afterward denied it, declaring that they had been but were so no longer, some of them having recanted many years before, and more than one so long as twenty years back. They all worshiped your image and the statues of the deities, and cursed the name of Christ. But they declared that the sum of their guilt or their error only amounted to this, that on a stated day they had been accustomed to meet before daybreak and to recite a hymn among themselves to Christ, as though he were a god, and that so far from binding themselves by oath to commit any crime, their oath was to abstain from theft, robbery, adultery, and from breach of faith, and not to deny trust money placed in their keeping when called upon to deliver it. When this ceremony was concluded, it had been their custom to depart and meet again to take food, but it was of no special character and quite harmless, and they had ceased this practice after the edict in which, in accordance with your orders, I had forbidden all secret societies. I thought it the more necessary, therefore, to find out what truth there was in these statements by submitting two women, who were called deaconesses, to the torture, but I found nothing but a debased superstition carried to great lengths. So I postponed my examination, and immediately consulted you. The matter seems to me worthy of your consideration, especially as there are so many people involved in the danger. Many persons of all ages, and of both sexes alike, are being brought into peril of their lives by their accusers; and the process will go on. For the contagion of this superstition has spread not only through the free cities, but into the villages and the rural districts, and yet it seems to me that it can be checked and set right. It is beyond doubt that the temples, which have been almost deserted, are beginning again to be thronged with worshipers, that the sacred rites which have for a long time been allowed to lapse are now being renewed, and that the food for the

Trajan's bath, Italica

sacrificial victims is once more finding a sale, whereas, up to recently, a buyer was hardly to be found. From this it is easy to infer what vast numbers of people might be reclaimed, if only they were given an opportunity of repentance.

JUVENAL (DECIMUS JUNIUS JUVENALIS)

(C. A.D. 60–C. 130)

Satires

~~⌒~~

The most important Roman satirist in the tradition of Lucilius, Horace, and Persius, Juvenal was born of an affluent family in Aquinum, Italy, in the Volscians. We know little of his life except that he was a minor army officer who also held office in Aquinum in Latium; and he was exiled from Rome around the age of thirty, probably to military service in Aswan, Egypt, because he'd offended Domitian by lampooning the emperor's favorite comedian. Hadrian seems to have restored him to Roman circles, where he depended on his patrons for his meager living. Martial was among his friends.

- Juvenal published, between A.D. 110 and 130, sixteen satires, in pyrotechnically varied dactylic hexameters, expressing his outrage at the decline of Roman culture under Domitian, Nerva, Trajan, and Hadrian. His subjects include greed, hypocritical Stoics, abuses of the patronage system, the misery of intellectuals, the fast-talking Greek entrepreneurs who'd taken over aristocratic circles in Rome, the cult of hereditary nobility, the sexual depravity of Roman women, marriage, parental responsibilities, homosexuality, the misuse of wealth, embezzlement, the discomforts and traffic jams of the overcrowded city, and the vice and corruption of Roman high society.
- His passionately concise style, used as a model of precision throughout the Medieval, Renaissance, and Romantic periods, is a unique rhetorical mixture of biting sarcasm, philosophical cynicism, irony, innuendo, and lofty moral invective. The detail with which he paints the vices he castigates made his critics believe his interests in sin were more than purely academic.

SATIRE I

Must I always be stuck in the audience at these
    poetry-readings, never
Up on the platform myself, taking it out on
    Cordus
For the times he's bored me to death with rant-
    ing speeches
From that Theseid of his? Is X to get off scot-
    free
After inflicting his farces on me, or Y his ele-
    gies? Is there
No recompense for whole days wasted on prolix
Versions of Telephus? And what about that
    Orestes—
Each margin of the roll crammed solid, top
    and bottom,
More on the back, and still it wasn't finished!
I know all the mythical landscapes like my
    own back-room:
The grove of Mars, that cave near Aeolus' island
Belonging to Vulcan. The stale themes are bel-
    lowed daily
In rich patrons' colonnades, till their marble
    pillars
Crack with a surfeit of rhetoric. The plane-trees
    echo
Every old trope—what the winds are up to,
    whose ghosts
Aeacus has on his hellish rack, from what far
    country
The other fellow is sneaking off with that
    golden sheepskin,
The monstrous size of those ash-trees the Cen-
    taurs used for spears:
You get the same stuff from them all, estab-
    lished poet
And raw beginner alike. I too have winced
    under the cane

And concocted "Advice to Sulla": Let the
    despot retire
Into private life, take a good long sleep, and
    so on. When you find
Hordes of poets on each street-corner, it's mis-
    placed kindness
To refrain from writing. The paper will still be
    wasted.
Why then have I chosen to drive my team down
    the track
Which great Lucilius blazed? If you have the
    leisure to listen
Calmly and reasonably, I will enlighten you.
       When a flabby eunuch marries, when
    well-born girls go crazy
For pig-sticking up-country, bare-breasted,
    spear in fist;
When the barber who rasped away at my
    youthful beard has risen
To challenge good society with his millions;
    when Crispinus—
That Delta-bred house-slave, silt washed down
    by the Nile—
Now hitches his shoulders under Tyrian purple,
    airs
A thin gold ring in summer on his sweaty finger
("My dear, I couldn't bear to wear my heavier
    jewels")—
Why then, it is harder not to be writing satires;
    for who
Could endure this monstrous city, however cal-
    lous at heart,
And swallow his wrath? Look: here comes a
    brand-new litter,
Crammed with its corpulent owner, some chis-
    eling advocate.
Who's next? An informer. He turned in his
    noble patron,

And soon he'll have gnawed away that favorite
bone of his,
The aristocracy. Lesser informers dread him, grease
His palm with ample bribes, while the wives of
trembling actors
Grease him the other way. Today we are
elbowed aside
By men who earn legacies in bed, who rise to
the top
Via that quickest, most popular route—the satisfied desires
Of some rich old matron. Each lover will get
his cut,
A twelfth share in the estate, or eleven-twelfths,
depending
On the size of his—services rendered. I suppose
he deserves
Some recompense for all that sweat and exertion: he looks
As pale as the man who steps barefoot on a
snake—or is waiting
His turn to declaim, at Lyons, in Caligula's
competitions.
      Need I tell you how anger burns in my
heart when I see
The bystanders jostled back by a mob of
bravos
Whose master has first debauched his ward,
and later
Defrauded the boy as well? The courts condemned him,
But the verdict was a farce. Who cares for reputation
If he keeps his cash? A provincial governor,
exiled
For extortion, boozes and feasts all day, basks
cheerfully

In the wrathful eye of the Gods; it's still his
province,
After winning the case against him, that feels
the pinch.
      Are not such themes well worthy of
Horace's pen? Should I
Not attack them too? Must I stick to the usual
round
Of Hercules' labors, what Diomede did, the
bellowing
Of that thingummy in the Labyrinth, or the
tale of the flying
Carpenter, and how his son went splash in the
sea?
Will these suffice in an age when each pimp of
a husband
Takes gifts from his own wife's lover—if she is
barred in law
From inheriting legacies—and, while they
paw each other,
Tactfully stares at the ceiling, or snores, wide
awake, in his wine?
Will these suffice, when the young blade who
has squandered
His family fortune on racing-stables still reckons to get
Command of a cohort? Just watch him lash
his horses
Down the Flaminian Way like Achilles' charioteer,
Reins bunched in one hand, showing off to his
mistress
Who stands beside him, wrapped in his riding-
cloak!
Don't you want to cram whole notebooks with
scribbled invective
When you stand at the corner and see some
forger carried past

On the necks of six porters, lounging back like
    Maecenas
In his open litter? A counterfeit seal, a will, a
    mere scrap
Of paper—these were enough to convert him to
    wealth and honor.
Do you see that distinguished lady? She has
    the perfect dose
For her husband—old wine with a dash of
    parching toad's blood:
Locusta's a child to her; she trains her untu-
    tored neighbors
To ignore all unkind rumors, to stalk through
    angry crowds
With their black and bloated husbands before
    them on the hearse.
If you want to be someone today you must
    nerve yourself
For deeds that could earn you an island exile,
    or years in jail.
Honesty's praised, but honest men freeze.
    Wealth springs from crime:
Landscape-gardens, palaces, furniture, antique
    silver—
Those cups embossed with prancing boats—all,
    all are tainted.
Who can sleep easy today? If your greedy
    daughter-in-law
Is not being seduced for cash, it'll be your
    bride: mere schoolboys
Are adulterers now. Though talent be wanting,
    yet
Indignation will drive me to verse, such as I—
    or any scribbler—
May still command. All human endeavors,
    men's prayers,
Fears, angers, pleasures, joys and pursuits,
    these make

The mixed mash of my verse.
               Since the days of the Flood,
When Deucalion anchored his ship on a moun-
    tain peak
To search for a sign, the days when hard stones
    quivered
To living softness and warmth, and Pyrrha
    confronted
The first men with their naked mates, has there
    ever
Been so rich a crop of vices? When has the
    purse
Of greed yawned wider? When was gambling
    more frantic
Than it is today? Men face the table's
    hazards
Not with their purse but their strong-box open
    beside them.
Here you'll see notable battles, with the
    croupier for squire,
Holding stakes instead of a shield. Is it not
    plain lunacy
To lose ten thousand on a turn of the dice, yet
    grudge
A shirt to your shivering slave? Which of your
    grandfathers
Would have built himself so many country
    houses, or dined
Off seven courses, alone? Clients were guests in
    those days.
But now Roman citizens are reduced to scram-
    bling
For a little basket of scraps on their patron's
    doorstep.
He peers into each face first, scared stiff that
    some imposter
May give a false name and cheat him: you
    must be identified

Before you get your ration. The crier has his
orders:
Each man to answer his name, nobility
included—
Oh yes, our Upper-Ten are scrounging with the
rest.
"The praetor first, then the Tribune—" But a
freedman blocks
Their way. "I got here first," he says, "why
shouldn't I keep
My place? I don't give that *for you. Oh, I know*
I'm foreign:
Look here, at my pierced ears, no use denying
it—born
Out East, on the Euphrates. But my five shops
bring in
Four hundred thousand, see? So I qualify for
the gentry.
What's in a senator's purple stripe, if true-blue
nobles
Are reduced to herding sheep up-country, while
I have more
Stashed away in the bank than any Imperial
favorite?"
So let the Tribunes wait, and money reign
supreme;
Let the Johnny-come-lately, whose feet only
yesterday were white
With the chalk of the slave-market, flout this
sacrosanct office!
Why not? Though as yet, pernicious Gash, you
lack
A temple of your own, though we have raised
no altars
To Sovereign Gold (as already we worship
Honor,
Peace, Victory, Virtue, or Concord—whose
roosting storks

Rattle and flap on the roof when you salute
their nest),
Still it is Wealth, not God, that compels our
deepest reverence.
    When the Consul himself tots up, at the
end of his year,
What the dole is worth, how much it adds to
his income, how
Are we poor dependants to manage? Out of
this pittance
We must pay for decent clothes and shoes—not
to mention our food
And the fuel for heating. But plenty who can
afford
A litter still queue up for their bob-a-day; some
husbands
Go the rounds with a sick or pregnant wife in
tow,
Or better (a well-known dodge) pretend she's
there when she isn't,
And claim for both, displaying a curtained,
empty sedan.
"My Galla's in there," he says. "Come on, let
us through! You doubt me?
Galla! Put out your head, girl! I'm sorry, she
must be asleep—
No, don't disturb her, please—!"
                    And so the day wears on
With its prescribed routine, its fascinating
round.
Dole in pocket, we next attend my lord to the
Forum;
Stare, bored, at all those statues—Apollo
beside the Law Courts
(He must be an expert by now) or that jumped-
up Egyptian
Pasha who's had the nerve to gate-crash Tri-
umph Row:

His *effigy's only fit for pissing on—or worse.*
[Experienced clients follow their patron home
    again],
Hoping against hope for that dinner-
    invitation
Which never comes: worn out, they drift away
    to purchase
(Poor souls) their cabbage and kindling. But
    he meanwhile will loll
Alone at his guestless meal, wolfing the choic-
    est produce
Of sea and woodland. These fellows will gob-
    ble up
Whole legacies at one course, off fine big
    antique tables:
Soon there won't be a parasite left. But who
    could stomach
Such measures in gourmands? What a grossly
    ravening maw
That man must have who dines off whole roast
    boar—a beast
Ordained for convivial feasting! But you'll pay
    the price
All too soon, my friend, when you undress and
    waddle
Into the bath, your belly still swollen with
    undigested
Peacock-meat—a lightning heart-attack, with
    no time
To make your final will. The story circulates
As a dinner-table joke, the latest thing. But no
    one
Cares about you. Your corpse is borne out to
    ironical
Cheers from your cheated friends. Posterity can
    add
No more, or worse, to our ways; our grandchil-
    dren will act

As we do, and share our desires. Today every
    vice
Has reached its ruinous zenith. So, satirist,
    hoist your sails,
Cram on every stitch of canvas! But where, you
    may ask,
Is a talent to match the theme? and where our
    outspoken
Ancestral bluntness, that wrote what burning
    passion dictated?
"Show me the man I dare not name," Lucilius
    cried,
"What odds if the noble Consul forgive my libel
    or not?"
But name an Imperial favorite, and you will
    soon enough
Blaze like those human torches, half-choked,
    half-grilled to death,
Those calcined corpses they drag with hooks
    from the arena,
And leave a broad black trail behind them in
    the sand.
    But what, you may ask, about the man
    who has poisoned
Three uncles with belladonna—are we to let
    him ride
In his feather-bedded litter, and look down his
    nose at us?
Yes; and when he approaches, keep mum, clap
    a hand to your mouth—
Just to say That's the man will brand you as
    an informer.
It's safe enough to retell how Aeneas fought
    fierce Turnus;
No one's a penny the worse for Achilles' death,
    or the frantic
Search for Hylas, that time he tumbled in after
    his pitcher.

But when fiery Lucilius rages with satire's
    naked sword
His hearers go red; their conscience is cold with
    crime,
Their innards sweat at the thought of their
    secret guilt:
Hence wrath and tears. So ponder these things
    in your mind
Before the trumpet sounds. It's too late for a
    soldier
To change his mind about fighting when he's
    armed in the battleline.
For myself, I shall try my hand on the famous
    dead, whose ashes
Rest beside the Latin and the Flaminian Ways.

SATIRE X

Search every land, from Cadiz to the dawn-
    streaked shores
Of Ganges, and you'll find few men who can
    distinguish
A false from a worthwhile objective, or slash
    their way through
The fogs of deception. Since when were our
    fears or desires
Ever dictated by reason? What project goes so
    smoothly
That you never regret the idea, let alone its
    realization?
What you ask for, you get. The Gods aren't
    fussy, they're willing
To blast you, root and branch, on request. It's
    universal,
This self-destructive urge, in civilian and soldier
Alike. The gift of the gab, a torrential facility,
Has proved fatal to so many; so has excessive
    reliance

On muscle and physical beef. But more are
    strangulated
By the capital they amass with such expense of
    spirit,
Those bloated fortunes that dwarf any normal
    inheritance,
Till they look like some puny dolphin beside a
    British whale.
So during the Reign of Terror, at Nero's com-
    mand,
Longinus was banished, Seneca—grown too
    wealthy—
Lost his magnificent gardens, storm-troopers
    besieged
Lateranus' ancestral mansion. Garrets are very
    seldom
The object of military raids. When you go on a
    night journey,
Though you may have only a few small trea-
    sures with you,
You'll take every stirring shadow, each moonlit
    reed
For a sword or a cudgel. But the empty-
    handed
Traveler whistles his way past any highway-
    man.
    The most popular, urgent prayer, well-
    known in every temple,
Is for wealth. Increase my holdings, please
    make my deposit account
The largest in town! But you'll never find
    yourself drinking
Belladonna from pottery cups. The time you
    should worry is when
You're clutching a jeweled goblet, when your
    bubbly gleams with gold.
They had a point—don't you agree?—those
    two old philosophers:

*One of them helpless with laughter whenever
    he set foot
Outside his house, the other a weeping fountain.
The cutting, dismissive sneer comes easily to us
    all—
But wherever did Heraclitus tap such an eye-
    brimming
Reservoir of tears? Democritus' sides shook
    non-stop,
Though the cities he knew had none of our
    modern trappings—
Togas bordered or striped with purple, sedans,
    the tribunal,
The rods and axes. Suppose he had seen the
    praetor
Borne in his lofty carriage through the midst
    of the dusty
Circus, and wearing full ceremonial dress—
The tunic with palm-leaves, the heavy Tyrian
    toga
Draped in great folds round his shoulders; a
    crown so enormous
That no neck can bear its weight, and instead
    it's carried
By a sweating public slave, who, to stop the
    Consul
Getting above himself, rides in the carriage
    beside him.
Then there's the ivory staff, crowned with an
    eagle,
A posse of trumpeters, the imposing procession
Of white-robed citizens marching so dutifully
    beside
His bridle-rein, retainers whose friendship was
    bought
With the meal-ticket stashed in their wallets.
    Democritus long ago*

*Found occasion for laughter in all human
    intercourse,
And his wisdom reveals that the greatest men,
    those destined
To set the highest examples, may still be born
In a land with a sluggish climate, a country of
    muttonheads.
The cares of the crowd he derided no less than
    their pleasures,
Their griefs, too, on occasion: if Fortune was
    threatening,
"Up you," he'd say, and give her the vulgar
    finger. So
If our current petitions are pointless—destruc-
    tive, even—
What should we ask for, what message leave on
    the knees of the Gods?
Some men are overthrown by the envy their
    great power
Arouses; it's that long and illustrious list of
    honors
That sinks them. The ropes are heaved, down
    come the statues,
Axes demolish their chariot-wheels, the unof-
    fending
Legs of their horses are broken. And now the
    fire
Roars up in the furnace, now flames hiss under
    the bellows:
The head of the people's darling glows red-hot,
    great Sejanus
Crackles and melts. That face only yesterday
    ranked
Second in all the world. Now it's so much
    scrap-metal,
To be turned into jugs and basins, frying-pans,
    chamber-pots.*

*Hang wreaths on your doors, lead a big white
    sacrificial
Bull to the Capitol! They're dragging Sejanus
    along
By a hook, in public. Everyone cheers. "Just
    look at that
Ugly stuck-up face," they say. "Believe me, I
    never
Cared for the fellow." "But what was his
    crime? Who brought
The charges, who gave evidence? How did they
    prove him guilty?"
"Nothing like that: a long and wordy letter
    arrived
From Capri." "Fair enough: you need say no
    more."*

                                            *And what
Of the commons? They follow fortune as
    always, and detest
The victims, the failures. If a little Etruscan
    luck
Had rubbed off on Sejanus, if the doddering
    Emperor
Had been struck down out of the blue, this
    identical rabble
Would now be proclaiming that carcase an
    equal successor
To Augustus. But nowadays, with no vote to
    sell, their motto
Is "Couldn't care less." Time was when their
    plebiscite elected
Generals, Heads of State, commanders of
    legions: but now
They've pulled in their horns, there's only two
    things that concern them:
Bread and the Games.*
                "I hear that many are to be purged."

*"That's right, they're turning the heat on, and
    no mistake."*
                                            *"My friend
Bruttidius looked somewhat pale when I met
    him in town just now—
Our slighted Ajax, I fear, is out for blood: dis-
    loyal
Heads will roll."*
        *"Come on, then, quickly, down to the river—
Boot Caesar's foe in the ribs while his corpse is
    still on show."
"Yes, and make our slaves watch us—eyewit-
    nesses can't deny it,
Can't drag their wretched masters into court at
    a rope's end."
That's how they talked of Sejanus, such was the
    private gossip
After his death. Would you really choose to be
    courted as
He was? To own his wealth? To hand out offi-
    cial appointments—
Consulships, army commands? To be known as
    the "protector"
Of an Imperial recluse squatting on Capri's
    narrow
Rocks with his fortune-tellers? You'd certainly
    enjoy
Having the Guards Brigade and the Household
    Cavalry
At your beck and call, and a barracks with you
    as Commandant.
Why not? Even those who lack the murderer's
    instinct
Would like to be licensed to kill. Yet what fame
    or prosperity
Are worth having if they bring you no less dis-
    aster than joy?*

Would you rather assume the mantle of the
  wretch who's being dragged
Through the streets today, or lord it over some
  sleepy
Rural backwater, an out-at-elbows official
Inspecting weights, giving orders for the
  destruction
Of short-measure pint-pots? Admit, then, that
  Sejanus
Had no idea what to pray for. His interminable
  pursuit
Of excessive wealth and honors built up a tow-
  ering
Edifice, story by story, so that his final down-
  fall
Was that degree greater, the crash more cata-
  strophic.
Take men like Pompey or Crassus—and that
  other tyrant
Who cowed Rome's citizens, brought them
  under the lash:
What proved their downfall? Lust for ultimate
  power
Pursued without scruple—and the malice of
  Heaven
That granted ambition's prayers. Battle and
  slaughter
See most kings off; few tyrants die in their
  beds.
    Eloquence, that's what they're after, all of
  them: even the schoolboy
—With one small houseslave to carry his
  satchel behind him,
And only a penny to spare for an offering to
  Minerva—
Spends all his holidays praying that one day
  he'll become

As good—and successful—as Cicero, or
  Demosthenes. And yet
Both of these perished because of their elo-
  quence, both
Were destroyed by their own overflowing and
  copious talent.
That talent alone cost Cicero his severed head
  and hand:
What third-rate advocate's blood ever stained
  the rostra?
O fortunate Roman State, born in my great
  Consulate—
Had he always spoken thus, he could have
  laughed Antony's
Swords to scorn. I prefer such ridiculous verses
To you, supreme and immortal Second Philip-
  pic. And then
Violent, too, was the end of Demosthenes, who
  held
All Athens spellbound with his torrential oratory
In the crowded theater. Under an evil-fated
  star
He was born, and the Gods were against him,
  that ardent boy
Whom his father—swart and bleary with work-
  ing red-hot ore—
Sent away from the coals and the pincers, the
  grime of the smithy,
The sword-forging anvil, to learn the rhetori-
  cian's trade.
    Consider the spoils of war, those trophies
  hung on tree-trunks—
A breastplate, a shattered helmet, one cheek-
  piece dangling,
A yoke shorn of its pole, a defeated trireme's
Flagstaff or figurehead, the miserable frieze of
  prisoners

On a triumphal arch—such things are coveted
As the zenith of human achievement. These are
    the prizes
For which every commander, Greek, barbarian,
    Roman,
Has always striven; for them he'll endure toil
And danger. The thirst for glory by far out-
    strips the
Pursuit of virtue. Who would embrace poor
    Virtue naked
Without the rewards she bestows? Yet countries
    have come to ruin
Not once, but many times, through the vain-
    glory of a few
Who lusted for power, who wanted a title that
    would cling
To the stones set over their ashes—though a
    barren
Fig-tree's rude strength will suffice to crack the
    stone asunder,
Seeing that sepulchres, too, have their allotted
    fate.
    Put Hannibal in the scales: how many
    pounds will that peerless
General mark up today? This is the man for
    whom Africa
Was too small a continent, though it stretched
    from the surf-beaten
Ocean shores of Morocco east to the steamy Nile,
To Ethiopian tribesmen—and new elephants'
    habitats.
Now Spain swells his empire, now he surmounts
The Pyrenees. Nature throws in his path
High Alpine passes, blizzards of snow: but he
    splits
The very rocks asunder, moves mountains—
    with vinegar.

Now Italy is his, yet still he forces on:
"We have accomplished nothing," he cries, "till
    we have stormed
The gates of Rome, till our Carthaginian stan-
    dard
Is set in the City's heart."
                            A fine sight it must have been,
Fit subject for caricature, the one-eyed com-
    mander
Perched on his monstrous beast! Alas, alas for
    glory,
What an end was here: the defeat, the igno-
    minious
Flight into exile, everyone crowding to see
The once-mighty Hannibal turned humble
    hanger-on,
Sitting outside the door of a petty Eastern
    despot
Till His Majesty deign to awake. No sword, no
    spear,
No battle-flung stone was to snuff the fiery
    spirit
That once had wrecked a world: those crushing
    defeats,
Those rivers of spilt blood were all wiped out
    by a
Ring, a poisoned ring. On, on, you madman,
    drive
Over your savage Alps, to thrill young school-
    boys
And supply a theme for speech-day recitations!
    One globe seemed all too small for the
    youthful Alexander:
Miserably he chafed at this world's narrow
    confines
As though pent on some rocky islet. Yet when
    he entered

Brick-walled Babylon, a coffin was measure
    enough
To contain him. Death alone reveals the puny
    dimensions
Of our human frame. A fleet, we are told, once
    sailed
Through Athos (the lies those old Greek histo-
    rians
Got away with!), the sea was spanned with a
    bridge of boats
And chariots drove across it: deep streams and
    rivers
Were drunk dry by the Persians at breakfast-
    time. (The rest
You can hear when some tame poet, sweating
    under the armpits,
Gives his wine-flown recital.) Here was a bar-
    barian
Monarch who flogged the winds with a rigor
    they'd never known
In Aeolus' prison-house, who clapped chains on
    Poseidon
And thought it an act of mercy, no doubt, to
    spare the God
A branding as well: what God would serve this
    master?
But mark his return from Salamis—the single
    unescorted
Vessel, the blood-red sea, the prow slow-
    thrusting
Through shoals of corpses. Such was the price
    he paid
For that long-cherished dream of glory and
    conquest.
    "Grant us a long life, Jupiter, O grant us
    many years!"
In the bloom of youth it's this which, pale with
    anxiety,

You pray for, and this alone. Yet how grisly,
    how unrelenting
Are longevity's ills! Look first at your face,
    you'll see an ugly
And shapeless caricature of its former self: your
    skin
Has become a scaly hide, you're all chapfallen,
    the wrinkles
Scored down your cheeks now make you resem-
    ble nothing so much
As some elderly female baboon in darkest
    Africa.
Young men are all individuals. A will have bet-
    ter looks
Or brains than B, while B will beat A on muscle;
But old men all look alike, all share the same
    bald pate,
Their noses all drip like an infant's, their voices
    tremble
As much as their limbs, they mumble their
    bread with toothless
Gums. It's a wretched life for them, they
    become a burden
To their wives, their children, themselves; the
    noblest and best of them
Become so loathsome a sight that even legacy-
    hunters
Turn queasy. Their taste-buds are ruined, they
    get scant pleasure
From food or wine, sex lies in long oblivion—
Or if they try, it's hopeless: though they labor
    all night long
At that limp and shriveled object, limp it
    remains.
What can the future hold for these impotent
    dodderers?
Nothing very exciting. Sex is a pretty dead
    loss—

The old tag's true—when desire outruns perfor-
    mance.
       Other senses deteriorate: take hearing, for
    instance.
How can the deaf appreciate music? The stan-
    dard
Of the performance eludes them: a top-line
    soloist,
Massed choirs in their golden robes, all mean
    less than nothing.
What does it matter to them where they sit in
    the concert-hall
When a brass band blowing its guts out is
    barely audible?
The slave who announces the time, or a visitor,
    must bawl
At the top of his lungs before they take in the
    message.
       The blood runs thin with age too; now
    nothing but fever
Can warm that frigid hulk, while diseases of
    every type
Assault it by battalions. (If you asked me their
    names
I'd find it less trouble to list all Oppia's lovers,
The number of patients Doc Themison kills
    each autumn,
The partners that X, the wards that Y has
    defrauded,
The times tall Maura goes down in a day, the
    pupils
Hamillus has off; I could sooner list all the
    country-houses
Owned by the barber who shaved me when I
    was a lad.)
One has an arthritic hip, another sciatica,
Lumbago plagues a third, while the totally
    sightless

Envy the one-eyed. Here's a fellow whose jaws
    would open
Wide, once long ago, at the prospect of din-
    ner—but now
Those leaden lips must mumble the tit-bits
    another hand
Feeds to him; when he gapes today, he's like a
    baby
Swallow that sees its mother approaching, her
    beak
Well-crammed with grubs. But worse than all
    bodily ills
Is the senescent mind. Men forget what their
    own servants
Are called, they can't recognize yesterday's host
    at dinner,
Or, finally, the children they begot and
    brought up. A heartless
Codicil to the will disinherits their flesh and
    blood,
And the whole estate is entailed to some whore,
    whose expert mouth
—After years in that narrow archway—earns
    her a rich reward.
       If he keeps his wits intact, though, a fur-
    ther ordeal awaits
The old man: he'll have to bury his sons, he'll
    witness
His dear wife's end, and his brother's, he'll see
    the urns
Filled with his sisters' ashes. Such are the
    penalties
If you live to a ripe old age—perpetual
    grief,
Black mourning, a world of sorrow, ever-
    recurrent
Family bereavements to haunt your declining
    years.

Nestor, the King of Pylos, if we can trust great
    Homer,
Lived longer than any creature save the prover-
    bial crow—
Happy, no doubt, to have postponed his death
    for so many
Generations of men, to have sampled the new-
    made wine
So many times, to have passed beyond his hun-
    dredth year.
But wait a moment—just look at the way he
    went on
About Fate's decrees, and his too-long threat of
    life, while
The funeral flames were licking up round his
    son,
His Antilochus: look how he asked all his fel-
    low-mourners the reason
He'd survived till now, what crime he'd ever
    committed
To deserve such longevity. So Peleus, mourning
    the dead
Achilles; and so his father at Odysseus the sea-
    farer's passing.
If Priam had died at a different time, before
The building of those ships for Paris' reckless
    venture,
He might have gone down to the shades while
    Troy still stood, with
Magnificent obsequies—his coffin shoul-
    dered
By Hector and Hector's brothers, while Ilion's
    womanhood
Wept, and Cassandra keened, and Polyxena
    rent her garments.
So what did length of days bring him? He saw
    his world

In ruins, saw its destruction by fire and the
    sword;
Then put off his crown, took arms, and—a
    dotard, but a soldier—
Fell before Jove's high altar, like some ancient
    ox
Turned off from the plough, whose stringy neck
    is severed
By his master's knife. This at least was a
    manly death:
But Hecuba lived on, stark crazy, grinning and
    barking
Like a mad dog.
                      I'll pass over Mithridates
And Croesus (warned by the wise and eloquent
    Solon
To beware of his final years): let our own coun-
    trymen
Provide an example. What else brought great
    Marius
To exile and prison, to an outlaw's life in the
    marshes,
To begging his bread through the streets of
    conquered Carthage?
But suppose he'd expired at the climax of his
    triumphal
Procession, after parading those hordes of cap-
    tured Teutons,
Just as he stepped from his chariot—what
    more fortunate
Paragon, men would say, had Rome, or the
    world, to show?
Pompey's Campanian fever came as a provi-
    dential
Blessing in disguise; but the public prayers of
    so many
Cities prevailed. Rome's destiny, and his
    own,

*Kept him alive for defeat and decapitation—a
  fate*
*Such as not even Catiline or his fellow-
  conspirators*
*Suffered: at least they died whole, without
  mutilation.*
  *When a doting mother passes the shrine of
  Venus, she'll whisper*
*One prayer for her sons, and another—louder,
  more fanciful—*
*For her daughters to have good looks. "And
  what's wrong with that?"*
*She'll ask you. "Didn't Latona rejoice in
  Diana's beauty?"*
*Perhaps; but the fate of Lucretia should warn
  us against our urge*
*To pray for a face like hers; Virginia would be
  happy*
*To take on poor Rutila's hump, to give Rutila
  best. A handsome*
*Son keeps his wretched parents in constant
  anxiety:*
*Good looks and decent behavior too seldom are
  found*
*In the same person. However old-fashioned his
  background,*
*However strict the morality on which he was
  brought up—*
*And even if Nature, with generous, kindly
  hand has*
*Turned him out a pure-minded, modestly
  blushing*
*Youth (and what greater gift, being more pow-
  erful*
*Than any solicitous guardian, could she
  bestow?)—*
*Manliness still is denied him. A seducer will
  not scruple*

*To lay out lavish bribes, corrupt the boy's very
  parents:*
Cash always wins in the end. But no misshapen
*Stripling was ever unsexed by a tyrant in his
  castle,*
*No Nero would ever rape a clubfooted adoles-
  cent—*
Much less one with hump, pot-belly, or scrofula.
  So you're proud of your handsome son?
  Fair enough—but don't ever forget
*The extra hazards that face him. He'll become
  a notorious*
*Layer of other men's wives, always scared that
  some husband's*
*Hot on his tail for revenge. He'll have no better
  luck*
*Than Mars did, he can't expect to steer clear of
  the toils for ever—*
*And sometimes an outraged cuckold will go far
  beyond*
*All legal sanctions, will horsewhip his rival to
  ribbons,*
*Stick a knife in his heart, or a mullet up his
  backside.*
*Maybe the first time your dream-boy goes with
  a married*
*Woman he'll really love her. But when she gets
  in the habit*
*Of giving him little presents, it won't be long
  before*
*He's become the perfect gigolo, taking them all
  for their eyeteeth—*
*And remember, there's nothing these women
  won't do to satisfy*
*Their ever-moist groins: they've just one obses-
  sion—sex.*
*"But what's wrong with good looks if you're
  chaste?" Try out that question*

On Hippolytus or Bellerophon: did stern self-
restraint
Benefit them? The women whose love they'd
spurned,
Phaedra and Sthenoboea, both hot with
shame, flared up
And lashed themselves into a fury. Pure femi-
nine ruthlessness
Thrives best on hatred and guilt.
          What advice, do you suppose,
Should one give the young man whom Caesar's
wife is determined
To marry? This blue-blooded sprig of the
higher nobility—
Wonderfully handsome, too—is raped and
doomed by one glance
From Messalina's eyes. She sits there, waiting
for him,
Veiled as a bride, while their marriage-bed is
prepared
In the public gardens. A big traditional
dowry
Will be handed over, the ceremony witnessed in
due form,
The omens taken. Did you think these were
secret doings
Known only to intimate friends? But the lady's
determined
On a proper, official wedding. So what's your
decision? If
You refuse her commands, you'll die before
lighting-up time;
If you do the deed, you'll get a brief respite,
until
Your liaison is so well known that it reaches the
Emperor's ears:
He'll be the last to learn of this family scandal.
Till then

Better do what you're told, if a few more days'
existence
Matter that much. But whichever you reckon
the quicker
And easier way, your lily neck still gets the
chop.
      Is there nothing worth praying for, then?
If you want my advice,
Let the Gods themselves determine what's most
appropriate
For mankind, and what best suits our various
circumstances.
They'll give us the things we need, not those we
want: a man
Is dearer to them than he is to himself. Led
helpless
By irrational impulse and powerful desires
We ask for marriage and children. But the
Gods alone know
What they'll be like, our future wives and off-
spring!
Still, if you must have something to pray for, if
you
Insist on offering up the entrails and conse-
crated
Sausages from a white pigling in every shrine,
then ask
For [a sound mind in a sound body,] a valiant
heart
Without fear of death, that reckons longevity
The least among Nature's gifts, that's strong to
endure
All kinds of toil, that's untainted by lust and
anger,
That prefers the sorrows and labors of Hercules
to all
Sardanapalus' downy cushions and women
and junketings.

What I've shown you, you can find by yourself:
  there's one
Path, and one only, to a life of peace—
  through virtue.

Fortune has no divinity, could we but see it:
  it's we,
We ourselves, who make her a goddess, and set
  her in the heavens.

(GAIUS) PETRONIUS (ARBITER) (1ST CENTURY A.D.)

Satyricon

*T*he author of the *Satyricon* is probably the Petronius Arbiter who served well as governor of Asian Bithynia and later as consul and arbiter of festivities at Nero's court. Tacitus tells us that Petronius spent his days asleep and his nights "in the business and pleasures of life." After being falsely implicated by the emperor's guard Tigellinus in the failed conspiracy of Piso in A.D. 66, Petronius made his suicide appear to be death by natural causes—after first sending Nero a catalog of the emperor's sexual perversions, listing his male and female sexual partners.

- The *Satyricon* is a sprawling picaresque novel, composed in the Menippean satire form in a vulgar Latin reminiscent of Plautus; only parts of Books 14, 15, and 16 survive. The novel chronicles with vivid realism and satirical precision the hedonistic exploits of the bright but amoral Encolpius and his two dropout pals as they make their way through the taverns and brothels of Campania and Magna Graecia.
- The profligate banquet hosted by the nouveau riche freedman Trimalchio and his wife Fortunata forms the centerpiece of the most intriguing surviving fragment of Petronius' *Saturae*, giving us an irreplaceable view of Roman decadence. Trimalchio's character is said to have been based in part on Nero himself. The novel is a masterpiece of dialogue and characterization, the most important example of Roman plebeian literature.

Though its borrowings from earlier works can be traced, the comic romantic *Satyricon* creates its own place in the literary canon. Its own influence through the ages has extended to Rabelais, Fielding, North, Balzac, Flaubert, Maupassant, and Fellini's film of the same title.

From this up rose Trimalchio, and went to the close-stool; we also being at liberty, without a tyrant over us fell to some table-talk.

When presently one calling for a bumper, "The day," said he, "is nothing, 'tis night e're the scene turn, and therefore nothing is better than to go straight from bed to board. We have had a great deal of frost, the bagnio has scarce heated me; but a warm drinking is my wardrobe-keeper: For my part, I have spun this days thread; the wine is got into my noddle, and I am down-right—"

Selucus went on with the rest, "And I," said he, "do not bathe every day, for he where I use to bathe is a fuller: Cold water has teeth in it, and my head grows every day more washy than others, but when I have got my dose in my guts, I bid defiance to cold: Nor could I well do it to day, for I was at a funeral, a jolly companion, and a good man was he, Crysanthus has breathed his last: 'Tis not long since we were together, and methinks I talk with him now. Alas, alas! we are but blown bladders, less than flies, yet they have somewhat in them: But we are meer bubbles. You'll say he would not be rul'd; not a drop of water, or crumb of bread went down his throat in five days: And yet he's gone, or that he died of the doctor. But I am of opinion his time was come; for a physician is a great comfort. However, he was well carried out of his house upon a rich bed, and mightily lamented, he made some of his servants free; but his wife seem'd not much concerned for him. You'll say again he was not kind to her; but women are a kind of kites; whatever good is done them, 'tis the same as if it were thrown in a well; and old love is as bad as a goal."

At this Philaos grew troublesome, and cried out, "Let us remember the living: He had what was due to him; as he liv'd so he dy'd; and what has he now that any man moans the want of it? He came from nothing, and to his dying-day would have taken a farthing from a dunghil with his teeth; therefore as he grew up, he grew like a honey-comb. He dy'd worth the Lord knows what, all ready money. But to the matter; I have eaten a dog's tongue and dare speak

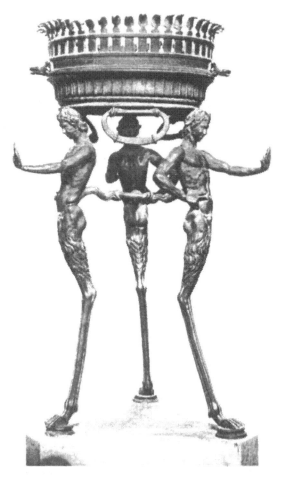

Tripod of satyrs

truth: He had a foul mouth, was all babble; a very make-bate, not a man. His brother was a brave fellow, a friend to his friends, of an open hand, and kept a full table: He did not order his affairs so well at first as he might have done; but the first vintage made him up again; for he sold what wine he would; and what kept up his chin was the expectation of a reversion; the credit of which brought him more than was left him; for his brother taking a pelt at him, devised the estate to I know not whose bastard: He flies far that flies his relations. Besides, this brother of his had whisperers about him, that were back-friends to the other: but he shall never do right that is quick of belief, especially in matter of business; and yet 'tis true, he'll be counted wise while he lives, to whom the thing whatever it be is given, nor he that ought to have had it. He was without doubt, one of fortune's sons; lead in his hand would turn to gold, and without trouble too, where there are not rubbs in the way. And how many years think ye he liv'd? Seventy-odd: but he was as hard as horn, bore his age well, and as black as a crow.

"I knew him some years ago an oilman, and to his last a good womans man; but withal such a miser, that (so help me Hercules) I think he left not a dogg in his house. He was also a great whore-master, and a jack of all trades; nor do I condemn him for't, for this was the only secret he kept to himself and carry'd with him."

Thus Phileros and Gammedes, as followeth: "Ye talk of what concerns neither Heaven nor Earth, when in the mean time no man regards what makes all victuals so scarce: I could not (so help me Hercules) get a mouthful of bread

to day: and how? The drought continues: For my part, I have not fill'd my belly this twelve-month: A plague on these clerks of the market, the baker and they juggle together; take no notice of me, I'll take no notice of thee; which make the poorer sort labor for nothing, while those greater jaw-bones make festival every day. Oh that we had those lyons I now find here, when I first came out of Asia, that had been to live: The inner part of Sicily had the like of them, but they so handled the goblins, even Jupiter bore them no good-will. I remember Safinius, when I was a boy, he liv'd by the old arch; you'd have taken him for pepper-corn rather than a man; where-ever he went the earth parched under him; yet he was honest at bottom; one might depend on him; a friend to his friend, and whom you might boldly trust in the dark. But how did he behave himself on the bench? He toss'd every one like a ball; made no starch'd speeches, but downright, as he were, doing himself what he would persuade others: But in the market his noise was like a trumpet, without sweating or spueing. I fancy he had somewhat, I know not what, of the Asian humor: then so ready to return a salute, and call every one by his name, as if he had been one of us. In his time corn was as common as loam; you might have bought more bread for half a farthing, than any two could eat; but now the eye of an ox will cost you twice as much: Alas! alas! we are every day worse and worse, and grow like a cows tail, downward: And why all this? We have a clerk of the market not worth three figgs, and values more the getting of a doit himself, than any of our lives: 'Tis this makes him laugh in his sleeve; for he gets more money in a day than many an honest man's whole estate: I know not how he got the estate he has; but if we had any thing of men about us, he would not hug himself as he does, but now the people are grown to this pass, that they are lyons at home, and foxes abroad: For my part, I have eaten up my cloaths already, and if corn holds at the rate it does, I shall be forc'd to sell house and all: For what will become of us, if neither gods nor men pity us? Let me never enjoy my friends more, than I believe all this comes from Heaven; for no one thinks there is any such thing; no one keeps a fast, or value Jupiter a hair, but shuts his eyes and reckons what he is worth. Time was, when matrons went bare-foot with dishevel'd hair, pure minds, and pray'd him to send rain, and forthwith it rained pitcher-fulls, or then or never, and every one was pleased: Now the gods are no better than mice; as they tread, their feet are wrapt in wooll; and because ye are not superstitious your lands yield nothing."

"More civilly, I beseech ye," said Echion the hundred-constable; "it is one while this way, and another while that, said the country-man when he lost his speckled hogg: What is not to day may be to morrow; and thus is life hurried about, so help me Hercules, a country is said not to be the better that it has many people in it, tho' ours at present labors under that difficulty, but it is no fault of hers: We must not be so nice, Heaven is equally distant every where; were you in another place you'd say hoggs walked here ready dress'd: And now I think on't, we shall have an excellent show these holy-days, a fencing-prize exhibited to the people; not of slaves bought for that purpose, but most of them freemen. Our patron

Titus has a large soul, but a very devil in his drink, and cares not a straw which side gets the better: I think I should know him, for I belong to him; he's of a right breed both by father and mother, no mongril. They are well provided with weapons, and will fight it out to the last: the theater will look like a butchers shambles, and he has where-withal to do it; his father left him a vast sum, and let him make ducks and drakes with it never so much, the Estate will bear it, and he always carries the reputation of it. He has his waggon horses, a woman-carter, and Glyco's steward, who was taken a-bed with his mistress; what a busle's here between cuckolds and cuckold-makers! But this Glyco a money-broker, condemned his steward to fight with beasts; and what was that but to expose himself for another? where lay the servant's crime, who perhaps was oblig'd to do what he did: She rather deserv'd to be brain'd, than the bull that tossed her; but he that cannot come at the arse, thrashes at the pack-saddle: yet how could Glyco expect Hermogine's daughter should make a good end? She'd have pared the claws of a flying kite; a snake does not bring forth a halter: Glyco might do what he would with his own; but it will be a brand on him as long as he lives; nor can any thing but Hell blot it out; however, every man's faults are his own. I perceive now what entertainment Mammea is like to give us; he'll be at twopence charges for me and my company; which if he does, he will pull Narbanus clean out of favor; for you must know, he'll live at the full height; yet in truth what good has he done us? He gave us a company of pittiful sword-players, but so old and decrepid, that had you blown on them, they'd have fallen of themselves: I have seen many a better at a funeral pile; he would not be at the charge of lamps for them; you'd have taken them for dunghil cocks fighting in the dark; one was a downright fool, and withal gouty; another crump-footed, and a third half dead, and hamstrung: There was one of them a Thracian, that made a figure, and kept up to the rule of fighting; but upon the whole matter, all of them were parted, and nothing came of this great block-headed rabble, but a downright running away: And yet, said he, I made ye a show, and I clap my hands for company; but cast up the account, I gave more than I received; one hand rubs another. You Agamemnon seem to tell me what would that trouble some fellow be at; because you that can speak, and do not, you are not of our form, and therefore ridicule what poor men say; tho', saving the repute of a scholar, we know you are but a meer fool. Where lies the matter then? let me persuade you to take a walk in the country, and see our cottage, you'll find somewhat to eat; a chicken, some eggs, or the like: The tempestuous season had like to have broke us all, yet we'll get enough to fill the belly. Your scholar, my boy Cicero, is mightily improved, and if he lives, you'll have a servant of him; he is pretty forward already, and whatever spare time he has, never off a book: He's a witty lad, well-featur'd, takes a thing without much study, tho' yet he be sickly: I killed three of his linnets the other day, and told him the weasels had eaten them; yet he found other things to play with, and has a pretty knack at painting: He has a perfect aversion to Greek, but seems better inclined to Latin; tho' the master he has now humors him in the other; nor can he be kept to one thing, but is still craving more, and will not

take pains with any. There is also another of this sort, not much troubled with learning, but very diligent, and teaches more than he knows himself: He comes to our house on holidays, and whatever you give him he's contented; I therefore bought the boy some ruled books, because I will have him get a smattering in accounts and the law; it will be his own another day: He has learning enough already, but if he takes back to it again, I design him for a trade, a barber, a parson, or a lawyer, which nothing but the devil can take from him: How oft have I told him, Thou art (Sirrah) my first begotten, and believe thy father, whatever thou learnest 'tis all thy own: See there Philero the lawyer, if he had not been a scholar he might have starved; but now see what trinkums he has about his neck, and dares nose Narbanus. Letters are a treasure, and a trade never dies."

Thus, or the like, we were bandying it about when Trimalchio return'd, and having wip'd the slops from his face, wash'd his hands, and in a very little time, "Pardon me, my friends," said he, "I have been costive for several days, and my physicians were to seek about it, when a suppository of pomegranate wine, with the liquor of a pine-tree and vinegar relieved me; and now I hope my belly may be ashamed if it keep no better order; for otherwise I have such a rumbling in my guts, you'd think an ox bellowed; and therefore if any of you has a mind, he need not blush for the matter; there's not one of us born without some defect or other, and I think no torment greater than wanting the benefit of going to stool, which is the only thing even Jupiter himself cannot prevent: And do you laugh, Fortunata, you that break me so often of my sleep by nights; I never denied any man do that in my room might pleasure himself, and physicians will not allow us to keep any thing in our bodies longer than we needs must; or if ye have any farther occasion, every thing is ready in the next room: Water, chamber-pots, close-stools, or whatever else ye may need; believe me, this being hard-bound, if it get into the head, disturbs the whole body; I have known many a man lost by it, when they have been so modest to themselves as not to tell what they ailed."

We thank'd him for his freeness, and the liberty he gave us, when yet to suppress our laughter, we set the glasses about again; nor did we yet know that in the midst of such dainties we were, as they say, to clamber another hill; for the cloth being again taken away, upon the next musick were brought in three fat hogs with collars and bells about their necks; and he that had the charge of them told us, the one was two years old, the other three, and the third full grown. I took it at first to have been a company of tumblers, and that the hogs, as the manner is, were to have shewn us some tricks in a ring, till Trimalchio breaking my expectation, "Which of them," said he, "will ye have for supper? for cocks, pheasants, and the like trifles are but country fare, but my cooks have coppers will boil a calf whole"; and therewith commanding a cook to be called for, he prevented our choice by ordering him to kill the largest, and with a loud voice, asked him, Of what rank of servants in that house he was? to which he answering, of the fortieth: "Were you bought," said the other, "or born in my house?" "Neither," said the cook, "but left you by Pansa's testament." "See then," said Trimalchio, "that you dress it as it should be, or I'll send you to the galleys." On which the cook, advertised of his power, went into the kitchin to mind his charge.

But Trimalchio turning to us with a pleasanter look, asked if the wine pleased us, "If not," said he, "I'll have it changed, and if it does, let me see it by your drinking: I thank the gods I do not buy it, but have everything that may get an appetite growing on my own grounds without the city, which no man that I know but my self has; and yet it has been taken for Tarracino and Taranto. I have a project to joyn Sicily to my lands on the continent, that when I have a mind to go into Africa, I may sail by my own coasts. But prithee Agamemnon tell me what moot-point was it you argued to day; for tho' I plead no causes my self, yet I have had a share of letters in my time; and that you may not think me sick of them now, have three libraries, the one Greek, the other two Latin; therefore as you love me tell me what was the state of the question:" "The poor and the rich are enemies," said Agamemnon: "And what is poor," answered Trimalchio? "Spoke like a gentleman," replyed Agamemnon. But making nothing of the matter, "If it be so," said Trimalchio, "where lies the dispute? And if it be not so, 'tis nothing."

While we all humm'd this and the like stuff, "I beseech ye," said he, "my dear Agamemnon, do you remember the twelve labors of Hercules, or the story of Ulysses, how a Cyclop put his thumb out of joint with a mawkin? I read such things in Homer when I was a boy; nay, saw my self the Sybil of Curna hanging in a glass bottle: And when the boys asked her, 'Sybil, what wouldst thou?' She answered, 'I would die.' "

He had not yet run to the end of the rope, when an over-grown hog was brought to the table. We all wondered at the quickness of the thing, and swore a capon could not be dress'd in the time; and that the more, because the hog seemed larger than was the boar, we had a little before: When Trimalchio looking more intent upon him, "What, what," said he, "are not his guts taken out? No, (so help me Hercules) they are not! Bring hither, bring hither this rogue of a cook." And when he stood hanging his head before us, and said, he was so much in haste he forgot it. "How, forgot it," cry'd out Trimalchio! "Do ye think he has given it no seasoning of pepper and cummin? Strip him:" When in a trice 'twas done, and himself set between two tormentors: However, we all interceded for him, as a fault that might now and then happen, and therefore beg'd his pardon; but if he ever did the like, there was no one would speak for him; tho' for my part, I think he deserved what he got: And so turning to Agamemnon's ear, "This fellow," said I, "must be a naughty knave; could any one forget to bowel a hog? I would not (so help me Hercules) have forgiven him if he had served me so with a single fish." But Trimalchio it seems, had somewhat else in his head; for falling a laughing, "You," said he, "that have so short a memory, let's see if you can do it now." On which, the cook having gotten his coat again, took up a knife, and with a feigned trembling, ripp'd up the hog's belly long and thwart, when immediately its own weight tumbled out a heap of hogs-puddings and sausages.

After this, as it had been done of it self, the family gave a shout, and cry'd out, "Health and prosperity to Caius!" The cook also was presented with wine, a silver coronet, and a drinking goblet, on a broad Corinthian plate: which Agamemnon more narrowly viewing; "I am," said Trimalchio, "the only person that has the true Corinthian vessels."

I expected, that according to the rest of his haughtiness, he would have told us they had been brought him from Corinth: But he better: "And perhaps," said he, "you'll ask me why I am the only person that have them. And why, but the copper-smith from whom I buy them, is called Corinthus? And what is Corinthian but what is made by Corinthus? But that ye may not take me for a man of no sence, I understand well enough whence the word first came. When Troy was taken, Hannibal, a cunning fellow, but withal mischievous, made a pile of all the brazen, gold and silver statues, and burnt them together, and thence came this mixt metal; which workmen afterwards carried off; and of this mass made platters, dishes, and several other things; so that these vessels are neither this nor that metal, but made of all of them. Pardon me what I say; however others may be of another mind, I had rather have glass ware; and if it were not so subject to breaking, I'd reckon it before gold; but now it is of no esteem.

"There was a copper-smith that made glass vessels of that pliant harness, that they were no more to be broken than gold and silver ones: It so happened, that having made a drinking-pot, with a wide mouth of that kind, but the finest glass, fit for no man, as he thought, less than Caesar himself; he went with his present to Caesar, and had admittance: The kind of the gift was praised, the hand of the workman commended, and the design of the giver accepted. He again, that he might turn the admiration of the beholders into astonishment, and work himself the more into the Emperor's favor, pray'd the glass out of the Emperor's hand; and having received it, threw it with such a force against the paved floor, that the most solid and firmest metal could not but have received some hurt thereby. Caesar also was no less amazed at it, than concerned for it; but the other took up the pot from the ground, not broken but bulg'd a little; as if the substance of metal had put on the likeness of a glass; and therewith taking a hammer out of his pocket, he hammer'd it as it had been a brass kettle, and beat out the bruise: And now the fellow thought himself in Heaven, in having, as he fansied, gotten the acquaintance of Caesar, and the admiration of all: But it fell out quite contrary: Caesar asking him if any one knew how to make this malleable glass but himself? And he answering, there was not, the Emperor commanded his head to be struck off: 'For,' said he, 'if this art were once known, gold and silver will be of no more esteem than dirt.'

"And for silver, I more than ordinarily affect it: I have several water-pots more or less, whereon is the story how Cassandra killed her son's, and the dead boys are so well embossed, you'd think them real. I have also a drinking cup left me by an advocate of mine, where Daedalus puts Niobe into the Trojan horse, as also that other of Hermerotes; that they may stand as a testimony, there's truth in cups, and all this massy; nor will I part with what I understand of them at any rate."

While he was thus talking, a cup dropt out of a boy's hand; on which, Trimalchio looking over his shoulder at him, bad him begone, and kill himself immediately; "for," said he, "thou art careless and mind'st not what thou art about." The boy hung his lip, and besought

him; but he said, "What! dost thou beseech me, as if I required some difficult matter of thee? I only bid thee obtain this of thy self, that thou be not careless again." But at last he discharged him upon our entreaty. On this the boy run round the table and cry'd, "Water without doors, and wine within." We all took the jest, but more especially Agamemnon, who knew on what account himself had been brought thither.

Trimalchio in the mean time hearing himself commended, drank all the merrier, and being within an ace of quite out, "Will none of you," said he, "invite my Fortunata to dance? Believe me, there's no one leads a country dance better:" And with that, tossing his hands round his head, fell to act a jack-pudding; the family all the while singing, "youth it self, most exactly youth it self;" and he had gotten into the middle of the room, but that Fortunata whispered him, and I believe told him, such gambols did not become his gravity. Nor was there any thing more uneven to it self; for one while he turned to his Fortunata, and another while to his natural inclination: But what disturbed the pleasure of her dancing, was his notaries coming in; who, as they had been the acts of a common council, read aloud:

"VII. of the Calends of August born in Trimalchio's manner of cumanum, thirty boys and forty girls, brought from the threshing-floor into the granary, five hundred thousand bushels of wheat. The same day broke out a fire in a pleasure-garden that was Pompey's, first began in one of his bayliffs houses."

"How's this," said Trimalchio: "When were those gardens bought for me?" "The year before," answered his notary, "and therefore not yet brought to account."

At this Trimalchio fell into a fume; and "whatever lands," said he, "shall be bought me hereafter, if I hear nothing of it in six months, let them never, I charge ye, be brought to any account of mine." Then also were read the orders of the clerks of the markets, and the testaments of his woodwards, rangers, and park-keepers, by which they disinherited their relations, and with ample praise of him, declare Trimalchio their heir. Next that, the names of his bayliffs; and how one of them that made his circuits in the country, turned off his wife for having taken her in bed with a barber; the door-keeper of his baths turn'd out of his place; the auditor found short in his accounts, and the dispute between the grooms of his chamber ended.

At last came in the dancers on the rope; and a gorbelly'd blockhead standing out with a ladder, commanded his boy to hopp every round singing, and dance a jigg on the top of it, and then tumble through burning hoops of iron, with a glass in his mouth. Trimalchio was the only person that admir'd it, but withal said, he did not like it; but there were two things he could willingly behold, and they were the flyers on the high rope, and quails; and that all other creatures and shows were meer gewgaws: "For," said he, "I bought once a sett of stroulers, and chose rather to make them merry-andrews than comedians; and commanded my bag-piper to sing in Latin to them."

While he was chattering all at this rate, a boy chanced to stumble upon him, on which the family gave a shriek, the same also did the guests; not for such a beast of a man, whose neck they could willingly have seen broken, but for fear the supper should break up ill, and they be forc'd to wail the death of the boy.

Whatever it were, Trimalchio gave a deep groan; and leaning upon his arm as if it had been hurt, the physicians ran thick about him, and with the first, Fortunata, her hair about her ears, a bottle of wine in her hand, still howling, miserable unfortunate woman that she was! Undone, undone. The boy on the other hand, ran under our feet, and beseeched us to procure him a discharge: But I was much concern'd, lest our interposition might make an ill end of the matter; for the cook that had forgotten to bowel the hog was still in my thoughts. I began therefore to look about the room, for fear somewhat or other might drop through the ceiling; while the servant that had bound up his arm in white, not scarlet-color flannel, was soundly beaten: Now was I much out, for instead of another course, came in an order of Trimalchio's by which he gave the boy his freedom; that it might not be said, so honorable a person had been hurt by his slave. We all commended the action, but chatted among our selves with what little consideration the things of this world were done. "You're in the right," said Trimalchio; "nor ought this accident to pass without booking"; and so calling for the journal, commanded it to be entered; and with, as little thought, tumbled out these verses:

What's least expected falls into our dish,
And fortune's more indulgent than our wish:
Therefore, boy, fill the generous wine about.

This epigram gave occasion to talk of the poets, and Marsus, the Trachian, carry'd the bays a long while: till Trimalchio (turning to some wit amongst them) "I beseech ye, master of mine," said he, "tell me what difference take

ye between Cicero the orator, and Publius the
poet? for my part I think one was more eloquent, the other the honester man; for what
could be said better than this."

Now sinking Rome grows weak with luxury,
To please her appetite cram'd peacocks die:
Their gaudy plumes a modish dress supply.

For her the guinnea hen and capon's drest:
The stork it self for Rome's luxurious taste,
Must in a caldron build its humbl'd nest.

That foreign, friendly, pious, long-leg'd thing,
Grateful, that with shrill sounding notes dost
   sing

All winter's gone; yet ushers in the spring.
Why in one ring must three rich pearls be
   worn,
But that your wives th' exhausted seas adorn,
Abroad t' increase their lust, at home their
   scorn?

Why is the costly emerald so desir'd,
Or richer glittering carbuncle admir'd,
Because they sparkle, is't with that you're
   fir'd?
Well, honesty's a jewel. Now none knows
A modest bride from a kept whore by 'er
   cloaths;
For cobweb lawns both spouse and wench
   expose. . . .

(PUBLIUS CORNELIUS) TACITUS (A.D. 56–117)

Annals: The Mutiny of the Pannonian Legions

*Q*uaestor in A.D. 81, praetor in 88, consul in 97, the great historian and prose stylist Tacitus, a close friend of Pliny the Younger, received senatorial rank from Vespasian and was also patronized by the emperors Titus and Domitian. He studied law under Marcus Aper and Julius Secundus, two distinguished orators. In 78 he married the daughter of the consul and general Gnaeus Julius Agricola. We know that he served as governor of Asia from A.D. 112 to 113, and that his oratorical eloquence led to his selection to deliver the funeral oration for Verginius Rufus in 97 under the emperor Nerva. Tacitus' attitude toward the Empire was heavily influenced by his experience during Domitian's savage reign of terror against the aristocracy.

- His major historical works, composed under the rule of Trajan and Hadrian, included the affectionate and brilliant biography *Life of Agricola* (A.D. 98); *Histories*; the *Annals* (between them covering A.D. 14 to 96, from Augustus' death to Domitian's); and the *Germania,* comparing the tribes north of the Rhine, generally known to the Romans as "Germanic," favorably with the Romans of his day.
- In the pages of these works we get glimpses of both the major events of these remarkable times and the lives of ordinary Roman soldiers, of senators, members of the imperial family, and barbarian princes as Tacitus takes us from the forums of the capital to the camps of the provincial armies.
- Tacitus, made gloomy and pessimistic by the imperial decadence that he witnessed in the capital's courts, believed that the shape of history is determined by powerful individuals, and that the Empire he had helped to form would be doomed unless the emperors after Augustus displayed the old Roman republican strength of character. Augustus himself he viewed not with the reverence accorded him by later history but with a more contemporary eye, as one of the "warlords" to hold sway over the Republic. Longing for what he saw as the contrasting robustness and simplicity of the provinces, Tacitus himself displayed that republican strength in the dignified way in which his writing pursues the truth of character and events.
- One of the great masters of Latin eloquence, Tacitus wrote in a self-conscious elevated "sublime style" prescribed by the Greek Longinus. His carefully polished, syntactically surprising language is intense, rhythmic, rapid, complex, colorful, psychologically subtle, and politically incisive, yet typically concise and compressed. Filled with witty inventiveness, innuendo, and irony, the *Annals* compels today's reader along from first to last.

Tacitus saw it as the historian's responsibility not only to determine the causality of epoch-making events but also faithfully to reward virtue and punish vice "at the bar of posterity." The *Annals* pass harsh judgment on Augustus' successor, the suspicious Tiberius, who reigned from A.D. 14 to 37, and who Tacitus considered the prototype of the decadent Domitian. No sooner had Tiberius taken the crown than a rebellion broke out in the province of Pannonia.

(ANNALES, I., 16–30.)

Such was the situation of affairs at Rome when a fierce and violent mutiny broke out among the legions in Pannonia. For this insurrection there was no other motive than the licentious spirit which is apt to show itself in the beginning of a new reign, and the hope of private advantage in the distractions of a civil war. A summer camp had been formed for three legions under the command of Junius Blaesus. The death of Augustus and the accession of Tiberius being known to the army, the general granted a suspension of military duty as an interval of grief or joy. The soldiers grew wanton in idleness; dissensions spread amongst them; the vile and profligate had their circles of auditors; sloth and pleasure prevailed; and all were willing to exchange a life of toil and discipline for repose and luxury. There happened to be in a camp a busy incendiary, by name Percennius, formerly a leader of theatrical factions, and now a common soldier; a man fluent in words, and by his early habits versed in the arts of exciting tumults and sedition. Over the weak and ignorant, and such as felt their minds alarmed with doubts and fears about the future condition of the service, this meddlesome fellow began to exert his influence. In the dead of the night he mixed in cabals, and never failed at the close of day, when the sober and well disposed retired to their tents, to draw together the idle and most abandoned. Having gained a number of proselytes, he stood forth the orator of sedition, and harangued his confederates in the following manner:

"How long, my fellow-soldiers, must we obey a small and despicable set of centurions? How long continue slaves to a wretched band of military tribunes? If we mean to redress our grievances, what time so fit as the present, when the new emperor is not yet settled on the throne? Relief may now be obtained, either by remonstrances, or sword in hand. By our passive spirit we have suffered enough; we have been slaves in thirty or forty campaigns; we are grown gray in the service, worn out with infirmities and covered with wounds. In that condition we are still condemned to the toils of war. Even the men who have obtained their discharge still follow the standard under the name of veterans: another word for protracted misery. A few, indeed, by their bodily vigor have surmounted all their labors; but what is their reward? They are sent to distant regions, and, under color of an allotment of lands, are settled on a barren mountain or a swampy fen. War of itself is a state of the vilest drudgery without an adequate compensation. The life and limb of a soldier are valued at ten *asses* a day: out of that wretched pittance he must find his clothing, his tent equipage, and his arms; with that fund he must bribe the centurion; with that must purchase occasional exemptions from service; and with that must pay for a remission of punishment. But blows and stripes from our officers, wounds from the enemy, intense cold in winter and the fatigue of summer campaigns, destructive war, in which everything is hazarded, and peace, by which nothing is gained, are all the soldier's portion.

"For these evils there is but one remedy left. Let us fix the conditions of our service; let every soldier receive a *denarius* a day, and at the end of sixteen years let him be entitled to his discharge; beyond that term no further service. Without detaining any man whatever, and without forcing him to follow the colors as a veteran, let every soldier receive the arrears that may be due to him; let him be paid in ready money on the spot, and in the very camp where he signalized his valor. The praetorian cohorts receive two *denarii* for their daily pay; at the end of sixteen years they return to their families. Is superior merit the ground of this distinction? Do they encounter greater dangers? It is theirs to mount guard within the city, and the service may be honorable; but it is our lot to serve amidst savage nations in a state of perpetual warfare. If we look out of our tents the barbarians are in view."

This speech was received with acclamations. Various passions heaved in every breast.

Some presented their bodies seamed with stripes; others pointed to their heads grown gray in the service; numbers showed their tattered clothing, and their persons almost naked. At length the frenzy of the malcontents knew no bounds. Their first design was to incorporate the three legions into one; but which should give its name to the united body was the question. Mutual jealousy put an end to the project. Another plan was carried out: the eagles of the three legions, with the colors of the cohorts, were crowded together without preference or distinction. They threw up sods of earth, and began to raise a tribunal. Amidst the tumult Blaesus arrived. He called aloud to all, laid hold of individuals, offered himself to their swords. "Here," he said, "behold your victim; imbrue your hands in the blood of your general. Murder is a crime less horrible than treason to your prince. I will either live to command the legions intrusted to me; or, if you are determined to revolt, despatch me first, that, when the frenzy is over, you may wake to shame, horror, and remorse."

The work of raising a tribunal, in spite of all his efforts, still went on. Heaps of turf were thrown up, and rose breast high. Conquered at length by the perseverance of their general, the mutineers desisted. Blaesus exerted all his eloquence: "Sedition and revolt," he said, "could not serve the cause; the remonstrances of the army ought to be conveyed to the ear of the prince with respect and deference. The demands which they now made were new, unknown to former armies, and with the deified Augustus never attempted. In the present juncture, when the prince had just undertaken the cares of government, was that a time to add to his solicitude by tumult and insurrection? If they would still persist, in the season of profound peace, to urge a claim never demanded even by the conquerors in a civil war, why incur the guilt of rebellion? Why, in violation of all military discipline, urge their pretensions sword in hand? They might depute their agent to treat with the prince, and, in the presence of their general, give their instructions on the spot." This proposal was accepted: with one voice they called for the son of Blaesus, then a military tribune. The young officer undertook the charge. His directions were to insist that at the expiration of sixteen years the soldier should be discharged from the service. That point settled, it then would be time to enumerate other grievances. With this commission the general's son went forward on his journey. A calm succeeded, and lasted for some days. But the minds of the soldiers were still in agitation: their pride was roused; the general's son was now the orator of the army; and force, it was manifest, had at length extorted what by gentle measures could never have been obtained.

Meanwhile the detached companies, which before the disturbance had been sent to Nauportum, having heard of the commotion in the camp, seized the colors, and, after ravaging the adjacent villages, plundered Nauportum, a place little inferior to a municipal town. They treated the centurions with derision, from derision proceeded to opprobrious language, and in the end to blows and open violence. Aufidienus Rufus, the prefect of the camp, was the chief object of their fury: they dragged him out of his carriage; and, laying a heavy load on his back, obliged him to march in the foremost ranks, asking him with contemptuous insolence how he liked his burden and the length of his journey. Rufus had risen from a common soldier to the rank of centurion, and was afterward made prefect of the camp. In that station he endeavored to recall the rigor of ancient discipline. A veteran in the service and long inured to fatigue, he was strict and rigorous in his duty, expecting from others what he had practised himself.

The return of this tumultuous body renewed the troubles of the camp. The soldiers, without control, left the lines, and pillaged the country round. Some, more heavily loaded with booty than their comrades, were apprehended by the orders of Blaesus, and, after receiving due correction, thrown into prison, as an example to the rest. The authority of the general was still in force with the centurions and such of the common soldiers as retained a sense of their duty. The delinquents, however, refused to submit: they were dragged along, resisting with all their strength; they clasped the knees of the multitude round them; they called on their fellow-soldiers by name; they implored the protection of the company to which they belonged; they invoked the cohorts and the legions, crying out to all that the same lot would shortly be their portion. Against their general they omitted nothing that calumny could suggest; they appealed to heaven; they implored their gods; they tried by every topic to excite compassion, to inflame resentment, to awaken terror, and rouse the men to acts of violence. A general insurrection followed: the soldiers in a body rushed to the prison, burst the gates, unchained the prisoners, and associated with themselves the vilest of the army, a band of deserters, and a desperate crew of malefactors,

then under condemnation for the enormity of their crimes.

The flame of discord raged with redoubled fury. New leaders joined the mutiny. Amidst the crowd, one of the common soldiers, a fellow known by the name of Vibulenus, mounted on the shoulders of his comrades before the tribunal of Blaesus, and addressed the multitude, all wild with fury, and eager to hear the language of sedition. "My friends," he said, "you have bravely interposed to save the lives of these innocent, these much-injured men; you have restored them to new life; but who will restore my brother? Who will give him to my arms? Sent hither from the German army, in concert with you to settle measures for our common safety, he was last night basely murdered by the hand of gladiators whom Blaesus arms for your destruction. Answer me, Blaesus, where have you bestowed the body? The very enemy allows the rites of sepulture. When I have washed my brother with my tears, and printed kisses on his mangled body, then plunge your poniard in this wretched bosom. I shall die content, if these my fellow-soldiers perform the last funeral office, and bury in one grave two wretched victims, who knew no crime but that of serving the common interest of the legions."

This speech Vibulenus rendered still more inflammatory by the vehemence of his manner, by beating his breast, by striking his forehead, and pouring a flood of tears. A way being opened through the crowd, he leaped from the men's shoulders, and groveling at the feet of individuals, excited the passions of the multitude to the highest pitch of frenzy. In their fury some fell on the gladiators retained by Blaesus, and loaded them with irons; others seized the general's domestic train, while numbers dispersed themselves on every side in quest of the body; and if it had not been speedily known that no corpse could be found, that the slaves of Blaesus averred under the torture that no murder had been committed, and, in fact, that the incendiary never had a brother, Blaesus must have fallen a sacrifice. The tribunes and the prefect of the army were obliged to save themselves by flight. Their baggage was seized and plundered. Lucilius the centurion was put to death. This man, by the sarcastic pleasantry of the soldiers, had been nicknamed, "Give me another"; because, in chastising the soldiers, when one rod was broken, he used to call for "Another," and then "Another." The rest of the centurions lay concealed. Out of the whole number, Julius Clemens, a man of promptness and energy, was the favorite of the insurgents. He was spared as a fit person to negotiate the claims of the army. Two of the legions, the eighth and the fifteenth, were on the point of coming to the decision of the sword: the former bent on the destruction of Sirpicus, a centurion, and the latter determined to protect him. The quarrel would have resulted in a scene of blood, if the soldiers of the ninth legion had not, by entreaties or menaces, appeased the fury of both parties.

When the account of these transactions reached Tiberius, that abstruse and gloomy prince, who loved to brood in secret over all untoward events, was so deeply affected, that he resolved to despatch his son Drusus and other nobles, together with two praetorian cohorts, to quell the insurrection. In their instructions no decisive orders were given: they were left to act as emergencies might require. To the cohorts

was added a select detachment, with a party of the praetorian horse, and the flower of the Germans, at that time the body-guard of the emperor. In the train which accompanied Drusus, Aelius Sejanus was appointed to guide the inexperience of the young prince. Sejanus, at that time in a joint commission with his father Strabo, had the command of the praetorian bands, and stood high in favor with Tiberius. The army would of course consider him as the fountain of rewards and punishments. As soon as they approached the camp, the discontented legions, by way of doing honor to Drusus, advanced to meet him; not, indeed, with colors displayed, as is usual on such occasions, but in deep and solemn silence, their dress neglected, and their whole appearance uncouth and sordid. In their looks was seen an air of dejection, and at the same time a sullen gloom, that plainly showed a spirit of mutiny still working in their hearts.

Drusus was no sooner within the entrenchments than the malcontents secured the gates. Sentinels were posted at different stations, while the rest gathered in a body round the tribunal. Drusus stood in act to speak, with his hand commanding silence. The soldiers felt a variety of contending passions: they looked around, and viewing their numbers grew fierce at the sight, rending the air with shouts and acclamations; they turned to Drusus, and were covered with confusion. An indistinct and hollow murmur was heard, a general uproar followed, and soon afterward a deep and awful silence. The behavior of the men varied with their passions, by turns inflamed with rage or depressed with fear. Drusus seized his moment, and read his father's letter, in substance stating that Tiberius had nothing so much at heart as the interest of the gallant legions with whom he had served in so many wars. As soon as his grief for the loss of Augustus allowed him leisure, it was his intention to refer the case of the army to the wisdom of the Senate. In the mean time he sent his son to grant all the relief that could then be applied. Ulterior demands he reserved for the deliberation of the fathers. To enforce authority, or to relax it, was the lawful right of that assembly, and the Senate, beyond all doubt, would distribute rewards and punishments with equal justice.

The soldiers made answer that they had appointed Julius Clemens to speak in their behalf. That officer claimed a right of discharge from the service at the end of sixteen years, all arrears to be settled then; in the mean time a *denarius* to be the soldier's daily pay, and the practice of detaining the men beyond the period of their service, under the name of veterans, to be abolished forever. In a business of so much moment, Drusus observed, the Senate and the emperor must be consulted. A general clamor followed. "Why did he come so far, since he had no authority to augment their pay, or to mitigate their sufferings? The power of doing good was not confided to him, while every petty officer inflicted blows and stripes, and even death. It had been formerly the policy of Tiberius to elude the claims of the army, by taking shelter under the name of Augustus; and now Drusus comes to play the same farce. How long were they to be amused by the visits of the emperor's son? Could that be deemed an equitable government that kept nothing in suspense but the good of the army? When the soldier is to be punished, or a battle to be fought, why not consult the Sen-

ate? According to the present system reward is to be always a subject of reference, while punishment is instant and without appeal."

The soldiers, in a tumultuous body, rushed from the tribunal, breathing vengeance, and wherever they met either men belonging to the praetorian bands, or friends of Drusus, they threatened violence, in hopes of ending the dispute by a sudden conflict. Gnaeus Lentulus, whose age and military character gave him considerable weight, was particularly obnoxious, he being regarded as the chief adviser of Drusus, and an enemy to the proceedings of the army. For the security of his person he went aside with Drusus, intending to repair to the winter camp. The mutineers gathered round him, demanding, with insolence, "Which way was he going? to the Senate? perhaps to the emperor? Was he there to show himself an enemy to the demands of the legion?" Nothing could restrain their fury. They discharged a volley of stones, and Lentulus, wounded and covered with blood, had nothing to expect but instant death, when the guards that attended Drusus came up in time, and rescued him from destruction.

The night that followed seemed big with some fatal disaster, when an unexpected phenomenon put an end to the commotion. In a clear and serene sky the moon was suddenly eclipsed. This appearance, its natural cause not being understood by the soldiers, was deemed a prognostic announcing the fate of the army. The planet in its languishing state represented the condition of the legions; if it recovered its former luster, the efforts of the men would be crowned with success. To assist the moon in her labors, the air resounded with the clangor of brazen instruments, with the sound of trumpets, and other warlike music. The crowd in the mean time stood at gaze. Every gleam of light inspired the men with joy, and the sudden gloom depressed their hearts with grief. The clouds condensed, and the moon was supposed to be lost in utter darkness. A melancholy horror seized the multitude, and melancholy is sure to engender superstition. A religious panic spread through the army. The appearance in the heavens foretold eternal labor to the legions, and all lamented that by their crimes they had called down on themselves the indignation of the gods. Drusus took advantage of the moment. The opportunity was the effect of chance, but, rightly managed, might conduce to the wisest purpose.

He gave orders that the men who by honest means were most in credit with the malcontents should go round from tent to tent. Among these was Clemens the centurion. They visited every part of the camp, applied to the guards on duty, conversed with the patrol, and mixed with the sentinels at the gates. They allured some by promises, and by terror subdued the spirit of others. "How long shall we besiege the son of the emperor? Where will this confusion end? Must we follow Percennius and Vibulenus? And shall we swear fidelity to those new commanders? Will their funds supply the pay of the legions? Have they lands to assign to the veteran soldier? For them shall the Neros and the Drusi be deposed? Are they to mount the vacant throne, the future sovereigns of Rome? Let us, since we were the last to enter into rebellion, be the first to expiate our guilt by well-timed repentance. Demands in favor of all proceed but slowly; to individuals indulgence is more easily granted; deserve it separately,

and the reward will follow." This reasoning had its effect. Suspicion and mutual distrust began to arise; the soldiers recently recruited went apart from the veterans; the legions separated; a sense of duty revived in the breasts of all; the gates were no longer guarded; and the colors, at first promiscuously crowded together, were restored to their proper stations.

At the return of day Drusus called an assembly of the soldiers. Though unused to public speaking, he delivered himself with the eloquence of a man who felt his own importance and the dignity of his rank. He condemned the past, and applauded the present. It was not, he said, a part of his character to yield to menaces, or to shrink from danger. If he saw them penitent, if he heard the language of remorse, he would make a report in their favor, and dispose his father to listen to their petition. The soldiers answered in humble terms. At their request the younger Blaesus, mentioned above, with Lucius Apronius, a Roman knight in the train of Drusus, and Justus Catonius, a centurion of the first rank, were despatched as the delegates of the army. In the councils afterward held by Drusus various opinions were entertained, and different measures proposed. To wait the return of the deputies, and meanwhile to win the affections of the men by moderation, was the advice of many: others were for immediate coercion. "Lenity," they said, "makes no impression on the vulgar herd. Common soldiers, when not kept in subjection, are fierce and turbulent, yet ever ready to bend and crouch under proper authority. It was now the time, while they were overwhelmed with superstition, to infuse another fear, and teach them to respect their general. The authors of the late sedition ought to be made a public example." Drusus, by the bent of his nature prone to vindictive measures, desired that Percennius and Vibulenus should be brought before him. By his orders they were put to death; according to some writers, in his own tent, and there buried; according to others, their bodies were thrown over the entrenchments, a spectacle for public view.

Diligent search was made for the most active incendiaries. Some were found roving on the outside of the lines, and were instantly cut off by the centurions or the praetorian soldiers. Others were delivered up to justice by their respective companies, as an earnest of their own conversion. The rigor of the winter, which set in earlier than usual, added to the afflictions of the army. Heavy rains ensued, and fell with such violence that the men could not venture from their tents. To meet in parties, and converse with their comrades, was impossible. The colors, borne down by torrents that rushed through the camp, were with difficulty secured. Superstition still continued to fill the mind with terror. In everything that happened imagination saw the anger of the gods: it was not without reason that the planets suffered an eclipse, and storms and tempests burst from the angry elements; the guilt of the army was the cause of all. To avert impending vengeance, the only expedient was to depart at once from an inauspicious camp, and by due atonement expiate their past offenses in their winter quarters. In this persuasion the eighth legion departed; the fifteenth followed. The ninth remained behind, declaring aloud that they would wait for orders from Tiberius, but they soon saw themselves deserted, and therefore struck their tents, willing to do by choice what in a little time would be an act of necessity. Peace and good order being thus restored, Drusus, deeming it unnecessary to wait for the return of the deputies, immediately set out for Rome.

(GAIUS) SUETONIUS (TRANQUILLUS) (C. A.D. 69–C. 140)

from *The Lives of the Twelve Caesars:* Julius Caesar

~⌒

*B*orn to the equestrian and tribune Suetonius Laetus, the biographer Gaius Suetonius Tranquillus was himself an equestrian, as well as attorney and friend to Pliny the Younger and Septicius Clarus; he also served as cultural secretary to the emperor Hadrian. He lost his job because of his familiarity with the emperor's wife Sabina, and retired to a literary life, concentrating on expanding his notes on philology and linguistics, physical science, biography, and Roman antiquities.

- Written in a compelling yet simple style, his *The Lives of the Twelve Caesars* (*De vita Caesarum*, from Julius Caesar to Domitian) and parts of his *Lives of Famous Men* (*De viris illustribus*, including poets, grammarians, rhetoricians, orators, and historians) survive.
- Each of his lives includes archival fact and imperial gossip on:

  - the subject's family history;
  - early life;
  - public career;
  - minute particulars of physical appearance;
  - private life;
  - death; and
  - anecdotes recording his subject's vices and virtues.

- *The Lives of the Twelve Caesars* was probably published for the first time in A.D. 121.

Suetonius isn't known for his critical judgment of his sources or depth of analysis of his subjects. He's more interested in the private lives and scandals of men and women than in the shattering events of empire, yet he provides us with material, as a result, that would otherwise be entirely lost.

JULIUS CAESAR

I. Julius Caesar, the divine, lost his father when he was in the sixteenth year of his age; and the year following, being nominated to the office of high-priest of Jupiter, he repudiated Cossutia, who was very wealthy, although her family belonged only to the equestrian order, and to whom he had been contracted when he was a mere boy. He then married Cornelia, the daughter of Cinna, who was four times consul; and had by her, shortly afterward, a daughter named Julia. Resisting all the efforts of the dictator Sylla to induce him to divorce Cornelia, he suffered the penalty of being stripped of his sacerdotal office, his wife's dowry, and his own patrimonial estates; and, being identified with the adverse faction, was compelled to withdraw from Rome. After changing his place of concealment nearly every night, although he was suffering from a quartan ague, and having effected his release by bribing the officers who had tracked his footsteps, he at length obtained a pardon through the intercession of the vestal virgins, and of Mamercus Aemilius and Aurelius Cotta, his near relatives. We are assured that when Sylla, having withstood for a while the entreaties of his own best friends, persons of distinguished rank, at last yielded to their importunity, he exclaimed—either by a divine impulse, or from a shrewd conjecture:

"Your suit is granted, and you may take him among you; but know," he added, "that this man, for whose safety you are so extremely anxious, will, some day or other, be the ruin of the party of the nobles, in defense of which you are leagued with me; for in this one Caesar, you will find many a Marius."

II. His first campaign was served in Asia, on the staff of the praetor, M. Thermus; and being dispatched into Bithynia, to bring thence a fleet, he loitered so long at the court of Nicomedes, as to give occasion to reports of a criminal intercourse between him and that prince; which received additional credit from his hasty return to Bithynia, under the pretext of recovering a debt due to a freedman, his client. The rest of his service was more favorable to his reputation; and when Mitylene was taken by storm, he was presented by Thermus with the civic crown.

X. In his edileship, he not only embellished the Comitium, and the rest of the Forum, with the adjoining halls, but adorned the Capitol also, with temporary piazzas, constructed for the purpose of displaying some part of the superabundant collections he had made for the amusement of the people. He entertained them with the hunting of wild beasts, and with games, both alone and in conjunction with his colleague. On this account, he obtained the whole credit of the expense to which they had jointly contributed; insomuch that his colleague, Marcus Bibulus, could not forbear remarking, that he was served in the manner of Pollux. For as the temple erected in the Forum to the two brothers went by the name of Castor alone, so his and Caesar's joint munificence was imputed to the latter only. To the

other public spectacles exhibited to the people, Caesar added a fight of gladiators, but with fewer pairs of combatants than he had intended. For he had collected from all parts so great a company of them, that his enemies became alarmed; and a decree was made, restricting the number of gladiators which any one was allowed to retain at Rome.

XIV. After he was chosen pretor, the conspiracy of Catiline was discovered; and while every other member of the Senate voted for inflicting capital punishment on the accomplices in that crime, he alone proposed that the delinquents should be distributed for safe custody among the towns of Italy, their property being confiscated. He even struck such terror into those who were advocates for greater severity, by representing to them what universal odium would be attached to their memories by the Roman people, that Decius Silanus, consul-elect, did not hesitate to qualify his proposal, it not being very honorable to change it, by a lenient interpretation; as if it had been understood in a harsher sense than he intended, and Caesar would certainly have carried his point, having brought over to his side a great number of the senators, among whom was Cicero, the consul's brother, had not a speech by Marcus Cato infused new vigor into the resolutions of the Senate. He persisted, however, in obstructing the measure, until a body of the Roman knights, who stood under arms as a guard, threatened him with instant death, if he continued his determined opposition. They even thrust at him with their drawn swords, so that those who sat next him moved away; and a few friends, with no small difficulty, protected him, by throwing their arms round him, and covering him with their togas. At last, deterred by this violence, he not only gave way, but absented himself from the Senate-House during the remainder of that year.

[At the end of his pretorship, Caesar drew Farther Spain. After quieting his creditors, he hurried off to his province. When peace was restored there, he hastened back to Rome to stand for the consulship. To this office he was elected with Bibulus.]

XX. Having entered upon his office, he introduced a new regulation, that the daily acts both of the Senate and people should be committed to writing, and published. He also revived an old custom, that an officer should precede him, and his lictors follow him, on the alternate months when the fasces were not carried before him. Upon preferring a bill to the people for the division of some public lands, he was opposed by his colleague, whom he violently drove out of the forum. Next day the insulted consul made a complaint in the Senate of this treatment; but such was the consternation, that no one having the courage to bring the matter forward or move a censure, which had been often done under outrages of less importance, he was so much dispirited, that until the expiration of his office he never stirred from home, and did nothing but issue edicts to obstruct his colleague's proceedings. From that time, therefore, Caesar had the sole management of public affairs; insomuch that some wags, when they signed any instrument as witnesses, did not add "in the consulship of Caesar and Bibulus," but, "of Julius and Caesar"; putting the same person down twice, under his name and surname. The following

verses likewise were currently repeated on this occasion:

Non Bibulo quidquam nuper, sed Caesare factum est;
Nam Bibulo fieri consule nil memini.
   Nothing was done in Bibulus's year:
   No; Caesar only then was consul here.

The land of Stellas, consecrated by our ancestors to the gods, with some other lands in Campania left subject to tribute, for the support of the expenses of the government, he divided, but not by lot, among upward of twenty thousand freemen, who had each of them three or more children. He eased the publicans, upon their petition, of a third part of the sum which they had engaged to pay into the public treasury; and openly admonished them not to bid so extravagantly upon the next occasion. He made various profuse grants to meet the wishes of others, no one opposing him; or if any such attempt was made, it was soon suppressed. Marcus Cato, who interrupted him in his proceedings, he ordered to be dragged out of the Senate-House by a lictor, and carried to prison. Lucius Lucullus, likewise, for opposing him with some warmth, he so terrified with the apprehension of being criminated, that to deprecate the consul's resentment, he fell on his knees. And upon Cicero's lamenting in some trial the miserable condition of the times, he the very same day, by nine o'clock, transferred his enemy, Publius Clodius, from a patrician to a plebeian family; a change which he had long solicited in vain. At last, effectually to intimidate all those of the opposite party, he by great rewards prevailed upon Vettius to declare, that he had been solicited by certain persons to assassinate Pompey; and when he was brought before the rostra to name those who had been concerted between them, after naming one or two to no purpose, not without great suspicion of subornation, Caesar, despairing of success in this rash stratagem, is supposed to have taken off his informer by poison.

XXV. During nine years in which he held the government of the province, his achievements were as follows: he reduced all Gaul, bounded by the Pyrenean forest, the Alps, mount Gebenna, and the two rivers, the Rhine and the Rhone, and being about three thousand two hundred miles in compass, into the form of a province, excepting only the nations in alliance with the Republic, and such as had merited his favor; imposing upon this new acquisition an annual tribute of forty millions of sesterces. He was the first of the Romans who, crossing the Rhine by a bridge, attacked the Germanic tribes inhabiting the country beyond that river, whom he defeated in several engagements. He also invaded the Britons, a people formerly unknown, and having vanquished them, exacted from them contributions and hostages. Amidst such a series of successes, he experienced thrice only any signal disaster; once in Britain, when his fleet was nearly wrecked in a storm; in Gaul, at Gergovia, where one of his legions was put to the rout; and in the territory of the Germans, his lieutenants Titurius and Aurunculeius were cut off by an ambuscade.

THE CIVIL WAR

XXXI. When intelligence, therefore, was received, that the interposition of the tribunes in his favor had been utterly rejected, and that they themselves had fled from the city, he immediately sent forward some cohorts, but privately, to prevent any suspicion of his design; and, to keep up appearances, attended at a public spectacle, examined the model of a fencing-school which he proposed to build, and, as usual, sat down to table with a numerous party of his friends. But after sun-set, mules being put to his carriage from a neighboring mill, he set forward on his journey with all possible privacy, and a small retinue. The lights going out, he lost his way, and wandered about a long time, until at length, by the help of a guide, whom he found toward day-break, he proceeded on foot through some narrow paths, and again reached the road. Coming up with his troops on the banks of the Rubicon, which was the boundary of his province, he halted for a while, and, revolving in his mind the importance of the step he was on the point of taking, he turned to those about him, and said: "We may still retreat; but if we pass this little bridge, nothing is left for us but to fight it out in arms."

XXXII. While he was thus hesitating, the following incident occurred. A person remarkable for his noble mien and graceful aspect, appeared close at hand, sitting and playing upon a pipe. When, not only the shepherds, but a number of soldiers also flocked from their posts to listen to him, and some trumpeters among them, he snatched a trumpet from one of them, ran to the river with it, and sounding the advance with a piercing blast, crossed to the other side. Upon this, Caesar exclaimed, "Let us go whither the omens of the Gods and the iniquity of our enemies call us. The die is now cast."

XXXIII. Accordingly, having marched his army over the river, he shewed them the tribunes of the people, who, upon their being driven from the city, had come to meet him; and, in the presence of that assembly, called upon the troops to pledge him their fidelity, with tears in his eyes, and his garment rent from his bosom. It has been supposed, that upon this occasion he promised to every soldier a knight's estate; but that opinion is founded on a mistake. For when, in his harangue to them, he frequently held out a finger of his left hand, and declared, that to recompense those who should support him in the defense of his honor, he would willingly part even with his ring; the soldiers at a distance, who could more easily see than hear him while he spoke, formed their conception of what he said, by the eye, not by the ear; and accordingly gave out, that he had promised to each of them the privilege of wearing the gold ring, and an estate of four hundred thousand sesterces.

XXXIV. Of his subsequent proceedings I shall give a cursory detail, in the order in which they occurred. He took possession of Picenum, Umbria, and Etruria; and having obliged Lucius Domitius, who had been tumultuously nominated his successor, and held Corsinium with a garrison, to surrender, and dismissed him, he marched along the coast of the Upper Sea, to Brundusium, to which place the consuls and Pompey were fled with the intention of crossing the sea as soon as possible. After vain attempts, by all the obstacles he could oppose, to prevent their leaving the harbor, he turned his steps toward Rome, where he appealed to the Senate on the present state of public affairs; and then set out for Spain, in which province Pompey had a numerous army, under the command of three lieutenants, Marcus Petreius, Lucius Afranius, and Marcus Varro; declaring amongst his friends, before he set forward, "That he was going against an army without a general, and should return thence against a general without an army." Though his progress was retarded both by the siege of Marseilles, which shut her gates against him, and a very great scarcity of corn, yet in a short time he bore down all before him.

XXXV. Thence he returned to Rome, and crossing the sea to Macedonia, blocked up Pompey during almost four months, within a line of ramparts of prodigious extent; and at last defeated him in the battle of Pharsalia. Pursuing him in his flight to Alexandria, where he was informed of his murder, he presently found himself also engaged, under all the disadvantages of time and place, in a very dangerous war, with king Ptolemy, who, he saw, had treacherous designs upon his life. It was winter, and he, within the walls of a well-provided and subtle enemy, was destitute of every thing, and wholly unprepared for such a conflict. He succeeded, however, in his enterprise, and put the kingdom of Egypt into the hands of Cleopatra and her younger brother; being afraid to make it a province, lest, under an aspiring prefect, it might become the center of revolt. From Alexandria he went into Syria, and thence to Pontus, induced by intelligence which he had received respecting Pharnaces. This prince, who was son of the great Mithridates, had seized the opportunity which the distraction of the times offered for making war upon his neighbors, and his insolence and fierceness had grown with his success. Caesar, however, within five days after entering his country, and four hours after coming in sight of him, overthrew him in one decisive battle. Upon which, he frequently remarked to those about him the good fortune of Pompey, who had obtained his military reputation, chiefly, by victory over so feeble an enemy. He afterward defeated Scipio and Juba, who were rallying the remains of the party in Africa, and Pompey's sons in Spain.

XXXVI. During the whole course of the Civil War, he never once suffered any defeat, except in the case of his lieutenants; of whom Caius Curio fell in Africa, Caius Antonius was made prisoner in Illyricum, Publius Dolabella lost a fleet in the same Illyricum, and Cneius Domitius Calvinus, an army in Pontus. In every encounter with the enemy where he himself commanded, he came off with complete success; nor was the issue ever doubtful, except on two occasions: once at Dyrrachium, when, being obliged to give ground, and Pompey not pursuing his advantage, he said that "Pompey knew not how to conquer"; the other instance occurred in his last battle in Spain, when, despairing of the event, he even had thoughts of killing himself.

CAESAR'S ABILITY AS AN ORATOR

LV. In eloquence and warlike achievements, he equaled at least, if he did not surpass, the greatest of men. After his prosecution of Dolabella, he was indisputably reckoned one of the most distinguished advocates. Cicero, in recounting to Brutus the famous orators, declares, "that he does not see that Caesar was inferior to any one of them"; and says, "that he had an elegant, splendid, noble, and magnificent vein of eloquence." And in a letter to Cornelius Nepos, he writes of him in the following terms: "What! Of all the orators, who, during the whole course of their lives, have done nothing else, which can you prefer to him? Which of them is more pointed or terse in his periods, or employs more polished and elegant language?" In his youth, he seems to have chosen Strabo Caesar for his model; from whose oration in behalf of the Sardinians he has transcribed some passages literally into his Divination. In his delivery he is said to have had a shrill voice, and his action was animated, but not ungraceful. He has left behind him some speeches, among which are ranked a few that are not genuine, such as that on behalf of Quintus Metellus. These Augustus supposes, with reason, to be rather the production of blundering short-hand writers, who were not able to keep pace with him in the delivery, than publications of his own. For I find in some copies that the title is not "For Metellus," but "What he wrote to Metellus"; whereas the speech is delivered in the name of Caesar, vindicating Metellus and himself from the aspersions cast upon them by their common defamers. The speech addressed "To his soldiers in Spain," Augustus considers likewise as spurious. We meet with two under this title; one made, as is pretended, in the first battle, and the other in the last; at which time, Asinius Pollio says, he had not leisure to address the soldiers, on account of the suddenness of the enemy's attack.

CAESAR'S LITERARY WORKS

LVI. He has likewise left Commentaries of his own actions both in the war in Gaul, and in the

Civil War with Pompey; for the author of the Alexandrian, African, and Spanish wars is not known with any certainty. Some think they are the productions of Oppius, and some of Hirtius; the latter of whom composed the last book, which is imperfect, of the Gallic war. Of Caesar's Commentaries, Cicero, in his Brutus, speaks thus: "He wrote his Commentaries in a manner deserving of great approbation: they are plain, precise, and elegant, without any affectation of rhetorical ornament. In having thus prepared materials for others who might be inclined to write his history, he may perhaps have encouraged some silly creatures to enter upon such a work, who will needs be dressing up his actions in all the extravagance of bombast; but he has discouraged wise men from ever attempting the subject." Hirtius delivers his opinion of these Commentaries in the following terms: "So great is the approbation with which they are universally perused, that, instead of rousing, he seems to have precluded, the efforts of any future historian. Yet, with respect to this work, we have more reason to admire him than others; for they only know how well and correctly he has written, but we know, likewise, how easily and quickly he did it." Asinius Pollio thinks that they were not drawn up with much care, or with a due regard to truth; for he insinuates that Caesar was too hasty of belief in regard to what was performed by others under his orders; and that, he has not given a very faithful account of his own acts, either by design, or through defect of memory; expressing at the same time an opinion that Caesar intended a new and more correct edition. He has left behind him likewise two books on Analogy, with the same number

under the title of Anti-Cato, and a poem entitled The Itinerary. Of these books, he composed the first two in his passage over the Alps, as he was returning to the army after making his circuit in Hither-Gaul; the second work about the time of the battle of Munda; and the last during the four-and-twenty days he employed in his journey from Rome to Farther-Spain. There are extant some letters of his to the Senate, written in a manner never practised by any before him; for they are distinguished into pages in the form of a memorandum book: whereas the consuls and commanders till then, used constantly in their letters to continue the line quite across the sheet, without any folding or distinction of pages. There are extant likewise some letters from him to Cicero, and others to his friends, concerning his domestic affairs; in which, if there was occasion for secrecy, he wrote in cyphers; that is, he used the alphabet in such a manner, that not a single word could be made out. The way to decipher those epistles was to substitute the fourth for the first letter, as *d* for *a*, and so for the other letters respectively. Some things likewise pass under his name, said to have been written by him when a boy, or a very young man; as the Encomium of Hercules, a tragedy entitled Oedipus, and a collection of Apophthegms; all which Augustus forbad to be published, in a short and plain letter to Pompeius Macer, who was employed by him in the arrangement of his libraries.

CAESAR'S ASSASSINATION

LXXXII. When he had taken his seat, the conspirators stood round him, under color of paying their compliments; and immediately Tullius

Cimber, who had engaged to commence the assault, advancing nearer than the rest, as if he had some favor to request, Caesar made signs that he should defer his petition to some other time. Tullius immediately seized him by the toga, on both shoulders; at which Caesar crying out, "Violence is meant!" one of the Cassii wounded him a little below the throat. Caesar seized him by the arm, and ran it through with his style; and endeavoring to rush forward, was stopped by another wound. Finding himself now attacked on all hands with naked poniards, he wrapped the toga about his head, and at the same moment drew the skirt round his legs with his left hand, that he might fall more decently with the lower part of his body covered. He was stabbed with three and twenty wounds, uttering a groan only, but no cry, at the first wound; although some authors relate, that when Marcus Brutus fell upon him, he exclaimed, "What! art thou, too, one of them! Thou, my son!" The whole assembly instantly dispersing, he lay for some time after he expired, until three of his slaves laid the body on a litter, and carried it home, with one arm hanging down over the side. Among so many wounds, there was none that was mortal, in the opinion of the surgeon Antistius, except the second, which he received in the breast. The conspirators meant to drag his body into the Tiber as soon as they had killed him; to confiscate his estate, and rescind all his enactments; but they were deterred by fear of Mark Antony, and Lepidus, Caesar's master of the horse, and abandoned their intentions.

HADRIAN (PUBLIUS AELIUS HADRIANUS)
(A.D. 76–138; EMPEROR 117–138)

To His Soul

*T*he childless Trajan became Hadrian's guardian when the boy lost his father, Aelius Hadrianus Afer, the emperor's first cousin, in A.D. 85, at the age of ten. By the time Domitian died in 96, the young Hadrian was already tribune of a Roman legion. Though he'd alienated himself from Trajan because of his wild spending, Hadrian through the maneuvering of the empress Plotina, married Trajan's grand-niece Vibia Sabina in 100, and subsequently became again a beloved close associate of the emperor.

In quick succession, he was appointed imperial quaestor, staff-officer in the First Dacian War, praetor, governor of Lower Pannonia, and consul. In 112 he became archon of Athens, and in 114 gover-

The Pons Aelius leading to Hadrian's tomb, Castel Sant'Angelo

nor of Syria. At the siege of Arabian Atria, Trajan put Hadrian in command of the Roman army. When Trajan neared death in Cilicia, he allegedly adopted Hadrian who, in any case, took over the imperial government when Trajan died in 117.

- His first accomplishment as emperor was peace initially with the Persians, based on making the Euphrates the boundary between the Roman and Persian Empires, then with the Parthians.
- After a triumphant return to Rome, where he ensured that Trajan receive proper credit for his triumphs and that his senatorial enemies be executed, Hadrian received the title *"Pater Patriae"* ("Father of his country") and imperial powers from the Senate, and set about consolidating his rule by winning over the populace.
- He spent much of his reign traveling from one end of the Empire to another, in each place inspecting the local administration, constructing public works (such as Hadrian's Wall, separating Scotland from England; and completing the Temple of Olympian Zeus in Athens), and

tightening Rome's hold on the provinces. His tour included Gaul, Britain, the Rhine, Holland, and Spain; but also Phrygia, the Troad, Caria, Cappadocia, Syria, Greece, the Propontis, and the Nile. He is said to have climbed Mt. Aetna in Sicily just to watch the sunrise.

- With a lifelong interest in Greek antiquities, Hadrian founded the Athenaeum in Rome to encourage the classical development of Latin literature. At Athens he had himself initiated into the Eleusinian Mysteries and preserved the ancient Acropolis building; he constructed a magnificent portal between the old and new cities (one side inscribed, "Through me is the ancient city of Theseus"; the other, "Through me is the City of Hadrian").

- Although he ordered that the persecution of Christians be stopped, he used the harshest of measures against the Jewish revolts and erected a temple to Jupiter on the site of the ancient temple in Jerusalem, forbidding the Holy City to Jews except one day a year, the anniversary of its destruction. Judaea became Syria Palestina, making the Jews homeless.

- Patron of the arts and philosophy, though hardly of literature, Hadrian formed a circle of intelligentsia around him wherever he went. He built the Pantheon, the Tivoli gardens, elaborate villas on Capri, the Temple of Venus and Roma, the Temple of Trajan, and his own mausoleum (modern Castel Sant'Angelo) in Rome. He himself wrote orations, letters, a history of his own time, decrees, and epigrams. Only one of his poems, written on his death bed, survives.

Little soul, like a cloud, like a feather,
My body's small guest and companion,
Where now do you rest, in what places—

Stripped naked, and rigid, and pallid,
Do you play as before, little jester?

SORANUS (A.D. 98–138)

Gynecology

～

Although he studied medicine in Alexandria and wrote in his beloved native Greek, Soranus of Ephesus was one of the most important physicians in Rome. Practicing gynecology, pediatrics, and obstetrics under Trajan and Hadrian, Soranus was renowned for his knowledge, observation, methodology, and sound judgment; he was critical of his Roman hosts.

- Soranus' straightforward and clearly written books, translated immediately into Latin, deal with the history of medicine, hygiene, problems of terminology, fracture surgery, symptomology, nervous disorders, methodology, and diagnostics, and include the oldest known biography of Hippocrates.
- His four-volume *Gynecology* (also known as *On Midwifery and the Diseases of Women*) gives us insight into Roman thought on normalities and abnormalities of the female reproductive system as well as on midwifery, fertility, birth control, abortion, and family planning. His commonsense opinion was the standard for women's and infants' care until the end of the Renaissance.

CONCEPTION

34. One must judge the majority from the ages of fifteen to forty to be fit for conception, if they are not mannish, compact, and oversturdy, or too flabby and very moist. Since the uterus is similar to the whole [body], it will in these cases either be unable, on account of its pronounced hardness, easily to accept the attachment of the seed, or by reason of its extreme laxity and atony [let it fall again]. Furthermore they seem fit if their uteri are neither very moist or dry, nor too lax or constricted, and if they have their catharsis regularly, not through some moisture or ichors of various kinds, but through blood and of this neither too much nor, on the other hand, extremely little. Also those in whom the orifice of the uterus is comparatively far forward and lies in a straight line (for an orifice deviated even in its natural state and lying farther back in the vagina, is less suited for the attraction and acceptance of the seed).

36. The best time for fruitful intercourse is when menstruation is ending and abating, when urge and appetite for coitus are present, when the body is neither in want nor too congested and heavy from drunkenness and indigestion, and after the body has been rubbed down and a

little food been eaten and when a pleasant state exists in every respect. (1) "When menstruation is ending and abating," for the time before menstruation is not suitable, the uterus already being overburdened and in an unresponsive state because of the ingress of material and incapable of carrying on two motions contrary to each other, one for the excretion of material, the other for receiving.

39. (2) In order that the offspring may not be rendered misshapen, women must be sober during coitus because in drunkenness the soul becomes the victim of strange fantasies; this furthermore, because the offspring bears some resemblance to the mother as well not only in body but in soul . . .

40. (3) Together with these points it has already been stated that the best time is after a rubdown has been given and a little food been eaten. The food will give the inner turbulence an impetus toward coitus, the urge for intercourse not being diverted by appetite for food; while the rubdown will make it possible to lay hold of the injected seed more readily. For just as the rubdown naturally aids the distribution of food, it helps also in the reception and retention of the seed, yesterday's superfluities, as

one may say, being unloaded, and the body thoroughly cleansed and in a sound state for its natural processes. Consequently, as the farmer sows only after having first cleansed the soil and removed any foreign material, in the same manner we too advise that insemination for the production of man should follow after the body has first been given a rubdown.

CONTRACEPTION

60. A contraceptive differs from an abortive, for the first does not let conception take place, while the latter destroys what has been conceived . . . And an expulsive some people say is synonymous with an abortive; others, however, say that there is a difference because an expulsive does not mean drugs but shaking and leaping . . . For this reason they say that Hippocrates, although prohibiting abortives, yet in his book "On the Nature of the Child" employs leaping with the heels to the buttocks for the sake of expulsion. But a controversy has arisen. For one party banishes abortives, citing the testimony of Hippocrates who says: "I will give to no one an abortive"; moreover, because it is the specific task of medicine to guard and preserve what has been engendered by nature. The other party prescribes abortives, but with discrimination, that is, they do not prescribe them when a person wishes to destroy the embryo because of adultery or out of consideration for youthful beauty; but only to prevent subsequent danger in parturition if the uterus is small and not capable of accommodating the complete development, or if the uterus at its orifice has knobbly swelling and fissures, or if some similar difficulty is involved. And they say the same about contraceptives as well, and

we too agree with them. And since it is safer to prevent conception from taking place than to destroy the fetus, we shall now first discourse upon such prevention.

61. For if it is much more advantageous not to conceive than to destroy the embryo, one must consequently beware of having sexual intercourse at those periods which we said were suitable for conception. And during the sexual act, at the critical moment of coitus when the man is about to discharge the seed, the woman must hold her breath and draw herself away a little, so that the seed may not be hurled too deep into the cavity of the uterus. And getting up immediately and squatting down, she should induce sneezing and carefully wipe the vagina all round; she might even drink something cold. It also aids in preventing conception to smear the orifice of the uterus all over before with old olive oil or honey or cedar resin or juice of the balsam tree, alone or together with white lead; or with a moist cerate containing myrtle oil and white lead; or before the act with moist alum, or with galbanum together with wine; or to put a lock of fine wool into the orifice of the uterus; or, before sexual relations to use vaginal suppositories which have the power to contract and to condense. For such of these things as are styptic, clogging and cooling cause the orifice of the uterus to shut before the time of coitus and do not let the seed pass into its fundus. [Such, however, as are hot] and irritating not only do not allow the seed of the man to remain in the cavity of the uterus, but draw forth as well another fluid from it.

62. And we shall make specific mention of some. Pine bark, tanning sumach, equal quan-

tities of each, rub with wine and apply in due measure before coitus after wool has been wrapped around; and after two or three hours she may remove it and have intercourse. Another: Of Cimolian earth, root of panax, equal quantities, rub with water separately and together, and when sticky apply in like manner. Or: Grind the inside of fresh pomegranate peel with water, and apply. Or: Grind two parts of pomegranate peel and one part of oak galls, form small suppositories and insert after the cessation of menstruation. Or: Moist alum, the inside of pomegranate rind, mix with water, and apply with wool. Or: Of unripe oak galls, of the inside of pomegranate peel, of ginger, of each 2 drachms, mold it with wine to the size of vetch peas and dry indoors and give before coitus, to be applied as a vaginal suppository. Or: Grind the flesh of dried figs and apply together with natron. Or: Apply pomegranate peel with an equal amount of gum and an equal amount of oil of roses. Then one should always follow with a drink of honey water. But one should beware of things which are very pungent, because of the ulcerations arising from them. And we use all these things after the end of menstruation . . .

ABORTION

64. In order that the embryo be separated, the woman should have [more violent exercise], walking about energetically and being shaken by means of draught animals; she should also leap energetically and carry things which are heavy beyond her strength. She should use diuretic decoctions which also have the power to bring on menstruation, and empty and purge the abdomen with relatively pungent clysters;

sometimes using warm and sweet olive oil as injections, sometimes anointing the whole body thoroughly therewith and rubbing it vigorously, especially around the pubes, the abdomen, and the loins, bathing daily in sweet water which is not too hot, lingering in the baths and drinking first a little wine and living on pungent food. If this is without effect, one must also treat locally by having her sit in a bath of a decoction of linseed, fenugreek, mallow, marsh mallow, and wormwood. She must also use poultices of the same substances and have injections of old oil, alone or together with rue juice or maybe with honey, or of iris oil, or of absinthium together with honey, or of panax balm or else of spelt together with rue and honey, or of Syrian unguent. And if the situation remains the same she must no longer apply the common poultices, but those made of meal of lupines together with ox bile and absinthium, [and she must use] plasters of a similar kind.

65. For a woman who intends to have an abortion, it is necessary for two or even three days beforehand to take protracted baths, little food and to use softening vaginal suppositories; also to abstain from wine; then to be bled and a relatively great quantity taken away. For the dictum of Hippocrates in the *Aphorisms*, even if not true in a case of constriction, is yet true of a healthy woman: "A pregnant woman if bled, miscarries." For just as sweat, urine or feces are excreted if the parts containing these substances slacken very much, so the fetus falls out after the uterus dilates. Following the venesection one must shake her by means of draught animals (for now the shaking is more effective on the parts which previously have

been relaxed) and one must use softening vaginal suppositories. But if a woman reacts unfavorably to venesection and is languid, one must first relax the parts by means of hip-baths, full baths, softening vaginal suppositories, by keeping her on water and limited food, and by means of aperients and the application of a softening clyster; afterward one must apply an abortive vaginal suppository. Of the latter one should choose those which are not too pungent, that they may not cause too great a sympathetic reaction and heat. And of the more gentle ones there exist for instance: Of myrtle, wallflower seed, bitter lupines equal quantities, by means of water, mold troches the size of a bean. Or: Of rue leaves 3 drachms, of myrtle 2 drachms and the same of sweet bay, mix with wine in the same way, and give her a drink. Another vaginal suppository which produces abortion with relatively little danger: Of wallflower, cardamom, brimstone, absinthium, myrrh, equal quantities, mold with water. And she who intends to apply these things should be bathed beforehand or made to relax by hip-baths; and if after some time she brings forth nothing, she should again be relaxed by hip-baths and for the second time a suppository should be applied. In addition, many different things have been mentioned by others; one must, however, beware of things that are too powerful and of separating the embryo by means of something sharp-edged, for danger arises that some of the adjacent parts be wounded. After the abortion one must treat as for inflammation.

(MARCUS CORNELIUS) FRONTO (C. A.D. 100–166)
Correspondence with Marcus Aurelius

ℬorn in Numidian Cirta, Fronto was educated in rhetoric, law, and grammar at Carthage and Alexandria and came to Rome in the time of Hadrian. Though he became the foremost orator and *literatus* of his century, ranked by his contemporaries with Cato, Cicero, and Quintilian, none of his speeches survive.

- Antoninus Pius appointed him tutor of Marcus Aurelius and Lucius Verus, impressed by his speeches on politics and law and as an advocate before the imperial courts. Fronto served as consul in 143. We learn more about his character from Aulus Gellius' *Attic Nights,* in which Fronto appears as one of the banqueters.

His correspondence with the leading figures of his day, rediscovered only in 1815, included letters to and from his student, the future emperor Marcus Aurelius. His letters, offering rare glimpses of the private life of the imperial court, reveal both his gentleness and a conceitedness well enough developed to allow him to scold even the emperor. They also illustrate what Fronto called his *elocutio novella* ("new style") of prose, blending in a curious though sometimes stultified fashion the ancient Latin of Cato and Gracchus with Greek phrases and with the colloquialisms of vulgar Latin speech. The greatest testimony to Fronto's influence is that of Marcus Aurelius, who wrote that he learned from Fronto what envy, deceit, and hypocrisy meant in a tyrant.

FRONTO TO MARCUS AURELIUS AS CAESAR

To my Lord.   A.D. 139?

Gratia came home last night. But to me it has been as good as having Gratia, that you have turned your "maxims" so brilliantly; the one which I received to-day almost faultlessly, so that it could be put in a book of Sallust's without jarring or shewing any inferiority. I am happy, merry, hale, in a word become young again, when you make such progress. It is no light thing that I shall require; but what I remember to have been of service to myself, I cannot but require of you also. You must turn the same maxim twice or thrice, just as you have done with that little one. And so turn longer ones two or three times diligently, boldly. Whatever you venture on, such are your abilities, you will accomplish: but, indeed, with toil have you coveted a task that is truly toilsome, but fair and honorable and attained by few . . . you have got (it) perfectly out. This exercise will be the greatest help to you in speech making; undoubtedly, too, the excerpting of some sentences from the *Jugurtha* or the

Catiline. If the Gods are kind, on your return to Rome I will exact again from you your daily quota of verses. Greet my Lady, your mother.

MARCUS AURELIUS TO FRONTO

To my master.   A.D. 139?

I have received two letters from you at once. In one of these you scolded me and pointed out that I had written a sentence carelessly; in the other, however, you strove to encourage my efforts with praise. Yet I protest to you by my health, by my mother's, and yours, that it was the former letter which gave me the greater pleasure, and that, as I read it, I cried out again and again *O happy that I am! Are you then so happy,* someone will say, *for having a teacher to shew you how to write a maxim more deftly, more clearly, more tersely, more elegantly?* No, that is not my reason for calling myself happy. What, then, is it? It is that I learn from you to speak the truth. That matter—of speaking the truth—is precisely what is so hard for Gods and men: in fact, there is no oracle so truth-telling as not to contain within itself something

Temple of Antoninus and Faustina, Roman Forum

strive to put it beyond my power to pay. If you will have no return made, how can I requite you like with like, if not by obedience? Disloyal, however, to myself, I preferred that you, moved by excess of care . . . since I had those days free, I had the chance . . . of doing some good work and making many extracts . . . Farewell, my good master, my best of masters. I rejoice, best of orators, that you have so become my friend. My Lady greets you.

MARCUS AURELIUS TO FRONTO

Hail my best of masters.   A.D. 139?

If any sleep comes back to you after the wakeful nights of which you complain, I beseech you write to me and, above all, I beseech you take care of your health. Then hide somewhere and bury that "axe of Tenedos," which you hold over us, and do not, whatever you do, give up your intention of pleading cases, or along with yours let all lips be dumb.

You say that you have composed something in Greek which pleases you more than almost anything you have written. Are you not he who lately gave me such a castigation for writing in Greek? However, I must now, more than ever, write in Greek. Do you ask *why*? I wish to make trial whether what I have not learnt may not more readily come to my aid, since what I have learnt leaves me in the lurch. But, an you really loved me, you would have sent me that new piece you are so pleased with. However, I read you here in spite of yourself and indeed that alone is my life and stay.

It is a sanguinary theme you have sent me. I have not yet read the extract from Coelius which you sent, nor shall I read it until I, on my

ambiguous or crooked or intricate, whereby the unwary may be caught and, interpreting the answer in the light of their own wishes, realize its fallaciousness only when the time is past and the business done. But the thing is profitable, and clearly it is the custom to excuse such things merely as pious fraud and delusion. On the other hand, your fault-findings or your guiding reins, whichever they be, shew me the way at once without guile and feigned words. And so I ought to be grateful to you for this, that you teach me before all to speak the truth at the same time and to hear the truth. A double return, then, would be due, and this you will part, have hunted up my wits. But my Caesar-speech grips me with its hooked talons. Now, if never before, I find what a task it is to round and shape three or five lines and to take time over writing. Farewell, breath of my life. Should I not burn with love of you, who have written to me as you have! What shall I do? I cannot refrain. Last year it befell me in this very place, and at this very time, to be consumed with a passionate longing for my mother. This year you inflame that my longing. My Lady greets you.

FRONTO TO MARCUS AURELIUS AS CAESAR
A DISCOURSE ON LOVE   A.D. 139?

1. This is the third letter, beloved Boy, that I am sending you on the same theme, the first by the hand of Lysias, the son of Kephalus, the second of Plato, the philosopher, and the third indeed by the hand of this foreigner, in speech little short of a barbarian, but as regards judgment, as I think, not wholly wanting in sagacity. And I write now without trenching at all upon those previous writings, and so do not you disregard the discourse as saying what has been already said. But if the present treatise seem to you to be longer than those which were previously sent through Lysias and Plato, let this be a proof to you that I can claim in fair words to be at no loss for words. But you must consider now whether my words are no less true than new.

2. No doubt, O Boy, you will wish to know at the very beginning of my discourse how it is that I, who am not in love, long with such eagerness for the very same things as lovers. I

will tell you, therefore, first of all how this is. He who is ever so much a lover is, by heaven, gifted with no keener sight than I who am no lover, but *I* can discern your beauty as well as anyone else, aye, far more accurately, I might say, even than your lover. But, just as we see in the case of fever patients, and those who have taken right good exercise in the gymnasium, the same result proceeds from different causes. They are both thirsty, the one from his malady, the other from his exercise. It has been my lot also to suffer some such malady from love . . .

3. But me you shall not come near to your ruin, nor associate with me to any detriment, but to your every advantage. For it is rather by non-lovers that beautiful youths are benefited and preserved, just as plants are by waters. For neither fountains nor rivers are in love with plants, but by going near them and flowing past them they make them bloom and thrive. Money given by me you would be right in calling a gift, but given by a lover a quittance. And the children of prophets say that to Gods also is the thank-offering among sacrifices more acceptable than the sin-offering, for the one is offered by the prosperous for the preservation and possession of their goods, the other by the wretched for the averting of ills. Let this suffice to be said on what is expedient and beneficial both for you and for him.

4. But if it is right that he should receive aid from you . . . you set this on a firm basis . . . you framed this love for him and devised Thessalian love-charms . . . owing to his insatiable desire . . . unless you have manifestly done wrong.

5. And do not ignore the fact that you are yourself wronged and subjected to no small

outrage in this, that all men know and speak openly thus of you, that he is your lover; and so, by anticipation and before being guilty of any such things, you abide the imputation of being guilty. Consequently the generality of the citizens call you the man's darling; but I shall keep your name unsullied and inviolate. For as far as I am concerned you shall be called *Beautiful,* not *Darling.* But if the other use this name as his by right because his desire is greater, let him know that his desire is not greater, but more importunate. Yet with flies and gnats the especial reason why we wave them away and brush them off is because they fly at us most impudently and importunately. It is this, indeed, that makes the wild beast shun the hunter most of all, and the bird the fowler. And, in fact, all animals avoid most those that especially lie in wait for and pursue them.

6. But if anyone thinks that beauty is more glorified and honored by reason of its lovers, he is totally mistaken. For you, the beautiful ones, through your lovers, run the risk of your beauty winning no credence with hearers, but through us non-lovers you establish your reputation for beauty on a sure basis. At any rate, if anyone who had never seen you were to enquire after your personal appearance, he would put faith in my praises, knowing that I am not in love; but he would disbelieve the other as praising not truthfully but lovingly. As many, then, as are maimed or ugly or deformed would naturally pray for lovers to be theirs, for they would find no others to court them but those who approach them under the madness and duress of love; but you, such is your beauty, cannot reap any greater advantage from a lover. For non-lovers

have need of you no less than they. And indeed, to those who are really beautiful, lovers are as useless as flatterers to those who deserve praise. It is sailors and steersmen and captains of warships and merchants, and those that in other ways travel upon it, who give excellence and glory and honor and gain and ornament to the sea—not, heaven help us, dolphins that can live only in the sea: but for beautiful boys it is we who cherish and praise them disinterestedly, not lovers, whose life, deprived of their darlings, would be unlivable. And you will find, if you look into it, that lovers are the cause of the utmost disgrace. But all who are right-minded must shun disgrace, the young most of all, since the evil attaching to them at the beginning of a long life will rest upon them the longer.

7. As, then, in the case of sacred rites and sacrifices, so also of life, it behoves above all those who are entering upon them to have a care for their good name ... For indeed by such adornments lovers do them no honor, but are themselves guilty of affectation and display, and, as it were, dance away the mysteries of love. Your lover, too, as they say, composes some amatory writings about you in the hope of enticing you with this bait, if with no other, and attracting you to himself and catching you; but such things are a disgrace and an insult and a sort of licentious cry, the outcome of stinging lust, such as those of wild beasts and fed cattle, that from sexual desire bellow or neigh or low or howl. Like to these are the lyrics of lovers. If, therefore, you submit yourself to your lover to enjoy where and when he pleases, awaiting neither time that is fitting nor leisure nor privacy, then, like a beast in the frenzy of desire,

will he make straight for you and be eager to "go to it" nothing ashamed.

8. I will add but one thing before I conclude my discourse, that we are formed by nature to praise and admire, but not to love, all the gifts of the Gods and their works that have come for the use and delight and benefit of men—those indeed of them which are wholly and in every way divine, I mean the earth and sky and sun and sea—while in the case of some other beautiful things of less worth, and formed to fulfill a less comely part, these at once are the subject of envy and love and emulation and desire. And some are in love with wealth, others again with rich viands, and others with wine. In the number and category of such is beauty reckoned by lovers, like wealth and viands and strong drink; but by us, who admire, indeed, but love not, like sun and sky and earth and sea, for such things are too good for any love and beyond its reach.

9. One thing more will I tell you, and if you will pass it on to all other boys, your words will seem convincing. Very likely you have heard from your mother, or from those who brought you up, that among flowers there is one that is indeed in love with the sun and undergoes the fate of lovers, lifting itself up when the sun rises, following his motions as he runs his course, and when he sets, turning itself about; but it takes no advantage thereby, nor yet, for all its love for the sun, does it find him the kinder. Least esteemed, at any rate, of plants and flowers, it is utilized neither for festal banquets nor for garlands of Gods or men. Maybe, O Boy, you would like to see this flower. Well, I will shew it you if we go for a walk outside the city walls as far as the Ilissus. . . .

MARCUS AURELIUS TO FRONTO

Hail, my best of masters.   A.D. 139?

1. Go on, threaten as much as you please and attack me with hosts of arguments, yet shall you never drive your lover, I mean me, away; nor shall I the less assert that I love Fronto, or love him the less, because you prove with reasons so various and so vehement that those who are less in love must be more helped and indulged. So passionately, by heaven, am I in love with you, nor am I frightened off by the law you lay down, and even if you shew yourself more forward and facile to others, who are non-lovers, yet will I love you while I have life and health.

For the rest, having regard to the close packing of ideas, the inventive subtilties, and the felicity of your championship of your cause, I hardly like, indeed, to say that you have far outstripped those Atticists, so self-satisfied and challenging, and yet I cannot but say so. For I am in love and this, if nothing else, ought, I think, verily to be allowed to lovers, that they should have greater joy in the triumph of their loved ones. Ours, then, is the triumph, ours, I say. Is it . . . preferable to talk philosophy under ceilings rather than under plane-trees, within the city bounds than without its walls, scorning delights than with Lais herself sitting at our side or sharing our home? Nor can I "make a cast" which to beware of more, the law which an orator of our time has laid down about this Lais, or my master's dictum about Plato.

2. This I can without rashness affirm: if that Phaedrus of yours ever really existed, if he was ever away from Socrates, Socrates never felt for Phaedrus a more passionate longing than I for

the sight of you all these days: days do I say? months I mean ... unless he is straightway seized with love of you. Farewell, my greatest treasure beneath the sky, my glory. It is enough to have had such a master. My Lady mother sends you greeting.

FRONTO TO MARCUS AURELIUS AS CAESAR

To my Lord.   A.D. 139?

1. As to the simile, which you say you are puzzling over and for which you call me in as your ally and adjutant in finding the clue, you will not take it amiss, will you, if I look for the clue to that fancy within your breast and your father's breast? Just as the island lies in the Ionian or Tyrrhenian sea, or, maybe, rather in the Adriatic, or, if it be some other sea, give it its right name—as then that sea-girt island (Aenaria) itself receives and repels the ocean waves, and itself bears the whole brunt of attack from fleets, pirates, sea-monsters and storms, yet in a lake within protects another island safely from all dangers and difficulties, while that other nevertheless shares in all its delights and pleasures (for that island in the inland lake is, like the other, washed by the waters, like it catches the health-giving breezes, like it is inhabited, like it looks out on the sea), so your father bears on his own shoulders the troubles and difficulties of the Roman Empire while you he safeguards safely in his own tranquil breast, the partner in his rank and glory and in all that is his. Accordingly you can use this simile in a variety of ways, when you return thanks to your father, on which occasion you should be most full and copious. For there is nothing that you

can say in all your life with more honor or more truth or more liking than that which concerns the setting forth of your father's praises. Whatever simile I may subsequently suggest will not please you so much as this one which concerns your father. I know this as well as you feel it. Consequently I will not myself give you any other simile, but will shew you the method of finding them out for yourself. You must send me any similes you search out and find by the method shewn you for that purpose, that if they prove neat and apt I may rejoice and love you.

2. Now, in the first place, you are aware that a simile is used for the purpose of setting off a thing or discrediting it, or comparing, or depreciating, or amplifying it, or of making credible what is scarcely credible. Where nothing of the kind is required, there will be no room for a simile. Hereafter when you compose a simile for a subject in hand, just as, if you were a painter, you would notice the characteristics of the object you were painting, so must you do in writing. Now, the characteristics of a thing you will pick out from many points of view, the likenesses of kind, the likenesses of form, the whole, the parts, the individual traits, the differences, the contraries, the consequences and the resultants, the names, the accidents, the elements, and generally everything from which arguments are drawn, the point in fact so often dwelt upon when we were dealing with the commonplaces of the arguments of Theodorus. If any of them have slipped your memory, it will not be amiss for us to go over them afresh when time serves. In this simile, which I have sketched out about your father and you, I have taken one of the accidentals of the subject, the identity of the safety and the enjoyment. Now it

remains for you, by those ways and paths which I have pointed out above, to discover how you may most conveniently come at your Aenaria.

3. The pain in my elbow is not much better. Farewell, my Lord, with your rare abilities.

Give my greeting to my Lady your mother. On another occasion we will follow out, with more care and exactness, the whole art of simile-making; now I have only touched upon the heads of it.

(AULUS) GELLIUS (A.D. 123–165; OR A.D. 130–180)

Attic Nights

We know little about the life of this minor Roman grammarian, whose legal career in private practice in Rome was overshadowed by twenty books of miscellaneous observations, notes, and essays that he composed during his days in Athens studying philosophy under Favorinus. Gellius studied oratory with Antonius Julianus and Sulpicius Apollinaris in Rome.

- *Attic Nights,* edited in his old age, from a lifetime of journal-writing, to instruct and entertain his children, ranges serendipitously across topics as diverse as history and metaphysics, poetry and anecdotes about the rich and famous, law and textual criticism, grammar and geometry.
- Aside from the colorful insight it provides into second-century A.D. Roman life and manners, Gellius' work is important for preserving countless fragments from previous Roman and Greek writers that would otherwise have been lost to us.

BOOK I
XVII

The patience with which Socrates endured his wife's shrewish disposition; and in that connection what Marcus Varro says in one of his satires about the duty of a husband.

Xanthippe, the wife of the philosopher Socrates, is said to have been ill-tempered and quarrelsome to a degree, with a constant flood of feminine tantrums and annoyances day and night. Alcibiades, amazed at this outrageous conduct of hers toward her husband, asked Socrates what earthly reason he had for not showing so

Wine pitcher

that kind in a wife cannot be corrected, it should be tolerated, in so far of course as a man may endure it honorably; for faults are less serious than crimes. . . .

BOOK II
XXI

About the constellation which the Greeks call ἅμαξα and the Romans septentriones; and as to the origin and meaning of both those words.

Several of us, Greeks and Romans, who were pursuing the same studies, were crossing in the same boat from Aegina to the Piraeus. It was night, the sea was calm, the time summer, and the sky bright and clear. So we all sat together in the stern and watched the brilliant stars. Then those of our company who were acquainted with Grecian lore discussed with learning and acumen such questions as these: what the ἅμαξα or "Wain," was, and what Boötes, which was the Great, and which the Little Bear and why they were so called; in what direction that constellation moved in the course of the advancing night, and why Homer says that this is the only constellation that does not set, in view of the fact that there are some other stars that do not set.

Thereupon I turned to our compatriots and said: "Why don't you barbarians tell me why we give the name of *septentriones* to what the Greeks call ἅμαξα. Now 'because we see seven stars' is not a sufficient answer, but I desire to be informed at some length," said I, "of the meaning of the whole idea which we express by the word *septentriones*."

shrewish a woman the door. "Because," replied Socrates, "it is by enduring such a person at home that I accustom and train myself to bear more easily away from home the impudence and injustice of other persons."

In the same vein Varro also said in the *Menippeau Satire* which he entitled *On the Duty of a Husband*: "A wife's faults must be either put down or put up with. He who puts down her faults, makes his wife more agreeable; he who puts up with them, improves himself." Varro contrasted the two words *tollere* and *ferre* very cleverly, to be sure, but he obviously uses *tollere* in the sense of "correct." It is evident too that Varro thought that if a fault of

Then one of them, who had devoted himself to ancient literature and antiquities, replied: "The common run of grammarians think that the word *septentriones* is derived solely from the number of stars. For they declare that *triones* of itself has no meaning, but is a mere addition to the word; just as in our word *quinquatrus*, so called because five is the number of days after the Ides, *atrus* means nothing. But for my part, I agree with Lucius Aelius and Marcus Varro, who wrote that oxen were called *triones*, a rustic term it is true, as if they were *terriones*, that is to say, adapted to ploughing and cultivating the earth. Therefore this constellation, which the early Greeks called ἅμαξα merely from its form and position, because it seemed to resemble a wagon, the early men also of our country called *septentriones*, from oxen yoked together, that is, seven stars by which yoked oxen *(triones)* seem to be represented." After giving this opinion, Varro further added, said he, "that he suspected that these seven stars were called *triones* rather for the reason that they are so situated that every group of three neighboring stars forms a triangle, that is to say, a three-sided figure."

Of these two reasons which he gave, the latter seemed the neater and the more ingenious; for as we looked at that constellation, it actually appeared to consist of triangles. . . .

BOOK III
XV

That it is recorded in literature and handed down by tradition, that great and unexpected joy has brought sudden death to many, since the breath of life was stifled and could not endure the effects of an unusual and strong emotion.

Aristotle the philosopher relates that Polycrita, a woman of high rank in the island of Naxos, on suddenly and unexpectedly hearing joyful news, breathed her last. Philippides too, a comic poet of no little repute, when he had unexpectedly won the prize in a contest of poets at an advanced age, and was rejoicing exceedingly, died suddenly in the midst of his joy. The story also of Diogoras of Rhodes is widely known. This Diogoras had three young sons, one a boxer, the second a pancratist, and the third a wrestler. He saw them all victors and crowned at Olympia on the same day, and when the three young men were embracing him there, and having placed their crowns on their father's head were kissing him, and the people were congratulating him and pelting him from all sides with flowers; there in the very stadium, before the eyes of the people, amid the kisses and embraces of his sons, he passed away.

Moreover, I have read in our annals that at the time when the army of the Roman people was cut to pieces at Cannae, an aged mother was overwhelmed with grief and sorrow by a message announcing the death of her son; but that report was false, and when not long afterward the young man returned from that battle to the city, the aged mother, upon suddenly seeing her son, was overpowered by the flood, the shock, and the crash, so to speak, of unlooked-for joy descending upon her, and gave up the ghost. . . .

BOOK IV
XII

Instances of disgrace and punishment inflicted by the censors, found in ancient records and worthy of notice.

If anyone had allowed his land to run to waste and was not giving it sufficient attention, if he had neither ploughed nor weeded it, or if anyone had neglected his orchard or vineyard, such conduct did not go unpunished, but it was taken up by the censors, who reduced such a man to the lowest class of citizens. So too, any Roman knight, if his horse seemed to be skinny or not well groomed, was charged with *inpolitiae*, a word which means the same thing as negligence. There are authorities for both these punishments, and Marcus Cato has cited frequent instances.

XIII

On the possibility of curing gout by certain melodies played in a special way on the flute.

I ran across the statement very recently in the book of Theophrastus *On Inspiration* that many men have believed and put their belief on record, that when gouty pains in the hips are most severe, they are relieved if a flute-player plays soothing measures. That snake-bites are cured by the music of the flute, when played skillfully and melodiously, is also stated in a book of Democritus, entitled *On Deadly Infections*, in which he shows that the music of the flute is medicine for many ills that flesh is heir to. So very close is the connection between the bodies and the minds of men, and therefore between physical and mental ailments and their remedies.

XIV

A story told of Hostilius Mancinus, a curule aedile, and the courtesan Manilia; and the words of the decree of the tribunes to whom Manilia appealed.

As I was reading the ninth book of the *Miscellany* of Ateius Capito, entitled *On Public Decisions*, one decree of the tribunes seemed to me full of old-time dignity. For that reason I remember it, and it was rendered for this reason and to this purport. Aulus Hostilius Mancinus was a curule aedile. He brought suit before the people against a courtesan called Manilia, because he said that he had been struck with a stone thrown from her apartment by night, and he exhibited the wound made by the stone. Manilia appealed to the tribunes of the commons. Before them she declared that Mancinus had come to her house in the garb of a reveler; that it would not have been to her advantage to admit him, and that when he tried to break in by force, he had been driven off with stones. The tribunes decided that the aedile had rightly been refused admission to a place to which it had not been seemly for him to go with a garland on his head; therefore they forbade the aedile to bring an action before the people. . . .

BOOK V
XIV

The account of Apion, a learned man who was surnamed Plistonices, of the mutual recognition, due to old acquaintance, that he had seen at Rome between a man and a lion.

Apion, who was called Plistonices, was a man widely versed in letters, and possessing an extensive and varied knowledge of things Greek. In his works, which are recognized as of no little repute, is contained an account of almost all the remarkable things which are to be seen and heard in Egypt. Now, in his account of what he professes either to have heard or read he is perhaps too verbose through a reprehensible love of display—for he is a great self-advertiser in parading his learning; but this incident, which he describes in the fifth book of his *Wonders of Egypt,* he declares that he neither heard nor read, but saw himself with his own eyes in the city of Rome.

"In the Great Circus," he says, "a battle with wild beasts on a grand scale was being exhibited to the people. Of that spectacle, since I chanced to be in Rome, I was," he says, "an eye-witness. There were there many savage wild beasts, brutes remarkable for their huge size, and all of uncommon appearance or unusual ferocity. But beyond all others," says he, "did the vast size of the lions excite wonder, and one of these in particular surpassed all the rest. This one lion had drawn to himself the attention and eyes of all because of the activity and huge size of his body, his terrific and deep roar, the development of his muscles, and the mane streaming over his shoulders. There was brought in, among many others who had been condemned to fight with the wild beasts, the slave of an ex-consul; the slave's name was Androclus. When that lion saw him from a distance," says Apion, "he stopped

short as if in amazement, and then approached the man slowly and quietly, as if he recognized him. Then, wagging his tail in a mild and caressing way, after the manner and fashion of fawning dogs, he came close to the man, who was now half dead from fright, and gently licked his feet and hands. The man Androclus, while submitting to the caresses of so fierce a beast, regained his lost courage and gradually turned his eyes to look at the lion. Then," says Apion, "you might have seen man and lion exchange joyful greetings, as if they had recognized each other."

He says that at this sight, so truly astonishing, the people broke out into mighty shouts; and Gaius Caesar called Androclus to him and inquired the reason why that fiercest of lions had spared him alone. Then Androclus related a strange and surprising story. "My master," said he, "was governing Africa with proconsular authority. While there, I was forced by his undeserved and daily floggings to run away, and that my hiding-places might be safer from my master, the ruler of that country, I took refuge in lonely plains and deserts, intending, if food should fail me, to seek death in some form. Then," said he, "when the midday sun was fierce and scorching, finding a remote and secluded cavern, I entered it, and hid myself. Not long afterward this lion came to the same cave with one paw lame and bleeding, making known by groans and moans the torturing pain of his wound." And then, at the first sight of the approaching lion, Androclus said that his mind was overwhelmed with fear and dread. "But when the lion," said he, "had entered what was evidently his own lair, and saw me cowering at a distance, he approached me mildly and gently, and lifting up his foot, was evidently showing it to me and holding it out as if to ask for help. Then," said he, "I drew out a huge splinter that was embedded in the sole of the foot, squeezed out the pus that had formed in the interior of the wound, wiped away the blood, and dried it thoroughly, being now free from any great feeling of fear. Then, relieved by that attention and treatment of mine, the lion, putting his paw in my hand, lay down and went to sleep, and for three whole years from that day the lion and I lived in the same cave, and on the same food as well. For he used to bring for me to the cave the choicest parts of the game which he took in hunting, which I, having no means of making a fire, dried in the noonday sun and ate. But," said he, "after I had finally grown tired of that wild life, I left the cave when the lion had gone off to hunt, and after traveling nearly three days, I was seen and caught by some soldiers and taken from Africa to Rome to my master. He at once had me condemned to death by being thrown to the wild beasts. But," said he, "I perceive that this lion was also captured, after I left him, and that he is now requiting me for my kindness and my cure of him."

Apion records that Androclus told this story, and that when it had been made known to the people by being written out in full on a tablet and carried about the Circus, at the request of all Androclus was freed, acquitted and presented with the lion by vote of the people. "Afterward," said he, "we used to see Androclus with the lion, attached to a slender leash, making the rounds of the shops throughout the city; Androclus was given money, the lion was sprinkled with flowers, and everyone who met them anywhere exclaimed: 'This is the lion that was a man's friend, this is the man who was physician to a lion.'"

XV

That it is a disputed question among philosophers whether voice is corporeal or incorporeal.

A question that has been argued long and continuously by the most famous philosophers is whether voice has body or is incorporeal; for the word *incorporeus* has been coined by some of them, corresponding exactly to the Greek ἀσώματος. Now a body is that which is either active or passive: this in Greek is defined as τὸ ἤτοι ποιοῦν ἤ πάσχον, or "that which either acts or is acted upon." Wishing to reproduce this definition the poet Lucretius wrote:

Naught save a body can be touched or touch.

The Greeks also define body in another way, as τὸ τριχῇ διάστατον, or "that which has three dimensions." But the Stoics maintain that voice is a body, and say that it is air which has been struck; Plato, however, thinks that voice is not corporeal: "for," says he, "not the air which is struck, but the stroke and the blow themselves are voice." Democritus, and following him Epicurus, declare that voice consists of individual particles, and they call it, to use their own words, ῥεῦμα ἀτόμων, or "a stream of atoms." When I heard of these and other sophistries, the result of a self-satisfied cleverness combined with lack of employment, and saw in these subtleties no real advantage affecting the conduct of life, and no end to the inquiry, I agreed with Ennius' Neoptolemus, who rightly says:

Philosophizing there must be, but by the few;
Since for all men it's not to be desired.

XVI

On the function of the eye and the process of
vision.

I have observed that the philosophers have
varying opinions about the method of seeing
and the nature of vision. The Stoics say that the
causes of sight are the emission of rays from
the eyes to those objects which can be seen,
and the simultaneous expansion of the air. Epicurus believes that there is a constant flow
from all bodies of images of those bodies themselves, and that these impinge upon the eyes
and hence the sensation of seeing arises. Plato
is of the opinion that a kind of fire or light
issues from the eyes, and that this, being
united and joined either with the light of the
sun or with that of some other fire, by means of
its own and the external force makes us see
whatever it has struck and illumined. But here
too we must not dally longer, but follow the
advice of that Neoptolemus in Ennius, of whom
I have just written, who advises having a
"taste" of philosophy, but not "gorging oneself
with it."

GAIUS (C. A.D. 110–180)

Institutes

～⌒)

$\mathscr{T}$he *patria potestas,* the power of the father over his family, a fundamental principle of Roman law,
is reflected in these observations on adoption and *manus* by one of the earliest imperial jurists. Gaius,
originally from Greece or Asia Minor, wrote and taught in Rome during the time of Hadrian.

- His treatises on Roman law included the seven-volume *Rerum cotidianarum* and analyses of
  various legal matters.
- His most important work was the *Institutes,* four comprehensive books on social law, completed around A.D. 161. Though he was not recognized or even cited in his own time, his
  work became the basis for the *Institutes* of Justinian, who called him *"Gaius noster"* ("our
  Gaius").

Staircase, Italica

Not only are the children of our bodies in our *potestas* according as we have stated, but also those whom we adopt. Adoption takes place in two ways, either by authority of the people or by the *imperium* of a magistrate, such as a praetor . . . The former kind of adoption, that by authority of the people, can be performed nowhere but at Rome, whereas the latter kind is regularly performed in the provinces before the provincial governors. Further, females cannot be adopted by authority of the people, for this opinion has prevailed; but before a praetor or, in the provinces, before the proconsul or legate, females are regularly adopted . . . But women cannot adopt by any method, for they do not hold even the children of their bodies in their *potestas*. . . .

Let us proceed to consider persons who are in *manus*, which is another right peculiar to Roman citizens. Now, while both males and females are found in *potestas*, only females can come under *manus*. Of old, women passed into *manus* in three ways, by *usus*, *confarreatio*, and *coemptio*. A woman used to pass into *manus* by *usus* if she cohabited with her husband for a year without interruption, being as it were acquired by a usucapion of one year and so passing into her husband's family and ranking as a daughter. Hence it was provided by the Twelve Tables that any woman wishing not to come under her husband's *manus* in this way should stay away from him for three nights in each year and thus interrupt the *usus* of each year. But the whole of this institution has been in part abolished by statutes and in part obliterated by simple disuse. Entry of a woman into *manus* by *confarreatio* is effected by a kind of sacrifice offered to Jupiter Farreus, in which the spelt cake is employed, whence the name *confarreatio*. In the performance of this ceremony a number of acts and things are done, accompanied by special formal words, in the presence of ten witnesses. This institution still exists at the present day. For the higher flamens, that is those of Jupiter, Mars, and Quirinus, and also the *rex sacrorum*, can only be chosen from those born of parents married by *confarreatio*; indeed, no person can hold the priesthood without being himself so married. Entry of a woman into *manus* by *coemptio* takes the form of a mancipation, that is a sort of imaginary sale: in the presence of not less than five witnesses, being Roman citizens above puberty, and of a scale-holder, the woman is bought by him into whose *manus* she is passing. It is, however, possible for a woman to make a *coemptio* not only with her husband, but also with a stranger; in other words, *coemptio* may be performed for either matrimonial or fiduciary purposes. A woman who makes a *coemptio* with her husband with the object of ranking as a daughter in his household is said to have made a *coemptio* for matrimonial purposes, while one who makes, whether with her husband or a stranger, a *coemptio* for some other object, such as that of evading a tutorship, is said to have done so for fiduciary purposes. What happens is as follows: a woman wishing to get rid of her existing tutors and to get another makes a *coemptio* with the *auctoritas* of her existing tutors; after that she is remancipated by her *coemptionator* to the person of her own choice and, having been manumitted *uindicta* by him, comes to have as her tutor the man by whom she has been manumitted. This person is called a fiduciary tutor, as will appear below. Formerly too fiduciary *coemptio* used to be performed for the purpose of making a will. This was at a time when women, with certain exceptions, had not the right to make a will unless they had made a *coemptio* and had been remancipated and manumitted. But the Senate on the authority of the late emperor Hadrian has dispensed from this requirement of a *coemptio* . . . But if a woman makes a fiduciary *coemptio* with her husband, she nevertheless acquires the position of his daughter. For it is the accepted view that, if for any reason whatever a wife be in her husband's *manus*, she acquires a daughter's rights.

We have still to explain what persons are *in mancipio*. All children, male or female, who are in a parent's *potestas* can be mancipated by him in just the same manner as slaves. . . .

Also, women cease to be in their father's *potestas* by passing into *manus*. But in the case of the *confarreate* marriage of the wife of a flamen of Jupiter a decree of the Senate passed on the proposal of Maximus and Tubero has provided that she is to be considered to be in *manus* only for sacral purposes, while for all other purposes she is to be treated as though she had not entered *manus*. On the other hand, a woman who enters *manus* by *coemptio* is freed from her father's *potestas*, and it makes no difference whether she be in her husband's or a stranger's *manus*, although only women who are in their husband's *manus* rank as daughters.

Women cease to be in *manus* in the same ways as those by which daughters are freed from their father's *potestas*. Thus, just as daughters pass out of their father's *potestas* by a single mancipation, so women in *manus* cease by a single mancipation to be in *manus*, and if manumitted from that mancipation become *sui iuris*. Between a woman who has made a *coemptio* with a stranger and one who has done so with her husband there is, however, this difference, that the former can compel her *coemptio* to remancipate her to the person of her choice, whereas the latter can no more compel her husband to do this than a daughter can compel her father. But, while a daughter, even if adoptive, is absolutely incapable of compelling her father, a woman in the *manus* of her husband can, if she has sent him notice of divorce, compel him to release her, just as though she had never been his wife.

MARCUS AURELIUS (ANTONINUS)

(A.D. 121–180; EMPEROR 161–180)

Meditations

*B*orn of a Roman-Spanish father, Annius Verus, whose own father was consul prefect of Rome, and an affluent tile-manufacturer's daughter, Domitia Lucilla, Marcus Aurelius was because of his precociousness designated by the emperor Hadrian as his potential successor at the age of eight and given the finest education in grammar, rhetoric, law, literature, and especially the Stoic philosophy of Epictetus as revised by Posidonius. Moral philosophy came to preoccupy his interests, leading him to abandon the rest of his studies in its favor. His tutor, Fronto, became a lifelong friend; the letters between them have survived (see pages 298–305).

When Antoninus Pius adopted him at Hadrian's request in A.D. 138, Marcus Aurelius served at the emperor's right hand until his own succession in 161. Upon his designation as emperor by the Senate, Marcus Aurelius appointed his adoptive brother Lucius Verus as his co-emperor. He married his cousin Anna Galeria Faustina the Younger, daughter of Antoninus Pius, in 145. She bore him Commodus, the next emperor. Marcus Aurelius' bronze statue stands today on Rome's Capitoline Hill.

- His reign witnessed one catastrophe after another, providing his Stoicism with the fullest test. Faced with barbarian invasions from German tribes to the north and rebellions and plague at home and in the east, he spent his time trying to rebuild the Roman frontier defenses on the Danube and died in an army tent at Vindobona (Vienna).
- Marcus Aurelius wrote his twelve-book *Meditations* in Greek while traveling on his various military campaigns. This remarkably intense journal of thoughts and observations, written in notebooks by an emperor who felt he had no one to talk to except himself, reveals:

  ▴ an absolute faith in an intelligent, governing providence;
  ▴ reverence for divine-given reason as the ruling principle of human life;
  ▴ affirmation that the human soul is part of divine intelligence; and
  ▴ a belief in the absolute insignificance of human affairs in the context of space and time.

Though considered as one of the great books of all time, the *Meditations* also has been criticized as the hysterical rantings of a drug-influenced and bewildered emperor with a chronic ulcer, longing for an afterlife he doesn't believe in.

Marcus Aurelius

XII

1. All those things to which you wish to attain sooner or later, you can have now, if you do not refuse them; if only you will take no notice of the past, and trust the future to providence, and direct the present in harmony with piety and justice. In harmony with piety that you may be content with the lot which is assigned to you, for nature designed it for you and you for it. In harmony with justice, that you may always speak the truth freely and without disguise, and do the things which are agreeable to law and according to the worth of each. And let neither another man's wickedness hinder you, nor opinion, nor voice, nor any persuasion of the flesh; for let that which suffers look to itself. If then, whatever the time may be when you shall be near

your departure, you shall respect only your ruling faculty and the divinity within you, neglecting everything else, and if you are afraid—not that you shall some day cease to live but that you shall never have begun to live according to nature—then you will be a man worthy of the universe which has produced you, and you will cease to be a stranger in your native land, and to wonder at things which happen daily as if they were something unexpected and to be dependent on this event or that.

2. God sees the ruling principles of all men bared of the material vesture and rind and impurities. With his mental being he touches the intelligence which has flowed and been derived from himself into these bodies. If you accustom yourself to the same habit, you will rid yourself of much trouble. For he who looks not to his poor fleshly shell surely will not trouble himself by looking after raiment, houses, fame, and such externals and show.

3. You are composed of three things: body, life, intelligence. Of these the first two are yours, inasmuch as it is your duty to take care of them; but the third alone is really yours. Therefore if you will separate from yourself, that is, from your understanding, whatever others do or say, and whatever you have done or said yourself, and whatever future things trouble you because they may happen, and whatever in the body which envelops you or in the breath which is by nature associated with the body is attached to you independent of your will, and whatever the external circumfluent vortex whirls round, so that the intellectual power, exempt from the things of fate, can live pure and free by itself, doing what is just and accepting what happens and saying the truth; if you will separate, I say, from this ruling faculty the things which are attached to it by the impressions of sense, and the things of time to come and of time that is past, and will make yourself like Empedocles' sphere,

All round, and in its joyous rest reposing;

and if you strive to live only what is really your life, that is, the present—then you will be able to pass that portion of life which remains for you up to the time of your death, free from perturbations, nobly, and obedient to your own deity within.

4. I have often wondered how it is that every man loves himself more than all the rest of men, but yet sets less value on his own opinion of himself than on the opinion of others. For if a god or a wise teacher should present himself to a man and bid him to think of nothing and to design nothing which he would not express as soon as he conceived it, he could not endure it even for a single day. So much more respect have we for what our neighbors think of us than for what we think of ourselves.

5. How can it be that the gods, after having arranged all things well and benevolently for mankind, have overlooked only this, that some men and very good men, and men who through pious acts and religious observances have had most intimate communion with the divinity, when they have once died should never exist again, but should be completely extinguished?

But if this is so, be assured that if it ought to have been otherwise, the gods would have done it. For if it were just, it would also be possible; and if it were according to nature, nature would have had it so. But because it is not so, if in fact it is not so, be assured that it ought not

to have been so: for you see that in this inquiry you are disputing with the deity; and we could not thus dispute with the gods unless they were most excellent and just; but if this is so, they would not have allowed anything in the ordering of the universe to be neglected unjustly and irrationally.

6. Practice even at the things which you despair of accomplishing. For even the left hand, which is ineffectual for all other things for want of practice, holds the bridle more vigorously than the right hand; for it has been practiced in this.

7. Consider in what condition both in body and soul a man should be when he is overtaken by death; and consider the shortness of life, the boundless abyss of time past and future, the feebleness of all matter.

8. Contemplate the formative principles of things, bare of their coverings; the purposes of actions; consider what pain is, what pleasure is, and death, and fame; who is to himself the cause of his uneasiness; how no man is hindered by another; that everything is opinion.

9. In the application of your principles you must be like the pancratiast, not like the gladiator; for the gladiator lets fall the sword which he uses and is killed; but the other always has his hand, and needs to do nothing else than use it.

10. See what things are in themselves, dividing them into matter, form and purpose.

11. What a power man has to do nothing except what God will approve, and to accept all that God may give him.

12. With respect to that which happens in harmony with nature, we ought to blame neither gods, for they do nothing wrong either voluntarily or involuntarily, nor men, for they do

nothing wrong, except involuntarily. Consequently we should blame nobody.

13. How ridiculous and how strange to be surprised at anything which happens in life!

14. Either there is a fatal necessity and invincible order, or a kind of providence, or a confusion without a purpose and without a director. If then there is an invincible necessity, why do you resist? But if there is a providence which allows itself to be propitiated, make yourself worthy of the help of the divinity. But if all is confusion without a governor, be content that in such a tempest you have in yourself a certain ruling intelligence. And even if the tempest carry you away, let it carry away the poor flesh, the breath, everything else; for the intelligence at least it will not sweep away.

15. Does the light of the lamp shine without losing its radiance until it is extinguished? Shall the truth and justice and temperance which is in you be extinguished?

16. When a man gives the impression of wrongdoing, say to yourself, "How do I know that it is a wrongful act?" And even if he has done wrong, how do I know that he has not condemned himself—like the mourner tearing his own face? Remember that he who would not have the bad man do wrong is like one who would not have the fig tree bear juice in its figs and infants to cry and horses to neigh, and whatever else must of necessity be. For what must a man do who has such a character? If then you are irritable with a man, amend his disposition.

17. If it is not right, do not do it; if it is not true, do not say it.

18. In everything always observe what the thing is which produces an appearance, and resolve it by dividing it into the causal, the material, the purpose, and the time within which it must end.

19. Perceive at last that you have within you something better and more divine than the things which cause the various effects, and, as it were, pull you around by strings. What is there now in your mind? Is it fear, or suspicion, or desire, or anything of the kind?

20. First, do nothing thoughtlessly or without a purpose. Secondly, see that your acts are directed to a social end.

21. Consider that before long you will be nobody and nowhere, nor will any of the things exist which you now see, nor any of those who are now living. For all things are formed by nature to change and be turned and to perish in order that other things in continuous succession may exist.

22. Consider that everything is opinion, and opinion is in your power. Disown opinion when you choose; and like a mariner, who has doubled the promontory, you will find calm, still waters and a waveless bay.

23. Any one activity, whatever it may be, when it has ceased at its proper time, suffers no evil because it has ceased; nor he who has done this act, does he suffer any evil for this reason that the act has ceased. In like manner then the whole which consists of all the acts, which is our life, if it cease at its proper time, suffers no evil that it has ceased; nor he who has terminated this series at the proper time, has he been ill dealt with. But the proper time and the limit nature fixes, sometimes as in old age the peculiar nature of man, but always the universal nature, by the change of whose parts the whole universe continues ever young and perfect. And everything which is useful to the universal is always good and in season. Therefore the termination of life for every man is no evil, because it is nothing shameful, since it is both independent of the will and not opposed to the general interest, but it is good, since it is seasonable and profitable to the universal. For thus man becomes one with the deity, moved in the same manner with the deity in tendency and intent.

24. These three principles you must have in readiness. Do nothing either inconsiderately or otherwise than as justice herself would act; but with respect to what may happen to you from without, consider that it happens either by chance or according to providence, and you must neither blame chance nor accuse providence. Second, consider what every being is from the seed to the time of its receiving a soul, and from the reception of a soul to the giving back of the same, and of what things every being is compounded and into what things it is resolved. Third, if you should suddenly be raised up above the earth, and should look down on human things, and observe the variety of them how great it is, and at the same time also should see at a glance how great is the number of beings who dwell all around in the air and the ether, consider that as often as you should be raised up you would see the same things, sameness of form and shortness of duration. Are these things any ground for pride?

25. Cast away opinion: you are saved. Who hinders you from casting it away?

26. When you are troubled about anything, you have forgotten this, that all things happen according to the universal nature, and that a man's wrongful act is nothing to you; and further you have forgotten this, that everything which happens always happened so, and will happen so, and now happens so everywhere;

forgotten this too, how close is the kinship between a man and the whole human race, for it is a community, not of a little blood or seed, but of intelligence. And you have forgotten this too, that every man's intelligence is a god, and is an efflux of the deity; and that nothing is a man's own, but that his child and his body and his very soul came from the deity; that everything is opinion; and lastly, that every man lives the present time only, and loses only this.

27. Constantly bring to your recollection those who have complained greatly about anything, those who have been most conspicuous by the greatest fame, or misfortunes and enmities, or fortunes of any kind; then think where are they all now? Smoke and ash and a tale and not even a tale. And let there be present to your mind also things of this sort, how Fabius Catullinus lived in the country, and Lucius Lupus in his gardens, and Stertinius at Baiae, and Tiberius at Capri, and Rufus at Velia; and, in short, think of the eager pursuit of anything joined together with pride; and how worthless everything is after which men strain violently; and how much more philosophical it is for a man in the opportunities presented to him to show himself just, temperate, obedient to the gods, and to do this with all simplicity: for the pride which is proud of its want of pride is the most intolerable of all.

28. To those who ask, "Where have you seen the gods and how do you know they exist, that you worship them as you do?" I answer: "In the first place, they may be seen even with the eyes; in the second place, neither have I seen even my own soul and yet I honor it. Thus then with respect to the gods, from what I constantly experience of their power, from this I comprehend that they exist and I venerate them."

29. The safety of life is this, to examine everything all through, what it is itself, what is its material, what the causal part; and with all your soul to do justice and to speak the truth. What remains except to enjoy life by joining one good thing to another so as not to leave even the smallest gap between?

30. There is one light of the sun though it is distributed over walls, mountains, and other things infinite. There is one common substance, though it is distributed among countless bodies which have their several qualities. There is one soul, though it is distributed among infinite natures and individuals. There is one intelligent soul, though it seems to be divided. Now in the things which have been mentioned all the other parts, such as those which are air and substance, are without sensation and have no fellowship: and yet even these parts the intelligent principle holds together and they gravitate toward the same. But intellect in a peculiar manner tends to that which is of the same kin, and combines with it, and the feeling for communion is not interrupted.

31. What do you wish? To continue to exist? Well, do you wish to have sensation, movement, growth? And then again to cease to grow, to use speech, to think? What is there of all these things which seems to you worth desiring? But if it is easy to set little value on all these things, turn to that which remains, which is to follow reason and God. But it is inconsistent with honoring reason and God to be troubled because by death a man will be deprived of the other things.

32. How small a part of the boundless and unfathomable time is assigned to every man! In a moment it is swallowed up in the eternal. And how small a part of the whole substance, and how small a part of the universal soul! And on what a small clod of the whole earth you creep! Reflecting on all this, consider nothing to be great, except to act as your nature leads you and to endure that which the common nature brings.

33. How does the ruling faculty make use of itself? For all lies in this. But everything else, whether it is in the power of your will or not, is only lifeless ashes and smoke.

34. This reflection is most adapted to move us to contempt of death, that even those who think pleasure to be a good and pain an evil still have despised it.

35. The man to whom that only is good which comes in due season, and to whom it is the same thing whether he has done more or fewer acts conformable to right reason, and to whom it makes no difference whether he contemplates the world for a longer or a shorter time—for this man neither is death a terrible thing.

36. Man, you have been a citizen in this great state:

What difference does it make to you whether for five years or three? For that which is conformable to the laws is just for all. Where is the hardship then, if no tyrant nor yet an unjust judge sends you away from the state, but nature who brought you into it? The same as if a praetor who has employed an actor dismisses him from the stage. "But I have not finished the five acts, but only three of them." Good, but in life the three acts are the whole drama. For what shall constitute a complete drama is determined by him who first caused its composition, and now its dissolution: but you are the cause of neither. Depart then serenely, for he who releases you is also serene. . . .

(LUCIUS) APULEIUS (C. A.D. 123)

The Golden Ass

~~◦

*B*orn into a wealthy family of Madaurus in African Numidia, Apuleius was sent to Carthage and Athens for his education. He was widely traveled as an investigator of the mystery cults and worked in Rome as a legal advocate and teacher of rhetoric. In African Oea he married Aemilia Pudentilla, an affluent widow, mother of his friend Sicinius Pontianus, and immediately found himself involved in a legal action brought by her former in-laws. In his brilliantly eccentric apologia, *Pro se de Magia,* Apuleius defended himself before the proconsul Claudius Maximus against charges of seduction by black magic. Acquitted, he returned to Carthage, where he continued his career as poet, Platonic philosopher, priest, public speaker, and all-around latter-day sophist.

- Apuleius will forever be remembered for his partly autobiographical *Metamorphosis,* popularly known as *The Golden Ass,* the only Latin novel to survive intact and a predecessor of the picaresque novel popular during the Renaissance. Based on a Greek source and written in the "new style" invented by his friend Marcus Cornelius Fronto, *The Golden Ass* is a romantic fantasy in eleven books. It tells the story of Lucius, the sorcerer's apprentice who's turned into an ass, and his various encounters with the human comedy until the goddess Isis restores him to his original form by initiating him into the mysteries of Osiris.
- *The Golden Ass,* a profanely entertaining source for an insight into the life of African Rome, also contains the allegorical fable of Cupid and Psyche, and eloquent passages on Isis. Though artificial, its style is yet compelling for its rich texture and explosions of imagery. Apuleius' influence can be seen in authors as diverse as Boccaccio, Rabelais, and Cervantes.

But now it is time that I told you about the waves of fortune on which I was being tossed. The soldier who had taken unquestioned possession of me without paying a farthing, was instructed by his tribune to carry letters to the great Potentate of Rome. He therefore sold me for elevenpence to two brothers, servants of a nearby landowner who was extremely wealthy. One of these men was a confectioner who baked sweet-breads and dainties; the other was a cook who specialized in appetizing messes succulently seasoned with mixed herbs. These two, living in common, bought me for the purpose of loading me with the abundant vessels that were needed for their master's use during his travels. I was thus received as a kind of third brother; and in all my metamor-phosed peregrinations I never had such a good time as now. For in the evening after supper (which was always a luxurious affair) my masters usually brought home to their little apartment a toothsome head of scraps. The cook brought large slabs of roast-pig, chicken, fishes, and other good meats. The confectioner brought rolls, pastries, tartlets, hook-cakes, lizard-loaves, and all kinds of honeyed flawns. Then, after they had fastened the chamber door and departed to refresh themselves at the Baths, I crammed my guts with these heaven-sent delicacies; for I was not such a fool of an ass as to neglect these most delicious foods and to jar my teeth upon dry prickly hay.

For a long time my artful thefts succeeded beautifully. For I pilfered cautiously and frugally, taking only a small proportion; and the brothers did not suspect an ass of being such an epicure. But after a time habit begot boldness; and I gobbled up all the choicest scraps, nosing through the heaps for the best oddments and leaving only the least desirable. Then a growing suspicion entered the minds of the brothers, and they made diligent efforts to detect the agent of their daily loss; but me they never suspected. At length they began to believe each other guilty of playing a mean trick; and keeping a shrewder eye open, they counted and noted the dishes that they brought.

Finally, dropping all reserve, one of them accused the other outright. "Now look here," he said, "this isn't fair, it isn't like a man, to sneak the finest eatables aside, to sell them on the sly for your private profit, and then to insist on a full half-share of what's left. If you're tired of our partnership we can still be brothers as far as

things in general are concerned, but we can drop this share-and-share-alike idea. For I can see that if this kind of thing goes on getting worse and worse, we'll end up bitterest enemies."

"By Hercules," answered the other, "I certainly do admire your brazen cheek. Here you have been stealing the food day after day, and then you get in first with a complaint, while all this long time I've been submitting in sorrowful silence rather than face the fact that my brother was a scurvy sneak-thief. It's a good thing that the subject has been broached between us and a stop can be put to this leakage. Otherwise we'd have brooded ourselves into a grudge as bad as Eteocles."

After they had thus exchanged reproaches for a while, they both of them seriously took an

Tripod from the Temple of Isis at Pompeii

oath that they had stolen nothing whatsoever, not a single surreptitious mouthful; and they decided that they must try every conceivable trap for the thief who was embroiling them in this common loss. It was impossible (they said) for the ass, who was shut in the room alone, to fancy such food; yet daily the best morsels disappeared. Flies could not be the culprits, since only flies as large as the Harpies that plundered the banquet of Phineus could have removed the articles; and no such flies penetrated the room.

Meanwhile, liberally fed and farced with human food, I found that I was plumply filling out, larding and supplying the hide, and showing a sleek glossy coat. But this bodily grace was the cause of my discredit. For the brothers' suspicion was stirred by my uncommon breadth in the beam; and when they had further noticed that the hay remained daily untouched, they directed all their attention toward me. They shut the door as usual at the hour for the Baths, and peeped in at me through a hole in the door as I began busily chewing the scattered scraps. At the sight they forgot all about the havoc I was creating; they stared in wonderment at the unnatural sweet-toothed ass and split their sides with laughter. They called one and then another of their fellow servants, and then a whole tribe of them; and they gave them each a peep at the memorable monster, the beast with a refined appetite. Indeed, so loud and infectious a mood of laughter seized them all that the sound reached their master who was passing near. He inquired what jest was amusing the household. Being informed what it was, he came himself and put his eye to the hole. At once he laughed broadly until his very entrails

quaked; and then, opening the door, he approached and inspected me at close quarters. For my part, beholding the face of Fortune benignantly smiling upon me, I continued eating at my ease without turning a hair, encouraged by the applauding merriment.

Charmed by the novelty of the spectacle, the master of the house ordered me to be led (nay, led me with his own hands) to the dining-room; and as soon as the meal was served he bade all kinds of solid victuals and untasted dishes to be laid before me. Although I had eaten a pretty bellyful already, I wished to make myself socially agreeable and to ingratiate myself with my host; so I appreciatively champed every delicacy that was offered. The diners racked their wits to think out every dish likely to be unpalatable to an ass, and offered them to me to test my manners: things such as vinegared beef, peppered pullet, and exotically pickled fish. And all this while the banquet-chamber was one roar of laughter.

Finally the buffoon of the party suggested, "Give our friend a sip of wine."

"All joking apart," answered the host, "I have a notion that our fellow-diner would not refuse a cup of honeyed wine. Here, lad," he went on, "give that golden cup a good rinse, fill it with honeyed wine, and present it to my guest—and at the same time say that I have pledged him."

A thick hush of expectation filled the room as I unconcernedly emptied the trough-like cup at one draught, gathering up my lips into the shape of a tongue and airily acting the part of boon companion. There was a yell of laughter, and the company with one accord toasted my health.

The master, rapturously enchanted, summoned the two servants who had bought me, and gave orders that they should receive four times my purchase-money. He then handed me over to a certain man (a favorite freedman who was in easy circumstances) and asked him to take good care of me. This man treated me with all humanity and civility; and to earn the praises of his diverted patron he took great pains to teach me a repertoire of tricks. For instance, he taught me to recline at table, leaning on my elbows; to wrestle and dance with lifted forefeet; and (a specially admired attainment) to converse by raising my head as a sign of Yes and by lowering it as a sign of No. He also taught me to look toward the cupbearer, when I was thirsty, and to wink first with one eye and then with the other. In all these acquirements I displayed myself a ready-learner, since I could have done them all without any lessons. But I was afraid that, if I showed knowledge of the human routine without being first taught, people would think that some horror was portended and that I should have my head amputated and my carcass thrown out to feast vultures.

Meanwhile the tale spread rapidly far and wide; and my marvelous exploits had consequently made my master an illustrious personage. "There goes the man," folk said, "who dines with an ass at his table, a wrestling ass, a dancing ass, an ass that understands human speech and answers with signs."

But I must now mention (as I should have at the beginning) who this man was, and whence he came. Thiasus (that was the name by which he went) was a native of Corinth, the capital of the province of Achaia. Gradually climbing the ladder of civic success, as his worth and birth warranted, he arrived at nomination to the office of five-yearly magistrate. Then, to show himself equal to the calls of that position, he promised to finance a three-day gladiatorial display. Munificence could go no further.

It was, in fact, his zeal to please the public which had brought him to Thessaly; for he was now engaged in collecting troupes of genuine wild beasts and prominent gladiators. When his dispositions and purchases were completed satisfactorily, he arranged for the homeward journey. But scornfully repudiating the glittering chariots and luxurious coaches which, some covered and some open, were herded along in the rear—ignoring his Thessalian steeds and his Gallic gennets, whose flawless pedigree demonstrated their valuable rarity—he rode affectionately upon me—me, trimmed with trappings of gold, bearing a painted saddle, hung with purple, bridled with silver, girthed with embroideries, and prinked with tintinnabulating bells. As we went he spoke to me confidentially. Among other remarks I remember him expressing his delight at possessing in me at one and the same time a nag and a nob.

At last after traveling by land and sea we arrived at Corinth, where the citizens streamed jostling out to greet us, not so much to pay their respects to Thiasus as to catch a glimpse of me. For my fame had preceded me so loudly that I was the source of considerable profit to my keeper. When he perceived that crowds of people were enthusiastically keen to see me amusing myself, he shut the gates and admitted the populace one at a time, charging a stiff price for the privilege. The daily gate-money soon amounted to a fair sum.

Among the visitors there was a rich and respected lady who after once paying for a view was so tickled by my manifold gambols that her flustered wonder drifted into a wondrous lust. Unable to cool her turbulent blood, she took heart at the example of Pasiphae and decided to act the she-ass. In short, she won my keeper over, by a heavy bribe, to surrender me to her mercies for a single night; and the corrupt servant, considering his own gain more than my amenities, assented.

Therefore, when I had supped as usual with my master, we left the parlor and went up to my bedroom. There we lighted upon this woman, whose nerves were already ragged with awaiting us. Good gods! how lordly were the preparations. Four eunuchs strewed the ground with mattresses of down and air-filled bolsters. The coverlet was of cloth-of-gold and broideries of Tyrian dye; and the pillows were small but wide enough for their purpose, and soft like those on which delicate ladies lay their lazy cheeks or necks. The eunuchs, anxious not to delay the pleasures of their mistress a moment longer, closed the bedroom-doors and went away; but there were tall wax-candles that banished every shadow from the glowing room. Then the woman stripped full-length (even to the band that upheld her darling breasts) and standing close to the light she rubbed herself from top to bottom with balmy unguents. After that she turned to me and anointed me likewise all over, expending particular care in scenting my nose.

That done, she gave me a lingering kiss; not the kind that you met in the stews, in the whore-shops and the open markets of venery. No, it was a sisterly and sincere salutation, accompanied with such remarks as "I love you," "I want you," "You're the only one in the world," "I can't live without you," and other phrases of the kind that women use to lead-on their lovers and to express their emotions. Then she took me by the neck-rope and placed me on the bed; and as she was a very beautiful woman, and as I was flushed with excellent wine and soused in fragrant ointments, I had no difficulty in meeting her half-way.

But I was deeply harrowed, uncertain how I could embrace so flower-like a lady with my clumsy legs; or how I could touch her gleaming tender milk-and-honey body with my coarse hooves; or how my enormous slavering jaws and rows of teeth like stones could kiss her small and scarlet lips dewed with ambrosia; or (to sum up) how she, who was still a woman even if she were itching to the very tips of her little fingernails, could manage to receive me. "Woe's me," I thought, "if I hurt this fine lady, I shall be thrown out for the beasts of prey to devour."

But, looking on me with burning eyes, she redoubled her enticing nicknames, assiduous kisses, and sweet moans, till at last, crying, "I take you, I take you, my dovelet, my heart's sparrow," she demonstrated that all my fears were falsely grounded. She embraced me successfully; and so far from finding her ass-journey troublesome she it was who set the pace and showed that she had no timidities or doubts as to the final destination. Indeed, I soon discovered that the only apprehensions I needed to entertain were on my own account; and I thought that the mother of the Minotaur knew what she was doing when she chose a lowing lover.

At last this laborious and sleepless night was concluded; and the woman, to avoid the eye of day, left me in haste—not neglecting, however, to contract with my keeper for another night later on at the same price. The fellow was willing to fall in with her schemes, partly because of the large sums she offered, and partly because of the chance he saw of providing a new side-show for his master. He, therefore, incontinently disclosed the whole episode to the latter, who, after richly rewarding him, decided to put the act on as a public spectacle. But as my winsome wife could not be employed for the job on account of her social position, and as no one else would volunteer, a certain debased woman (whom the prefect had condemned to be eaten alive by wild beasts) was procured to mate with me in the arena before the populace. Of this woman I heard the following story:

THE TALE OF THE JEALOUS WIFE

She had a husband whose father had been once called away from home. Before leaving he gave strict injunctions to his wife (the young man's mother) whose belly was swelling roundly, that if the babe turned out to be one of the frailer sex it should at once be strangled. While he was still absent, the wife gave birth to a girl; but overcome by the impulses of mother-love she disobeyed her husband and arranged for a neighbor to rear the child. Then on the husband's return she admitted that she had borne a daughter but said that it had been duly destroyed.

When, however, the girl had grown to a nubile age, the mother realized that she was unable to give her a dowry suitable to her birth without the father knowing; and in desperation she told the whole tale to her son. A further reason for this step was the fear that he might in the heats of youth fortuitously seduce the girl, since neither knew of the relationship. The young man, who loved his mother ardently, religiously followed her suggestions, acted in brotherly fashion, and kept the family secret so well that he seemed to any observer merely a good friend to the girl. But he undertook to fulfill his obligations by receiving her into his house as if she was an orphan girl from the neighborhood who needed parental protection; and he proposed to marry her soon to a beloved and trusty friend of his, after settling a liberal dowry upon her out of his own estate.

But these excellent and innocent dispositions could not escape the distorting rancor of Fortune. They sowed the seeds of bitter jealousy in the household and drove the wife to the crimes for which she was later condemned. For the wife first suspected the sister to be a rival who had ravished her husband from her; next she hated her; and finally she resolved to murder her with the cruelest tortures. In pursuance of this she devised the following trap. She stole her husband's signet-ring and went to a farm of theirs in the country. Thence she despatched a servant of hers (a faithful villain who deserved death for such fidelity) to inform the girl that the husband was come to the farm and wished to see her alone as soon as possible. To remove any doubts that might breed delay, she gave the messenger the stolen ring as a token of the message's truth.

The girl, obedient to her brother's request (for she was the only other one in the secret of her birth) and convinced by the signet which was shown her, instantly set out unaccompanied for the farm. When she had been thus basely lured into the wife's clutches, the latter goaded by lustful frenzy stripped her naked and madly flogged her. In vain the screaming girl confessed the truth; in vain she declared that she was the husband's sister. The wife was too overcome by jealous rage to listen; she considered the confession mere trumped-up evasion; and thrusting a burning brand between the girl's thighs, she cruelly murdered her.

When the brother of the dead girl (and spouse of the murderess) heard what had happened, he hastened to the scene of the crime. Deeply affected, he saw to all the burial arrangements; and then, distracted by the girl's unhappy death at the hands of the woman who should most have cherished her, and racked through and through with regret, he fell into a dangerous fever. Some medical attention was clearly indicated; and the wife (if we can still give her that honorable title) went straightway to a notoriously corrupt doctor, who, victor in many a stricken field, could boast (if he so wished) of the golden trophies reared upon his palm in consequence. Meaning to remove her husband, she offered fifty goldpieces for guaranteed effective poison.

No sooner said than done. She and the doctor pretended that they were about to administer a drug (called Sacred by the learned) which was never known to fail in alleviating intestinal trouble and carrying off the bile. But the drug which they poured out was one Sacred to the needs of the Lady of Death. Before the assembled household and a number of friends and relatives, the doctor himself sagely stirred the cup and offered it to the sick man; but the relentless woman, planning to get rid of her accomplice and to save the money that she owed him, stayed his hand.

"My dear doctor," she said, "you must not give my beloved husband the potion without taking a good pull at it yourself. How do I know that there isn't poison in it? I'm sure that you as a sensible and well-read man won't be offended if I as a true-hearted wife take every rightful precaution for my husband's safety."

The doctor, quite demoralized by the woman's truculent assurance, was deprived of all power of thought by the necessity of decision at so short a notice. If he showed any signs of doubt or fear, he would at once be suspected; and in his dilemma he drank deeply. The husband thereupon confidently received and drained the cup.

That part of the business completed, the doctor was making-off as fast as he could, in the hope of finding an antidote at home to counteract the fatal effects of the poison; but the persistent woman, determined not to be beaten, refused to let him get a nail's-breadth away till the potion was digested and its results apparent. However, after he had prayed and protested, she at length relented so far as to dismiss him.

But the virulent poison had already tainted his blood and was fast gnawing at his vitals. Walking in a trance of anguish he just managed to totter home and tell his wife what had happened (instructing her not to forget to claim the fee for this twin-murder) before he died in convulsions. Such was the violent end of this notable doctor.

Nor did the husband survive him many hours. He died of the same complaint, amid the fictitious tears of his false wife. After a few days (taken up by the performance of the obsequies) the doctor's widow came to demand the fee owing for the duplicated deaths; but the other relict, consistently deceitful, answered with a pretence of open honesty and friendliness and with promises that she would pay the agreed sum without further demur if the other on her side would complete the pact by handing over a small additional quantity of the drug.

So that's that. Duped by the woman's fraudulent assurance, the doctor's widow readily assented. She hurried home in her eagerness to curry favor with the wealthy woman, and returned at once with the whole box of poisons. The murderess, now possessed of the potent means of destruction, spread her bloody web further abroad for victims. She had borne a young daughter to her lately poisoned husband; and she was annoyed that the laws should make this child the heir to the estate. As the child stood between her and this property, she resolved to remove the child. Ascertaining that a widow inherits what is left her child under such circumstances, she showed herself as worthy a mother as she had been a wife. For, preparing breakfast one day, she grasped an opportunity to poison both her own daughter and the doctor's widow.

The child, being young and frail, died at the first shock of the encroaching venom; but the woman, feeling the powerful virus coagulate in her lungs, immediately suspected the truth. She knew her life was choking fast away; but faster she fled to the house of the provincial governor, screaming that she had horrible mischiefs to reveal. Her protesting voice attracted a large crowd, and the governor admitted her to an instant audience where she exposed the career of the infamous woman in all its atrocious details. That done, a sudden dizziness clouded blackly over her mind; her mouth, opened to speak, closed with a click; she ground her teeth furiously; and then she dropped dead at the governor's feet.

The capable official did not allow the horror of the accursed poisoner's multiple crimes to languish by delay. He forthwith ordered the chambermaids to be summoned; by torture he extracted the truth from them; and then, as a punishment less than her deserts but at least worse than any other he could invent, he sentenced the woman to be thrown to the wild beasts.

This was the woman with whom they decided to join me publicly in wedlock. . . .

(JULIUS) PAULUS (FL. A.D. 215)

Opinions

~~❧~~

One of the third century's leading jurists, Paulus served in the "kitchen cabinet" of the emperor Caracalla. He studied law under Scaevola Cirvinius, and served as an advocate, then as legal secretary to Aemilius Papinianus (Papinian), legal assessor for Septimius Severus. He had been banished by the emperor Elagabalus, but recalled to Rome by Severus Alexander, who appointed him to the Praetorian Guard with Ulpian.

- In great demand as a respondent in the courts, he wrote commentaries on the work of other jurists.
- Paulus' more than three hundred books on Roman law are noted for their brevity and clarity of style and their effectiveness in compiling and synthesizing the vast corpus of juridical literature.

In the second chapter of the *lex Julia* concerning adultery, either an adoptive or a natural father is permitted to kill an adulterer caught in the act with his daughter in his own house or in that of his son-in-law, no matter what his rank may be.

If a son under paternal control, who is the father, should surprise his daughter in the act of adultery, while it is inferred from the terms of the law that he cannot kill her, still, he ought to be permitted to do so.

Again, it is provided in the fifth chapter of the *lex Julia* that it is permitted to detain witnesses for twenty hours, in order to convict an adulterer taken in the act.

A husband cannot kill anyone taken in adultery except persons who are infamous, and those who sell their bodies for gain, as well as slaves, and the freedmen of his wife, and those of his parents and children; his wife, however, is excepted, and he is forbidden to kill her.

It has been decided that a husband who kills his wife when caught with an adulterer, should be punished more leniently, for the reason that he committed the act through impatience caused by just suffering.

After having killed the adulterer, the husband should at once dismiss his wife, and publicly declare within the next three days with what adulterer, and in what place he found his wife.

An angry husband who surprises his wife in adultery can only kill the adulterer when he finds him in his own house.

It has been decided that a husband who does not at once dismiss his wife whom he has taken in adultery can be prosecuted as a pander.

It should be noted that two adulterers can be accused at the same time with the wife, but more than that number cannot be.

It has been decided that adultery cannot be committed with women who have charge of any business or shop.

Anyone who debauches a male who is free, against his consent, shall be punished with death.

It has been held that women convicted of adultery shall be punished with the loss of half of their dowry and the third of their estates, and by relegation to an island. The adulterer, however, shall be deprived of half his property, and shall also be punished by relegation to an island; provided the parties are exiled to different islands.

It has been decided that the penalty for incest, which in case of a man is deportation to an island, shall not be inflicted upon the woman; that is to say when she has not been convicted under the *lex Julia* concerning adultery.

Fornication committed with female slaves, unless they are deteriorated in value or an attempt is made against their mistress through them, is not considered an injury.

If a delay is demanded in a case of adultery it cannot be obtained.

JULIAN THE APOSTATE (FLAVIUS CLAUDIUS JULIANUS) (A.D. 331–363; EMPEROR 360–363)

Hymn to the Mother of the Gods

*T*his remarkable oration was written and delivered by one of the most colorful figures in the history of imperial Rome. Julian reigned as sole emperor from A.D. 360 to 363, and like Akhenaten of Egypt, dared to attempt a religious revolution, returning the Empire to its pagan roots because he thought Christianity was sapping the vitality of the Roman character. The youngest son of Julius Constantius, Julianus and his brother escaped the murder of his family in 337. Imprisoned in Macellum castle, in Cappadocia, for seven years, he turned his thoughts to the avid study of the Greek classics—studies he continued in later years under the tutelage of Libanius and Themistius after his passion for the clear-mindedness and self-sufficiency of the Greeks had led him to convert secretly to paganism.

He was named emperor in 355 after his brother was murdered, and set out to repel the Alemanni invaders pouring in from Gaul. He succeeded not only in pushing back the attack but also in restoring Roman defenses along the Rhine and financial stability to the Gallic provinces. When he became sole emperor in 360, he released his true feelings in policies aimed at repressing Christian privileges and restoring Rome's ancient pagan culture—along with modern variations, like the imported Phrygian cult of Cybele-Attis, which was popular in the capital at the time. His religious reform was cut short when Julian was killed at Ctesiphon in his expedition against Persia.

Julian was a prolific writer, leaving behind eight orations and eighty letters.

Ought I to say something on this subject also? And shall I write about things not to be spoken of and divulge what ought not to be divulged? Shall I utter the unutterable? Who is Attis or Gallus, who is the Mother of the Gods, and what is the manner of their ritual of purification? And further why was it introduced in the beginning among us Romans? It was handed down by the Phrygians in very ancient times, and was first taken over by the Greeks, and not by any ordinary Greeks but by Athenians who had learned by experience that they did wrong to jeer at one who was celebrating the Mysteries of the Mother. For it is said that they wantonly insulted and drove out Gallus, on the ground that he was introducing a new cult, because they did not understand what sort of goddess they had to do with, and that she was that very Deo whom they worship, and Rhea and Demeter too. Then followed the wrath of the goddess and the propitiation of her wrath. For the priestess of the Pythian god who guided the Greeks in all noble conduct, bade them propitiate the wrath of the Mother of the Gods. And so, we are told, the Metroum was built, where the Athenians used to keep all their state records. After the Greeks the Romans took over the cult, when the Pythian god had advised them in their turn to bring the goddess from Phrygia as an ally for their war against the Carthaginians. And perhaps there is no reason why I should not insert here a brief account of what happened. When they learned the response of the oracle, the inhabitants of Rome, that city beloved of the gods, sent an embassy to ask from the kings of Pergamon who then ruled over Phrygia and from the Phrygians themselves the most holy statue of the goddess. And when they had received it they brought back their most sacred freight, putting it on a broad cargo-boat which could sail smoothly over those wide seas. Thus she crossed the Aegean and Ionian Seas, and sailed round Sicily and over the Etruscan Sea, and so entered the mouth of the Tiber. And the people and the Senate with them poured out of the city, and in front of all the others there came to meet her all the priests and priestesses in suitable attire according to their ancestral custom. And in excited suspense they gazed at the ship as she ran before a fair wind, and about her keel they could discern the foaming

Crowned goddess, ivory

wake as she cleft the waves. And they greeted the ship as she sailed in and adored her from afar, everyone where he happened to be standing. But the goddess, as though she desired to show the Roman people that they were not bringing a lifeless image from Phrygia, but that what they had received from the Phrygians and were now bringing home possessed greater and more divine powers than an image, stayed the ship directly she touched the Tiber, and she was suddenly as though rooted in mid-stream. So they tried to tow her against the current, but she did not follow. Then they tried to push her off, thinking they had grounded on a shoal, but for all their efforts she did not move. Next every possible device was brought to bear, but

in spite of all she remained immovable. Thereupon a terrible and unjust suspicion fell on the maiden who had been consecrated to the most sacred office of priestess, and they began to accuse Claudia—for that was the name of that noble maiden—of not having kept herself stainless and pure for the goddess; wherefore they said that the goddess was angry and was plainly declaring her wrath. For by this time the thing seemed to all to be supernatural. Now at first she was filled with shame at the mere name of the thing and the suspicion; so very far was she from such shameless and lawless behavior. But when she saw that the charge against her was gaining strength, she took off her girdle and fastened it about the prow of the ship, and, like one divinely inspired, bade all stand aside: and then she besought the goddess not to suffer her to be thus implicated in unjust slanders. Next, as the story goes, she cried aloud as though it were some nautical word of command, "O Goddess Mother, if I am pure follow me!" And lo, she not only made the ship move, but even towed her for some distance up stream. Two things, I think, the goddess showed the Romans on that day: first that the freight they were bringing from Phrygia had no small value, but was priceless, and that this was no work of men's hands but truly divine, not lifeless clay but a thing possessed of life and divine powers. This, I say, was one thing that the goddess showed them. And the other was that no one of the citizens could be good or bad and she not know thereof. Moreover the war of the Romans against the Carthaginians forthwith took a favorable turn, so that the third war was waged only for the walls of Carthage itself.

As for this narrative, though some will think it incredible and wholly unworthy of a philosopher or a theologian, nevertheless let it here be related. For besides the fact that it is commonly recorded by most historians, it has been preserved too on bronze statues in mighty Rome, beloved of the gods. And yet I am well aware that some over-wise persons will call it an old wives' tale, not to be credited. But for my part I would rather trust the traditions of cities than those too clever people, whose puny souls are keen-sighted enough, but never do they see aught that is sound.

I am told that on this same subject of which I am impelled to speak at the very season of these sacred rites, Porphyry too has written a philosophic treatise. But since I have never met with it I do not know whether at any point it may chance to agree with my discourse. But him whom I call Gallus or Attis I discern of my own knowledge to be the substance of generative and creative Mind which engenders all things down to the lowest plane of matter, and comprehends in itself all the concepts and causes of the forms that are embodied in matter. For truly the forms of all things are not in all things, and in the highest and first causes we do not find the forms of the lowest and last, after which there is nothing save privation coupled with a dim idea. Now there are many substances and very many creative gods, but the nature of the third creator, who contains in himself the separate concepts of the forms that are embodied in matter and also the connected chain of causes, I mean that nature which is last in order, and through its superabundance of generative power descends even unto our earth through the upper region from the stars,—this is he

whom we seek, even Attis. But perhaps I ought to distinguish more clearly what I mean. We assert that matter exists and also form embodied in matter. But if no cause be assigned prior to these two, we should be introducing, unconsciously, the Epicurean doctrine. For if there be nothing of higher order than these two principles, then a spontaneous motion and chance brought them together. "But," says some acute Peripatetic like Xenarchus, "we see that the cause of these is the fifth or cyclic substance. Aristotle is absurd when he investigates and discusses these matters, and Theophrastus likewise. At any rate he overlooked the implications of a well-known utterance of his. For just as when he came to incorporeal and intelligible substance he stopped short and did not inquire into its cause, and merely asserted that this is what it is by nature; surely in the case of the fifth substance also he ought to have assumed that its nature is to be thus; and he ought not to have gone on to search for causes, but should have stopped at these, and not fallen back on the intelligible, which has no independent existence by itself, and in any case represents a bare supposition." This is the sort of thing that Xenarchus says, as I remember to have heard. Now whether what he says is correct or not, let us leave to the extreme Peripatetics to refine upon. But that his view is not agreeable to me is, I think, clear to everyone. For I hold that the theories of Aristotle himself are incomplete unless they are brought into harmony with those of Plato; or rather we must make these also agree with the oracles that have been vouchsafed to us by the gods.

But this it is perhaps worth while to inquire, how the cyclic substance can contain the incorporeal causes of the forms that are embodied in matter. For that, apart from these causes, it is not possible for generation to take place is, I think, clear and manifest. For why are there so many kinds of generated things? Whence arise masculine and feminine? Whence the distinguishing characteristics of things according to their species in well-defined types, if there are not pre-existing and pre-established concepts, and causes which existed beforehand to serve as a pattern? And if we discern these causes but dimly, let us still further purify the eyes of the soul. And the right kind of purification is to turn our gaze inward and to observe how the soul and embodied Mind are a sort of mold and likeness of the forms that are embodied in matter. For in the case of the corporeal, or of things that though incorporeal come into being and are to be studied in connection with the corporeal, there is no single thing whose mental image the mind cannot grasp independently of the corporeal. But this it could not have done if it did not possess something naturally akin to the incorporeal forms. Indeed it is for this reason that Aristotle himself called the soul the "place of the forms," only he said that the forms are there not actually but potentially. Now a soul of this sort, that is allied with matter, must needs possess these forms potentially only, but a soul that should be independent and unmixed in this way we must believe would contain all the concepts, not potentially but actually. Let us make this clearer by means of the example which Plato himself employed in the Sophist, with reference certainly to another theory, but still he did employ it. And I bring forward the illustration, not to prove my argument; for one must not try to grasp it by demonstration, but

only by apprehension. For it deals with the first causes, or at least those that rank with the first, if indeed, as it is right to believe, we must regard Attis also as a god. What then, and of what sort is this illustration? Plato says that, if any man whose profession is imitation desire to imitate in such a way that the original is exactly reproduced, this method of imitation is troublesome and difficult, and, by Zeus, borders on the impossible; but pleasant and easy and quite possible is the method which only seems to imitate real things. For instance, when we take up a mirror and turn it round we easily get an impression of all objects, and show the general outline of every single thing. From this example let us go back to the analogy I spoke of, and let the mirror stand for what Aristotle calls the "place of the forms" potentially.

Now the forms themselves must certainly subsist actually before they subsist potentially. If, therefore, the soul in us, as Aristotle himself believed, contains potentially the forms of existing things, where shall we place the forms in that previous state of actuality? Shall it be in material things? No, for the forms that are in them are evidently the last and lowest. Therefore it only remains to search for immaterial causes which exist in actuality prior to and of a higher order than the causes that are embodied in matter. And our souls must subsist in dependence on these and come forth together with them, and so receive from them the concepts of the forms, as mirrors show the reflections of things; and then with the aid of nature it bestows them on matter and on these material bodies of our world. For we know that nature is the creator of bodies, universal nature in some sort of the All; while that the individual nature of each is the creator of particulars is plainly evident. But nature exists in us in actuality without a mental image, whereas the soul, which is superior to nature, possesses a mental image besides. If therefore we admit that nature contains in herself the cause of things of which she has however no mental image, why, in heaven's name, are we not to assign to the soul these same forms, only in a still higher degree, and with priority over nature, seeing that it is in the soul that we recognize the forms by means of mental images, and comprehend them by means of the concept? Who then is so contentious as to admit on the one hand that the concepts embodied in matter exist in nature—even though not all and equally in actuality, yet all potentially—while on the other hand he refuses to recognise that the same is true of the soul? If therefore the forms exist in nature potentially, but not actually, and if also they exist potentially in the soul, only in a still purer sense and more completely separated, so that they can be comprehended and recognized; but yet exist in actuality nowhere at all; to what, I ask, shall we hang the chain of perpetual generation, and on what shall we base our theories of the imperishability of the universe? For the cyclic substance itself is composed of matter and form. It must therefore follow that, even though in actuality these two, matter and form, are never separate from one another, yet for our intelligence the forms must have prior existence and be regarded as of a higher order. Accordingly, since for the forms embodied in matter a wholly immaterial cause has been assigned, which leads these forms under the hand of the third creator—who for us is the lord and father not only of these forms

but also of the visible fifth substance—from that creator we distinguish Attis, the cause which descends even unto matter, and we believe that Attis or Gallus is a god of generative powers. Of him the myth relates that, after being exposed at birth near the eddying stream of the river Gallus, he grew up like a flower, and when he had grown to be fair and tall, he was beloved by the Mother of the Gods. And she entrusted all things to him, and moreover set on his head the starry cap. But if our visible sky covers the crown of Attis, must one not interpret the river Gallus as the Milky Way? For it is there, they say, that the substance which is subject to change mingles with the passionless revolving sphere of the fifth substance. Only as far as this did the Mother of the Gods permit this fair intellectual god Attis, who resembles the sun's rays, to leap and dance. But when he passed beyond this limit and came even to the lowest region, the myth said that he had descended into the cave, and had wedded the nymph. And the nymph is to be interpreted as the dampness of matter; though the myth does not here mean matter itself, but the lowest immaterial cause which subsists prior to matter. Indeed Heracleitus also says: "It is death to souls to become wet." We mean therefore that this Gallus, the intellectual god, the connecting link between forms embodied in matter beneath the region of the moon, is united with the cause that is set over matter, but not in the sense that one sex is united with another, but like an element that is gathered to itself.

Who then is the Mother of the Gods? She is the source of the intellectual and creative gods, who in their turn guide the visible gods: she is both the mother and the spouse of mighty Zeus; she came into being next to and together with the great creator; she is in control of every form of life, and the cause of all generation; she easily brings to perfection all things that are made; without pain she brings to birth, and with the father's aid creates all things that are; she is the motherless maiden, enthroned at the side of Zeus, and in very truth is the Mother of all the Gods. For having received into herself the causes of all the gods, both intelligible and supra-mundane, she became the source of the intellectual gods. Now this goddess, who is also Forethought, was inspired with a passionless love for Attis. For not only the forms embodied in matter, but to a still greater degree the causes of those forms, voluntarily serve her and obey her will. Accordingly the myth relates the following: that she who is the Providence who preserves all that is subject to generation and decay, loved their creative and generative cause, and commanded that cause to beget offspring rather in the intelligible region; and she desired that it should turn toward herself and dwell with her, but condemned it to dwell with no other thing. For only thus would that creative cause strive toward the uniformity that preserves it, and at the same time would avoid that which inclines toward matter. And she bade that cause look toward her, who is the source of the creative gods, and not be dragged down or allured into generation. For in this way was mighty Attis destined to be an even mightier creation, seeing that in all things the conversion to what is higher produces more power to effect than the inclination to what is lower. And the fifth substance itself is more creative and more divine than the elements of our earth, for this

reason, that it is more nearly connected with the gods. Not that anyone, surely, would venture to assert that any substance, even if it be composed of the purest ether, is superior to soul undefiled and pure, that of Heracles for instance, as it was when the creator sent it to earth. For that soul of his both seemed to be and was more effective than after it had bestowed itself on a body. Since even Heracles, now that he has returned, one and indivisible, to his father one and indivisible, more easily controls his own province than formerly when he wore the garment of flesh and walked among men. And this shows that in all things the conversion to the higher is more effective than the propensity to the lower. This is what the myth aims to teach us when it says that the Mother of the Gods exhorted Attis not to leave her or to love another. But he went further, and descended even to the lowest limits of matter. Since, however, it was necessary that his limitless course should cease and halt at last, mighty Helios the Corybant, who shares the Mother's throne and with her creates all things, with her has providence for all things, and apart from her does nothing, persuaded the Lion to reveal the matter. And who is the Lion? Verily we are told that he is flame-colored. He is, therefore, the cause that subsists prior to the hot and fiery, and it was his task to contend against the nymph and to be jealous of her union with Attis. (And who the nymph is, I have said.) And the myth says that the Lion serves the creative Providence of the world, which evidently means the Mother of the Gods. Then it says that by detecting and revealing the truth, he caused the youth's castration. What is the meaning of this castration? It is the checking of the unlimited. For now was generation confined within definite forms checked by creative Providence. And this would not have happened without the so-called madness of Attis, which overstepped and transgressed due measure, and thereby made him become weak so that he had no control over himself. And it is not surprising that this should come to pass, when we have to do with the cause that ranks lowest among the gods. For consider the fifth substance, which is subject to no change of any sort, in the region of the light of the moor: I mean where our world of continuous generation and decay borders on the fifth substance. We perceive that in the region of her light it seems to undergo certain alterations and to be affected by external influences. Therefore it is not contradictory to suppose that our Attis also is a sort of demigod—for that is actually the meaning of the myth—or rather for the universe he is wholly god, for he proceeds from the third creator, and after his castration is led upward again to the Mother of the Gods But though he seems to lean and incline toward matter, one would not be mistaken in supposing that, though he is the lowest in order of the gods, nevertheless he is the leader of all the tribes of divine beings. But the myth calls him a demigod to indicate the difference between him and the unchanging gods. He is attended by the Corybants who are assigned to him by the Mother; they are the three leading personalities of the higher races that are next in order to the gods. Also Attis rules over the lions, who together with the Lion, who is their leader, have chosen for themselves hot and fiery substance, and so are, first and foremost, the cause of fire. And through the heat derived from fire they are the causes of motive force and of preservation for all other things

that exist. And Attis encircles the heavens like a tiara, and thence sets out as though to descend to earth.

This, then, is our mighty god Attis. This explains his once lamented flight and concealment and disappearance and descent into the cave. In proof of this let me cite the time of year at which it happens. For we are told that the sacred tree is felled on the day when the sun reaches the height of the equinox. Thereupon the trumpets are sounded. And on the third day the sacred and unspeakable member of the god Gallus is severed. Next comes, they say, the Hilaria and the festival. And that this castration, so much discussed by the crowd, is really the halting of his unlimited course, is evident from what happens directly mighty Helios touches the cycle of the equinox, where the bounds are most clearly defined. (For the even is bounded, but the uneven is without bounds, and there is no way through or out of it.) At that time then, precisely, according to the account we have, the sacred tree is felled. Thereupon, in their proper order, all the other ceremonies take place. Some of them are celebrated with the secret ritual of the Mysteries, but others by a ritual that can be told to all. For instance, the cutting of the tree belongs to the story of Gallus and not to the Mysteries at all, but it has been taken over by them, I think because the gods wished to teach us, in symbolic fashion, that we must pluck the fairest fruits from the earth, namely, virtue and piety, and offer them to the goddess to be the symbol of our well-ordered constitution here on earth. For the tree grows from the soil, but it strives upward as though to reach the upper air, and it is fair to behold and gives us shade in the heat, and casts before us and bestows on us its fruits as a boon; such is its superabundance of generative life. Accordingly the ritual enjoins on us, who by nature belong to the heavens but have fallen to earth, to reap the harvest of our constitution here on earth, namely, virtue and piety, and then strive upward to the goddess of our forefathers, to her who is the principle of all life. . . .

(DECIMUS MAGNUS) AUSONIUS (C. A.D. 310–394)

Lyrics

~~

Son of the imperial physician of Valentinian I, and educated in Tolosa (modern Toulouse) and his native Burdigala (modern Bordeaux), Ausonius, the most important Latin poet of the fourth century, served as an advocate for nearly thirty years and taught rhetoric and grammar in his hometown. In A.D. 364, the reputation of his learnedness led to Ausonius' appointment as tutor, in Treviri (Trier on the Moselle), to Valentinian I's son Gratian, whom he accompanied on the emperor's campaign against the Alemanni in 368–69. Ausonius soon became adviser to Valentinian as well. After spending some time in public service, including as consul and as governor of Gaul appointed by the new emperor Gratian, he retired to Burdigala when Gratian was assassinated in 383.

- In addition to his poetry and correspondence with important people of his time, including Paulinus of Nola, Ausonius wrote a collection of accounts of twenty great cities of the Roman Empire.
- L. R. Lind, translator of Virgil's *Aeneid,* calls him "the first secular Christian-Latin poet to compose literature, not propaganda or polemic, in Western Europe." As a poet, he wrote prolifically though not brilliantly in a variety of meters and on many subjects:

  - His *Ephemeris* describes his daily routine;
  - *Parentalia* praises his ancestors and deceased friends;
  - His *Mosella* was a popular long hexameter narrative on the splendors of the Rhine and Moselle Rivers.

- Though nominally a Christian (converted, probably, upon accepting his appointment at the imperial court), Ausonius is the last pagan Latin author of note to revere the Roman classics. He wrote over one hundred epigrams, in both Greek and Latin, many showing the influence of Virgil and Ovid. Lind notes that he is the link between classical Rome and the Middle Ages.

TO HIS WIFE

Love, let us live as we have lived, nor lose
The little names that were the first night's
   grace,
And never come the day that sees us old,
I still your lad, and you my little lass.
Let me be older than old Nestor's years,
And you the Sibyl, if we heed it not.
What should we know, we two, of ripe old age?
We'll have its richness, and the years forgot.

ON NEWBLOWN ROSES

Spring, and the sharpness of the golden dawn.
Before the sun was up a cooler breeze
Had blown, in promise of a day of heat,
And I was walking in my formal garden,
To freshen me, before the day grew old.

I saw the hoar frost stiff on the bent grasses,
Sitting in fat globes on the cabbage leaves,
And all my Paestum roses laughing at me,
Dew-drenched, and in the East the morning
   star,
And here and there a dewdrop glistening white,
That soon must perish in the early sun.

Think you, did Dawn steal color from the
   roses,
Or was it new born day that stained the rose?
To each one dew, one crimson, and one
   morning,

To star and rose, their lady Venus one.
Mayhap one fragrance, but the sweet of Dawn
Drifts through the sky, and closer breathes the
   rose.
A moment dies: this bud that was new born
Has burgeoned even fold on even fold;
This still is green, with her close cap of leaves,
This shows a red stain on her tender sheath,
This the first crimson of the loosened bud;
And now she thinks to unwind her coverings,
And lo! the glory of the radiant chalice,
Scattering the close seeds of her golden heart.
One moment, all on fire and crimson glowing,
All pallid now and bare and desolate.
I marveled at the flying rape of time;
But now a rose was born: that rose is old.
Even as I speak the crimson petals float
Down drifting, and the crimsoned earth is
   bright.

So many lovely things, so rare, so young,
A day begat them, and a day will end.
O Earth, to give a flower so brief a grace!
As long as a day is long, so long the life of a
   rose.
The golden sun at morning sees her born,
And late at eve returning finds her old.
Yet wise is she, that hath so soon to die,
And lives her life in some succeeding rose.
O maid, while youth is with the rose and
   thee,
Pluck thou the rose: life is as swift for thee.

CLAUDIAN (CLAUDIUS CLAUDIANUS)

(C. A.D. 370–C. 404)

The Rape of Proserpine

*T*he last noteworthy poet in the classical Latin tradition, Claudian by 395 had abandoned his native Alexandria and Greek language to become, in his adopted city of Rome, more Roman than the Romans. Eulogizing his way into favor first with the consuls Probinus and Olybrius, then with the Vandal Stilicho, regent in Mediolanum (modern Milan) of the western emperor Flavius Honorius, Claudian was granted the positions of court poet and of tribune. By A.D. 400, he had returned to Rome where, in 404, Stilicho's wife Serena arranged an affluent marital alliance for him. A statue was erected for Claudian in the forum of Trajan (its inscribed pedestal survives).

- Claudian's output, reflecting the decline of the Western empire, included epistles, epigrams, historical epics, and idylls, as well as longer panegyrics praising Stilicho, Honorius, and Mallius Theodorus and invectives against the enemies of Honorius. His longer poems include "The Old Man of Verona" and "The Battle of the Giants." Though he may be regarded today as over-rhetorical, poets of the Middle Ages ranked Claudian with Lucan and Statius.
- His unfinished mythological epic (of which only 1,100 lines survive), *The Rape of Proserpine,* retells in highly descriptive and accomplished hexameters one of the most familiar of the Greco-Roman myths: that of Ceres' daughter Proserpina (in Greek mythology: Demeter's daughter Persephone) being snatched to the underworld by Jupiter's brother Hades while her mother's back was turned as she went about her agricultural duties. The poem may have been inspired by the corn shortage of 395–97, and meant as a mythical explanation (Ceres punished mankind with famine until Proserpina was restored by the intervention of Hercules).

BOOK III
(XXXVI)

. . . But, far from Sicily, no uncertain suspicions of the loss she had suffered alarmed Ceres, where long she had dwelt peaceful and secure beneath the rocky roof of the cave resounding with arms. Dreams doubled her dread and a vision of Proserpine lost troubled her every sleep. Now she dreams that an enemy's spear is piercing her body, now (oh horror!) that her raiment is changed and is become black, now that the infecund ash is budding in the midst of her house. Moreover, there stood a laurel, loved above all the grove, that used with maiden leaf to o'ershadow the virgin bower of Proserpine. This she saw hewn down to the roots, its straggling branches fouled with dust, and when she asked the cause of this disaster weeping dryads told her that the Furies had destroyed it with an axe of Hell.

Next her very image appeared in the mother's dreams, announcing her fate in no uncertain manner. She saw Proserpine shut in the dark confines of a prison-house and bound with cruel chains. Yet not so had she entrusted her to the fields of Sicily, not so had the wondering goddesses beheld her in Etna's flowery meadows. Foul was now that hair, more beauteous erstwhile than gold; night had dimmed the fire of her eyes and frost banished the roses from her pale cheeks. The gracious flush of her skin and those limbs whose whiteness matched the hoar-frost are alike turned to hell-tinctured grain. When, therefore, she was at last able to recognize her daughter, albeit with doubtful gaze, she cried: "What crime hath merited these many punishments? Whence comes this dreadful wasting away? Who hath power to wreak such cruelty upon me? How have thy soft arms deserved fetters of stubborn iron, scarce fitted for beasts? Art thou my daughter or does a vain shadow deceive me?"

Thus she answered: "Cruel mother, forgetful of thy daughter's fate, more hard of heart than the tawny lioness! Could'st thou be so heedless of me? Didst thou hold me cheap for that I am thy sole daughter? Dear indeed to thee must be the name of Proserpine who now, shut in this vast cavern, as thou seest, am plagued with torment! Hast thou heart to dance, cruel mother? Canst thou revel through the cities of Phrygia? If thou hast not banished the mother from thy breast, if thou, Ceres, art really my mother and 'twas no Hyrcanian tiger gave me birth, save me, I pray thee, from this prison and restore me to the upper world. If the fates forbid my return come thou down at least and visit me."

So spake she and strove to hold out her trembling hands. The iron's ruthless strength forbade it, and the clangor of the chains awoke her sleeping mother. Ceres lay stiff with terror at the vision, rejoices that it was not true, but grieves that she cannot embrace her daughter. Maddened with fear she rushes out of the cavern and thus addresses Cybele: "No longer now will I tarry in the land of Phrygia, holy mother; the duty of protecting my dear daughter calls me back after so long an absence, for she is of an age that is exposed to many dangers. I put not complete trust in my palace, though built with iron from the Cyclopes' furnace. I fear lest rumor disclose her hiding-place and Sicily too lightly guard my trust. The fame of that place too widely bruited abroad alarms me; needs must I find elsewhere some obscurer abode. Our retreat must be on all men's tongues by reason of the groanings of Enceladus and the neighbor flames. Ill-omened dreams, too, with diverse visions often give me pause, and no day passes but brings some inauspicious hap. How often has my crown of golden ears fallen of itself! How often blood flowed from my breast! In mine own despite streams of tears course down my cheeks and unbidden my hands beat my astonished breast. Would I blow up the flute, funereal is the note; do I shake the cymbals, the cymbals echo a sound of mourning. Alas! I fear there is some trouble in these portents. This long sojourn has wrought me woe."

"May the wind carry far away thy vain words," replies Cybele; "not such the Thunderer's want of care that he would not hurl his bolt in his daughter's defense. Yet go and return, dismayed by no evil hap."

This said, Ceres left the temple; but no speed is enough for her haste; she complains that her sluggish dragons scarce move, and, lashing the wings now of this one and now of that (though little they deserved it), she hopes to reach Sicily e'er yet out of sight of Ida. She fears everything and hopes nothing, anxious as the bird that has entrusted its unfledged brood to a low-growing ash and while absent gathering food has many fears lest perchance the wind has blown the fragile nest from the tree, lest her young ones be exposed to the theft of man or the greed of snakes.

When she saw the gate-keepers fled, the house unguarded, the rusted hinges, the overthrown doorposts, and the miserable state of the silent halls, pausing not to look again at the disaster, she rent her garment and tore away the shattered corn-ears along with her hair. She could not weep nor speak nor breathe and a trembling shook the very marrow of her bones; her faltering steps tottered. She flung open the doors and wandering through the empty rooms and deserted halls, recognized the half-ruined warp with its disordered threads and the work of the loom broken off. The goddess' labors had come to naught, and

what remained to be done, that the bold spider was finishing with her sacrilegious web.

She weeps not nor bewails the ill; only kisses the loom and stifles her dumb complaints amid the threads, clasping to her bosom, as though it had been her child, the spindles her child's hand had touched, the wool she had cast aside, and all the toys scattered in maiden sport. She scans the virgin bed, the deserted couch, and the chair where Proserpine had sat: even as a herd, whose drove the unexpected fury of an African lion or bands of marauding beasts have attacked, gazes in amaze at the vacant stall, and, too late returned, wanders through the emptied pastures, sadly calling to the unreplying steers.

And there, lying in the innermost parts of the house, she saw Electra, loving nurse of Proserpine, best known among the old Nymphs of Ocean; she who loved Proserpine as did Ceres. 'Twas she who, when Proserpine had left her cradle, would bear her in her loving bosom and bring the little girl to mighty Jove and set her to play on her father's knee. She was her companion, her guardian, and could be deemed her second mother. There, with torn and disheveled hair, all foul with gray dust, she was lamenting the rape of her divine foster-child.

Ceres approached her, and when at length her grief allowed her sighs free rein: "What ruin is here?" she said. "Of what enemy am I become the victim? Does my husband yet rule or do the Titans hold heaven? What hand hath dared this, if the Thunderer be still alive? Have Typhon's shoulders forced up Inarime or does Alcyoneus course on foot through the Etruscan Sea, having burst the bonds of imprisoning Vesuvius? Or has the neighboring mountain of Etna oped her jaws and expelled Enceladus? Perchance Briareus with his hundred arms has attacked my house? Ah, my daughter, where art thou now? Whither are fled my thousand servants, whither Cyane? What violence has driven away the winged Sirens? Is this your faith? Is this the way to guard another's treasure?"

The nurse trembled and her sorrow gave place to shame; fain would she have died could she so escape the gaze of that unhappy mother, and long stayed she motionless, hesitating to disclose the suspected criminal and the all too certain death. Scarce could she thus speak: "Would that the raging band of Giants had wrought this ruin! Easier to bear is a common lot. 'Tis the goddesses, and, though thou wilt scarce credit it, her own sisters, who have conspired to our undoing. Thou seest the devices of gods and wounds inflicted by sisters' jealousy. Heaven is a more cruel enemy than Hell.

"All quiet was the house, the maiden dared not o'erstep the threshold nor visit the grassy pastures, close bound by thy commands. The loom gave her work, the Sirens with their song relaxation—with me she held pleasant converse, with me she slept; safe delights were hers within the halls. Then suddenly Cytherea came (who showed her the way to our hid abode I know not), and, that she might not rouse our suspicions, she brought with her Diana and Minerva, attending her on either side. Straightway with beaming smiles she put on a pretense of joy, kissed Proserpine many a time, and repeated the name of sister, complaining of that hard-hearted mother who chose to condemn

such beauty to imprisonment and complaining that by forbidding her intercourse with the goddesses she had removed her far from her father's heaven. My unwitting charge rejoiced in these evil words and bade a feast be spread with plentiful nectar. Now she dons Diana's arms and dress and tries her bow with her soft fingers. Now crowned with horse-hair plumes she puts on the helmet, Minerva commending her, and strives to carry her huge shield.

"Venus was the first with guileful suggestion to mention fields and the vale of Henna. Cunningly she harps upon the nearness of the flowery mead, and as though she knew it not, asks what merits the place boasts, pretending not to believe that a harmless winter allows the roses to bloom, that the cold months are bright with flowers not rightly theirs, and that the spring thickets fear not there Boötes' wrath. So with her wonderment, her passion to see the spot, she persuades Proserpine. Alas! how easily does youth err with its weak ways! What tears did I not shed to no purpose, what vain entreaties did my lips not utter! Away she flew, trusting to the sisters' protection; the scattered company of attendant nymphs followed after her.

"They went to the hills clothed with undying grass and gather flowers 'neath the twilight of dawn, when the quiet meads are white with dew and violets drink the scattered moisture. But when the sun had mounted to higher air at noon, behold! murky night hid the sky and the island trembled and shook beneath the beat of horses' hoofs and the rumble of wheels. Who the charioteer was none might tell—whether he was the harbinger of death or it was Death himself. Gloom spread through the meadows, the rivers stayed their courses, the fields were blighted, nor did aught live, once touched with those horses' breath. I saw the bryony pale, the roses fade, the lilies wither. When in his roaring course the driver turned back his steeds the night it brought accompanied the chariot and light was restored to the world. Proserpine was nowhere to be seen. Their vows fulfilled, the goddesses had returned and tarried not. We found Cyane half dead amid the fields; there she lay, a garland round her neck and the blackened wreaths faded upon her forehead. At once we approached her and inquired after her mistress's fortune, for she had been a witness of the disaster. What, we asked, was the aspect of the horses; who their driver? Naught said she, but corrupted with some hidden venom, dissolved into water. Water crept amid her hair; legs and arms melted and flowed away, and soon a clear stream washed our feet. The rest are gone; the Sirens, Achelous' daughters, rising on rapid wing, have occupied the coast of Sicilian Pelorus, and in wrath at this crime now turned their lyres to man's destruction, tuneful now for ill. Their sweet voices stay ships, but once that song is heard the oars can move no more. I alone am left in the house to drag out an old age of mourning."

Ceres is still a prey to anxiety; half distraught she fears everything as though all were not yet accomplished. Anon she turns her head and eyes to heaven and with raging breast inveighs against its denizens; even as lofty Niphates shakes to the roaring of the Hyrcan tigress whose cubs the terrified horseman has carried off to be the playthings of Persia's king. Speedier than the west wind that is her paramour rushes the tigress, anger blazing from her stripes, but just as she is about to engulf the terrified hunter in her capacious maw, she is checked by the mirrored image of her own form: so the mother of Proserpine rages over all Olympus crying: "Give her back; no wandering stream gave me birth; I spring not from the Dryad rabble. Towered Cybele bare me also to Saturn. Where are the ordinances of the gods, where the laws of heaven? What boots it to live a good life? See, Cytherea dares show her face (modest goddess!) even after her Lemnian bondage! 'Tis that chaste sleep and a loverless couch have given her this courage! This is, I suppose, the reward of those maidenly embraces! Small wonder that after such infamy she account nothing disgraceful. Ye goddesses that have known not marriage, is it thus that ye neglect the honor due to virginity? Have ye so changed your counsel? Do ye now go allied with Venus and her accomplice ravishers? Worthy each of you to be worshipped in Scythian temples and at altars that lust after human blood. What hath caused such great anger? Which of you has my Proserpine wronged even in her slightest word? Doubtless she drove thee, Delian goddess, from thy loved woods, or deprived thee, Triton-born, of some battle thou hadst joined. Did she plague you with talk? Break rudely upon your dances? Nay, that she might be no burden to you, she dwelt far away in the solitudes of Sicily. What good hath her retirement done her? No peace can still the madness of bitter jealousy."

Thus she upbraids them all. But they, obedient to the Father's word, keep silence or say they know nothing, and make tears their answer to the mother's questionings. What can she do? She ceases, beaten, and in turn descends to humble entreaty. "If a mother's love swelled too high or if I have done aught more boldly than befitted misery, oh forgive! A suppliant and wretched I fling me at your feet; grant me to learn my doom; grant me at least this much—sure knowledge of my woes. Fain would I know the manner of this ill; whatsoever fortune ye have visited upon me that will I bear and account it fate, not injustice. Grant a parent the sight of her child; I ask her not back. Whosoever thou art, possess in peace what thine hand has taken. The prey is thine, fear not. But if the ravisher has thwarted me, binding you by some oath, yet do thou, at least, Latona, tell me his name; to thee mayhap Diana hath confessed her knowledge. Thou hast known childbirth, the anxiety and love for children; to offspring twain hast thou given birth; this was mine only child. So mayest thou ever enjoy Apollo's locks, so mayest thou live a happier mother than I."

Plenteous tears then bedewed her cheeks. She continued: "Why these tears? why this silence? Woe is me; all desert me. Why tarriest thou yet to no purpose? Seest thou not 'tis open war with heaven? were it not better to seek again thy daughter by sea and land? I will gird myself and scour the world, unwearied I will penetrate its every corner, nor ever stay my search, nor rest nor sleep till I find my reft treasure, though she lie whelmed in the Spanish Ocean bed or hedged around in the depths of the Red Sea. Neither ice-bound Rhine nor Alpine frosts shall stay me; the treacherous tides of Syrtes shall not give me pause. My purpose holds to penetrate the fastnesses of the South and to tread the snowy home of Boreas. I will climb Atlas on the brink of the sunset and illumine Hydaspes' stream with my torches. Let wicked Jove behold me wandering through towns and country, and Juno's jealousy be sated with her rival's ruin. Have your sport with me, triumph in heaven, proud gods, celebrate your illustrious victory o'er Ceres' conquered daughter."

So spake she and glides down upon Etna's familiar slopes, there to fashion torches to aid her night-wandering labors. . . .

AVIANUS (FL. A.D. 400)

Fables

Roman love for succinct wisdom extended from Ennius through Lucilius and Horace to the latter-day fabulist Avianus.

- The introduction to his collection of forty-two fables in elegiac verse credits as sources Phaedrus and Babrius. His style was influenced by Ovid and Virgil, though his command of Latin was no match for theirs.
- Avianus' fables—visual, descriptive, but sometimes stylistically strained—were found in standard schoolbooks throughout the Middle Ages.

THE WOMEN AND THE WOLF

A country-nurse once told her weeping boy
"A wolf will eat you if you cry again."
A credulous wolf, who overheard with joy,
Remained all night before the doors, in vain.
The weary child soon drifted into sleep;
With disappointed hope the listener burned—
Back to his forest-lair he had to creep;
His bitch perceived that fasting he'd returned.
"Where is the usual snack?" she asked. "And
*   why*
With wasted jaws come crawling in dismay?"
"Don't stare," he said. "I heard a wicked lie.
It's luck that, famished out, I got away.
What profit could I ever hope to gain
When hearkening to the prattle of a nurse?"
Thus often must a worried man complain,
Who, trusting woman, finds her art a curse.

THE CRAB

A crab once tried to turn and bumped
*   instead*
On washing rocks his rugged carapace.
His mother, who desired to go ahead,
Admonished thus her son with moral face:
"Come, leave these crooked ways and mend
*   your gait;*
Don't dodge aside on any weak pretence:
With ready effort take the road that's
*   straight;*
And tread the unwinding path of
*   innocence."*
The son replied: "Then go in front of me
And show me what is right. I'll do it
*   then."*
A man, defaulting, is a fool if he
Accuses faults revealed by other men.

(AMBROSIUS THEODOSIUS) MACROBIUS (FL. A.D. 400)

Commentary on the Dream of Scipio

*A*lmost nothing is known for certain of Macrobius' life. He may have been prefect of Africa, was certainly of high rank, and was also known as a grammarian whose second tongue was Latin. Only two works survive, though he is known to have composed a third, *On the Differences and Similarities of the Greek and Latin Verb.*

- The seven-volume *Convivia Saturnalia,* a three-day banquet dialogue among aristocratic Roman intellectuals at the house of Vettius Praetextatus, a favorite of the emperor Valentinian, held at the winter festival in 384. Modeled on Plato's *Symposium,* reminiscent of Athenaeus' *Deipnosophiae* and especially of Gellius' *Attic Nights,* and no doubt written to instruct Macrobius' son Eustachius in manners, the discussion focuses on criticism and praise of Virgil as the ultimate poet-philosopher but also ranges freely and miscellaneously over popular science, mythology, dance, history, literature, critical theory, and philology. Among other things, the *Saturnalia* is important for preserving otherwise unknown fragments of Ennius and Lucilius.

- The *Commentary on the Dream of Scipio* is based on the last book of Cicero's *De Republica* and heavily influenced by religious philosopher Porphyry's commentary on Plato's *Timaeus.* Dealing with the soul, dreams, a classification of the virtues, a condemnation of suicide, and astronomy, the *Commentary* is an important expression of late-Roman Neo-Platonism. Considered a basic sourcebook by medieval scholastics and scientists, it continued to be influential through the Renaissance. Comparing Plato's *Republic* with Cicero's *De Republica* (the last section of which, known as "Scipio's Dream," is consciously modeled on the "vision of Er" at the close of Plato's dialogue), Macrobius provides insight into the difference between the Greek and Roman minds. Plato's utopian republic is the product of philosophical reasoning; Cicero's is modeled on Roman constitutions and values.

Before broadening his discussion into the dogmas of Neo-Platonism, Macrobius classifies dreams into five types:

- the enigmatic dream, *somnium*
- the prophetic dream, *visio*

- the oracular dream, *oraculum*
- the nightmare, *insomnium*
- the apparition, *visum*

His distinction between oracular and prophetic dreams is characteristic of Roman practical logic: A dream is oracular if it predicts the future; it's prophetic if the prediction proves accurate.

Central to the commentary is the belief in the immortality of the soul and life beyond the grave.

CHAPTER III

... [4] Nightmares may be caused by mental or physical distress, or anxiety about the future: the patient experiences in dreams vexations similar to those that disturb him during the day. As examples of the mental variety, we might mention the lover who dreams of possessing his sweetheart or of losing her, or the man who fears the plots or might of an enemy and is confronted with him in his dream or seems to be fleeing him. The physical variety might be illustrated by one who has overindulged in eating or drinking and dreams that he is either choking with food or unburdening himself, or by one who has been suffering from hunger or thirst and dreams that he is craving and searching for food or drink or has found it. Anxiety about the future would cause a man to dream that he is gaining a prominent position or office as he hoped or that he is being deprived of it as he feared.

[5] Since these dreams and others like them arise from some condition or circumstance that irritates a man during the day and consequently disturbs him when he falls asleep, they flee when he awakes and vanish into thin air. Thus the name *insomnium* was given, not because such dreams occur "in sleep"—in this respect nightmares are like other types—but because they are noteworthy only during their course and afterward have no importance or meaning.

[6] Virgil, too, considers nightmares deceitful: "False are the dreams *(insomnia)* sent by departed spirits to their sky." He used the word "sky" with reference to our mortal realm because the earth bears the same relation to the regions of the dead as the heavens bear to the earth. Again, in describing the passion of love, whose concerns are always accompanied by nightmares, he says: "Oft to her heart rushes back the chief's valor, oft his glorious stock; his looks and words cling fast within her bosom, and the pang withholds calm rest from her limbs." And a moment later: "Anna, my sister, what dreams *(insomnia)* thrill me with fears?"

[7] The apparition *(phantasma* or *visum)* comes upon one in the moment between wakefulness and slumber, in the so-called "first cloud of sleep." In this drowsy condition he thinks he is still fully awake and imagines he sees specters rushing at him or wandering vaguely about, differing from natural creatures in size and shape, and hosts of diverse things, either delightful or disturbing. To this class belongs the incubus, which, according to popular belief, rushes upon people in sleep and presses them with a weight which they can

feel. [8] The two types just described are of no assistance in foretelling the future; but by means of the other three we are gifted with the powers of divination.

We call a dream oracular in which a parent, or a pious or revered man, or a priest, or even a god clearly reveals what will or will not transpire, and what action to take or to avoid. [9] We call a dream a prophetic vision if it actually comes true. For example, a man dreams of the return of a friend who has been staying in a foreign land, thoughts of whom never enter his mind. He goes out and presently meets his friend and embraces him. Or in his dream he agrees to accept a deposit, and early the next day a man runs anxiously to him, charging him with the safekeeping of his money and committing secrets to his trust. [10] By an enigmatic dream we mean one that conceals with strange shapes and veils with ambiguity the true meaning of the information being offered, and requires an interpretation for its understanding. We need not explain further the nature of this dream since everyone knows from experience what it is. There are five varieties of it: personal, alien, social, public, and universal. [11] It is called personal when one dreams that he himself is doing or experiencing something; alien, when he dreams this about someone else; social, when his dream involves others and himself; public, when he dreams that some misfortune or benefit has befallen the city, forum, theater, public walls, or other public enterprise; universal, when he dreams that some change has taken place in the sun, moon, planets, sky, or regions of the earth. [12] The dream which Scipio reports that he saw embraces the three reliable types mentioned above, and also has to do with all five varieties of the enigmatic dream. It is oracular since the two men who appeared before him and revealed his future, Aemilius Paulus and Scipio the Elder, were both his father, both were pious and revered men, and both were affiliated with the priesthood. It is a prophetic vision since Scipio saw the regions of his abode after death and his future condition. It is an enigmatic dream because the truths revealed to him were couched in words that hid their profound meaning and could not be comprehended without skillful interpretation.

It also embraces the five varieties of the last type. [13] It is personal since Scipio himself was conducted to the regions above and learned of his future. It is alien since he observed the estates to which the souls of others were destined. It is social since he learned that for men with merits similar to his the same places were being prepared as for himself. It is public since he foresaw the victory of Rome and the destruction of Carthage, his triumph on the Capitoline, and the coming civil strife. And it is universal since by gazing up and down he was initiated into the wonders of the heavens, the great celestial circles, and the harmony of the revolving spheres, things strange and unknown to mortals before this; in addition he witnessed the movements of the stars and planets and was able to survey the whole earth.

[14] It is incorrect to maintain that Scipio was not the proper person to have a dream that was both public and universal inasmuch as he had not yet attained the highest office but, as he himself admitted, was still ranked "not much higher than a private soldier." The critics say that dreams concerning the welfare of the state

are not to be considered significant unless military or civil officers dream them, or unless many plebeians have the same dream. [15] They cite the incident in Homer when, before the assembled Greeks, Agamemnon disclosed a dream that he had had about a forthcoming battle. Nestor, who helped the army quite as much with his prudence as all the youth with their might, by way of instilling confidence in the dream said that in matters of general welfare they had to confide in the dream of a king, whereas they would repudiate the dream of anyone else. [16] However, the point in Scipio's favor was that although he had not yet held the consulship or a military command, he—who himself was destined to lead that campaign— was dreaming about the coming destruction of Carthage, was witnessing the public triumph in his honor, and was even learning of the secrets of nature; for he excelled as much in philosophy as in deeds of courage.

[17] Because, in citing Virgil above as an authority for the unreliability of nightmares, we excerpted a verse from his description of the twin portals of dreams, someone may take the occasion to inquire why false dreams are allotted to the gate of ivory and trustworthy ones to the gate of horn. He should avail himself of the help of Porphyry, who, in his *Commentaries*, makes the following remarks on a passage in Homer presenting the same distinction between gates: "All truth is concealed. [18] Nevertheless, the soul, when it is partially disengaged from bodily functions during sleep, at times gazes and at times peers intently at the truth, but does not apprehend it; and when it gazes it does not see with clear and direct vision, but rather with a dark obstructing veil

interposed." [19] Virgil attests that this is natural in the following lines: "Behold—for all the cloud, which now, drawn over thy sight, dulls thy mortal vision and with dank pall enshrouds thee, I will tear away." [20] If, during sleep, this veil permits the vision of the attentive soul to perceive the truth, it is thought to be made of horn, the nature of which is such that, when thinned, it becomes transparent. When the veil dulls the vision and prevents its reaching the truth, it is thought to be made of ivory, the composition of which is so dense that no matter how thin a layer of it may be, it remains opaque.

CHAPTER IV

[1] Now that we have discussed the types to which *Scipio's Dream* belongs, and before we examine the words of the dream itself, let us try to reveal its design and purpose, its *skopos*, as the Greeks call it. Once again we must affirm, as we did at the opening of this discourse, that the purpose of the dream is to teach us that the souls of those who serve the state well are returned to the heavens after death and there enjoy everlasting blessedness.

[2] It was the following occasion, indeed, that impelled Scipio to relate his dream, which, he says, he had kept secret for a long time. When Laelius was deploring the fact that no statues of Nasica had been set up in public in recognition of his slaying a tyrant, Scipio replied among other things: "Though for wise men the fullest reward for virtue is consciousness of the merit of their deeds, still that Divine Virtue does not long for statues held together with lead nor for triumphs with their withering laurels, but for rewards of a more

substantial and enduring character." "What are they?" Laelius inquired. [3] Scipio then answered, "Grant me your indulgence since this is the third day of our holiday festival," together with other introductory words. Then he began to narrate his dream, showing by words like the following that the rewards which he saw in the sky reserved for the outstanding men of public affairs were more substantial and lasting: [4] *That you may be more zealous in safeguarding the commonwealth, Scipio, be persuaded of this: all those who have saved, aided, or enlarged the commonwealth have a definite place marked off in the heavens where they may enjoy a blessed existence forever.*

A little later, in describing the sort of place it was, Paulus said: *But, Scipio, cherish justice and your obligations to duty, as your grandfather here and I, your father, have done; this is important where parents and relatives are concerned, but is of utmost importance in matters concerning the commonwealth. This sort of life is your passport into the sky, to a union with those who have finished their lives on earth and who, upon being released from their bodies, inhabit that place at which you are now looking,* meaning the Milky Way.

[5] You must know that the place where Scipio thought he was in his dream is the Milky Way, called by the Greeks *galaxias*. We may be assured of this because in the first part of the dream Scipio uses these words: *From our lofty perch, dazzling and glorious, set among the radiant stars, he pointed out Carthage.* And a little later he spoke more clearly: *Furthermore, it was a circle of surpassing brilliance gleaming out amidst the blazing stars, which takes its name, the Milky Way, from the Greek word. As I looked out from this spot everything appeared splendid and wonderful. . . .*

(FLAVIUS) VEGETIUS (RENATUS) (FL. C. A.D. 400)
Military Institutions of the Romans

～♪

*T*he only manual of Roman military practices to survive in its entirety was written sometime in the late fourth or early fifth century, probably in the reign of Theodosius and possibly under the emperor's direct orders. In a time when foreign mercenaries and cavalry had replaced the tightly disciplined legion on the battlefield, Vegetius, in the characteristically Roman tradition of bemoaning the present in favor of the past, preaches a return to the traditional organization of the cohesive legion. His work is divided into four books:

- Book 1 discusses the recruiting and training process and camp construction, including commentary on the famous Roman discipline, selection of recruits, proper age for recruits, initial training, swimming, sword training, special drill, use of bow, sling, javelin, vaulting and burden carrying, "arms of the ancients," troops in action, entrenched camps, and marches.
- Book 2 deals with the organization of the legion, the relationship between the legions and the auxiliaries, causes of legion decay, duties of cohorts, legion officers, tribunes of the soldiers, legionary horse, and order of battle.
- Book 3 covers logistics, tactics and strategy, and everything having to do with the operations of an army in the field.
- Book 4 focuses on siege fortifications and naval tactics.

An uncritical hodgepodge of a compilation of practices belonging to many different periods, the book is yet logical and informative. Vegetius' acknowledged sources include Cato the Censor, Sallust, Cornelius Celsus, Frontinus, Paternus, and the constitutions of the emperors Trajan, Hadrian, and Augustus. The *Art of War* of its time, *Military Institutions* was the bible of European warfare during the Middle Ages and Renaissance and has been called the single most influential military treatise in the Western world for its fundamental role in transforming warfare from its aristocratic ancestry to its modern dimensions. The same author may have written the more popular *Mulomedicina,* a study of equine veterinary practice.

ATTACKING THE ENEMY

He should regulate his march so as to fall upon them while taking their refreshments or sleeping, or at a time when they suspect no danger and are dispersed, unarmed and their horses unsaddled. He should continue these tactics till his soldiers have imbibed a proper confidence in themselves. For troops that have never been in action or have not for some time been used to such spectacles, are greatly shocked at the sight of the wounded and dying; and the impressions of fear they receive dispose them rather to fly than fight.

If the enemy makes excursions or expeditions, the general should attack him when fatigued by a long march, fall upon him unexpectedly, or harass his rear. He should detach parties to endeavor to carry by surprise any quarters established at a distance from the hostile army for the collection of forage or provisions. For such measures should be pursued at first as can produce no very bad effects if they

Testudo ("tortoise"): siege machine

should happen to miscarry, but be of great advantage if attended with success. A prudent general will also try to sow dissention among his adversaries, for no nation, no matter how weak in itself, can be completely ruined by its enemies unless its fall be facilitated by its own acts. In civil dissensions men are so intent on the destruction of their private enemies that they are entirely regardless of the public safety.

One maxim must be remembered throughout this work: that no one should ever despair of effecting what has been already accomplished. It may be said that our troops for many years past have not even fortified their permanent camps with ditches, ramparts or palisades. The answer is plain. If those precautions had been taken, our armies would never have suffered by surprises of the enemy both by day and night.

The Persians, after the example of the old Romans, surround their camps with ditches and, as the ground in their country is generally sandy, they always carry with them empty bags to fill with the sand taken out of the trenches and raise a parapet by piling them one on the other. All the barbarous nations range their vehicles round them in a circle, a method which bears some resemblance to a fortified camp. They thus pass their nights secure from surprise.

RESTORING ANCIENT DISCIPLINE

Are we afraid of not being able to learn from others what they before have learned from us? At present all this is to be found in books only, although formerly constantly practiced. Inquiries are now no longer made about customs that have been so long neglected, because in the midst of peace, war is looked upon as an eventuality too distant to merit consideration. But former instances will convince us that the reestablishment of ancient discipline is by no means impossible, although now so totally in disuse.

In former ages the art of war, often neglected and forgotten, was as often recovered from books and reestablished by the authority and attention of our generals. Our armies in Spain, when Scipio Africanus took the command, were in bad condition and had often been beaten under preceding generals. He soon reformed them by severe discipline and obliged them to undergo the greatest fatigue in the different military works, reproaching them by the remark that since they would not wet their hands with the blood of their enemies, they should soil them with the mud of the trenches. In short, with these very troops he afterward took the city of Numantia and burned it to the ground with such destruction of its inhabitants that not one escaped.

In Africa an army, which under the command of Albinus had been forced to pass under the yoke, was by Metellus brought into such order and discipline, by forming it on the ancient model, that they afterward vanquished those very enemies who had subjected them to that ignominious treatment. The Cimbri defeated the legions of Caepio, Manilus and Silanus in Gaul, but Marius collected their shattered remnants and disciplined them so effectually that he destroyed an innumerable multitude of the Cimbri, Teutones and Ambrones in one general engagement. Nevertheless it is easier to form young soldiers and inspire them with proper notions of honor than to reanimate troops who have been once disheartened.

PREPARATIONS FOR A GENERAL ENGAGEMENT

Having explained the less considerable branches of the art of war, the order of military affairs naturally leads us to the general engagement. This is a conjuncture full of uncertainty and fatal to kingdoms and nations, for in the decision of a pitched battle consists the fullness of victory. This eventuality above all others requires the exertion of all the abilities of a general, as his good conduct on such an occasion gains him greater glory, as the reverse exposes him to greater danger and disgrace. This is the moment in which his talents, skill and experience show themselves in their fullest extent.

Formerly to enable the soldiers to charge with greater vigor, it was customary to order them a moderate refreshment of food before an engagement, so that their strength might be the better supported during a long conflict. When the army is to march out of a camp or city in the presence of their enemies drawn up and ready for action, great precaution must be observed lest they should be attacked as they defile from the gates and be cut to pieces in detail. Proper measures must therefore be taken so that the whole army may be clear of the gates and form in order of battle before the enemy's approach.

If they are ready before you can have quitted the place, your design of marching out must either be deferred till another opportunity or at least dissembled, so that when they begin to taunt you on the supposition that you dare not appear, or think of nothing but plundering or retiring and no longer keep their ranks, you may sally out and fall upon them while in confusion and surprise.

Troops must never be engaged in a general action immediately after a long march, when the men are fatigued and the horses tired. The strength required for action is spent in the toil of the march. What can a soldier do who charges when out of breath? The ancients carefully avoided this inconvenience, but in later times some of our Roman generals, to say nothing more, have lost their armies by unskillfully neglecting this precaution. Two armies, one tired and spent, the other fresh and in full vigor, are by no means an equal match.

TROOPS' PRE-BATTLE SENTIMENT

It is necessary to know the sentiments of the soldiers on the day of an engagement. Their confidence or apprehensions are easily discovered by their looks, their words, their actions and their motions. No great dependence is to be placed on the eagerness of young soldiers for action, for the prospect of fighting is attractive to those who are strangers to it. On the other hand, it would be wrong to hazard an engagement, if old experienced soldiers testify to a disinclination to fight. A general, however, may encourage and animate his troops by proper exhortations and orations, especially if by his prophecies of a favorable result of the approaching action he can persuade them into the belief of an easy victory. With this view, he should lay before them the cowardice or unskillfulness of their enemies and remind them of any former advantages they may have gained over them. He should employ every argument capable of exciting rage, hatred and indignation against the adversaries in the minds of his soldiers.

It is natural for men in general to be affected with some sensations of fear at the beginning of an engagement, but there are without doubt some of a more timorous disposition who are disordered by the very sight of the enemy. To diminish these apprehensions before you venture on action, draw up your army frequently in order of battle in some safe situation, so that your men may be accustomed to the sight and appearance of the enemy. When opportunity offers, they should be sent to fall upon them and endeavor to put them to flight or kill some of their men. Thus they will become acquainted with their customs, arms and horses. The objects with which we are once familiarized are seldom longer capable of inspiring us with terror.

CHOICE OF THE BATTLE FIELD

Good generals are acutely aware that victory depends much on the nature of the field of battle. When you intend to engage, endeavor to draw the chief advantage from your position. The highest ground is reckoned the best. Weapons thrown from a height strike with greater force; and the party above their antagonists can repulse and bear them down with greater impetuosity, while they who struggle with the ascent have both the ground and the enemy to contend with.

There is, however, this difference: If you depend on your foot against the enemy's horse, you must choose a rough, unequal and mountainous situation. But if, on the contrary, you expect your cavalry to act with advantage against the enemy's infantry, your ground must indeed be higher, but level and open, without any obstructions such as woods or morasses. . . .

GENERAL MAXIMS

It is the nature of war that what is beneficial to you is detrimental to the enemy and what is of service to him hurts you. It is therefore a maxim never to do, or to omit doing anything as a consequence of his actions, but to consult invariably your own interest only. And you depart from this interest whenever you imitate such measures as he pursues for his benefit. For the same reason it would be wrong for him to follow such steps as you take for your advantage.

The more your troops have been accustomed to camp duties on frontier stations and the more carefully they have been disciplined, the less danger they will be exposed to in the field.

Men must be sufficiently tried before they are led against the enemy.

It is much better to overcome the enemy by imposing upon him famine, surprise or terror than by general actions, for in the latter instance fortune has often a greater share than valor.

Those designs are best of which the enemy are entirely ignorant till the moment of execution. Opportunity in war is often more to be depended on than courage.

To seduce the enemy's soldiers from their allegiance and encourage them to surrender is of especial service, for an adversary is more hurt by desertion than by slaughter.

It is better to have several bodies of reserves than to extend your front too much.

A general is not easily overcome who can form a true judgment of his own and the enemy's forces.

Valor is superior to numbers.

The nature of the ground is often of more consequence than courage.

Few men are born brave; many become so through training and force of discipline.

An army is strengthened by labor and enervated by idleness.

Troops are not to be led to battle unless confident of success.

Novelty and surprise throw an enemy into consternation, but common incidents have no effect.

He who rashly pursues a flying enemy with troops in disorder, seems bent upon throwing away that victory which he had before obtained.

An army unsupplied with grain and other necessary provisions risks being vanquished without striking a blow.

A general whose troops are superior both in number and bravery should engage in the oblong square, which is the first formation.

He who judges himself inferior should advance his right wing obliquely against the enemy's left. This is the second formation.

If your left wing is strongest, you must attack the enemy's right according to the third formation.

The general who can depend on the discipline of his men should begin the engagement by attacking both the enemy's wings at once, the fourth formation.

He whose light infantry is good should cover his center by forming them in its front and charge both the enemy's wings at once. This is the fifth formation.

He who cannot depend either on the number or courage of his troops, if obliged to engage, should begin the action with his right and endeavor to break the enemy's left, the rest of his army remaining formed in line perpendicular to the front and extended to the rear like a javelin. This is the sixth formation.

If your forces are few and weak in comparison to the enemy, you must make use of the seventh formation and cover one of your flanks either with an eminence, a city, the sea, a river or some protection of that kind.

A general who trusts to his cavalry should choose the proper ground for them and employ them principally in the action.

He who depends on his infantry should choose a situation most proper for them and make full use of them.

When an enemy's spy lurks in the camp, order all your soldiers in the day time to their tents, and he will instantly be apprehended.

On finding that the enemy has notice of your designs, you must immediately alter your plan of operations.

Consult with many on proper measures to be taken, but communicate the plans you intend to put in execution to few, and those only of the most assured fidelity. Or better, trust no one but yourself.

Punishment, and fear thereof, are necessary to keep soldiers in order in quarters; but in the field they are more influenced by hope and rewards.

Good officers never engage in general actions unless induced by opportunity or obliged by necessity.

To distress the enemy more by famine than the sword is a mark of consummate skill.

Many instructions might be given with regard to the cavalry. But as this branch of the service has been brought to perfection since the ancient writers and considerable improvements have been made in their drills and maneuvers, their arms, and the quality and management of their horses, nothing can be collected from those writers' works. Our present mode of discipline is sufficient.

Dispositions for action must be carefully concealed from the enemy, lest they should counteract them and defeat your plans by proper expedients.

This abridgment of the most eminent military writers, invincible Emperor, contains the maxims and instructions they have left us, approved by different ages and confirmed by repeated experience. The Persians admire your skill in archery; the Huns and Alans endeavor in vain to imitate your dexterity in horsemanship; the Saracens and other eastern warriors cannot equal your activity in the hunt; and even the masters-at-arms pique themselves on only part of that knowledge and expertness of which you give so many instances in their own profession. How glorious it is therefore for Your Majesty with all these qualifications to unite the science of war and the art of conquest, and to convince the world that by your conduct and courage you are equally capable of performing the duties of the soldier and the general!

ANONYMOUS (DATE UNKNOWN)

The Vigil of Venus

❧

*T*his beautiful hymn, the *Pervigilium Veneris,* materialized out of the ether sometime between the late second and early fourth centuries. Written in the tradition of festival hymns and set in Sicily, the sophisticated unknown poet celebrates in seven-foot trochaic lines familiar to Roman folk songs the springtime power of Venus, patron goddess of the Romans and source of all life and fertility. Its ardently romantic and sensuous description of nature is perhaps the most delicate and moving in the entire span of Roman literature. The poem's refrain, *Cras amet qui numquam amavit, quique amavit cras amet,* "Tomorrow he will love / Who has never loved. / Tomorrow he who has loved / Will love again," is musical and haunting.

Tomorrow he will love
Who has never loved.
Tomorrow he who has loved
Will love again.

Spring is new, the spring of birdsong.
In the spring our earth was born.
In the spring hearts come together.
In the spring the birds all mate.
And the trees undo their tresses to the rain.

Tomorrow he will love
Who has never loved.
Tomorrow he who has loved
Will love again.

Tomorrow Father Heaven
Held his marriage feast.
He made the whole year bloom
Out of his springtime showers,
Falling as husband rain
To the lap of his lovely wife,
Mixing the seeds to nourish all
In the warmth of her broad body.

Tomorrow he will love
Who has never loved.
Tomorrow he who has loved
Will love again.

Venus herself rules mind and matter
With an inward-stealing spirit.
The creatress governs all
With her secret strength.

Over the land, the heavens,
Over the deep-dug sea,
She sows her path of seed
In a straight and perfect course,
As she orders the world to know
The silent ways of birth.

Tomorrow he will love
Who has never loved.
Tomorrow he who has loved
Will love again.

Desire makes our world bear fruit;
It feels the spell of love.
We must hold the dark night back
And keep her vigil with our songs.

Tomorrow he will love
Who has never loved.
Tomorrow he who has loved
Will love again.

(FLAVIUS PETRUS SABBATIUS JUSTINIANUS)
JUSTINIAN (C. A.D. 482–565)

Institutes

~~⌒

*T*he last great emperor was born to a Latin-speaking Illyrian family in a village named Tauresium near Dardanian Naissus (modern Yugoslavia). He was educated in Constantinople and began his rule at the age of forty-five as co-emperor with his uncle and adopted father Justin I. He married the free-thinking actress Theodora, who, despite her loyalty and support of his best ambitions, has been blamed for some of the cruelties of his otherwise model career.

During his thirty-eight-year reign, Justinian's objective was to restore the Roman Empire to its former greatness by recovering the western provinces that had fallen to the barbarians in A.D. 476, reforming imperial administration, and modernizing and codifying the vast body of imperial law. He and his generals Narses, Belisarius, and Germanus managed to bring the endless war with Persia to a truce, reoccupy Rome, wrest Africa from the Vandals, route the Langobards on the Danube, overthrow the Italian kingdom of the Ostrogoth Theodoric, free Spain from the Visigoths, and quash another Persian incursion. Justinian had succeeded in reuniting the old Empire of the Caesars.

With the energy of Octavian, the education and literary bent of Julius Caesar, and the self-discipline of Marcus Aurelius, this "emperor who never sleeps," as he was called, lavishly patronized the arts and reconstructed forts, walls, bridges, roads, churches, and monuments (including Constantinople's St. Sophia) throughout the east and west. The dark side of his reign lay in his fierce suppression of paganism, heresies like Arianism, and Judaism, and his attempt to institute his own brand of Christian orthodoxy.

- Justinian's greatest achievement, his codification of Roman law known since the sixteenth century as the *Corpus Juris Civilis,* was commissioned in 528 and accomplished at his direction by the lawyer Tribonianus of Sidé.
- The *Corpus Justinianus,* as it is also called, is the primary source for preserving classical Roman jurisprudence. In addition to the *Institutes,* it consists of:

  - The twelve-book *Codex,* published in 534, a revised edition of a previously published code that is no longer extant—a compilation of previous imperial law from Hadrian to the time of Justinian;

- *Digesta,* a fifty-book subject-organized anthology of the thought of classical jurists;
- The *Novellae constitutiones (New Ordinances),* over 150 new codes made by Justinian himself;
- The *Institutiones,* from which the following excerpts were taken, was a handbook of jurisprudence for the use of law students.

1.9 FAMILY AUTHORITY

The people within our authority are our children, the offspring of a Roman law marriage. 1. Marriage, or matrimony, is the union of a man and a woman, committing them to a single path through life. 2. Our authority over our children is a right which only Roman citizens have. Nobody else has such extreme control over children. 3. Any child born to you and your wife is in your authority. The same is true of one born to your son and his wife. That is to say, your grandson and granddaughter are equally within your authority, and your great grandson and great granddaughter, and so on. Your daughter's child is not in your authority but in its father's.

1.10 MARRIAGE

A Roman law marriage is a marriage between Roman citizens who meet the law's requirements. Males must have reached puberty. Females must be sexually mature. They may be independent persons or dependents within authority. In the latter case they must have the consent of the head of their family. Logic and law alike require this. His approval must be given in advance. Can the daughter of someone who is insane marry, or can his son take a wife? There used to be differences of opinion about the son. Our own ruling settled the matter: we

took the case of the insane person's daughter as the model and extended permission to a son to contract a marriage without the father's co-operation, subject to restrictions set out in the pronouncement. 1. Next, we cannot marry any and every woman. Some unions have to be avoided. Marriage cannot be contracted between people in the relation of parent and child, for instance father and daughter or grandfather and granddaughter or mother and son or grandmother and grandson and so on up and down the line. A union within these degrees is evil and incestuous. If their relationship as parent and child is based on adoption, they still cannot marry; the same applies after the adoptive tie is broken. You cannot marry a girl who has become your daughter or granddaughter by adoption, not even if you have emancipated her. 2. A similar but less stringent regime applies to collaterals. Marriage is obviously forbidden between brother and sister, whether they have the same father and mother or are siblings with one common parent. There can be no marriage during the currency of the adoptive relationship between you and your adopted sister, but you can marry her once the adoptive tie is broken by her emancipation. If you yourself are emancipated the bar to marriage also goes. A man who wants to adopt his son-in-law must first emancipate his daughter, and one who wants to adopt his daughter-in-law should first emancipate his son. 3. One may not marry the daughter of one's brother or sister. Nor may one marry the granddaughter of one's brother or sister, despite the fact that that is a relationship in the fourth degree. A bar to marriage with a daughter always extends to the granddaughter. There is judged to be no bar to marrying the daughter of a woman adopted by your father, since in that case you are not related naturally or in the eyes of the law. 4. The children of two brothers or two sisters, or of a brother and sister, can marry. 5. Next, a man may not marry his paternal aunt even if the tie is only adoptive; nor his maternal aunt. These count as ascendants. On the same ground, marriage with a great aunt, paternal or maternal, is forbidden. 6. Respect for relationships created by marriage also obstructs some marriages. A man may not marry his step-daughter or his daughter-in-law because these both count as daughters. Obviously this bar must be taken to apply to someone who has at any time been your step-daughter or daughter-in-law. If she is still your daughter-in-law—she is married to your son—there is another bar to your marrying her: the same woman cannot be married to two men. If she is still your step-daughter—her mother is married to you—the reason you cannot marry her is that a man may not have two wives at once. 7. Marriage to a mother-in-law or step-mother is forbidden, since they count as mothers. This bar applies after the relationship through the marriage has ended. If the woman is still your step-mother, married to your father, the bar is the general rule against bigamy. If she is still your mother-in-law, in that her daughter is currently married to you, the mar-

riage would again be bigamous. 8. The law allows a husband's son or daughter by a former wife to marry a wife's daughter or son by a former husband. This is true even if they have a brother or sister born of the later marriage. 9. If you and your wife are divorced and then she has a daughter by another man, the girl is not of course your step-daughter. Yet Julian says that you ought not to marry her. In the same way he says that though a woman engaged to your son is not a daughter-in-law and one engaged to your father is not a mother-in-law the right and proper thing is not to contemplate marrying them. 10. There is no doubt that blood-relationship among slaves is also a bar to marriage. A father and daughter or brother and sister cannot marry after being freed. 11. There are also other people who for a variety of reasons are barred from marrying. We have agreed to these being listed in the Digest or Pandects, in which the classical law has been collected. 12. In a union which breaks these rules the law recognizes no husband, no wife, no wedding, no marriage, and no dowry. Children born of such a relationship are not in the authority of their father but so far as concerns family authority are in the same position as those conceived casually. They are considered fatherless, their fathers being unknown. Such sons are called spurious. The word comes from the Greek *sporaden*, meaning "scattered around," or perhaps from the letters of "sine patre filii" (sons without a father). When such a relationship breaks down there is no basis for claiming back a dowry. Those who enter these forbidden unions are also liable to punishments set out in imperial pronouncements. 13. Sometimes children excluded from family authority at birth are brought in later. One case is the natural son brought within paternal authority by virtue of being presented to his local council. Another is the son born to a free woman whom the father could lawfully have married but only lived with. Under our own pronouncement the subsequent execution of a marriage settlement brings such a son into his father's authority. Similar provision is made for other children too, so long as they are born of the same union. . . .

1.16 STATUS-LOSS

Status-loss is the exchange of one status for another and happens in three ways, namely in the first, the second—also called intermediate—or the third degree. 1. Status-loss in the first degree happens when a person loses his citizenship and his liberty together, as by the very harsh sentence of penal slavery, or where a freedman is found guilty of ingratitude to his patron, or where a man allows himself to be sold to share the price. 2. Second degree or intermediate status-loss means loss of citizenship but not liberty, as where a man is banished from home and hearth or transported to an island. 3. Third degree status-loss occurs where a man keeps both citizenship and freedom but alters his personal standing, as where an independent person passes into the authority of another, or vice versa. 4. A slave's manumission does not count as a status-loss, because as a slave he had no standing at all. 5. Where people suffer a set-back in honor rather than status, there is no status-loss. So, removal from the Senate is accepted not to be

a status-loss. 6. The proposition that cognate ties survive status-loss holds good only for the third degree. Then the tie does survive. But a status-loss in the first degree destroys even the cognatic link. This happens for instance where one's relative is enslaved. It does not even revive if he is manumitted. Transportation to an island also breaks cognatic relationship. 7. Though guardianship belongs to the agnatic relations, it does not devolve on all of them at once but only on the closest, or on all of them if they do all happen to be of the same degree.

1.17 STATUTORY GUARDIANSHIP
BY PATRONS

Again by virtue of the Twelve Tables, guardianship of freedmen and freedwomen is vested in their patrons and their patrons' descendants. This too is called statutory guardianship, not because provisions for it are spelled out in that code but because it has been evolved by an interpretation which treats it as though there were express provisions for it. The old jurists held that the fact that the code vested the estates of intestate freedmen and freedwomen in their patrons and their patrons' descendants meant that it intended to vest the guardianship in them too. They inferred this from its treatment of agnates: the code made them heirs and also imposed guardianship upon them. Generally the burden of guardianship ought to go with the benefit of succession. "Generally" is used advisedly, because if a child is given his freedom by a woman she is made heir but another person becomes guardian.

1.18 STATUTORY GUARDIANSHIP BY HEADS OF FAMILIES

Modeled on the case of patrons, another species of guardianship, also called statutory, has been evolved. If someone emancipates his son, or his daughter, or his grandchild through his son, and so on, and the person emancipated is still a young child, he himself becomes its statutory guardian.

1.19 FIDUCIARY GUARDIANSHIP

There is yet another case of guardianship, called fiduciary. If the head of the family emancipates his son, his daughter, or his grandchild, and the person emancipated is still a young child, he himself becomes statutory guardian. When he dies, his male children, if any, then become fiduciary guardians of their own son or sister or brother, and so on. By contrast where a patron is a statutory guardian and dies his children follow him as statutory guardians. The son of a person now dead, had he not been emancipated by his father in the father's life, would have become independent after the father's death. Authority over him would not have passed to the brother. Nor can the guardianship. By contrast if the freedman had stayed a slave the children of the owner would have stepped into the same relationship to him as their father before his death. The people in this category are only called upon to act as guardians if they are of full age. That is a rule which by our own pronouncement we have extended to every kind of guardianship and supervision. . . .

1.21 GUARDIAN'S ENDORSEMENT

A child needs his guardian's endorsement in some matters but not in others. If he takes a stipulation for a conveyance to himself he needs no endorsement. But if he makes a promise to someone else he must have it. The principle which applies is that he may improve his position without his guardian's endorsement but cannot make it worse without that backing. Where reciprocal obligations arise, as from sale, hire, mandate, and deposit, the outsider contracting with the child therefore becomes bound but the child incurs no obligation unless the guardian endorses. 1. A child cannot accept an inheritance, apply for estate-possession, or receive an inheritance under a trust without his guardian's endorsement, even though they may be profitable and not involve him in loss. 2. The guardian must be present when the business is done and give his backing there and then if he thinks it to the child's advantage. An endorsement given after an interval or by letter is a nullity. 3. A guardian cannot give his endorsement where his own interest is involved. If a matter between the child and the guardian has to go to trial the former practice was for the praetor to appoint someone to act as guardian, but now a supervisor is assigned instead. The case can proceed once he has taken over, and when it is finished his office ends.

2.1 THE CLASSIFICATION OF THINGS

. . . After persons in the previous book, we turn to things. They are either in the category of private wealth or not. Things can be: everybody's by the law of nature; the state's; a corporation's; or nobody's. But most things belong to individuals, who acquire them in a variety of ways, described below. 1. The things which are naturally everybody's are: air, flowing water, the sea, and the sea-shore. So nobody can be stopped from going on to the sea-shore. But he must keep away from houses, monuments, and buildings. Unlike the sea, rights to those things are not determined by the law of all peoples. 2. Rivers and harbors are state property. So everybody shares the right to fish in them. 3. The sea-shore extends as far as the highest winter tide. 4. The law of all peoples allows public use of river banks, as of the rivers themselves: everybody is free to navigate rivers, and they can moor their boats to the banks, run ropes from trees growing there, and unload cargo. But ownership of the banks is vested in the adjacent landowners. That also makes them owners of the trees which grow there. 5. The law of all peoples gives the public a similar right to use the sea-shore, and the sea itself. Anyone is free to put up a hut there to shelter himself. He can dry his nets, or beach his boat. The right view is that ownership of these shores is vested in no one at all. Their legal position is the same as that of the sea and the land or sand under the sea. 6. Corporate, as opposed to individual, property consists in things in towns like theaters, racecourses and so on, in fact in all the things vested in the citizen-body. 7. Sacred, religious, and sanctified things are owned by nobody. Things under divine law cannot belong to individuals. 8. Sacred things are those which have been ceremonially consecrated to God by priests, for instance churches, and also gifts solemnly dedicated to the service of God. Under our pronouncement such things must not be alienated or charged except for redeeming prisoners. If anyone tries to make something sacred himself for his own purposes, it does not become sacred but remains secular. The ground on which a church has been built remains sacred even after the building comes down. That is in Papinian. 9. Anyone can make a site religious by deciding to bury a dead body on land which he owns. A co-owner of land which is not religious cannot use it as a burial place without his colleague's consent. With a shared tomb it is different: burial by one does not need the others' consent. Where someone has ausufruct in the land the law is that the owner cannot make it religious unless the usufructuary consents. The land of a third party may be used for burial if its owner consents; the site does become religious even if his approval is given after the burial. 10. Sanctified things, such as city walls and gates, are also in a certain sense under divine law; they cannot become private property. We call them sanctified because anyone who offends against them faces a capital penalty. We use the word "sanctions" to describe the parts of statutes which specify the punishment for those who break their provisions. 11. Things become the property of individuals in many ways, some by the law of nature, which, as we have said, can be described as the law of all peoples, and others by our state law. It is easier to begin with the older law. Obviously natural law is earlier. It is the product of the natural order, as old as man himself. Systems of state law did not start to develop until cities were founded, magistracies were established, and law began to be written. 12. Wild animals, birds and fish, the creatures of land, sea and sky, become the property of the taker as soon as they are caught. Where something has no owner, it is reasonable that the person who takes it should have it. . . .

ROMAN GODS/HEROES AND THEIR GREEK COUNTERPARTS

ROMAN GODS/HEROES	GREEK COUNTERPART
Aesculapius	*Aesclepios*
Ajax	*Aias*
Apollo	*Apollo*
Ceres	*Demeter*
Cupid	*Eros*
Diana, Trivia	*Artemis*
Dis, or Pluton	*Hades*
Discordia	*Eris*
Faunus	*Pan*
Hercules	*Herakles*
Juno	*Hera*

ROMAN GODS/HEROES	GREEK COUNTERPART
Jupiter (Jove)	Zeus
Latona	Leto
Mars	Ares
Mercury	Hermes
Minerva	Athena
Neptune	Poseidon
Pollux	Polydeukes
Proserpina	Persephone
Saturn	Kronos
Sol Invictus	Helios
Ulysses	Odysseus
Venus	Aphrodite
Vesta	Hestia
Victoria	Nike
Vulcan	Hephaestus

LANDMARKS OF ROMAN HISTORY

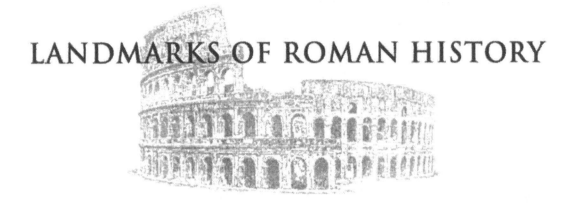

EARLY ROME

8th century B.C.	**Rome founded, Romulus, Remus**
753 B.C.	**April 21, traditional date for founding of Rome by Romulus**
753–715 B.C.	**Rule of Romulus**
753–509 B.C.	**PERIOD OF KINGS**
7th century B.C.	**Tarquinius Priscus**
616–579 B.C.	**Tarquinius Priscus**
6th century B.C.	**Servius Tullius, Tarquinius Superbus, Foundation of the Republic, Treaty with Carthage, Horatio Cocles**
579–534 B.C.	Servius Tullius
	Military reforms; creation of *comitia centuriata* to give more power to affluent plebians
	Treaty with the Latins
	Founding of Temple of Diana on the Aventine Hill
534–509 B.C.	Tarquinus Superbus ("the Proud")
	Forum drained to create urban center
509 B.C.	Tarquin expelled, last of the Etruscan kings
	Republic established

A Roman aqueduct, Costa del Sol, Spain, still in use

THE REPUBLIC

508 B.C.	First treaty with Carthage
	Founding of Temple of Jupiter on Capitoline Hill
	Horatius Cocles holds back Etruscan army at the Sublician Bridge
5th century B.C.	**Cincinnatus, Laws of the Twelve Tables**
498 B.C.	Temple of Saturn built
496 B.C.	Latins defeated at Battle of Lake Regillus
494–440 B.C.	Struggle of the Orders
493 B.C.	Latin League Treaty signed
491 B.C.	"Tribune of the plebs" established
458 B.C.	Cincinnatus called from his plowing to the dictatorship
451–450 B.C.	Laws of the Twelve Tables
445 B.C.	Canuleian Law gives plebs right of intermarriage with patricians
405–396 B.C.	Siege and conquest of Veii

4th century B.C.	War with Gauls, Second Treaty with Carthage, First Samnite War, Latin War, Conquests of Alexander the Great
390 B.C.	Roman army defeated by Gauls at Allia River
	After seven-month siege, Rome sacked
366 B.C.	First plebeian consul
348 B.C.	Second treaty with Carthage
343–341 B.C.	First Samnite War
340–338 B.C.	Latin War; Latin League dissolved
338 B.C.	Campania incorporated into Roman state
336 B.C.	Alexander the Great becomes king of Macedonia
335 B.C.	Alexander sacks Thebes
	Darius III becomes king of Persia
334 B.C.	Alexander crosses into Asia
	Battle of Granicus, conquest of Asia Minor
333 B.C.	Alexander defeats Dariuis at Battle of Issus
332 B.C.	Alexander lays siege to Tyre and Gaza
	Alexander enters Egypt
331 B.C.	Founding of Alexandria
	Alexander defeats Darius in Battle of Gaugamela, takes Mesopotamia, enters Babylon, Persepolis, and Pasargadae
330–328 B.C.	Alexander campaigns in Bactria and Sogdiana
327 B.C.	Alexander enters India
326 B.C.	Alexander crosses the Indus, wins battle of Hydaspes
	Conquest of Punjab; Alexander sails down the Indus to the Indian Ocean
325 B.C.	Alexander returns through Baluchistan, suffering great hardships in the desert
323 B.C.	Death of Alexander, age 32
321 B.C.	Roman army surrenders to Samnites at Caudine Forks
312 B.C.	Construction of the Via Appia, first Roman highway
	Acqua Appia begun, first aqueduct
	Plebs win right to become senators
310 B.C.	Murder of Alexander IV, son of Alexander the Great, and last member of the dynasty
	Rome advances into Etruria
307 B.C.	Demetrius the Besieger, son of Antigonus, conquers Athens
306–304 B.C.	Antigonus, Ptolemy, and Seleucus call themselves kings
301 B.C.	Destruction of power of Antigonus and Demetrius at Battle of Ipsus
	Antigonus killed

3rd century B.C.	**Ennius, Plautus, Hannibal, Livius Andronicus, Scipio Africanus**
298–290 B.C.	Third Samnite War; Rome's victory ensures its control of central Italy
297 B.C.	Death of Cassander, ruler of Macedon
297–272 B.C.	Career of Pyrrhus of Epirus
293 B.C.	Cult of Aesculapius introduced to Rome
290 B.C.	Final victory over the Samnites, completing Rome's domination of central Italy
287 B.C.	Hortensian law moves legislative power from aristocrats to plebeians, from the *Comitia Centuriata* to the *Comitia Tributa.*
285 B.C.	Demetrius the Besieger captured by Seleucus
283 B.C.	Ptolemy I Soter dies; Ptolemy II Philadelphus succeeds
281 B.C.	Lysimachus killed; Seleucus assassinated; his son Antiochus I succeeds
280–275 B.C.	War with Pyrrhus, who crosses into southern Italy to aid the Greek city-states against Rome
	Earliest Roman coinage
	Rome unrivaled power in southern Italy
279 B.C.	Invasion of Macedon and Greece by Gauls
276 B.C.	Antigonus Gonatas, son of Demetrius, defeats the Gauls; becomes king of Macedon, founding the Macedonian dynasty
275 B.C.	Pyrrhus defeated at Benevento, leaves Italy
	Romans control southern Italy
274–271 B.C.	First Syrian War between Ptolemy II and Antiochus I
267–262 B.C.	Chremonidean War; Ptolemy unsuccessfully supports Greek independence from Macedon; Antigonus Gonatas enters Athens
266 B.C.	Rome completes conquest of Italy to the Rubicon
264 B.C.	First gladiatorial contests in Rome
	Roman army enters Sicily to aid Mamertines against Carthage
	First Punic War (264–241) begins
263 B.C.	Hiero of Syracuse allies with Rome
261 B.C.	Antiochus II succeeds to Seleucid kingdom
260 B.C.	First Roman naval victory, at Mylae
260–253 B.C.	Second Syrian War between Ptolemy II and Antiochus II
c. 250 B.C.	Plautus born
246 B.C.	Ptolemy III succeeds to kingdom of Egypt
	Seleucus II succeeds to Seleucid kingdom
241 B.C.	Roman victory off Aegates Islands ends First Punic War
240 B.C.	Plays of Livius Andronicus staged
239 B.C.	Ennius born

235 B.C.	Doors of Janus' temple closed: Rome at peace with all nations
234 B.C.	Cato the Elder born
229–228 B.C.	First Illyrian War, against pirates along Illyrian coast
226 B.C.	Treaty of Ebro River with Carthage
225 B.C.	Invading Gauls defeated at battle of Telamon
221 B.C.	Hannibal, 25, takes command of Carthage's forces in Spain
	Rome allies with Saguntum in Spain
	Circus Flaminius built
220 B.C.	Via Flaminia begun
219 B.C.	Hannibal lays siege to and conquers Saguntum, then marches from Spain toward Italy
	Second Illyrian War against pirates
218–201 B.C.	Second Punic War: Hannibal invades Italy
218 B.C.	Hannibal crosses the Alps into Italy, defeats Romans at Trebia.
217 B.C.	Hannibal defeats Romans at Lake Trasimene; 15,000 Romans killed
216 B.C.	Hannibal defeats Romans at Cannae; 50,000 Romans killed
215 B.C.	Philip V of Macedon allies with Carthage
	Hannibal in southern Italy
	Roman victories in Spain
	Lex Oppia restricts women's jewelry
214–205 B.C.	First War of Rome with Philip V of Macedon
213 B.C.	Rome besieges Syracuse
212 B.C.	Rome besieges Capua
211 B.C.	Rome allies with Aetolian League
	Hannibal marches on Rome
	Capua and Syracuse fall
	Rome suffers defeats in Spain
211–206 B.C.	Scipio Africanus defeats Hasdrubal in Spain; Spain divided into two provinces
209 B.C.	Attalus I of Pergamum allies with Rome against Philip V
206–185 B.C.	Revolt and independence of Upper Egypt
c. 207 B.C.	Actors' guild founded
c. 205 B.C.	Production of Plautus' *Braggart Soldier*
205–204 B.C.	Scipio invades Africa
	Philip V of Macedon defeated
	Ennius arrives in Rome
203–200 B.C.	Philip V and Antiochus secretly ally against Egypt
	Fifth Syrian War: Antiochus seizes Syria
203 B.C.	Hannibal forced to leave Italy

202 B.C.	Scipio defeats Hannibal at Battle of Zama
	End of Second Punic War
	Carthage becomes dependent of Rome
2nd century B.C.	**Bion, Cato, Lucilius, Marius, Meleager, Nicander, Plautus, Polybius, Sulla, Terence, Tiberius Gracchus**
200–197 B.C.	Second Macedonian War between Rome and Philip V
	Philip V defeated at Cynoscephalae
196 B.C.	Rome declares the freedom of the Greeks at the Isthmus of Corinth
196–179 B.C.	Philip V rebuilds the power of Macedon
195 B.C.	*Lex Oppia* repealed
194 B.C.	Rome evacuates Greece
192–188 B.C.	Syrian War between Rome and Antiochus III after Antiochus invades Greece in 192
191 B.C.	Romans victorious at Thermopylae
	War against Antiochus III, who is forced out of Greece
190 B.C.	Romans invade Asia Minor, defeat Antiochus III at Magnesia
187 B.C.	Antiochus III dies
186 B.C.	Senate forbids Bacchic rites throughout Italy
185 B.C.	Birth of Terence
184 B.C.	Plautus dies
	Cato the Elder becomes censor
179 B.C.	Philip V of Macedon dies, succeeded by his son Perseus
175 B.C.	Antiochus IV Epiphanes succeeds to Seleucid Empire
172–167 B.C.	Third Macedonian War; Rome ends Macedonian kingdom at Battle of Pydna (168); divides territory into four republics.
	Rome orders Antiochus IV out of Egypt
	Rome declares Delos a free port
	Desecration of the temple at Jerusalem brings Jewish resistance to a head against Antiochus' hellenizing policy
169 B.C.	Ennius dies
	Lex Voconia restricts financial freedom of women
167 B.C.	Polybius brought to Rome, with 1,000 Greek hostages
166 B.C.	Terence's *Andria* produced at *Ludi Megalenses*
164 B.C.	Death of Antiochus IV
	Maccabean Revolt
161 B.C.	Greek philosophers expelled from Rome
160 B.C.	Cato's *On Agriculture*

	Terence's *Brothers* produced at funeral games of Aemilius Paulus
159 B.C.	Terence dies
149 B.C.	Third Punic War begins
	Rebellion in Macedonia
	Cato the Elder dies
148 B.C.	Fourth Macedonian War, and war against Achaian League
146 B.C.	Rome razes Carthage, ending Third Punic War
	Rome destroys Corinth, dissolves Achaian League
142 B.C.	Independence of the Jews
141 B.C.	Parthians attack Babylon
137 B.C.	Roman army defeated at Numantia in Spain

THE LATE REPUBLIC

136–132 B.C.	First Sicilian Slave War, ended by Roman army
134–133 B.C.	Numantia besieged and destroyed by Scipio
133 B.C.	Tiberius Gracchus initiates land reforms
131 B.C.	Lucilius' *Satires* published
130 B.C.	Antiochus VII dies fighting the Parthians
129 B.C.	Attalus III of Pergamum bequeaths his kingdom to Rome, as Asian province
125 B.C.	M. Fulvius Flaccus proposes enfranchising the Latins
123–122 B.C.	Tribunates of Caius Gracchus
121 B.C.	First use of *senatus consultum ultimum* to authorize massacre of Gracchus and Gracchan supporters
	Gallia Narbonensis becomes Roman province
118–117 B.C.	Roman campaigns in Dalmatia
116 B.C.	Varro born
112–105 B.C.	War against Jugurtha of Numidia ended by Marius
107–100 B.C.	Marius consul six times, reforms the army
	Marius campaigns against Jugurtha in Africa
106 B.C.	Cicero born
105 B.C.	Roman army destroyed at Orange by invading Germans
	Marius defeats Numidians
104–102 B.C.	Second Sicilian Slave War
102–101 B.C.	Marius defeats Teutones and Cimbri at Aquae Sextiae and Vercellae
100 B.C.	Julius Caesar born

1st century B.C.	Agrippa, Antony, Brutus, Cassius, Catullus, Julius Caesar, Cicero, Cleopatra, Crassus, Diodorus Siculus, Horace, Decimus Laberius, Lepidus, Livy, Lucretius, Maecenas, Octavian, Ovid, Pompey, Propertius, Publilius Syrus, Sallust, Seneca the Elder, Spartacus, Strabo, Sulla, Sulpicia, Tiberius, Tibullus, Varro, Virgil, Vitruvius
99–98 B.C.	Lucretius born
91–88 B.C.	Reforms of Livius Drusus lead to Social War between Rome and Italian allies demanding citizenship; Rome defeats allies by force and offers of citizenship
88 B.C.	Sulla marches on Rome
	Mithridates of Pontus invades Asia Minor
88–85 B.C.	Mithridates conquers Greece
	Greece conquered by Sulla
88–82 B.C.	Civil War between Marius and Sulla
87 B.C.	Sulla receives Greek command, moves to besiege Athens
	Violence between plebs and aristocrats
	Marius and Cinna sieze Rome
86 B.C.	Marius dies
	Sallust born
	Sulla defeats Mithridates, captures Athens
83–82 B.C.	Sulla returns to Italy: Civil War
	Second Mithridatic War
82 B.C.	Sulla appointed dictator of Rome, undertakes reforms and restores Senate's powers
80 B.C.	Cicero delivers first oration, defending Sextus Roscius against parricide charges
80 B.C.	Sulpicia flourishes
80–79 B.C.	Sulla resigns
78 B.C.	Sulla dies
77 B.C.	Cicero quaestor of Sicily
74–63 B.C.	Third Mithridatic War
73–71 B.C.	Slave revolt of Spartacus, put down by Pompey and Crassus
	Verres governor of Sicily
70 B.C.	Consulate of Crassus and Pompey
	Virgil born
	Cicero, as aedile, prosecutes Verres for extortion from his province
66–62 B.C.	Pompey's eastern campaign gains new territories for Rome; he reaches Jerusalem

66 B.C.	Cicero unanimously elected praetor
65 B.C.	Horace born
63 B.C.	Octavian born
	Caesar elected *Pontifex Maximus*
	Consulship of Cicero
	Pompey takes Jerusalem
	Catilian conspiracy
	Mithridates dies
62 B.C.	Pompey returns to Italy, disbands army
	Catullus arrives in Rome?
	Catiline arrested and executed
61 B.C.	Trial and acquittal of P. Clodius on religious charge
60 B.C.	First Triumvirate formed: Pompey, Crassus, and Caesar
59 B.C.	Consulate of Caesar: legislation in favor of triumvirs
	Pompey marries Caesar's daughter Julia
	Livy born
58–57 B.C.	Cicero's exile and return
	Cicero strives to alienate Pompey and Caesar
58–49 B.C.	Caesar campaigns in and conquers Gaul
58 B.C.	Clodius tribune, distributes free grain
56 B.C.	Triumvirate renewed at Luca
55–54 B.C.	Caesar invades Britain
55 B.C.	Theater of Pompey, first stone theater in Rome, constructed
	Lucretius dies
	Seneca the Elder born
54 B.C.	Julia dies, severing link between Caesar and Pompey
	Crassus campaigns in Syria
	Catullus dies
	Tibullus born
53 B.C.	Crassus' army defeated at Carrhae; he is killed by the Parthians. End of First Triumvirate
52 B.C.	Clodius murdered by Milo in gang warfare
	Pompey elected sole consul
51–50 B.C.	Cicero, governor of Cilicia, writes *De Republica*
	Caesar publishes *Commentaries on the Gallic Wars*
	Publilius Syrus flourishes
49 B.C.	On January 10, Caesar crosses Rubicon, defying Senate's orders
	Pompey leaves for Greece

49–45 B.C.	Civil War
48 B.C.	Caesar defeats Pompey at Pharsalus
	Pompey murdered in Egypt
	Great Library of Alexandria destroyed by fire
	Caesar meets Cleopatra
47–44 B.C.	Dictatorship of Julius Caesar
	He campaigns against republicans in Spain, Africa, and the east
47 B.C.	Battle of Zela
	Caesar appoints Varro public librarian
46 B.C.	Cato commits suicide at Utica
	Caesar victorious at Thapsus
	Forum Julius dedicated
45 B.C.	Caesar defeats republicans at Munda; returns from Spain
	Publilius Syrus defeats mimist Laberius in public contest
	January 1: Julian calendar introduced
44 B.C.	Caesar is assassinated on the Ides of March
	Marc Antony controls Rome
	Cicero's *Philippics* attack Marc Antony
	Civil War begins between assassins and Mark Antony and Octavian, Caesar's heir

THE SECOND TRIUMVIRATE AND THE AGE OF AUGUSTUS

43 B.C.	First consulate of Octavian
	Antony campaigns in Cisalpine Gaul
	Senate declares Antony enemy of the state
	Octavian defeats Antony at Mutina
	Senate refuses consulship to Octavian
	Octavian marches on Rome
	Octavian reconciles with Antony, forming Second Triumvirate with him and Lepidus; their opponents, including Cicero, murdered
	Ovid born
42 B.C.	Lepidus consul
	Octavian and Antony defeat republicans at Philippi: Brutus and Cassius commit suicide
	Tiberius born
	Cisalpine Gaul incorporated into Italy

41–40 B.C.	Perusia rebels against Octavian; is besieged and quashed
41–32 B.C.	Antony in the east, meets Cleopatra
c. 41 B.C.	Sallust publishes history of Jugurthan War
40 B.C.	Antony marries Octavian's sister Octavia
	Pact of Brundisium
	Lepidus commands Africa, Antony the east, and Octavian the west
39 B.C.	First public library established
38 B.C.	Octavian marries Livia Drusilla
37 B.C.	Renewal of Second Triumvirate
36 B.C.	Sacrosanctity of tribunate conferred on Octavian
	Lepidus's attempted coup fails; he's allowed to retire, as *Pontifex Maximus*
	Antony defeated by Parthians
36–35 B.C.	Campaigns against Sextus Pompeius
34 B.C.	Sallust dies
33 B.C.	Maecenas gives Horace farm in Sabine Hills
	Octavian returns from Dalmatia for second consulship
	Second Triumvirate ends
32 B.C.	Final breach between Octavian and Antony
31 B.C.	Senate strips Antony of his powers
	Octavian sent to war against Cleopatra, defeats her and Antony at Actium, September 2
31–23 B.C.	Octavian consul; he controls Roman world
30 B.C.	Civil War between Octavian and Antony ends
	Antony and Cleopatra commit suicide at Alexandria
	Rome annexes Egypt
	Horace publishes *Epodes*
29 B.C.	Octavian returns from Egypt; celebrates his victories at Illyricum, Actium, and Egypt
	Marcus Crassus' expedition against the Dacians triumphant
	Virgil completes *Georgics*
28 B.C.	Census held: 4,063,000 citizens
	82 Roman temples restored

IMPERIAL OR JULIO-CLAUDIAN PERIOD

27 B.C.	*Imperium* for ten years conferred on Octavian in his seventh consulship
	Title of "Augustus" bestowed

	Augustus "restores" the Republic
	Provinces divided into imperial and senatorial
27–25 B.C.	Agrippa completes Pantheon
	Varro dies
27–24 B.C.	Augustus in Spain and Gaul
25 B.C.	Marcellus marries Julia
	Galatia made a province
	Expedition to Arabia Felix
	Augustus reorganizes Africa
23 B.C.	Augustus confirmed as *proconsular imperium,* with *tribunicia potestas* for life and special privileges
	Marcellus dies
	Horace publishes first three books of *Odes*
22 B.C.	Augustus declines dictatorship and perpetual censorship, accepts *cura annonae*
22–19 B.C.	Augustus campaigns in Greece and Asia
21 B.C.	Agrippa made *praefectus urbi,* marries Julia
20 B.C.	Strabo's *Historical Sketches*
	Peace with Parthians, who return standards captured at Carrhae
	Building of Temple of Mars
19 B.C.	Agrippa defeats Cantabri, completes conquest of northwest Spain
	Virgil and Tibullus die
	Aeneid published by Augustus
18 B.C.	*Leges Juliae* regulate marriage and adultery
	Augustus organizes corn supply
	Agrippa made *proconsul imperium* and *tribunicia potestas*
17 B.C.	Augustus adopts grandsons Gaius and Lucius Caesar and Agrippa Postumus
	Holds *Ludi saeculares* (secular games), celebrated by Horace's *Carmen Saeculare*
16 B.C.	Death of Lollius in Gaul
	Alpine tribes and Raetians subdued
15–13 B.C.	Augustus campaigns in Gaul
13 B.C.	Tiberius consul
	Agrippa campaigns in Pannonia
12 B.C.	Agrippa dies
	Augustus becomes *Pontifex Maximus* when Lepidus dies
12–9 B.C.	Drusus in Germany, *legatus of Tres Galliae*
	Tiberius campaigns in Pannonia

12 B.C.	Tiberius forced to divorce Vipsania Agrippina and marry Augustus' daughter Julia
11 B.C.	Octavia dies
9 B.C.	Tiberius receives *proconsul imperium*
	Drusus dies
8 B.C.	Census: 4,233,000 citizens
	Tiberius campaigns in Germany
	Maecenas and Horace die
6 B.C.	Tiberius receives *tribunicia potestas*. Retires to Rhodes
5 B.C.	Gaius Caesar enters public life
4 B.C.	Herod the Great, King of Judaea, dies
	Jesus Christ born
	Seneca the Younger born
2 B.C.	Augustus consul for the thirteenth time
	Lucius Caesar enters public life
	Augustus receives title *Pater Patriae*; he exiles Julia
	He dedicates the Forum of Augustus
1st century A.D.	Agricola, Agrippina, Augustus, Britannicus, Celsus, Claudius, Columella, Corbulo, Domitian, Frontinus, Galba, Germanicus, Josephus, Juvenal, Livy, Lucan, Martial, Nero, Nerva, Persius, Petronius, Piso, Pliny the Elder, Pliny the Younger, Poppaea, Quintilian, Seneca the Younger, Silius Italicus, Statius, Suetonius, Tacitus, Tiberius, Titus, Trajan, Valerius Maximus, Vespasian
2	Lucius Caesar dies
	Tiberius returns from Rhodes
4	Gaius Caesar dies
	Augustus adopts Tiberius, invests him with *tribunicia potestas* for ten years
	Tiberius adopts Germanicus
	Tiberius campaigns in Germany
6–9	Campaign against the Marcomanni
	Pannonia and Dalmatia rebel
8	Ovid exiled to Tomis
9	Ambush and massacre of Varus by Arminius
	Pannonian Revolt
13	Tiberius receives power equal to Augustus
14	Census: 4,937,000 citizens
	Augustus dies

44	Herod Agrippa, King of Judaea, dies
47	*Ludi Saeculares* held
49	Claudius marries Agrippina
	Seneca recalled from exile by Agrippina to tutor Nero
50	Claudius adopts Nero
	Basilica built at Porta Maggiore
51	Burrus appointed prefect of the Praetorian Guard
53	Nero marries Octavia
54	Claudius dies, poisoned by Agrippina, Nero's mother
	Nero emperor (54–68)
	Parthian War
	Corbulo begins command in east
55	Britannicus dies
56	Tacitus born
57	Corbulo advances into Armenia
58	Corbulo captures Artaxata
	Otho sent to Lusitania
59–61	Suetonius Paulinus campaigns in Britain
59	Nero murders his mother Agrippina
60	Britain, under Boudicca, rebels
61	Paulinus quashes Boudiccan rebellion
62	Nero has wife Octavia killed; marries Poppaea Sabina
	Burrus dies
	First books of Lucan's *Bellum Civile* published
64	Rome burns for nine days: Christians blamed and persecuted
	Josephus arrives in Rome, befriended by Poppaea Sabina
65	Conspiracy of Piso: Seneca, Lucan, Petronius Arbiter, and Poppaea die at Nero's order
66	Nero campaigns in Greece
66–73	Jewish revolt
67	Corbulo dies
	Vespasian campaigns against Jews, captures Jerusalem
68	Revolt of Vindex
	Galba proclaimed emperor
	Nero commits suicide
	House of Caesar ends

FLAVIAN DYNASTY (69–96)

69	Year of the Four Emperors: Galba, Otho, Vitellius, Vespasian (69–79; proclaimed emperor July 1)
70	Vespasian campaigns in Italy, Titus in Judaea
	Titus captures and destroys Jerusalem
71	Triumph of Vespasian and Titus in Italy
	Plague and fire in Rome
73	Vespasian and Titus censors
75	Vespasian dedicates Forum of Peace
77–78	Agricola arrives in Britain
	Pliny the Elder publishes *Natural History*
78–85	Agricola campaigns in Britain
79	Vespasian dies
	Titus emperor
	Vesuvius' eruption destroys Herculaneum and Pompeii (August 24)
	Pliny the Elder dies exploring the aftermath of the eruption.
80	Rome burns; Vespasian's Temple of Jupiter on the Capitoline destroyed
	Colosseum inaugurated
81	Titus dies
	Domitian emperor (81–96)
	Tacitus quaestor
82	Arch of Titus constructed celebrating Jewish victory
83–84	Domitian defeats Agri Decumates, takes title "Germanicus"; recalls Agricola from Britain
85–89	War against the Dacians
85	Victory at Battle of Mons Graupius
	Domitian's palace built on Palatine Hill
86	Martial publishes *Epigrams*
88	*Ludi Saeculares* held
	Tacitus praetor
88–89	Rebellion of army commander Saturninus quashed
92	Marcomanni, Quadi, and Iazyges attack Pannonia
	Statius publishes *Thebaid*
93	Agricola dies
95	Flavius Clemens executed
96	Domitian dies
	Statius dies

	Nerva emperor
	Trajan campaigns on northern frontier
97	Nerva adopts Trajan
	Tacitus *consul suffectus*
	Nerva appoints Frontinus superintendent of waterworks
98	Nerva dies
	Soranus born
	Trajan emperor
	Tacitus' *Germania* and *Agricola* published
99	Trajan arrives in Rome

AGE OF THE ANTONINES

2nd century A.D.	Antoninus Pius, Apollodorus, Apuleius, Aulus Gellius, Commodus, Epictetus, Fronto, Gaius, Galen, Hadrian, Justin Martyr, Juvenal, Lucian, Lucius Verus, Marcus Aurelius, Pausanius, Pliny the Younger, Ptolemy, Septimius Severus, Soranus, Suetonius, Tertullian, Trajan
100	Hadrian marries Trajan's grandniece Vibia Sabina
	Juvenal's first satires appear
	Quintilian dies
101	Silius Italicus dies
101–2	First Dacian War, conducted by Trajan
105–6	Trajan's Second Dacian War
109–11	Pliny the Younger serves in Bithynia
112	Trajan's Forum dedicated
	Hadrian archon of Athens
113	Trajan campaigns in the east
	Pliny the Younger dies
114	Hadrian governor of Syria
114–17	Trajan's Parthian War: Rome annexes Armenia and Mesopotamia
115	Trajan captures Parthian capital Ctesiphon
115–17	Jewish revolt
	Empire reaches widest expanse
117	Trajan dies
	Tacitus dies
	Hadrian emperor, abandons Parthian territory

ANTONINE PERIOD

168–75	German wars of Marcus Aurelius
169	Lucius Verus dies
170	Galen granted position in imperial court
	German tribes invade northern Empire
176	Commodus becomes emperor consort
178	Marcus Aurelius campaigns on northern frontier
180	Marcus Aurelius dies
	Commodus emperor
	Gaius dies
192	Commodus murdered on December 31
193	Four emperors compete for power
	Column of Marcus Aurelius completed
193–97	Civil wars
197	Septimius Severus defeats Clodius Albinus, last of the competing emperors, at Lyon
	Tertullian defends Christians
197–98	Severus wars against Parthians

SEVERAN DYNASTY

3rd century A.D.	**Athenaeus, Aurelian, Caracalla, Diocletian, Heliodorus, Longus, Paulus, Plotinus, Severus**
208–11	Severus campaigns in Britain, dies at York
212	Constitution of Antoniniana grants citizenship to all free inhabitants of the Empire
213	Caracalla campaigns against Alamanni at the Rhine-Danube border
215	Caracalla campaigns in Asia Minor against Parthians but is defeated in Armenia
216	Baths of Caracalla completed
226	Ardashir the Sassanian, King of kings in Iran, begins four hundred years of war with the Roman Empire
235–85	Fifty years of anarchy
244	Plotinus begins teaching in Rome
247–70	Army declares thirty generals emperors
250	Christians persecuted by Decius
251	Goth invasions in northern Empire begin
267	Heruli Goths invade Greece

270	Plotinus dies
	Aurelian (270–75) builds wall around Rome
272	Aurelian captures Palmyra

THE LATE EMPIRE

274	Aurelian recaptures Gallic empire
283	Carus captures Persian capital Ctesiphon
287	Carausius proclaims his own empire in Britain
293	Diocletian (284–305) establishes the Tetrarchy (four-man rule), with himself ruling the east and Maximian the west.
296	Britain reassimilated into western Empire
4th century A.D.	**Ausonius, Claudian, Constantine, Diocletian, Julian, Theodosius**
301	Diocletian's edict on wage and price controls
303	Christians persecuted
305	Diocletian and Maximian abdicate
306–37	Constantine the Great
312	Constantine I invades Italy
	Defeats Maxentius at battle of Milvian Bridge under the "sign of the cross": Edict of Milan declares Christianity a legitimate religion
315	Arch of Constantine constructed
324	Constantine defeats Licinius, becomes sole emperor; founds Constantinople
325	Council of Nicaea
330	Constantine transfers seat of Empire to Constantinople
331	Julian born
355	Julian emperor
357	Julian forces Germanic tribes back across Rhine
	Julian defeats Alemanni at Battle of Argentorate
360–63	Julian sole emperor, tries to revive paganism
364	Ausonius named tutor to Gratian
367	Theodosius suppresses invasion of Britain
376	Valens allows Visigoths to enter Empire to strengthen frontier zone.
378	Valens campaigns against Visigoths, but is routed—and killed—at the battle of Adrianople
378–95	Theodosius the Great emperor
382	St. Jerome arrives in Rome to work on new version of Bible
383	Gratian assassinated

391	Theodosius bans paganism, closes ancient temples
395	Empire divided into east and west by sons of Theodosius
	Alaric's Visigoths invade Thrace and Macedonia
5th century A.D.	**Alaric, Avianus, Honorius, Macrobius, Odoacer, Romulus Augustulus, Stilicho, Theodoric, Vegetius**
401	Alaric invades Italy
402	Stilicho and Vandals repel Visigoths
	Honorius (395–423) moves imperial court to Ravenna
403	Alaric invades Italy again
406	Vandals invade Gaul
407–8	Constantine III crosses from Britain into Gaul, establishes court at Arles; creates new Gallic empire; pacifies Britain, Gaul, Germany, and Spain
408	Stilicho executed by Honorius, for supposed alliance with Alaric
409	Vandals invade Spain
410	Rome abandons Britain; end of Roman Britain
	On August 24, Alaric sacks Rome
412	Visigoths seize southwestern Gaul
413–26	Augustine's *City of God* defines Christian perfection
419	Visigoths form kingdom within Roman Gaul
429	Gaiseric's Vandals cross the Straits of Gibraltar into Africa
438	Law code of Theodosius
439	Vandals conquer Carthage and Africa
451	Visigoths and Romans under Aetius defeat Attila's Huns in Gaul.
452	Attila and the Huns invade Italy, dissuaded from sacking Rome by Pope Leo I
455	Vandals under Gaiseric sack Rome
476	Romulus Augustulus deposed by Odoacer: end of Roman Empire in the west
c. 482	Justinian born
489	Zeno asks Theodoric, King of Ostrogoths, to reclaim Italy for the eastern empire
493	Theodoric defeats Odoacer and becomes King of Italy (493–526)
6th century A.D.	**Justinian**
527–65	Justinian, eastern emperor, reconquers Italy, Dalmatia, parts of Spain, and Africa
528	Justinian commissions new codification of Roman law
532	Justinian achieves truce with Persia
533	Justinian recovers Africa from Vandals

534	Justinian publishes his *Digest* of laws
540	Justinian overthrows Italian kingdom of Ostrogoth Theodoric
552	Justinian frees Spain from Visigoths
7th century A.D.	
633–55	Arabs conquer Syria, Egypt, and the Sassanid Empire
15th century A.D.	
1453	Ottoman Turks conquer Constantinople and end eastern Roman Empire

GLOSSARY

Accius. Latin tragic poet, 170–c. 86 B.C.; author of *Bacchae*, based on Euripides' play of the same name.

Acestes. Legendary king of Seqesta (Greek: Eqesta) in Sicily; welcomed the Trojans in their wanderings.

Achaia (Achaians, Achaea, Achaeans). Generic word for "Greeks" in the Homeric epics, referring to southeast Thessaly and the north coast of the Peloponesian peninsula. Achaians, Argives, and Danaans are all used indiscriminately by Homer and the tragic dramatists to denote the people later called Hellenes.

Achates. Faithful comrade of Aeneas.

Achelous. The longest and most celebrated river in Greece, rising on Mount Pindus in central Epirus, flowing through Acarnania, and emptying into the Ionian Sea at the entrance to the Corinthian Gulf. Also the god of this river, who was one of the most important of the numerous river-gods.

Acheron. A river in southern Epirus, known for its wild gorge that was considered to be the entrance to Hades.

Achilles (Greek: Achilleus). King of the Myrmidons; son of the mortal Peleus and sea nymph Thetis; father of Neoptolemus; the preeminent Greek warrior at Troy; and the principal hero of Homer's *Iliad*. The Trojan War had its start at the wedding feast of this hero's parents. Eris ("Discord") was the one grace not invited. In her anger, she dropped a golden apple onto the dance floor, inscribed "to the fairest." Hera, Aphrodite, and Athena reached to pick it up simultaneously. The judgment of Paris was the aftermath, and the awarding of the apple to Aphrodite in exchange for the love of Helen. When Paris came to Menelaos' court, met and wooed her, then returned with her to Troy, Menelaos appealed to his brother Agamemnon, king of Mycenae and of the Achaian confederacy. Agamemnon led the Greek fleet against Troy to bring her back. Insulted in the ninth year of the war by Agamemnon, Achilles withdrew from the fighting only to return to battle to avenge the death of his best friend Patroklos, slain by Hector. The death of Hector at Achilles' hands virtually ended the Trojan

War, returning Helen to her Achaean husband Menelaos. Achilles, as was predicted to his mother Thetis, was finally slain by Paris the archer, whose arrow hit him in the one part of his body that she had not protected with magic: his "Achilles' tendon."

Actaeon. Legendary hunter and grandson of Cadmus, who witnessing Artemis and her nymphs bathing, was changed by the goddess into a stag and torn to pieces by his own dogs.

Actium. Promontory on the west coast of Greece where Octavian defeated Antony and Cleopatra in 31 B.C.

Adherbal. Numidian prince, son of Micipsa, slain by Jugurtha.

Admetus (Greek: Admetos). King of Pherae in Thessaly; husband of Alcestis; son of Pheres. Hero of Euripides' *Alcestis*, granted a new lease on life if he could find someone who loved him enough to die in his stead. Alcestis, his wife, agreed to the bargain, making him promise never to marry again. The result was grief for his entire kingdom, a situation remedied by the coming of Hercules in Euripides' play.

Adonis. Beautiful youth brought up by the Nymphs and so beloved by Aphrodite that after his death, from a boar's wound or by the arrow of Artemis, she was allowed to bring him back to earth for half of each year. Symbolizes the agricultural cycle. Annual festivals, the Adonia, were presided over by women in various parts of Greece.

Adrastus. King of Argos, one of the famous "Seven" who fought against Thebes to support Polyneices' claim on its throne.

Aeacus. King of Aegina; grandfather of Achilles; later a judge of the dead.

aedile. Civic administrative office, below praetor, dealing with temples, streets, corn supply, and the organization of public games.

Aedui. Powerful Gallic tribe.

Aeneas. Trojan hero in the *Iliad*, son of Aphrodite and the mortal Anchises, protected by her in battle. After the fall of Troy, according to the legend made famous by Virgil's *Aeneid*, he led a band of Trojan survivors to Italy, where his descendants founded Rome.

Aeolus. Ruler of the winds, described in Homer's *Odyssey* as living on a floating island with his intermarried sons and daughters. Also, the first ruler of Thessaly, ancestor of the Aeolians.

Aesculapius. God of healing; son of Apollo and the nymph Coronis. A temple was built for him in 293 B.C. on an island in the Tiber. His festival is celebrated in January.

Aeson. King of Thessaly; father of Jason, who drank fatal bull's blood when it seemed that the Argonauts were lost.

Aetolia. North of Achaia and Locris, and east of Acarnania, wild and mountainous region in

View of stadium floor, amphitheater, Italica

western Greece, scene of many hunting legends, including the famous Caledonian boar hunt. Its favorite gods were Artemis, Apollo, and Athena.

Africus. The southwest wind.

Agamemnon. Son of Atreus; brother of Menelaos; king of Mycenae; leader of the Greek forces against Troy. His insult to Achilles is the inciting incident of Homer's *Iliad.* Upon his return to Mycenae after the war, with Priam's daughter Cassandra in tow as his trophy bride, Agamemnon was slain by his wife Klytaimnestra and her lover Aegisthus. The regicide, in turn, provoked vengeance by their children Orestes and Elektra.

Aganippe. Naiad, her sacred spring on Mount Helicon in Boeotia; associated with the Muses.

Agenor. Father of Cadmus and an ancestor of Dido. "Agenorean" is sometimes used instead of "Theban."

Agricola. The father-in-law of Tacitus and governor of Britain.

Agrippa. (1) Marcus Vipsanius (63–12 B.C.) Noted military commander under Augustus and one of his chief counselors. He helped Augustus defeat Sextus Pompeius and Marc Antony, and built the Pantheon. (2) Postumus. Son of the former, put to death early in the reign of Tiberius.

Agrippina. Mother of Nero, murdered at his order.

Aias (Roman: Ajax). Son of Telamon of Salamis, a powerful hero in Homer's *Iliad.* Sophocles made his suicide the subject of his *Aias.*

Alba. Mountain near Rome, considered sacred by the early Romans; later associated with the Muses.

Alban Lake. Fifty miles southeast of Rome, famous for its wines.

Alba Longa. Mother city of Rome founded c. 1152 B.C. by Ascanius, situated in the hills south of Rome.

Alcestis. Daughter of Pelias; wife of Admetus of Pherae, heroine of Euripides' play *Alcestis,* which tells the story of her death on behalf of her husband.

Alcibiades. Athenian, son of Cleinias; known for his charismatic good looks; born around 450 B.C. Socrates saved his life at the Battle of Potidaea, in 432. Of a noble and wealthy family and raised in Pericles' household, Alcibiades was frustrated in his ambitions to become one of Athens' greatest leaders because his lack of self-discipline never allowed him to win the citizens' complete confidence.

Alcides. Hercules.

Alexander the Great. Son of Philip of Macedon, succeeded his father as king in 336 B.C. He became a phenomenal conqueror who spread Hellenic culture and civilization over a large part of the Near East.

Alexandria. City in Egypt renamed after himself by Alexander, center of "Alexandrian" culture from the third century B.C. Here Alexander's general Ptolemy I established his central government and the great library that preserved most of what we have of Greek texts, containing in its heyday over half a million volumes. The library's "museum" was a residential center for writers, scientists, and scholars.

Althaea. Wife of Oeneus, king of Calydon; mother of Meleager. When Meleager slew her brothers during a boar hunt, she took revenge by burning the firebrand on which his life depended.

Ammon. A name of Jupiter. There was a shrine to him in an oasis in the Libyan desert.

Amphiaraus. Priest and prophet of Argos, one of the Seven against Thebes.

Amphion. Son of Jupiter and Antiope; brother of Zethus; founder king of Thebes; and husband of Niobe. He played the lyre so beautifully the stones of Thebes moved into place at his music.

Amphitryon. Grandson of Perseus; son of Alcaeus; husband of Alcmena. Hercules called "Amphitryon's son."

Anchises. Son of Capys; member of the royal house of Troy. His marriage to Venus (Aphrodite) led to the birth of Aeneas, Trojan hero and founder of Rome.

Ancus (Ancus Marcius). Fourth of the seven kings of Rome (640–16 B.C.).

Anna. Sister of Dido; heroine of Virgil's *Aeneid.*

Antiochus. Seleucid king of Asia.

Antiope. Mythical Theban heroine; mother by Jupiter of Amphion and Zethus, who killed her tormentors; also a play by Pacuvius.

Antony (Marcus Antonius) (c. 82–30 B.C.). Friend of Julius Caesar; member of the Second Triumvirate. He and Cleopatra were defeated by Octavian at the Battle of Actium, 31 B.C.

Anubis. Dog- or jackal-headed attendant god of the Egyptian goddess Isis and her brother and consort, the god Osiris. As god of the dead, his cult was brought to Rome during the Empire.

Appius Claudius. Consul in 451 B.C., one of the decemvirs appointed to draw up a written code of laws. His attempted rape of Virginia is said to have led to the overthrow of the decemvirs.

Apollo. Son of Jupiter (Zeus) and Latona (Leto); brother of Diana (Artemis); father of the singer Linus; god of the sun who kept his name among the Romans, primarily as the god of poetry but also as a healer, patron of shepherds, and god of prophecy, inspiration, and divination. The Cumaean Sibyl celebrated by Virgil was a priestess of Apollo. Also known as Phoebus.

Apulia. Wild territory in southeast Italy.

Aquarius. The water carrier; one of the signs of the zodiac.

Aquilo. North wind.

Arachne. A Lydian maiden, skillful at weaving. Minerva changed her into a spider.

Arbuscula. Well-known actress of Cicero's circle.

Arcadia. Mountainous territory in the middle of the Greek Peloponnesus, idealized by Roman poets for its hill pastures and hunting lands and its worship of the shepherds' god Pan.

Areopagus (Ares' hill). In Athens, seat of the first Athenian law court, where Ares was tried for murdering Poseidon's son. The oldest council in Athens.

Arethusa. Nymph turned into a fountain to escape the amorous Alpheus. As a fountain she flowed under the Ionian Sea to resurface on the island of Ortygia, off Sicily's Syracuse. Invoked by Virgil as patroness of Sicilian pastoral.

Argo. Ship of Jason and the Argonauts, which carried them on their quest for the Golden Fleece.

Argus (Greek: Argos, Argolid, Argives). (1) City in the northeast corner of the Peloponnesus; the territory, south of Corinth, in which this city was situated; a center of Mycenaean civilization. (2) Builder of the ship Argo. (3) A son of Gaia, had 100 eyes and was sent by Hera to watch over Io until he was slain by Hermes at the command of Zeus (his eyes then transformed to the tail of a peacock). In the Roman version, hundred-eyed giant who was set to watch Io after Jupiter metamorphosed into a heifer. After Mercury killed him at the command of Jupiter, Juno placed his hundred eyes in the tail of the peacock.

Ariadne. Daughter of Minos and Pasiphae. She fell in love with Theseus, was deserted by him on the island of Naxos, where Dionysus found her.

Arion. Seventh-century B.C. Greek poet and player of the lyre, whose playing was so powerful it led the dolphins to rescue him at sea.

Ariovistus. A powerful German king, defeated by Caesar.

Aristophanes. (1) Athenian playwright, author of eleven extant comedies that hugely influenced Roman comedy. (2) Grammarian (fl. 264 B.C.) and librarian at Alexandria.

Aristotle. Student of Plato; most distinguished Athenian philosopher (384–322 B.C.).

Aristus Fucus. Noted poet and rhetorician; friend of Horace.

Ascanius. Son of Aeneas.

Assaracus. King of Troy; son of Tros and grandfather of Anchises.

Assemblies. Though much governmental power was actually controlled by the Senate, in theory it resided, during the Republic, in the hands of the assemblies:

- *Comitia Curiata.* The oldest assembly; originally consisted entirely of patricians and elected the kings of Rome. By the time of the Republic it had become a primarily religious organization with merely formal and little real power.
- *Comitia Centuriata.* Established by Servius Tullius in the last days of the monarchy, this assembly based its membership on affluence and bloodlines. With rich plebians as its most powerful members, it elected high government officials and served as the chief legislative body until 287 B.C. when the Hortentian Law gave this power to the:
- *Comitia Tributa.* This assembly, effectively controlled by the largest landholders, consisted of district representatives, from the four districts of the city and thirty-one exurban districts.

Assyria. General name for the territory bounded by the Tigris and Euphrates.

Athena (Athene; Roman: Minerva). Also called Pallas, virgin goddess; daughter of Zeus; special protectress of Athens. Although regularly thought of as a warrior goddess, she was also the patroness of peaceful arts and of wisdom and the sciences. Her epithet Polias means "guardian of cities." Athens was named after her because it chose her gift of the olive over Poseidon's gift of water.

Atlas. Titan condemned, for rebelling against the gods, to hold the heavens on his hands and neck.

Atreus. Son of Pelops; husband of Aerope; father of Agamemnon; brother of Thyestes. The curse on his house began when he fed his brother's children to his brother for dinner, hoping to win the royal succession. He won the scepter, but also more pain than he could imagine when the curse on the house of Atreus led to the killing of his son Agamemnon by Klytaimnestra.

Atrides. Agamemnon and Menelaus, the sons of Atreus.

Atticus. Literary patron and good friend of Cicero. Many of their letters are extant.

Attis. Emasculated devotee (or consort) of the goddess Cybele; subject of compositions by Catullus and Nero. His symbol was the pine tree, which was felled annually to commemorate his castration.

Augusta. Honorary title of distinguished Roman matrons, especially empresses.

Augustus. Title reserved for the emperor, or when there were two emperors, for the senior emperor.

Augustus, Octavius Caesar. Grandnephew of Julius Caesar and first Emperor of Rome. Died in A.D. 14.

Aurora. Goddess of dawn (Greek: Eos).

Auster. South wind.

Aventine. One of the seven hills of Rome.

Avernus. Lake near Cumae on the site of an extinct volcano. Nearby was the Sibyl's cave through which Aeneas descended to the lower world.

Bacchus. God of wine, associated with Greek Dionysus. Son of Zeus (Jupiter) and Semele; originally Thracian (Phrygian) god of wine, wildlife, vegetation, and of the fertile power of nature; patron of drama at Athens. He was the god of the poor. His orgiastic worship, depicted in Euripides' *The Bacchae*, was strongly opposed by the powers that be for its savagery (involving the tearing of flesh and drinking of animal blood). He had an oracular shrine in Thrace. His cult in Greece and Rome celebrated the unity of all life, the cycle of death and rebirth, the conception of the daimon or collective soul immanent in the community, which may transcend in its ecstatic ritual any individual's potential. The orgiastic Bacchanalia festival was suppressed in 186 B.C. His temple in Rome was built by the emperor Severus.

Baiae. Popular resort in the Bay of Naples.

Barca. Famous family in Carthage, to which Hamilcar and Hannibal belonged.

Barce. Nurse of Sychaeus who accompanied Dido to Carthage.

Baucis. Wife of Philemon, both of whom were metamorphosed into trees.

Belial. Principal evil spirit.

Bellerophon. Rider of the winged steed Pegasus, by whose aid he slew the Chimera.

Bellona (Bellola). Roman goddess of war (Greek: Enyo); wife or sister of Mars; her temple in the Campus Martius, her festival on June 3 was celebrated with frenzied self-mutilation. Also called Duellona; later identified with the Cappadocian war goddess Ma.

Bestia (Lucius Bestia Calpurnius). Consul sent against Numidian Jugurtha, by whom he was bribed to make a peace which was, when he returned to Rome, canceled. He was banished.

Biblis. Daughter of Miletus and Cyane; fell in love with her brother but was repulsed and then became a fountain.

Bibulus, Marcus Calpurnius. Consul with Julius Caesar in 59 B.C., married to Porcia, Cato's daughter (who later married Brutus).

Boethius, Anicius Manlius Severinus (c. A.D. 480–524). Statesman, poet, and theologian; famous for his *Consolation of Philosophy*.

Bona Dea. Earth fertility goddess, sometimes confused with Fauna. During her festival on December 3, she was worshipped by women.

Brennus. A leader of the Gauls who defeated the Romans and sacked Rome in 390 B.C.

Brittanicus, Tiberius Claudius Caesar "Germanicus" (A.D. 41–55). Son of the emperor Claudius and Messalina and designated heir. He was given the name "Brittanicus" after his father invaded England in 43. He was probably poisoned by his successor Nero.

(1) Brutus, Lucius Junius. Traditional leader of the movement resulting in the expulsion of the Tarquins in 509 B.C., and therefore known as the founder of the Roman Republic. **(2) Marcus Junius Brutus.** Friend of Cicero who fought on Pompey's side at Pharsalus in 48 B.C.; one of the assassins, with Cassius, of Caesar. When Octavian defeated him at the second battle of Philippi, he committed suicide.

Cadmus (Kadmos). Legendary founder of Thebes; son of Agenor of Tyre; brother of Europa.

Caecilius Statius (fl. 179 B.C.). Comic playwright before Terence; famous for adopting the style of Greek New Comedy.

Caecina (Aulus). Friend and correspondent of Cicero.

Caelestis. Carthaginian goddess.

Caelius Rufus. Pupil and friend of Cicero; famous orator and lawyer; defended by Cicero against Catullus' lover Clodia's charge that he'd tried to poison her. Made praetor in 48 B.C. by Julius Caesar.

Caenis. (1) Maiden changed by Neptune into a man. In the sixth book of the *Aeneid,* Caeneus (masculine of Caenis) is represented as again restored to womanly form. (2) Vespasian's concubine, who amassed great wealth by administering the sale of offices for him.

Calabria. The heel of the Italian "boot."

Calends (Kalends). First day of the Roman month.

Caligula, Gaius Julius Caesar Germanicus. Infamous emperor A.D. 37–41; protégé of Tiberius; responsible for the fiercest reign of terror in Roman history.

Gladiators' entrance, amphitheater at Italica

Callimachus (c. 305–c. 240 B.C.). Famous Greek poet of Alexandria; enormously influential on Roman elegy.

Calliope. Muse of epic poetry; mother, by Oeagrus, of Orpheus.

Camillus. Conquered Veii, a town in Etruria, and saved Rome from the Gauls in 390 B.C.

Campania. Province in southern Italy surrounded by Latium, Samnium, and Lucania, its principal cities Capua, Pompeii, and Herculaneum.

Campus Martius. Plain outside the original walls of Rome, surrounded by the Quirinal, Capitoline, and Pincian hills; named for its temple to Mars; used for gymnastic and military training in early Rome and as the site for Augustus' temple to Neptune, Statilius Taurus' stone amphitheater, Agrippa's baths, and the Pantheon.

Cannae. Town in southern Italy where the Romans were severely defeated by Hannibal in 216 B.C.

Cantabri. Warlike tribe in the north of Spain.

Capua. Principal city of the Campania district, located near the river Volturnus.

Caracalla (Marcus Aurelius Antoninus). Bellicose ruler of Rome from A.D. 211–217; a Syrian born in Gaul. He ruled jointly with his father, Septimius Severus, from 198 to 211.

Cardea. Goddess of hinges.

Casca (Servilius). Struck the first blow in the assassination of Julius Caesar. Committed suicide at Philippi, rather than face punishment.

Cassius (Gaius Cassius Longinus). Chief conspirator in Julius Caesar's assassination; married to Brutus' half-sister Junia Tertulla; killed at the defeat at Philippi, at his own request, by his own men.

Castor. Son of Leda and Zeus; with his twin brother Pollux, worshipped by the Romans on January 27 and August 13; known for his horsemanship. When they died, the brothers were placed among the stars as the constellation Gemini.

Censor. Republican officer in charge of the census, the Senate rolls, citizen lists, and public morality; elected every five years for an eighteen-month term.

Centaurs. Race dwelling in the mountains of Thessaly with the heads and torsos of men and the bodies of horses.

Cerberus. The three-headed dog that guarded the entrance to the underworld.

Ceres. Italian goddess-patroness of farmers; goddess of agriculture and grain (Greek: Demeter); daughter of Saturn; sister of Jupiter; mother of Proserpina (Persephone). Worshipped originally at Cumae, depicted holding sheaves of corn. Her festival was April 12–19.

Cethegus. One of the Catilinian conspirators.

Charon. Ferryman of the Styx, who conveyed souls into Hades for a price (leading to the Roman custom of placing coins, first on the mouths, later on the eyes of the dead).

Charybdis. Whirlpool in the Straits of Messina across from the cave of the monster Scylla; confronted by Homer's Odysseus.

Chimaera. A monster with the head of a lion, the body of a goat, and the tail of a dragon.

Chios. Greek island whose wines were favored by the Romans.

Chrysanthius. Neoplatonic philosopher; mentor of the emperor Julian.

Chrysippus (c. 280–c. 207 B.C.). Stoic philosopher, often credited with founding Stoicism (instead of Zeno).

Cincinnatus (Lucius Quinctius). When Minucius was besieged by the Aequi, he was summoned from his plowing to assume the dictatorship in 458 B.C. Defeating the Aequi, he saved the Roman army, resigned the dictatorship, and returned to his plowing sixteen days later.

Cinna (Lucius Cornelius). (1) Served as praetor in 44 B.C. and, along with Cassius, Casca, and Brutus, one of the assassins of Julius Caesar. (2) Gaius Helvius Cinna. Late-republican poet; born at Brixellum; friend of Catullus and Virgil; known for his epic *Smyrna* and as leader of the New Poets; after Caesar's assassination murdered, by mistake, by an angry mob that confused him with Lucius Cornelius Cinna.

Circus. Stadium designed for public races and spectacles, especially the Circus Maximus in Rome, which was built by Tarquin and restored by Julius Caesar and which held 150,000.

Claudius Marcellus. (1) First general successful against Hannibal. (2) Son of Octavia, sister of Augustus.

Claudius (Tiberius Claudius Drusus Nero Germanicus). Emperor from A.D. 41–54, succeeding the insane Caligula, and known also for his oratory and forty-one-book histories. Poisoned with a plate of mushrooms by his fourth "wife" Agrippina.

Cleopatra. Last queen of Egypt (51–30 B.C.); loved by Julius Caesar (their son, Caesarion) and then Antony. She and Antony were defeated by Octavian at the Battle of Actium, 31 B.C., ending the Ptolemaic dynasty in Egypt.

Clio. Muse of history.

Clodia. The most beautiful woman in Rome: wife of Metellus Celer for one year until he died; sister of Clodius; the "Lesbia" of the poems of Catullus.

Clodius Pulcher (Publius). Patrician of the Claudian *gens*; enemy of Cicero; killed by Milo in gang fighting (52 B.C.).

Cocytus. River of the underworld.

Codrus. The last king of Athens.

Comitia Centuriata. *See:* Assemblies.

Comitia Curiata. *See:* Assemblies.

Comitia Tributa. *See:* Assemblies.

Concordia. Goddess of peace and concord, her festival in July.

Consul. One of the two chief administrative executives with power to summon and preside over the Senate and *Comitia Centuriata*, and commanding the army.

Coriolanus. A Roman patrician of the first half of the fifth century B.C.

Coroebus. A Phrygian; ally of Priam; suitor of Cassandra; killed at Troy.

Corybantes. Priests of the goddess Cybele.

Cotys. Thracian goddess, her orgiastic cult associated with that of Cybele.

Crassus (Marcus Licinius) (c. 115–53 B.C.). Republican leader of great wealth and influence; ally of Sulla; as praetor in 72–71 B.C., quashed the slave revolt led by Spartacus; in 60 B.C., Caesar, Pompey, and Crassus formed the First Triumvirate; died during the disastrous defeat of his army at Carrhae, in Mesopotamia.

Cremona. Northern Italian town, not far from Mantua; it became a Roman colony in 218 B.C. but fought against Octavian in the Civil War; he then redistributed its lands to his veterans.

Cremutius Cordus (Aulus) (d. A.D. 25). Historian forced to starve himself to death by Tiberius for praising Brutus' assassination of Julius Caesar.

Creusa. First wife of Aeneas; daughter of Priam.

Crispinilla, Calvia. Nero's mistress; granted the office of caretaker of the imperial wardrobe in A.D. 67, used her position to amass great wealth.

Cupid. Arrow-bearing son of Venus and Vulcan (Greek: Eros); symbol of erotic love, life, and death.

Cura Aquarum. Founded by Augustus in 11 B.C., Rome's department of water supply, in charge of maintaining wells and aqueducts.

Curia. (1) Ancient division of the Roman people, as early as the monarchy, equivalent to the Athenian *deme*. Originally there were thirty *curiae*, ten for each of the tribes of Romulus. (2) Senate meeting house, originally in the seventh century B.C. Curia Hostilia, later in the Curia Julia begun by Julius Caesar and completed by Augustus.

Curialis. Inherited title for a member of the city councils, the *curiae*, local representatives of the imperial government known mostly for their role in tax collection.

Cursus honorum. "Course of honors"; the cycle of public service appointments by which a magistrate rose in the ranks, normally: tribune, quaestor (minimum age thirty), aedile, praetor (forty), consul (forty-three), and censor.

Cybele. Asian "Great Mother" goddess; Anatolian (Phrygian) fertility deity identified with Rhea; associated with her lover Attis. Her worship was wild and orgiastic in nature, and her cult statue, of black meteorite, was brought to Rome from Phrygia by the Senate during the Punic War. The great Megalesia

Games were held in her honor and her priests, known as Galli, were initiated in a ritual castration.

Cynic (-ism). Philosophical sect founded by Socrates' associate Antisthenes and/or Diogenes of Sinope (nicknamed *kuon*, "dog"), and centered at the Cynosarges gymnasium in Athens. Its primary belief was in immunity from life's pains by practicing independence from all worldly concerns. The sect, which had faded from lack of leadership, was reborn in the first century A.D. among the Romans. Roman Cynics, especially under Demetrius the Cynic in the rule of Vespasian, wandered the streets in rags, preaching their opposition to all authority.

Cynthia. Name for Diana.

Dacians. Tribe inhabiting territory north of the Danube, allied with Antony against Augustus.

Dama. Name used by Horace to indicate a person of no importance.

Danuvius. The Danube River.

Daphne. Her symbol the laurel branch, Greek goddess worshipped in Rome for her dignified virginity. Apollo saw her, fell in love, pursued her, but she refused and asked her mother Gaia for aid in resisting him. Gaia turned her into a laurel tree.

Dardanus (Dardanians). Mythical ancestor of the Trojans. Another term for "Trojans."

Daunus. Legendary king of Apulia.

Dea Dia. Harvest goddess; associated with corn; worshipped in a May festival.

Decemvirs. Fifth-century B.C. panel of ten administrators who composed the Twelve Tables of traditional Roman law.

Delatores. Informers, who received one quarter of those they successfully accused.

Delos. Small island in the Aegean, the center of the Cyclades. Birthplace of Apollo and Artemis, and the place where the Delian League held its treasury before it was shifted to Athens.

Delphi. Town in Phocis, on the lower slopes of Mount Parnassus, site of the most important oracle of Apollo and the Pythian Games. Delphi was considered to be "the navel of the earth."

Demetrius. (1) An actor who, in the opinion of Quintilian, played the role of matrons very well. (2) Demetrius the Cynic (fl. first century A.D.). Friend of Seneca, leader of the popular movement harshly critical of authority under Gaius and Nero. Exiled in A.D. 66 but returned to Rome under Vespasian to continue his attacks until he was once again banished. His writings from exile finally provoked the emperor, who called him a "barking dog," to have him executed.

Democritus (c. 460–c. 370 B.C.). Founder of the materialist Atomist school of philosophy; he was later known as "the Laughing Philosopher."

Denarius. Silver coin originally worth ten asses (a denis assibus).

Deucalion. Son of Prometheus; at his father's advice built an ark to survive the flood Zeus sent on humanity.

Diana (Greek: Artemis). Virgin goddess of the hunt, wild nature, the moon, and childbirth; sister of Apollo; protector of women; her sacred grove was near Aricia; her temple on the Aventine Hill.

Dictator. Also known as magister populi ("master of the people"); exceptional republican supreme office, appointed by consuls advised by the Senate for a six-month term under the post-monarchical constitution only in times of national emergency. The office was abolished under the Empire.

Dido. Queen of Carthage; legendary daughter of the king of Tyre called Belus (in Virgil's Aeneid); when Aeneas and his Trojan comrades sought refuge in Carthage, he became enamored of her but was forced by his duty to found Rome to abandon her; she committed suicide in despair.

Dinochares. Builder of a pyramid which, according to Ammianus Marcellinus, dwindled like a flame to a point.

Diocletian. Chosen emperor (A.D. 284) by the army after he personally executed the murderer of Numerian; one of the most controversial and glorious of Rome's rulers. Shortly before his retirement (in 305) he launched a major persecution against Christianity.

Dione. Mother of Venus; Zeus' (Jupiter's) consort at Dodona.

Dionysius (Dionysus). Greek god of wine and fertility. See Bacchus.

Dis (Greek: Hades). Husband of Proserpina (Persephone); god of the underworld and the dead; known also as Dis Pater, Dives, Aides, Hades, and Pluto or Plouton.

Discordia. Goddess of strife; daughter of Jupiter and Juno.

Diverbium. The dialogue in a comic play, as distinct from the sung lines, cantica.

Divitiacus. Noble leader of the Aeduans and friend of Caesar; brother of Dumnorix.

Dodona. Ancient oracle of Zeus in Epirus. The sounds made by the wind in the sacred oaks were interpreted by the priests.

Domitian (Titus Flavious Domitianus). Son of Vespasian and brother of Titus; emperor (A.D. 81–96); conspicuous for his tyranny, cruelty, and military prowess.

Drusilla, Julia (d. 38 A.D.). Daughter of Germanicus, she rose to prominence through an incestuous relationship with her brother Caligula. Deified by him after her death.

Dryads. Nymphs of the trees, along with the Hamadryads.

Duellona. See Bellona.

Dymas. Devoted squire of Parthenopaeus; committed suicide when trapped during an attempt to bring his chief's body off the battlefield.

Egeria. Nymph of Latium; legendary consort of King Numa.

Elektra (Electra). Daughter of Agamemnon and Klytaimnestra, who, so great was her love for her father in Euripides' version of the myth, conspired with her brother Orestes to kill their mother in revenge for her slaying of their father.

Elissa. Another name for Dido, the founder of Carthage.

Elysium. The abode of the blessed in the Greek underworld, in whose fields the heroic dead followed patterns of earthly life.

Emancipatio. Release of a son or daughter from family ties, making the emancipated male a *pater familias* in his own right.

Endymion. Youth beloved by the moon-goddess Selene, who spent his immortal life in sleep.

Epicurus (341–270 B.C.). Athenian philosopher; founder of the Epicurean school, whose most significant teaching was that the highest good in life is in simple pleasures, to be achieved by wise and virtuous living; pleasure he defined as absence of pain and achievement of equanimity; the most influential Roman epicure was Lucretius.

Epithalimium. Song sung by young men and women during a wedding festival, at the door of the bridal chamber. The most famous surviving epithalamia are those of Catullus.

Equites. "Horsemen," "knights," "equestrians," "cavalry"; title given in the first century B.C. to the wealthiest nonsenatorial class (upper middle class).

Erasistratus. Noted physician of the third century B.C.; founder of a medical school at Alexandria.

Erato. Muse of amorous poetry and the lyre.

Erebus. The darkness surrounding the Underworld.

Eros. Greek god of love; son of Aphrodite; Roman: Cupid.

Eryx. Mountain in Sicily; site of a temple to Aphrodite.

Etna. The great volcano in Sicily, under which the Cyclopes forged the thunderbolts of Jupiter.

Etruria. Central Italian territory of the Etruscans, finally conquered by the Romans in 283 B.C.

Etruscans. Also known as Tyrrheni; one of the earliest tribes to inhabit the territory between the Tiber and the Arno taken over by Rome.

Euhoe! A Bacchic cry.

Europa. Mother of Cretan King of Minos and of Rhadamanthys; Zeus, disguised as a bull, kidnapped her and took her to Mount Ida in Crete.

Eurus. The southeast wind.

Eurydice. Dryad; wife of Orpheus.

Euterpe. Muse of flute-playing.

Evander. Greek hero; son of Hermes (Mercury); said to have emigrated from Arcadia to Italy, there, as the first settler of Rome, founding Pallanteum on the Tiber; he welcomed Aeneas to his home on the Palatine Hill.

Exsilium. Voluntary self-banishment, a practice that substituted for the death penalty by allowing a condemned criminal to escape with his life by leaving Roman territory.

Faber. Artist, craftsman, or mechanic who works with hard materials such as stone, metal, or wood in his *fabrica* (English: workshop or factory).

Fabianus Papirius (fl. first century A.D.). Philosopher; mentor of Seneca; famous for his studies of rhetoric and natural history.

Fabius (Quintus Maximus Cunctator). Consul 215, 214, 209 B.C.; famous for wearing down the invading Carthaginian forces of Hannibal with delaying tactics; fabio was named after him.

Fabricius (Gaius Luscinus). Consul 282, 278 B.C.; victorious general; Roman symbol of austerity.

Falernus. Territory in Campania famous for its outstanding wines.

Fasces. Symbolic bundle of birch rods and axes tied together with a red strap and carried over the left shoulder by the *lictores*. The rods reminded wrongdoers of minor crimes and the ax of capital punishment.

Fascinum. Enchantment by spells, the evil eye, or curses; especially applied to the *phallus*, used as a countercharm.

Fates. Known to the Romans as "Parcae," three sisters who determined the length of a man's life, represented as a thread of varying length.

Fauna. Fertility goddess; consort of Faunus; sometimes confused with Bona Dea.

Faunus. King of Latium; father of Latinus; worshipped as protecting deity of husbandmen and agriculture and sometimes identified with Pan, and also with Inuus, a god of fertility; called *Fatuus* ("speaker") for his oracular powers; his festival, the *Faunalia*, is celebrated on February 13, December 5, and at the Lupercalia.

Faustulus. Shepherd who found Romulus and Remus being suckled by the wolf, and brought them home to raise them properly.

Favonius. The west wind.

Februus. Ancient Etruscan underworld divinity; god of purification; later identified with Dis.

Fecial (Fetial). The priestly college of *fetiales* undertook diplomatic missions prior to a declaration of the war, and were responsible for the ratification of the treaty at the conclusion of hostilities.

Felicitas. Goddess of luck; her temple on the Velabrum; her face used on coins; she was represented as an older woman, holding the cornucopia and the caduceus.

Felsina. Etrurian city renamed Bononia by the Romans (modern Bologna); alternate residence of the emperors; Octavian, Antony, and Lepidus created the Second Triumvirate at Felsina.

Feretrius. An epithet of Jupiter, from the verb *ferire*, "to strike"; those who took oaths called on him by this surname to strike them dead as they struck a sacrificial animal, if what they swore was untrue; to him also were dedicated the *spolia opima*, the arms taken from a conquered general and his army.

Feriae. Roman holidays dedicated to various gods.

Ferona. Ancient Italian goddess of flowers, later identified with Flora; her festival: November 13.

Fides. Goddess of honor, good faith, and contracts; her temple on the Capitoline Hill; her festival: October 1.

Fiscus. The emperor's private treasury, his discretionary funds based on provincial taxation, unclaimed estates, and special levies and confiscations.

Flamen. Priest of a particular deity, such as the *flamen Martialis* ("priest of Mars").

Flaminius (Gaius). Consul 223, 220, 217 B.C.; commander at Lake Trasimene (217 B.C.), where he died.

Flavians. Family and supporters of Vespasian, Titus, and Domitian (Vespasian's full name was Titus Flavius Sabinus Vespasianus).

Flora. Lascivious goddess of spring and flowers; her April 28 festival still celebrated in Rome's *Campo dei Fiori*.

Florentia. Florence, originally a city of Etruria, colonized by the Romans.

Florentinus. Prefect of Rome, A.D. 395–97; patron of Claudian.

Fons. God of springs; his festival: October 13.

Formiae. Town in Latium, source of good wine.

Formulus. Finest painter of the empire; flourished under Nero.

Fortuna. Goddess of good luck, fate, chance, and fortune (Greek: Tyche); usually depicted with wheel or rudder; very popular in suburban Rome; her festivals were on May 25 and June 24.

Forum. Like the Greek *agora*, an open space in the city used for meetings and markets.

Franks. Germanic people who overran Gaul at the end of the western empire (476 B.C.).

Frumentarii. Imperial secret service built by Hadrian from the grain collectors (*frumentarii*) in the provinces; the institution was abolished by Diocletian.

Fulvia. Daughter of Marcus Fulvius Bambalio; Marc Antony's fanatically supportive and scheming wife who served as his representative when he was away from Rome.

Gades. Modern Cádiz, in Spain.

Gaia. Greek earth goddess worshipped by the Romans on December 8.

Galateia. Sea nymph; daughter of Doris and Nereus; loved by the Cyclops Polyphemos.

Galba. Roman emperor (A.D. June 68–January 69).

Galla (Gaul). Territory bounded by the Alps, the Pyrenees, the Rhine, and the ocean; divided into several Roman provinces after being conquered in the Gallic Wars (58–51 B.C.) by Julius Caesar.

Gallia Cisalpina (Cisalpine Gaul). Northern Italian territory between the Apennines and the Alps annexed by Rome by 222 B.C. and made part of Italy in 42 B.C.

Gallia Comata (Long-haired Gaul). Organized after the conquest by Julius Caesar into three provinces—Aquitania, Ludgdunensis, and Belgia—the "Three Gauls," including parts of modern France, Belgium, and Germany.

Gallia Transalpina (Transalpine Gaul). Sometimes known only as "Gaul," the territory in the south of France that provided passage to Spain.

Gallia Transpadana (Transpadane Gaul). Territory of Cisalpine Gaul north of the River Po.

Galli. Castrated priests of Cybele-Attis.

Garganus. Mountain in Apulia.

Gaul. *See:* Galla.

Genius. A founding or protecting demigod, similar to the Greek *daemon* or the Christian guardian angel; associated with Hercules and particular to each family; each person had his own *genius*, who died when he died. Festival of the *Genius Publicus* ("public spirit") was celebrated on October 9.

Gens. Clan united by reverence to a common ancestor and bearing a common name.

Germania. Roman province east of the Rhine and north of the Danube, extending to the Elbe.

Germanicus Julius Caesar, Nero Claudius (15 B.C.–A.D. 19). Son of Drusus the Elder and Antonia; general under the emperor Tiberius, who adopted him but later grew jealous of his popularity; married to Agrippina.

Geryon. Three-bodied giant whose oxen were stolen by Hercules.

Gracchus. (1) Tiberius Sempronius Longus, consul 218 B.C., one of the Roman commanders at the Battle of the Trebia; (2) Tiberius Sempronius, consul 215, 213 B.C.; killed by the Carthaginians in 212 B.C. Both brothers were noted reformers and orators.

Graces. Beautiful and gracious maidens; commonly held to be three in number; attendants to the Muses.

Gratian, Flavius. Son of Valentinian; pupil and patron of Ausonius; co-emperor A.D. 367–83.

Hades. Son of Cronos; brother of Zeus and Poseidon; husband of Persephone; Greek god of the underworld; (Roman: Pluto).

Hadria. The Adriatic Sea.

Hannibal (247–183 B.C.). Son of Hamilcar, sworn to eternal hatred for Rome, Hannibal was the great Carthaginian general in the Second Punic War; invaded Italy with an army of 26,000, defeating the Romans at Cannae in 216 B.C.

Harmonia (Harmony). Daughter of Ares and Aphrodite; wife of Cadmus.

Harpax. Grappling hook fired by the Roman navy at an enemy ship; the ship would then be reeled in and boarded.

Harpies. Monstrous god-birds with heads of maidens, associated with the winds.

Hecate. Greek goddess of the moon and the underworld, and of magic and witchcraft, spells and incantations; often represented with three heads; daughter of Perses and Asteria; sister of Latona; identified with Diana, Luna, and Proserpina.

Hecuba (Greek: Hekabe). Daughter of Phrygian Dimas; Queen of Troy; wife of Priam; mother of Hector and Paris.

Hector (Greek: Hektor). Son of Priam and Hecuba; brother of Paris; husband of Andromache; father of Astyanax; principal hero of the Trojans; killed by Achilles in revenge for Hector's killing of Patroklos.

Helen. Daughter of Zeus and Leda; sister of the Dioscuri; Paris' abduction of her from Menelaos, at the behest of Aphrodite, instigated the Trojan War.

Helicon. Mountain in Boeotia; residence of the Muses.

Helvetia. Western part of modern Switzerland; territory of the Helvetii.

Herculaneum. City of Campania (near Naples) destroyed by the eruption of Vesuvius on August 24, A.D. 79, which also destroyed Pompeii.

Hercules (Greek: Herakles). Popular hero, later deified, his name synonymous with strength; son of Zeus and Alcmena; Romans considered him god of victory and enterprise, and patron of gladiators; through the trickery of the jealous Hera, Eurystheus was given power over Hercules and ordered him to perform twelve labors. The festival of Hercules *Invictus* ("unconquered") is held on August 12–13.

Herillus (Erillus). Stoic philosopher who flourished in the middle of the third century B.C.

Hermaphroditus. Also known as Aphroditus; son of Hermes and Aphrodite who became half man and half woman through bathing in the fountain of the enamored nymph Salmacis.

Pompeii fresco

hero. Half god and half human, ancient "heroes" included Achilles (son of the nymph Thetis and the mortal Peleus); the Dioscuri (twin sons of Zeus and Leda); Helen (daughter of Leda and Zeus); Hercules (son of Zeus and Alcmena); and the Trojan warrior Aeneas (son of Venus and Anchises), the mythical founder of Rome.

Hesperides. Daughters of Hesperis and Atlas (or Night and Erebus); goddess-guardians of the golden apples in the garden of the gods beyond the Atlas Mountains at the western shore of the Ocean.

Hesperus (Vesper). The evening star, depicted as a youth bearing a torch.

Hestia. Greek equivalent of Roman Vesta, goddess of the hearth.

Hibernia (Iverna, Juverna). Roman name for Ireland.

Hills of Rome. Aventine, Caelian, Capitoline, Esquiline, Palatine, Quirinal, and Viminal; three other nearby hills are the Janiculum, the Pincian, and the Vatican.

Hirtius, Aulus. Friend and officer of Julius Caesar, killed with his fellow consul, Vibius Pansa, while fighting Antony at Mutina in 43 B.C.; he may have written the eighth book of Caesar's *Gallic War*.

Hispania. Roman name for the province now known as Spain.

Horatius Cocles. Roman soldier who held off single-handedly the Etruscan army of Lars Porsenna, until a vital bridge was destroyed.

Hortensius, Quintus. Noted orator, contemporary with Cicero.

Huns. Most famous of the nomadic barbarian tribes that attacked the Roman Empire, they were originally from central Asia.

Hybla. Town on the slopes of Sicily's Mount Etna, known for its honey.

Hydra. Many-headed monster slain by Hercules.

Iapetus. A Titan, son of Heaven and Earth, hurled into Tartarus by Jupiter; father of Prometheus and Epimetheus.

Iberia. (1) Roman name for Spain. (2) Territory in the southern Caucasus (approximately modern Georgia), between the Black and Caspian Seas.

Icarus. Son of the craftsman Daedalus; held captive by Minos on Crete; they escaped by mounting feathered wings to their shoulders with wax, but Icarus flew too near the sun and his wax melted and he fell into the Icarian Sea.

Ides. The middle day of the Roman month, sacred to Jupiter.

Ilia. Rhea Silvia, daughter of Numitor and the mother by Mars of Romulus and Remus. Roman poets tell how she threw herself into the Anio, or Tiber, and was taken by the river god to be his wife.

Ilium. Name for Troy.

Illyria. Modern territory of the Balkan countries facing Italy across the Adriatic Sea.

Illyrian Sea. The part of the Adriatic facing Illyria (also known as Dalmatia).

Imagines. Death masks made of wax reverenced by the family.

Imperium. Highest administrative power.

Interrex. Temporary office, appointed by Senate to a five-day term, to fill a vacant consular position.

Io. Daughter of Inachus; seduced by Jupiter, who turned her into a heifer to avoid suspicion; tormented by a gadfly sent in jealousy by Juno, she wandered the world until she returned to Egypt and became a woman once again. Her Egyptian connections facilitated her assimilation to Isis.

Iphigeneia. Daughter of Agamemnon and Klytaimnestra; sacrificed by her father, at the suggestion of the prophet Calchas, at Aulis, so that the Greek expedition might sail for Troy; Agamemnon convinced Klytaimnestra to send her to Aulis on the promise that she would be married to Achilles.

Iris. Messenger and rainbow goddess; wife of Zephyros; the west wind. In the *Iliad* she announces the will of Zeus to mortals.

Isis. Egyptian fertility goddess and symbol of the universal mother; sister and consort of Osiris; mother of Horus; whose cult the Roman Senate attempted to expel from Italy toward the end of the Republic; later her worship spread through the Roman Empire, and Caligula built a temple to her in the Campus Martius.

Ismarus. Mountain in Thrace associated with Orpheus.

Istria (Histria). Northern Adriatic territory, extending from Venetia to Illyricum on the River Arsia.

Italia. Roman homeland; originally the southern half of the Italian peninsula, but eventually extending from Sicily to the Alps.

Iuga/Juga. Goddess of marriage, a title of Juno.

Ius civile (Jus civile). Civil law, governing Roman citizens throughout the Empire.

Ius gentium (Jus gentium). Governing Roman relations with foreigners, known as *peregrini*.

Ixion. King of the Lapiths; father of Pirithous; after killing his father-in-law and trying to rape Hera, Zeus had him chained to a revolving wheel in Hades for all eternity.

Janiculum. Hill on the west bank of the Tiber, site of an ancient temple to Fons, son of Janus.

Janus. Ancient Roman god of gates and doorways, and of beginnings (hence January) and morning; he was depicted with two faces, one staring forward, one behind; his temple in Rome was built by King Numa; its doors were open in time of war. His festival was celebrated on New Year's Day, the first day of the month dedicated to him.

Jove. Alternate name for Jupiter (from the Latin: Jupiter [nominative], Jovis [genitive]).

Juba. King of Numidia, who sided with Pompey and the Senate against Julius Caesar and obtained control of Libya; he ordered himself slain by a slave after losing the battle of Thapsus (46 B.C.).

Julia. (1) d. 51 B.C.; sister of Julius Caesar; mother of Atia, who was mother of Augustus. (2) c. 83–c. 54 B.C.; Julius Caesar's daughter

with Cornelia; wife of Pompey. After her death in childbirth, Caesar and Pompey drifted back into enmity. (3) 39 B.C.–14 A.D.; daughter of Augustus and Scribonia, wife of Tiberius (also of Agrippa and M. Marcellus), notorious for her promiscuity.

Juno (Greek: Hera; Etruscan: Uni). Daughter of Saturn; wife of Jupiter; queen of heaven; protectress of women; her most important festival, the Matronalia, was March 1; as Juno Moneta she was patroness of Roman finance; the first of each month was sacred to her.

Jupiter (Greek: Zeus). Sky god; father of the gods; protector of Rome; god of weather, agriculture, justice, war and peace, and treaties. His first temple was built on the Capitoline Hill by the Etruscans. His titles included *Divis pater* ("Father of Heaven"), *Imperator* ("Emperor of Heaven"), and *Tonans* ("Sender of Thunder").

Justice. Astraea or Nemesis, who left the earth with Chastity (Pudicitia) in the later years of the Silver Age, when mankind had deteriorated from the primal innocence of the Golden Age.

Juturna. Italian goddess of springs; her temple in the Campus Martius.

Juvenalia. Youth Games established by Nero in A.D. 59 to celebrate the Roman coming of age beard-cutting ritual.

Juventas. Daughter of Juno and Jupiter; also known as Hebe, goddess of youth and nectar-bearer of the gods.

Kalends (Calends). First day of the Roman month.

Labeo, Attius. Translator of Homer.

Labienus, Titus. Julius Caesar's chief lieutenant in the Gallic Wars, who supported Pompey and the senatorial cause in the Civil War and was killed at the Battle of Munda (45 B.C.).

Lamia. Female monster who feeds on children.

Lara. Talkative nymph who married Mercury and bore him the Lares. Jupiter cut her tongue out.

Lar(es). Sons of Mercury and Lara, according to Ovid; but more anciently the protective household and tutelar gods around which Roman family worship revolved; generally depicted as young men dancing; they symbolized the benign force of nature and were the patrons of travelers.

Lateranus (Plautius). Rich senator, implicated in a plot against Nero and forced to kill himself in 65 A.D.

Latiaris. Jupiter's title as protector of Latium and presider over the *Feriae Latinae,* the Latin festival.

Latin. Originally the language of Rome and the plain of Latium, eventually spreading throughout Italy and the Empire.

Latini. Early tribe inhabiting the plain of Latium.

Latium. Middle Italian region that includes Rome; its inhabitants, the Latini, displaced the original Pelasgians.

Latona (Greek: Leto). Mother, by Jupiter, of Apollo and Diana.

Laurentines. Inhabitants of Laurentum or Latium in general; supporters of Aeneas; another name for the Romans.

Laverna. Goddess of thieves.

Legatus ("legate"). Imperial lieutenant, of senatorial rank, with both military and political responsibilities.

Legion. Basic military division of the Roman army, backbone of imperial conquest.

Lemures. Ghosts of the dead, who wandered the earth, haunting crossroads, to trouble the living.

Lepidus, Marcus Aemilius. Supporter of Julius Caesar against Pompey; praetor, consul, and commander of horses; and member with Octavian and Antony of the Second Triumvirate; married to Junia. After trying to acquire Sicily for himself, Lepidus was defeated by Octavian, stripped of all offices except that of *Pontifex Maximus,* and kept under guard until his death about 13 B.C.

Lesbos. Greek island off the coast of Asia Minor, birthplace of the great lyric poet Sappho.

Lethe. River in Hades, from which the souls of the dead drank water that made them forget their lives.

Liber ("Liberator"). Italian god of fertility, as *Liber Pater,* identified with wine and Bacchus; his cult on the Aventine Hill; his festival: March 17.

Libera. Consort of Liber, associated with the Greek Persephone.

Liberators. Name taken by the assassins of Julius Caesar, led by Cassius and Brutus.

Libertas. Goddess of personal liberty, associated with Jupiter; her temple built in 238 B.C. on the Aventine Hill.

Libertus. A "freedman," formerly a slave.

Libitina. Goddess of death.

Lictors. Bodyguards, attendants, and executioners serving Roman magistrates and high officials. The lictors traced their authority back to Romulus. They walked in front of their employers bearing the *fasces,* symbolic of their punitive role.

Linus. Son of Apollo, poet and singer who caused the trees to uproot themselves to follow his music.

Lipara. Island off the coast of Sicily.

Livia Drusilla (58 B.C.–29 A.D.). Wife of Octavian's opponent Tiberius Claudius Nero, by whom she became mother of the future emperors Tiberius and Drusus. Octavian (later the emperor Augustus) forced her husband to divorce her so that he himself might marry her even though she was six months pregnant by Tiberius. In return for her loyalty to him, Augustus adopted her sons. She was accused of the murder of Marcellus, Augustus' nephew and designated heir, and even of Augustus himself. When Tiberius became emperor she was given the title of *Julia Augusta,* and served as his co-regent.

Lollius (Marcus Lollius Palicanus). Died about 1 B.C.; associate of Augustus, instrumental in Romanizing Galatia; under his command Roman arms sustained losses in Germany in 17 B.C.; dismissed by Gaius Caesar for accepting bribes from Eastern tribes.

Lombards. Germanic tribe described by Tacitus as warlike and fierce.

Londinum. Modern London; trade gateway city in Roman Britannia.

Lucina. Goddess of childbirth; associated with Juno and Diana.

Lucretia. Legendary Roman heroine; wife of Tarquinius Collatinus. Her rape by Sextus Tarquin (son of Tarquin the Proud) in 510 B.C. led to the expulsion of the Etruscan kings from Rome and the establishment of Rome as a Republic. Symbol of old-fashioned Roman chastity, she took her own life after telling her husband of the outrage.

Lucullus, Lucius Licinius. General under Sulla. He warred eight years against Mithridates. When his troops revolted, he returned to Rome to live in luxury that became proverbial.

Lucusta (Locusta). Notorious imperial poisoner, who prepared the fatal plate of mushrooms for the emperor Claudius at Agrippina the Younger's direction. Nero later commissioned her to poison Claudius' son Britannicus. She was executed by Galba in A.D. 69.

Ludi (Games). Public games similar to those held by the ancient Greeks were held in Rome from earliest times, organized by the various priesthoods. The oldest, *ludi Romani,* held in honor of Jupiter, dated back to the time of the kings.

Luna. Goddess of the moon; associated with Diana.

Lupercalia. Fertility festival held on February 15, beginning with the sacrifice of goats to the god Faunus at the Lupercal, a cave at the base of the Palatine Hill.

Luperci. Priests of Lycean Pan; in the festival of Lupercalia, they paraded wearing only loin cloths, flogging women with goatskins to ensure their fertility.

Lusitania. Region of modern Portugal and western Spain, territory of the Lusitani tribe.

Lutetia (Lutecia). Capital city of the Gallic Parisii (modern Paris); later a Roman colony situated on an island in the Sequana (Seine).

Lycaeus. Mountain in Arcadia associated with Pan.

Macedon (Macedonia). District of northern Greece bordering on the Balkans, brought to imperial greatness by Philip and Alexander; it became a Roman province after the Battle of Pydna, in 168 B.C., when Lucius Paullus defeated King Perseus.

Maecenas, Gaius Cilnius (74 or 64–8 B.C.). Loyal friend of Augustus; literary patron of Virgil, Horace, and Propertius. He himself wrote much, but it has survived only in fragments; his name became synonymous with "patron of the arts."

Maenalus. Mountain range in Arcadia associated with Pan.

Magister equitum. "Master of horse"; cavalry commander, an important office as assistant to the *dictator* in the Republic and late Empire.

Magistrates. Ordinary magistrates:

- *Higher:*

  ▲ Consuls (2)
  ▲ Praetors (8)
  ▲ Censors (2)
  ▲ Curile aediles (2)

- *Lower:*

  ▲ Plebian aediles (2)
  ▲ Quaestors (20)

Extraordinary magistrates:

  ▲ Dictator
  ▲ Magister equitum
  ▲ Interrex

Magnus (the Great). Title given to Pompey by Sulla; Lucan's favorite term for him.

Maia. Italian goddess associated with Vulcan; mother of Mercury, by Jupiter; her festival celebrated in May.

Manes. Hostile spirits of the dead.

Manius. Common name for a beggar or vagabond.

Mantua. Market town on an island in the River Mincius in northern Italy.

Marcellus, Marcus Claudius. (42–23 B.C.); son of Octavia; nephew of Augustus; betrothed to Augustus' daughter Julia; groomed to be emperor. His sudden, perhaps suspicious death, in 23 placed the succession in question.

Mare internum (internal sea). Roman designation for the Mediterranean.

Marius, Gaius (c. 157–86 B.C.). General whose military achievements in Spain, against King Jugurtha in Africa, and against the Celtic Cimbri in upper Italy (102–101 B.C.) made him an important political figure (consul seven times between 107 and 86 B.C.). His new model army, recruited partly from the lower classes, became an instrument for future military coups. His political feud with Sulla—marked by failures, exile, a flight to Carthage, and successes—prompted the first of the civil wars. He died of ill health before he could consolidate his temporary ascendancy in Rome.

Mars (Greek: Ares). Symbolized by the wolf, the lance, and the woodpecker. Although originally an Italian god of agriculture, he became the Roman god of war and father of Romulus, the founder of Rome; second in power only to Jupiter. March 1 was one of his special holidays in Rome, his altar in the Campus Martius and his temple, of *Mars Ultor* ("Mars the Avenger") built by Augustus in the Forum.

Matinum. Coastal region in Apulia.

Mediolanum. Modern Milan; by the late third century A.D., it had become an important center of Roman culture and administration.

Melpomene. Muse of tragedy, or of poetry in general.

Mercury (Greek: Hermes). Son of Maia and Jupiter; god of travelers, boundaries, merchants, success, the arts, and thieves; messenger of the gods; escorter of souls from this world to the next. His mercantile festival was held on May 25. His temple was on the Aventine Hill. He is depicted carrying the caduceus, a herald's staff around which two snakes are entwined.

Messalina, Valeria (d. A.D. 48). Notoriously unfaithful wife of the emperor Claudius; mother of his daughter Octavia and son Britannicus, who was poisoned during the second year of Nero's reign (A.D. 55).

Mettius. Latin general of Alba Longa who broke his word to Rome. For punishment, he was tied to two chariots and torn apart.

Mincius. River in northern Italy, tributary of the Po; beloved of Virgil.

Minerva (Greek: Athena; Etruscan: Menrva). Born from Jupiter's head fully formed, she was goddess of reason, wisdom, war, crafts, trade guilds, and the arts; and was worshipped in her own chapel within the temple of Jupiter on the Capitoline Hill. She was depicted carrying a shield and spear.

Minos. Legendary king of Crete for whom Daedalus built the labyrinth; with his brother Rhadamanthys, one of the judges of the underworld.

Mithras. Ancient Indo-Iranian god of light, who became a Roman cult figure from the first to the fourth centuries A.D.

Mnester (d. A.D. 48). Famous actor executed by Claudius for his affair with Empress Messallina.

Moneta. Epithet of Juno as patroness of finances.

Moors. Arabian-Berber nomadic peoples from Mauretania in North Africa.

Munda. Southern Spanish city where the last battle of the Civil War was fought in 46 B.C., leaving Julius Caesar in undisputed control.

Muses. Daughters of Zeus and Mnemosyne; patronesses of the arts and sciences; lived on Mount Helicon, where they appeared to Hesiod. The Romans identified Calliope as the Muse of epic, Clio of history, Euterpe of flutes, Terpsichore of dance, Erato of lyric poetry, Melpomene of tragedy, Thalia of comedy, Polyhymnia of pantomime, and Urania of astronomy.

Mycenae. Chief city of Argos, in the Greek Peloponnesus; its king, Agamemnon, led the expedition against Troy to recover the wife of his brother Menelaos of Sparta.

Mytilene. City on the Greek island of Lesbos.

Naiads. Greek nymphs of fresh waters—lakes, springs, rivers.

Nar. Modern Nera; sulfurous river in central Italy, emptying into the Tiber.

Narcissus. (1) Son of the Boetian river god Cephisus and the nymph Liriope, a beautiful young man who rejected the love of the nymph Echo, fell in love with his own image in the water, and pined away to his death; he was changed into the flower by the same name. (2) Powerful freedman of the emperor Claudius, who amassed a fortune at the Empire's expense. Agrippina forced him to commit suicide after she poisoned Claudius.

Neapolis. Modern Naples, "new city"; port city in Campania, on the western slope of Mt. Vesuvius.

Necessitas (Greek: Ananke). Goddess of the inevitable; her symbol was the nail, by which the decrees of Fate are made realities.

Negotiatores. Citizens of the provinces who loaned money for interest to buy grain on speculation.

Nemausus. Modern Nîmes; important town of Gallia Narbonensis, a Roman colony situated west of the Rhone on the road from Spain to Italy. Site of the Maison Carrée, the well-preserved Roman Corinthian temple and the Pont du Gard, one of the finest surviving Roman aqueducts.

Nenia. A funeral dirge in honor of the dead; a goddess of the same name whose temple was near the Porta Viminalis.

Neptunus (Neptune); (Greek: Poseidon; Etruscan: Nethun). Italian god of the sea (originally of wells, springs, rivers, and fountains); husband of Salacia, goddess of saltwater; his temple was originally in the Circus Flaminius, later in the Campus Martius; his festival was celebrated July 23.

Nero, Claudius Caesar Drusus Germanicus. Born Lucius Domitius Ahenobarbus; A.D. 37–68. The fifth emperor, A.D. 54–68; son of Gnaeus Domitius Ahenobarbus and Agrippina the Younger; stepson of Claudius, who married Agrippina after the execution of the empress Messalina; nephew of Caligula. Famous for his interest in the arts (he was an actor, and spent much of his reign on stage) and nefarious crimes and persecution of Christians; he was under the control of his ambitious and shameless mother Agrippina. His first marriage was to Claudius' daughter Octavia. After a promising early reign under the influence of Seneca and Burrus, his debauched tendencies took over. Crimes he was accused of include murdering Claudius' son Britannicus, murdering his mother, poisoning Burrus, killing his pregnant second wife Poppaea Sabina with a kick, and the burning of Rome, which he blamed on the Christians. Gaius Calpurnius Piso's conspiracy against him was met with wholesale executions, including those of Lucan and Seneca. When the army and Senate finally rebelled against him, Nero ordered his own death.

Nerva, Marcus Cocceius (A.D. 30–98). Emperor (A.D. 96–98), who shaped a policy of imperial succession (through adoption of heirs by the reigning emperor) that brought stability to the empire for nearly 100 years.

Nones. Fifth or seventh day of the Roman month (depending on the number of days), falling nine days before the Ides.

Goblet, with skeletons and masks, first century A.D.

Notus. The south wind.

Novus homo. "New man"; one who had not yet won curile office.

Nox (Greek: Nyx). "Night"; daughter of Chaos, spouse of her brother Erebus; mother of Day and the Light; her symbols: a black sheep and a cock.

Numa of Pompilius. Successor of Romulus; second king of Rome (715–673 B.C.); a peace-loving lawmaker; legendary ancestor of the Pisos addressed by Horace in his *Ars Poetica.*

Numidia. Territory southwest of Carthage.

Nymphae (Nymphs). Minor female divinities of the field, stream, mountain, and forest.

Octavia (d. 11 B.C.). Sister of Octavian (later the emperor Augustus); daughter of Gaius Octavius and Atia; married to consul Gaius Marcellus, by whom she had three children. When Gaius died, she was married to Marc Antony to cement his alliance with Octavian; they had two daughters before he fell in love with Cleopatra and divorced her. When he and Cleopatra died she remained loyal to his memory and cared for all their children.

Octavia Claudia (c. A.D. 41–62). Nero's first wife, daughter of Claudius and Messalina; first divorced when he became enamored of the freedwoman Acte; then accused of treason, exiled, and executed by the emperor and his new wife Poppaea.

Octavian. *See* Augustus.

Octavius, Gaius. Affluent father of the emperor Augustus, first praetor, then governor of Macedonia; his second wife Atia, daughter of Julius Caesar's sister Julia, bore the future emperor as well as Octavian's sister Octavia.

Odoacer (d. A.D. 493). Chieftain and king of the Sciri (or Heruli), declared "King of Italy" by the Roman army in A.D. 476 and overthrew the Empire, ruling until he was defeated in battle and then slain by the Ostrogoth Theodoric in 493.

Odysseus (Roman: Ulysses). Trojan warrior, hero of Homer's *Odyssey,* whose wanderings en route home to Ithaca and his faithful Penelope form the basis of the great Greek epic.

Ops. Fertility, abundance, and harvest goddess; wife of Saturn. Her festival, called the *Opalia,* was held on December 19.

Optimates. Roman nobles, consisting of all those who had won a magistrate's office. Since all magistrates, after their term of office, automatically became senators, *optimates* were virtually indistinguishable from senators (though the children of *optimates* were automatically *optimates,* where senators held their office only for life).

Orcus. God of the underworld; death.

Orpheus (Orphism). Husband of Eurydice; legendary Thracian poet and student of Pythagoras; a musician, whose fifth-century B.C. cult shifted focus from the earth to heaven, practicing asceticism to release the soul from earthly desire and allow it to experience godhead. Orphics believed that all men are brothers, and in the unity of all living beings from the lowliest organism to God. The "sorrowful wheel" of reincarnation can be escaped only by initiation into the cult's purifications. Although rooted in Dionysian religion, Orphism believed that spiritual, not physical, rituals led to ecstasy. Orpheus has been called Dionysus "Apollonized."

Osiris. Egyptian god of the underworld who was identified with Bacchus; consort of Isis, he was associated with fertility. When he was killed and dismembered, Isis searched for his remains. Like Isis, he was the subject of cult worship in Rome.

Ostia. Gateway port and naval base of Rome, at the mouth of the Tiber about sixteen miles from the capital.

Ostrogoths. The "eastern" Goths who along with the Visigoths overran the Roman Empire in the third and fourth centuries A.D.; they were annihilated by the Huns.

Pacuvius (b. 220 B.C.). Tragedian, after his uncle Ennius.

Padus. Modern Po; the chief river of the territory that was to become northern Italy, dividing Cisalpine Gaul into Cispadine Gaul and Transpadane Gaul.

Paean. Ancient Greek god of healing, physician of the Olympians; later associated with Apollo, for whom Paean became another name. Also used for hymns of thanksgiving in his honor.

Paganalia. Movable agricultural festival, celebrated in two days in January with sacrifices to Ceres and Tellus.

Pagus. Administrative designation for a country district with scattered *vici* ("hamlets").

Palatine (Palatium). One of the seven hills of Rome, site of the earliest city; later it rose above the Roman Forum and was the site of the main imperial residence after Augustus (hence the word meant "palace").

Pales. Italian goddess of pastoral life and shepherds, her festival, the Parilia, was celebrated on April 21.

Palinurus. Pilot of Aeneas' ship who fell into the sea, giving his name to Cape Palinuro on the west coast of Lucania in southwest Italy.

Palla. Mantle worn by women over the *stola*, consisting of a square piece of cloth.

Pallas (Palladium). Title for Athena (Roman: Minerva), patroness of fortified cities. The Palladium was a sacred image of Athena sent by Zeus to Dardanus, the founder of Troy. When it was stolen by Odysseus and Diomedes, Troy's doom was sealed. One tradition says that Aeneas brought it with him to Rome.

Pallor and Pavor. "Paleness" and "Terror"; companions of Mars, the war god.

Palma. Palm branch given to victors in athletic contests.

Pamphila. An historian quoted by Aulus Gellius, who lived in Nero's reign and wrote an historical miscellany. Nothing of her work survives.

Pan. Son of Hermes, originally Arcadian goat-footed god of flocks and shepherds; inventor of the reed pipe. Sudden terror (panic) was caused by him, giving rise to "pandemonium." Since pan in Greek also means "all" or "whole," he later became a "universal" god. Depicted with horns and the hind legs of a goat.

Panaetius (c. 185/180–c. 109 B.C.). Stoic philosopher from Rhodes, mentor of Scipio Africanus the Younger. Cicero's *De Officiis* is also influenced by Panaetius' *Treatise on Duty*.

Pannonia. Province between the Alps and the Danube, conquered by Augustus by 33 B.C.

Panormus. Modern Palermo; commercially important city in northern Sicily conquered from the Carthaginians in the First Punic War.

Pansa, Gaius Vibius. Friend of Julius Caesar; successor of Brutus as governor of Cisalpine Gaul.

Pantheon. Most perfectly preserved temple of ancient Rome, and one of its greatest architectural accomplishments, built in 27–25 B.C.

by M. Vipsanius Agrippa, dedicated to all the gods. It was preserved and enlarged by Domitian and Hadrian.

Pantomimus ("pantomime"). Dramatization through dancing and rhythmic gestures.

Paris (Alexander; Alexandros). Trojan archer-prince, son of Hecuba and Priam, who carried off Helen, the wife of Menelaos. Aphrodite promised Helen to him if he gave her the award for beauty in her contest with Hera and Athena. Seeking revenge for the death of his brother Hector, he killed Achilles by wounding him in the one place where he was not invulnerable.

Parma. Town in Cispadane Gaul known for its wool.

Parnassus. Mountain of the Pindus range near Delphi, sacred to Apollo, Dionysius, and the Muses.

Parrhasia. Town of Arcadia in southern Greece from where Evander led his people to settle what was later to be the site of Rome.

Parthia. Unconquered kingdom on the Roman frontiers in Asia Minor southeast of the Caspian Sea; successor to Persia's power; perceived as a constant military threat, the Parthians figured frequently in Roman historical writings. Famous for their archers, who continued shooting as they retreated (hence, "Parthian shot," corrupted to "parting shot").

Patavium. Modern Padua; most important town in northern Italy, especially for its wool trade.

Pater Familias ("Family Father"). The master of a house.

Patricii ("Patricians"). Roman citizens from ancient landed families, the hereditary aristocracy that formed its own ruling party opposed to the plebeians.

Paullus, Lucius Aemilius. Aristocratic son of consul Marcus Paullus and himself consul in 219 and 216 B.C. As a general, he advised against the battle of Cannae but chose to die rather than to fly from the battlefield.

Pavor. *See* **Pallor.**

Pax Romana. Pax was the Roman goddess of peace, her temple the Via Sacra; and the Pax Romana was the term given to designate a period of peace during the Empire. The years of peace initiated with Octavian's final victory over the Liberators at Actium in 31 B.C. was known as the Pax Augusta.

Peculium. Allowance given by the Pater Familias to a son or slave.

Pegasus. Winged horse, son of Medusa, tamed by Bellerophon. Associated with Zeus' thunderbolt.

Pelasgus (Pelasgians). Mythical king of Argos. Greeks in general were often called Pelasgians because of a legend that Pelasgus was their earliest ancestor. Homer also uses the term to refer to a tribe allied with Troy.

Penates. Household gods who guarded the pantry *(penus)*. Associated with the *lar(es)*.

Penelope. Daughter of Icarius; wife of Ulysses, who faithfully awaited his return on Ithaca after the Trojan War. Roman model of wifely virtue.

Penthesilea. Daughter of Ares; queen of the Amazons; ally of Troy; slain by Achilles.

Peregrinus ("pilgrim"). Legal term for a "resident alien" in Roman territory.

Peripatetics. Philosophers of the school of Aristotle, who delivered their instruction while walking. The Greek verb from which the name is derived means "to walk about."

Persephone. *See* **Proserpina.**

Perseus. (1) Mythical hero; son of Zeus and Danae; slayer of Medusa. (2) Last king of Macedonia (179–168 B.C.), decisively defeated by the Romans at Pydna in 168.

Persona. Mask worn by actors, and used to cover the faces of the dead.

Pervigilium. Nighttime festival in honor of a god or goddess.

Phallus. Male procreative organ. As a symbol of fertility and of the god Priapus, it was worn as a potency charm in ancient Rome.

Pharsalus. Town in Thessaly near which Caesar defeated Pompey in the decisive battle of 48 B.C.

Philippi. Modern Filibah; town in Macedonia famous for the battle (42 B.C.) in which the assassins of Julius Caesar, Brutus and Cassius, were defeated by Marc Antony and Octavian.

Phoebus. *See* Apollo.

Pictura. Painting.

Picumnus. Ancient Italian god of agriculture; married to Danae; inventor of manure; associated with Picus.

Pieria. District on the southeast coast of Macedonia (Thessaly) on the northern side of Mount Olympus, sacred to the Muses in preclassical times.

Pietas. Goddess of devotion and loyalty.

Pindus. Mountain range in northern Greece, associated with the Muses.

Piper (pepper). Used as a seasoning, imported from India.

Pisae. Modern Pisa; ancient city of the Etrurians.

Piso. Famous plebeian family, originally known for their agricultural pursuits. C. Piso was the ringleader of a conspiracy against Nero in A.D. 65 uncovered by a freedman of one of the conspirators. He died by opening his own veins rather than face execution by the emperor.

Pleiades. Constellation made of the seven daughters of Atlas and Pleione who were turned into stars when Orion pursued them.

Pluto (Pluton). Supreme god of the underworld, another name for Hades.

Poeni (Phoenicians). Alternate name for the Carthaginians, because their city was founded by the Phoenicians.

Pollio, Gaius Asinius. Friend of Virgil; a poet, as well as orator and historian. He fought on Caesar's side during the Civil War, and later with Marc Antony against the Liberators. When in charge of Transpadane Gaul, he

helped Virgil recover his ancestral farm. He served as consul in 40 B.C.

Pollio, Vedius. A knight and friend of Augustus of such cruelty that he tossed slaves who displeased him to his lampreys. Unable to temper his friend's wrath, the emperor ordered his fish pond filled up.

Pollux (Greek: Polydeukes). One of the Gemini "twins" (Greek: Dioscuri); brother of Kastor; son of Zeus and Leda (or Leda and Tyndareus); brother of Helen.

Pomona. Italian goddess of fruit trees.

Pompeii. City of Campania, in the shadow of Vesuvius, destroyed by an eruption in A.D. 79.

Pompey, Gnaeus Pompeius Magnus ("the Great") (106–48 B.C.). Republican general who served Sulla and then the Senate with great military successes in Spain, Africa, and the Middle East. A member of the first triumvirate, his alliance with Julius Caesar failed and he became, instead, the military leader of the senatorial party. Defeated by Caesar at Pharsalus, he fled to Egypt, where he was captured and executed by the eunuch regent of Egypt, Pothinus.

Pons (Bridge). Also a term for towns or military posts strategically placed at river crossings.

Pontifex. Member of the college of high-priests.

Pontus. Territory in Asia Minor, south of the Black Sea.

Populares (Commoners). The "common people" of Rome, specifically all those who had not served as a magistrate.

Porcia (d. 42). Daughter of Cato and loyal wife of Brutus, assassin of Julius Caesar; she killed herself when she learned of her husband's death.

Porsenna, Lars. King of Etruscan Clusium, who besieged Rome in order to restore the exiled Tarquin the Proud but was stopped at the bridge between the Janiculum and Rome by Horatius.

Porta (Gate). City gate, usually flanked by bastions.

Pompeii: the House of Loreius Tiburtinus

Porticus. Colonnade.

Portunus. God of harbors.

Poseidon (Roman: Neptune). Son of Cronos and Rhea; brother of Zeus; father of the Cyclopes; god of the sea; his name literally: "spouse of the rivers"; also the cause of earthquakes. Horse racing was under his patronage. After the fall of Minoan civilization through earthquakes and tidal waves, the predominant preclassical ocean god until his primacy was usurped by Zeus.

Pothinus. Eunuch regent of Egypt in 48 B.C., who ordered the execution of Pompey and was himself executed by Caesar for conspiring against him.

Praefectus. One of twelve officers appointed by the consuls to command allied troops. The warden of the city of Rome was known as the *Praefectus urbi.*

Praetor. Originally a title of the consul, it came to designate, after the consulship became open to the plebs, the chief administrator of justice in the various courts of Rome. The praetor sometimes served as assistant consul.

Priam. Son of Laomedon; last king of Troy during the Trojan War; husband of Hecuba; according to Homeric tradition father of fifty sons and many daughters, including Hector, Cassandra, and Paris (Alexandros).

Priapus (Priapos). Son of Dionysus and Aphrodite (Venus); god of fertility, animal husbandry; protector of gardens; usually represented with erect penis. The city of Priapus in Mysia was the center of his worship.

Proconsul. Official who represents the consul in a district outside Rome.

Proculus. Senator instructed by the ghost of Romulus to announce that he was to be worshipped as Quirinus, a god.

Prometheus. Demigod who created humanity from clay and who, for stealing fire from Olympus to give to his creations, was punished for eternity by Zeus by being chained to a rock while an eagle fed daily on his liver.

Proserpina (Greek: Persephone). Daughter of Ceres (Demeter); wife of Pluto; queen of the underworld.

Provincia. The territory ruled by a single magistrate; the conquered territory ruled by a Roman governor.

Proteus. Greek sea god and shape-shifter, associated with the elusiveness of truth.

Publicola, Publius Valerius (d. 503 B.C.). Roman leader active in expelling the Tarquins from Rome.

Pudicitia (Greek: Aidos). Goddess of chastity and modesty.

Punic Wars. The three wars between Rome and Carthage, 264–146 B.C., ending with the complete destruction of Carthage.

Pyrrha. Sole survivor, with her husband Deucalion, of the ancient flood.

Pyrrho. Founder of the Skeptical school of philosophy, which maintained that certainty was unattainable and that the greatest good was a life of virtue.

Pyrrhus. King of Epirus, whose invasion of Italy was stopped at Asculum in 279 B.C., though he won the battle (hence "Pyrrhic victory").

Pythagoras. Greek philosopher of the sixth century B.C., whose sect was established in Croton, Magna Graecia; believed in transmigration of the soul and asceticism.

Pytho. Ancient name for Delphi, where the python priestess gave oracular answers to pilgrims' prayers, before she was replaced by the Delphic Apollo whose totem was the dolphin *(delphos)*.

Quadragesima. Fortieth part (2.5 percent) of imported goods, collected as provincial tax.

Quadriga. Four-horse chariot used in games and battles.

Quaestio. Court of inquiry.

Quaestor. Lowest-ranking official in the *cursus honorum*, held by all those seeking a senatorial career. The quaestor's office was usually a financial one, managing treasuries and assisting the proconsul in his absence.

Quies. Goddess of rest and relaxation.

Quintilius Varus. Friend of Horace and Virgil, whose death Horace mourns in his *Odes*.

Quirinus. Lance-wielding Sabine deity (his wife: Hora) later identified with Romulus, and with his father Mars. His festival, the Quirinalia, was held on February 17 (the day Romulus was assumed into heaven).

Quirites. Term of uncertain derivation, referring to "Roman citizens." When applied to soldiers, it was an insult.

Recitatio. Public reading of a literary work by the author.

Rectus (d. 40 A.D.). Stoic philosopher executed by Caligula.

Rediculus. God honored in Rome for causing Hannibal to stop short of the city gates; his temple was at the Porta Capena.

Res Privata Principis. Term used to designate the personal treasury of the emperor.

Rhadamanthys. Son of Zeus and Europa; brother of Minos; ruler of Phaistos in Crete; appointed with his brother a judge of the dead.

Rheims. Principal city of the Gallic Rhemi, Roman capital of Gallia Belgica.

Rhine (Rhenus). Frontier river between Roman and "barbarian" German territory.

Rhodes (Rhodus). Easternmost Aegean island, near the Carian mainland; attached to the province of Asia after Vespasian. Tiberius made it his home away from home.

Rhodope. Mountain range in Thrace; legendary homeland of Orpheus.

Robigus. God of nature and crops, manifesting his displeasure through rust and blight. Sheep and dogs were sacrificed to placate him. His April 25 festival was known as the Robigalia.

Roma. Divine personification of the city, depicted on coins as a beautiful woman. Her temple in Rome was constructed by Hadrian.

Romulus. Son of Mars and Rhea Silvia; brother of Remus, suckled with him by a she-wolf; mythical founder and first king of Rome.

Romulus Augustulus (late fifth century A.D.). Last emperor of the western empire, ruling 475–76, reigning through the military power of his father Orestes. Romulus was deposed by Odoacer and allowed to live out his life in the Campania countryside.

Rostra. Platform in the Forum from which speeches were delivered, so called because it was decorated with the prows *(rostra)* of conquered ships.

Rubicon (Rubico). North Italian "Red River," near Ravenna, boundary between Italy and Gallia Cisalpina. When Julius Caesar crossed it, in 49 B.C., with his army, against the direct orders of the Senate, the Civil War had begun.

Rufina, Pomponia (d. A.D. 213). Vestal Virgin, executed by being buried alive, allegedly for her impurity.

Rusticus, Arulenus. Stoic philosopher who, according to Suetonius, was put to death by Domitian for writing a panegyric on Thrasea, a Roman senator who met his end at Nero's order.

Sabina, Vibia (d. A.D. 128?). Wife of Hadrian; empress 117–136; known for her infidelities with praetorian prefect Septicius Clarus and imperial secretary Suetonius Tranquillus.

Sabines. Tribe inhabiting the territory directly north of Rome.

Sacramentum. Loyalty oath sworn by the legions.

Saguntum. Modern Sagunto; city in Spain which fell to Carthage at the outset of the Second Punic War.

Salii. "Jumpers," "leapers"; name given to the college of dancing priests serving the god Mars.

Salus. Italian goddess of health, associated with the Greek goddess Hygiea (Hygieia); her festival was on August 5.

Salutatio. Custom of greeting important leaders each morning in Rome, a time for asking and bestowing favors. Also used for the troops' salutation to their generals, in recognition of their status as *imperator*.

Saturn (Saturnus). Early Italian god of agriculture and sowing, later associated with Greek Cronos; god of time; father of Jupiter, who deposed him as king of heaven; husband of Ops. His temple at the foot of the Capitoline Hill served as the state treasury.

Saturnalia. Festival of Saturn celebrated with great merriment at the winter solstice, December 17–19; gifts were exchanged and social status discarded for the duration.

Satyrs. Mythic race of beings, sons of Hermes and Iphthima, with goatlike characteristics; followers of Pan and/or Dionysus, who symbolized the animal vitality of human nature. On vases they are frequently painted with penis erect, attacking nymphs from behind.

Scaevola, Quintus Mucius (c. 140–82 B.C.). Famous orator, published the first systematic treatise on civil law.

Scipio, Publius Cornelius Scipio Aemilianus (c. 185–129 B.C.). Served as consul in 147, then put in military charge of the Third Punic War, destroying Carthage in 146.

Scorpus. Famous charioteer of Martial's time.

Scribonia. Sister of Lucius Scribonius Libo, Pompey's father-in-law; married to Octavian. In 39 B.C., on the day she bore him his daughter Julia, he divorced her in favor of Livia Drusilla. In 2 B.C., when he banished Julia, Scribonia accompanied her daughter into exile. Augustus said he couldn't stand her nagging.

Scylla. Homeric sea monster confronted by Odysseus (Ulysses); she barked like a dog and had long necks and twelve feet, living in a cave on the Italian side of the straits between Italy and Sicily, across from the whirlpool Charybdis.

Scythia. Remote territory in what is now southern Russia.

Segovia. Town in Hispania Lusitania (Spain); site of one of the greatest Roman acqueducts.

Sejanus, Lucius Aelius (d. A.D. 31). From distinguished Etruscan origins, he quickly rose to power as prefect of the Praetorian Guard A.D. 14–31 under Tiberius and ruled Rome in the emperor's absence after A.D. 27. He was accused of poisoning Tiberius' son Drusus in 23 A.D. His brutality when Tiberius retired to Capri in 26 made him many enemies; their influence with Tiberius finally brought the emperor to charge Sejanus with treason and to execute him.

Semele. Daughter of Cadmus, mother of Dionysus.

Sempronius. Consul defeated by Hannibal at the river Trebia, in 218 B.C.

Senate (Senatus). Originally composed of patricians advising the monarch, the Senate evolved into the chief legislative and executive body elected by the consuls or the censors. After Sulla, any man who had served as *quaestor* was entitled to a senatorial seat. The Senate shaped the laws for the assembly to vote on and pass. Its powers included:

- nominating magistrates for election by the assemblies;
- deciding on revenues and expenditures;
- determining foreign policy and government of the provinces;
- directing the religious worship in Rome.

Septemviri. "The board of seven," the most influential priesthood in Rome in charge of organizing festivals for the Capitoline gods.

Septimius Severus, Lucius (A.D. 146–211). Emperor 193–211; father of the emperors Caracalla and Geta; founder of the "Severan Dynasty."

Serapis (Sarapis). Egyptian god, later associated with Zeus, whose worship spread throughout the Roman empire. Imported into the capital by Caligula.

Seres. Roman name for the Chinese.

Servius. Fourth- to fifth-century A.D. grammarian noted for his commentary on Virgil.

Severa, Aurelia. One of the Vestal Virgins buried alive by Caracalla in A.D. 213 for her alleged sins against chastity.

Sibyl. Divinely inspired prophetess, usually of Apollo; the most important was at Cumae.

Silenus. Known as "Papa-Silenus"; the jolly old satyr who raised and taught the infant Dionysus.

Silvanus. Originally Italian, then Roman god of woodlands, wilderness, boundaries, and gardens.

Simo. Stock character of Roman comedy.

Sirens. Sea nymphs, daughters of Phorcys, who had the power of charming and luring to destruction all who heard their songs. Odysseus evades them by tying himself to his mast.

Sirius. The dog star.

Sisyphus. Son of Aeolus and Enarete; king of Corinth, and founder of the royal house there. For his avarice he was punished in Hades by being forced to roll a stone uphill for all eternity as depicted in Virgil's *Aeneid*. Antony named his pet dwarf after him.

Socrates. Athenian philosopher; mentor of Plato; put to death for his refusal to kow-tow to the gods of the city.

Solidus. Most important gold coin of the late Empire, initiated to replace the *aureus* by Constantine the Great.

Sol Invictus (Unconquered Sun). Originally a god of the Sabines, later associated with the Greek Helios and Apollo; his temple was on the Quirinal Hill, his feast: August 8. Aurelian made him the universal deity of the entire Roman Empire.

Sophocles. Classical Athenian playwright, whose plays included *Antigone* and *Oedipus the King*.

Soracte. Mountain north of Rome, associated with the Muses.

Sosii. Family name of two brothers who were booksellers and publishers in Rome.

Spartacus. Thracian gladiator slave; led the murderous slave rebellion that ravaged south-ern Italy in 73–71 B.C. Crassus and Pompey defeated and executed him.

Spes. God of hope; his festival: August 1.

Sphinx. Monster with a winged lion's body and a woman's breast and head who proposed a riddle to the Thebans, killing all who could not solve it. When Oedipus answered correctly, she killed herself. The riddle: "What goes on four feet in the morning, two at noon, and three in the evening?" Answer: Man.

Sportula. Literally "a little basket." A term used to indicate the gifts, often very trifling, given by a Roman to his clients.

S.P.Q.R. Still seen throughout the city today, where modern Romans tell you they stand for *"Sono porci questi romani"* ("These Romans

Detail of sewer, Neapolis, Italica

are pigs"), the letters stood for *Senatus popu-lusque romanus* ("the Senate and the Roman people") and were inscribed on coins, monuments, standards, and public buildings to remind citizens of their nation's power.

Spurinna. Augur who warned Caesar, "Beware the Ides of March."

Stella, Lucius Arruntius. Consul A.D. 101; close associate of the emperor Domitian; patron of Martial and Statius.

Stilicho, Flavius (c. A.D. 365–408). *Magister militum*, "Master of the soldiers," 394–408, ruled the western empire for Honorius. Half Roman, half Vandal by birth, he was married to Serena, niece of Emperor Theodosius I; their daughter married Honorius. Later, accused of selling out to the Visigoth Alaric, he was executed by Honorius.

Stoics. Members of a school of philosophy that originated with the Greek Zeno toward the end of the fourth century B.C. and was introduced into Rome by Panaetius in the second century B.C. It placed an emphasis on duty instead of pleasure, the latter held by the Epicureans to be the greatest good. The Stoics maintained that nature was the embodiment of the mind of god and that wisdom lay in conformity with nature. Famous Roman Stoics included Scaevola, Scipio Aemilianus, Seneca the Younger, and Marcus Aurelius.

Strabo. First-century B.C. Greek geographer, whose travels throughout the Roman world he recorded in seventeen books of observations.

Strenia. Goddess of health and vigor. Twigs taken from her grove in Rome were exchanged as presents at New Year's to bring good luck.

Styx. Daughter of Oceanus and Tethys; the principal river of Hades which flows around the underworld seven times and which souls of the dead had to cross to gain entrance.

Suadela. Goddess of persuasiveness.

Subura (Suburra). The commercial and red-light district, in a valley created by the Esquiline, Quitrinal, and Viminal Hills.

Sulla, Lucius Cornelius (c. 138–78 B.C.). General famed for victories in Africa, Germany, Gaul, and Asia. In a civil war, Sulla captured Rome and was, in 82 B.C., elected dictator. He restored constitutional government, and served as consul in 80.

Sura, Lucius Licinius. Consul A.D. 97, 102, 107; governor of Germany; a patron of Martial.

Taenarus. Town in Laconia, the southernmost promontory of the Greek Peloponnesus, near which was an entrance to Hades.

Tamesis. Modern Thames, the most important river in Britain.

Tanaquil. Fortune-telling Etruscan wife of Tarquinius Priscus, the fifth king of Rome (c. 600 B.C.).

Tantalus. Son of Zeus and the Titaness Pluto; father of Pelops, Broteas, and Niobe; grandfather of Atreus. Variously king of Lydia, Argos, or Corinth. For divulging secrets entrusted to him, and for serving them a dish of his son's flesh, he was punished in Hades by reaching forever for the receding fruit of an overhanging tree.

Tarentum. Modern Taranto; city on the heel of the Italian "boot," where Marc Antony and Octavian signed an uneasy treaty in 37 B.C. reaffirming the triumvirate.

Tarquin the Proud (Tarquinius Superbus). Etruscan (and last) king of Rome; expelled in 510 B.C.

Tartarus. Son of Aether and Gaia; father of the Giants. In Homer "Tartarus" is the deepest pit of Hades; to the Romans, synonymous with the underworld in general.

Telegonus. Son of Ulysses, whom he killed by mistake; founder of Latian Tusculum.

Tellus. Goddess of the earth, honored at agricultural festivals in January and April.

Tempestates. Goddess of weather, her temple was in Rome.

Terminus. God of boundaries and boundary stones, worshipped in the Temple of Jupiter on the Capitoline Hill.

Tessera (Ticket). For admission to circuses, theater, and games.

Tethys. Daughter of Ouranos and Gaia; wife of Oceanus.

Teutons. Germanic tribe from the Baltic region; destroyed by Marius in 102 B.C. at the Battle of Aquae Sextiae; term used to identify Germans in general.

Thalia. Muse of pastoral poetry and comedy.

Themis. Daughter of Ouranos and Gaia; goddess of law, and of custom.

Theodosius I (d. A.D. 395). Flavius "the Great"; eastern emperor 378–92; sole emperor of east and west 392–95; father of the emperor Honorius; ardent defender of Christianity and foe of paganism; banished the Visigoths to Thrace; after his death, the Empire was divided permanently into east and west.

Theodosius II (A.D. 401–50). Flavius; nephew of Honorius; longest reigning emperor in Roman history (408–50); grandson of Theodosius I. His daughter married the western emperor Valentinian III.

Theseus. Legendary king of Attica; son of Aegeus and Aethra; father of Hippolytus, Demophoon, Acamas, and Melanippus; defeated the Centaurs at the wedding feast of Pirithous; volunteered to go to Knossos and destroy the Minotaur that demanded annual tribute from the Greeks. After succeeding with the help of Ariadne's golden thread, he abandoned her on Naxos.

Thespis. Legendary founder of tragedy, who won the prize at the first tragic festival in c. 536–533 B.C.

Thessalia (Thessaly). Largest region in Greece. south of Macedonia; liberated by Rome in 196 B.C.; incorporated into the Roman province of Macedonia in 148 B.C.

Thetis. Daughter of Nereus and Doris; a sea nymph; wife of Peleus, mother of Achilles.

Thrace. Region north of the Aegean, south of the Danube, east of Macedonia, and west of the Black Sea; its inhabitants among Rome's fiercest mercenaries.

Thunderer. Jupiter or Jove, the Roman sky god, whose symbol was the thunderbolt.

Thurii. Town in southern Italy.

Tiber. Originally called the Albula, the chief river of Italy upon whose banks Rome was founded. Its festival was celebrated on May 14.

Tiberinus. (1) God of the River Tiber; his festival: December 8. (2) Alban king drowned in the Albula, which then became known as the Tiber.

Tiberius (Tiberius Claudius Nero Caesar) (42 B.C.–37 A.D.). Son of Livia Drusilla and Tiberius Claudius Nero; emperor (A.D. 14–37); stepson and successor of Augustus (Augustus married Livia); married Augustus' daughter Julia; father of the emperor Claudian.

Tibur. Town north of Rome, site of Horace's estate.

Ticinus. River in the far north of Italy and location of a battle in the Second Punic War.

Tigris. Along with the Euphrates, a principal river of Mesopotamia; boundary between the Parthian and Persian empires.

Timavus. Northeastern Italian river forming the boundary between Venetia and Istria.

Tiphys. Helmsman of the *Argo* in the quest for the Golden Fleece described in the *Argonautica* of Apollonius of Rhodes.

Titans. Twelve sons and daughters of Gaia and Ouranos—including Oceanus, Tethys, Hyperion, Cronos, Rhea, Themis, Phoebe, Mnemosyne, and Iapetus—who made war against the gods.

Tithonus (Tithonos). Mortal loved by Aurora, who begged Zeus to give him eternal life but forgot to add "eternal youth" to her prayer.

Titus (Titus Flavius Vespasianus) (A.D. 41–81). Son of the emperor Vespasian; brother of Domitian; captured in Jerusalem in A.D. 70; Emperor 79–81.

Tivoli. Hilltop town fifteen miles from Rome where Hadrian constructed a magnificent villa.

Toga. White woolen outer garment worn by Roman citizens.

Tomis. Town of Moesia on the west coast of the Black Sea, to which Augustus banished the poet Ovid.

Tophet. Literary name for hell.

Trajan (Marcus Ulpius Traianus) (A.D. 53–117). Adopted son of Nerva; governor of Germany; militant emperor A.D. 98–117; campaigned against the Dacians and the Parthians.

Trasimene. Lake in Etruria and site of a battle in the Second Punic War (217 B.C.).

Trebatius. Distinguished attorney in the circle of Cicero, Caesar, and Augustus.

Trebia. River in upper Italy, by which a battle was fought in the Second Punic War (218 B.C.).

Tribune. In charge of summoning and presiding over the *Comitia Tributa*, the tribune was a defender of the plebs with powerful rights of veto.

Triton. Sea god; son of Poseidon and Amphitrite; his trumpet calmed the sea.

Triumvirates. First: alliance of Julius Caesar, Pompey, and Crassus. Second: Augustus, Marc Antony, and Lepidus.

Trivia. Diana.

Tullius, Servius (578–535 B.C.). Born to a slave mother, he became the sixth king of Rome.

Turbo. A small gladiator famous for courage disproportionate to his size.

Tuscan. Etruscan.

Twelve Tables. First codification of traditional Roman law, c. 450 B.C.

Tyndareus. King of Sparta; husband of Leda; and at least the foster father of Castor, Polydeuces, Helen, and Klytaimnestra.

Tyros (Tyre). Famous port of Phoenicia (modern Lebanon) in the Roman province of Syria; noted for its purple dye.

Tyrrhenian Sea (Tyrrhene). Sea west of Rome and roughly east of Sardinia and Corsica, north of Sicily; also known as the Tuscan Sea.

Ulpian (Domitius Ulpianus) (c. A.D. 170–228). Born in Tyre, he was a leading jurist of the third century A.D. and, with Paulus, prefect of the Praetorian Guard under Lucius Septimus Severus and Elagabalus. His most important works were *Ad Edictum*, eighty-one books on the praetorian law, and *Ad Sabinum*, fifty-one books on civil law.

Ultor (Avenger). Epithet of Mars; his temple was built in the Forum Augustum by Octavius in honor of his vengeance on the murderers of Octavius' uncle, Julius Caesar.

Ulysses (Greek: Odysseus). Subject of Homer's *Odyssey*, Greek warrior whose wanderings back to his home in Ithaca took him through twenty years of adventures and became the model for the first six books of Virgil's *Aeneid*.

Umbra. Ghost or "shade," inhabitant of the underworld in the same shape it occupied in life.

Umbria. Mountainous territory in central Italy south of Cisalpine Gaul; one of its chief towns was Umbrium (modern Urbino). Originally home of the Umbri, who were defeated by the Etruscans.

Uncia (Ounce). A measurement: a twelfth part of anything.

Urania (Greek: Ourania). Daughter of Zeus and Mnemosyne; the Muse of astronomy.

Uranus (Greek: Ouranos). Husband of Gaia (Earth) and father of Oceanus, Hyperion, Cronos, Mercury, Venus, and others.

Ustica. Valley near Horace's Sabine farm.

Valentinian I (A.D. 321–75). Last successful emperor of the western Empire (A.D. 364–75); renowned for his military leadership; appointed his brother Valens emperor of the east. Rebuilt the Rhine fortifications and pacified Britain.

Valerian (Publius Licinius Valerianus) (d. A.D. 260). Emperor 253–60; known for his fierce purge of Christians. After the Battle of Edessa, he was captured and executed by the Persian king Shapur who stuffed his body and put it in display.

Vallonia. Goddess of valleys.

Vandals. Powerful Germanic tribe from the Baltic coast, then Hungary, that swept over Western Europe and eventually established a kingdom in Africa.

Vatican. Westernmost of the hills of Rome, across the Tiber; site of the upside-down crucifixion of St. Peter, where Constantine erected a basilica in A.D. 326.

Varenus. In the *Punica*, a warrior fighting on the Roman side at the Battle of Trebia.

Varius, Lucius Rufus. Poet of the Augustan age; friend of Virgil, Horace, and Maecenas; author of epics and a tragedy, *Thyestes*, which Quintilian lauded.

Veii. Important Etruscan city north of Rome; its inhabitants, called Veientes, hated Rome; captured by the dictator Camillus in 396 B.C.

Venetia. Territory in northern Italy; the "tenth region" in Augustus' reorganization of Italy; its cities included Patavium (Padua), Aquileia, and, from the fifth century A.D., Venetia (Venice).

Venus. Wife of Mars; goddess of sexual love (corresponding to the Greek Aphrodite); mother of Aeneas and Cupid; protectress of Rome. The emperor Augustus and the Julian family claimed descent from her through Aeneas' son, Julus. The temple of Venus Erycina (her title derived from her shrine on Mount Eryx in Sicily) was dedicated on the Capitoline Hill in 217 B.C. The festival of Venus Genetrix ("Universal Mother") was celebrated on September 26; her temple was dedicated by Julius Caesar in 46 B.C. The Veneralia, celebrated April 1, was dedicated to Venus Verticordia, "Turner of Hearts."

Venusia. Town in Apulia; birthplace of Horace.

Vercingetorix. Chieftain of the Arverni who united Gaul to oppose Caesar and his legions. In 52 B.C. the Gauls were defeated at Alesia. Vercingetorix was taken captive and later put to death in Rome some time after Caesar's triumph in 45 B.C.

Verona. Major city of northern Italy, north of Mantua and west of Patavium (Padua); gateway to the Alps.

Vertumnus (Vortumnus). Husband of Pomona; ancient Italian god of the changing year and of fruit orchards; his festival: August 13.

Verus, Lucius (Lucius Aelius Aurelius Commodus) (A.D. 130–169). Adopted son of Antoninus Pius, at the insistence of Hadrian; co-emperor with Marcus Aurelius A.D. 161–69.

Vespasian (Titus Flavius Sabinus Vespasianus) (A.D. 9–79). Soldier emperor A.D. 69–79; restored stability after Nero and the civil war of 69; father, by Flavia Domitilla, of the emperors Titus and Domitian.

Vesper. The evening star.

Vesta. Goddess of the hearth and of the city; her cult, centered on tending her eternal flame, was served by the Vestal Virgins whose house was in the Forum. In early Rome, honored each day at the hearth by the entire family. Her temple in the Forum housed the eternal flame tended by the Vestal Virgins.

Vesuvius. Volcano in Campania near the Bay of Naples that erupted on August 24, 79 A.D., burying Pompeii, Herculaneum, and Stabiae.

Vettius, Lucius. Knight bribed (allegedly by Caesar) to implicate distinguished Romans, including Cicero, in a conspiracy to assassinate Pompey.

Vexillarii. Divisions of the legions entirely made up of veterans who chose not to retire after their full term of service.

Victoria (Greek: Nike). Daughter of Styx and Pallas Athena; goddess of victory and success; protectress of heroes; her festivals: July 17 and August 1; she was also worshipped during games and circuses.

Vigiles. The imperial fire brigade organized by Augustus; commanded by the *praefectus vigilum*.

Vinalia. Annual wine festival; celebrated August 19–20 when the first grapes of the new vintage were cut.

House of the Vestal Virgins, in the Old Forum

Vindobona. Modern Vienna; strategically important, originally Celtic, market city on the Danube, in the province of Pannonia Superior.

Virginia. Legendary heroine; stabbed to death by her centurion father to save her from the advances of the decemvir Appius Claudius. Her death marked Rome's return to nontyrannical government.

Virtus. God of physical and moral virtue; his festival: July 17.

Visigoths. These "western Goths" (as opposed to the Ostrogoths) besieged Rome in A.D. 409 and sacked it on August 24, 410, defeating the meager defenses of the emperor Honorius.

Volturnus. Alternate name for the river god Tiber. His festival, the Volturnalia, was celebrated on August 27.

Vulcan (Volcanus). God of fire; identified with Greek Hephaestus; god of the arts and of the forge; patron god of Ostia. His festivals were celebrated on May 23 and August 23.

Xanthus. Modern Gunik; capital of the province of Lycia, destroyed in 42 B.C. by its own citizens in a mass suicide when Marcus Brutus tried to exact tribute from them for his war against Augustus and Antony.

Xenophon. Born on the Greek island of Cos, he became, at the invitation of Agrippina, final physician to the emperor Claudius; he assisted her in murdering him (with a feather dipped in poison).

Zama. Town in Numidia where the final battle in the Second Punic War was fought.

Zephyrus. The Greek god of the west wind.

Zeus. Supreme god of the Greeks. *See* **Jupiter.**

SOURCES & RECOMMENDATIONS

Adkins, Lesley, and Roy A. Adkins. *Handbook to Life in Ancient Rome.* New York: Facts On File, 1994.

Andreae, B. *The Art of Rome.* London: Macmillan, 1978.

Atchity, Kenneth J., ed. *The Classical Greek Reader.* New York: Henry Holt, 1996.

Balsdon, J. P. V. D. *Life and Leisure in Ancient Rome.* London: Bodley Head, 1962.

Barnstone, Aliki, and Willis Barnstone. *A Book of Women Poets from Antiquity to Now.* New York: Schocken Books, Inc., 1992.

Bickerman, E. J. *Chronology of the Ancient World.* 2nd edition. London: Thames and Hudson, 1980.

Boardman, J., J. Griffin, and O. Murray. *The Roman World.* Oxford: Oxford University Press, 1986.

Bonner, S. F. *Education in Ancient Rome from the Elder Cato to the Younger Pliny.* London: Methuen, 1977.

Boyle, A. J., and J. P. Sullivan. *Roman Poets of the Early Empire.* London: Penguin Books Ltd., 1991.

Bradley, P. *Ancient Rome: Using Evidence.* Victoria: Edward Arnold, 1990.

Bunson, Matthew. *Encyclopedia of the Roman Empire.* New York: Facts On File, 1994.

Clarke, M. L. *The Roman Mind: Studies in the History of Thought from Cicero to Marcus Aurelius.* New York: W. W. Norton & Company, Inc., 1968.

Cornell, T., and J. Matthews. *Atlas of the Roman World.* Oxford: Phaidon, 1982.

Cowell, F. R. *Cicero and the Roman Republic.* Harmondsworth, Middlesex: Penguin Books, 1948.

Duckworth, George E. *The Complete Roman Drama.* New York: Random House, Inc., 1942.

Dupont, F. *Daily Life in Ancient Rome.* Oxford: Blackwell, 1992.

Edman, Irwin. *Marcus Aurelius and His Times: The Transition from Paganism to Christianity.* Roslyn, NY: Walter J. Black, Inc., 1945.

Grant, Michael. *Roman Literature.* Middlesex, England: Penguin Books, 1954.

———. *Roman Myths.* London: Weidenfeld & Nicolson, 1971.

Guinagh, Kevin, and Alfred P. Dorjahn. *Latin Literature in Translation*. New York, London, and Toronto: Longmans, Green and Co., 1942.

Hadas, Moses. *Imperial Rome*. New York: Time Incorporated, 1965.

Hamilton, Edith. *The Roman Way*. New York: W. W. Norton & Company, 1932.

Hammond, N. G. L., and H. H Scullard, eds. *The Oxford Classical Dictionary*. 2nd edition. Oxford: Clarendon Press, 1970.

Harsh, Philip Whaley. *An Anthology of Roman Drama*. New York: Holt, Rinehart and Winston, 1962.

Holland, Jack, and John Monroe. *The Order of Rome*. New York: HBJ Press, 1980.

Howe, George and Gustave Adolphus Harrer. *Roman Literature in Translation*. New York: Harper & Brothers, 1959.

Howatson, M. C. *The Oxford Companion to Classical Literature*. 2nd edition. New York: Oxford University Press, 1989.

Isbell, Harold. *The Last Poets of Imperial Rome*. Middlesex, England: Penguin Books Ltd., 1971.

Keppie, L. *The Making of the Roman Army: From Republic to Empire*. London: Batsford, 1984.

Laing, Gordon Jennings. *Masterpieces of Latin Literature*. Boston: Houghton Mifflin Company, 1903.

Lang, D. M., and D. R. Dudley. *The Penguin Companion to Classical, Oriental & African Literature*. New York: McGraw-Hill Book Company, 1969.

Lefkowitz, Mary R., and Maureen B. Fant. *Women's Life in Greece and Rome*. Baltimore: The Johns Hopkins University Press, 1982.

Lind, L. R. *Latin Poetry in Verse Translation*. Boston: Houghton Mifflin Company, 1957.

MacKendrick, Paul, and Herbert M. Howe, eds. *Classics in Translation: Volume II: Latin Literature*. Madison, WI: University of Wisconsin Press, 1966.

Ogilvie, R. M. *The Romans and Their Gods*. London: Chatto & Windus, 1969.

Peck, Harry Thurston. *Harper's Dictionary of Classical Literature and Antiquities*. New York: Cooper Square Publishers, Inc., 1965.

Pottier, T. W. *Roman Italy*. London: British Museum Publications, 1987.

Rawson, B. *Marriage, Divorce and Children in Ancient Rome*. Oxford: Oxford University Press, 1991.

Rose, H. J. *A Handbook of Latin Literature*. New York: E. P. Dutton & Co., Inc., 1960.

Salmon, E. T. *Roman Civilization Under the Republic*. London: Thames and Hudson, 1969.

Scullard, H. H. *A History of the Roman World 753–146 B.C.* 4th edition. London and New York: Routledge, 1980.

Seyffert, Oskar. *Dictionary of Classical Antiquities*. Cleveland and New York: Meridian Books/The World Publishing Company, 1956–62.

Shelton, J.-A. *As the Romans Did: A Sourcebook in Roman Social History*. New York: Oxford University Press, 1988.

Solomon, Jon, and Julia Solomon. *Ancient Roman Feasts and Recipes: Adapted for Modern Cooking*. Miami: E. A. Seeman Publishing, Inc., 1977.

Todd, M. *The Walls of Rome*. London: Paul Elek, 1978.

Wacher, J. *The Roman World*. London and New York: Routledge & Kegan Paul, 1987.

Wells, J., and R. H. Barrow. *Short History of the Roman Empire*. New York: Barnes & Noble Inc., 1931.

Yavetz, Z. *Slaves and Slavery in Ancient Rome*. New Brunswick, NJ: Transaction Books, 1988.

Yonah, Michael Avi, and Israel Shatzman, eds. *Illustrated Encyclopedia of the Classical World*. New York: Harper & Row, 1975.

ACKNOWLEDGMENTS

Anonymous. "Vigil of Venus": Adapted from James J. Wilhelm's translation in *The Cruelest Month*. New Haven: Yale University Press, 1965. By permission of Yale University Press.

Apicius. Translated by Barbara Flower and Elisabeth Rosenbaum. *The Roman Cookery Book.* London, Toronto, Wellington, Sydney: George G. Harrap & Co. Ltd., 1958.

Apuleius. From *The Golden Ass*, translated by Jack Lindsay. Bloomington: Indiana University Press, 1960. © 1960 by Jack Lindsay.

Augustus. Translated by Frederick W. Shipley. *Velleius Paterculus and Res Gestae Divi Augusti*, edited by G. P. Goold. Cambridge: Harvard University Press, 1924. By permission of the publishers and the Loeb Classical Library.

Ausonius. Translated by Helen Waddell, from *Latin Poetry in Verse Translation*, edited by L. R. Lind. Houghton Mifflin Company. Copyright © L. R. Lind. Originally from Helen Waddell, *Mediaeval Latin Lyrics*, Constable and Co., London, 1929.

Avianus. Translated by Jack Lindsay from *Song of a Falling World: Culture During the Break-Up of the Roman Empire*, 1947. By permission of Andrew Dakers Ltd., London.

Caesar. Translated by H. J. Edwards. From *Caesar: The Gallic War*, edited by G. P. Goold. Cambridge: Harvard University Press, 1917–1986. Reprinted by permission of the publishers and the Loeb Classical Library.

Cato. Translated by Fairfax Harrison. From *Roman Literature in Translation*. Revised Edition. Selected and edited by George Howe and Gustave Adolphus Harrer. Copyright © 1924, 1959 by Harper Brothers. Copyright 1952 by Mrs. Gustave A. Harrer. By permission of the Macmillan Company.

Catullus. Translated by Roy Arthur Swanson. *Odi et Amo: The Complete Poetry of Catullus.* New York: The Liberal Arts Press, 1959. © 1959 by the Liberal Arts Press.

Celsus. *De Medicina.* Translated by W. G. Spenser, edited by T. E. Page. Cambridge: Harvard University Press, 1948. Reprinted by permission of the publishers and the Loeb Classical Library.

Cicero. "Oration Against Catiline": Translated by K. Guinagh, from *The Speeches*, edited by T. E. Page. Cambridge: Harvard University Press, 1922. Reprinted by permission of the publishers and the Loeb Classical Library. "Letters to His Wife and Family in Rome, to Caesar in Gaul," translated by E. S. Shuckburg, in *Masterpieces of Latin Literature*, edited by Gordon Jennings Laing. Boston: Houghton Mifflin Company, 1903.

Claudian. Translated by Maurice Platnauer, *Claudian*, Vol. II, edited by T. E. Page. Cambridge: Harvard University Press, 1922–1956. Reprinted by permission of the publishers and the Loeb Classical Library.

Columella. *On Agriculture and Trees*, Vol. III, edited by T. E. Page. English translation by E. S. Forster and Edward H. Heffner. London: William Heinemann, 1955. Reprinted by permission of the publishers and the Loeb Classical Library.

Diodorus. *Diodorus of Sicily*, Vol. I, edited by T. E. Page. Translated by C. H. Oldfather. Cambridge: Harvard University Press, 1946. Reprinted by permission of the publishers and the Loeb Classical Library.

Ennius. Translated by John Wright. From Richard Eberhart and Selden Rodman, *War and the Poet*. New York: Devin-Adair Company, 1945.

Frontinus. *The Two Books on the Water Supply of the City of Rome of Sextus Julius Frontinus, Water Commissioner of the City of Rome, A.D. 97*. Translated by Clemens Herschel. Boston: Dana Estes & Company, Publishers. Copyright 1898 by Clemens Herschel.

Fronto. *The Correspondence of Marcus Cornelius Fronto with Marcus Aurelius Antoninus, Lucius Verus, Antoninus Pius, and Various Friends*, Vol. I, edited by T. E. Page, translated by C. R. Haines. Cambridge: Harvard University Press, 1919/1928/1955. Reprinted by permission of the publishers and the Loeb Classical Library.

Gaius. Translated by F. de Zulueta, as quoted in Mary R. Lefkowitz and Maureen B. Fant, *Women's Life in Greece & Rome*. Baltimore: Johns Hopkins University Press, 1982. © 1982 by M. B. Fant and M. R. Lefkowitz.

Gellius. From *The Attic Nights of Aulus Gellius*, Vol. I, translated by John C. Rolfe. London: William Heinemann, 1927.

Hadrian. Translated by Elinor Wylie. From *Latin Poetry in Verse Translation*, edited by L. R. Lind. Boston: Houghton Mifflin Company/The Riverside Press Cambridge. Copyright © 1957 L. R. Lind.

Horace. *Horace's Satires and Epistles*. Translated by Jacob Fuchs. New York: W. W. Norton & Company, 1977. Copyright © 1977 by Jacob Fuchs.

Josephus. From *The Jewish War*, translated by G. A. Williamson. Baltimore: Penguin Books, 1959/1970. Copyright © G. A. Williamson, 1959, 1969.

Julian. *The Works of the Emperor Julian*, Vol. I, translated by Wilmer Cave Wright. Cambridge: Harvard University Press, 1949. By permission of the publishers and the Loeb Classical Library.

Justin Martyr. From *Marcus Aurelius and His Times*. Roslyn, New York: Walter J. Black, Inc. Copyright © 1945 by Walter J. Black, Inc.

Justinian. *Justinian's Institutes*. Translated with an introduction by Peter Birks and Grant McLeod. Ithaca: Cornell University Press, 1987. Copyright © 1987 Peter Birks and Grant McLeod.

Juvenal. From *Roman Poets of the Early Empire*, edited with introductions, notes, and glossary by A. J. Boyle and J. P. Sullivan. New York: Penguin Books, 1991.

Laberius. Translated by J. V. Cunningham, from *Latin Poetry in Verse Translation,* edited by L. R. Lind. Boston: Houghton Mifflin Company. Copyright © L. R. Lind. Originally from *The New Mexico Quarterly Review,* Vol. 16, 1946.

Livy. *The Early History of Rome,* translated by Aubrey de Sélincourt. Baltimore, Maryland: Penguin Books, 1960, 1969. Copyright © the Estate of Aubrey de Sélincourt.

Lucan. *Pharsalia: Dramatic Episodes of the Civil Wars.* Translated by Robert Graves. Baltimore, Maryland: Penguin Books, 1957. © 1957 by Robert Graves.

Lucilius. Translated by Willis Barnstone, in his *Greek Lyric Poetry.* Bloomington & London: Indiana University Press. By kind permission of Willis Barnstone and Indiana University Press.

Lucretius. *The Nature of Things,* translated by Frank O. Copley. New York: W. W. Norton & Company, Inc., 1977. Copyright © 1977 by W. W. Norton & Company, Inc. Reprinted by permission of W. W. Norton & Company, Inc.

Macrobius. *Commentary on the Dream of Scipio,* translated with an introduction and notes by William Harris Stahl. New York: Columbia University Press, 1952. Copyright 1952 by Columbia University Press, New York.

Marcus Aurelius. From *Marcus Aurelius and His Times.* Roslyn, New York: Walter J. Black, Inc. Copyright © 1945 by Walter J. Black, Inc. Reprinted by permission of Platinum Press Inc.

Martial. From *Roman Poets of the Early Empire,* edited by A. J. Boyle and J. P. Sullivan. London: Penguin Books, 1991. Copyright © 1991 by A. J. Boyle and J. P. Sullivan.

Ovid. Translated by Rolfe Humphries. *Ovid: The Loves, The Art of Beauty, The Remedies for Love, and The Art of Love.* Bloomington: Indiana University Press/A Midland Original, 1957/1966. Copyright © 1986 by Allen Mandelbaum.

Paulus. Translated by S. P. Scott, as quoted in Mary R. Lefkowitz and Maureen B. Fant, *Women's Life in Greece & Rome.* Baltimore: Johns Hopkins University Press, 1982. Copyright © 1982 by M. B. Fant and M. R. Lefkowitz.

Persius. Translated by Robert A. Brooks, in *Latin Poetry in Verse Translation,* edited by L. R. Lind. Boston: Houghton Mifflin Company/The Riverside Press Cambridge. Copyright © 1957 by L. R. Lind.

Petronius. *The Satyricon of Petronius Arbiter,* translated by William Burnaby. Random House: Modern Library. Date unknown.

Plautus. Translated by Cleveland K. Chase, from *An Anthology of Roman Drama,* edited by Philip Whaley Harsh. New York: Holt, Rinehart and Winston, 1906/1962. Copyright © by Philip Whaley Harsh.

Pliny the Elder. From *The Natural History of Pliny,* Vol. 1. Translated by John Bostock and H. T. Riley. London: Henry G. Bohn, 1855.

Pliny the Younger. Translated by Firth. From *Masterpieces of Latin Literature,* edited by Gordon Jennings Laing. Boston: Houghton Mifflin Company, 1903.

Propertius. Translated by Goldwin Smith and Thomas Gray. From *Masterpieces of Latin Literature,* edited by Gordon Jennings Laing. Boston: Houghton Mifflin Company, 1903.

Publilius. Translated by Gilbert Highet, in *Latin Poetry in Verse Translation,* edited by L. R. Lind. Boston: Houghton Mifflin Company/The Riverside Press Cambridge. Copyright © 1957 by L. R. Lind. Originally from Highet's *Roman Drama in Translation: Illustrative Material for Comparative Literature 252,* Columbia University, mimeograph.

Quintilian. Translated by H. E. Butler. *The Institutio Oratoria of Quintilian*, Vol. I. Cambridge: Harvard University Press; London: William Heinemann Ltd., 1953. By permission of the publishers and the Loeb Classical Library.

Sallust. From *Sallust: The Histories*, Vol. 1. Translated by Patrick McGushin. Oxford: Clarendon Press, 1992. © Patrick McGushin, 1992.

Seneca the Elder. *The Elder Seneca: Declamations*, Vol. 2. Translated by M. Winterbottom. Cambridge: Harvard University Press, 1974. © The President and Fellows of Harvard College 1974.

Seneca the Younger. *Seneca's Apocolocyntosis*. Translated by Allan Perley Ball. New York & London: Garland Publishing, Inc., 1978. Reprinted by permission.

Silius Italicus. *Punica*, with an English translation by J. D. Duff. Cambridge: William Heinemann/Harvard University Press, 1934.

Soranus. Translated by O. Temkin, as quoted in Mary R. Lefkowitz and Maureen B. Fant, *Women's Life in Greece & Rome*. Baltimore: Johns Hopkins University Press, 1982. Copyright © 1982 by M. B. Fant and M. R. Lefkowitz.

Statius. *The Thebaid of Statius*. Translated by George Calder. Cambridge: University Press, 1922. Reprinted with the permission of Cambridge University Press.

Suetonius. From *Latin Literature in Translation*, by Kevin Guinagh and Alfred P. Dorjahn. New York: Longmans, Green and Co. Copyright © 1942 by Longmans, Green and Co., Inc.

Sulpicia. From *A Book of Women Poets, from Antiquity to Now*, by Aliki Barnstone & Willis Barnstone, editors. New York: Schocken Books, 1992. © 1980, 1992 by Schocken Books, Inc. Reprinted by permission of Schocken Books and Willis and Aliki Barnstone; published by Pantheon Books, a division of Random House, Inc.

Tacitus. From *Masterpieces of Latin Literature*, edited by Gordon Jennings Laing. Boston: Houghton Mifflin Company, 1903.

Terence. From *The Brothers (Adelphoe), The Complete Comedies of Terence: Modern Verse Translations*. Palmer Bovie, Constance Carrier, and Douglas Parker. New Brunswick: Rutgers University Press, 1974. Copyright © 1974 by Rutgers University, the State University of New Jersey. Reprinted by permission of Rutgers University Press and Constance Carrier.

Tibullus. Translated by James Grainger. From *Masterpieces of Latin Literature*, edited by Gordon Jennings Laing. Boston: Houghton Mifflin Company, 1903.

Valerius Maximus. Translated by Maureen B. Fant, as quoted in Mary R. Lefkowitz and Maureen B. Fant, *Women's Life in Greece & Rome*. Baltimore: Johns Hopkins University Press, 1982. Copyright © 1982 by M. B. Fant and M. R. Lefkowitz.

Varro. From *Varro on Farming*, translated Lloyd Storr-Best. London: G. Bell and Sons, Ltd., 1912.

Vegetius. *The Military Institutions of the Romans*, translated by Lieutenant John Clark. Harrisburg, PA: The Military Service Publishing Company, 1944.

Virgil. *The Aeneid: An Epic Poem of Rome*. Translated by L. R. Lind. Bloomington & London: Indiana University Press, 1963.

Vitruvius. Translated by Frank Granger, in *Vitruvius On Architecture*, Vol. 1. Cambridge: Harvard University Press; London: William Heinemann Ltd., 1945. By permission of the publishers and the Loeb Classical Library.

ILLUSTRATION CREDITS

Aqueduct: Photograph by Kenneth J. Atchity.

Entrance to the theater at Italica: Photograph by Kenneth J. Atchity.

The arch of Titus: Lazio. Courtesy of Art Resource.

Graffiti: Alinari. 1935. Courtesy of Art Resource.

Entrance to Hadrian's Neapolis, Italica: Photograph by Kenneth J. Atchity.

Theater tickets: Museo Nazionale. Copyright Archivi Alinari, 1989. Courtesy of Art Resource.

Theater at Italica: Photograph courtesy of Chi-Li Wong.

Ruins of Forum: Photograph by Kenneth J. Atchity.

Roman war machines: Mostra Augustea, Roma. Editorial Photocolor Archives, Inc. Courtesy of Art Resource.

Temple to Julius Caesar: Photograph by Kenneth J. Atchity.

Entrance to theater, Italica: Photograph by Kenneth J. Atchity.

"The Aldobrandini Nuptials": Copyright Archivi Alinari, 1989. Courtesy of Art Resource.

Young Bacchus: Roman sculpture, Museo Nazionale. Copyright Archivi Alinari, 1989/1991. Courtesy of Art Resource.

The Comitium well: Photograph by Kenneth J. Atchity.

Roman temple: Photograph by Kenneth J. Atchity.

Drinking fountain: Photograph courtesy of Chi-Li Wong.

Processional staircase: Photograph by Kenneth J. Atchity.

Augustus, Prima Porta: Roman Sculpture, Vatican Museum. Courtesy of Archivi Alinari and Art Resource.

Diocletian's palace: Alinari, 1938. Courtesy of Editorial Photocolor Archives and Art Resource.

Mirror, bronze, from Pompeii: Museo Nazionale. Copyright Archivi Alinari, 1989. Courtesy of Art Resource.

Temple of Saturn: Photograph by Kenneth J. Atchity.

Pharmacy: Copyright Archivi Alinari, 1989. Courtesy of Art Resource.

Pompeii, fountain: Copyright Archivi Alinari, 1989. Courtesy of Art Resource.

Gladiators' corridor: Photograph courtesy of Chi-Li Wong.

Domitian, cameo on 16th-century crucifix: Foto Marburg/Art Resource, NY.

Archives, Forum, Rome: Photograph by Kenneth J. Atchity.

Rome in the time of Constantine: Mostra Augustea, Roma. Alinari. Courtesy of Art Resource.

Detail of sewer system: Photograph by Kenneth J. Atchity.

Trajan's bath, Italica: Photograph by Kenneth J. Atchity.

Tripod: Archivi Alinari. Courtesy of Art Resource.

Hadrian's tomb: Copyright Archivi Alinari, 1990. Courtesy of Art Resource.

Hermaphrodite vase: Museo Nazionale. Anderson, Roma. Courtesy of Art Resource.

Temple of Antoninus and Faustina: Photograph by Kenneth J. Atchity.

Wine pitcher: Paris, Louvre. Alinari. Courtesy of Art Resource.

Staircase: Photograph by Kenneth J. Atchity.

Marcus Aurelius: Museo Nazionale. Copyright Archivi Alinari, 1989. Courtesy of Art Resource.

Tripod: Museo Archeologico Nazionale, Naples. Alinari/Art Resource, NY.

Musical instruments: Museo Nazionale, Anderson. Courtesy of Art Resource.

Goddess, ivory: Musee du Moyen Age (Cluny), Paris. Giraudon. Courtesy of Art Resource.

Circular oven: Museo Nazionale, Anderson, Roma. Courtesy of Art Resource.

Testudo: Copyright Alinari 1938. Alinari-Scala. Courtesy of Art Resource.

Via Sacra: Photograph by Kenneth J. Atchity.

Detail of stadium floor: Photograph courtesy of Chi-Li Wong.

Gladiators' entrance: Photograph courtesy of Chi-Li Wong.

Pompeii fresco: Photograph by Kenneth J. Atchity.

Goblet: Louvre, Lauros-Giraudon. Courtesy of Art Resource.

House of Loreius Tiburtinus: Fratelli Alinori. Courtesy of Art Resource.

Detail of sewer: Photograph courtesy of Chi-Li Wong.

House of the Vestal Virgins: Photograph by Kenneth J. Atchity.

INDEX

Note: Page numbers in boldface refer to profiles of authors or to excerpts.

Made in the USA
Lexington, KY
20 January 2017